Weird Sports and Wacky Games around the World

Weird Sports and Wacky Games around the World

From Buzkashi to Zorbing

VICTORIA WILLIAMS

GREENWOOD™

An Imprint of ABC-CLIO, LLC

Santa Barbara, California • Denver, Colorado

Library of Congress Cataloging-in-Publication Data

Williams, Victoria.
   Weird sports and wacky games around the world : from Buzkashi to Zorbing / Victoria Williams.
      pages cm
   Includes bibliographical references and index.
   ISBN 978-1-61069-639-5 (acid-free paper) — ISBN 978-1-61069-640-1 (ebook)
1. Sports.   2. Games.   I. Title.
   GV706.8.W55   2015
   796—dc23   2014040274

ISBN: 978-1-61069-639-5
EISBN: 978-1-61069-640-1

19 18 17 16 15   1 2 3 4 5

This book is also available on the World Wide Web as an eBook.
Visit www.abc-clio.com for details.

Greenwood
An Imprint of ABC-CLIO, LLC

ABC-CLIO, LLC
130 Cremona Drive, P.O. Box 1911
Santa Barbara, California 93116-1911

This book is printed on acid-free paper ∞

Manufactured in the United States of America

Contents

Alphabetical List of Entries

Geographic Guide to Entry Origins by Region

Africa and Middle East
Camel Racing
Varzesh-e Bastani

Asia (Central and North)
Buzkashi
Mongolian Wrestling
Yak Racing

Asia (South and Southeast)
Korean Wrestling
Sepak Takraw
Sumo Wrestling
Thai Boxing

Australia and Pacific
Aussie Rules Football
Boomerang Throwing
Heli-Skiing
Rogaining
Sheepdog Trials
Yabbie Races

Continental Europe and Russia
Bearbaiting
Bossaball
Bull Running
Bunnock
Camel Wrestling
Canal Jumping
Cockfighting
Cresta Run
Croquet
Futnet
Horseball
Jacks and Knucklebones
Korfball

Lapta
La Soule
Parkour
Pelota
Pétanque
Pigeon Racing
Real Tennis
Rhythmic Gymnastics
Schwingen
Spanish Bullfighting
Ultramarathons
Wingsuiting
Yagli Gures

India
Gilli-Danda
Kabaddi
Mallakhamb
Pehlwani/Kushti
Snooker
Yoga

International
Badger Baiting
Barrel Races
Celtic Wrestling
Chess Boxing
Elephant Sports
Foxhunting
Handball
Nonlethal Bullfighting
Round-the-World Yacht Races
Shoe Throwing
Skittles
Stone Skimming
Trampolining
Zorbing

North America
Kin-Ball
Paintball
Quidditch
Street Luge
Synchronized Skating

Scandinavia
Brännboll
Glima
Kubb
Kyykkä
Mölkky
Nordic Walking
Orienteering
Pesäpallo
Wife Carrying

South and Central America
Capoeira
Footvolley
Lucha Libre
Pato
Volcano Boarding

United Kingdom and Ireland
Aunt Sally
Bandy
Bog Snorkeling World Championship
Cheese Rolling
Conkers
Cotswold Olimpicks
Cricket
Curling
Dwile Flonking
Eton Wall Game
Extreme Ironing
Fell Running
Fives
Hare Coursing
Haxey Hood Game
Highland Games
Hurling
Kitesurfing
Lawnmower Racing
Netball
Nipsy
Pancake Races
Rounders
Rugby League
Shin Kicking
Shinty
Shove Ha'penny
Swimming the English Channel
Underwater Hockey

Thematic Guide to Entries

Animal Sports
Bearbaiting and Badger Baiting
Bull Running
Buzkashi
Camel and Yak Racing
Camel Wrestling
Cockfighting
Elephant Sports
Foxhunting
Hare Coursing
Nonlethal Bullfighting
Pato and Horseball
Pigeon Racing
Sheepdog Trials
Spanish Bullfighting
Yabbie Races

Ball and Bat Sports
Aussie Rules Football
Bandy
Bossaball
Brännboll and *Pesäpallo*
Cricket
Croquet
Fives
Footvolley and Futnet
Handball
Hurling
Kin-Ball
Korfball
Lapta
Netball
Nipsy
Pelota
Pétanque
Real Tennis
Rounders
Sepak Takraw
Shinty
Snooker

Competitive Transport
Canal Jumping
Cresta Run
Heli-Skiing
Kitesurfing
Lawnmower Racing
Round-the-World Yacht Races
Street Luge

Contact and Combat Sports
Aussie Rules Football
Capoeira
Celtic Wrestling
Chess Boxing
Eton Wall Game
Glima
Kabaddi
Korean Wrestling
La Soule
Lucha Libre
Mongolian Wrestling
Pehlwani/Kushti
Quidditch
Rugby League
Schwingen
Shin Kicking
Sumo Wrestling
Thai Boxing
Varzesh-e Bastani
Yagli Gures

Events
Bog Snorkeling World Championship
Cotswold Olimpicks
Highland Games
Swimming the English Channel

Extreme Sports
Extreme Ironing
Volcano Boarding

Preface

Play is an essential part of the human experience that has existed since time immemorial and occurs in all cultures. Play proves that what can seem frivolous is actually a source of joy and sometimes of great commercial value. One of the main ways people play is through participating in sports and games. This single-volume encyclopedia concentrates on sporting activities and pastimes enjoyed around the world that may be less familiar to American readers. Therefore, this book does not contain entries on baseball, basketball, American football, ice hockey, track and field, or soccer. These sports are all mentioned but in relation to other activities, some of which are enjoyed by many millions of people and have a huge cultural significance (such as cricket), while others are played by a handful of participants only (such as the Eton Wall Game). It was something of an eye-opener for me as a Londoner born and bred to consider what sports Americans might consider unusual. For instance, in England cricket is played at every level from village sides and school physical education classes to international competitions such as the Ashes, an ultracompetitive multimatch contest between England and Australia, while cricket is probably the most popular sport in India, with players such as Sachin Tendulkar achieving the status of idols. Also, it was interesting to consider that netball and rounders (both of which I played at school) are not mainstream elements of physical education classes in the United States, though both are very similar to sports that are played throughout America.

In general, I opted to write about activities that included elements of history, folklore, politics, art, literature, and science. The scope of this book takes in North America, South America, Europe, Africa, Asia, the Middle East, and Oceania and covers games played by men, women, and children in teams or as individuals. Animal sports are also featured, including controversial so-called blood sports. I have also included a number of entries on traditional British pub games and other pastimes that tend not to receive much coverage in reference books but are known in the United Kingdom. Similarly, I have included British folk sports such as the Haxey Hood Game and activities including cheese rolling and pancake races, which, I was surprised to learn, had parallel events in other countries; I had erroneously presumed that they were uniquely English events, the product of the famously eccentric British mentality.

This book is primarily aimed at researchers, though I have purposely kept the writing as jargon-free as possible so that the general reader can also read the book from cover to cover for entertainment. However, with the researcher in mind, every entry can be looked at as a stand-alone item or as part of an overarching theme, and each entry is followed by a "See also" section that enables cross-referencing as well as a brief "Further Reading" list (there is also a select bibliography at the back of the book). Each entry details the known history and evolution of each pastime and specifies governing bodies and championships where applicable. I have also detailed the myths and legends that lie at the heart of several of the sports and games, and I have tried, where space allows, to note artworks, literature, and films that depict the various activities detailed in the entries.

The writing of this publication would not have been possible without the seemingly ceaseless enthusiasm of Kaitlin Ciarmiello, senior acquisitions editor at ABC-CLIO. I would like to thank Kaitlin for trusting me to produce this book on time and for putting up with the many questions I have e-mailed to her from across the Atlantic. I would also like to thank my family and friends for feigning interest when I came out with random facts about obscure activities, for helping me locate pubs where Aunt Sally is still played, and for accompanying me on a day trip to Chipping Campden to visit a windswept Dover's Hill, site of the Cotswold Olimpicks. In particular my Mum, Rosemary Williams, deserves a special mention for alerting me to newspaper articles on unusual sports and the like. Thank you also to Dr. Nida Suri for her input on Indian sports and games and to Roger and Cynthia Levicki who, as Brits living in the south of France, provided a valuable insight into the mysteries of *pétanque*.

Introduction

The terms "sports" and "games" refer to a myriad of casual or organized competitive activities usually of a physical nature. Hundreds of different sports and games exist often under several names and with multiple variations, plus there are those activities such as yoga that are not usually practiced as sports but rather as part of a healthy lifestyle, though this too can be organized as competition.

Such pastimes are often thought of as nonserious, voluntary pursuits that exist purely for enjoyment or as a way to get fitter or leaner, but in actuality many sports are embedded in everyday life interconnected with social customs, war, politics, commerce, education, entertainment, national identity, internationalism, morality, and so on. Indeed, even those people who claim to have no interest in sports of any kind will find that they are aware of certain sports because sport is ubiquitous, and nonsporty types living in today's multimedia information age have no choice but to absorb information through a process of osmosis, however disinterested they may be. Social networks such as Twitter mean that news and sports updates are delivered almost instantaneously and are read by Web site users even if the user does not follow the source of the updates. Further, Twitter feeds from media outlets such as the BBC and Huffington Post often cover odd or localized sports and games in tweets accompanied by a link to a longer article on, say, Dorset knob throwing or *pehlwani/kushti,* meaning that potentially these activities will become more widely known.

For the ease of play and enjoyment of both players and spectators, sports and games are usually governed by rules and customs that serve to ensure fair play and allow for the adjudication of victory. However, some, such as *buzkashi,* the Haxey Hood Game, and several types of wrestling, evolved from preexisting social customs and are therefore classed as folk sports, by which is meant traditional sports tied directly to specific folk or ethnic cultures. Interestingly, it is the emergence of newer sports that throws into sharper relief exactly what is meant by the term "folk sports." Modern mainstream sports tend to be extremely organized at local, national, and international levels, with competition structured around formal written rules that are legitimized by a body of authority. These governing bodies also standardize the equipment to be used, the dimensions of playing areas, the duration of competition, and so on. Folk sports differ greatly from this mainstream model. Folk sports tend to be loosely structured, with little in the way of formal organization. Such sports do not have written rules but instead employ simple rules expressed using local terminology and passed down by oral tradition. The rules of folk sports become established over time and exhibit ritualistic overtones.

Sumo wrestling and Mongolian wrestling are very good examples of this ritualized form of sport, as both these styles of wrestling see competitors perform highly symbolic prematch rituals as well as postmatch rites.

Competitors in formal, organized sport tend to exhibit a high level of emotional control, so there is little or no violence during play. For example, in cricket the slightest show of dissent or disagreement with an umpiring decision is liable to land a cricketer in trouble, even to the point that the player may be fined half of his match fee. Similarly, if a soccer player shows dissent he can be punished by the showing of a card that may remove him from the game, while dissent is also punishable in lawn tennis. This is in contrast to folk sports such as the French game *la soule,* which in times past had a reputation for descending into violence akin to rioting, and the rowdy Haxey Hood Game, which features much drinking of alcohol and sees a participant tested by fire.

Another important factor of modern mainstream sports is that competitors take part through choice and compete in order to display their sporting prowess—in mainstream sports skill is nearly always emphasized over strength and power. This is reflected in the earning power of professional sportspeople. According to *Forbes,* none of the highest-paid athletes of 2013 came from any sport in which power and physical strength are the most important attributes—three boxers make the *Forbes* top 50, but only one of these, Wladimir Klitschko, is a heavyweight; and it could be argued that power is not the primary attribute needed by a successful boxer, even a heavyweight. By contrast, contestants in strongman competitions are required to possess great physical strength, as these events tend to feature exaggerated versions of everyday tasks—heaving logs, carrying cars, lifting rocks—and strongman competitors often have to take second jobs to pay their expenses. Like strongman events (but unlike mainstream sports), folk sports often place emphasis on power rather than skill. For example, in the Swiss sport *steinstossen,* competitors vie to see which of them can throw a huge stone the farthest. Also like strongman competitions, folk sports are often so niche that competitors do not become widely known through competing and do not earn great financial rewards.

Another difference between mainstream modern sport and folk sports is that participants in folk sports often face pressure to compete because it is part of their cultural heritage, even if this means sublimating their own personal identity to fit in with their society's demands to compete. This is exemplified by land diving, which takes place on Pentecost Island, part of the South Pacific nation of Vanuatu. Land diving is a coming-of-age ritual that sees men jump headfirst off specially erected wooden towers fitted with multiple diving platforms between 60 and 100 feet high. When they jump the men encounter speeds of up to 45 miles per hour, but they do not wear any safety equipment except for two thin vines tied around their ankles in the manner of the equipment worn during bungee jumping. Though a social custom with a long history, land diving is also a sport, for a man's expertise at land diving is viewed as a measure of his manliness and bravery. Land diving also fulfills another criteria of folk sports, for, like most folk sports, land diving does not have a professional form and therefore manifests the best of sport in general's most basic and purest principles—the desire to test oneself and strive to improve with each competition for the sake of personal achievement. Land diving also shows how folk sports perform an important function in helping to preserve established values and help both participants and spectators connect to old ways and ancient rites. Though land diving attracts tourists to Vanuatu, the event reveals local values—ideals of masculinity, politics, and the perceived correlation of ritual to risk.

Folk sports often have their roots in ancient history. For example, *pétanque* is thought to have originated from a game played by Roman soldiers stationed in France circa 125 BCE, while *varzesh-e bastani*, meaning "sport of ancients," is an early form of wrestling predating the culture of Persia (now Iran). Not all folk sports have long histories, however. For instance, the English pub game dwile flonking appears to be a recent attempt to fashion a folk sport, for the game has its own vernacular, customs, and clothing. However, dwile flonking's apparent lack of history and very newness mean that some view the game as lacking authenticity, and it is regarded as a spoof folk sport by some critics.

Combat sports such as the numerous forms of wrestling tend to be ancient in origin, though strangely the Greco-Roman wrestling as performed at the Summer Olympics is not related to the forms of wrestling practiced in ancient Greece or Rome. The wrestling practiced in these ancient civilizations was much more like *varzesh-e bastani* or the various types of wrestling found in modern-day Turkey. There are many different styles of wrestling in Europe, such as Icelandic *glima*, Turkish *yagli gures*, Swiss *schwingen*, and the various forms that make up Celtic wrestling, including Cumberland and Westmorland wrestling, Breton *gouren*, and Scottish backhold. Wrestling is not confined to Europe, however; there are other famous folk wrestling styles, including Japanese sumo and Mexican luche libra. Indigenous wrestling can also be found in Mongolia and Korea, among other countries. Wrestling need not, however, be confined to humans—camel wrestling is a traditional cultural event in Turkey.

Not all forms of sporting combat are ancient, however. Chess boxing is a relatively new sport, while sports in which participants use weapons, such as paintball, tend to be newly invented—paintball evolved in the 1970s. Moreover, one of the world's newest sporting tournaments is the Battle of the Nations, in which participants use medieval-style metal weapons in competitive categories such as Professional Fight as well as nonbattle competitions, including the Contest for Best Set of Armor and Weapons, the Contest for Best Authentic Field Camp, and an archery tournament.

Several British pub games can be classed as folk sports. Games have been integral to pubs for as long as there have been inns and hostelries in Britain—the Ye Olde Trip to Jerusalem pub in Nottingham dating from 1189 claims to be England's oldest inn, as does the Bingley Arms in Leeds, which has roots dating back to 953. However, according to the *Guinness Book of Records*, the oldest pub in England is Ye Olde Fighting Cocks in St. Albans to the north of London, the capital of England, which is an 11th-century building located on a site circa 793. The name of this pub was changed during the 19th century to reflect the fact that cockfighting took place in the main bar within an area called the Cock Pit that was donated to the pub by the local abbey.

Pub games tend to absorb players. This pleases pub owners, as it means that players remain in the bar and, of course, drink more than they would ordinarily. However, in the past authority has frowned upon some pub games, as they have been perceived as part of a problematic pub culture. This means that many pubs have removed gaming equipment from their premises. This, together with the closure of many pubs in recent years for various reasons and the introduction of weekly pub quizzes (in which drinkers form regular teams to answer general knowledge questions in order to win prizes), has had a direct impact on the number of pub games being played in the United Kingdom, and today some games face extinction or near extinction. However, all is not lost, for in recent years a number of brewers have harked back to traditional pub values and started to support pub games by way of sponsorship. These include Hook Norton, supporters of several Aunt Sally leagues; John Smith's, promoters of local and national darts competitions as well as darts leagues; Theakston, which provides financial backing for various quoits leagues; and Blackthorn, which sponsors skittles tournaments and leagues. Some pub owners are also starting to notice the moneymaking potential of pub games and have reintroduced game equipment. Further to this, several pubs in London now offer drinkers the chance to play board games such as chess, checkers, Scrabble, and bridge, while a dedicated board games café opened in London on November 15, 2014, following a trend for similar establishments in Oxford, England, and Toronto, Canada.

Like folk sports and pub games, ball sports, meaning sports that feature a ball that can be played either with the hand, feet, a bat or other device, also have a very long history. In Mesoamerica, the region extending from Mexico to Costa Rica, a sport called simply the ball game was invented around 2500–100 BCE and went on to become hugely important for many civilizations, including the Aztecs and Mayans. However, ball game was much more than just a sport. In Mesoamerican mythology, ball game is an intrinsic element in the story of the Mayan brother gods Hun Hunahpú and Vucub Hunahpú. The pair played ball game noisily, thereby incurring the wrath of the gods of the underworld, and consequently the two were hoodwinked into descending into the underworld, Xibalba, where they were challenged to a ball game contest. Hun Hunahpús was defeated and was punished by being beheaded. This is significant, for in reality prisoners of war were often forced to take part in ball game, and those who lost would sometimes become the victims of human sacrifice. Indeed, while winners would receive trophies, losers (individuals or entire teams) would be sacrificed to the gods. The Mayans also played a similar game in which captives who had lost at ball game took the place of the ball by being tied up and rolled down the stone steps of the ball game court.

Many ball games that are still played today evolved many centuries ago. For instance, *jeu de palme,* the forerunner of real tennis, was invented by French monks during the 12th century. While peasants had played ball sports before this time, the monks standardized play, leading to the uptake of the game by the aristocracy, who moved ball games indoors by building palatial courts. The Middle Ages was also a time when ball games, such as *la soule,* were mass participation events. It was around this time that the British started to greatly influence ball sports. The British too had a mass-participation ball game in the form of Shrovetide football, but this had unclear rules and was often violent (as too was *la soule*). The violence inherent in these early ball games meant that they tended to attract the opprobrium of those in authority. Later British innovations in ball sports, such as the invention of soccer, would be more bourgeois in nature with sports disseminated through the English public school system, where rules and other important elements were standardized. The migration of British and Irish immigrants to the United States and Canada brought ball games such as shinty to the New World, and 19th-century British colonialism spread cricket across the globe, with the first-ever international cricket match played in 1844 between the United States and Canada at the St. George's Cricket Club in Manhattan. Meanwhile, elsewhere in Europe ball games such as *pétanque* and *pelota* were evolving in the Basque region of Spain/France. Ball games were busy being invented in the United States too. For instance, the creation of basketball in Springfield, Massachusetts, led to the evolution of netball in England, with both games becoming popular sports. Contrastingly, a similar ball game, korfball, which is played by mixed-sex teams, never took off internationally and is popular only in the country of its birth, the Netherlands.

More recently technical and scientific developments have helped ball games evolve. For instance, the invention of both manufactured rubber and the lawnmower at the start of the 19th century eventually led real tennis to evolve into lawn tennis, as it is known today. Not all ball games are old however. Kin-ball, for instance, is a fairly new sport, as it was developed in 1986 as a way of increasing children's aerobic fitness, coordination, and teamwork skills. Today kin-ball is played in schools in order to tackle childhood obesity levels and to allow people with disabilities to participate in sports.

Perhaps the oldest sports, games, and activities are, however, those that require little or no equipment, such as walking, running, yoga, and sports involving animals. However, over time several of these sports have fallen out of fashion on the grounds that they are cruel to the animals involved. Those who wish to see an end to such sports, including animal welfare groups and animal charities, class these sports as blood sports. It could be argued that some animal sports are not cruel, as they either revolve around animals doing what comes naturally to them, such as snail racing and worm charming, or see animals matched in fair competition, such as in sheepdog trials. Meanwhile, some other animal sports are not classified as blood sports but see people engage in direct and dangerous confrontation with the animals. The famous Pamplona Bull Run falls into this category, as does the Indian bull-taming spectacle *jallikattu*. Certain sports involving animals, however, attract a great deal of controversy to the extent that they become known as blood sports. Brutal sports such as bearbaiting and foxhunting have existed since medieval times in England but in the main have died out largely because of pressure from animal charities and animal rights groups as well as a general softening in the public's attitude toward animals. This is despite the efforts of prohunting groups such as the Countryside Alliance, a British pressure group founded in 1997 partly in response to the newly elected Labour government's pledge to outlaw hunting with dogs. The Countryside Alliance maintains that there is no evidence that hunting with dogs is objectionable on the grounds of animal welfare and has fought a long battle against the banning of hunting with dogs, arguing that such a ban endangers rural economies, traditions, and communities. Hunting and blood sports are extremely controversial topics in the United Kingdom, arousing strong opinions in those who are for and against such pursuits. Part of the reason that the subject of hunting is so contentious in the United Kingdom is that the British have a reputation for being animal lovers. This is evinced by research conducted in 2013 that discovered that while figures have dropped in recent years, 43 percent of UK households kept a pet of some kind. Indeed, there are 71 million pets in the United Kingdom (with dogs and cats being equally popular). This makes it all the more surprising that the United Kingdom is presently experiencing an upsurge in the frequency of illegal badger baiting, and England in particular is witnessing the evolution of a new blood sport—cat coursing—in which pet cats are used as sporting bait by dog owners. However, blood sports are not confined to the United Kingdom, where they are often banned and occur covertly. For instance, cockfighting takes place in the United States, the Middle East, the Far East, Pakistan, and Latin America. Perhaps the most controversial animal sport, however, is Spanish bullfighting. This style of bullfighting is highly controversial, as it nearly always results in the death of an animal that has previously been baited and ceremoniously fought for the amusement of spectators. Those in favor of the sport, including the Spanish government, claim that the activity is a ritualistic spectacle central to Spanish identity. However, those who are against the activity claim that bullfighting is merely a form of animal cruelty.

Just as animals feature in many minority sports, so too do various forms of transport. Walking and running are perhaps the most natural sports to participate in, as most people walk as part of everyday life. Also, walking sports do not cost a lot to enjoy, as there is little needed in the way of equipment. Thus, sports such as Nordic walking, orienteering, rogaining, and pedestrianism are really extensions of everyday activities. Some people like to add a little mystery to their walk by taking up geocaching, a sort of 21st-century treasure hunt that, despite involving modern equipment such as the Internet and GPS, has its roots in 19th-century England. Other transport-based activities include Birdman Rallies (competitions held for human-powered flying machines) and lawnmower racing, which though sounding eccentric, is taken seriously by competitors, who see the sport as a less expensive form of motor racing.

Additionally, some transport-based activities are so intrinsically hazardous that they fall into the category of extreme sports, also known as adventure sports. For example, in wingsuiting participants soar above the landscape after jumping from mountaintops and the like, in heli-skiing skiers are helicoptered to mountain summits and then ski downward, and in volcano boarding participants ride a surfboard-like piece of equipment down the sides of craters. Meanwhile, the ultraglamorous though exceptionally dangerous Cresta Run is so likely to lead to injury or worse that participants must sign a liability disclaimer before attempting the course. Interestingly, it could be argued that land diving in Vanuatu is simultaneously a folk sport, a transport-based sport, and an extreme sport, for competitors have to avoid crashing into the ground during their dive and strive to graze the ground with their shoulders. Therefore, it is clear that while blood sports place animals in danger, extreme sports see competitors choose to participate in activities that are at the very least challenging and more often than not inherently perilous. Extreme sports are so called because they involve high levels of risk to participants. Such activities test the limit of human capacity and often see competitors risk their lives for the thrill of the sport. As a result, many extreme sports are individual activities because by their very nature they set out to challenge personal boundaries and test the limits of a competitor's endurance. The individualistic nature of extreme sports is exemplified by wingsuiting and by ultramarathons, in which competitors face the challenge of completing an extra–long-distance run usually against an inhospitable natural landscape such as a desert. A team aspect can exist within the realm of extreme sports, however. For instance, the less serious adventure activity of extreme ironing can be practiced solo or as part of a team.

Another facet of many extreme sports is that they consist of tricks and freestyle events that give rise to their own vernacular. This distinct language helps foster an extreme sports culture that extends to extreme sports clothing, music, and specialist magazines. *Parkour* exemplifies this, for the sport has partly developed through word of mouth and social networking, has given rise to an MTV television program, and has originated niche magazines such as *Breathe Parkour* and *Spiked*.

Interestingly, although many extreme sports seem to be recently invented, this is not necessarily the case. For example, the popular extreme sport of kayaking has been used as a fishing method for over 4,000 years, and surfing has been practiced by Polynesians living in the South Pacific region for millennia but was only classified as an extreme sport once the activity took hold in Hawaii in the 1900s. Extreme sports received a boost with the advent of ESPN's annual X Games, an extreme sports tournament launched in 1995 that features various extreme sports, including street luge. However, another extreme transport-based sport, modified shovel racing, proved just too hazardous for the X Games and was dropped from the schedule.

It might seem likely that children's games are at the completely opposite end of the spectrum compared to inherently hazardous extreme sports. However, not all children's pastimes are gentle. For instance, conkers has been banned from being played on school grounds by some British municipal authorities in case a fiercely swinging nut hurts a child. Moreover, the rough tag-style schoolyard game British Bulldog is frequently banned from UK schools because of its violent nature. There are, however, many gentle pastimes enjoyed by children. Pooh-sticks, inspired by the Winnie the Pooh stories by A. A. Milne, is perhaps the epitome of a relaxed pastime, for there is perhaps no other sport on Earth that is as leisurely; participants have to do little other than drop a wooden stick into a stream and let nature decide the outcome.

In the United Kingdom during the latter half on the 19th century, children's games became increasingly popular both in schools and in events organized by churches and other associations. These games were designed to teach discipline, promote physical fitness, and encourage a sense of team spirit and fair play—all qualities regarded as desirable in the face of growing anxieties about the perceived misbehavior of the young and deemed necessary to ensure the longer-term survival of the British Empire. However, many of these games fell outside the realm of adult supervision, for the children playing these games were not overseen by grown-ups. Therefore, these games are testimony to the ingenuity, imagination, and spontaneity of children, who gradually modified games without resorting to formal play equipment or asking adult permission. Children's games also reveal a child's ability to enforce fair rules and devise winning tactics. These games are also testimony to the power of oral tradition, through which complex game rules are established and disseminated. However, children's games and play in general have changed greatly over the years. Whereas once children in the United Kingdom might play outdoors, they now tend to play inside, partly because of increased traffic and also because of parental fears for children's safety during play and so-called stranger danger—the fear that an unknown person will abduct or harm their child. Another reason for changes in children's play is that the very nature of childhood has changed. A century ago it was common for 12-year-olds to go out to work, and age 14 used to be the school-leaving age. While some rue that children are maturing early, in fact adulthood is deferred as never before, as children do not have to become working adults as early in life as they once did. Today, children in many countries do not have to move straight from childhood to adulthood virtually overnight but can instead enjoy adolescence and often a time at university that bridges the gap between the teenage years and adult life. However, just because youth has been extended does not mean that the games of childhood continue to be played during teenage years. In fact, research has found that in general UK children stop playing childhood games when they reach 11 years of age. This is generally the age at which children move to secondary school, leaving behind childhood and assuming a teen mentality. That said, while it may be apparent that children grow out of playing childhood games earlier than they used to and while the media may suggest that today's children (and adults) are more concerned with playing the latest computer games and watching television than participating in sports and games, it is perhaps a nod to the enduring popularity of old-fashioned leisure activities that children still participate in pastimes such as Pooh-sticks, and some even hold world records for activities such as worm charming (the sport of attracting earthworms from beneath the ground to the surface). Also, in the United Kingdom and elsewhere the increasingly popular vintage trend means that some adults view playing nostalgic childhood games as actually quite trendy. This is evinced by a look at the Etsy Web site in which retro games paraphernalia is available to buy, either as equipment to use in play or fashioned into jewelry, home accessories, and so on.

This book has an encyclopedia format and thus is foremost a reference book that can be used as a general resource to research specific topics by examining the list of entries at the front. In addition, each individual entry can be read as either a stand-alone article or as part of a larger theme, such as ball games, folk games, or sports involving animals. Further, the "See also" section at the end of each entry aims to help the researcher cross-reference material. That said, this book can also be read cover to cover for entertainment, as both the entries and the short sidebar items aim to offer compelling yet informative insight into a wide selection of different sports, games, and activities set within a global context.

Further Reading

Badenhausen, Kurt. "The World's Highest-Paid Athletes 2013: Behind the Numbers." *Forbes,* June 5, 2013, http://www.forbes.com/sites/kurtbadenhausen/2013/06/05/the -worlds-highest-paid-athletes-2013-behind-the-numbers/ (accessed August 4, 2014).

Bale, John. *Sports Geography.* 2nd ed. London: Routledge, 2003.

Blanchard, Kendall. *The Anthropology of Sport: An Introduction.* Revised ed. Westport, CT: Bergin and Garvey, 1995.

Cartwright, Mark. "The Ball Game of Mesoamerica." Ancient History Encyclopedia, September 16, 2013, http://www.ancient.eu.com/article/604/ (accessed July 20, 2014).

Chaplin, Patrick. "Pub Games—The Lifeblood of the English Pub?" The Guardian, August 29, 2011, http://www.theguardian.com/commentisfree/2011/aug/29/pub-games-closures (accessed August 5, 2014).

Coldwell, Will. "London's First Board Game Cafe to Open in Hackney." The Guardian, July 16, 2014, http://www.theguardian.com/travel/2014/jul/16/london-first-board-game -cafe-to-open-in-hackney (accessed August 9, 2014).

Collins, Tony, John Martin, and Wray Vamplew. *Encyclopedia of Traditional British Rural Sports.* Abingdon, UK: Routledge, 2005.

Craig, Steve. *Sports and Games of the Ancients.* Westport, CT: Greenwood, 2002.

Crossingham, John, and Bobbie Kalman. *Extreme Sports.* New York: Crabtree, 2004.

East Midlands Oral History Archive. *Toys and Games: An Oral History.* http://www.le.ac.uk /emoha/schools/pdf/toysandgames.pdf (accessed August 9, 2014).

Jordan, Tom. "Britain's Oldest Pub—Who Deserves the Crown?" CNN Travel, November 11, 2013, http://travel.cnn.com/britains-oldest-pub-which-inn-deserves-crown-740196 (accessed August 10, 2014).

Nauright, John, and Charles Parrish, eds. *Sports around the World: History, Culture and Practice,* Vol. 1, *General Topics, Africa, Asia, Middle East, and Oceania.* Santa Barbara, CA: ABC-CLIO, 2012.

"Pet Population 2013." Pet Food Manufacturers Association, 2010, http://www.pfma.org. uk/pet-population/ (accessed August 8, 2014).

Roud, Steve. *The Lore of the Playground: One Hundred Years of Children's Games, Rhymes & Traditions.* London: Random House, 2010.

Wells, Stephen. "What Goes Around, Comes A-rounders." The Guardian, July 27, 2004, http://www.theguardian.com/sport/2004/jul/27/cricket.comment (accessed August 3, 2014).

"What Is Life Like as a 'Strongman'?" BBC News Magazine, August 7, 2013, http://www .bbc.co.uk/news/magazine-23574005 (accessed August 4, 2014).

Ye Olde Fighting Cocks. "About." Ye Olde Fighting Cocks, http://fightingcocks.fl1hosting. com/staff/ (accessed August 10, 2014).

"Ye Olde Fighting Cocks Public House." Allaboutstalbans.com, 2008–2014, http://www .allaboutstalbans.com/having-fun/nightlife/ye-olde-fighting-cocks-public-house (accessed August 10, 2014).

AUNT SALLY

Aunt Sally is a traditional pub game played between May and September in the counties of Berkshire, Buckinghamshire, Warwickshire, and, most especially, Oxfordshire in southern and central England, with the towns of Abingdon and Oxford particular epicenters of the game. Though Aunt Sally can be played one-on-one, the modern version of the game is usually played by two opposing teams that throw wooden batons at a wooden target from a set distance, typically in the back garden of public houses located in country villages. The game consists of a wooden ball or skittle—that is, a wooden pin as used in a game of skittles or pin bowling—known as a dolly that is about 6 inches tall and 2.75 inches in diameter. The dolly is placed on a hollow metal rod known as the iron or swivel. The iron is driven into the grass playing surface and holds the dolly between 2.5 and 3 feet off the ground, with players aiming to knock the dolly off the iron without hitting the iron. Since large, heavy wooden objects are thrown through the air during a game of Aunt Sally it is necessary to provide protection from the missiles for players and onlookers, so a sheet of PVC, leather, canvas, or other material able to absorb impact is used as a backdrop.

A game of Aunt Sally sees two teams of typically six (but sometimes eight) players take turns to throw six round-ended wooden projectiles roughly 18 inches long and 2 inches in diameter, known as sticks, at the dolly. Players have to throw from behind a line known as the hockey, which is marked 10 yards from the iron. The game is played over three legs, known as horses, with a leg won by the team that scores the highest number of points, or dolls. If the scores are tied after the third and decisive leg, each team can throw three sticks and then one more until a result is achieved. However, Aunt Sally games are often part of a league system so a tie is permitted, with two points awarded for a leg win and one point for a draw. The failure of a player to score in a leg is called a blob, and it is considered extremely embarrassing for a player to fail in three consecutive legs.

The origins of Aunt Sally are unknown, though some authors suggest that the game was invented by King Charles I's Royalist soldiers when they were staying in Oxford during the English Civil War (1642–1651). Another theory proposes that the game is a development of a medieval pastime called club kayles, derived from the French word *quilles,* meaning "skittles." In club kayles, players used an under-arm motion to throw a club-shaped skittle at a larger, differently shaped skittle. A third theory is that Aunt Sally is a humane development of the blood sport of throwing at cocks, in which a cock was tethered by one leg to a stake driven into the ground, and players paid to take it in turns to throw small clubs known as cok-steles at the bird. If the bird's leg was broken before it died, it would be propped up and so remain a target. The player who killed the bird was declared the winner, and the prize was to take the bird home to cook. By 1801, the live cock had been replaced by a wooden replica at which players paid to aim.

The heyday of Aunt Sally came during the reign of Queen Victoria (1838–1901). The first written reference to the game dates back to the mid-19th century, when Aunt Sally was played as a popular parlor game and was also a fairground attraction akin to the traditional coconut shy. In Victorian times the dolly was usually painted to look like an old black woman, often with a clay pipes hanging from her mouth, nose, and ears. In this instance, the aim of the game was either to break the pipes or knock them from the dolly's face. An interesting alternative version of the wooden dolly was employed at large social gatherings such as the Derby Day horse-racing meeting, where a woman's head made of rags was used and players aimed to remove a pipe from the face. It has been suggested that this was intended as a deterrent to women smokers.

By the 1930s, the offensive racist and misogynistic overtones had been removed from Aunt Sally as rural pub teams began to compete in leagues, though why and how the transition from funfair attraction to pub game took place is uncertain. The earliest written reference to Aunt Sally as a pub game can be found in the records of the Oxford Aunt Sally League dating from World War II. The impact of the war can be seen in these records, as they show that no game took place between 1939 and 1941, though from 1942 onward no years were missed.

Today there are around 120 teams divided into 12 sectors affiliated to the Oxford and District Aunt Sally Association, with up to 1,400 players registered to play. This makes Aunt Sally one of the most geographically concentrated sports or games in the world. However, at the same time it is noteworthy that several English universities boast Aunt Sally teams, including the northern universities of Leeds Metropolitan and Sheffield Hallam, the centrally located Cambridge University, and Reading and Bournemouth Universities in the south of the country. That these universities range throughout England suggests that Aunt Sally's popularity may continue to spread. Such student participation also suggests that Aunt Sally will continue to be played by future generations.

The inaugural World Aunt Sally Open Singles Championship took place in Oxfordshire in 2011 during the Charlbury Beer Festival, thus highlighting that these days Aunt Sally is essentially a pub game. British prime minister David Cameron opened the event by throwing the first stick, and over 3,000 spectators watched it as part of a festival that also featured traditional English folk music and Morris dancing. Thirty-two top league players battled for the title of world champion, and the winner, Trevor Dyer, received £100. Dyer's win proved controversial, as he did not live in Oxfordshire but rather in the neighboring county of Gloucestershire.

In England the term "Aunt Sally" is used to denote a person or thing that has been established as the target of abuse, blame, or criticism. In political circles it refers to something used to deflect attention from another issue. In British popular culture, the name "Aunt Sally" is particularly associated with a character from the classic children's television show *Worzel Gummidge* (1979–1981). In the program Aunt Sally is the living personification of a rosy-cheeked fairground dolly wearing a floral dress and bonnet who considers herself to be superior to her would-be lover, Worzel, who is a lowly scarecrow.

See also: Bunnock; Dwile Flonking; *Kyykkä; Mölkky;* Skittles

Further Reading

Ayton, Eric G. *Clay Tobacco Pipes*. Princes Risborough, UK: Shire Publications, 2002.

Bradley, Lloyd. *The Rough Guide to Cult Sport*. London: Rough Guides, 2011.

CNIASL. "World Singles Champion." CNIASL, 2011, http://www.chippyauntsally.co.uk /the-world-singles-champion/4553584603 (accessed July 12, 2013).

Cotswolds Info. "Aunt Sally Game." Cotswolds Info, 2005–2014, http://www.cotswolds .info/strange-things/aunt-sally-game.shtml (accessed July 11, 2013).

Elsfield Village. "Aunt Sally." Elsfield Village, http://www.elsfield.net/history/elsfield-in-the -20th-century/aunt-sally-1/aunt-sally-3 (accessed July 12, 2013).

Masters, James. "Aunt Sally." The Online Guide to Traditional Games, 1997–2014, http:// www.tradgames.org.uk/games/Aunt-Sally.htm (accessed July 11, 2013).

Oxford & District Aunt Sally Association. "Home Page." Oxford & District Aunt Sally Association, http://www.oxfordauntsally.co.uk (accessed July 12, 2013).

AUSSIE RULES FOOTBALL

Aussie Rules Football, known colloquially as footy and more properly as Australian Football, is a contact ball game played by two teams of 18 players on the playing field and 4 interchange players who may be swapped for any player on the field at any time. Although Aussie Rules is related to rugby and Gaelic football, the sport is undeniably Australian and is played in every Australian state. However, Aussie Rules has yet to become popular in other countries. Aussie Rules teams are made up of males or females, from around the age of six upward, and the sport is played at all levels from amateur to professional. The Australian Football League (AFL) is the highest level of Aussie Rules competition.

An Aussie Rules match consists of four 20-minute quarters with time added on to the end of each quarter for the amount of time the ball has been out of play during that quarter—usually between 5 and 10 minutes. There is a 10-minute break between the first and third quarters and a 20-minute break at halftime for which all the players leave the field. In total, an Aussie Rules game lasts around two hours. During the two hours an unlimited number of interchanges of players may occur. Indeed, it is common for 100 interchanges to take place per game.

The match is officiated by three field umpires who start play, award marks, and enforce rules; two goal umpires who judge and record all match scores; and two boundary umpires who determine when the ball is out of play. The umpires are assigned the role of villain during the match, and as such it is traditional for spectators to boo the umpires as the officials leave the pitch.

Aussie Rules is played either on a specific Aussie Rules ground that is oval in shape, on a modified cricket pitch, or on any other suitably sized sports ground.

Formula 1 drivers Adrian Sutil and Christijan Albers play Aussie Rules Football in South Melbourne, Australia, on March 13, 2007. Aussie Rules Football is a contact ball game similar to rugby and Gaelic football that is played by males and females in every Australian state. (AP Photo/Oliver Multhaup)

The sport is unusual, for it does not require grounds to be uniform in size. The playing field for an Aussie Rules game may have a width of 110 to 155 meters (around 120 to 170 yards) and a length of between 135 and 185 meters (roughly 145 and 200 yards).

A match begins when the field umpire bounces the ball in the center of the field and players jump in order to knock the ball downfield to a teammate. The aim of the game is to move the ball, which like the pitch is also oval and weighs 450 to 480 grams (between 16 and 17 ounces), down the field of play and kick the ball through the goal toward which the ball is being maneuvered. The goalposts are not less than 20 feet in height, and a line painted on the field between the goalposts is called the goal line. The goalposts are placed at each end of the pitch, and to the side of each goalpost are shorter posts called behind posts. The section of the goal line that extends to the behind posts is known as the behind line.

The traditional player formation sees five lines of three players extend from one end of the field to the other. Players located closest to the goal they are defending are known as the backs, while those attacking the opposing team's goal are called forwards. The players in between the backs and the forwards follow the play, though recently a more fluid, less structured formation has gained popularity. The quick pace of Aussie Rules demands that players in general possess great aerobic

capacity as well as stamina, agility, coordination, and quick thinking. The physiological demands faced by players do, however, depend on which position that
player holds—backs and forwards tend to perform lots of short sprints, while on-
ball players can cover up to 12 miles per game, with the distance made up of walking, running, and sprinting.

The principal method of scoring points in Aussie Rules is for a member of the
attacking side to score a goal by kicking the ball through the goalposts. A goal is
worth six points. One point is scored by a behind. A behind occurs when the ball
crosses a behind line or when the ball crosses the goal line without meeting all the
requirements for a goal to be scored; for example, if the ball touches a goalpost.
After a goal is scored the ball is bounced in the center of the playing arena (as it is
at the start of the game), while when a behind is scored the team against whom the
behind was awarded is allowed to kick the ball into play from its own goal. An
Aussie Rules score is written in a distinctive way, with the number of goals scored
noted first, then the number of behinds, and then the total number of points
scored. The numbers are separated by colons. The team that scores the highest
number of points by the end of the game is declared the winner. If scores are even
at the end of the game, then a draw is declared.

Aussie Rules predates other modern football games, as the sport was the first to
introduce an official code of play, and the world's oldest football clubs, Melbourne
and Geelong, founded in 1858 and 1859, respectively, are Aussie Rules clubs. The
sport originated in Melbourne, Southern Australia, and was at first known as Melbourne Rules Football or Victorian Rules Football after Victoria, the state in which
Melbourne is located. Indeed, the AFL was originally called the Victorian Football
League. Aussie Rules was invented in 1858 by a cricketer named Thomas Went-
worth Wills. Wills was born in Australia but had been educated at Rugby School in
England. Wanting a way to keep himself and his teammates fit during cricket's winter off-season, he created Aussie Rules as an amalgam of various ball sports played
in English public schools. Wills put his suggestion for a new sport to the Melbourne
Cricket Club, which agreed with Wills that the game would be a good way to keep
players active during the winter and appointed a committee to create a standardized
set of rules for the new game. On May 17, 1859, the committee ratified a code of
play that was a combination of the football games played at Winchester, Harrow,
and Rugby public schools. The popularity of Aussie Rules grew rapidly during the
1870s, with matches drawing crowds in excess of 10,000 paying spectators, and in
1876 the first facility was constructed specifically for Aussie Rules on land leased
from Melbourne University. With the increase in interest in the sport came increasingly large crowds so that by the mid-1880s, matches attracted audiences of more
than 30,000.

In 1866 H. C. A. Harrison, Wills's cousin, rewrote the rules to say that there
should be no limit on the number of players in a game, and then in the 1880s this
rule was changed so that 20 players per side became the norm. It soon became evident that players were worried that landing on the hard, sunbaked Australian soil
might result in injury and so were reluctant to tackle. Therefore, a rule was introduced outlawing the deliberate kicking or tripping of an opponent, a characteristic

of the Rugby School game called hacking. Today Aussie Rules remains a contact sport in which players may tackle members of the opposing team using their hands and are permitted to obstruct the opposition using their own bodies. Aussie Rules allows greater body contact than Association Football (soccer) but less contact than American football or rugby. Players are allowed to shepherd or check opponents using hip, shoulder, hand, chest, or arm as long as the ball is closer than 16 feet from the player who is checked. However, play that is considered to be deliberately dangerous, such as pushing a player in the back, is illegal and is punished by awarding free kicks or distance penalties or, as a more severe punishment, suspension for a fixed number of games. Free kicks are awarded if a player tackles an opponent in the back, above the shoulders, or below the knees. Interfering with marking and deliberately slowing down the game are also punishable offenses, as the fast pace of the game and fierce marking are the main attributes of the game.

Samoa Rules

Samoa Rules, a combination of Aussie Rules Football and Rugby Union and governed by the Samoa Australian Rules Football Association (SARFA), is played on the South Pacific island nation of Samoa. Game rules are very similar to those of Aussie Rules, though each team consists of 15 players as in rugby union (5 forwards, 5 backs, and 5 onballers) and is played on a rugby pitch rather than an oval field. Players are restricted to certain zones except for the onballers, who play anywhere on the field. Kicking is encouraged, as players may only bounce the ball once while running.

Soon after Aussie Rules was invented, it began to evolve into a sport distinct from the games from which it originated. One of the major distinctions between Aussie Rules and other football games is the provision that players who catch the ball in the air from the kick of a player who is not less than 15 meters (about 50 feet) away, a move called a mark, are awarded a free kick. A mark is one of only two instances in a game of Aussie Rules in which possession of the ball is undisputed, for during an Aussie Rules match both teams constantly vie for possession of the ball. The player who makes the mark is allowed to kick the ball at the goal, without interference from the opposing team, from anywhere behind the spot where the mark occurred. A high mark occurs when three or four competing players leap together to catch the ball and thus claim a free kick. A high mark is considered the most spectacular move in Aussie Rules. The only other time possession of the ball is undisputed is when a free kick is awarded for illegal play. Another key distinction between Aussie Rules Football and other similar sports is that Aussie Rules does not have an offside rule.

In modern Aussie Rules, players may use any part of the marked pitch and move the ball with any part of their body, though kicking, handballing, and running with the ball are the most frequently used ways of moving the ball downfield. Handballing sees a player hold the ball in one hand and hit it with the clenched fist of the opposite hand. When running with the ball, a player must touch it to the ground or bounce it at least every 15 meters (50 feet). This is in contrast to the sport's early rules, which stated that the ball must touch the ground around every 33 feet. If a player running with the ball is caught by an opponent, the ball must be disposed of immediately. Also, players must not throw the ball or be caught while in possession of the ball.

The sport's most prestigious competition is the AFL, which culminates in the AFL Grand Final. The AFL season starts in March and ends in August and consists of 22 matches leading up to a month of finals in September. Games tend to be played on weekends, with junior and reserve matches played before the main games. The AFL Finals is Australia's most popular sporting competition in terms of both attendance at matches and the number of people watching on television. In order to maintain a high level of interest in Aussie Rules in the future, the AFL has launched the Auskick program. Auskick aims to interest children and their parents in Aussie Rules by teaching children the skills needed to play the game at school and at club level, with parents acting as coaches and volunteer coordinators.

See also: Cricket; Eton Wall Game; Rugby League; Yabbie Races

Further Reading

"Australian Football (AFL) for Kids." Active Activities, http://www.activeactivities.com.au /directory/category/sports/ball-sports/aussie-rules-afl/article-australian-football-afl -for-kids-24.html (accessed May 4, 2014).

"Australian Rules Football." Australian Sports Commission, 2014, http://www.ausport.gov. au/ais/nutrition/factsheets/sports/australian_rules_football (accessed July 29, 2013).

"Australian Rules Football." BBC, 2002, http://news.bbc.co.uk/dna/place-lancashire/plain /A812639 (accessed July 29, 2013).

Blainey, Geoffrey. *A Game of Our Own: The Origins of Australian Football.* Melbourne: Black, 2003.

Harvey, Darryl. "Frequently Asked Questions." Footy Tipping Software, 1998, http://www .footy.com.au/dags/FAQ1v1-5.html (accessed September 15, 2013).

Stewart, Bob, Matthew Nicholson, Aaron Smith, and Hans Westerbeek. *Australian Sport: Better by Design? The Evolution of Australian Sporting Policy.* Abingdon, UK: Routledge, 2004.

B

BANDY

Bandy, also known as banty or bandy ball and sometimes referred to as winter soccer, is a stick and ball game played on ice outdoors between two teams of 11 men or women players that combines elements of ice hockey, field hockey, and soccer. The sport is particularly popular in Scandinavia, Russia, the Balkan region of Eastern Europe, and Mongolia and is also played in the United States, Ukraine, and Japan. The name "bandy" derives from the Teutonic word *bandja,* meaning "curved stick," and is used to refer to both the sport and the stick used in the game. Bandy is governed by the International Bandy Federation, which was founded in 1955.

Bandy is very similar to shinty and field hockey. Indeed, during the 18th and 19th centuries in Britain, the terms "bandy" and "field hockey" were interchangeable. Bandy is also seen as the precursor of ice hockey, with the two main differences being that bandy is played on a frozen field about the size of a soccer field rather than inside on a rink and that, instead of a puck, bandy employs a bouncing ball roughly the size of a tennis ball that is made of cork and plastic and is brightly colored in order to be visible against the ice playing surface. There is also a strong similarity between bandy and soccer, for as in soccer, bandy teams consist of 11 players, with 5 players available as substitutes, and each team seeks to maneuver the ball toward the opposing side's goal, which measures 7 feet by 11 feet. In bandy, players move the ball by dribbling, passing, and striking it in order to score, and teams aim to score more goals than they concede. A game of bandy, like a soccer match, is divided into two halves lasting 45 minutes, with a short break between the halves. Scores may be tied at the end of a bandy game unless the match is a championship decider, in which case, as in a championship-deciding game of soccer, two 15-minute periods of extra time are played with the possibility of a sudden-death period if scores remain even.

Bandy players, like soccer players, are divided into three types: forwards, who seek to score goals; midfield players, who both dispossess the opposition and keep possession of the ball; and defenders, who try to prevent the opposition from scoring. A bandy match, like a soccer game, is officiated by a referee and up to two assistants, and in general the rules are the same as the rules of soccer, with an offside rule, corners, penalties, goal throws (as opposed to the goal kicks found in soccer), and free strokes (as opposed to free kicks) for rule infringements. There are, however, two major differences between bandy and soccer. First, no tackling is permitted in bandy (though a player may challenge an opponent), so it is forbidden to push, kick, hold, or trip members of the opposition or to raise

Players vie for control of the ball in a gold medal deciding match between Russia and Sweden during the Bandy World Championships held in Kazakhstan on February 5, 2012. Bandy is a game similar to field hockey that is also viewed as a forerunner of ice hockey. (AP Photo/Pavel Mekheyev)

the bandy stick above shoulder height. If a player flouts this rule repeatedly during a match, then the player is expelled from the game. The strict enforcement of the no tackling rule means that incidents of injury playing bandy are roughly half that of ice hockey. The other major difference between bandy and soccer is that in bandy, goalkeepers may not touch the ball with their arms, hands, or head despite being the only member of a bandy team not equipped with a stick.

The roots of bandy reach back to ancient times, for the ancient Egyptians, Romans, and Greeks all played sports similar to bandy, while 9th-century Icelandic literature refers to a similar game called *knattlekr*. However, the actual sport of bandy itself originated in Britain, though quite when is unknown. A 13th-century stained glass window at Canterbury Cathedral, in southeast England, depicts a boy holding a curved stick and a ball that appears very similar to the type of stick and ball used in bandy. In the 16th century in the counties of Devon and Wiltshire, southwestern England, bandy was played on Palm Sunday, though in these areas the game was played differently, for in Devon and Wiltshire men and boys would endeavor to hit the ball up a hill rather than toward a goal. Bandy was also played in the eastern English counties of Suffolk and Norfolk at this time, though in Suffolk the game was known as hawkey and in Norfolk as bandy-hoshoe. Later in the same century William Shakespeare referred to the sport in his play *Romeo and Juliet* (first published in 1597).

During the 18th and 19th centuries a form of bandy was played in eastern England on the flat, low-lying areas of marsh known as the Fens, with the bandy stick made from extremely hard wood or metal or from animal horn or hoof and the ball fashioned from a tree trunk or from rubber. Local teams would use a ball to play a variation of field hockey when the Fens froze in winter, thus creating the game of bandy. During the 19th century frozen village greens were also used as bandy pitches. This was particularly true in the eastern counties of Lincolnshire and Cambridgeshire. In the county of Nottinghamshire in central England, bandy was so popular that in 1865 the Nottingham Forrest Football and Bandy Club was founded, highlighting the similarity between bandy and soccer. Later the club would be renamed Nottingham Forrest Football Club and go on to become a championship winning soccer team. The 1860s also saw the export of bandy to Canada, for in 1867 British troops played bandy in Ontario—this event would eventually lead to the development of ice hockey.

In 1891 the National Bandy Association of Britain was founded, and a Cambridgeshire resident, James Tebbutt, established the formal rules of the sport. Tebbutt then decided to travel across Northern Europe in the hope of popularizing the game. That same year the first international bandy match took place between the English team Bury Fen Club and the Dutch team Haarlem. In 1894 Tebbutt traveled from the Netherlands to Sweden, and the sport achieved a foothold in Scandinavia. Indeed, by 1926 there were over 200 bandy clubs in Sweden, and by 2003 there were over 500 Swedish teams. Bandy was introduced to Russia in 1898 and quickly became popular, with the sport occasionally challenging soccer as the country's favorite team game. In Russia, bandy is often played in extremely cold weather. One standout instance of this came during the 1999 world championship held in Arkhangelsk, northwestern Russia, when temperatures dipped to –37°F. Such was the intensity of the cold that championship matches had to be played over three periods of 30 minutes rather than the standard format of two lengthy halves. Russian winters are so cold that in Russia, spectators used to drink copious amounts of alcohol in order to keep warm during matches. However, Russian authorities have banned the consumption of alcohol at matches, and subsequently attendance figures for bandy matches have dropped significantly from the 50,000 who often attended games during the Soviet era (1922–1990). One Russian team, Dynamo Moscow, plays matches indoors, but this too is unpopular, drawing crowds of only a few hundred, as Russians feel that the indoor version of the sport is inferior.

During the 19th century bandy was also introduced to Denmark, Germany, and Switzerland, though the game did not thrive in these countries and eventually died out. The popularity of bandy came to an end in England too, mainly due to a lack of sufficiently cold winters to freeze the Fens, and the sport never became hugely popular in the United States because of the popularity of ice hockey, though an urban version of the sport played on dry ground, street hockey, is played in America.

The first major bandy tournament to be held was the European Championships that took place in 1913 in which teams from Austria, Belgium, England, France, Germany, Italy, Holland, and Switzerland competed. The tournament was won by

England. However, the outbreak of World War I put an end to the development of bandy as a Europe-wide sport. The bandy world championships began in 1957 and ever since have been dominated by Sweden and Russia. This is partly because for many years only four teams took part in the tournament—Russia, Sweden, Finland, and Norway—with the United States participating since the mid-1980s. In bandy world championships history, Russian and Soviet teams have won 21 gold medals, Sweden has won 11, and Finland has won 1. Since the breakup of the Soviet Union, Kazakhstan has become a leading bandy-playing nation and has fielded a number of formerly Russian players.

The popularity of bandy in Scandinavia, the Balkans, and Russia means that there have been attempts to include bandy in the Winter Olympic Games. However, though bandy was included as a demonstration sport at the Oslo Olympics of 1952, the sport has yet to achieve official medal status, as the number of bandy-playing nations is too small to meet the International Olympic Committee's requirements.

See also: Aussie Rules Football; Curling; *Glima; Kubb; Lapta;* Shinty; Synchronized Skating; Underwater Hockey

Further Reading

Burchell, Helen. "A Handy Bandy Guide." BBC, April 2008, http://www.bbc.co.uk/cambrid geshire/content/articles/2006/02/15/bandy_sport_feature.shtml (accessed October 27, 2013).

Collins, Tony, John Martin, and Wray Vamplew, eds. *Encyclopedia of Traditional British Rural Sports.* Abingdon, UK: Routledge, 2005.

Crego, Robert. *Sports and Games of the 18th and 19th Centuries.* Westport, CT: Greenwood, 2003.

Levinson, David, and Karen Christensen, eds. *Encyclopedia of World Sport: From Ancient Times to the Present.* Oxford: Oxford University Press, 1996.

Trisvyatsky, Ilya. "Bandy: A Concise History of the Extreme Sport." Russia beyond the Headlines, February 14, 2013, http://rbth.co.uk/arts/sport/2013/02/14/bandy_a _concise_history_of_the_extreme_sport_22867.html (accessed January 7, 2014).

BARREL RACES

Competitive barrel races are informal endurance events for individuals and teams in which competitors roll or carry a barrel along a set route with the aim of being the first to complete the course. Barrel races take place in the United Kingdom, France, Italy, and the United States.

Several barrel-rolling events are held in the United Kingdom, particularly as a folk calendar custom, that is, events that happen on certain dates each year. One such event is the Hedley Barrel Race. Every Easter Monday in the village of Hedley on the Hill in Northumberland, northern England, an exhausting barrel race is held in which teams of three carry an empty nine–imperial gallon metal beer barrel over a steep uphill course 1.5 miles in length, journeying through fields as they go. The finishing line is marked on the road outside the Feathers pub, and the winning team gets a nine-gallon barrel filled with ale. In 2008 18 teams of three participants competed, with the winning team of three men completing the course in 9 minutes

35 seconds. A barrel race in which the barrels are rolled rather than carried is also part of the Westleton Barrel Fair in the village of Westleton in Suffolk, an annual event that began in 1951 as part of the Westleton Carnival. Originally the barrels used in the race were wooden and were pushed down the town's main street, which proved quite dangerous when the barrels went out of control. Subsequent races saw aluminum barrels pushed up the street, which proved much safer. Another annual barrel race is the race held in Grantchester near Cambridge in eastern England, the village said to have the world's highest concentration of Nobel Prize winners. The Grantchester race traditionally takes place on December 26, the national holiday known as Boxing Day in the United Kingdom. The race was first held during the 1960s, only to go into hiatus until it was revived in 2003. Since then the event has grown in popularity and now attracts spectators from as far afield as the United States and South Korea. In the Grantchester race, teams from four of the village's pubs (color-coded red, blue, green, and yellow) compete at rolling a whiskey barrel specially imported from the Orkney Islands in Scotland along the 100-meter (328-foot) course lined with hay bales in a relay race format. This barrel race is then followed by the county championships barrel race in which the winning Grantchester team takes on three other teams, one from each of Grantchester's neighboring villages of Barton, Coton, and Newnham. This intervillage race sees competing teams roll their barrel up and down Grantchester's high street in a relay race. In total the races take about 40 minutes to complete.

Carrying Flaming Barrels

The custom of carrying flaming barrels occurs in various parts of Britain. One of the most celebrated events occurs each November in Ottery St. Mary in Devon, England. The occasion sees 17 flaming barrels, ranging in size from small to large, carried on the shoulders of participants, known as barrel rollers, from afternoon to night. Barrels are set alight at various pubs and hotels around the town, and the final barrel is brought into the town square at midnight. Similar November events in southern England take place in Hatherleigh, Devon, and Lewes, Sussex.

In France, competitors at events such as the Bordeaux Wine Festival Competitive Barrel Rolling transport wine barrels rather than beer barrels. The Bordeaux event is organized by the Lussac Saint-Emilion Club in order to symbolize the skill of local barrel makers. Similarly, wine barrels are raced in a contest held annually at 7:00 p.m. on the last Sunday in August in Montepulciano, Italy. The race has changed significantly since it began, for in its earliest days the barrels were maneuvered by riders on horseback. This changed in 1974 so that today the barrels, which weigh 80 kilograms (176 pounds), are rolled around the town by eight teams of two men. The size and weight of the barrels means that this race is a contest of strength as well as speed. During the race the barrels are rolled uphill for about 1 kilometer (3,281 feet) through the picturesque streets of the historic town center until they reach the end of the course in the Piazza Grande. Race winners are awarded the Bravio, a painted cloth bearing the image of San Giovanni De-collato, the town's patron saint.

Barrel races in the United States include the annual charity Barrel to Keg Relay held in Oregon each July that is now in its fourth year. The race features teams of two to seven runners that split the 69-mile distance into 14 legs, plus teams of two to seven walkers who divide the course into 7 legs. Solo ultramarathon runners also take part. The barrel race starts at the Harris Bridge Vineyard in Philomath and then continues along the Oregon Coast Range, crosses the Yaquina Bay Bridge, and ends at the Rogue Ales Brewery at Newport's South Beach Marina.

Barrels also feature in the sport of keg tossing, a highlight of the World's Strongest Man contest. In this event competitors pitch squat metal barrels of varying weights over a high barrier employing a specific technique. The keg toss is based on the weight-for-height event that makes up part of the Highland Games and sees competitors rely on a combination of technique and explosive power to toss several kegs over a fixed height in the fastest possible time. Strongman athletes adopt a variety of different techniques to toss the kegs. Some hold the barrels horizontally, others hold them vertically (this technique is better suited to taller competitors), and a keg can be tossed one-handed if a competitor wishes to show off. The world record for the highest keg toss is 7.30 meters (almost 24 feet). However, keg toss records achieved at strongman events are sparse, since competitions are not sufficiently standardized to allow for official records to be established. At the World's Strongest Man Competition Finals of 2012 the kegs used in the keg toss event ranged in weight from 40 to 55 pounds, and the event was won by four-time World's Strongest Man champion Zydrunas Savickas, who tossed eight kegs in 19.12 seconds.

See also: Highland Games; Ultramarathons; Wife Carrying

Further Reading

"Block/Keg Toss." The World's Strongest Man, July 4, 2011, http://www.theworldsstrong-estman.com/individual-event/block-keg-toss/ (accessed July 1, 2014).

Brown, Raymond. "Blues Sweep Grantchester's Boxing Day as Hundreds Flock to Event." Cambridge News, December 26, 2013, http://www.cambridge-news.co.uk/News /Blues-sweep-Grantchesters-Boxing-Day-as-hundreds-flock-to-event-201312261401 26.htm (accessed July 1, 2014).

CafTours.com. "Barrels of Fun in Montepulciano!" *CAF Magazine,* August 20, 2013, http:// www.caftours.com/magazine/barrels-fun-montepulciano/ (accessed July 1, 2014).

Community Services Consortium. "Barrel to Keg Relay—July 12, 2014." Community Services Consortium, 2014, http://www.communityservices.us/barrel-to-keg/ (accessed July 1, 2014).

Coulter, David. "Easter Offers a Barrel of Laughs." *Hexham Courant,* March 26, 2008, http:// www.hexhamcourant.co.uk/news/2.2978/easter-offers-a-barrel-of-laughs-1.61434# (accessed August 1, 2014).

"The History of the Barrel Fair." Westleton Barrel Fair, http://www.westletonbarrelfair.com /history.htm (accessed August 1, 2014).

"Keg Toss." Strongman.org, 2014, http://www.strongman.org/events/keg-toss/ (accessed August 1, 2014).

Shepherd, A. C. "Hedley Barrel Race." Calendar Customs, 2010, http://calendarcustoms
.com/articles/hedley-barrel-race/ (accessed August 1, 2014).

Winter, Gregor. "2012 World's Strongest Man Keg Toss." All Things Gym, September 28,
2012, http://www.allthingsgym.com/2012-worlds-strongest-man-keg-toss-mikhail-
koklyaev/ (accessed July 1, 2014).

BEARBAITING AND BADGER BAITING

Bearbaiting is a blood sport in which a captive bear is tormented and attacked by a pack of dogs. This form of bearbaiting is not related to the method of bear hunting called bearbaiting that occurs in many areas of the United States. The sport also takes place in rural Pakistan, despite the activity being banned. Indeed, in the face of the continued existence of bearbaiting in Pakistan, the country's then-president, Pervez Musharraf, issued a decree in 2001 calling for the enforcement of the existing ban on bearbaiting, thereby reinforcing Pakistan's Prevention of Cruelty Act. Bearbaiting also occurs in the Ukraine and Russia.

Bearbaiting has a very long history. The sport was introduced to England from Italy during the 12th century, with one of the earliest accounts of the sport documenting a bearbaiting event held in Leicestershire, central England, in 1183. Though a very popular pastime in medieval England, bearbaiting was a fairly rare occurrence because bears were no longer native to Britain, so every bear had to be imported for bouts. The need to import bears gave the sport an air of exoticism that eventually led to it attracting royal patronage with Queen Elizabeth I (1533–1603), said to have attended an event featuring 12 bears held in London, England's capital city, in 1575. The queen also created an official appointment, the "Master of the Bears." Indeed, during the 16th century bearbaiting became the height of fashion in London, with baiting arenas, such as the Bear Garden, built in the borough of Southwark, and the Paris Garden, which in 1583 saw the grandstand holding over 1,000 spectators collapse, with many spectators injured or killed. However, bearbaiting did face opposition from Puritan critics who deplored the fact that good Christians could enjoy the spectacle of animals fighting against each other, while fans of other sports, such as archery, worried that the popularity of bearbaiting might lead to diminished interest in other pastimes and the subsequent extinction of some sports.

During the 17th century views on bearbaiting began to change in England, and during the Great Plague of 1665, when deadly and highly infectious bubonic plague swept through England, the sport began to decline, as public gatherings were cancelled to prevent the plague from spreading. Also during the century, it became increasingly expensive to import bears for fights, as the animals were becoming rare across Europe. During the 18th century the sport attracted criticism from moral reformers for two reasons. First, critics felt that bearbaiting was cruel to animals and therefore conflicted with Christian values. Second, reformers worried that the sport was associated with immorality and would ultimately have a detrimental effect on the working classes. Bearbaiting participants clashed with reformers during the 18th and 19th centuries, but ultimately the reformers prevailed, with the sport banned under the Cruelty to Animals Act of 1835, alongside cockfighting and dogfighting. By this time bearbaiting had largely fallen out of fashion, as spectators preferred human blood sports such as boxing. Also, there was a general consensus that as the bear used in bearbaiting did not have a so-called sporting chance, the sport went against the British ideal of fair play.

Until it was outlawed, public bearbaiting competitions known by participants as bear bays were known to take place in Spartanburg, Hickory Grove, and Travelers Rest in South Carolina, with backyard events reported to occur throughout rural areas of northwestern South Carolina throughout the year. According to an investigation by the Humane Society of the United States, bear-baying events in South Carolina saw captive black bears set upon by teams of dogs. Prior to a bout, a bear would have its claws and teeth either removed or filed down. During the fight the bear was tethered to a stake in the corner of a fenced area so that it was unable to defend itself and had little freedom of movement as one to three dogs bayed at the bear simultaneously. In theory, when the dogs bayed at the bear it means that the dogs barked at the bear, make eye contact with it, and generally worry the larger animal. However, in actuality in bearbaiting displays the dogs torment the bear by jumping and biting. This behavior can go on for as long as four hours, with the bear having to face around 300 dogs in total. In South Carolina bear-baying events, teams of dogs competed at keeping the bear at bay, or in place. The owners of the dogs that were rated highest on their ability to keep the bear at bay were awarded trophies and sometimes cash prizes. Meanwhile, the bear was forced to fight in other bays throughout the year.

Bearbaiting was introduced to Pakistan by British colonizers during the 19th century, when the country was still part of India. In Pakistan there are estimated to be fewer than 300 Asiatic black bears living in the wild. For the purposes of bearbaiting, adult bears are killed and the cubs are sold to Gypsies, who then force them to fight specially trained dogs at around 50 events during the period November–April. Fights, which are hosted by landlords in rural areas, last for three minutes, and the aim of each fight is to see whether one of the two trained dogs can force the bear to roll over. The dog usually succeeds, as prior to the fight the bear will (usually) have had its teeth and claws removed, and during the bout the bear is tied to a stake and is therefore helpless and trapped as the dogs attack. However, the bears rarely die but do suffer horrific bite wounds and other injuries to their ears and muzzles. According to the World Society for the Protection of Animals (WSPA), Pakistani bearbaiting events, which are often part of annual village festivals such as that in Shah Jewiena in the Jhang district of Punjab Province, can consist of 20 fights involving 30 bears and over 100 dogs. The WSPA has spent more than £100,000 (US$150,000) on the construction of a sanctuary for rescued bears at Kund Park, in the North-West Frontier Province of Pakistan.

There are thought to be around four to six bearbaiting events in the Ukraine per year, with 15 to 20 brown bears used in baiting events, such as that held near Vinnytsia, central Ukraine. According to the animal welfare group Four Paws, despite the fact that in the Ukraine brown bears are officially protected by law, wild bear cubs are snatched from their mothers at just a few months old. The cubs' claws are removed, and they are housed in small cages, with the only time the bears are allowed out of the cages being when they are training or for fights. It has also been claimed that the bears are kept deliberately undernourished to keep them weak. During a Ukrainian bearbaiting display several dogs attack the chained bear simultaneously, while the bear's movements are limited by several men tugging on its chain. Trophies are awarded to the owner of the most aggressive dogs in the competition. Meanwhile in Russia, the *laika* breed of dog is used in a contest that includes bearbaiting for a *laika* can prove its pedigree by taking part in hunting tests, including the hunting of captive bears. This form of bearbaiting dates back to the late 19th century. Today a 100-point scoring system is used by trained judges to assess dogs on grounds of courage (worth up to 20 points), skill (15 points), aggression (30 points), and so on. Russia's captive bearbaiting takes place at designated grounds and features adult male bears weighing 80 kilograms (12.5 stones). The bear is tied to a line, and the dogs' owners are not allowed to encourage their animals to attack.

In Russia, dogs including *laikas* are also assessed by a scoring system on their ability to hunt captive badgers that are released into paddocks into which are placed the hunting dogs. This is not strictly speaking badger baiting, as the badger is not tethered or otherwise prevented from moving. Traditionally there are two forms of badger baiting: one in which a badger is tied by its tail to a stake driven into the ground so that it cannot escape while it is attacked by dogs and another in which a badger is placed inside a box and a dog is sent out to fight it. The sport takes place illegally in the United Kingdom, despite being banned under the Cruelty to Animals Act of 1835 and the Badgers Act of 1973 that was enacted with the specific intention of protecting badgers. Indeed, since the late 1990s there has been an upsurge in badger baiting across England and Scotland. Today, however, additional forms of badger baiting have evolved. One sees a declawed badger thrown into a pit to fight against hunting terriers. A second innovation sees a badger dug from its sett by dog owners and thrown to the dogs, often bull lurchers or terriers, that then play tug-o-war with the badger. This not only causes serious harm or death to the badger but can also lead to the dogs receiving severe injuries to their lower jaws, lips, nose, and teeth. Despite the potential for injury to their own animals, the dogs' owners see the fight as a form of competition that determines whose dog is the strongest and fiercest. Those found guilty of badger baiting in the United Kingdom face prosecution under the Protection of Badgers Act of 1992. However, whereas the illegality of baiting used to mean that the sport was arranged by word of mouth, today participants use social media and cell phones to broadcast news of upcoming baiting meets and post graphic pictures of their trophies. This can, however, work against dog owners, as a number of participants have been convicted on the strength of images found on computers and the like.

Meanwhile, a new trend in blood sports in the United Kingdom is cat coursing, in which pet cats are stolen and pitted against fighting dogs, with the outcome that the dogs always win. In Scotland, cats have been forced into trash cans to fight against dogs, with the result that the dog becomes used to killing and being injured and also discovers a bloodlust that makes it want to fight again. It is believed that 15 pet cats have been snatched from a single neighborhood in Blackburn in northern England in order to feed this new and increasingly popular underground sport. An alternative version of cat coursing sees specially trained dogs hunt pet cats close to the cat's home. In Darlington in northeastern England in 2011, groups of lurcher owners were witnessed throwing their dogs over garden fences to track and kill pet cats, resulting in several pets being maimed, killed, or having to be euthanized because of the severity of their injuries.

See also: Bull Running; *Buzkashi;* Camel and Yak Racing; Camel Wrestling; Cockfighting; Cotswold Olimpicks; Elephant Sports; Foxhunting; Hare Coursing; Nonlethal Bullfighting; *Pato* and Horseball; Pigeon Racing; Sheepdog Trials; Spanish Bullfighting; Yabbie Races

Further Reading

"Badger Baiting Father and Son Given 10 Year Dog Ban." BBC News Glasgow & West Scotland, April 8, 2014, http://www.bbc.co.uk/news/uk-scotland-glasgow-west-26947863 (accessed July 15, 2014).

"The Baiting of Wild Animals in Russia." One Voice, November 2013, http://www.one-voice.fr/wp-content/uploads/2013/11/The-baiting-of-wild-animals-in-Russia.pdf (accessed July 15, 2014).

Barkham, Patrick. "Badger Baiting Has Been Outlawed since 1835—So Why Is It Making a Comeback?" *The Guardian,* January 3, 2012, http://www.theguardian.com/world/2012/jan/03/badger-baiting-on-increase (accessed July 15, 2014).

"Bear Baiting Competitions." The Humane Society of the United States, 2014, http://www.humanesociety.org/issues/campaigns/wildlife_abuse/bear_baiting_fact_sheet.html (accessed July 15, 2014).

Bekoff, Marc, and Carron A. Meaney, eds. *Encyclopedia of Animal Rights and Animal Welfare.* Abingdon, UK: Routledge, 1998.

Collins, Tony, John Martin, and Wray Vamplew, eds. *Encyclopedia of Traditional British Rural Sports.* Abingdon, UK: Routledge, 2005.

Gayle, Damien. "Food Giant Mars under Fire after It Is Linked to Bear Baiting Event in the Ukraine." MailOnline, July 29, 2013, http://www.dailymail.co.uk/news/article-2380315/Food-giant-Mars-bear-baiting-event-Ukraine-sponsored-pet-food-subsidiary.html (accessed July 15, 2014).

Hough, Andrew. "Police Investigate Disturbing New 'Cat Coursing' Crimes." *The Telegraph,* October 31, 2011, http://www.telegraph.co.uk/news/uknews/crime/8859061/When-dogs-attack-cats-Police-investigate-disturbing-new-cat-coursing-crimes.html (accessed July 15, 2014).

Pacelle, Wayne. "Uncovered in South Carolina: Bear Abuse for Show." Huffington Post, August 23, 2010, http://www.huffingtonpost.com/wayne-pacelle/uncovered-in-south-caroli_b_691434.html (accessed July 15, 2014)

"Pakistan Halts Bear-Baiting Event." BBC News, May 18, 2005, http://news.bbc.co.uk/1/hi/world/south_asia/4558165.stm (accessed July 15, 2014).

"Pakistan's Baited Bears Wait for Rescue." BBC News, January 4, 2001, http://news.bbc.co.uk/1/hi/sci/tech/1100555.stm (accessed July 15, 2014).

Schoon, Nicholas. "When Baiting Bears and Bulls Was Legal . . ." *The Independent,* June 17, 1997, http://www.independent.co.uk/news/when-baiting-bears-and-bulls-was-legal-1256374.html (accessed July 15, 2014).

Simpson, Jacqueline, and Steve Roud. *A Dictionary of English Folklore.* Oxford: Oxford University Press, 2001.

"Voters to Decide Whether to Ban Bear Baiting." NECN.com, July 14, 2014, http://www.necn.com/07/14/14/Voters-to-decide-whether-to-ban-bear-bai/landing_politics.html?blockID=869200&feedID=4212 (accessed July 15, 2014).

"What Is Bloodsport?" Anti-Fur Society, http://www.antifursociety.org/Bloodsport_in_the_United_States.html (accessed July 15, 2014).

BOG SNORKELING WORLD CHAMPIONSHIP

The Bog Snorkeling World Championship is a minor sporting event held in Wales in which competitors traverse a mud-filled quagmire wearing a snorkel and flippers. The championship was created by Gordon Green, MBE, in 1986 in a bid to attract tourists to the town of Llanwrtyd Wells, the smallest town in Britain, an initiative that proved highly successful, for each year hundreds of spectators travel from around the United Kingdom to watch the snorkelers, while competitors travel to Wales from all over the world. Indeed, past entrants have come from Russia, Australia, and New Zealand as well as England and Ireland. Media interest in the event is also international, for the championship garners television coverage in

A participant at the 2014 Irish Bog Snorkelling Championship. Bog snorkelling is a lighthearted, though exhausting, activity in which participants traverse a mud-filled bog wearing a snorkel and flippers. The annual Bog Snorkelling World Championship is held in Wales and attracts an international field of competitors. (Charles McQuillan/Getty Images)

Belgium, Russia, China, Australia, and Germany as well as in the United Kingdom, where the event also appears in newspapers and magazines. Other bog snorkeling contests are also held in Ireland and Australia.

The Bog Snorkeling World Championship is held annually on the August Bank Holiday and sees competitors complete two lengths of a trench through a peat bog in the fastest time possible. The trench measures 60 yards in length and is about 4 feet deep. Competitors must wear flippers and a snorkel, and many entrants choose to wear a wetsuit too, as the bog is muddy and often freezing cold and has an extremely unpleasant smell. The championship's official rules state that competitors are not allowed to use any known swimming stroke to travel the lengths but instead must rely on the power generated by their flippers to navigate the course. However, it is common practice to employ a form of doggy paddle to negotiate the bog. The average time for completing the course is about five minutes, though championship winning times are usually less than two minutes. If competitors tie for the winning time, then a bog off is held in which each contender for the title completes the course for a second time. Though the championship is generally a lighthearted affair, the event is nonetheless quite grueling. Indeed, each year a number of competitors fail to finish the course. The current world record for completing the course is held by Kristy Johnson, with a time of 1 minute 22 seconds.

Around 100 to 150 competitors participate in the Bog Snorkeling World Championship, each of whom pays a small entrance fee to take part in one of several categories, which include races for men and women, junior races, and fancy dress competitions. Each winner receives the title of world champion of their respective discipline as well as cash and other prizes. All funds raised by the championship go to charity.

The World Bog Snorkeling Championship has proved so successful that it has spawned two spin-off events held in July, the World Bog Mountain Bike Championship and the World Bog Triathlon, which are also held in Llanwrtyd Wells. The World Mountain Bike Championship began in 2005 and sees entrants ride a specially adapted mountain bike along the bottom of a trench cut through the Waen Rhydd peat bog that is 6 feet deep and 45 yards long. Competitors must complete two lengths of the trench. Entrants must provide their own snorkel and wear a wetsuit and a lead-filled belt, which prevents competitors from floating off the bike that is especially prepared for the event with a lead-filled frame and tires filled with water. Filling the tires with water allows them to grip the bottom of the bog. Underwater marshals known as scuba drivers are present to ensure the safety of competitors. A winning time is usually under one minute.

Many entrants into the World Bog Mountain Bike Championship use the event as a warm-up for the World Bog Triathlon, which takes place the day after the bog biking. The triathlon was first held in 2005 and comprises a contest for individuals as well a team event. Those competing for the title of world champion bog snorkeling triathlete must complete a 7-mile fell run and then snorkel their way along two lengths of the peat bog, as in the World Bog Snorkeling Championship. Having traversed the bog, competitors must next complete a mountain bike ride of about 19 miles that crosses wooded areas and several streams, fords, and rivers. In addition to the triathlon for individuals, an optional team relay event is also held in which teams of three enter one team member for each discipline of the triathlon. Competitors entered into the individual's triathlon are permitted to use the fell run section of that triathlon as their entry into the team event.

Coincidentally, Llanwrtyd Wells also hosts another minority sporting event, for each June the towns holds the Man versus Horse Race.

Man versus Horse Race: Llanwrtyd Wells's Other Sporting Oddity

The first annual Man versus Horse Race was held in Llanwrtyd Wells in 1980 to settle a barroom debate as to whether a man or a horse was faster over a long distance. The race sees runners compete with riders on horseback over a 22-mile route consisting of city streets, hills, forests, moorland, and open countryside. Over time the margin by which horses outpace runners has dropped from 30 minutes to a few seconds, and in 2004 athlete Huw Lobb became the first human to win the race.

The world's first-ever dry bog snorkeling competition was held in Shrewsbury, in the north of England, in August 2013. A dry indoor bog was constructed at the headquarters of the Shropshire Wildlife Trust in order to highlight the biodiversity of the area's landscape. Entrants in adult and junior contests wore kneepads, a mask, and, of course, a snorkel to compete and laid facedown on a converted skateboard to negotiate the short course.

See also: Fell Running; Swimming the English Channel; Underwater Hockey

Further Reading

"Biking Bog Snorkelers Get Dirty." BBC, July 5, 2008, http://news.bbc.co.uk/1/hi /wales/7491518.stm (accessed August 12, 2013).

"Bog Champion Offers Trade Secrets." BBC, August 29, 2006, http://news.bbc.co.uk/1/hi /wales/mid/5287194.stm (accessed August 12, 2013).

"Bog Snorkeling Creator Dives in." BBC, August 31, 2009, http://news.bbc.co.uk/1/hi /wales/8230601.stm (accessed August 12, 2013).

"Bog Snorkelling." Internet Archive, http://web.archive.org/web/20071214181427/http:// llanwrtyd-wells.powys.org.uk/bog.html (accessed August 12, 2013).

"Bogsnorkelling Triathlon." World Alternative Games, http://www.worldalternativegames. co.uk/events/bog-snorkelling-triathlon/ (accessed August 9, 2013).

"Shrewsbury's Snorkeling Day Hailed a Success." *Shropshire Star,* August 5, 2013, http:// www.shropshirestar.com/news/2013/08/05/shrewsburys-snorkelling-day-hailed-a -success/ (accessed August 9, 2013).

"The 3rd World Bog Snorkelling Triathlon Will Take Place on Sunday 8th July 2007." Internet Archive, http://web.archive.org/web/20080116041515/http://llanwrtyd-wells .powys.org.uk/bogtriathlon.htm (accessed August 12, 2013).

"World Bog Snorkelling Championships." World Alternative Games, http://www.worldalter nativegames.co.uk/events/bog-snorkelling/ (accessed August 9, 2013).

BOOMERANG THROWING

Boomerang throwing is an indoor or outdoor activity enjoyed by adults and children involving the throwing of a boomerang, a tool used in hunting and entertainment. The boomerang is typically associated with Australia, and though the sport of boomerang throwing was once exclusively Australian, there are now hundreds of boomerang throwing clubs throughout the world practicing the sport as both a competitive and leisure pursuit. Boomerang throwing is particularly thriving in the United States, where the United States Boomerang Association boasts over 500 members and almost 40 boomerang throwing tournaments are held annually. The sport is also increasingly popular in Japan, Brazil, and Russia and across Europe and Asia. The sport is loosely governed by the World Boomerang Association, which has around 25 member nations. Boomerangs are traditionally made of wood, but competition boomerangs manufactured from synthetic materials such as carbon fiber, polypropylene, and Paxolin also exist.

In the most basic terms, a boomerang is given lift and the ability to hover by the two uneven wings at either end of the boomerang, which spin horizontally in a manner similar to the blades of a helicopter's rotor. The mechanics of a boomerang's flight is, however, scientifically very complex, involving the gyroscopic motion of Earth's rotation, the ratio of lift to drag in flight, and aerodynamics. These processes result in the boomerang spinning about its axis following an elliptical path. Although it is often thought that boomerangs always return to their thrower, this is not the case, as both returning and nonreturning boomerangs exist.

The origins of the boomerang are unknown. While the boomerang is commonly thought of as the invention of native Australians known as Aborigines, a boomerang discovered in Poland is thought to be the world's oldest, having been fashioned out of mammoth tusk 23,000 years ago, while King Tutankhamen of Egypt (ca. 1332–1323 BCE) was known to have a collection of boomerangs. The earliest depiction of a boomerang in Australia can be found painted on rock in the Arnhem Land located on Australia's Northern Coast. It is thought that the artwork is around 15,000 years old. Meanwhile, the oldest boomerang to be found in Australia (discovered in the Wyrie Swamp in Southern Australia) is made of wood and is thought to be around 10,000 years old. For millennia Australian Aborigines have used the boomerang as both a tool for hunting animals and for use in games. Indeed, since ancient times the Aborigines have thrown boomerangs as part of a sporting tournament known as a *prun*, seeking to determine which participant could throw the boomerang the farthest or the most accurately. Another Aborigine pastime involving boomerang throwing is a common game in which six or more men would form a line, standing with their arms outstretched and their hands on the shoulders of the man in front. Another player would then stand facing the lined-up men and throw a boomerang over their heads, and each man in the line would then have to dodge the flying boomerang.

However, despite the long history of the boomerang, competitive boomerang throwing as an organized sport began as recently as the 1970s in Australia and the United States. Competitive boomerang throwing takes place on a field marked with concentric circles that indicate 10 meters, 20 meters, 30 meters, 40 meters, and 50 meters (roughly 33 feet, 66 feet, 98 feet, 131 feet, and 164 feet). The innermost circle is 2 meters (6.5 feet) in diameter, and it is from inside this circle that competitors stand to the launch their boomerang for most events. Inside the first 10-meter circle are concentric rings denoting every 2 meters that are worth varying numbers of points in accuracy events.

The rules of boomerang throwing have been standardized by the Boomerang Association of Australia and the U.S. Boomerang Association, and it is these rules that are employed at most boomerang competitions. Boomerang competitions usually consist of eight events: accuracy, Australian Round, trick catch/doubling, endurance, fast catch, juggling, and maximum time aloft (MTA). Accuracy is the oldest of all competitive boomerang events and is similar in concept to darts. To begin with, a competitor in an accuracy event stands in the center circle and throws her or his boomerang to or beyond the 20-meter circle line. The thrower then waits for the boomerang to return to the 2-meter circle and collects points depending on where in the innermost circle the boomerang lands. A boomerang that lands in the center circle earns the thrower 10 points, landing on the next circle earns 8 points, then 6 points, 4 points, and 2 points; thus, the maximum possible score in an accuracy event is 50 points, as each competitor has five throws that can each potentially score 10 points. In an accuracy event, competitors must not touch their returning boomerang or stop it in flight. Australian Round, sometimes known as Aussie Round, is often thought of as the most prestigious boomerang throwing event, as it comprises accurate throwing, distance throwing, and catching. In the Australian Round, competitors aim to throw their boomerang past the 50-meter line, earning 6 points, and then catch the boomerang while standing in the center circle, thus earning 4 points for the catch and 10 points for the boomerang returning to the center circle. Competitors each have five throws, with each throw potentially worth 20 points. Thus, theoretically, 100 points can be achieved in this event. The endurance event sees a competitor stand inside the center circle and then throw and catch the boomerang as many times as possible within a five-minute time limit. Similarly, in the fast catch event competitors aim to make five catches as quickly as possible, usually within a one-minute time limit. In this event the score is given either as the time taken to make the catches or the number of catches achieved within the one minute. Conversely, in the MTA event competitors try to keep the boomerang in the air for as long as possible and then catch it. Many variations of this event exist, but the most frequently used in competition is the MTA-100 in which participants must throw and subsequently catch the boomerang within a field of play measuring 100 meters in diameter. It is usual for each competitor to take five throws, with the throw that resulted in the boomerang staying in the air for the longest time counting.

In the trick catch/doubling event, a series of extravagant catches are made that are each worth a certain number of points. The event begins the trick catch section in which participants attempt the following catches: left- and right-hand catches (worth 2 points each), behind-the-back catch (3 points), under-the-leg catch (3 points), an eagle catch in which the competitor uses a swooping motion to come over the boomerang and catch it with one hand (4 points), and the hackey sack catch in which the competitor must kick the boomerang up in the air before catching it (6 points). Also worth 6 points is the tunnel catch, in which the competitor catches the boomerang using a hand placed between the legs while keeping both feet on the ground. A one-hand-behind-the-back catch is worth 7 points, as is a one-hand-under-the-leg catch. The catch that earns the most points is the foot catch. This is worth 10 points and sees a competitor catch the boomerang with the foot. Therefore, the maximum number of points a competitor can earn for this section of the event is 50 points. In the second section of the event, doubling, competitors throw two boomerangs simultaneously and attempt the following catches: behind the back and under the leg, left-hand catch and hackey sack catch, right-hand catch and tunnel catch, one-hand-behind-the-back catch and one-hand-under-the-leg catch, and eagle catch and foot catch. The pairs of catches may be made in any order, but repeating a catch will not earn a competitor points. The maximum combined score for the trick catch/doubling event is 100 points. The juggling event also sees two boomerangs used at the same time. However, in this event the boomerangs are kept in the air alternately for as long as possible without touching the ground.

Another possible boomerang throwing event is a team event called Relay Race Rang. In this event each team lines up single file but far enough apart so that the throwers do not get in each other's way. When the race begins, the first thrower in each line runs to a spot marked 30 meters (98 feet) in front of the line and throws the boomerang. The thrower must then catch the boomerang, tag the marker, return to the team, and tag the next teammate in line, who runs out to the marker and throws the boomerang. However, if the first thrower does not catch the boomerang, then the thrower must throw once more. After the second throw the thrower must tag the marker and return to the team whether or not the thrower has caught the boomerang.

A number of boomerang throwing championships are held every year, including international team cup challenges, world team championships, and world individual championships. However, these tournaments have not been dominated by Australia. Instead, since the 1980s the United States, Japan, Germany, and France have prevailed. Indeed, such is the U.S. dominance in the field of competitive boomerang throwing that Ohio is known as the Boomerang Capital of the World because it has produced so many champion throwers. The U.S. domination of the sport dates from 1981, when a 10-member team of U.S. boomerang throwers traveled to Australia to challenge Australians at their indigenous sport in the first-ever international boomerang throwing contest, which the Americans won by winning all three tests of the series. Three years later in 1984, the Australians traveled to the United States to take part in the Land's End Boomerang Cup, winning the tournament. Australia's lack of international prowess is perhaps due to the fact that though many thousands of boomerangs are sold in Australia every year, these are usually bought by tourists, and competitive boomerang throwing is not widely practiced in Australia. Conversely, in Japan, where boomerang throwing is growing in popularity, the Japanese buy thousands of boomerangs each year. The majority of boomerangs bought in Japan are made of foam and intended for use indoors, which is extremely important for the Japanese market, as outside space is severely limited in Japan.

See also: Aussie Rules Football; Cricket; Paintball; Stone Skimming; Yabbie Races

Further Reading

Blanchard, Kendall. *The Anthropology of Sport: An Introduction.* Revised ed. Westport, CT: Bergin and Garvey, 1995.

"Boomerang Competition Events." Boomerang Association of Australia, http://boomerang .org.au/wp/articles/boomerang-competition-events/ (accessed June 30, 2014).

"Boomerang Societies around the World." About Boomerangs, 2012–2013, http://about -boomerangs.com/boomerang-societies-around-the-world/ (accessed June 30, 2014).

Bushell, Mike. *Bushell's Best Bits: Everything You Needed to Know about the World's Craziest Sports.* London: John Blake, 2013.

"Competitions and Games." Boomerangs.org, 2005, http://www.boomerangs.org/comp .html (accessed July 2, 2014).

Craig, Steve. *Sports and Games of the Ancients.* Westport, CT: Greenwood, 2002.

Jones, Philip. *Boomerang: Behind an Australian Icon.* Kent Town, Australia: Wakefield, 2004.

Levinson, David, and Karen Christensen, eds. *Encyclopedia of World Sport: From Ancient Times to the Present.* Oxford: Oxford University Press, 1996.

"Origins of the Boomerang." Owens & Sons Boomerangs, 2011, http://owensboomerangs .com/styled-7/ (accessed September 29, 2013).

Sisson, Richard, Chris Zacher, and Andrew Cayton, eds. *The American Midwest: An Interpretive Encyclopedia.* Bloomington: Indiana University Press, 2007.

Thomas, Jacques. "Why Boomerangs Boomerang (and Why Killing-Sticks Don't)." *New Scientist* 99(1376) (September 22, 1983): 838–843.

BOSSABALL

Bossaball is a competitive sport that combines elements of volleyball, soccer, gymnastics, trampolining, and capoeira. Bossaball was invented in Spain by Belgian Filip Eyckmans and is played in Brazil, Germany, Spain, the Netherlands, Portugal, Romania, Singapore, Ecuador, Kuwait, and Saudi Arabia. Shortly after its inception a bossaball league was established in Belgium, and further leagues have become established in countries as diverse as Romania, Saudi Arabia, and Singapore.

A game of bossaball is contested by two teams of three to five players standing opposite each other on an inflatable court featuring an integrated, circular trampoline on either side of the net. The trampolines are separated from the rest of the court by knee-high inflatable rings about 1 meter (just over 39 inches) wide known as the bossawalls that act as a safety zone on which the ball may bounce or roll. Players are not allowed to touch the net, the height of which can be adjusted to suit men, women, children, professionals, or amateurs; and players must keep at least one body part on their own side of the net. The ball, which is round and about the size of a soccer ball, can be maneuvered using one of two touch techniques—a volleyball touch, in which a player hits the ball using hands or lower arms, or a soccer touch utilizing the feet and head, which allows the player to employ double contact but only counts as one touch. It is usual for a maximum of five touches to be allowed per team, though this is increased to six for amateur players.

The object of the game is to ground the ball on the opposing team's side of the court or hit the ball so that it cannot be returned. Points can be awarded for scoring or because of an opponent's fault. One point is scored for employing a volleyball touch to ground the ball in the opponent's playing area, while 3 points are scored for a volleyball touch that propels the ball directly onto the opposite side's trampoline. Three points are also scored for using a soccer touch to hit the opposing side's half of the court, while 5 points are scored for using a soccer touch to hit the opposite trampoline directly. A point is also awarded if the ball lies still on the bossawall. The first team to score 25 points by 2 clear points wins the set, and each bossaball match consists of three sets.

Music is an intrinsic element of bossaball, for matches are accompanied by a soundtrack consisting of different styles of Brazilian music, most especially bossa nova and samba. Indeed, bossaball officials are known as samba referees, as they not only ensure that players adhere to the rules of the game but also provide the music played during the match and have access to a variety of musical equipment, including turntables, microphones, and drums.

The first Bossaball World Cup was held in Turkey in 2009, with the Brazilian team crowned champions, while the following year saw the first European Indoor Bossaball Championships held in the Netherlands.

See also: Aussie Rules Football; Capoeira; Footvolley and Futnet; Rhythmic Gymnastics; Trampolining

Further Reading

Brooks, T. "Brazilian Bossaball Bounces on the Beach." The National, November 27, 2009, http://www.thenational.ae/news/uae-news/brazilian-bossaball-bounces-on-to-the-beach (accessed August 11, 2013).
Connolly, Paul. *The World's Weirdest Sports.* Millers Point, Australia: Pier 9, 2007.
"Home." Bossaball Sports, http://www.bossaballsports.com (accessed July 16, 2013)
Jumbro. "W2FY Recommends: Bossaball International." W2FY, June 1, 2010, http://www.welcometofreshmanyear.com/b/archives/2602 (accessed August 11, 2013).
"World of Weird Sports: Bossaball." ABC, 2009, http://www.abc.net.au/rollercoaster/dash/wowsports/bossaball.htm (accessed August 11, 2013).

BRÄNNBOLL AND PESÄPALLO

Brännboll, known as *brennball* and *slåball* in Norway and *rundbold* in Denmark, is a bat and ball game similar to baseball and rounders played at an amateur level throughout Scandinavia and Germany, either as part of school physical education classes or on fields and in public parks. The name *brännboll* derives from the act of trapping a player between two bases at the end of batting, for this is known as *bränna* ("burning") and is the equivalent of being out in rounders/baseball. *Brännboll* is not an organized sport; there are no *brännboll* leagues, nor is there a governing body. Rather, *brännboll* is an informal sport most appreciated by schoolchildren or played by groups of friends after work as a fun pastime. Indeed, the sport has been described as baseball for anarchists.

The annual Brännboll World Championship, Brännbollscupen, has been held in the northern Swedish city of Umeå, as is the Brännboll World Championship, which began in 1974 and is played using standardized rules. A *brännboll* festival called Brännbollsyran is also held. Meanwhile, the most significant *brännboll* event in Germany is the International Brennball Tournament that has been held since the mid-1990s in the town of Würzburg, which is twinned with Umeå.

Unlike cricket and baseball, there is no bowler or pitcher in a game of *brännboll*. Instead, the batter must throw or bounce the ball (typically a tennis ball) and then hit it with the bat, which is usually a baseball bat made of metal or wood. However, if players are new to the game, then a bat similar to a cricket bat or a tautly strung racquet may be used. A batter who fails to hit the ball after the three attempts moves to the first base and runs once the next batter makes a valid hit.

The batter must hit the ball within the playing area, which in *brännboll* is denoted either by natural features such as trees or by a prearranged imaginary boundary. The number of players playing and their skill level usually determine the size of the playing area. The batter, after hitting the ball, drops the bat and runs clockwise around the four bases. Meanwhile, members of the opposing side stop the ball and throw it back to the player designated as the catcher, who is positioned by the *brännplatta*, or outing base. If the catcher makes contact with the *brännplatta* while holding the ball then the catcher shouts "*brand*," meaning "burned," to indicate that a player is out. If a player is caught between bases, that player must retreat either to the last base reached or the first base, depending on the rules decided before the game began. In this instance the fielding side earns one point.

In *brännboll* no restrictions exist on the number of players at each base. Also, if a batter fails to rejoin the queue of batters waiting to play because the batter failed to reach the fourth base and there is no batter on strike, then the batting side is said to be *utebrända*, or out. In this instance, depending on the rules being used, the fielding side is rewarded by either being awarded extra points or being allowed to swap sides, since it is easier to win points by batting than by fielding. Each team fields and bats at least once (usually twice).

Pesäpallo, often called *pesis* and sometimes referred to as Finnish baseball, is a fast-paced bat and ball game for men, women, and children that is very similar to *brännboll* (and therefore akin to rounders and baseball). The national sport of Finland, *pesäpallo* is also played elsewhere. For instance, the 2012 Pesäpallo World Cup was held in Australia, and participating nations at previous World Cups have included Sweden, Switzerland, and Germany as well as Australia and Finland. *Pesäpallo* is also played in Canada, Japan, New Zealand, and the United Kingdom. In domestic competition the top *pesäpallo* division, the Superpesis, was founded in 1990. The Superpesis is divided into a men's league consisting of 11 teams and a women's league made up of 10 teams.

Pesäpallo was invented by Lauri "Tahko" Pihkala in the 1920s. Today the game is a popular spectator sport, as it is unique combination of athleticism and teamwork and is deeply ingrained in the Finnish national psyche, for it is played in schools and as leisure activity in parks.

A game of *pesäpallo* is contested by two teams that take turns at offense (batting) and defending (fielding). Each team has nine players, though the batting side may also use three extra players known as designated hitters. The teams aim to score as many runs as possible, for the team that scores the most runs is declared the winner. When a player is in, the player stands on the circular home base facing the pitcher. The pitch is delivered by pitching the ball directly upward above the home plate so that it reaches a height of at least 1 meter (3 feet) over the head of the pitcher, and the batter then hits the ball. The batter is allowed three strikes and does not have to run just because he or she has hit the ball—the batter can use all three strikes before advancing. However, if the batter's third strike is a foul, then the batter is out.

A pitch is deemed a strike if the batter swings at the ball or if the match umpire judges it to be legal. If a bad ball is delivered, the batter is allowed to walk to first base if there are no other batters on the field. A bad pitch occurs if the ball does not fall on the home base, if it travels too low to the ground, or if the pitcher commits a rule violation. A hit is said to be a foul if the ball bounces outside the boundaries of the playing area. When a foul occurs, neither the batter nor the runners may proceed.

When the batter sets off from home base he or she assumes the role of runner. The runner attempts to run around the bases in turn and return to the home base without being out—the runner reaches a base safely by touching the base before the ball is thrown to a fielder standing by the base. However, if the ball arrives at the base first, then the runner is out and has to leave the field. It should be noted also that a runner must leave a base and advance if the next runner arrives safely on the same base.

If the runner manages to advance through all three bases and return to the home base without getting out, then the batter's scores one run. A home run is scored if the batter reaches the third base on his or her own single hit. The defending side tries to stop the runner from getting around the bases by catching the ball before it touches the field of play. If the ball is caught by a member of the defending side, the runner is said to be wounded and cannot continue the run. Indeed, all runners who tried to proceed on that play are deemed caught. Caught players must leave the field, but they do not count as an out. Defenders may also throw the ball to the base at which the runner is aiming before the runner reaches the base. Similarly, a runner is out if he or she is touched by the ball while running. After three members of the batting side are out the teams swap roles, with the defending team now batting. The role reversal also occurs when all players on the attacking side have batted but have been unable to score a run. When both teams have had a go at both batting and fielding, an innings has been played.

The main difference between *pesäpallo* and baseball is that vertical pitching occurs in *pesäpallo*. This means that it is easier for batters to strike the ball and control the direction in which it is hit so they can hit the ball in a variety of ways and at different speeds. Consequently, batters can play much more tactically than they can in baseball. The fielding team has to counteract the varied batting by employing various defensive schemes and anticipating the batters' hitting strategy. In this way *pesäpallo* is also a thought-provoking game. The mental aspect of *pesäpallo* means that role of team manager is very important, as the manager must devise both offensive and defensive strategies. The manager of the batting team communicates tactics using a multicolored fan, while the manager of the fielding side uses hand signals. The constant need for the manager to communicate with the players means that teamwork is a major part of *pesäpallo*.

Competitive *pesäpallo* is played in two periods of four innings for each team, and the side that scores the most runs in its batting half of the innings wins the period. If both sides win a period, each then receives an extra period consisting of one inning. If scores are still level after this, then a special scoring contest is held to break the deadlock.

Pesäpallo was caught in the center of a match-fixing controversy at the end of the 1990s. This scandal saw 17 people sentenced to 3 to 5 months of conditional imprisonment and 3 others fined after betting on *pesäpallo* matches that they knew to be fixed.

See also: Cricket; *Gilli-Danda; Kubb; Lapta*; Nipsy; Rounders

Further Reading

European Commission. *Match-Fixing in Sport: A Mapping of Criminal Law Provisions in EU 27*. March 2012, http://ec.europa.eu/sport/library/studies/study-sports-fraud-final-version _en.pdf (accessed July 28, 2014).

"Introduction to the Game." Pesäpalloliitto, 2014, http://www.pesis.fi/pesapalloliitto /international_site/introduction/ (accessed July 28, 2014).

Kraus, Ulrich. "Brennball." June 23, 2013. Brennball, http://www.brennball.de/english/index .htm (accessed July 28, 2014).

"National Sports of the Lovely Planet." The Lovely Planet, July 30, 2012, http://www.the lovelyplanet.net/tag/pesapallo/ (accessed July 28, 2014).

Pullinen, Jari, ed. "Internet Introduction to Finnish Baseball: Pesapallo," NIC Funet, http:// www.nic.funet.fi/index/sports/pesapallo/pesapallo.introduction.ver102 (accessed July 28, 2014).

"Two Traditional Swedish Summer Games." Totally Swedish, http://www.totallyswedish .com/en/calendar/two-traditional-swedish-summer-games (accessed July 28, 2014).

BULL RUNNING

Bull running, also known as the running of the bulls, is a controversial activity in which people run through the streets of a town ahead of a group of charging bulls. Bull running is most closely associated with Spain, where the spectacle is called *encierro,* which translates from Spanish as the corralling of the bulls, and is synonymous with the town of Pamplona. However, bull running also occurs in southern France, Portugal, Mexico, Peru, and, in modified form, in the United States.

The Pamplona Bull Run is part of the Sanfermines Festival (the Fiesta of San Fermin, the patron saint of Navarra), held annually during July 6–14, with the bull running occurring during July 7–14. Though the bull run is only part of the

Runners try to stay clear as a bull charges through the streets of Pamplona, Spain, home of the world's most famous bull running event. The Pamplona Bull Run is part of the Sanfermines Festival and has been held in the town for 400 years. The best bull runners are known as Los Divinos meaning "The Divine Ones." (AP Photo/Jon Dimis)

festivities, it is considered by many to be the highlight and is broadcast live on Spanish television. The event is also aired on the Internet and attracts media interest from around the world. The medieval setting of the Pamplona Bull Run reflects the event's history, for the bull run is 400 years old, dating back to a time when wild bulls were driven into town. However, the bull run became an official part of the Sanfermines Festival as recently as 1876. The exact origins of the Pamplona event are unknown, but one theory as to how the event originated is that during the Middle Ages when only the aristocracy were permitted to attend bullfights, a group of daring young men who wished to participate in the bullfight in any way they could began the custom of running in front of the bulls as they traveled to the fighting arena. Another theory suggests that Pamplona bull running began as an ancient way of transporting the animals from the corral to the bullring, where they would subsequently take part in a bullfight. However, the Pamplona Bull Run in its present form (in which people run in front of the bulls) is thought to date from as recently as the latter half of the 19th century. Prior to this the bulls followed riders on horseback who cleared a path for the bulls. During the *encierro* the runners both run ahead of the bulls and also choose one particular bull to run alongside for as long as possible. An often overlooked element of the Pamplona Bull Run is that the people involved participate with the objective of leading the bulls rather than to run from the animals. The best runners are known as *los divinos* ("the divine ones").

The Sanfermines Festival begins at noon on July 6 when the *chupinazo,* or inaugural rocket, is launched from the second-floor balcony of the town hall in the Plaza Consistorial and 12,500 onlookers declare first in Spanish and then in Basque "Viva San Fermín! Gora San Fermín!" (which translates as "Long Live San Fermín!"). At 8:00 a.m. on each day of the festival the runners, dressed in the traditional runners' outfit of white trousers and top and a red sash, go to the corral housing the bulls, and with five minutes, three minutes, and one minute to go before the gates open, a prayer to San Fermin is said aloud: "A San Fermin pedimos, por se nuestro patron, nos guie en el encierro dandos su bendicion" ("We ask San Fermin, being our patron saint, to guide us in the bull run and give us his blessing"). The prayer is directed toward an image of the saint placed in a niche in a wall. The runners then shout "Viva San Fermín! Gora San Fermín!" and the gates open. Then the run begins with the launching of two rockets—one to signal the release of the bulls and the other to signal that the last of the bulls has left its pen. The runners then lead six bulls weighing around 1,300 pounds each, the kind used in Spanish-style bullfighting, plus two nonfighting bulls called *mansos* that act as steers directing the bulls to the bullring, 902 yards from their pens in Calle Santo Domingo to the bullring along Pamplona's medieval cobbled streets. A 12-foot-high double barrier protects spectators and property along the route. After two minutes three additional *mansos* are released to run down the route to guide any bulls that may have become separated from the previous group. However, it is the job of a group of spectators called the *pastores,* who wear green and carry a long pole, to ensure that bulls do not stop en route, run back to where they came from, or become separated from their fellow bulls. Another group of onlookers, the *dobladores,* who await the bulls in the bullring, are charged with using capes to navigate the bulls into the corral. When all the bulls have reached the bullring and are corralled, a fourth rocket signals that the bull run has ended. The entire run takes very little time to complete, usually around three minutes.

The Pamplona Bull Run became globally famous after the publication of Ernest Hemingway's novel *The Sun Also Rises* (1926) and today attracts up to 2,000 participants per day. Human deaths are uncommon during the bull running, with 15 fatalities occurring since 1924—the most recent death, that of a 62-year-old Spaniard, occurred in 2003. However, around 200 people are injured during the Sanfermines Festival each year usually as a result of being gored by the bulls or trampled by the animals and other runners as the run passes through the town's narrow streets. The event also attracts animal rights protestors who oppose the event, particularly the fact that the six fighting bulls that are run through the town die later the same day at the hands of bullfighters. To highlight their opposition to the bull run in 2002, People for the Ethical Treatment of Animals (PETA) inaugurated an annual tradition called the Running of the Nudes, an alternative event during the Sanfermines Festival in which participants wearing little more than plastic bull horns and a red scarf run through the streets of Pamplona, to the delight of ever-increasing numbers of spectators. Other mock bull runs include the San Fermin in Nueva Orleans, in which the Big Easy Roller Girls and other U.S. Roller Derby players adopt the part of the bulls in an annual event in New Orleans. Meanwhile in Ballyjamsduff, Ireland, an annual running of the pigs takes place with wild boar rather than bulls, and in Te Kuiti, New Zealand, a running of the sheep is held. In London, England's capital city, the running of the bulls is an annual pub crawl in which participants wearing horned helmets race from pub to pub on Hampstead Heath.

Bull running has taken place in France since the 16th century and is centered on the southern French region of the Camargue, Western Europe's largest river delta (where the Rhône River meets the Mediterranean Sea), which is home to three breeds of bull including a particularly small breed known as Camargue bulls. A unique breed of horse called Camargue also lives in the region, as do 40,000 pink flamingos.

The main difference between French and Spanish bull runs is that in France the bull is not killed. Indeed, the bull is the real star in a French bull run, often entering into the bullring to music from the opera *Carmen*. Camargue bull running takes place from spring through autumn and is most associated with the towns of Arles, Nimes, Béziers, and Palavas, and so entrenched is bull culture in the region that a specific name is used to describe it—*tauromachie*. However, while Pamplona-style bull running takes place as part of some southern French village festivals, the more common form of Camargue bull running is called *course Camarguaise* meaning "Camargue racing," and is sometimes known as *course provençale* or *course à la co-carde*. In *course camarguaise* 12 young men wearing white, called the *razeteurs,* face a number of Camargue bulls during a 15-minute spectacle. The *razeteurs* run at the bull and use a special handheld hook to remove a selection of small objects including a rosette, tassels, and ribbons that are tied to the bull's horns—the more objects the *razeteurs* remove the more money they earn. The *razeteurs* tire the bull by allowing it to chase them right up to the barriers of the arena and leaping over barriers at the last minute, though sometimes the bull does not give up the chase and jumps over the barrier too. At the end of each round of bull running, music from *Carmen* is played, then when the event finishes the bull's owner earns around €3,000, and the bull is released to continue its semiwild existence on the marshland of the Camargue. When a bull has served around eight seasons it is retired to roam the countryside.

Famous bulls become big box-office draws, with their names placed prominently on posters advertising bull running events, and the most popular bulls are revered, as seen by the fact that a statue of Vovo, a famed bull that starred in bull runs from 1947 to 1954, stands outside the arena at Les Saintes-Maries-de-la-Mer, the capital of the Camargue. The artwork is by British sculptor Peter Eugene Ball, who usually specializes in religious works. Les Saintes-Maries-de-la-Mer is the location for the Festival of Abrivado in which every November 11, 1,000 horses and their owners guide a herd of bulls at trotting pace over a four-mile course from the beach to the bull arena.

The most prestigious of the *course Camarguaise* events is La Cocade d'Or (Golden Rosette) that is held annually on the first Monday of July in Arles. At the end of this prestigious event, prizes are awarded to the year's best bull breeder and the bravest *razeteur.*

A number of bull runs take place in the United States, most famously at Cave Creek in Arizona. The Arizona event, known as Running with the Bulls USA, is a three-day spectacle hosting six runs per day, with $500 cash prizes for the top runner in each race. A run is held every hour during the event, and before each run event staff walk runners along the track, explaining the rules as they go. Runners position themselves on the track according to their perceived skill level—those who believe themselves adept at bull running start the run near the center of the track, while the less confident start near a fence so that they can escape the animals more easily.

Unlike the Pamplona Bull Run, Cave Creek bull running takes place on a wide track a quarter of a mile in length with exits every 100 feet to allow runners to escape the bulls if necessary. However, such safety measures have not prevented participants from being hurt, for in 2012 eight runners were injured after especially large hostile bulls capable of running at 15 miles per hour were introduced after complaints from runners that the bulls used in previous years had lacked aggression. The injuries incurred by runners caused an outcry in the national media. Meanwhile, animal rights groups object to Running with Bulls USA on the grounds that the event is cruel to bulls.

See also: Bearbaiting and Badger Baiting; *Buzkashi;* Camel and Yak Racing; Camel Wrestling; Cockfighting; Elephant Sports; Foxhunting; Hare Coursing; Nonlethal Bullfighting; *Pato* and Horseball; *Pelota;* Pigeon Racing; Sheepdog Trials; Spanish Bullfighting; Yabbie Races

Further Reading

"The Camargue (Rhône Delta)." Midi-France, www.midi-france.info, http://www.midi-france .info/07020201_camargue.htm#bulls (accessed July 19, 2014).

"The Chupinazo." Ayuntamiento de Pamplona: Tourist Portal of the City Council Pamplona, http://sanfermin.pamplona.es/VerPagina.asp?IdPag=30&Idioma=5 (accessed July 19, 2014).

"The Course Camarguaise (Camargue Bullfighting)—Camargue Traditions." Avignon-et-Provence, 1996–2014, http://www.avignon-et-provence.com/camargue-provence/cou rse-camarguaise.htm#.U8p-ExavvR0 (accessed July 19, 2014).

del Valle, Teresa. *Korrika: Basque Ritual for Ethnic Identity.* Reno: University of Nevada Press, 1994.

"FAQs." Running with the Bulls USA, 2013, http://runningwiththebullsusa.com/faqs/ (accessed July 19, 2014).

Galvan, Javier A., ed. *They Do What? A Cultural Encyclopedia of Extraordinary and Exotic Customs from around the World.* Santa Barbara, CA: ABC-CLIO, 2014.

Goodale, Greg, and Jason Edward Black, eds. *Arguments about Animal Ethics.* Lanham, MD: Lexington Books, 2010.

Haldiman, Philip. "Annual Cave Creek Bull Run to Expand to 2 Days." AZ Central, July 12, 2013, http://www.azcentral.com/community/scottsdale/articles/20130708annual-cave -creek-bull-run-expand-days.html (accessed July 19, 2014).

Let's Go Spain & Portugal: The Student Travel Guide. Cambridge, MA: Let's Go, 2012.

Nauright, John, and Charles Parrish, eds. *Sports around the World: History, Culture and Practice,* Vol. 1, *General Topics, Africa, Asia, Middle East, and Oceania.* Santa Barbara, CA: ABC-CLIO, 2012.

Office de Tourisme Les Saintes-Maries-de-la-Mer. "Festival of Abrivado." Festivities and
    Feria, http://www.saintesmaries.com/en/home/festivities-and-feria/festival-of-abrivado
    .html (accessed July 19, 2014).
Peregrine, Anthony. "Bullfighting: When Blood Sport Spoils a Good Party." *The Telegraph*,
    March 18, 2014, http://www.telegraph.co.uk/travel/destinations/europe/france/107051
    61/Bullfighting-when-blood-sport-spoils-a-good-party.html (accessed July 19, 2014).
PETA. Running of the Nudes, 2014, http://www.runningofthenudes.com/index.asp (ac-
    cessed July 19, 2014).
Powder Blue Ltd. "Course Camarguaise." See Provence, 1998–2014, http://www.see
    provence.com/events/calendar/course-camarguaise.html (accessed July 19, 2014).
Small, James. "About the Event." The Running of the Bulls, 2014, http://www.runningbulls
    .co.uk/about (accessed July 19, 2014).
Smith, Oliver. "San Fermin, Pamplona: Has Bull Running Had Its Day?" *The Telegraph*,
    July 5, 2013, http://www.telegraph.co.uk/travel/travelnews/10162753/San-Fermin
    -Pamplona-has-bull-running-had-its-day.html (accessed July 19, 2014).

BUNNOCK

Bunnock, also known as the game of bones, is an outdoor game akin to a cross
between bowling and horseshoes that uses horse anklebones instead of a ball and
pins. Bunnock is played in Canada by males and females of all ages, usually as a
team game involving two team of eight players but sometimes by pairs or by teams
of more than eight. Bunnock is similar in nature to *kyykkä*, *mölkky*, and *kubb*.

A bunnock set comprises 4 black guard pieces called the black bones, 40 white
soldier pieces known as the white bones, and 8 colored thrower pieces known as
the bunnocks (or 4 colored pieces if the set is intended for novice players). A
game of bunnock begins with the toss either of a coin or a bunnock piece to decide which team throws first, and the team that wins the toss has to decide if it
wishes to choose the side from which the team throws or whether to throw last
and therefore gain a possible advantage. The last throw of the game is known as
the hammer.

The bunnock must be thrown underarm, and the usual throwing action sees the
bunnock held facedown in the palm of the hand with the index finger hooked into
the bottom of the bunnock. A spinning motion is then employed so that the bunnock lands just short of the target piece and then continues to spin on contact with
the ground, continuing on to knock down both the target piece and others around
it. The 40 soldier pieces are placed in two parallel rows set about 32 feet apart and
with a guard piece placed at either end about 16 inches from the soldiers. The aim
of the game is to knock down first the black bones and then the white bones inside
the guards before the other team does so. The guard pieces must be knocked over
first. If soldier pieces are knocked down before the guard pieces, then those soldier
pieces are reset one bunnock's width inside the nearest standing guard piece. However, if there is no room for the soldier pieces to be replaced inside the guard piece,
then the soldier must be placed a bunnock's width behind the guard. Should the
soldier be knocked down again before the guard, then it is reset on the outside of
the nearest guard piece. If the soldier piece is knocked down for a third time before

the guard piece, then the soldier piece is placed upright pointing in the direction that it fell. Players are not permitted to touch any of the playing pieces until all the throws have been taken from one end, and when an end has been completed all the pieces must be collected from the playing area. If a piece is knocked down and rolls into the pile of collected pieces, then that piece is considered down and inactive. Similarly, if a player accidently makes physical contact with an active piece and it is knocked down, then it too shall be considered dead. As players are not permitted on the field of play during an end, they should seldom come into contact with pieces.

To start the game, the first player to throw stands either with the feet behind the throw line or with both feet on the throw line and then steps forward one pace. Players are not permitted to take more than one step beyond the throw line. Each player in each team has two throws to knock down the bones using a throwing piece, and the team that takes the fewest number of throws to knock down all the bones is declared the winner. A tie is declared if the team throwing last uses the same number of throws to knock down all the opposing team's pieces. In the event of a tie a deciding game must be played, with the teams changing ends but keeping the same throwing order.

Bunnock pieces need to be placed on a hard, even surface, and so the game tends to be played on finely crushed gravel, grass, dirt, or snow. Since it is advantageous to get the thrown bunnock to spin on the ground, it is inadvisable to play bunnock on concrete, as spinning on such a hard surface damages the playing pieces.

The game of bunnock is thought to have been invented by Russian soldiers stationed in Siberia 200 years ago who, looking for something to entertain themselves amid the tundra landscape, tried to play horseshoes but that found the frozen ground was too hard to allow pegs to be driven into it. However, the soldiers then realized that the anklebones of dead horses were plentiful in the region and could be set to stand on the frozen ground. Thus, the soldiers invented bunnock using what meager resources they had. When Russian German settlers immigrated to Canada in the early 20th century, they brought with them the game of bunnock. Many German Catholics from Russia and the United States settled in the town of Macklin in the province of Saskatchewan, and bunnock quickly became popular in the area. The popularity of the game eventually led to the Bunnock World Championships being founded in Macklin, with the inaugural tournament held in 1993. The Bunnock World Championships are held every Civic holiday, commonly known in Canada as the August long weekend, at Macklin Lake Regional Park, with around 320 teams competing for both the title and the prizes, which in 2013 had a total value of over CAN$30,000.

Macklin's association with bunnock is marked by a folk monument called the World's Largest Bunnock. The monument rises over 30 feet above the prairies surrounding Macklin and takes the form of a horse anklebone enlarged 98 times and fashioned from metal pipe, fiberglass, and chicken wire. The monument houses a tourist information office in its base and is lit bright orange at night so that it can be seen for miles around.

See also: Aunt Sally; *Kubb; Kyykkä; Mölkky;* Skittles

Further Reading

"About Bunnock—The Game of Bones." The Original Bunnock, 2004–2014, http://www.bunnock.com/index.php?page=about-bunnock (accessed July 28, 2013).

"The Game of Bunnock," http://www.macklin.ca/bunnock.htm (accessed July 30, 2013).

"History of Bunnock—The Game of Bones." The Original Bunnock, September 9, 2006, http://www.bunnock.com/uploads/File/Bunnock%20instructions.pdf (accessed July 30, 2013).

McLennan, David. "Macklin." The Encyclopedia of Saskatchewan, http://esask.uregina.ca/entry/macklin.html (accessed December 11, 2014).

Wishart, David J., ed. *Encyclopedia of the Great Plains.* Lincoln: University of Nebraska Press, 2004.

BUZKASHI

Buzkashi, or *bozkashi,* meaning "goat dragging," is an equestrian sport played by men in which players compete for control of the carcass of a goat or calf. *Buzkashi* is the national sport of Afghanistan, where it is played in the capital city, Kabul, and in the north of the country by the nomadic Turkic tribes consisting of the Kazak, Kyrgyz, Turkmen, and Uzbek peoples as well as non-Turkic peoples including the Persian (Dari)-speaking Tajiks and Hazaras and the Pashtuns. *Buzkashi* is also played in the Muslim republics to the north of Afghanistan such as Kazakhstan,

Horsemen vie for the carcass of a goat in a game of *buzkashi* held in Tursunzade, Tajikistan, on January 8, 2012. *Buzkashi* is the national sport of Afghanistan. Often the dead animal that is the focus of the game is beheaded and has its legs severed at the knee before a game of *buzkashi* begins. (Nozim Kalandarov/Reuters/Corbis)

where the sport is considered to have a cultural significance. Areas of northwestern China also hold *buzkashi* competitions, as do areas of Pakistan in which Afghan refugees settle.

Buzkashi has a significance beyond that of sport for many Afghan people. Indeed, Afghans are proud of their national sport, for they believe that *buzkashi* represents their way of life and demonstrates the importance of communication and teamwork. In contrast to Spain and Mexico, where some inhabitants object to bullfighting, *buzkashi* is not considered cruel in Afghanistan.

There are two main theories as to how *buzkashi* originated. One suggestion is that the sport evolved among the Turkic peoples as an entertaining variant on traditional goat herding. However, it has also been suggested that *buzkashi* began as a nocturnal training regime for horseman responsible for defending their territory from marauding enemies. In this instance the corpse of an enemy tribesman was used instead of that of an animal. Today *buzkashi* contests are accompanied by wrestling matches, as in earlier times expert horsemen had to be adept at hand-to-hand combat as well as horsemanship.

Today there are two main forms of *buzkashi*—*tudabaray* (*tudaberai*) and *qarajay* (*qarajai*)—though there is also a variation called *darya-yi-buzkashi* that takes place in the middle of a river and a version in which individuals compete one-on-one. *Tudabaray* translates from Persian as "coming out of the crowd" and is the traditional version of the game, while *qarajay,* which means "black place," is a modern variation of the sport that is sponsored by the Afghan government. Both forms of the sport feature competitors mounted on horseback vying for control of a dead goat or calf, usually by grabbing the carcass with their hands. It is usual for the dead animal to have been beheaded and its legs severed from the knee. The carcass is soaked in cold water for 24 hours to make the flesh tough enough to withstand rough handling during play, and sometimes the carcass is gutted or stuffed with sand. This treatment results in an animal corpse weighing between 40 and 100 pounds. The animal's head is not always wasted, for it has been known for spectators to attach balloons to their backs and run around the edge of the game carrying the head of the animal in a *buzkashi* version of cheerleading.

Both *tudabaray* and *qarajay* have few formal rules, though *buzkashi* etiquette prohibits players from using weapons, commandeering an opponent's horse, biting an opponent, or pulling an opponent's hair. It is also forbidden for opponents to trip one another using ropes, to whip an opponent, or to claim the animal carcass by tying it to a saddle. This etiquette is not necessarily adhered to at grassroots level, and it is even permissible to attempt to drown an opponent should a contest take place in water, as in *darya-i-buzkashi*. Recently the Afghan Olympic Federation has sought to establish more rules for all types of *buzkashi*, but these only truly apply to games held in Kabul of the *qarajay* variety. The new rules include the condition that the game be played on a square surface area with sides measuring 400 meters (1,312 feet) with two circles, the starting circle and the scoring circle, drawn inside the square. The new version of the game begins at the starting circle, and players then have to drop the animal carcass into the scoring circle, with two points awarded for each goal. At one end of the field stands a row of flags showing the minimum distance the carcass must be carried before returning to the scoring circle to claim a goal. The team that crosses the line of flags earns one point. In championship games held in Kabul, teams consist of 10 players. Five players take part in the first half lasting 45 minutes, and the other 5 players compete in the second half of the contest. In between the two halves is a halftime break of 15 minutes. An official known as the field master presides over the game and has the authority to add extra time and allow the substitution of players and horses.

Traditional *tudabaray buzkashi* does not involve teams but instead has many opposing players, all of whom have the right to compete against one another. It is not uncommon for a game of *tudabaray buzkashi* to feature several hundreds riders all competing at once, though expert riders known as *chapandazan* dominate play, which in *tudabaray* games is not governed by any spatial boundaries. When playing the *tudabaray* version of *buzkashi,* play starts with a circular mounted scrum and then players aim to gain sole control of the animal carcass by claiming it and riding free and clear of all other competitors. Once a player has claimed the carcass, he must ride out to a predetermined goal, usually a rock, hill, pole, or hand-drawn circle, at full speed. Though in theory any player may claim the carcass, only a *chapandaz,* that is, an individual expert horseman, has a realistic chance of winning a *buzkashi* competition. As the *chapandaz* claims a win he usually places his whip between his teeth so as to leave his hands free to hold the carcass. The *chapandaz's* triumph is often the high point of a contest and is accompanied by a roar from spectators, who usually sit on a nearby hill. Since spectators often bet on a specific *chapandaz* to win, there is much cheering when the *chapandazan* are involved in play. It is not uncommon for spectators to have to run away when horses gallop toward their viewing position.

The lack of rules in a *tudabaray*-style game often results in violence as players argue over whether the animal carcass has been taken away free and clear of all other riders. The game's lack of formality also means that contests can last as long as a week. The aggressive nature of *buzkashi* together with the sport's absence of protective clothing means that it is quite common for players to incur fractures, broken bones, cuts, and bruises. Rather than protective clothes, *buzkashi* players wear thick hats as well as quilted smocks tied with strong sashes. The only safety equipment worn by players is their long boots, which have a very high heel that can be locked into stirrups to prevent falls.

Horsemen must train for many years to become *chapandazan,* with the result that most are over the age of 40. Many *chapandazan* achieve iconic status within their own lifetime, and it is a role to which many Afghan boys aspire. Aspiring *chapandazan* must start playing *buzkashi* as boys, riding on the fringe of games and observing play in the hope that one day they will be allowed to play in major *buzkashi* competitions such as those played on the Desert of Happiness (Daht-i-Shadian) near Mazar-i-Sharif or in the Kunduz Stadium. The horses used in *buzkashi* are exchanged for around US$2,500, yet *chapandazan* may earn salaries (plus goal bonuses) that enable them to buy their own horses.

Like the *chapandazan,* the horses used in *buzkashi* take years of intensive training by a trainer, known as a *mehta* or *sayez,* to reach competition standard. Indeed,

5 years is the usual time it takes for a horse to complete its training. Two breeds of Afghan horse are used principally in *buzkashi,* the Tatar and the Habash. The Tartar is a small, swift, strong breed native to the provinces of Badakhaahan, Baghlan, Kunduz, Samanga, and Takhar. The Habash is larger and found on the vast plains of the Turkistan region of Central Asia. In addition to the Tartar and the Habash, the Arabi, Borta, Tazi, and Waziri breeds are also used. Only male horses are selected to play *buzkashi,* and the horses are taught several key skills. These include knowing to wait for their riders to remount should they become unseated during competition, to gallop away at high speed as soon as their rider has control of the animal carcass target, to swerve away from collisions, and to never tread on a fallen player. During the *buzkashi* playing season in winter and early spring, the horses are fed a special diet consisting of barley twice per day, melons, and occasionally a special meal of barley mixed with raw eggs and butter. In late spring and summer when it is too hot to play *buzkashi,* the horses are taken to fields to graze. It is common for successful *buzkashi* horses to play the sport for up to 20 years. A few days before a *buzkashi* contest, horses are kept hungry and taken for long-distance rides in order to make them especially lean, fit, and ready for competition. The horses are not given individual names but instead are sorted into nine color classifications: *ablaq* (mixed), *gul badam* (spotted), *jerand* (red), *kabood* (gray), *kahar* (yellow), *mushki* (black), and *toroq* (dark red).

There is a strong political element to both *tudabaray* and *qarajay* forms of *buzkashi.* The political component of *qarajay buzkashi* is clear, since that form of *buzkashi* is sponsored by the government, and under previous political regimes *qarajay*-style *buzkashi* was often officiated by military officers, with any player questioning the decision of the referees risking imprisonment. At the start of the 1950s the Afghan government began to hold *buzkashi* competitions across the country to celebrate the birthday of King Mohammad Zahir Shar. As the political regime of Afghanistan changed, *buzkashi* competitions were held on various days throughout the year that were considered to have a political importance, and by 1977 every element of *buzkashi* was controlled by the government. However, when the authority of the Marxist central government of Afghanistan diminished during the Soviet-Afghan War (1979–1989), authorities found it increasingly difficult to stage *buzkashi* competitions, particularly in Kabul. Thus, from 1982 onward the government stopped hosting *buzkashi* competitions, which severely damaged the regime's standing among its people. Noting this, opposition mujahideen commanders stationed in rural areas began to sponsor *buzkashi* competitions of their own in order to curry favor with villagers.

After recent political upheaval in Afghanistan *tudabaray buzkashi* is played in an exceedingly political context, for the sport's patrons, consisting of the traditional elite known as the khans living in the north of the country, sponsor *buzkashi* in a bid to both demonstrate and strengthen their political control in a land in which the political landscape is ever shifting. The khans breed and train the horses used in *buzkashi,* employ the *chapandazan,* and provide the prizes. *Buzkashi* competitions form the centerpiece of large ceremonial social gatherings called *tu is* that are held to demonstrate the social, political, and economic power of the sponsoring khan. During the *tu is* several rounds of *buzkashi* are played, with the patron awarding to the winner of each round prizes ranging from money to expensive turbans and clothes to rifles. The *tu is* is considered a success if the event passes off successfully, that is, without violence, and thus the status of the khan is enhanced. However, should the patron's financial resources run out before all the winners are awarded prizes and the event degenerates into violence, the *tu is* is deemed a failure, and the khan's reputation is diminished or even ruined.

Buzkashi is the focus of the Academy Award–nominated documentary short *Buzkashi Boys* (2012) and the feature film *The Horsemen* (1971).

See also: Bearbaiting and Badger Baiting; Bull Running; Camel and Yak Racing; Camel Wrestling; Cockfighting; Elephant Sports; Foxhunting; Hare Coursing; Nonlethal Bullfighting; Sheepdog Trials; Spanish Bullfighting; Yabbie Races

Further Reading

"Afghan National Sport (Buzkashi)." Afghanistan Online, 1997, http://www.afghan-web.com/sports/buzkashi.html (accessed August 12, 2013).

"Buzkashi: The National Game of Afghans." Embassy of Afghanistan, Canberra, http://www.afghanembassy.net/buz.php (accessed August 12, 2013).

"Buzkashi—National Sport of Afghanistan." Kidzworld, http://www.kidzworld.com/article/1944-buzkashi-national-sport-of-afghanistan (accessed August 12, 2013).

Lambert, Larry B. "Buzkashi." Afghan-Network.Net, http://www.afghan-network.net/Culture/buzkashi.html (accessed August 12, 2013).

Levine, Emma. *A Game of Polo with a Headless Goat and Other Bizarre Sports Discovered across Asia.* London: André Deutsch, 2003.

Scriber, Brad. "Nat Geo Photographer Tells All about Buzkashi, the Afghan Sport Involving a Headless Goat (and the Subject of an Oscar-Nommed Film)." *National Geographic,* February 22, 2013, http://newswatch.nationalgeographic.com/2013/02/22/nat-geo-photographer-tells-all-about-buzkashi-the-afghan-sport-involving-a-headless-goat-and-the-subject-of-an-oscar-nommed-film/ (accessed August 12, 2013).

C

CAMEL AND YAK RACING

Camel racing is the sport of riding camels over a course in a race format. Camel racing tends to involve the Dromedary species of camel, the name of which is derived from the Greek verb *dramein,* meaning "to run." The sport is extremely popular on the Arabian Peninsula, an area of western Asia to the northeast of Africa, where camel racing has spread due to a variety of cultural and geographical factors, with the United Arab Emirates the camel racing heartland of the region. Camel racing also takes place regularly in the desert regions of Sudan, Egypt, Kenya, India, and Australia. One-off races, such as the Cotley Point to Point camel steeplechase, also take place in England and other European countries, such as Germany.

The history of camel racing can be traced to the Arabian Peninsula during the 7th century when camel racing was a folk sport practiced at social gatherings and festivals. An Arabian desert-dwelling ethnic group called the Bedouins traditionally cared greatly for their camels, treating them as much more than mere racing animals. Rather, camels represented both a means of transportation and a symbol of wealth, and camel racing and riding were major hobbies among Bedouin children. Camel racing existed as a somewhat informal form of competition until the latter half of the 20th century, when camel racing attracted tourists and gamblers and subsequently began to be planned along the lines of horse racing, with organizations established to control and govern events. The rapid expansion of camel racing as an organized entity can be seen in the fact that in less than 10 years the United Arab Emirates constructed 12 camel racing courses, and virtually every inhabited area could boast its own track. Camel racing also became a major source of employment at famous racetracks, and in areas where the sport is popular it is an industry of which the actual racing of the animals is just one part. The breeding, training, and scientific research of camel rearing are also important factors. Indeed, nowadays camels are specially raised for racing through particular methods of breeding, training, and nutrition. Moreover, special methods of artificial insemination and techniques of embryo transfer are used to hybridize select lineages of camel. In addition to this scientific approach to crossbreeding, in the United Arab Emirates sophisticated camel training methods, such as exercising camels in swimming pools and on treadmills, are employed to prepare camels physically for the rigors of competition. Such meticulous preparation is financially savvy, for the country's local government provides subsidies to successful camel owners and breeders, and a camel born of good racing stock or that has an excellent racing history can sell for a high price.

The rules of camel racing vary between countries. In the United Arab Emirates camel racing takes place during the cooler months of October through April. Each race has between 25 and 30 registered entrants. In preparation for a race, camels are fed on a diet of dates, milk, seeds, alfalfa, and honey (though not before a race, as camels are not given food for 12 hours before they run). On the day of a race the camels are covered in blankets to keep them warm and daubed with henna and saffron, which according to local custom are symbols of good luck. Just before a race begins, trainers and owners together with their camels congregate and determine how the race is to be handicapped on the basis of breed, age, and sex and also decide the distance to be raced, which depends on the age of the camels involved—camels begin racing at two or three years of age and in general race until they are eight or nine, though an exceptional animal may have a longer racing career. The distances of a camel race range from 2.5 miles (4 kilometers) for younger camels to the 6 miles (10 kilometers) covered by older animals, which can reach speeds of 20 to 25 miles per hour at a gallop and 40 miles per hour sprinting.

As male and female camels tend to be different weights they are run in separate races, with jockeys preferring to race females, as they are not only lighter but also faster and better disciplined. Geldings (castrated camels) and studs are also raced separately.

Once prerace decisions have been made, lightweight jockeys mount the camels and maneuver the animals into a line, and then the race begins. In order to prevent any underhandedness or subterfuge, racing camels have identification microchips implanted in their necks, and after the race urine samples are collected and tested for banned substances.

Akin to camel racing is yak racing, a slightly comical traditional sport that takes place in Mongolia, Pakistan, Kazakhstan, and Kyrgyzstan as well as in the Tibetan region of China. Yak racing is common in the areas of Tibet noted for agriculture and animal husbandry and also often takes place at festivals, such as the annual Shoton Festival that is held in August. Yak races feature 10 or 12 riders who mount their yaks—which are dressed in ornamental saddles, with their heads adorned with red flowers—and then race the animals to the opposite end of the racetrack at a sprint. Despite their cumbersome appearance, yaks can run surprisingly quickly over a short distance. The winner receives a number of traditional Tibetan scarves (*khatas*) in addition to a small amount of prize money. Tibetan yak racing also takes place at the yearly Yushu Horse Festival, the Darma Festival in Gyangtse, and the Damxung Horse Festival, also known as the Dajyur, where yak races are held to celebrate the harvest and pray for good farming weather for the year ahead.

Mongolia has the second-largest yak population after China, and the animals are celebrated at the annual Mongolian Yak Festival, held in Bat-Ulzii Soum, the area of the world with the highest concentrations of yaks. The festival begins with 20 minutes of yak racing, though as the yaks are untrained it is often the case that many of them either do not finish the race or walk or slowly trot to the finish line. After the races have ended the festival moves on to a yak lassoing competition in which men on horseback frighten the yaks into running fast and then men on the ground lasso the animals. On successfully lassoing a yak, a contestant then has to control the animal. The last stage of the festival is yak polo, in which untrained, untamed yaks are ridden around the playing area as their riders try to hit a ball with a mallet.

Similar to camel and yak racing is the lighthearted sport of pig racing, though in pig racing the animals are not ridden. Instead the pigs are encouraged to hurdle obstacles and race around a special grass 36-meter (118-foot) track by handlers. The first pig to reach a bucket of food placed at the end of the track is declared the winner. Pigs often complete a race in less than five seconds. Pig racing takes place at agricultural fairs, tourist attractions, and charity fund-raisers in the United Kingdom, the United States, and Australia, where pig diving also takes place. Pig diving sees pigs dive from a 4-meter (13-foot) platform into a pool of water.

See also: Bearbaiting and Badger Baiting; Bull Running; *Buzkashi*; Camel Wrestling; Cockfighting; Elephant Sports; Foxhunting; Hare Coursing; Nonlethal Bullfighting; *Pato* and Horseball; Pigeon Racing; Sheepdog Trials; Spanish Bullfighting; Yabbie Races

Further Reading

Moriarty, Christopher. "Pigs Do Fly: Pig Diving in Australia." Chilli Sauce, September 4, 2012, http://blog.chillisauce.co.uk/pigs-do-fly-pig-diving-in-australia/ (accessed April 16, 2014).

Nauright, John, and Charles Parrish, eds. *Sports around the World: History, Culture and Practice,* Vol. 1, *General Topics, Africa, Asia, Middle East, and Oceania.* Santa Barbara, CA: ABC-CLIO, 2012.

"Pig Racing." Joseph's Amazing Camels, 2014, http://www.jacamels.co.uk/index.php/pig/ (accessed April 16, 2014).

Rasmi, Adam. "Dubai's Camel Races Embrace Robot Jockeys." The Daily Beast, December 7, 2013, http://www.thedailybeast.com/articles/2013/12/07/dubai-s-camel-races-embrace-robot-jockeys.html (accessed April 16, 2014).

Watson, Leon. "Do You Think It Will Catch On? Crowds Flock to See Popular Saudi Sport of CAMEL RACING in Rural Somerset village." MailOnline, March 30, 2014, http://www.dailymail.co.uk/news/article-2592835/Do-think-catch-Crowds-flock-popular-Saudi-sport-CAMEL-RACING-rural-Somerset-village.html (accessed April 16, 2014).

"Yak Festival." Happy Camel Journey, 1999–2014, http://www.happycamel.com/mongolian_festivals/yak_festival.php (accessed April 16, 2014).

"Yak Racing, a Spectator Sport in Tibet." Tibet Travel, March 27, 2014, http://www.tibettravel.org/tibetan-local-customs/yak-racing-in-tibet.html (accessed April 16, 2014).

CAMEL WRESTLING

Camel wrestling is a traditional Turkish cultural and sporting event in which two specially trained male camels vie for supremacy. The sport is mainly associated with Turkey's Aegean region, particularly Aydin Province, but also occurs in the Marmara region of northwestern Turkey and the Mediterranean region to the southwest of the country. The breed of camel most commonly employed in camel wrestling is a Tülü, the hybrid offspring of a female single-hump Dromedary camel (*camelus dromedarius*) and a male double-hump Asian Bactrian camel (*camelus*

A camel wrestling match in Mugla, Turkey. Camel wrestling is a traditional Turkish sporting and cultural event in which two trained male camels vie for supremacy. During a camel wrestling bout spectators may have to flee from retreating camels. (Aydindurdu/Dreamstime.com)

bactrianus) that is reared especially for wrestling. Today there are around 1,200 Tülüs in Turkey, mainly bought from Iran and Afghanistan, as both countries have a long heritage of breeding camels for wrestling and, together with Pakistan, also hold occasional camel wrestling matches. While a wrestling event may last just one day (sometimes with traditional rituals in the evening), some owners take their camels to multiple events in a region, thereby making a circuit of a region's annual matches.

The history of camel wrestling dates back at least around 2,400 years, when the nomadic peoples of Turkey learned to take advantage of the male camels' natural mating instinct to fight for supremacy. Camel wrestling is frequently depicted in the art of the Persian and Mughal Empires, the ruling powers in geographic regions covering modern-day Iran, Turkey, Afghanistan, Bangladesh, India, and Pakistan, while a miniature attributed to celebrated Persian Islamic artist Bihzad from the 1540s illustrates two camels wrestling. The first recorded camel wrestling festival took place in the Turkish Hıdırbeyli village, in Aydin Province, around 200 years ago.

From the 19th century onward, the popularity of camel wrestling grew to the extent that the sport became a favorite pastime of the Turkish people. Indeed, such was the popularity of the sport during the 1920s that the Turkish National Aviation league used camel wrestling matches to raise funds to allow the government to buy airplanes. However, when the Ottoman Empire (the ruling power of Turkey and many other countries since the start of the 14th century) collapsed in 1922, leading to the establishment of the Turkish state, the new government heavily discouraged camel wrestling, as it went against the European notion of a modern nation. However, in the 1980s Turkey experienced a military coup, after which camel wrestling was encouraged as a celebration of traditional Turkish culture.

As the sport depends on the mating urges of the male camel, it is natural that camel wrestling takes place during the camel mating season, usually during the winter. During a camel wrestling match two male camels are led into a ring or other similar area cleared for the bout, while a female camel is paraded past the males to stimulate their natural urge to fight over a potential mate. Male camels may also be starved for months prior to a bout to make them irritable and therefore more inclined to fight. To further annoy the animals, during a match the camels' owners are permitted to goad their beasts with the use of sticks. Camels wrestle for a period of 10 minutes, after which time match referees declare which camel has won. This decision is based on which camel has managed to make its opponent retreat, scream, or fall or has injured its opponent to the extent that the opposing camel's owner has to withdraw the camel from the fight in order to preserve its health. The forfeiture of a match is signaled when the owner of the injured camel throws a rope into the ring.

Male camels are eligible to wrestle in tournaments from the age of 10. Once a camel reaches this age, it is entered into competitions that have different categories based on animals' weight and age. There are also categories for camels that are left- or right-side dominant. Camels display various fighting tactics, and tournament organizers match camels known to use certain tactics. For instance, some camels attempt to trip their opponents using a foot in a move called *cengelci,* others push against their competitors to try to force a retreat in a move called *tekci,* and others trap their rival's head beneath their chest and then try to sit down. This move is known as *bagci.*

Today there are approximately 30 annual camel wrestling events held across Turkey, with the most prestigious being the national camel wrestling championship held in an ancient stadium at Ephesus near Selcuk, a town on Turkey's Aegean coast. This event involves around 140 camels and attracts 20,000 spectators. Camels are brought to a tournament's location several days before the tournament starts so they can participate in all aspects of the contest, which tend to include events such as camel beauty pageants. Each camel is given a name that not only acts as a way of identifying it but also forms part of a prayer, as the camel's name is inscribed on the small cloth bag, called a *pes,* that hangs from the camel's saddle preceding the word "Maşallah," a petition for God to protect the camel during the fight.

The day before the camels wrestle they are decorated with ornamental rugs and bells in addition to their saddles and protective clothing, and their owners don festive attire consisting of pointed caps, scarves worn over jackets, trousers, and long leather boots. Both camels and owners then take part in a march through the town's streets, followed by musicians playing drums and special instrumental horns called *zurnas.* Such pageantry highlights the fact that during a tournament, both camels and owner are treated as celebrities. After the parade, camel owners and spectators unite in a festive gathering to sing folk songs, eat, drink, and dance.

Wrestling events begin in the morning. As spectators' excitement grows, the main announcer, called the *cazgır,* reads aloud each camel's name and recites a poem about it. Camels are then paired to fight, and the *urgancılar,* or rope handler, leads each pair of camels into the arena, their mouths having been muzzled to stop the animals from biting each other. Once in the arena, officials and referees ensure that all competitors adhere to the established rules and time the bouts. During camel wrestling, spectators, who may have to flee from a retreating camel, bet on which animals will win and eat camel sausage. Also during a match, onlookers need to be aware that camels are retromingent, meaning they urinate backward. Thus, spectators may have to avoid spraying urine as well as copious amounts of spittle flying from the camel's mouths, as camels foam at the mouth when excited.

Though Turkish tourist authorities and government officials regard camel wrestling as a way of continuing ancient traditions and a lucrative boon to the tourism industry, there is a growing amount of disquiet about the sport among Turkish animal rights groups, who argue that camel wrestling is technically illegal under Turkey's animal rights laws and vociferously call for the abolishment of the sport on the grounds that the camels are treated inhumanly. Such qualms coupled with the rising cost of buying wrestling camels—a prize-winning camel is valued at roughly US$30,000 in addition to training, boarding, and transportation costs—mean that the future of camel wrestling is in doubt.

See also: Bearbaiting and Badger Baiting; Bull Running; *Buzkashi;* Camel and Yak Racing; Cockfighting; Elephant Sports; Foxhunting; Hare Coursing; Nonlethal Bullfighting; *Pato* and Horseball; Pigeon Racing; Sheepdog Trials; Spanish Bullfighting; Yabbie Races; *Yagli Gures*

Further Reading

Adamova, Adel T., "The Iconography of the Camel Fight." In *Muqarnas,* Vol. 21, *Essays in Honor of JM Rogers: An Annual on the Visual Culture of the Islamic World,* 1–14. Leiden: Brill, 2004.

Aydin, Ali Fuat. "A Brief Introduction to the Camel Wrestling Events in Western Turkey." SOAS Camel Conference, May 24, 2011, https://www.soas.ac.uk/camelconference 2011/file75386.pdf (accessed July 22, 2014).

"Camel Wrestling." Selcuk Ephesus, http://www.selcukephesus.com/what-to-do/camel -wrestling.html (accessed July 22, 2014).

Christie-Miller, Alexander. "Turkey: Tradition of Camel Wrestling Making a Comeback." Eurasianet.org, January 27, 2011, http://www.eurasianet.org/node/62784 (accessed July 22, 2014).

Galvan, Javier A., ed. *They Do What? A Cultural Encyclopedia of Extraordinary and Exotic Customs from around the World.* Santa Barbara, CA: ABC-CLIO, 2014.

Robehmed, Sophie. "Do the Participants of Turkey's Annual Camel Wrestling Festival Enjoy It as Much as the Audience?" *The Independent,* January 16, 2014, http://www.independent .co.uk/news/world/europe/do-the-participants-of-turkeys-annual-camel-wrestling -festival-enjoy-it-as-much-as-the-audience-9065497.html (accessed July 22, 2014).

CANAL JUMPING

Canal jumping, or *fierljeppen* (meaning "far leaping"), is a traditional athletic sport found almost exclusively in the Netherlands. The heyday for canal jumping came in the years directly after World War II, but then the popularity of the sport waned. Today the sport is experiencing something of a revival.

Quite when canal jumping began is unknown, though the first written reference to the sport dates to the 13th century, with the sport's first written records dating to 1771. Canal jumping is generally agreed to have originated when Germanic Frisian farmers decided to vault across the many canals dissecting their fields via a pole rather than to trudge to the bridges provided, as the bridges were few and far apart. Another theory is that poachers developed the technique of hurdling the canals in order to escape farmers from whom they had stolen eggs. Vaulting the waterways gradually evolved into the sport of canal jumping, which involves competitors of all ages pole-vaulting across the canals for which the Netherlands is famous. Each competitor carries a pole called a *polsstok* that is made of aluminum, carbon fiber, or wood. A competitor has three turns at sprinting toward the waterway, which is around 40 feet deep, and then planting the pole into the muddy bed of the canal near to the opposite bank. The pole is a maximum of 43 feet in length, and at the bottom of the pole is a round flat disk that prevents the pole from sinking into the canal's bed. However, unlike mainstream pole vaulting, the objective in canal jumping is to achieve distance rather than height, so the competitor jumps up the pole and then tries to climb farther up the pole by correcting the pole's forward and lateral movements. Once a competitor reaches the top of the pole, he then has to try to jump from the pole to land on a sand bed on the opposite bank of the canal, which can be as far as 46 feet away. Unsurprisingly, it is quite common for 30 percent of competitors to get a soaking by either missing the pole or falling from it, hence many competitors bring a change of clothes with them to competitions.

The canal jumping season begins in May and ends in September with the National Canal Jumping Contest held every August 22. The winner receives the title "Dutch Champion Canal Jumper." Though the sport is most closely associated with the Netherlands, jumpers from Africa, South America, Asia, Australasia, and the rest of Europe have all competed.

Another related Dutch sport is *paalzitten*, or pole sitting. Pole sitting is particularly popular in Aruba, a Caribbean island that continues to be part of the kingdom of the Netherlands and where a pole sitting competition has been held for the past 18 years. The sport of pole sitting owes its origins to the habit of Dutch boat hands resting on the poles that lined the canals and onto which Dutch barges moored. The sport sees four competitors vie to see who can sit on top of wooden poles for the longest time. Bathroom breaks are the only permitted interruption. The winner has been known to sit atop the pole for over 87 hours.

See also: Mallakhamb

Further Reading

Rosen, Michael J., and Ben Kassoy. *No Dribbling the Squid: Octopush, Shin Kicking, Elephant Polo and Other Oddball Sports.* Kansas City: Andrews McMeel Publishing, 2009.

Shipside, Steve. *Extreme Sports: Brilliant Ideas for Taking Yourself to the Limit.* Oxford, UK: Infinite Ideas, 2012.

Tagliabue, John. "Dutch Sports Revival Puts Canal-Vaulting Back in the Spotlight." *New York Times,* July 18, 2012, http://www.nytimes.com/2012/07/19/world/europe/little-known-dutch-sports-experience-a-revival.html?_r=1& (accessed August 7, 2013).

CAPOEIRA

Capoeira is an Afro-Brazilian physical activity fusing dance and fighting that takes the form of ritualized combat and involves rhythm, movement, philosophy, and music. The many various elements of capoeira mean that it is difficult to categorize. For instance, while some practitioners of capoeira, known as capoeiristas, meaning "players of capoeira," claim that the activity is a martial art, others dispute this, as unlike most martial arts, capoeira involves a limited amount of physical contact. The enigmatic nature of capoeira means that capoeiristas use the neutral term "playing" to refer to capoeira rather than "fighting" or "dancing." Capoeira is thought to improve flexibility, balance, strength, coordination, and aerobic capacity. Over the past 20 years women have started to outnumber men in terms of those learning capoeira techniques, and it has been predicted that in the near future women will dominate the capoeira world. The upsurge of interest in capoeira by women is thought to be due to capoeira's unique blending of dance, stretching, conditioning moves, and self-defense.

Two capoeira practitioners, or capoeiristas, playing within the roda. Capoeira is an Afro-Brazilian activity that combines combat moves, philosophy, music and dance. (AP Photo/Brandi Jade Thomas.)

Capoeira is practiced worldwide but is especially associated with Brazil. During the 1960s and 1970s there was an attempt to establish a capoeira governing body to oversee competitive capoeira bound by rules and laws. This led many capoeiristas to fear that the activity was about to become akin to many other competitive martial arts and in so doing lose capoeira's unique blend of philosophical and ritualistic aspects. However, while capoeira competitions still take place, capoeira as a competitive sport failed to become generally popular, and the competitions have no real significance in the capoeira world today.

The origin of the word "capoeira" is disputed, as are the origins of the activity. It has been suggested that the name "capoeira" comes from the Brazilian

Tupi language and is derived from the words *caa,* meaning both "down" and "little," and *puoera,* meaning "grass," to form a term meaning "to escape detection by hiding in the grass." Another theory claims that the name evolved from the Portuguese word *capa,* a term used to describe a basket in which African slaves carried capons (castrated male chickens, called *capao* in Portuguese) to the marketplace, where capoeira was traditionally staged. A third suggestion, and one that perhaps has the most credence, is that the name "capoeira" derives from the word *kipura,* meaning to "flutter," and refers to the movements of a fighting rooster. *Kipura* is a word taken from the Kikongo language spoken in the African countries of the Democratic Republic of Congo, Angola, and the Republic of the Congo.

Each of these explanations of the etymology of the word "capoeira" reflects that the origins of the activity lie with the presence of African slaves in Brazil. However, it is important to note that capoeira did not evolve in every area to which African slaves were shipped—the history of capoeira harks back to the transportation of slaves from Africa to Brazil only. While it is generally agreed that the roots of capoeira relate to the history of African slavery in Brazil, quite how the activity came into being is unknown. There are three theories as to how capoeira was invented. On the one hand, it has been suggested that African slaves exported the activity to Brazil. This theory maintains that when slaves from various African countries and regions were housed together, they merged different elements of their cultures and in so doing invented a new art form, capoeira. The main problem with this theory is that it would have taken many years for different cultural aspects to merge into one to form capoeira, and since there are records of capoeira being practiced in Rio de Janeiro as early as 1770, there seems to have been insufficient time for the cultures to meld and for capoeira to develop. Another suggestion is that capoeira evolved as a means of self-defense, either among communities of escaped slaves living in the Brazilian jungles who wished to avoid recapture by Portuguese police or as a way of retaliating against cruel treatment by slave owners. Those who side with this theory believe that the music that accompanies capoeira was employed to fool slave owners into thinking that early slave capoeiristas were dancing rather than practicing fighting moves. However, this theory too has problems. First, capoeira would have been little defense against the guns and knives wielded by the police or slave owners, and second, slaves were not permitted to dance.

A third, still weaker, theory is that capoeira is derived from an African ritual practiced by pubertal males called Danca de Zebra or N'golo, which apes the fighting style of zebras. However, this theory lacks credibility, as capoeira is particular to Brazil and does not have roots in any other country to which African slaves were exported. Thus, capoeira must have developed in Brazil rather than having been transported as an existing entity from Africa.

However capoeira originated, during the 18th century it became associated with violence and illegal activity in the major cities of Brazil as gangs known as *maltas* and made up of freed slaves noted the potential violence inherent in capoeira and used the capoeira techniques to commit robbery and street crime. The image of capoeira was rehabilitated somewhat during the 19th century, first when the first-ever Brazilian police force was created and charged with curbing the ruffian capoeirista element and then when capoeiristas were conscripted to help Brazil fight Paraguay in a war during 1865. The capoeiristas fought with great valor during the war, and their reputation was enhanced. However, this newfound prestige was short-lived, and soon capoeira was again seen as a violent threat to society. Indeed, in 1890 legislation was passed threatening capoeiristas with corporal punishment or exile. However, soon the most revered exponents of capoeira, know as *mestres*, instituted changes within capoeira to the end that the activity was gradually accepted as a game. Chief among these innovators was Manoel dos Reis Machado, know as Mestre Bimba, who took capoeira away from the streets by establishing capoeira academies, where the game is taught within a strict structure and with a strong set of ethics alongside its cultural heritage. Mestre Bimba also helped make capoeira a respectable pastime by bringing capoeira to the attention of the Brazilian upper middle classes and intelligentsia and spreading knowledge of capoeira throughout Brazil.

Capoeira takes place within a circle formed by other capoeiristas and musical instruments known as the *roda*. Two capoeiristas enter the *roda* simultaneously, and while watching each other the players pivot clockwise or counterclockwise, an action that continues throughout the game. The capoeiristas then perform arched and spinning kicks and sweeps in a series of moves in which physical contact is almost but not quite achieved, all the while keeping their eyes fixed on one another. Though takedowns can occur in capoeira, there is no winner in a capoeira game (unless the game is competitive). Instead, the general aim of the capoeirista, that is, an individual practitioner of capoeira, is to balance movements of attack and defense within the context of the individual game of capoeira, known as the *jogo,* as effectively as possible. For instance, the spinning kick of one player may make space for the sweeping move of the opponent, but then in an instant the rhythm of the capoeiristas loses synchronicity, and the game suddenly sees the two players act in opposition to one another. Meanwhile, defensive moves such as blocking and counteracting take the form of ironic interpretations of aggressive tactics.

Though capoeiristas each develop their own individual style, there are three main types of capoeira: capoeira Angola, capoeira regional, and capoeira contemporanea. Capoeira Angola, the oldest and most traditional form of capoeira, was chiefly developed by Vicente Ferreira Pastinha, known as Mestre Pastinha. Capoeira Angola is played at a variety of speeds from slow to fast, and moves tend to be long and played close to the ground. This form of capoeira focuses on strategy and trickery, so games last longer than in other forms of capoeira, around 10 minutes. Originally known as Bahian Regional Martial Art, capoeira regional was invented by Mestre Bimba as a modified version of traditional capoeira with an emphasis on fighting technique. Games of capoeira regional see capoeiristas remain upright, and because the game is played at a faster speed than capoeira Angola, games are much shorter, lasting only 2 to 3 minutes. The third type of capoeira, capoeira contemporanea, evolved during the 1960s in Rio de Janeiro. This style of capoeira, with its emphasis on technique, is heavily influenced by capoeira regional, though games are even shorter, lasting an average of 1 minute. An important element of capoeira contemporanea is the act of buying, that is, the cutting into play by another player. In capoeira contemporanea, capoeiristas can augment their play with decorative flips either during play or as a means to enter the *roda*.

Each of these different types of capoeira involves different musical instruments and musical arrangements, though the use of the instruments differs depending on the individual game. In general, capoeira employs a range of percussion instruments—the *berimbau*, *pandeiro*, *atabaquê*, *agogô*, and *reco reco*—which are believed to tap into the deepest reaches of human consciousness and also reflect the rhythms of play taking place within the *roda*. Perhaps the quintessential capoeira instrument is the *berimbau*, which is a metal bow at the base of which is placed a hollow gourd called a *cabaça*. There are three different types of *berimbau*, each offering a different pitch: the bass pitch of the *berimbau berra-boi*, the middle pitch of the *berimbau gunga ou médio*, and the high- or sharp-pitched *berimbau* viola or *violinha*. The *berimbau* is thought to symbolize the dual nature of capoeira, for it is said that in the days of yore a small, sharp sickle would hang from the instrument so that in an instant the *berimbau* could be used as a deadly weapon. Thus, the *berimbau*, like capoeira, united antagonistic elements—beauty and violence, death and dance, music and fight.

A *pandeiro* is a tambourine-like instrument in the shape of a wooden circle covered in small cymbals, over which is stretched the skin of a goat or an ox. Animal hide is also stretched across the *atabaquê*, a very basic instrument with skin stretched across a hollow, bottomless wooden cone. Like the *berimbau*, there are three types of *atabaquê* offering three different sound pitches: the *rum*, which is bass pitched; the *rumpi*, which is middle pitched; and the high- or sharp-pitched *lé*. The *agogô*, like the *berimbau* and the *atabaquê*, is African in origin. The *agogô* resembles a cowbell in both appearance and sound and consists of two iron bells that are tapped by an iron stick. The *reco reco* is a simple instrument consisting of a wooden or bamboo stick covered in ridges over which a wooden stick is rubbed to produce a scratching sound. Capoeira Angola employs all these percussion instruments, usually three *berimbaus*, two *pandeiros*, one *agogô*, one *reco reco*, and an *atabaquê*. To these instruments are added three different types of song or chant, *ladainhas*, *chulas*, and *corridos*. Chanting is an essential element of capoeira, as it is felt that singing is not just a musical accompaniment to the rhythms created by the various percussion instruments but is also a way of creating the necessary energy level required for the capoeira to take place.

See also: Footvolley and Futnet; *Parkour*; Rhythmic Gymnastics; *Varzesh-e Bastani*; Yoga

Further Reading

Almeida, Ponciano. *Capoeira: The Essential Guide to Mastering the Art*. London: New Holland Publishers, 2007.

Almeida, Ubirajara G. "Brief Description of Capoeira." Capoeira: Mestre Acordeon, 1996, http://www.capoeira.bz/mestreacordeon/capoeira/capoeira.html (accessed January 15, 2014).

Assuncao, Matthias Rohrig. *Capoeira: The History of an Afro-Brazilian Martial Art*. Abingdon, UK: Routledge, 2005.

Capoeira Connection. "What Does Capoeira Mean?" Capoeira Connection, October 26, 2011, http://capoeira-connection.com/capoeira/2011/10/what-does-the-word-capoeira-mean/ (accessed January 15, 2014).

Capoeira, Nestor. *The Little Capoeira Book*. Revised ed. Berkeley, CA: Blue Snake Books, 2003.

Centro Cultural e Artes Marcials Brasileiros em Montreal. "Grand Masters." January 31, 2004, http://www.capoeirabrasileira.com/centro/index.php?option=com_content&view=article&id=10&Itemid=13&lang=en (accessed January 16, 2014).

Centro Cultural e Artes Marcials Brasileiros em Montreal. "Musical Instruments." January 31, 2004, http://www.capoeirabrasileira.com/centro/index.php?option=com_content&view=article&id=13&Itemid=15&lang=en (accessed January 16, 2014).

Centro Cultural e Artes Marcials Brasileiros em Montreal. "Women in Capoeira." August 19, 2009, http://www.capoeirabrasileira.com/centro/index.php?option=com_content&view=article&id=15&Itemid=17&lang=en (accessed January 16, 2014).

Dils, Ann, and Ann Cooper Albright, eds. *Moving History/Dancing Cultures: A Dance History Reader*. Middletown, CT: Wesleyan University Press, 2001.

Essien, Aniefre. *Capoeira beyond Brazil: From a Slave Tradition to an International Way of Life*. Berkeley, CA: Blue Snake Books, 2008.

Taylor, Gerard. *Capoeira Conditioning: How to Build Strength, Agility and Cardiovascular Fitness Using Capoeira Movements*. Berkeley, CA: Blue Snake Books/Frog, 2005.

CELTIC WRESTLING

Celtic wrestling is an umbrella term for various styles of folk wrestling found in areas in which a people known as the Celts live. Today the Celts are particularly associated with settlements along Europe's Atlantic coast, where limited numbers of inhabitants speak languages classed as Celtic—that is, Irish and Scottish Gaelic, Welsh, Breton, Cornish, and Manx—and where a Celtic cultural identity has been forged and Celtic traditions have been kept alive. The six areas considered as Celtic territories are Scotland, Ireland, Wales, and Cornwall in England; Brittany in France; and the Isle of Man, a self-governing British dependency. Celtic wrestling also takes place in Spain and Portugal, but these countries are not classed as Celtic nations, as no Celtic language is spoken in either country. Rather, the Spanish peoples known as the Asturians and Galicians as well as the Portuguese claim a Celtic cultural heritage, as their languages derive from continental Celtic roots. Celtic wrestling also occurs in the areas of the world in which Celts have settled. For example, there is a strong Celtic wrestling tradition in Australia and the United States.

Gaelic-speaking Scotland and Ireland share a long history of grappling styles of wrestling. Indeed, the first literary references to Celtic wrestling in Ireland appear in the ancient myth of Cú Chulainn, who is said to have donned a belt to wrestle a Scottish invader whom he killed, only to discover that the invader was in fact his own son. That a Celtic wrestling style has existed in Ireland since ancient times is also suggested by the fact that wrestling was included in the annual harvest festival held in the former settlement of Telltown in County Meath between around 632 BCE and 1169 CE. Also, a stone cross in Kells, County Meath, depicts two wrestlers grappling with each other. That the cross portrays Celtic wrestling rather than, say, the Icelandic wrestling style of *glima* is proven by the fact that the cross dates to around the eighth century, which predates any invasion of Ireland by the Vikings. Similarly, grappling-style wrestling is depicted in Scottish carvings thought to date from between the seventh and ninth centuries. Also in Scotland, Domhnuil Gruamach, chief of the Clan Donald and lord of the Isles, is known to have erected a gymnasium for wrestlers on the island of North Uist in 1400 CE. This means that the wrestling arena was the first Scottish building to be constructed exclusively for sporting events.

In modern Scotland the most common form of Celtic wrestling is Scottish backhold wrestling, which is closely related to the English wrestling–style Cumberland and Westmorland wrestling. The history of Scottish backhold wrestling is not known, though William Shakespeare refers to the sport in his play *As You Like It* (ca. 1599). In this form of Celtic wrestling, wrestlers stand chest to chest and grip each other around the back of the waist, with the right hand under the opponent's left arm and with the chin resting on the opponent's right shoulder. When the referee is certain the wrestlers have taken a firm grip of each other, he shouts "hold" and the bout starts. There is no ground-work section to a Scottish backhold bout, and with the exception of kicking, wrestlers are allowed to use every legal way to throw their opponent. Bouts are usually best of five falls, with a fall said to occur when a wrestler touches the ground with any part of his body except his feet. Two judges and a referee (who has the final say if the judges disagree) must decide each fall. A wrestler is also declared the loser if he breaks hold while his opponent retains his own grip.

Scottish backhold wrestling is an important part of the Highland Games both in Scotland and around the world, and in Australia the style is played in a round-robin format in which wrestlers match each other. After all wrestlers have faced each other, the total number of falls are added together in order to decide the ultimate winner. A variation of Scottish backhold wrestling, Carachd Uibhist, is practiced on the Scottish islands of North and South Uist and Benbecula. In Carachd Uibhist, the style of grip employed in the bout is decided by a toss of a coin, and the best two of three falls is declared the winner. In contrast Carachd Bharraidh, which takes place on the Isle of Barra, is a loosehold style of wrestling in which opponents do not grip each other at the start of a bout and may choose whichever grip they wish. Carachd Bharraidh includes a ground-work section, and the winner is the wrestler who manages to force his opponent from the designated wrestling area.

There are several styles of native Irish wrestling, but the most notable are collar and elbow wrestling, also known as Irish scuffling, and Coraiocht. The origins of collar and elbow wrestling are unknown, though an Irish legend states that the sport developed when a young wrestler called Laidir (meaning "The Strong") accepted the challenge of a fight from the champion wrestler of the town of Sligo, who had already killed several of his opponents. Laidir met the Sligo wrestler in public, and onlookers were astonished to see Laidir throw the Sligo wrestler to the ground, breaking his neck. In reality, it is thought that muscular farmers earned money from participating in organized bouts of collar and elbow wrestling as early as 1600 in Connacht. Those who performed in collar and elbow wrestling were known as scufflers, and fights were known as scuffling bees. The name "collar and elbow wrestling" refers to the area of the scuffler's body grabbed during a fight, for at the start of a bout each scuffler stands face to face and places his right hand on the opponent's neck and his left hand on the opponent's elbow. Such a stance means that there is ample opportunity for skillful, tactical maneuvering, and this in turn means that in collar and elbow wrestling, technique and agility are more important than physical strength. The initial gripping position must be broken by the opponent, and once this has happened scufflers may catch any grip possible. The beginning of the bout was often a test of strategy and balance, as the scufflers would circle each other clockwise while trying to unbalance their opponent, whom they would kick and trip. This stage of the match could last a very long time. Indeed, there are reports of the standing portion of a bout lasting over an hour. Inevitably a takedown would occur, however. Common takedown moves included the snap mare, in which the opponent's head was grasped rather than his arm. Once one of the scufflers hits the ground, the ground wrestling section of the bout could begin in which ground control techniques such as half nelsons and various grapevines are employed. In the earliest days of collar and elbow wrestling a bout was won when all four points of the body, that is, both shoulders and both hips, were pinned to the ground for the count of five. In the late 19th century, the requirement to win was lessened to a three-point touch.

Recently a modern colonial-Irish style of collar and elbow wrestling has evolved in Australia that forms a component of Australian Pan-Celtic wrestling. This modern style of collar and elbow wrestling is performed by scufflers with or without a jacket—collar and elbow wrestling is traditionally practiced shirtless, though occasionally wrestlers would wear a tight-fitting jacket sewn with reinforced seams. Scufflers were also barefooted, as it was thought that wearing shoes might prompt wrestlers to kick their opponents. This modern variation of collar and elbow wrestling features a wide array of pinning techniques and submissions that are decided by agreement on the day of the bout according to the skill level of both scufflers. In modern-style collar and elbow wrestling a whistle is used to start and finish a match, and victory is achieved by a five-second pin or when one scuffler yields. Matches can only be won or drawn, and no minor points are awarded during a bout.

There has been a resurgence of interest in collar and elbow wrestling in Ireland as well as in Australia. The history of collar and elbow wrestling in the United States reaches back to the 1700s when Irish immigrants settled in Vermont. Though viewed in Ireland as a sport for peasants, in America collar and elbow wrestling was considered a gentlemanly activity, with several U.S. presidents known to have practiced the sport, including George Washington, Zachary Taylor, Ulysses S. Grant, Chester Arthur, and Calvin Coolidge, while William H. Taft was a Yale University wrestling champion.

Coraiocht is a backhold wrestling style that is practiced in Connemara, Galway, and Donegal in western Ireland. At the start of each bout it is traditional for the referee to shout "Lamh an iochdair, lamh an uachdar," which translates as "One hand up, one hand down." The rules are very similar to the other backhold styles of wrestling.

Cumberland and Westmorland wrestling is a form of folk wrestling found in the north of England, especially in the areas of Cumbria, Lancashire and Northumberland, and in the south of Scotland, with Grasmere, in Cumbria, acting as the sport's home. Both males and females compete in Cumberland and Westmorland wrestling, which is very similar to the Scottish backhold style—both wrestling forms demand both skill and strength and see opponents come face-to-face with their arms around each other, one arm above the shoulder and one below, with their finger interlinked. The winner is the best of three falls.

Alternative English Wrestling

Toe wrestling sees two competitors sit opposite each other with their feet on a board, lock toes, and attempt to force their opponent's foot down, all the while keeping their other foot suspended in the air and their bottom on the ground. Contests are the best of three rounds, with each round known as a toe-down. The sport originated in a pub in Derbyshire, England, where the annual world championships have been held since the mid-1970s.

The World Thumb-Wrestling Championships also take place in a pub in England and were won by American James Isaacs in 2013.

The origins of Cumberland and Westmorland wrestling are uncertain but are intertwined with Celtic wrestling styles found in other areas, particularly Cornish wrestling and *gouren,* native to Brittany, hence Cumberland and Westmorland wrestling is classed as a Celtic wrestling style by the Federation Francaise de Lutte (French Wrestling Federation). During the 19th and 20th centuries wrestling was popular with English farmers, as the sport was seen as a way of earning both money and esteem, with formal tournaments beginning in 1904. Over the years Cumberland and Westmorland wrestling has become more organized in terms of competitions and official coaching, but much of the sport's skills are still passed on via oral transmission and demonstrations. During the 19th century a unique Cumberland and Westmorland competition uniform developed that consists of white long johns and vest and colored, embroidered velvet trunks with matching socks, with prizes awarded for the most elaborately decorated shorts. In recent times this outfit has deterred some wrestlers, particularly young men, and Cumberland and Westmorland wrestling, which was hugely popular in Victorian England, has declined in popularity. However, wrestlers are now permitted to wear a tracksuit to compete.

The Breton Celtic wrestling style of *gouren,* which dates from at least the 14th century, and that of the ancient summer sport of Cornish wrestling, or "wrasslin," are almost identical. The main differences are that in *gouren* competitors wear a tight jacket, and in Cornish wrestling the jacket is loose. Also, while ground wrestling does not occur in either style, in *gouren* a wrestler has to throw an opponent down onto two shoulders, while in Cornish wrestling wrestlers must achieve a three-point pin as in collar and elbow wrestling. In Brittany *gouren* is very important culturally. Many Breton men were killed during World War I, and the future of *gouren* looked uncertain. However, a chance encounter between a Breton doctor and a Cornish folklorist led to the creation of an international Celtic wrestling meeting, the Inter-Celtic, that was first held in Quimperlé, Brittany, in 1928. The popularity of Cornish wrestling peaked during the 19th century, and the sport spread to Australia, South Africa, and America when Cornish miners emigrated in search of work. Indeed, Cornish wrestling is part of Grass Valley St. Piran's Day celebrations in California—St. Piran being one of the patron saints of Cornwall. While the *gouren* revival has continued steadily, Cornish wrestling struggled to survive initially. However, the sport has made a strong comeback, with competitions for both children and adults held in villages across Cornwall.

The neighboring English county of Devon also has its own style of Celtic wrestling, which differs from Cornish wrestling in that a form of kicking and tripping similar to shin kicking, called outplay, is permitted. Devonian wrestling is somewhat scorned by Cornish wrestlers, and intercounty bouts are particularly bruising affairs.

See also: Fell Running; *Glima;* Highland Games; Hurling; Korean Wrestling; *La Soule; Lucha Libre;* Mongolian Wrestling; Nonlethal Bullfighting; *Pehlwani/Kushti; Schwingen;* Sheepdog Trials; Shin Kicking; Sumo Wrestling; *Varzesh-e Bastani; Yagli Gures*

Further Reading

Baxter, Willie. "New Vigour in Our Oldest Sport." *Renfrewshire Local History Forum Journal* 8 (1997), http://rlhf.info/wp-content/uploads/8.2-Wrestling-Baxter.pdf (accessed March 2, 2014).

"Colonial Grappling: Irish Scuffling." Australian Celtic Wrestling, http://celticwrestling .wordpress.com/irish-scuffling/ (accessed March 2, 2014).

Coomes, Phil. "Wrestling with the Past." BBC News in Pictures, December 14, 2011, http:// www.bbc.co.uk/news/in-pictures-16108841 (accessed March 4, 2014).

Dellinger, Bob. "A History of Wrestling in the United States." New Milford Green Wave Wrestling, Spring 2014, http://newmilfordgreenwavewrestling.stackvarsity.com/cpage .asp?id=163294 (accessed March 2, 2014).

Federation of Gouren of the FALSAB. *Gouren: Breton and Celtic Wrestling.* Brittany, France: Fédération de Gouren et Institut Culturel de Bretagne, 1985.

Green, Thomas A., and Joseph R. Svinth. *Martial Arts of the World: An Encyclopedia of History and Innovation,* Vol. 2. Santa Barbara, CA: ABC-CLIO, 2010.

Holden, Rebecca. "Cornish Wrestling." MyCornwall, August 27, 2013, http://www .thatsmycornwall.com/cornish-wrestling/ (accessed March 4, 2014).

Hurley, John W. *Shillelagh: The Irish Fighting Stick.* Pipersville, PA: Caravat, 2007.

Litt, W. *Wrestliana: Or, an Historical Account of Ancient and Modern Wrestling.* London: John Richardson, 1823.

Marshall, John Duncan, and John K. Valton. *The Lake Counties from 1830 to the Mid-Twentieth Century.* Manchester, UK: Manchester University Press, 1981.

McKinney, Gage. "The Most Cornish Spot in America." Downtown Grass Valley, 2013, http://www.downtowngrassvalley.com/grass-valley/st-pirans.html (accessed March 4, 2014).

Pfenger, Ken. "Wrestling in Celtic Culture." Celtic Wrestling, http://celtic-wrestling.tripod
.com/id12.html (accessed March 2, 2014).

Renwick, Jamie. "'Embarrassed' Wrestlers Drop Embroidered Pants to Save Sport from Dying." *The Independent,* April 13, 2005, http://www.independent.co.uk/news/uk/this
-britain/embarrassed-wrestlers-drop-embroidered-pants-to-save-sport-from-dying
-6148440.html (accessed January 1, 2014).

Robson, Roger. "Cumberland & Westmorland Wrestling: A Personal View of the Sport." BBC,
http://www.bbc.co.uk/cumbria/content/articles/2005/09/27/wrestling_2005_09_28
_feature.shtml (accessed January 1, 2014).

Tomlinson, Alan. *A Dictionary of Sport Studies.* Oxford: Oxford University Press, 2010.

Tripp, Michael. "Persistence of Difference: A History of Cornish Wrestling," Vol. 1. PhD
dissertation, University of Exeter, 2009, https://ore.exeter.ac.uk/repository/bitstream
/handle/10036/106560/TrippM_vol1.pdf?sequence=3 (accessed March 4, 2014).

CHEESE ROLLING

Cheese rolling is a competitive activity in which competitors either chase a rolling
cheese over a predetermined distance or roll a cheese along a course. The most celebrated cheese rolling competitions are traditional English folkloric events. The most
famous is the Cooper's Hill cheese rolling competition held in Brockworth in the
western county of Gloucestershire. Competitors chase a wheel of cheese measuring
one foot in diameter down a hillside, with the first person to reach the bottom of the
hill declared the winner and winning the cheese as a prize. The cheese rolling competition sees competitors chase an entire Double Gloucester cheese weighing eight
pounds down the hillside over a course measuring 600 feet long and with an average
gradient of 1:2 (and 1:1 in some places). The competition takes place at noon on
the last Monday in May as part of a festivity called the Cooper's Hill Wake that used
to include tug-of-war and shin kicking. The origins of the cheese rolling competition
are not known, but one theory is that Roman soldiers stationed at a fort at the top
of Cooper's Hill used to throw items from the building, though another theory suggests that the competition harks back to a pagan fertility rite that sought to ensure a
bountiful harvest, with the round yellow wheel of cheese symbolizing the sun. However, the cheese rolling competition as known today dates from the early 19th
century.

Double Gloucester Cheese

Double Gloucester has been made in the Cotswold area of England since at least
1498, when so much cheese was being produced in Gloucester that a dedicated market was instituted to sell the produce. Today Double Gloucester is made across the
United Kingdom both on farms and at large dairies. Since the 16th century, the milk
used to make the cheese has had annatto added to it to produce a characteristic pale
orange color. Double Gloucester is usually sold at four months of age, when it has
developed a firm texture and a buttery flavor.

The day of the Cooper's Hill cheese rolling competition sees five races held, including a ladies' race and uphill races for children. A cheese rolling event has taken place at Cooper's Hill every year within living memory except 1998, which was cancelled because 33 competitors had been injured the previous year; 2001, because of an outbreak of foot-and-mouth disease; and 2003, when emergency crews were called away to serve at the site of an earthquake in Algeria. However, whenever the cheese rolling competition has been cancelled, a Double Gloucester has been rolled down the hill to symbolize the event. It is important to note that since 2010, the Cooper's Hill cheese rolling competition has had to take place in an unofficial capacity. This is due to health and safety fears for both spectators and competitors. The year before the official competition was cancelled, 15,000 spectators massed on the hill to watch the competition despite the fact that the hill can only safely accommodate 5,000 people. This large number of spectators was due partly to the fact that the competition now attracts tourists from as far afield as Australia. Competitors also come from abroad, particularly from the United States, Australia, and Japan. Moreover, cheese rolling is a dangerous activity that often results in broken bones and other injuries incurred either by falling while chasing the cheese or by the cheese rolling out of control and crashing into competitors and spectators at high speed. Thus, the Cooper's Hill competition now takes place without medical cover or insurance and uses a lightweight replica cheese made of foam rather than a real cheese.

Another English cheese rolling competition is held in Stilton, home of the famous blue-veined cheese of the same name, on May Day, a national holiday that takes place on the first Monday in May. The origins of the Stilton cheese rolling competition are unknown, but the event used to be held on Easter Monday and involved competitors rolling a piece of wood shaped like a wheel of Stilton cheese through the town's streets from a starting line between the Stilton Cheese Inn and the Talbot pubs to the finish line outside another pub, the Bell Inn. The competition was exclusively for teams of men who would compete boisterously to roll the cheese to the finish line, with the first team to reach the end declared the winner. Today the race starts between the Bell Inn and the Angel pub, and the finish is located at a crossroads in the town. The competition is no longer exclusively male and sees contestants compete in teams of four men, women, or mixed juniors, with each team member having to roll the cheese at least once during the race. The competition is a knockout competition format with quarterfinals, semifinals, and a grand final.

A cheese rolling competition of a different kind occurs in the town of Gessopalena, in central Italy, as part of the annual September Buon Gusto Cheese Fair. Here the cheese rolling competition, Gara di Ruzzola, takes the form of a cross between yo-yoing and *pétanque,* for male competitors, either as individuals or as part of a team, use 2 meters (around 6.5 feet) of hemp twine to attach wheels of Italian pecorino cheese to their wrists and see who can roll the cheese the farthest along the town's street toward the local church. The event dates back to the times of the Etruscan civilization (ca. 700–4 BCE), and though the competition died out during World War II, Gara di Ruzzola became a national craze during the

1970s, and the event's postwar popularity means that it is now the focus of spread betting, with wagers laid on which team or individual will win the competition. A similar event takes place in the central Italian village of Panicale to celebrate the national holiday of Pasquetta (Little Easter), which commemorates the meeting between the women who went to Jesus's tomb after the crucifixion and the angel who told the women that the tomb was empty. Food is integral to the celebration of Pasquetta, and the Panicale cheese rolling competition reflects this, for during the competition players roll a whole pecorino weighing nine pounds around a course following the perimeter of the ancient walled village. Players launch the cheese using a leather strap wrapped around the cheese, and competitors maneuver the cheese around the course using a wooden stick. Officials run alongside the cheese to mark where it falls over, for the winner is the competitor who completes the course in the fewest strokes. The victor receives the cheese as a reward.

See also: Barrel Races; Cotswold Olimpicks; Fell Running; *La Soule;* Pancake Races; *Pétanque;* Shin Kicking; Skittles

Further Reading

"American Flies in to Win Gloucestershire Cheese Rolling Contest." *The Guardian*, May 27, 2013, http://www.theguardian.com/uk/2013/may/27/gloucestershire-cheese-rolling -race (accessed April 28, 2014).

Bradley, Lloyd. *The Rough Guide to Cult Sport.* London: Rough Guides, 2011.

Calta, Marialisa. "Roll That Cheese! It's Little Easter in Italy." *New York Times,* April 8, 2007, http://www.nytimes.com/2007/04/08/travel/08heads.html?pagewanted=all (accessed April 28, 2014).

"Cheese Rolling." Stilton Parish Council, 2003–2014, http://www.stilton.org/cheese -rolling/ (accessed April 28, 2014).

Connolly, Paul. *The World's Weirdest Sports.* Millers Point, Australia: Pier 9, 2007.

Dunham, Samantha. "Yo-Yo Cheese Rolling at Gessopalena." Life in Abruzzo, http://www .lifeinabruzzo.com/yo-yo-cheese-rolling-at-gessopalena/ (accessed April 28, 2014).

"Gloucestershire Cheese Rolling." So Glos, May 26, 2014, http://www.soglos.com/sport -outdoor/27837/Gloucestershire-Cheese-Rolling (accessed April 28, 2014).

Morris, Steve. "Gloucestershire's Annual Cheese Rolling Cancelled Due to Health and Safety Fears." *The Guardian*, March 12, 2010, http://www.theguardian.com/uk/2010 /mar/12/gloucestershire-cheese-rolling-cancelled (accessed April 28, 2014).

"Previous Years." Cheese-rolling.co.uk, April 27, 2013, http://www.cheese-rolling.co.uk /past_events.htm (accessed April 28, 2014).

Tabone, Paige, and Agencies. "Grandmother Won't Make Double Gloucester for Cheese-Rolling Event after 'Heavy-Handed Threats' from Police." *The Telegraph,* May 23, 2014, http://www.telegraph.co.uk/news/newstopics/howaboutthat/10076336/Grandmother -wont-make-Double-Gloucester-for-cheese-rolling-event-after-heavy-handed-threats -from-police.html (accessed April 28, 2014).

"2001 Event Cancelled." Cheese-rolling.co.uk, April 19, 2012, http://www.cheese-rolling. co.uk/what_happened_in_2001.htm (accessed April 28, 2014).

Winn, Christopher. *I Never Knew That about the English.* New York: Random House ebooks, 2009.

CHESS BOXING

Chess boxing is a relatively new hybrid sport for men and women in which the two seemingly incompatible activities of boxing and playing chess take place in alternating rounds. The sport is played in the United Kingdom, the United States, Japan, India, Iceland, France, Russia, Iran, Germany, Italy, and Spain.

There are several theories as to how chess boxing originated. Perhaps the best-known theory is that the sport was invented by French cartoonist Enki Bilal, who depicted a game of chess boxing in his 1992 graphic novel *Froid-Equateur* (*Cold Equator*). Bilal's concept was built upon by Dutch artist Iepe Rubingh, who in 2003 staged a chess boxing bout in Berlin. Rubingh competed in the fight and won. Subsequently he established the World Chess Boxing Organization (WCBO), which in 2005 organized the first European chess boxing title fight that was won by Tihomir Titschko, a professional chess player from Bulgaria. However, another theory purports that chess boxing was invented in Kidbrooke, London, in 1978 when young brothers James and Stewart Robinson discovered that the boxing class they attended regularly had been cancelled for a night and that a chess class was being held at the same venue. The Robinsons decided to combine the two activities, and over the next three years the combination of boxing and chess began to draw crowds. Eventually the Kidbrooke chess boxing became a regular event that was reported in local newspapers and billed as brain versus brawn. A year after the Robinson brothers first combined chess and boxing, a Chinese martial arts film, *Shuang ma lian huan* (known internationally as *Ninja Checkmate* and called *Mystery*

Chess boxers competing at the Bread & Butter Fair in Berlin, Germany, on January 19, 2011. A chess boxing match sees participants compete in alternate rounds of chess and boxing. Chess boxers must be proficient in both disciplines. (Paul Prescott/Dreamstime.com)

of *Chess Boxing* in America) combined chess and boxing in its title, for *Shuang ma lian huan* translates metaphorically as the joint double offensive power of the double knight pieces attack in chess strategy.

Chess boxing is governed by both the WCBO and the World Chessboxing Association (WCBA). Tim Woolgar, chief executive of London Chessboxing, founded the World Chessboxing Association after talks between the national chess boxing boards of the United Kingdom, Russia, Italy, and Spain in response to the rapid growth of chess boxing across the globe. The WCBA is a nonprofit body that aims to continue the development of the sport and has created a chess boxing code of practice.

A chess boxing match consists of 11 alternating rounds of chess and boxing made up of 6 chess rounds and 5 rounds of boxing. The match starts with a chess round that lasts for four minutes and is played on a table located in the center of the boxing ring. At the end of the first chess round the table and chess-playing equipment are removed from the ring, and competitors put on boxing gloves. Next a round of boxing begins that lasts two minutes. When the two minutes of boxing is over the chess paraphernalia is retuned to the ring, and another four-minute chess round begins. The match continues in this way until all 11 rounds have taken place.

Chess boxers must be proficient at both chess and boxing, as a win can be awarded for skill at either discipline. For instance, on the boxing side a win can be achieved by a knockout in the ring, a technical knockout, or a boxing points decision. If a match is drawn, for example, if a chess stalemate occurs, the decision as to which player has won is given to more than who has scored the most boxing points. If, however, a draw occurs at any time before the final round, then another round of boxing is held to conclude the match. A player can also achieve a win on chess grounds, for example, by achieving a chess checkmate. However, perhaps the most common reason for a win being awarded is because a player has exceeded the time limit in a chess round—six rounds of chess at 4 minutes equates to 24 minutes of chess playing per chess boxing match. This means that players each have 12 minutes in which to considered their strategy and complete their moves. In order that a player does not use the chess playing rounds of a match as a breather to recover from the physical exertion of boxing, a chess boxing match ends when a player's 12 minutes are over. A match official known as the arbiter acts as the chess referee by constantly assessing the play on the chessboard and judges whether time is being wasted. If the arbiter believes that a player is wasting time, then the arbiter may impose a 10-second time limit during which the player suspected of wasting time must make a chess move or be disqualified from the match.

Players can also win if their opponent is disqualified for cheating. During the chess rounds players wear closed-back headphones to prevent them from hearing advice shouted to them by spectators and also so that they are not distracted by background noise.

Players do not need to be expert chess players to take part in chess boxing. A player's chess ability is graded by Elo points, which are named after Arpad Elo, a Hungarian chess master who invented the system, and most chess boxing champions have an Elo rating of 1,700 or above. Most chess boxers begin with a lower Elo ranking than this, however, but once players have learned the basic strategies and tactics of chess, their rating improves rapidly. Chess boxers' chess abilities are split into divisions within an eight-tiered system based on Elo points, so as long as both chess boxers fall within the same Elo tier category, neither will have a major chess-playing advantage. Tier 1 of the Elo system is for beginners who have up to 1,000 Elo points. Players with 1,001 to 1,200 points are classed as social players, while an Elo score of 1,201 to 1,400 Elo points denotes an advanced social player. A weak club player is a chess boxer with 1,401 to 1,600 Elo points, while 1,601 to 1,800 Elo points equates to an average club player, and a player with an Elo score of 1,801 to 2,000 is classed as a strong club player. An Elo points score of 2,001 to 2,300 places a player within the class of nationally ranked players, while an internationally ranked player has an Elo points score of more than 2,301.

Just as players' chess-playing abilities are ranked, their boxing weights are also divided into classes. These range from straw weight for players weighing 108 pounds through players weighing more than 200.6 pounds, who are classed as heavyweight chess boxers.

See also: Celtic Wrestling; Footvolley and Futnet; Shin Kicking; Shove Ha'penny; Thai Boxing; *Varzesh-e Bastani*

Further Reading

Chandler, Mark. "Chessboxing—The Bizarre Craze That Started in a Kidbrooke Youth Club." News Shopper, September 17, 2012, http://www.newsshopper.co.uk/news/greenwich/9933055.Chessboxing___the_bizarre_craze_that_started_in_a_Kidbrooke_youth_club/ (accessed March 11, 2014).

Connolly, Paul. *The World's Weirdest Sports*. Millers Point, Australia: Pier 9, 2007.

"FAQ." World Chess Boxing Association, 2013, http://worldchessboxing.com/contact/wcba-chessboxing-faq/ (accessed March 11, 2014).

"Ninja Checkmate—Trivia." IMDB.com, 1990–2014, http://www.imdb.com/title/tt0199813/trivia?ref_=tt_trv_trv (accessed March 11, 2014).

Reilly, Rick. *Sports from Hell: My Search for the World's Most Outrageous Competition*. New York: Doubleday, 2010.

Stokel-Walker, Chris. "The Mystery of Chessboxing." BuzzFeed, November 21, 2013, http://www.buzzfeed.com/chrisstokelwalker/the-mystery-of-chessboxing (accessed March 11, 2014).

"World Chessboxing Association: Official Launch." World Chess Boxing Association, 2013, http://worldchessboxing.com/world-chessboxing-association-official-launch/ (accessed March 11, 2014).

COCKFIGHTING

Cockfighting is a blood sport in which two or more specially bred roosters fight each other in a ring called a cockpit. Cockfighting is a major sport in the Middle East, the Far East, Pakistan, and Latin America, where the activity is known as *pelea de gallos*. However, cockfighting is banned in many countries, including the United States, the United Kingdom, and Australia, though the activity does

A cockfighting enthusiast displays an aggressive Hatch cock in Oregon on March 7, 2003. Cockfighting sees specially bred roosters fight each other for the entertainment of spectators. The sport is prevalent in the Middle East, Far East, and Latin America but is banned in many countries on the grounds of animal cruelty. (AP Photo/John Gress)

continue in these countries. Cockfighting is also forbidden in much of Spain and France, where the pastime may be practiced only in areas that enjoy a long cock-fighting tradition. Cockfighting is a contentious issue, as proponents of the activity maintain that the sport is an important aspect of cultural heritage, while animal rights groups argue that the activity is sadistic. Where cockfighting is banned the activity tends to become an underground activity, as the sport enjoys such strong cultural ties that people are unwilling to give it up despite its illegality. As a result of being driven underground, the sport often becomes associated with other illegal activities such as drug trafficking and gambling.

Cockfighting is one of the world's oldest sports. There is evidence that birds were bred for sport by ancient peoples such as the Celts, Gauls, and Britons, and from 524 to 460 BCE roosters were used in sport in ancient Greece, from where the sport spread to Asia. Cockfighting also took place in ancient Rome, from where it spread to Italy, Germany, and Spain as well as to the Roman colonies of England, Wales, and Scotland. Indeed, cockfighting has been present in the United Kingdom for so long that terms associated with the activity are in common usage; for example, an overconfident person is described as cocky, while a disappointed person is said to be crestfallen.

Though the Romans imported cockfighting to Britain, the first documented evidence of the sport in the United Kingdom dates from the 12th century, when cockfighting took place in London, the capital of England, on Shrove Tuesday, the day that marked the beginning of Lent. Moreover, during medieval times cockfighting became a regular part of village fairs. However, King Edward III (1312–1377) banned the sport in 1366, as he wished to encourage archery instead of cockfighting, and King Henry VI (1421–1471) also outlawed the activity. However, the sport was revived under King Henry VIII (1491–1547), who approved of cockfighting to the extent that he had constructed the Royal Cockpit in Westminster, central London. The popularity of cockfighting in England peaked during the late 18th and early 19th centuries, when many purpose-built cockpits were constructed. Some of these cockfighting arenas were very large, such as the Lowther Street octagonal pit built in Carlisle, northern England, during the 18th century that had a diameter of 40 feet, and the pit built in Stamford in the eastern county of Lincolnshire, which could accommodate 500 spectators. During this time the activity was generally seen as a socially acceptable mainstream sport alongside horse racing that was enjoyed by all sections of society as both entertainment and a form of gambling. However, though cockfighting was generally accepted, dissenters began to argue against the sport as early as the reign of Queen Elizabeth I (1533–1603). Notable dissenters include famous diarist and politician Samuel Pepys (1633–1703), who deemed cockfighting barbaric; and celebrated artist William Hogarth (1697–1764) depicted cockfighting as a diabolical pursuit comparable to cruelty to cats and dogs in his 1751 illustration *The First Stage of Cruelty* and in *The Cockpit* (1759), which portrays cockfighting as the focus of immoral gambling activity. However, it was poet George Crabbe (1754–1832) who truly gave impetus to the anticockfighting movement in England when he described the sport in savage detail in his 1807 poem *The Parish Register*. From then on anticockfighting opinions gained ground, particularly among conformist and evangelical religious groups. The founding of the Society for the Prevention of Cruelty to Animals, later renamed the Royal Society for the Prevention of Cruelty to Animals (RSPCA) in 1824, spurred on the anticockfighting movement, and in 1835 cockfighting was outlawed under the Cruelty to Animals Act alongside bull- and bearbaiting. By 1840 horse racing publications had stopped advertising cockfights, though in some areas of England, particularly in the working-class north of the country and throughout rural areas, cockfighting circles continued as normal, with cockfighting clubs using issues of parish and county jurisdiction to evade prosecution by the police. The upper classes also continued to enjoy cockfighting either by hosting private cockfights in London or at their country estates or by traveling to Calais in northern France, where the activity still took place despite a ban. Today cockfighting continues in the United Kingdom. One reason for this is that some immigrants from countries where cockfighting is legal continue the activity when they move to the United Kingdom. However, undercover work by RSPCA officers often leads to the prosecution of those who organize cockfights. For example, in 2012 two men were sentenced to 20 weeks in jail for their part in one of the largest cockfighting operations ever in England in which hundreds of roosters were used in cockfights in northern France. The history of cockfighting in the United States followed a pattern similar to that in the United Kingdom. In the United States the sport's popularity peaked between 1750 and 1800, with the sport's fans, who resided between North Carolina and New York, reflecting their desire to behave in the manner of the British upper classes. During this time cockfighting in the United States involved specially bred birds developed for their strength, athleticism, and aggression that, prior to fights, were fed on a special diet, exercised, and kept segregated from other birds. In order to fight, the birds had small pointed metal blades strapped to their legs and would usually fight to the death, as this eliminated any question as to which bird was the winner.

American cockfights, which sometimes featured as many as 60 pairs of birds, tended to be very formal events advertised in newspapers and by word of mouth, and as in the United Kingdom, the fights attracted people from all classes of society. However, unlike in England, American cockfights did not take place at specially constructed venues. Rather, the fights took place in roped-off areas or on wasteland in urban areas and were associated with debauched behavior. The fights often appalled those who abhorred violence. For instance, 18th-century writer Elkannah Watson wrote of his bemusement that anyone of intelligence could enjoy the barbarity of the sport. Such sentiments helped fuel the anticockfighting movement in the United States, and authorities frequently tried to quash the activity. Indeed, cockfighting was outlawed in Georgia as early as 1775. Further to this, in the aftermath of the Revolutionary War, cockfighting was considered an unwanted relic of English culture. In addition, attitudes toward animal cruelty began to change, and by the 1830s cockfighting was deemed unsavory, with a law to outlaw cockfighting passed in Pennsylvania in 1830. Today cockfighting is illegal in all 50 states of the United States and is a felony offense in 40 states plus the District of Columbia. It is also forbidden to keep birds for fighting in 38 states as well as the District of Columbia. Yet despite these laws, cockfighting continues in America. Prior to a fight birds are put through months of training, sometimes involving running obstacle courses and on treadmills, and then just before a fight a bird will have most of his feathers plucked and his wattle, that is, the combs below his beak, severed so that his opponent cannot tear it off during the fight. Once in the cockpit, which is usually a circle drawn in the dirt, the birds, which are matched on the basis of equal weight, are fitted with knives or tapering metal blade attachments up to three inches long called gaffs that transform the birds' natural spurs into weapons. The blades are sufficiently sharp to puncture a bird's eye or lung and to break bones. Such weaponry is integral to cockfighting in America, for fights are classified by the style of weapon attached to the birds—fights are defined as a short-knife fight, a long-knife fight, or a gaff fight. Fights can last as long as 15 minutes and are supervised by a referee. Modern American cockfights need not end in the death of the birds, though this is often the outcome. As in the United Kingdom, illegal cockfighting is often associated with other criminal activity involving drugs and firearms and tends to involve ethnic minorities whose cultures do not frown upon cockfighting or who are native to countries where the sport is permitted. Illegal cockfighting in the United States is particularly prevalent among Puerto Ricans, Delta blacks, Cajuns, Mexican Americans, and rural whites.

Generally speaking cockfighting is a cyclical activity that involves the prefight preparation of birds, betting on the outcome of the fight, the fight itself, the declaration of a winning bird, the settling of bets, and then the initiation of the next fight. However, there are local, regional, and national differences in the specifics of the sport. For instance, in parts of India the birds simply fight each other using their claws as weapons. However, it is more usual for the birds to be equipped with some sort of weapon. In Bali, Indonesia, for instance, cockfighting is thought by many to have magical, spiritual powers, as the sport was originally part of a religious purification rite known as Tabuh Rah, meaning "pouring blood," in which various animals, including roosters, were sacrificed so that blood might spill upon temple ground. This history is reflected in the fact that today Balinese roosters are fitted with a metal blade called a *taji* attached to their legs with which to inflict bloody injury on each other. Today cockfighting is one of the main leisure activities among Bali's male population, viewed as both a source of entertainment and a gambling activity involving bets on houses, cars, and land. Meanwhile, in Latin America and the Philippines cockfighting roosters have a razor-sharp piece of metal called a slasher fitted to their claws so that when the birds are pitched into the cockpit, they slash at one another until one of the birds dies or is critically wounded, often in front of many spectators who have bet on the outcome of the fight. Fights may take some time to conclude, with hour-long fights not unknown, as the birds are often specially bred and trained to be aggressive and may be injected with steroids or painkillers to help prolong the fight. Meanwhile, in Puerto Rico a needlelike shard of plastic is attached to the heel of the bird.

Despite the sport's varying degrees of legality, cockfighting is so popular globally that dedicated cockfighting magazines exist, as do specialist jewelers who create the weaponry attached to the fighting birds.

See also: Bearbaiting and Badger Baiting; Bull Running; *Buzkashi;* Camel and Yak Racing; Camel Wrestling; Elephant Sports; Foxhunting; Hare Coursing; Nonlethal Bullfighting; *Pato* and Horseball; Pigeon Racing; Real Tennis; Sheepdog Trials; Spanish Bullfighting; Yabbie Races

Further Reading

Antenucci, Antonio, and Gabrielle Fonrouge. "70 Arrested in NY's Largest Cockfighting Bust." *New York Post,* February 10, 2014, http://nypost.com/2014/02/10/70-arrested -in-new-yorks-largest-ever-cockfighting-bust/ (accessed April 27, 2014).

ASPCA. "Cockfighting." ASPCA, 2014, http://www.aspca.org/fight-cruelty/animals-in -entertainment/cockfighting (accessed April 27, 2014).

Collins, Tony, John Martin, and Wray Vamplew, eds. *Encyclopedia of Traditional British Rural Sports.* Abingdon, UK: Routledge, 2005.

Crews, Ed. "Once Popular and Socially Acceptable: Cockfighting." Colonial Williamsburg, 2014, http://www.history.org/Foundation/journal/Autumn08/rooster.cfm (accessed April 27, 2014).

Dundes, Alan, ed. *The Cockfight: A Casebook.* Madison: University of Wisconsin Press, 1994.

Hernandez, Raymond. "A Blood Sport Gets in the Blood; Fans of Cockfighting Don't Understand Its Outlaw Status." *New York Times,* April 11, 1995, http://www.nytimes .com/1995/04/11/nyregion/blood-sport-gets-blood-fans-cockfighting-don-t-under- stand-its-outlaw-status.html?pagewanted=all&src=pm (accessed April 27, 2014).

Herrera-Sobek, María, ed. *Celebrating Latino Folklore: An Encyclopedia of Cultural Traditions,* Vol. 1. Santa Barbara, CA: ABC-CLIO, 2012.

Jarrett, Derek. *England in the Age of Hogarth.* New Haven, CT: Yale University Press, 1986.

Levinson, David, and Karen Christensen, eds. *Encyclopedia of World Sport: From Ancient Times to the Present.* Oxford: Oxford University Press, 1996.

RSPCA. "A Cockfighting Factory." Animal Fighting—Cockfighting in the 21st Century, 2014, http://www.rspca.org.uk/inaction/whatwedo/prosecution/report/cover/details/-/article/PROS_PAR_2012_Animal_Fighting_1 (accessed April 27, 2014).

Sadet, Guy. "Cockfighting in the North of France: The Name of Tradition." Gameness Till the End, January 21, 2011, http://gtte.wordpress.com/2012/05/15/france-cockfighting-the-name-of-tradition/ (accessed May 21, 2014).

Suryani, Tri Vivi. "Bali's Cockfighting Tradition Lives On." Jakarta Post, January 24, 2002, http://www.thejakartapost.com/news/2002/01/23/bali039s-cockfighting-tradition-lives.html (accessed April 27, 2014).

CONKERS

Conkers is a competitive pastime played especially in the United Kingdom but also in other European nations. The game is particularly associated with schoolchildren but is also enjoyed by adults. A conker is the nut of the horse chestnut tree, *aesculus hippocastanum,* which is native to the Balkan region of Europe and was introduced to Britain in the 16th century, spreading gradually across the countryside thereafter. There are now almost 500,000 horse chestnut trees growing all over the United Kingdom. The word "conkers" is used to denote both the fruit of the horse chestnut and the game conkers, in which two players hit each other's conker with their own with the aim of destroying the conker of the opposition. In America the conker fruit is known as buckeyes.

Though the horse chestnut colonized the British landscape over three centuries ago, the game of conkers did not evolve until about 160 years ago. It has been suggested that the name "conkers" may have entered the English language from the French word *conch,* meaning "shell," during the 14th century. However, there is no real evidence to support this theory. Another more credible theory regarding the word "conkers" is that it derives from earlier games in which objects found in nature were pitted against one another by squeezing or hitting. These previous games all featured the word "conqueror" in their titles, and so it seems that the generic name "conquerors" gradually evolved into "conkers," though different dialect names also evolved throughout England, including the northern names "coggers" and "cocks and hens" as well as "oblionker" in central regions.

In the early 19th century, snail shells were the most popular item to feature in conquerors. Each player would grasp a shell, and then each shell would be pressed against the other, point to point, until one of the shells broke. It is not known exactly when conkers took over from snail shells as the main component in the game, but by the middle of the 19th century conkers were frequently used in the game.

Conkers are usually picked off the ground where they have fallen from the tree in autumn. The hard brown fruits are housed in a spiky green casing that must be pried apart to obtain the hard, shiny brown conker. To play conkers, a hole is made through the middle of the fruit, and a string is threaded through the hole and tied in a knot at one end. The string must be long enough to be able to wrap around a player's hand twice and have at least 10 inches left free from which to dangle the conker. A shoelace is often used as a conker's string.

Though there are variations to the game, in general conkers is a very simple game. To start a game of conkers, either a coin is tossed or a player claims the first hit by shouting the phrase "Oblionker! My first conker!" or something similar. Then the player going first aims her or his own stringed conker at the conker belonging to the opponent, who lets her or his conker dangle from its string at almost arm's length, just above shoulder height. In nontournament conkers if the strings become tangled, then the first player to shout "snags" or "strings" is allowed an extra turn. Usually players take turns hitting each other's conkers until one falls apart or is knocked from its string, though common variations include allowing three swings per go or allowing a player to continue a turn until she or he swings and fails to make contact with the target, much like in snooker, billiards, croquet, or progressive shove ha'penny. The game is over when one player destroys the conker of the other. In nonchampionship conkers if a conker is knocked from a player's hand or the player drops it to the ground, the opponent is permitted to shout "stamps" and trample on the fallen fruit. However, if the player who lost the conker shouts "no stamps" before the opponent shouts "stamps," then the opponent is not allowed to squash the conker underfoot. The "stamps" rule is not applied in championship conkers, while causing the strings to intertwine and shouting "snags" is considered the height of bad sportsmanship in conkers tournaments—a player who snags three times is disqualified.

In nontournament games of conkers a winning nut is played again and again, each time inheriting the previous victories achieved by its vanquished opponent conker, with the score suffixed by the ending "er." For example, a conker that has beaten four others is called a fourer. However, if the fourer beats a conker that has beaten two others—that is, a twoer—then the fourer becomes a sevener. This is because the fourer absorbs the number of wins held by the beaten conker (two) and is given an extra point for beating the twoer: $4 + 2 + 1 = 7$. Thus, a successful conker can quickly achieve a large score. Since it is desirable to have a high scoring, conker players have been known to cheat by hardening their fruits. Conkers can be hardened by boiling or soaking in vinegar or saltwater, parbaking them, soaking them in paraffin, coating them in clear nail polish, or storing them in the dark for several years so that the fruits shrivel. One particularly extreme measure taken to harden a conker is to feed the conker to a pig, for the conker travels to the animal's stomach, where it is soaked in gastric juices, and then later the player retrieves the conker from the pig's excrement. Other legal techniques used to win at conkers include swinging the conker overarm, as this brings the conker down vertically upon that of the opponent. Players may also swing laterally or on the diagonal, as this means that the softest part of the opponent's conker is hit. Styles of diagonal swing include the side slash, the backhand side slash, and the forward side slash. Other elements to consider include the length of the string, for a shorter string is best for accurate aiming but does not provide the power of a longer string.

The player whose conker is being hit also has to decide how tightly to hold the string, for holding the string loosely allows the conker to absorb the force of the swing, but holding the string too loosely risks the chance of the conker being knocked to the ground and potentially breaking or being stamped on.

As conkers is a purely aggressive game in which defense plays no part, some local government authorities and school authorities in England have either banned or tried to ban the game on the grounds that it presents too many health and safety issues. Indeed, in the United Kingdom the cutting down of horse chestnut trees and the banning of conkers is often cited as the epitome of local government inter- ference in everyday life and the overprotection of children by school authorities. Schools in particular have acquired a reputation in England for banning conkers, with one in six teachers having outlawed the game for fear that they may be sued if a pupil is hit by a conker or if a child with a nut allergy comes into contact with a conker. Also, scout clubs have been known to stop children from playing the game unless their parents have given written consent, as scouting authorities deem the game too dangerous to play without taking legal precautions.

However, despite the recent paranoia directed at conkers, the World Conker Championships are held annually at Ashton Conker Club in Northamptonshire, northern England, attracting over 6,000 spectators and competitors from many different European countries, who each pay a registration fee to enter the tourna- ment, with proceeds going to charity. To prevent cheating, the Conker Club pro- vides all strings and conkers, and two stewards officiate each match. Other world championship officials include the chief umpire, whose decision is final; the ring- master, who presides over the rate of play; the competition secretary, who is as- sisted by the ushers; and the recorders, who keep score.

The championships play the three swings per turn variation of the game, and competitors must abide by several championship rules. For instance, any nut knocked from its string but not smashed may be rethreaded and resume play, a fragment of conker must be big enough to mount an attack, and if a game lasts longer than five minutes then the five-minute rule comes into effect. This rule means that each player is allowed nine further swings at the opponent's conker, with play alternating between the player's every three swings. If after the nine strikes neither conker has broken, then the player who has hit the opposing conker the most times is declared the winner.

Similar to championship conkers is the annual Egg Knocking Contest held on Easter Sunday in Marksville, Louisiana, since 1956. A parallel event is held in the neighboring town of Cottonport, and similar events take place throughout the Cajun areas of southern Louisiana. Some Cajun communities call the practice of egg knocking Pacques Pacques, which is doubly apt as the name translates form French as "Easter Easter" and also mimics the sound of two eggs being tapped together.

At the egg-knocking contests, two competitors armed with a boiled and dyed hen egg or guinea egg face each other and proceed to knock eggs. To knock eggs, a competitor will hold an egg by the small end while the opponent taps the held egg with the small end of her or his own egg. The tapping continues until one egg cracks. The competitor whose egg cracks first then has to forfeit the egg to the opponent. At the Marksville contest one person from each pairing of competitors is eliminated after each round. Winning competitors then face each other, and the eventual overall winner is the person who makes it through the competition with an egg that is still intact.

See also: Jacks and Knucklebones; Rounders; Shove Ha'penny

Further Reading

Ashton Conker Club. "All about Conkers." World Conker Championships, 1965–2013, http://www.worldconkerchampionships.com/html/conkers_about.html (accessed August 12, 2013).

Lane Dunbar, Sheri. "If Your Eggs Are Cracked, Please Step Down: Easter Egg Knocking in Marksville." Louisiana's Living Traditions, http://www.louisianafolklife.org/LT/Articles_Essays/creole_art_egg_knocking.html (accessed August 9, 2013).

"Official World Championships Rules." World Conker Championships, 1965–2013, http://www.worldconkerchampionships.com/html/conkers_rules.html (accessed August 12, 2013).

Paton, Graeme. "Schools Banning Conkers and Leapfrog over Safety Fears." *The Telegraph*, April 19, 2011, http://www.telegraph.co.uk/education/educationnews/8458526/Schools-banning-conkers-and-leapfrog-over-safety-fears.html (accessed August 9, 2013).

Pearson, Harry. "Conkers: The Game with Growing Support." *The Guardian*, October 12, 2002, http://www.theguardian.com/sport/2002/oct/12/comment.harrypearson (accessed August 12, 2013).

Roud, Steve. *The Lore of the Playground: One Hundred Years of Children's Games, Rhymes & Traditions.* London: Random House, 2010.

Tyzack, Anne. "Conkers Bonkers." *The Telegraph*, October 26, 2007, http://www.telegraph.co.uk/gardening/3345163/Conkers-bonkers.html (accessed August 12, 2013).

COTSWOLD OLIMPICKS

The Cotswold Olimpicks, or Robert Dover's Games as they are sometimes known, are a multisport tournament held on a natural amphitheater called Dover's Hill near Chipping Campden, Gloucestershire, in the Cotswolds area of south-central England. The games take place in May on the first Friday after the Spring Bank Holiday. The Cotswold Olimpicks are thought to be the first public sporting tournament to use the "Olympic" title since the ancient Greeks named their games some 1,200 years earlier. It has been argued that the Cotswold Olimpicks helped lead to the founding of the modern Olympic Games.

A local lawyer named Robert Dover devised the concept of the tournament, and the first Cotswold Olimpicks were held during the Pentecostal Week of 1612. Dover's tournament took the form of a country festival at which sporting events took place. To a certain extent, Dover believed that the physical exertions of a major sporting event would improve the fitness levels and agility of local people, something that would prove useful if ever the people needed to defend themselves and their land in battle. However, to a greater degree Dover envisaged the Cotswold

Olimpicks as a way of using sport and competition to unify communities in the face of political, religious, and social conflict, in much the same way as the modern Olympic Games are held up as a way of uniting nations through sport. The founding of the Cotswold Olimpicks reflected the fact that in England during the 16th and 17th centuries, sport had started to reflect social tensions, particularly strains related to religion. In simple terms, England was divided between those who wished to maintain the country's Catholic identity and those, known as Puritans, who wanted to impose a strict form of Protestantism upon the nation. Sports and games, like all elements of English life at the time, were dragged into arguments surrounding religion, as the Puritans took a dim view of pleasurable pastimes, with some Puritans even going so far as to suggest that sports, like games and fun in general, were satanic. The English king James I (1566–1625) stepped into the debate by publishing the *Book of Sports* (1618), in which he outlined those pastimes he considered permissible, such as archery, dancing, and vaulting, and those that were not, such as bowling, bearbaiting and bullbaiting, and any game played near pubs. For Robert Dover, as a Catholic, to launch a sporting event was both an anti-Puritan act and a statement of support for the king, and it is noteworthy that Dover would wear clothes formerly worn by the king during the Cotswold Olimpicks. The games were immortalized in a collection of 30 poems titled the *Annalia Dubrensis* (Annals of Dover) published in 1636, the frontispiece of which is a famous illustration depicting Dover dressed in the king's finery and presiding over a wide variety of traditional sports.

The early Cotswold Olimpicks were a grand spectacle, for the hillside on which the games took place is home to Dover's Castle, a temporary wooden structure equipped with cannons. The cannons were fired to announce the start of proceedings, and competitors were summoned to the hillside by a hunting horn. The sports that formed the core of the Cotswold Olimpicks tested strength and skill and harked back to the Olympics of ancient Greece while maintaining a particularly English nature. The main events, which were contested by men only, were horse racing, hunting, coursing, and athletic events, including jousting, handball, javelin throwing, running, jumping, tug-of-war, sledgehammer throwing, wrestling, fencing using sticks, fencing with cudgels (a short baton used as a weapon), and shin kicking. There were also contests for gurning (the traditional English pastime of deliberately making distorted facial expressions, usually by jutting the jaw as far forward and upward as possible), pipe playing, country dancing, singing, and playing chess. The prizes for victory in these events included silver trophies. Women were permitted to take part in gentler events such as dancing, and after the initial Cotswold Olimpicks, a women-only running race known as the smock race was invented in which women competed to win a beribboned tunic.

The Cotswold Olimpicks ran annually from 1612 to 1642, when they were suspended for the duration of the English Civil War (1642–1651). The games were revived in the 1660s but took place at irregular intervals. During the 19th century the Cotswold Olimpicks became extremely popular with people working and living in the overcrowded cities of central England who could reach the Cotswolds by the newly installed railways. Indeed, in 1851 over 30,000 people attended the

Cotswold Olimpicks. However, the crowds at the 1851 event behaved in a rowdy fashion—drinking, dancing, and fighting—and this lead to the cancellation of the Cotswold Olimpicks by an act of Parliament. The tournament was revived once more in 1951 as part of the Festival of Britain, an exhibition designed to improve British morale in the aftermath of World War II, but this revival did not last. However, the Cotswold Olimpicks were revived again in 1963, and in 1965 the Robert Dover's Games Society was established to ensure the continuation of the games. The Cotswold Olimpicks have continued to be held annually ever since.

Today all the events of the Cotswold Olimpicks take place on one day, with events divided between the upper and lower arenas. Occasionally pastimes such as dwile flonking, morris dancing, and poetry have been included, but events central to the games are a five-mile cross-country race known as the Olimpick Run, a tug-of-war contest for both men and women, and shin kicking, an event that garners much media attention. One of the highlights of the Cotswold Olimpicks is the Championship of the Hill contest. This event is made up of several relay races contested by teams representing local churches and pubs. The relay races include an obstacle race and a wheelbarrow race. Children also take part in their own Cotswold Olimpicks, known as the Scuttlebrook Wake races. The children's races are held on the Friday evening of the games on Chipping Campden High Street and include running races for boys and girls from under 5 years of age to 15 years of age and over as well as wheelbarrow races.

Wattolümpiade: The Muddy Olympics

Inaugurated in 2004, Wattolümpiade, which translates from Low German as "Mud-flats Olympics," is a multisport tournament held on mudflats in Brunsbüttel, Germany, funds from which contribute substantially to the Cancer Relief Organization of Schleswig-Holstein. Some of the sports at the Wattolümpiade are football, handball, and volleyball, relay races using an artificial eel instead of a baton, and mud sledding. Though all competitors can expect to become mud-covered, the sport of mud wrestling is not included in the tournament.

To celebrate the 400th anniversary of the Cotswold Olimpicks, the 2012 games were an extra special event that included the traditional contests of the Olimpick Run, tug-of-war, and shin kicking. In order to highlight the long history of the games, officials were dressed in Jacobean costumes, and traditional English folk music and dance accompanied the event. The 2012 Cotswold Olimpicks attracted a crowd of around 5,000 people, each paying a small entry fee in a year in which England's capital, London, hosted the 30th Summer Olympic Games.

London 2012 highlighted that the year was an especially apt year for the city to host the Olympics, as 2012 marked exactly 400 years since Britain's Olympic movement began with the first Cotswold Olimpicks. Further, it has also been argued that the Cotswold Olimpicks influenced the founding of another English multisport tournament, the Much Wenlock Games, also known as the Wenlock

Olympian Games, which in turn greatly influenced the creation of the international modern Olympic movement during the 19th century, with the first modern summer Olympic Games held in Athens in 1896. The Much Wenlock Games were invented by a doctor, William Penny Brookes, in 1850 and named after the town of Much Wenlock in the county of Shropshire in west-central England, which acts as a focal point for the multivenue games. The Much Wenlock Games stressed the moral and health benefits of exercise and sport with events including cricket, athletics, soccer, and quoits, a traditional game in which metal hoops are thrown over a predetermined distance so that they land on a metal pin that is set in the center of an area of soft clay. Brookes, who was well aware of the Cotswold Olimpicks, designed the Much Wenlock Games to encourage physical education for all, with the ethos that winning and losing were less important than taking part. This belief is known to have greatly influenced Pierre de Coubertin, the founder of the International Olympic Committee. Thus, it could be argued that the influence of the Cotswold Olimpicks on the founding of the modern Olympic Games is twofold. The Much Wenlock Games continue to be held each summer, and the varied sports incorporated in the games include athletic events such as a triathlon, a marathon, a long-distance walk, archery, badminton, swimming, fencing, cricket, clay pigeon shooting, golf, bowls, and gliding, among many others. In order to mark the influence of the Much Wenlock Games on the founding of the modern Olympics, one of the mascots for London 2012 was named Wenlock.

See also: Aunt Sally; Bearbaiting and Badger Baiting; Celtic Wrestling; Cheese Rolling; Conkers; Cresta Run; Cricket; Dwile Flonking; Foxhunting; Handball; Hare Coursing; Highland Games; *Schwingen;* Shin Kicking

Further Reading

Bingham, Jane. *The Cotswolds: A Cultural History*. New York: Oxford University Press, 2009.

"Cotswold Olimpicks Press Release 2012." Robert Dover's Cotswold Olimpicks, http://www.olimpickgames.co.uk/images/cotswold_olimpicks_press_release_2012.pdf (accessed November 11, 2013).

Goodheart, Benjie. "For the Real British Olympic Spirit, Visit the Cotswold Olimpicks." *The Guardian*, May 31, 2012, http://www.theguardian.com/sport/shortcuts/2012/may/31/british-olympic-cotswold-olympicks (accessed November 11, 2013).

Horne, John, and Gary Whannel. *Understanding the Olympics*. Abingdon, UK: Routledge, 2012.

Mallon, Bill, and Jeroen Heijmans. *Historical Dictionary of the Olympic Movement*. 4th ed. Lanham, MD: Scarecrow, 2011.

"Museum on the Move: Brookes' Much Wenlock." Discovering Shropshire's History, http://www.shropshirehistory.org.uk/html/search/verb/GetRecord/theme:20090401152819 (accessed June 24, 2014).

Polley, Martin. *The British Olympics: Britain's Olympic Heritage, 1612–2012*. London: English Heritage, 2011.

"Robert Dover's Games (The Cotswold Olimpicks)." Chipping Campden Online, May 31, 2012, http://www.chippingcampdenonline.org/robert-dovers-games-the-cotswold-olimpicks (accessed November 11, 2013).

Swaddling, Judith. *The Ancient Olympic Games*. 2nd ed. Austin: University of Texas Press, 2002.

CRESTA RUN

The Cresta Run is a toboggan run located in St. Moritz, in the Engadine Valley of eastern Switzerland. The run has been operated by an English private club, the St. Moritz Tobogganing Club (SMTC) since 1885, and riding the Cresta Run is often seen as the epitome of dangerous and daring sports. On its completion, the Cresta Run became the world's first ice run. Therefore, the original riding of the Cresta Run can be seen as the forerunner of winter sports such as bobsleigh, skeleton, and luge. Tobogganing on the Cresta Run is an almost exclusively male pursuit—women are only permitted to use the course on special occasions, such as the 125th anniversary celebration of the course held in February 2010. Formerly an Olympic sport, riding the Cresta Run is an amateur pursuit and receives no live television coverage. The Cresta Run opens in December and closes after a nine-week season in February or March. Tobogganing takes place on the Cresta Run every day of the season except Christmas Day.

The Cresta Run is a natural run that follows the contours and earth banks of a mountain valley and is built anew each year from snow that is then iced. The Cresta Run begins in St. Moritz and winds down a narrow valley to what used to be the village of Cresta but is now part of the hamlet of Celerina. The Cresta Run is about three-fourths of a mile long with a drop of 514 feet. The run's gradient varies from 1 in 2.8 to 1 in 8.7. The 1 in 2.8 section of the course makes the Cresta Run the world's steepest ice run. Riders can easily achieve speeds of around 80 miles

The start of the Olympic Skeleton Race on the Cresta Run at St. Moritz, Switzerland, on February 3, 1948. The Cresta Run is a natural run that is rebuilt each year from snow and ice. Riding the Cresta Run is often seen as the epitome of dangerous sport as riders can easily reach speeds of 80 miles per hour. (AP Photo)

per hour. This means that it takes less than a minute to drop 514 feet. Riders can do little to influence the steering of their toboggan once in motion, though they do wear special boots equipped with metal rakes that can influence the speed and direction of travel.

There are 10 corners on the Cresta Run, each of which is named. However, the most infamous corner is a six-foot-high ice wall called Shuttlecock. Anyone who falls from their toboggan at Shuttlecock automatically becomes a member of the Shuttlecock Club. The existence of the club points to the number of riders who have fallen afoul of the wall. Those wishing to race the Cresta Run may start from one of two starting points on the track: Top and Junction. Those tobogganing from Junction begin opposite the Clubhouse, which is located about a third of the way down from Top, which is, as the name would suggest, located higher up the course. Only experienced riders may race from Top. When the Cresta Run is constructed the section from Junction is built first, followed by the upper section of the run.

The first Cresta Run was built over a nine-week period between 1884 and 1885 by five British guests staying at the Kulm Hotel in St. Moritz. In 1884 the Davos Tobogganing Club invited a team from St. Moritz to compete against the Davos team on a toboggan run on a road spanning the distance from Davos to Klosters. The Davos team won the contest, and the St. Moritz team vowed to create a run in time for a rematch the following winter. Hence, the Cresta Run was invented. The first race on the Cresta Run took place on February 16, 1885, against Davos. Races against Davos are known as the Grand National and the centenary Grand National was run on February 13, 2010. The 1887 Grand National is particularly significant, for it was during this contest that a Mr. Cornish decided to adopt the now familiar head-first, prone position in which the rider's face lies just inches from the ice. Prior to Cornish's 1887 innovation, all riders rode in an upright position on the wooden sit-on toboggans. Another contest, a competition for women called the Freeman Trophy, was held separately from the Grand National. In the early years of the Cresta Run women were treated on a par with male competitors, but this gradually changed so that by 1925 women were banned from competing on the course, and then in 1929 they were barred from practicing on the run. No one reason for the gradual exclusion of women was given, though it was suggested at a club meeting that the vibrations and bangs on the chest experienced by the women as they rode the course might cause breast cancer, since at least two women riders had been diagnosed with the disease.

During the 1880s the various Cresta Run competitions gradually became more specialized and began to attract elite sportsmen. This is turn led to the emergence of the individual disciplines of bobsleigh, luge, and skeleton. Apart from the Grand National, the other classic races are the Curzon Cup (first run in 1910), the Morgan Cup (inaugurated in 1935), and the Brabazon Cup (established 1966). Any rider who wins all four classic races in one season is declared the "Winner of the Grand Slam." This feat has been achieved just 12 times since 1972.

Riding the Cresta Run is inherently dangerous. The aim of those who choose to toboggan on the course is to use their skill and judgment to negotiate the corners of the run without sacrificing speed. The desire to achieve the fastest time possible around a course made of ice means that there is always a risk of losing control of the toboggan. Indeed, some of the corners are deliberately designed to be convex so that a rider will fall out of the open-topped toboggan if he loses control. This is the opposite of bobsleigh and luge tracks that are specifically designed to be concave. This means that competitors in bob and luge events will fall onto the course rather than be thrown out. In order to demonstrate the difference in danger levels between these winter sports and the Cresta Run, it has been proven that a curling stone sent down a bobsleigh track will continue on to the finish line. However, a curling stone sent down the Cresta Run will be thrown off the track at the earliest opportunity. The level of danger involved in the Cresta Run cannot be underemphasized. There is always the chance of being injured or worse, and riders must sign a liability disclaimer before attempting the track. In addition to signing the disclaimer, would-be riders must sit through a so-called death talk and view images of the kind of bone breakages experienced by past riders. These breakages and fractures include injuries to legs, hips, collarbones, arms, shoulders, and the spine. Thus far four men have been killed riding the Cresta Run, a relatively small number, but hundreds of competitors have broken bones on the course, while others have lost limbs. There also exists an injury called an ice kiss that is specific to the Cresta Run. An ice kiss occurs when part of a competitor's face is shaved off by making glancing contact with an ice wall on the course.

As well as being synonymous with extreme, exhilarating, if dangerous sport, the Cresta Run has cultivated an image of luxury, glamour, and privilege; hence, an extended chase scene takes place on a specially constructed version of the Cresta Run in the James Bond film *On Her Majesty's Secret Service* (1969). The moneyed air of the Cresta Run is evident from the companies associated with the club. For instance, in 2008 the course timings were measured by Omega, and Krug champagne was one of the course sponsors. The association of wealth and the Cresta Run is emphasized by the course charges. As a private club the SMTC has around 1,300 members and also allows a limited number of riders to buy pay-as-you-go access to the course, which acts as a form of temporary seasonal membership. Currently supplementary riders, known as SLs, who are aged over 28 pay 500 Swiss francs for five rides and then 50 Swiss francs for each race after that. Riders aged under 28 pay 35 Swiss francs for additional rides. The cost includes hire of equipment and clothing, which includes boots with rakes, helmet, gloves, elbow and knee guards, and the toboggan. Beginners must pay 600 Swiss francs for five rides and then 50 Swiss francs for additional rides. In general, riders can expect to complete up to three runs per day.

Switzerland is also home to the world's largest amateur downhill ski race, an annual event held called the Inferno that takes place in the village of Mürren and was first held in 1928. The Inferno has been proclaimed the world's longest and arguably most arduous downhill race and sees 1,800 participants set off from the the summit of the 2,970-meter (9,744-foot) Schilthorn mountain to the bottom of the picturesque Lauterbrunnen Valley floor. The meandering course, which includes a vertical descent of 2,000 meters (roughly 6,562 feet), covers 15.8 kilometers (almost 10 miles) of varied terrain and topography and has very few gates. The

Inferno is more appropriate for all-round downhill skiers, for the upper section of the course is best suited to those with good turning technique able to achieve optimal line, the middle part of the course calls for fast gliding and optimal downhill positioning, and the lower section sees the best skiers prevail, as here the course demands arm power, optimal equipment, skating step, good positioning, and mental stamina. Indeed, the Inferno is so testing that having witnessed the race in 1949 and 1950, leading British Army officer Viscount Montgomery of Alamein persuaded the British Army to enter a team in the event in 1952 as a way of preparing for the eventuality of a third world war, which Montgomery felt might take place in Russia during the winter. Montgomery also persuaded the organizers of the race, the Kandahar Club, to create the Field Marshal Montgomery Cup to be awarded to the highest-placed British competitor to finish the course.

While competent skiers can complete the course in around 45 minutes, the winner of the Inferno takes less than 15 minutes from start to finish.

See also: Curling; Elephant Sports; Heli-Skiing; Kitesurfing; Lawnmower Racing; *Schwingen;* Stone Skimming; Street Luge; Synchronized Skating; Volcano Boarding; Wingsuiting; Zorbing

Further Reading

"About the SMTC & the Cresta Run." Cresta Run, http://www.cresta-run.com/?id=2 (accessed August 9, 2013).

"The Cresta Run." Royal Air Force, http://www.raf.mod.uk/rafcresta/crestarun/ (accessed August 9, 2013).

Davis, Simon. "The Cresta Run's 125th Anniversary." *Country Life,* December 27, 2009, http://www.countrylife.co.uk/countryside/article/435495/The-Cresta-Run-s-125th -anniversary.html (accessed August 9, 2013).

Grainger, Lisa. "Skiing in St Moritz: Head First Down the Cresta Run." Telegraph Ski and Snowboard, February 8, 2012, http://www.telegraph.co.uk/travel/snowandski /9069377 /Skiing-in-St-Moritz-head-first-down-the-Cresta-Run.html (accessed November 3, 2013).

"Henry Irvine-Fortescue—Obituaries." *The Daily Telegraph,* March 1, 2014, http://www .telegraph.co.uk/news/obituaries/10669042/Henry-Irvine-Fortescue-obituary.html (accessed March 1, 2014).

Inferno-Mürren. "What Is the Inferno Race?" Inferno-Mürren, http://www.inferno-muerren .ch/en/facts-and-figures/history/description (accessed March 1, 2014).

Nauright, John, and Charles Parrish, eds. *Sports around the World: History, Culture and Practice,* Vol. 1, *General Topics, Africa, Asia, Middle East, and Oceania.* Santa Barbara, CA: ABC-CLIO, 2012.

Schott, Ben. *Schott's Sporting, Gaming & Idling Miscellany.* London: Bloomsbury, 2004.

Tomlinson, Alan. *A Dictionary of Sports Studies.* Oxford: Oxford University Press, 2010.

CRICKET

Cricket is a bat and ball team game most commonly played by men but also by women and children. Teams consist of 11 players plus a reserve, known as the 12th man, who is used as a substitute fielder if a player is injured during play.

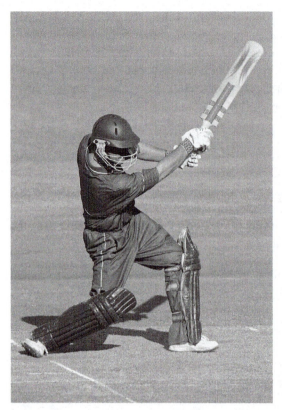

A batsman strikes out at the ball during a cricket match. The batsman aims to earn his team points called runs by hitting the ball but without being dismissed by the bowler. The rules of cricket are particularly complex but this has not prevented the sport from becoming highly popular in many countries. (iStockphoto.com)

Cricket is the national summer sport of England and is played in those areas of the world once colonized by the English, particularly India, Pakistan, Sri Lanka, South Africa, Australasia, and the West Indies, while Ireland, Scotland, the Netherlands, and the United Arab Emirates are emerging cricket nations. Different forms of cricket match exist, including a test match (an international match that lasts for a maximum duration of five days) as well as a one-day match and a Twenty20 game (both lasting for a predetermined limited number of overs). Cricket-playing nations tend to have their own domestic leagues and also play internationals. The Cricket World Cup is the international championship for One-Day Internationals and is organized by cricket's governing body, the International Cricket Council. It is traditional for sides to wear white trousers and tops during tests and brightly colored uniforms for limited-overs games.

The origins of cricket are unknown. While some historians believe that shepherds working on the Sussex Downs in southeastern England invented the game, another theory, which also helps explain how some of cricket's terminology evolved, suggests that cricket is a country game dating from the 13th century that began when boys bowled a stone at a tree stump or at a wicket, that is, the hurdle gate of a sheep pen, with a tree branch acting as a bat. The hurdle gate was formed by two upright posts called stumps on which rested a crosspiece called a bail. While the exact date of cricket's invention is not clear, manuscripts dating from 1697 describe an 11-a-side cricket match being played in Sussex.

Cricket gained in popularity when the upper classes joined in village cricket matches held across southern England, and during the 18th century cricket became organized and much codified. For instance, in 1774 a ball weighing between five and six ounces was introduced and the cricket bat evolved into its current shape of a long, heavy, broad, straight blade with a short handle. This new bat allowed the batter to play forward and to cut and drive the ball. Prior to this the ball had dominated the bat, as length bowling had already been developed at the Hambledon Club in Oxfordshire. In 1878 the Marylebone Cricket Club, commonly known as the MCC and based at Lord's Cricket Ground in London, which is regarded as the spiritual home of cricket, was founded and standardized the rules of cricket. Soon the game became a fixture in British public schools and universities, and national and international competitions developed. It was widely believed at this time that playing cricket was a character-building exercise and that values learned on the cricket field, such as the importance of fair play, could transfer to other areas of life, such as military combat. Cricket also helped forge the concept of athleticism, that is, the idea that a sport may have significance beyond the sphere of play. Cricket also demonstrated the snobberies of the era, however, for though cricket brought different social classes together, grounds were equipped with separate gates and facilities for the gentry, who did not mingle with working-class or professional players. The names of gentlemen amateurs also appeared on a separate team sheet.

As the British Empire grew, cricket spread across the colonies, where it became extremely popular and was often seen by indigenous peoples as a way in which to demonstrate a form of superiority over the English colonizers. Cricket still thrives on traditional international rivalries such as that between England and Australia, which forms the basis for the Ashes, a series of tests between the two national sides that occur at least every four years.

During the late 1970s Australian entrepreneur Kerry Packer bankrolled a revolution in cricket by establishing World Series Cricket. This initiative brought together the world's best players for televised matches and ultimately led to cricket becoming much more business-minded and to new forms of cricket competition developing, including Twenty20 and the all-star Indian Premiere League.

Cricket is played on an oval grass field at the center of which is a rectangular area known as the pitch, which measures 22 yards long by 10 feet wide. The ground is divided lengthways into two halves known as offside and onside or legside. When the batter takes a stand at the wicket, the offside is the portion of the ground to the right of a line drawn to the bowler's end opposite the batter. The leg or onside is the ground to the left. At each end of the pitch two sets of three sticks measuring 28 inches high, called wickets, are set in the ground. Across the top of each wicket lie 8-inch horizontal pieces called bails.

England Cricketers Triumph on Television Dance Show

England bowler Darren Gough and batsman Mark Ramprakash have both won the BBC television reality program *Strictly Come Dancing*, known worldwide as *Dancing with the Stars*. Gough won in 2005 partnering with Lilia Kopylova, while Ramprakash competed alongside Karen Hardy in 2006—the couple's Argentine Tango is often cited as the best dance in the show's history. Former England captain Michael Vaughan and spinner Phil Tufnell also performed well on the show—Tufnell also won the jungle-based reality show *I'm a Celebrity . . . Get Me Out of Here!* in 2003.

Each side takes turns at batting and fielding, with each turn called an inning.

The rules and regulations of cricket are numerous and notoriously convoluted, but in general depending on the nature of the match, each team has one or two innings each in which to become the side to score the most runs. The team with the highest number of runs wins, and it is common for scores to reach the hundreds. However, if both teams are unable to complete their innings before the match ends, then a draw is declared.

The batting team aims to score runs, while the fielding team aims to dismiss 10 batters, thus ending the batting team's innings—though there are 11 players in a side only 10 need be dismissed, as batting is done in pairs, and so a batter cannot bat alone. Bowlers deliver the ball from either their left or right hand with a straight arm, usually employing an overarm action, and try to hit the wicket with the ball so that the bails fall. Bowlers may take any number of paces as part of their delivery as long as they do not cross the popping crease, that is, a line running parallel with the bowling crease. The ball usually pitches, or hits, the ground before reaching the batter, and the bowler generally aims to pitch at or just in front of the batter's feet, though the location depends on the pace of the bowler and the state of the pitch. Direction is also important, for bowlers may vary the flight of the ball to confuse batters so that they do not know whether to play a stroke or be defensive. This is achieved through techniques including finger spin, in which the ball rotates on its axis as it moves toward the batter with the objective of obscuring the angle at which the ball will pitch, thereby making it difficult for the batter to anticipate how to strike the ball. Other techniques include altering the pace of the delivery and using the swerve, in which the ball curves toward or away from the batter on contact with the pitch, known respectively as an inswinger and an outswinger. In cricket there are several types of bowled ball. For instance, a full toss is a ball bowled in such a way that the batter can reach it before it hits the ground, while a long hop is bowled slightly short. A ball that pitches so close to the batter that the batter can drive it without having to move forward is called a half volley, while a yorker is a ball that pitches on or inside the popping crease very close to the batter's feet. A ball bowled with finger spin that veers unexpectedly in the opposite direction from that anticipated by the batter is called a googly. Meanwhile, a recent bowling innovation called reverse swing sees a ball delivered at a speed in excess of 85 miles per hour. Such speed allows the bowler to disguise how the ball will swing and thus confuses the batter as to how the ball will move, as there is no outward sign as to whether the bowler is delivering a swing or reverse swing delivery.

A bowler delivers six balls, known as an over, at one wicket, and then a different player from the bowling side bowls six balls at the opposite wicket. Meanwhile, the batting side defends its wicket. The batter being bowled to is known as the striker and tries to hit the ball away from the wicket using the bat in either a defensive or an offensive manner. A defensive hit protects the wicket but does not allow the batter time to run to the opposite wicket at the other end of the pitch. However, the batter does not have to run, and play resumes with another bowl. If the batter makes an offensive hit, that batter and the second batter (at the nonstriking end at the other wicket) swap places. A batter may hit right-handed or left-handed, and good batting is based on a vertical bat being presented to the ball with full face, though a horizontal (or cross) bat may be employed to cope with aggressive bowling. Other batting strokes include a forward stroke, in which the batter moves the front leg toward the bowled ball. This is in contrast to a backstroke, in which the batter moves the rear leg backward before playing the ball. A leg glance sees the batter deflect the ball behind the wicket on the leg side. A cut occurs when the batter strikes the ball after it has hit the ground on the offside either square of the wicket or behind it, and a pull or hook shot sees the batter hit a ball on the up through the leg side. A pull is struck when the ball is around waist high, and a hook is played off a short delivery when the ball is between chest and head height. The hook is considered the riskiest stroke in cricket because a hook shot causes the ball to be in the air for a few seconds, increasing the likelihood of the batter being caught and therefore dismissed.

A run is scored every time both batters reach the opposite wicket. To score a run, the batters cross back and forth between the wickets, earning a run for each time both swap ends, all the while being careful not to be run out and thus dismissed. A cricket field has an outside boundary, and if a ball is hit along the ground to that boundary, then 4 runs are scored (a four). If the batter hits the ball so that it travels through the air to beyond the boundary, then 6 runs are scored (a six). An umpire, of which there are two on the field and sometimes a third watching video evidence, signals a four or six via hand gestures. The umpire also adjudicates on dismissals, counts the number of balls in an over, and decides the suitability of playing conditions. Meanwhile, a match referee ensures that both the laws of cricket and the spirit of the game are upheld. A batter who is dismissed without scoring is said to have scored a duck, but an individual batter's score of 100 runs is called a century (200 runs is a double century). It is thought to be unlucky for a batter's or team's score to rest on a multiple of 111. This is called a nelson (222 is a double nelson, 333 a triple nelson, and so on).

Other types of runs can also be scored, including no balls, a wide, byes, and leg byes, though these runs are awarded to the batting team as extras rather than to the score of the individual batters. A no ball can be declared for many reasons, such as if the bowler delivers the ball from the wrong place, if the ball is declared dangerous (as happens when the ball is bowled full length at the batter's head or body), or if the ball bounces more than twice before reaching the batter. The batter may hit for runs a ball that has been declared a no ball but cannot be dismissed by a no ball except if the batter is run out, hits the ball twice, obstructs the field, or touches the ball with the gloved hand. A batter is awarded any runs scored from the no ball, and the team is awarded a run for the no ball itself. A wide is declared if the umpire decides that the batter did not have a reasonable opportunity to score from a bowled ball because it pitched too far beyond the batter's reach. Umpires are especially strict on wides in limited-overs cricket. A wide adds one run to the batting side's score plus any other runs scored by the batter, who cannot be dismissed by a wide delivery except if the batter is stumped, run out, hit the team's own wicket, handles the ball, or obstructs the fielding side. A bye occurs when a ball that is neither a no ball or a wide travels past the striking batter, with runs scored despite the batter not hitting the ball, while a leg bye occurs when runs are scored by hitting the batter rather than the bat, and the ball is neither a wide nor a no ball. Runs cannot be scored if the striking batter deliberately fails to attempt to play a shot.

There are numerous ways in which a batter may be dismissed, though the most common are bowled, caught, leg before wicket (usually referred to as LBW), stumped, and run out. A batter is bowled out when the ball is bowled and hits the striking batter's wicket so that at least one bail is dislodged, while a batter may also be dismissed if the batter touches the ball with the bat (or the gloved hand gripping the bat) and the ball is then caught by a member of the fielding side before it bounces. LBW occurs when the ball is bowled and hits the batter without hitting the bat. At its most basic for a batter to be dismissed LBW, the umpire must decide if the ball would have hit the wicket if the batter were standing in a different spot. However, the LBW rule is extremely complex, and the umpire must take into account numerous factors when giving such a decision. The complexity of the LBW rule is such that LBW decisions are often contentious and the cause of much controversy and discussion among players, commentators, and spectators. A batter is out stumped if the wicketkeeper (a member of the fielding side who stands behind the wicket of the batter who is on strike) knocks down a bail/the wicket while the batter is out of the crease and not attempting a run. If this occurs while the batter is running between the wickets, then a run out occurs. In order for a batter to be given out, a member of the fielding side must appeal to the umpire, usually by asking "How's that?"

Variations on cricket included high-speed Kwik cricket aimed primarily at children, French cricket in which the batter's legs are the stumps, and indoor cricket, which is played inside by teams of six players.

See also: Aussie Rules Football; *Gilli-Danda; Lapta*

Further Reading

"Cricket Game Rules." Cricket Rules, http://www.cricket-rules.com (accessed March 5, 2014).

"Glossary of Cricket Terms, Cricket Terminology, Cricketing Terms, and Cricketing Terminology." Cricker, 2014, http://cricker.com/glossary/#l (accessed August 4, 2014).

"History." Cricket Web, 2001–2012, http://www.cricketweb.net/resources/history/ (accessed August 4, 2014).

"The Hook Shot." BBC Cricket, 2009, http://news.bbc.co.uk/sport1/hi/cricket/skills/4174458.stm (accessed August 4, 2014).

Tomlinson, Alan. *A Dictionary of Sport Studies*. Oxford: Oxford University Press, 2010.

CROQUET

Croquet is a tactical lawn game played with wooden mallets in which individuals hit balls through hoops, either on a one-on-one basis or in teams of up to six per side. Croquet is played at club level and at national and international competitions and is also a recreational activity that is especially popular in England, the United

Players use wooden mallets to hit balls through hoops during a game of croquet. Croquet is played on a grass court featuring six hoops and a central peg. In order to score points players must strike the balls through the hoops in a certain order and then hit the peg. (Gannet77/iStockphoto.com)

States, Australia, and New Zealand, while the game is also played in South Africa, India, and Egypt, and individual players are also found in countries including Spain, Russia, Sweden, Portugal, Switzerland, Finland, and Latvia, among others. In addition, the multiball mallet and hoop game known as gateball, which originated in Japan, is related to croquet. There are several styles of the game, but the two main variations are association croquet and golf croquet. It is possible to buy indoor croquet sets consisting of balls, mallets, and hoops that tend to be re-creations of historic sets and are intended for noncompetitive play. The game is overseen by the World Croquet Federation (WCF), which consists of national associations recognized by the WCF.

Croquet was included as an official sport at the 1900 Olympic Games held in Paris, but the game is no longer an Olympic sport. The world's premier croquet event is the MacRobertson International Croquet Shield. Teams of individuals from England, Australia, New Zealand, and the United States contest the competition, which began in 1925.

Croquet is descended from the French game of *palle mall* in which players hit a ball called a *palla* through a series of metal rings using a mallet called a *maglio*. At the start of the 19th century the *palle mall* mallet gradually evolved into a unique mallet with a broomstick for a handle. Indeed, the name "croquet" derives from the French word *croc*, meaning something hooked or shaped like a crook. Croquet's popularity soon spread to Ireland, where the earliest recorded reference to croquet appeared in 1852. From Ireland croquet traveled to England, where the sport flourished during the 1860s. In England croquet was promoted by a number of individuals, most notably John Jaques and Walter James Whitmore. Jaques was a sporting goods manufacturer who produced the equipment necessary for croquet to be played regularly and also published the laws of croquet so that an increased number of individuals would know how to play. On the other hand, Whitmore both played croquet and promoted it as a sport, instituting a croquet championship. As a master tactician, he was the premier croquet player of his age and won the first (unofficial) croquet world championship, the Croquet Open Championship held in Moreton-in-Marsh in Gloucestershire, England, in 1867. Croquet soon became the in thing among the English fashionable society of the mid-19th century, and to display croquet hoops on a lawn was a sign of good taste and refinement. Today the sport is still regarded as an upper-class pursuit that can only be enjoyed by the wealthy. This is partly due to the fact that croquet club fees tend to be extremely expensive, as are croquet sets that can cost thousands of pounds. Indeed, Jaques's company, Jaques London, still sells croquet equipment, with the most expensive Jaques croquet set, the Balmoral, retailing at £3,999.99 at the time of writing. That the set is named Balmoral, the name of Queen Elizabeth II's Scottish residence, reinforces the notion that croquet is an elitist pastime. Another indicator of the game's exclusivity is that the English universities of Oxford and Cambridge, plus Yale and Harvard in the United States, all have university croquet clubs. However, to try to counter the charge of elitism often leveled at croquet, some croquet clubs such as the Ealing Croquet Club in west London, the capital of England, hold special open days so that nonmembers can experience the game and also allow people to pay a modest £5 per croquet session rather than take up club membership.

The year after Whitmore won the open championship the All England Croquet Club was established, though in 1875 the club would change its name to the All England Lawn Tennis and Croquet Club, which hosts the famous annual Wimbledon tennis tournament. This name change reveals much about the fortunes of croquet in England during the 1870s. While a number of Irish croquet players had come to England to help spread the game and while croquet had been deemed socially acceptable for women to play, the popularity of lawn tennis had outstripped that of croquet and led to much of the lawn available to croquet being used for home tennis courts. The popularity of croquet in England continued to fluctuate throughout the remainder of the 19th century and up until the start of World War I in 1914. The game did, however, make inroads into other countries during this time, particularly the United States, Australia, New Zealand, and South Africa. For instance, in 1866 a croquet club was established in Kyneton in Victoria, southeastern Australia, and in 1896 the Australian Croquet Association was founded. The Australian Croquet Council was launched in 1950, and today Australia boasts more croquet players than any other nation, with an excess of 6,000 registered players. Meanwhile in 1880, the American National Croquet League was founded despite resistance to the sport by publications such as the *American Christian Review*, which in 1878 expressed the fear that croquet might lead to the moral decline of American women and was but a short step to sexual disgrace. However, such moralizing went largely unheeded, and croquet soon became one of the first competitive sports that women could enjoy in the United States, though in America it was considered more respectable for women to play indoor versions of croquet, such as parlor croquet, table croquet, and carpet croquet, than any version played outside.

Croquet is played on a grass court on which are placed six hoops and a center peg. For association and golf croquet, the court should measure 105 feet long by 84 feet wide.

Croquet is an unusual game in that it is played solely by individuals on a one-on-one basis. Croquet is a very simple game, though it is often likened to more complex games such as chess because of its tactical nature. There are many different ways of playing croquet of which at least nine are recognized by the WCF, but the general aim of the game is for a player to score more points than the opponent. Points are scored by hitting the croquet ball through hoops in a certain order and hitting the peg, and each player in turn attempts to score a point or to roquet, meaning that the player hits a ball to try to strike the opponent's ball. If a player makes a point, then he or she takes another turn and keeps taking turns until failing to score a point, as in tiddlywinks and snooker. However, if the player fails to make a point, then the opponent may play.

International championships are played under the rules of one of two croquet variations—association croquet and golf croquet. The main difference between the two forms is the use of the croquet shot, that is, an extra shot taken with the striking player's ball touching the opponent's ball. Association croquet is a very tactical game in which players aim to maneuver both their own balls and the opponent's balls to win points for their own side while restricting their opponent's scoring chances. Association croquet is played with two pairs of four balls on a grass court—blue and black versus red and yellow. A game of association croquet can be played as singles or in a doubles format—pairs play alternately. In association croquet each ball must follow a set route through the hoops set out around the playing area. The balls must pass through each hoop twice and then hit the peg, and a ball scores a hoop point when it passes through the hoop designated to be played next by the order of play. The correct order of hoops to be played is bottom left, top left, top right, bottom right, bottom center, top center, top left, bottom left, bottom right, top right, top center, bottom center, and finally the peg. A point is scored whether the ball is struck directly by the player or is hit by another ball. Clips color-coded to match the balls are placed on the hoops or the peg to indicate the next target for each ball. For the first six hoops, clips are placed on the top of a hoop, and then during play the second six hoops clips are attached to the side of the hoop.

A turn consists initially of one stroke only, but extra strokes can be earned either when a player's ball runs a hoop or if the player's ball makes a roquet. In this case a player places his or her own ball in contact with the other ball and then strikes the ball so that the other ball moves, or takes croquet. After this the player is allowed another stroke. When a player runs a hoop he or she may roquet all three balls again. In this way it is possible to run several hoops in one turn. Skillful players frequently run all 12 hoops in one go. Thus, by a combination of taking croquet and running hoops, a series of points can be scored in a turn. This is known as making a break. A turn ends when the player has made all the strokes to which her or she is are entitled, directs a ball off the court, or infringes a game rule.

Twenty-six points are available to the winning pair: 12 points for passing through each hoop plus 1 point for each ball that hits the peg, for when a ball has scored its final hoop point it may score a peg point either by being hit onto the peg or by being hit onto the peg by another ball about to play its last hoop. When a ball hits the peg it is said to be pegged out and is removed from the court. The side that is first to complete the course with both balls is declared the winner.

If at any point during play a ball is driven off court it is placed a yard inside the boundary on the yard line nearest to where it left the court. Any ball that comes to lie between the boundary and the yard line is also placed on the yard line unless the ball is the player's own ball.

Association croquet competitions are governed by national organizations such as the British Croquet Association, which is based at the exclusive Hurlingham Club located in the southwest of London, England's capital city.

Golf croquet is as tactical as association croquet but is both much simpler to play and more interactive, as each playing turn lasts for just a single stroke. In golf croquet, players follow a course contesting each hoop in turn, and as soon as one hoop is scored all players move on to contest the next hoop. Golf croquet does not feature a croquet shot, so once a hoop has been won all players play to win the next hoop.

For a game enjoyed by a comparatively small number of players, croquet has a relatively strong presence in the arts and popular culture. For instance, painters Edouard Manet, Pierre Bonnard, and Norman Rockwell have all depicted the game in their work. Meanwhile, in the cult film *Heathers* (1988) a game of strip croquet takes place, and in *Savages* (1972) a group of primitive people find a croquet ball rolling through their forest and, following it whence it came, come upon a deserted estate where the primitives dress as the upper classes and play croquet. After the game has finished the primitive people begin to devolve and return to their forest. The film is intended to be an allegory of upper-class society and uses croquet as a symbol of elitism. However, perhaps the most celebrated depiction of croquet in the arts is in Lewis Carroll's 1865 novel *Alice's Adventures in Wonderland*, which was adapted into a feature-length Disney animation in 1951. In Carroll's story, live flamingos are used as mallets, and hedgehogs are used for balls.

See also: Conkers; Cotswold Olimpicks; *La Soule; Mölkky;* Real Tennis; Shove Ha'penny; Snooker

Further Reading

"About." Croquet Federation of India, 2012, http://croquet.in/about.asp (accessed March 26, 2014).

"Association Croquet—The Game and How It Is played." Oxford Croquet, 2004, http://oxfordcroquet.com/coach/capubs/index.asp (accessed August 4, 2014).

"Croquet Sets." Jaques London, http://www.jaqueslondon.co.uk/croquet/croquet-set.html?limit=all (accessed March 24, 2014).

"ECC Membership." Ealing Croquet Club, http://www.ealingcroquet.org/membership .html (accessed May 22, 2014).

Levinson, David, and Karen Christensen, eds. *Encyclopedia of World Sport: From Ancient Times to the Present*. Oxford: Oxford University Press, 1996.

Nauright, John, and Charles Parrish, eds. *Sports around the World: History, Culture and Practice*, Vol. 1, *General Topics, Africa, Asia, Middle East, and Oceania*. Santa Barbara, CA: ABC-CLIO, 2012.

"A Synopsis of Association Croquet." The Croquet Association, 2000–2004, 2014, https:// www.croquet.org.uk/association/ (accessed March 26, 2014).

"What Is the WCF?" World Croquet Federation, 2014, http://www.wcfcroquet.org/joomla/ (accessed March 26, 2014).

CURLING

Curling is a strategic winter team sport played by men and women in which players propel large, heavy, smooth stones across ice. The sport is included in the Winter Olympic Games and is similar to lawn bowling, *pétanque,* and shuffleboard. Curling can be played outside on natural ice, though national and international competitive curling takes place indoors on specially prepared rinks. Curling is so-named in reference to the way the stones travel over the ice. In Scotland and New Zealand curling is sometimes known as the roaring game because of the sound made by the stone as it slides over the frozen playing surface. Curling is played in Canada, China, South Korea, the United States, New Zealand, and Australia, and there are curling clubs in most countries of Western Europe and Scandinavia. Those who participate in curling matches are known as curlers.

It is not known exactly when or where curling was invented, but the sport is closely associated with Scotland, and it is known that a game of sliding stones on ice was played at Paisley Abbey in Renfrewshire, south-central Scotland, in 1541. Dutch painter Peter Breughel the Elder depicted curling being played in his 1565 work *Winter Landscape with Skaters and Bird Trap*. This painting was produced at a time when Scotland enjoyed strong trade links with the Netherlands. Also, a curling stone dating to 1511 has been discovered in Dunblane, central Scotland. Thus, it seems that curling may have been invented in Scotland during the medieval period. Scotland was also home to the first governing body of curling for the Grand Caledonian Curling Club, which was established in Edinburgh, Scotland's capital city, in 1838 with the intention of promoting and regulating the sport. Four years later a demonstration of curling was held for British queen Victoria (1819–1901) on the floor of the ballroom at Scone Palace near Perth, central Scotland. Queen Victoria was so impressed by the sport that the club was granted royal patronage and permitted to change its name to the Royal Caledonian Curling Club in 1843. It was also during the 19th century that curling became popular in Canada and the United States when Scottish immigrants exported the sport. For example, in 1852 a Canadian branch of the Royal Caledonian Curling Club was founded, though the Royal Montreal Curling Club was actually founded before any of the Scottish curling organizations, as the Montreal club was established in 1807. The first Canadian Championships was held in 1927 and soon became the world's biggest curling tournament. The first curling club to be founded in the United States was the Orchard Lake Club, which was set up in 1832 and located near Detroit, Michigan. An American club affiliated with the Royal Caledonian Curling Club was established in 1867, and the first U.S. championship was held in Chicago in 1957. A year after this the United States Curling Association was established to oversee 125 clubs, though the United States Women's Curling Association had been founded 11 years earlier in 1947. In 1966 the sport's first international governing body, the International Curling Federation, was established in Edinburgh.

The World Curling Championships began as a competitive curling series, the Scotch Cup, that was launched in 1959 and in which the men's teams of Canada and Scotland competed. The Scotch Cup attracted the interest of other curling nations, and soon the series was expanded to include teams from the United States, Sweden, Norway, Switzerland, France, and Germany. The results from the Scotch Cup from 1959 to 1967 are now recognized as part of the records for the World Men's Curling Championships.

Curling was first included at the Winter Olympics in 1924 when the Games were held in Chamonix, France, but the scores for this competition were not considered official until 2006, when the International Olympic Committee retroactively accepted the result. Curling was included as a demonstration sport at the Lake Placid Olympics of 1932 and again at the Winter Olympic Games in Calgary, Canada (1988), and Albertville, France (1992). Curling was given official medal status when the sport was included in the 1998 Winter Olympics at Nagano, Japan. Eight teams of men and women took part in the Nagano Games, with Canada winning the women's event and Switzerland winning the men's. Since the Salt Lake City Winter Olympics in 2002, 10 teams have participated in both the men's and women's events. The 2014 Winter Olympics held in Sochi, Russia, saw the Canadian men's team complete a hat trick of victories, starting with their win in Turin, Italy, in 2006.

One particularly noteworthy Olympic victory came in 2002 when the Scottish Women's curling team won the gold medal for Great Britain. This was the nation's first Winter Olympic gold medal in 18 years and was also a surprise television hit that led to a surge in the popularity of curling in the United Kingdom.

Wheelchair curling, in which teams must consist of both male and female players, was first demonstrated at the 2000 World Handi Ski Championship held in Switzerland and has been included in the Winter Paralympics since the 2006 Turin Games, where eight teams took part. Ten Paralympic teams took part in the Winter Olympics in Vancouver, Canada, in 2010.

In curling, it is usual for two teams of four players to take part, though mixed doubles curling also exists in which two teams of two players—one male and one female—compete. The teams slide specially carved stones across a sheet of ice that has deliberately been made slightly bumpy. The players in a four-person curling team are given the titles lead, second, third, and skip (who is also the team captain), and each has to slide a round stone across the designated playing area marked on the ice toward a fixed point, known as the tee or the button, in the center of a circle, called the house, which is marked on the playing area. The house is marked by rings of concentric bands. The object of the game is for each team to slide its stones as close as possible to the center of the house. Each player slides two stones alternating with their opposing number on the opposite team. The lead starts the game, followed by the second, then the third, and finally the skip. A point is scored for each stone that comes to rest closer to the encircled tee than its rival stone, so it is possible for a team to earn a maximum of 8 points per inning, the curling term for an end, of which there are usually 8 or 12 per curling match unless the match is a competition game, in which case it is mandatory to play 10 end. If points are level at the end of an inning, then extra ends are played until a team emerges victorious. No points are scored if a stone fails to enter the house or if rival stones are equidistant from the tee.

A skilled curler is able to make her or his stone turn toward the target, whether that is the tee or an opponent's stone, for blocking and knocking an opponent's stone from the house is an important strategic maneuver in curling. The curling of the stone toward its target can be influenced by the action of two sweeper players equipped with brooms who can affect the direction of the stone depending on how gently or vigorously they rub the ice. This element of teamwork is crucial, for in curling it is vital to choose the best path and placement of a stone.

The round stones used in curling must weigh 18.14 kilograms, nearly 40 pounds, and are made from granite; hence, in the United States the stones are known as rocks. The stones are polished to a shiny finish yet begin life as lumps of roughly hewn rock. One of the key producers of the granite used in the manufacture of curling stones is the uninhabited island of Ailsa Craig, a rocky outcrop in the Firth of Clyde 10 miles from the mainland of southwest Scotland. Ailsa Craig was formed by prehistoric volcanic activity and is the world's only source of two extremely hard types of granite, called Ailsa Craig common green granite and Ailsa Craig blue hone granite. These forms of granite are used to make curling stones, as they are both very hard wearing. However, each has its own important special property—the green granite, which makes up the body of the stone, is impact resistant and breathable, while the blue granite, which is both inserted into the green granite stone and used to make the stone's running band, has a denser structure, making it impervious to water. This is important, for the running band is the only part of a stone to make contact with the ice playing surface and is exposed to moisture as it moves across the playing area. Curling stone manufacturers Kays of Scotland have the exclusive right to use Ailsa Craig granite and have combined both types of granite in the manufacture of curling stones since 1851. The Ailsa Craig granite is so hard that a cutter made up of small particles of diamond must be used to hone the rock into the special curling stone shape, much like a whole cheese. Once both types of granite have been combined in a round shape, the stone is polished and a handle is attached. Finally, a unique serial number is printed on each stone so it can be tracked, for the stones produced by Kays of Scotland are in demand worldwide.

It is not just the type of stone used in curling that is significant, for the condition of the ice is of the upmost importance too. In curling it is vital that the ice is perfectly level but with tiny drops of frozen water deliberately made to form on the ice to give a slightly bumpy surface. This effect is achieved by leveling the ice with a blade and then sprinkling the ice's surface with tiny drops of water from a system that produces around 40 types of ice pebbles all of different sizes. These pebbles are important, for as the stones slide they produce friction that in turn slows the stone as it travels. Thus, the friction produced by the stones allows them to glide more easily. During a curling match the pebbles erode, increasing the friction and making the stones curl more. Friction is vital in curling, so the ice is resurfaced between matches, and it is for this reason that it is considered very bad form for a curler to place her or his knee or hand on the ice, for such contact would allow body heat to melt the ice, reducing friction.

See also: Bandy; Cresta Run; Heli-Skiing; Highland Games; *Kubb; Pétanque;* Shove Ha'penny; Stone Skimming; Synchronized Skating

Further Reading

"About Wheelchair Curling." World Curling Federation, http://www.worldcurling.org /about-wheelchair-curling (accessed January 5, 2014).

Branch, John. "Curlers Are Finicky When It Comes to Their Olympic Ice." *New York Times,* August 16, 2009, http://www.nytimes.com/2009/08/17/sports/17curling.html?ref=sports& _r=0 (accessed January 4, 2014).

Cumberpatch, Fiona. "Sliding Stones." *LandScape Magazine,* January–February 2014, 80–85.

"Curling at the Olympics." World Curling Federation, http://www.worldcurling.org/curling -at-the-olympic-winter-games (accessed January 4, 2014).

Hope, Nick. "Sochi 2014: Great Britain's Men Defeated in Olympic Curling Final." BBC, February 21, 2014, http://www.bbc.co.uk/sport/0/winter-olympics/26287263 (accessed May 18, 2014).

D

DWILE FLONKING

Dwile flonking, or dwyle flunking, is a lighthearted pub game played almost exclusively in the English counties of Norfolk and, most particularly, Suffolk on summer weekends. A dwile flonking match is contested by two opposing pub sides of 8 to 10 players who each take a turn to dance around the other while trying to avoid being hit by a beer-sodden rag. Both men and women may play, and traditional English country dress is encouraged, including (for men) a porkpie hat, a yeoman's smock, *lijahs* (trousers tied at the knees with twine), hobnail boots, and a clay pipe. It has been proposed that dwile flonking is a not entirely serious game but rather is a spoof of old English country pastimes.

The origins of dwile flonking are disputed. It has been suggested that the game began at the court of King Offa of Mercia (an Anglo-Saxon kingdom that later became the English Midlands) during the eighth century as an offshoot of the game of spile troshing in which a weight was attached to a rope wound around a wheel axle. The game's antiquity is further suggested by its seeming inclusion as a detail in the painting *Young Folk at Play* (1560) by Pieter Bruegel the Elder. However, a counterargument suggests that the game was created by two subversive Suffolk printers in the 1960s, hence the lack of any documentary evidence of dwile flonking before that time. Dwile flonking became headline news in 1967 when the Waveney Valley Dwile Flonking Association debuted the game on British television, attracting attention from as far afield as America, Australia, and Hong Kong.

The word "dwile" means a knitted cloth used to clean floors and is derived from the Dutch word *dweil,* meaning "floor cloth," most probably brought to England by Flemish weavers during medieval times, while the word "flonking" is thought most likely to be a corruption of the word "flong," an old term for the past tense of "fling." Before the game begins a *jobanowl,* or referee, is chosen. Election to the role of referee is not perhaps as great an honor as it may seem, as the rules of dwile flonking say that the referee should be a person generally considered to be of low intelligence. Also, before the match begins a sugar beet is tossed to decide which team will flonk and which will perform the girting, that is, holding hands with arms outstretched in a circle while simultaneously rotating clockwise and jumping about to try to avoid being touched by the dwile. Prior to the game the teams join together to sing the dwile flonking anthem "Here We 'em Be Together," and the game begins when the referee announces "Here y'go t'gether." The girting side encircles one member of the flonking side, who wields a pole two to three feet in length, on the end of which is the beer-soaked dwile. The pole is made from yew or hazel wood and is called a driveller. The flonker declares "Dwiles away" and then spins in a counterclockwise direction, flonking the dwile at the girting side and scoring points for hitting the opponents with the dwile. The points awarded vary depending on which part of the body is hit by the dwile. For example, a hit on the head is called a wonton and scores three points, while hitting above an opponent's waist or on the arms is known as a morther and scores two points. Striking below the waist or on the legs is known as a ripper and scores one point. As in cricket, different hand signals on the part of the match official denote the different number of points scored. For instance, a wonton is signaled by the referee patting his or her head with both hands, while a morther is shown by both the referee's hands being held aloft, and a ripper is signaled by one hand held high. The failure of the dwile to come into contact with a member of the opposing side is known as a swadger and is shown by the referee's hand waving from side to side.

When a swadger occurs, it is traditional for the girting side to break the circle and form a line, while the flonker wielding the driveller must drink a pot of ale containing a half to a pint of beer quicker than a dwile can pass from hand to hand down the line of the opposing team, whose members chant the word "pot" repeatedly. If the girting side manages to move the dwile from one end of their line to the other before the flonker finishes the pot of ale, then the flonking side is docked a point. However, if the girting side cheats by throwing the dwile down the line, then they are docked a point or made to restart the passing of the dwile. It should be noted, however, that such speed drinking may contravene new UK drinking laws and result in a heavy fine or even prison terms for landlords who allow such behavior. Thus, a cup of nonalcoholic ginger beer may be substituted for the ale, or the flonker may simply pour the beer over her or his head rather than drink it. Other dwile flonking penalties can also be awarded. For instance, if the girting side breaks the hand-holding deliberately, then a penalty flonk is awarded for which the girting side must stand still while the flonker hits them. The flonker may be penalized if he or she stops spinning while flonking.

When all the players in one team have flonked they then form a circle, and the girting side takes over the flonking. The winning team is the side that scores the most points, though points may be deducted for each player who remains sober at the end of a game. The winning side receives as a prize a pewter chamber pot called a *gazunder*.

See also: Aunt Sally; Conkers; Haxey Hood Game; Nipsy; Wife Carrying

Further Reading

"The Art of Dwile Flonking." BBC, September 11, 2003, http://www.bbc.co.uk/suffolk /going_out/pubs/2003/09/dwile_flonking/introduction.shtml (accessed September 23, 2013).

"Dwile Flonking Rules." The Norfolk Broads, http://www.thenorfolkbroads.org/Dwile%20 Flonking.html (accessed September 23, 2013).

Hobson, Jeremy. *Curious Country Customs.* Cincinnati: David and Charles, 2007.

Hough, Andrew. "Dwile Flonking: Council Bans Traditional Pub Sport under Health and Safety." *The Telegraph,* May 29, 2010, http://www.telegraph.co.uk/news/newstopics

/howaboutthat/7777836/Dwile-Flonking-council-bans-traditional-pub-sport-under -health-and-safety.html (accessed September 23, 2013).

Le Vay, Benedict. *Bradt Eccentric Britain.* 2nd ed. Chalfont St. Peter, UK: Bradt Travel Guides, 2005.

Schott, Ben. *Schott's Sporting, Gaming & Idling Miscellany.* London: Bloomsbury, 2004.

ELEPHANT SPORTS

Elephant sports include the sports of elephant polo, elephant soccer, and elephant racing. Polo is a team ball sport usually played on horseback. However, in a game of elephant polo, players sit atop elephants instead of horses. The game is popular in India, Nepal, Sri Lanka, and Thailand. Elephant polo has existed in India since around 1900, but it was as recently as 1982 that Britons James Manclark and Jim Edwards, who owned a lodge in Nepal, decided to create the World Elephant Polo Association, based in Tiger Tops Jungle Lodge, in Royal Chitwan Park, southern Nepal. It is here that three annual international tournaments are held as well as the World Elephant Polo Championships for which half the animals are provided by Nepal national parks and half by Tiger Tops Jungle Lodge.

The first game of elephant polo was played on a grass airstrip at Meghauly on the edge of the park, and it is here that the World Elephant Polo Tournament is played each December. Teams from throughout the world are invited to play in the tournament, but teams are based on sponsors rather than representing nations. A similar tournament, the King's Cup, is held at Hua Hin in Thailand.

In a game of elephant polo, players use a standard polo ball, which they hit with a special cane stick of 6 to 9 feet with a mallet at one end, though male players may use only one hand to hold the cane, while women are permitted to use two hands. Since elephants move more slowly than horses, an elephant polo pitch is three-quarters the size of a standard polo field. Each elephant is ridden by two players. One player, called the mahout, steers the elephant, while the other player tells the mahout which way to guide the elephant and also hits the ball. A game of elephant polo sees six elephants selected from a pool of elephants, each one marked with a letter from A through F. Three elephants are ridden per team, and it is considered a foul for a team to have more than two elephants in one half of the pitch.

As is the case with many sports involving animals, elephant polo attracts a degree of controversy. Those who advocate for the sport stress that the animals involved are trained and cared for by skilled handlers, who often stay with an elephant for many years, developing a loving bond with their charge. Advocates also claim that polo elephants are well fed, sheltered, and exercised in much the same way as they would be in the wild, unlike elephants belonging to a zoo. Proponents of the sport also argue that as intelligent, social animals, elephants enjoy the break from routine and the social opportunities provided by polo. Those in favor of the sport also assert that strict rules prevent the elephants from being treated badly, for elephant polo matches finish at midday to prevent the

Players sitting atop elephants play a game of elephant polo in Bardia, Nepal, on November 26, 2013. Elephant polo is popular in Nepal with an international competition held in Bardia each year. (Utopia_88/iStockphoto.com)

elephants from becoming too hot, and while elephants may play twice per day, they are not allowed to be played in two consecutive polo games. The elephants are also provided with food and water at halftime and are rested for an hour. In addition, an injured elephant is not played. Instead, the game takes place with only three elephants per side. However, animal rights groups such as People for the Ethical Treatment of Animals (PETA) claim that polo-playing elephants are torn away from their families, beaten, and trained through cruel methods, including being gouged with sharp-tipped metal rods and hooks. Meanwhile, authorities in India have voiced concern that polo elephants are not always properly registered as performing animals. As a result of such controversy, Guinness World Records has agreed to stop detailing records for wins in elephant polo matches, and companies such as beer giant Carlsberg India have ended their sponsorship of the Polo Cup in the northern Indian state of Rajasthan. Similarly, a charity elephant polo match in Jaipur, India, organized by Mark Shand, brother-in-law of heir to the British throne Price Charles and sponsored by luxury jewelers Cartier, faced condemnation from several animal welfare groups, including the World Society for the Protection of Animals and the Born Free Foundation. The animal welfare groups claimed that the match would serve to perpetuate the use of elephants in polo matches in countries where animal rights concerns are not addressed appropriately. Similarly, the foremost expert on the hand rearing of elephants, Dame Daphne Sheldrick, declared that the match was insensitive and cruel. Shand countered this criticism by asserting that the intention of the polo match was to give elephants back their dignity and to highlight the plight of elephants in the wild.

Chitwan, which is synonymous with Nepalese elephant polo, is also home to another elephant sport, elephant racing, for Chitwan is the base for Nepal's International Elephant Race. Nepal is home to about 200 elephants, of which 100 are wild. The country's indigenous Tharu people are celebrated for their ability to tame elephants and act as jockeys in the annual International Elephant Race. The International Elephant Race is held in Sauraha, a tourist area in the Chitwan district, as part of the Chitwan Elephant Festival. The first International Elephant Race was held in December 2005 with the intention of increasing tourism in the area and promoting elephant conservation. A particularly interesting feature of the race is that the riders and elephants are paired via a lottery system, so jockeys rarely get to ride their favored elephant. Once all the jockeys are paired with an elephant, the jockeys mount their animals and race them down a straight path measuring about 900 feet in length, turn them around, and then run the animals back to the starting line. The elephants take part in elimination rounds that whittle down the number of participants. Sixteen foreign teams and 8 national teams have been known to compete in the first round, though no more than 6 elephants race in each heat, with the winner being the first elephant to cross the finish line. The eventual winning jockey receives a trophy decorated with elephants. In addition to elephant racing, elephant beauty pageants also take place at the festival, while baby elephant soccer has been part of the Chitwan Elephant Festival since 2006. In elephant soccer, riders sit atop the elephants that kick around a ball until it is kicked into a goal. Elephant soccer also takes place at the David Sheldrick Wildlife Trust elephant orphanage in Tsavo National Park in Nairobi, Kenya. Here baby elephants move the ball about with their trunks, pass it between their front feet, tackle each other, and dribble the ball between their legs. According to the elephant pressure group Elephant Voices, elephants naturally kick things around and pick up rocks and sticks using their trunks and feet, particularly their back feet.

Elephant races are incredibly popular throughout Vietnam's Dak Lak Province. The country's Buon Don district is particularly associated with elephant racing, for the M'Nongs, the area's ethnic group, enjoy a proud heritage of training and hunting wild elephants. However, while demand for elephant trainers has diminished, Buon Don celebrates its history with elephant races held during the third lunar month (usually March) as part of the annual festival of Don Village. The festival is one of the biggest in the area and reflects the fighting spirit of the M'Nong people as well as their celebrated aptitude for hunting and training wild elephants. The Buon Don Elephant Races begin in the forests near the Sevepoi River and follow a one-mile-long racetrack wide enough to accommodate 10 elephants running side by side. On race day, elephants from neighboring villages gather at Don Village while inhabitants of the village look on to support the village's entrant. After a fanfare of musical instruments fashioned from horns known as the *tu va,* the elephant handlers line their elephants up along the starting line. The *tu vas* then blast again to signal the start of the race. At this signal the elephants rush forward through the onlooking crowds. As in elephant polo, each elephant is ridden by two riders— one jockey steers the elephant, while the other manages the speed of the elephant, which is surprisingly fast at around 25 miles per hour. The first elephant across the finish line is declared the winner and awarded a laurel wreath, sugarcane, and bananas by the spectators. To relax the elephants after their race, the animals are taken for a swim in the Serepok River, and they then take part in elephant tug-of-war and play elephant soccer.

Elephant racing is a tradition in India, though only two states hold elephant races. The small number of races is partly due to the elephant being revered in the Hindu religion, as the animal resembles the god Ganesh, who is depicted with an elephant's head on a human body. The Indian-born mayor of a German town brought elephant racing to Europe in the 21st century, for in 2009 Ravindra Gujjula, the mayor of Altlandsberg just to the east of the German capital of Berlin, instigated an elephant racing tournament consisting of six races contested by 14 circus elephants (7 Indian and 7 African elephants), with winning elephants rewarded with prizes of fresh fruit and vegetables. The event was well attended but attracted much criticism, with protests coming from the animal rights group Animal Peace as well as iconic French actress Brigitte Bardot.

See also: Bearbaiting and Badger Baiting; Bull Running; *Buzkashi;* Camel and Yak Racing; Camel Wrestling; Cockfighting; Fell Running; Foxhunting; Hare Coursing; Nonlethal Bullfighting; *Pato* and Horseball; Pigeon Racing; Sheepdog Trials; Spanish Bullfighting; Yabbie Races

Further Reading

Browning, William. "Nepal's Elephant Races Becoming Annual Tradition." Yahoo! Sports, November 7, 2011, http://sports.yahoo.com/top/news?slug=ycn-10378085 (accessed July 12, 2014).

Connolly, Paul. *The World's Weirdest Sports.* Millers Point, Australia: Pier 9, 2007.

"'Cruel' Elephant Polo Match Cancelled in Jaipur." *The Telegraph,* August 21, 2011, http://www.telegraph.co.uk/news/worldnews/asia/india/8714257/Cruel-elephant-polo-match-cancelled-in-Jaipur.html (accessed July 12, 2014).

Delaney, Tim, and Tim Madigan. *The Sociology of Sports: An Introduction.* Jefferson, NC: McFarland, 2009.

Foster, Peter. "Camilla's Brother Rides Out Polo Protest." *The Telegraph,* November 15, 2006, http://www.telegraph.co.uk/news/worldnews/1534252/Camillas-brother-rides-out-polo-protest.html (accessed July 12, 2014).

"International Elephant Race Starts." *Himalayan Times,* December 26, 2012, http://www.thehimalayantimes.com/fullNews.php?headline=International+elephant+race+starts&NewsID=359225 (accessed July 12, 2014).

"It's All about the Elephants." The Pukka Chukkas, 2014, http://www.pukkachukkas.com/elephants.html (accessed July 12, 2014).

Taneja, Anil. *World of Sports Outdoor,* Vol. 2. Delhi: Kalpaz Publications, 2009.

"Victory! Guinness Drops Elephant Polo Record." People for the Ethical Treatment of Animals, January 25, 2011, http://www.peta.org/blog/victory-guinness-drops-elephant-polo-record/ (accessed July 12, 2014).

Worrall, Simon. "Baby Elephants Have Sharp Soccer Skills, New Video Shows: World Cup Prospects? Probably Not." National Geographic: Daily News, June 23, 2014, http://news.nationalgeographic.com/news/2014/06/140623-world-cup-soccer-elephants-sheldrick-wildlife-trust-kenya/ (accessed July 12, 2014).

"A Year of Festivals: March—Buon Don Elephant Races, Vietnam." World Nomads, February 11, 2009, http://journals.worldnomads.com/worldfestivals/story/31518/Vietnam/March-Buon-Don-Elephant-Races-Vietnam#axzz37GFiQs9D (accessed July 12, 2014).

ETON WALL GAME

The Eton Wall Game is a contact ball game played by two teams of 10 boys and is similar to rugby union and soccer. The game originated at the famous English public school, Eton College, usually referred to as Eton, which is located near the town of Windsor just to the west of London, England's capital city. Indeed, the Eton Wall Game is perhaps the world's most exclusive sport, as it is played only on the school grounds and only by a select few of the school's 70 scholarship holders, known as Collegers, plus a small number of fee-paying pupils called Oppidans, who make up most of the school's students. In addition, a few former players are sometimes invited to make up a visiting side, and on very rare occasions teams of invited girls have been permitted to play. As the game is played by so few players, there is no Eton Wall Game league, nor does the game have a governing body. In fact, only one Eton Wall Game match really matters—the annual match between the Oppidans and the Collegers that takes place on the Saturday before St. Andrew's Day on November 30 and is often considered a contest of brain versus brawn.

The Eton Wall Game is not particularly spectator-friendly (especially for those who are not well versed in the game), as the game does not appear to involve much skill, and matches often end in 0–0 draws—it has even been suggested that the Eton Wall Game is not only brutal, pointless, and dangerous but is also the world's dullest sport. However, rather than clever or flamboyant play, the game revolves around the ceaseless application of pressure, with teams attempting to advance inch by inch through an

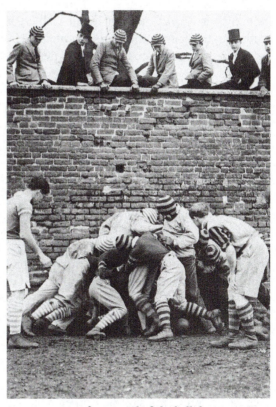

Teams compete for control of the ball during an Eton Wall Game match played at Eton College, England, on December 10, 1951. Players seek to move the ball towards a scoring zone called the calx and then kick at the goal. Players often suffer skin abrasions after grazing the wall during play. (AP Photo)

apparently impassable mass of opponents. The Eton Wall Game is extremely tiring to play, and many players, especially those positioned against the wall, suffer skin abrasions to their elbows, hips, and knees as they graze the wall. For this reason players usually wear long-sleeved tops, with players positioned next to the wall also sporting protective headgear.

It has been claimed that the Eton Wall Game is one of the oldest surviving forms of soccer. However, it is not known when the Eton Wall Game was invented, for while King Henry VI founded Eton College in 1440, the first reference to the game being played was recorded centuries later in 1766, and the red brick wall that is an important feature of the game was not built until 1717. The rules of the Eton Wall Game were published formally in 1849 and, except for a few minor alterations, have stayed the same ever since. Perhaps the most important amendment came after World War II when it was decided to change the number of players per side from 11 to 10.

The game, which consists of two halves lasting 30 minutes, is played on a narrow strip of ground measuring roughly 5 meters by 110 meters (approximately 16.5 feet by 361 feet) beside a gently curving brick wall that separates the college from Slough Road. Traditionally the wall belongs to the Collegers, and so the Collegers get to practice the game frequently. However, this advantage is leveled out by the fact that there are few Colleger pupils from which to select the Colleger team of 10 players.

Each end of the pitch has a landscape feature that acts as a goal—one end uses a door as a goal, while at the other end of the pitch an ancient elm tree is used. In addition to the goals, each end of the wall has a scoring zone called the calx. When play enters the calx the rules of the game change somewhat; for instance, it becomes legal to pass the ball backward.

The aim of the game is for each team to maneuver a ball, which is slightly smaller than a soccer ball, toward their opponents' calx in order to earn a kick at the goal. In the Eton Wall Game a kick at the opposing side's goal is known as a shy. The ball may only be passed sideways, and a strict offside rule is enforced to prohibit the ball being handled or moved forward or backward. Other rules state that no body part other than the players' hands and feet may touch the ground; players may not hold back one another, and violent conduct is prohibited, though it has been known for knuckling to occur whereby a player plants his or her fist in the face of an opponent (avoiding the eyes) and then rotates the fist, which mud-encrusted has the effect of sandpapering the opposing player's face.

Teams usually move the ball toward the goal by forming a rugby-style scrum, called a bully, that moves along the wall. In the Eton Wall Game each phase of play starts with a bully, during which around 6 of the 10 players from each side line up against the wall opposite each other. The ball is then rolled into the scrum, and play restarts. Usually a player gains possession of the ball during the bully by taking to all fours, with the ball at his feet or enclosed by his knees. The teammates of the player in possession of the ball then try to support him either by placing themselves in a position where they can receive the ball or by disrupting the opposition. When the ball emerges from the bully, the team in possession of the ball can make up ground by kicking the ball up the field and then out of play. Meanwhile, the opposing team aims both to obstruct the ball winner's progress by forcing him or her downward and trying to win the ball for themselves. Sometimes during the bully the ball runs free, allowing a player to kick it out of play. In this case the next bully is formed opposite where the ball stops or is captured. The Eton Wall Game differs from any other form of soccer, for when the ball is kicked out of play, the game restarts from a point parallel with where the ball stopped outside of the pitch rather than from where the ball crossed the touch line to leave the field of play.

Eventually the ball reaches the calx, allowing the attacking side to score. Within the calx a player can earn a shy (pl. shies), which is worth one point, by lifting the ball against the wall with his or her foot. The scoring player's teammate then touches the ball with his or her hand and shouts "Got it!" If the match umpire believes that the shy has been scored within the rules of the game, he then declares "Shy" and awards the point to the attacking team. After the shy is awarded, the scoring team may try to earn an extra nine points by scoring a goal. This is achieved by throwing the ball at one of the playing area's two goals—a garden door at one end of the field known as the Good Calx and a tree at the other end referred to as the Bad Calx. A player can also score a kicked goal, which is worth five points. It is quite common for a shy to be scored, with around six awarded each year. However, goals are extremely rare, with the last scored on St. Andrew's Day in 1909. This is partly because both targets are difficult to hit, since the angle to the garden door is acute and the tree is young and slender.

Eton College

Eton was founded in 1440 by King Henry VI of England (1421–1471) to provide free education to 70 poor boys who would continue on to King's College, Cambridge, which he founded in 1441. Pupils awoke at 5:00 a.m., prayed, and studied from 6:00 a.m., with all lessons in Latin. Boys were allowed 60 minutes of play, with soccer being the favorite game. King George III (1760–1820) visited frequently and entertained students at Windsor Castle. By 1891 Eton had over 1,000 pupils, rising to the present figure of 1,300 by the 1970s. Nowadays 20 percent of boys receive help with fees, and 50 boys study free.

The most important contest for players of the Eton Wall Game is the annual St. Andrew's Day match that takes place between the same two teams each year, the Oppidans and the Collegers. In order to be ready for the match, boys chosen to play in the contest practice throughout the Michaelmas Half by playing unofficial teams consisting of other boys, teachers, and Old Etonians (former Eton pupils).

Many famous men have played the Eton Wall Game, including British prime minister Harold Macmillan, London mayor Boris Johnson, writer George Orwell (as Eric Blair), and British royals Prince William and Prince Harry. In addition, legendary 19th-century Eton Wall Game player and later poet J. K. Stephen, for whom the Collegers hold a special memorial ceremony, was one of the suspects in the hunt for Victorian serial killer Jack the Ripper. The game has also appeared in literature, for according to the 2005 novel *SilverFin* written by Charlie Higson, James Bond played the Eton Wall Game as a schoolboy, and a version of the Eton Wall Game is played by the Ankh-Morpork Assassins Guild in Terry Pratchett's *Discworld* novels.

A second soccer-type game is also played at Eton, the Field Game, which is played throughout the school's Lent Half. The first rules for the field game were drawn up in 1847, and the game has survived largely unchanged for more than 150 years. As in soccer, the Field Game is played with a round ball, and a player is not allowed to pick up the ball. There is also an offside rule, though the version of the rule employed in the Field Game is more complicated than that used in soccer, as a Field Game player may be judged horizontal offside. An element of rugby also exists in the Field Game, for the game also includes a scrum called a bully that is made up of seven players, with a fly playing behind the bully players in a way similar to a rugby scrum-half, and there are three behinds.

The game's scoring system also marries soccer and rugby, for teams aim to score goals as in a soccer match as well as rouges, which are akin to the tries scored in rugby and, as in rugby, may be converted.

The Field Game is played by all Eton boys over the age of 13 regardless of sporting ability and is therefore not as elitist as the Eton Wall Game. Indeed, most Eton pupils play the Field Game for their school around three times per week in various competitions, including the Senior House knockout competition. However, in recent years some changes have been made to the game, including the removal of a violent move called the ram. In the ram, up to four boys lined up one behind the other and charged together at the opposing side from a distance of only 2.5 yards with the aim of scoring by getting the ball past the opposing team, whose members must remain immobile because the opposing players run toward them. The outlawing of the ram is part of a move to make the Field Game suitable for the mores of the 21st century, reminding players that fair play rather than aggression lies at the heart of the game, preventing players from intimidating one another, and making the game more enjoyable to play.

See also: Aussie Rules Football; Conkers; Croquet; Fives; Haxey Hood Game; *La Soule;* Rugby League

Further Reading

Davies, Caroline. "Harry Will Join Eton's 'Brutal and Violent' Wall Game." *The Telegraph,* November 23, 2001, http://www.telegraph.co.uk/news/uknews/1363187/Harry-will -join-Etons-brutal-and-violent-Wall-Game.html (accessed July 11, 2014).

"The Eton Wall Game: Shies, calx and bullies." *The Economist,* November 17, 2003, http:// www.economist.com/node/2204483 (accessed July 11, 2014).

"The Field Game." Eton College, 2014, http://www.etoncollege.com/FieldGame.aspx (accessed July 11, 2014).

Freinberg, Tony. "Just Don't Call Them the Eton Wallflowers." *The Telegraph,* July 24, 2005, http://www.telegraph.co.uk/news/uknews/1494720/Just-dont-call-them-the-Eton -Wallflowers.html (accessed July 11, 2014).

Le Vay, Benedict. *Eccentric Britain: Britain's Follies and Foibles.* 2nd ed. Chalfont St. Peter, UK: Bradt Travel Guides, 2005.

Nauright, John, and Charles Parrish, eds. *Sports around the World: History, Culture and Practice,* Vol. 1, *General Topics, Africa, Asia, Middle East, and Oceania.* Santa Barbara, CA: ABC-CLIO, 2012.

Pook, Sally. "Field Game Is Judged Too Rough for Eton's Modern Young Gentlemen." *The Telegraph,* February 21, 2002, http://www.telegraph.co.uk/news/uknews/1385508/Field-Game-is-judged-too-rough-for-Etons-modern-young-gentlemen.html (accessed July 11, 2014).

"The Wall Game." Eton College, 2014, http://www.etoncollege.com/wallgame.aspx (accessed November 17, 2013).

EXTREME IRONING

Extreme ironing, sometimes referred to as EI, is a lighthearted outdoor adventure sport-come-performance art that incorporates elements of activities such as rock climbing, scuba diving, skiing, skydiving, canoeing, trampolining, snowboarding, and running with ironing boards so that participants iron clothes in extreme situations. The sport is particularly popular in the United Kingdom, the United States, Japan, the Netherlands, South Africa, New Zealand, Croatia, Chile, and Germany. The men and women who participate in extreme ironing are known as ironists, and it is customary for participants to adopt monikers that reflect their love of ironing. There are estimated to be around 1,500 ironists worldwide who either act alone or in groups. Though extreme ironing is classed as an adventure sport, it could be argued that the sport's juxtaposition of adventure and sedate housework gently mocks the gung-ho culture often associated with adrenaline-fueled activities. Indeed, it has been claimed that ironists view extreme ironing as the tongue-in-cheek antidote to what they feel is the po-faced ultraseriousness of extreme sports.

The sport was invented in 1997 in Leicester, central England, by Phil Shaw, who one evening decided to iron his clothes in his garden and dubbed the activity extreme ironing. Shaw's housemate enjoyed the outdoor ironing, and the two adopted the nicknames "Steam" and "Spray." The pair invited their friends to join them in outdoor ironing, and soon the world's first extreme ironing governing body, the Extreme Ironing Bureau, was established with the intention of developing and promoting the sport. The popularity of extreme ironing spread after the formation of the German Extreme Ironing Section in 2000. The two extreme ironing factions, having organized their own individual competitions, eventually united to create the inaugural World Extreme Ironing Championships held in Munich, southern Germany, in 2002. The first world championships saw 80 teams from 10 countries tackle an iron-shaped obstacle course and climb a wall while ironing boxer shorts and blouses. Competitors also had to hang from trees and squeeze under the hood of cars. At this first world championships the individual event was won by a German ironist nicknamed "Hot Pants," while the team trophy was awarded to Shaw's team, GB1. In 2004 Shaw set out on an extreme ironing tour of the United States, visiting cities including New York and Boston.

There are various forms of extreme ironing. These variations include the rock-climbing style favored by ironists who also mountaineer, forest style in which ironists iron among the treetops, urban style in which ironists perform on top of statues or in the middle of busy streets, underwater style in which ironists perform under ice floes, and BASE style in which ironists iron while jumping from cliffs. Extreme ironing while sky diving and trampolining have also been attempted. One particularly noteworthy example of extreme ironing occurred in August 2003 when naked South African Anton Van De Venter ironed his country's flag at the summit of the dormant volcano Mount Kilimanjaro, in Tanzania, East Africa, which at 20,000 feet is Africa's highest peak. Another striking incident of extreme ironing was performed by Briton Geoff Reiss, who set the land speed record for ironing a shirt at 125 miles per hour after ironing at speed on the back of a BMW car.

In competitive extreme ironing, points are awarded for speed, style, and quality of ironing. Points for quality of ironing are marked out of a maximum of 60 points, style is marked out of 40 points, and speed is marked out of 20. Thus, the maximum number of points possible to accrue is 120. Level of adventure, difficulty, and style are also considered.

Judges tend to mark harshly, though it is accepted that participants may, for instance, sacrifice style or quality of pressing in order to increase the level of difficulty or speed. Different categories of iron also exist, ranging from the One Iron class for irons that are powered by 1,800 to 2,000 watts to the far less powerful Four Iron class for travel irons. The One Iron is used in situations necessitating a heavy, powerful iron such as locations in which strong winds are prevalent (e.g., at the top of a mountain). The lightweight Four Iron is useful in instances where a One Iron is too weighty and cumbersome, such as on a long-distance trek that culminates in extreme ironing. It has been known for ironists to bring electrical generators with them on ironing adventures, but it is more usual for irons to be heated on portable gas stoves. The sport's reliance on household goods means that the manufacturers of electrical goods sometimes sponsor ironists. For example, the German iron manufacturer Rowenta sponsored Phil Shaw's extreme ironing tour of the United States.

In 2003 extreme ironing inspired a group of musicians in Yorkshire, northern England, to invent extreme cello. In extreme cello musicians undertake long-distance walks while wearing their concert performance clothing and with their case-bound cellos strapped to their backs. The cellists then play their instruments in unusual locations, such as the roof of a cathedral. In order to raise money for charity, cellists have taken part in such endurance events as the London Marathon, the Sheffield Half Marathon, and the Four Peaks Challenge. Similarly, extreme knitting sees knitters knit while running or cycling, usually in order to raise money for charity. For instance, Susie Hewer holds the world record for running a marathon while knitting a scarf and for knitting while riding a tandem bicycle—she also holds the record for crocheting during a marathon.

Extreme ironing is the subject of a British television documentary, *Extreme Ironing: Pressing for Glory* (2003), and the 2009 children's novel *The Iron, the Switch and the Broom Cupboard* by Michael Lawrence.

See also: Lawnmower Racing; Pancake Races; *Parkour;* Shoe Throwing; Trampolining; Ultramarathons; Underwater Hockey; Volcano Boarding; Wingsuiting

Further Reading

Belluck, Pam. "Get Out Your Boards: Extreme Ironing May Soon Be Hot." *New York Times,* May 21, 2004, http://www.nytimes.com/2004/05/21/us/get-out-your-boards-extreme -ironing-may-soon-be-hot.html (accessed January 3, 2014).

Carter, Helen. "The Northerner: Hit and Miss." *The Guardian*, June 9, 2005, http://www .theguardian.com/uk/2005/jun/09/northerner.helencarter (accessed January 3, 2014).

Johnson Morgan, Melissa, and Jane Summers. *Sports Marketing.* Southbank, Victoria: Thomson, 2005.

Oldfield, Molly, and John Mitchinson. "QI: How Knitting Was Used as Code During WW2." *The Telegraph,* February 18, 2014, http://www.telegraph.co.uk/men/the-filter/qi/10638 792/QI-how-knitting-was-used-as-code-in-WW2.html (accessed February 21, 2014).

Shipside, Steve. *Extreme Sports: Brilliant Ways for Taking Yourself to the Limit.* Oxford, UK: Infinite Ideas, 2006.

Vale, Louise. "The History of Extreme Cello." Extreme Cello, http://www.extreme-cello .com/History.htm (accessed January 3, 2014).

"What Is Extreme Ironing?" TeamSteam, http://teamsteam.org/iron/what-is-extreme -ironing/ (accessed January 3, 2014).

F

FELL RUNNING

Fell running, also known as hill running and mountain running, sees participants run and race off-road, across an upland landscape at an altitude generally above 1,000 feet. Fell running takes place on rugged terrain, with the presence of the gradient a significant factor. The sport originated in the north of England, where hill areas are known as fells. Though England's Lake District is particularly associated with the sport, races take place all over the United Kingdom, including in the Yorkshire Dales and the Pennines, a range of hills that run from Derbyshire to the border between England and Scotland and effectively separate the northwest of England from the northeast. Fell running can take place only in areas classed as fell, hill, or mountain; otherwise, the run is known as a trail run. Fell running can be undertaken by individuals or can be raced by pairs or teams of four. Both men and women take part in fell running, with veteran races and junior events held too.

Fell running is more arduous than trail running, as fell running covers many ascents and descents and crosses many types of running surface, usually including grass, gravel, and soil and sometimes heather beds, boulders, and peat bogs. Since fell running usually takes place away from populated areas, fell courses are often unmarked, and so fell runners need good navigational skills, as in orienteering. Fell runners also need to make sure they take all necessary provisions and equipment with them when they set out on a run. Fell running often takes place during inclement weather, so race organizers can stipulate that it is essential for runners to carry with them windproof full-body cover, including a hat and gloves—this is particularly important for medium and long races and those where part of the course is located at high altitude. A map, a compass, a whistle, and an emergency food ration are also requisite. Fell running shoes are lightweight, with deeply studded soles that provide grip.

The length of a fell running course may be classified as long, medium, or short. A long race covers a distance in excess of 12 miles, a medium race covers 6 to 8 miles, and a short distance race is less than 6 miles in length. There are also three different classifications of incline rated A–C, with A being the greatest level of ascent. For a race to be rated as an A, it must include not less than 50 meters of climb per kilometer (not less than 164 feet per 3,281 feet). A run rated a B must include not less than 25 meters of incline per kilometer (not less than 82 feet of climb per 3,281 feet), and a category C race must include not less than 20 meters of climb per kilometer (not less than 66 feet of incline per 3,281 feet).

The history of fell running reaches back to Scotland in 1064, when King Malcolm Canmore organized for his footmen to race up the mountain Craig Choinnich in Braemar, eastern Scotland, in order to decide which of his men would be quickest at delivering his dispatches. Then in the 19th century the sport of guide racing became popular. Guide racing flourished in the Lake District and Yorkshire Dales of northern England, where local men, such as shepherds, enjoyed running up short, steep hill courses. The races were called guide races, as the competitors knew the terrain so well that they could act as tour guides for visitors to the fell regions, and races tended to be held as part of existing sport meetings or as part of local shows, such as the Wasdale Show. As the winners of the guide races won a cash prize, they were classed as professional runners. An amateur class of fell runner gradually evolved under the auspices of the Amateur Athletics Association. The new code of fell running combined the uphill running of guide racing with the upland element of fell walking.

Today fell running takes place throughout the year, including races on New Year's Eve and New Year's Day, and with notable races in the Lake District, including the Hawkshead Half Marathon in March and the Windermere Marathon in May. Another very popular fell run is the race at Burnsall in the Yorkshire Dales that has been held since 1882. The Burnsall race is particularly tough, as competitors must run 1.5 miles with an ascent of 900 feet followed by a descent that encompasses dense thickets of heather and boulders. Early runners of the Burnsall race completed the course in around 14 minutes, while the current record, set in 1977 by Fred Reeves, stands at just over 12 minutes. The Burnsall run is a short race at 1.5 miles. The race seems particularly brief when compared to runs such as the Old Counties Tops Race, which is 37 miles long, and the High Peak Marathon, which lasts for 40 miles. The latter is run by teams of four who start at around 11:00 p.m. and finish just after dawn the next morning.

Perhaps the most famous and arduous fell run, however, is the Bob Graham Round. The race is named after Bob Graham, who in 1932 managed to complete a circuit of 42 Lake District peaks in less than 24 hours. Graham started his run in Keswick, Cumbria, and traversed the peaks of Skiddaw, Helvellyn, Scafell, and Scafell Pike, among others, which all rise to heights above 3,000 feet. The Bob Graham Round covers a distance of 72 miles and involves 28,000 feet of climbing. Any runner who completes the round is entered into the Bob Graham 24 Hour Club, which was established in 1971. Similar round races include the Ramsay Round in Scotland, the South Wales Traverse, Ireland's Wicklow Round, and the Paddy Buckley Round in Wales.

An endurance activity related to fell running is the Three Peaks Challenge, in which entrants aim to conquer the highest mountains in a given area of Britain either within a 24-hour time limit or over three days, usually by walking. The National Three Peaks Challenge sees participants ascend peaks in England, Scotland, and Wales. The highest peak in England, Scafell Pike, is 978 meters (about 3,209 feet) high and takes around 4 hours to walk, as does the highest peak in Wales, Snowdon, measuring 1,085 meters (about 3,560 feet). The highest peak in Scotland is Ben Nevis, at 1,344 meters (about 4,410 feet), and takes around 5 hours to climb. These mountains are not, however, the 3 highest peaks in Britain, as over 100 Scottish peaks are higher than Scafell Pike, and over 50 are taller than Snowdon. To reach each summit within 24 hours, it is necessary to drive for 11 hours. However, a more environmentally friendly way to complete the challenge is to either run or cycle the route, though obviously this adds to the difficulty of the challenge and takes longer. Other walking Three Peaks Challenges include the Yorkshire Three Peak Challenge and the Welsh 3000s.

See also: Bog Snorkeling World Championship; Nordic Walking; Orienteering and Rogaining

Further Reading

Bradley, Lloyd. *The Rough Guide to Cult Sport.* London: Rough Guides, 2011.

Chase, Andy W., and Nancy Hobbs. *The Ultimate Guide to Trail Running.* Guilford, CT: Falcon Guides, 2010.

Holman, Tom. *A Lake District Miscellany.* London: Frances Lincoln, 2007.

Rose, Lesley Anne. *The Best of Britain: The Lake District.* Richmond, UK: Crimson Business, 2008.

Shevels, Keven. *An Introduction to Trail and Fell Running.* Darlington, UK: Trail Guides, 2010.

"Three Peaks Challenge." The Three Peaks Challenge, http://www.thethreepeakschallenge.co.uk (accessed December 22, 2013).

Williams, Morgan. "Fell Running: A Quick Guide (Part 1)." iRunFar, October 29, 2012, http://www.irunfar.com/2012/10/fell-running-a-quick-guide-part-1.html (accessed August 1, 2013).

Williams, Morgan. "Fell Running: A Quick Guide (Part 2)." iRunFar, October 30, 2012, http://www.irunfar.com/2012/10/fell-running-a-quick-guide-part-2.html (accessed August 3, 2013).

FIVES

Fives, also known as Eton Fives or hand tennis, is a unisex handball-type game for two teams of two players. The name "fives" is thought to derive from the five fingers of the player's hand, which is used instead of a bat, though this name was not applied to the game until the 17th century—prior to this time, fives was usually known as handball. Fives is played across England and is particularly associated with English public schools, meaning that the game is considered by some to be elitist. However, the advent of prefabricated cast cement fives courts mean that in recent years the sport has been taken up by a growing number of government-funded state schools in England. Fives is also played by a small number of players in New Zealand, Australia (at Geelong Grammar School), the United States, India (at St. Paul's School in Darjeeling), Austria, Germany, Malaysia (at Malay College in Perak), Argentina, France, and Switzerland (where the Zuoz Fives Club has operated since 1963) as well as in the north of Nigeria, where there are around 30 fives courts and where matches attract hundreds of spectators.

Fives is a sport that demands a high degree of physical fitness, as the game requires players to perform a great many twists and turns, sudden accelerations, and direction changes, as well as good hand-eye coordination. However, despite the game's somewhat exclusive image, no special clothing (apart from padded leather gloves) or equipment is needed to play the game. Rather, all that is required to play fives in terms of equipment is a fives ball (which is made of cork and leather and is about the size of a golf ball) and a fives court.

Fives is a very old game, as evidenced by the fact that in 1287 the Synod of Exeter banned fives, as players persisted in playing the game against church walls. However, at some point before the 19th century the game was adopted by the Catholic Church in southwestern England and was officially sanctioned by the church to be played at Easter. In addition, the ball used in fives became part of church Easter services. During the 19th century many churches had special shutters attached to their windows to prevent damage to the windows by fives balls, while other churches provided fives scoreboards and smoothed over their exterior walls so that the walls were better suited to fives play. In addition, in 1813 a church was built at West Pennard in the southwestern county of Somerset that included a fives court in its tower. Fives was also played throughout Wales from the 15th century onward and was home to champion fives player Richard Edwards, who during the 18th century was said to have played and won at fives on every church wall in the Welsh county of Denbighshire.

During the 19th century fives also became a pub game, with many pubs having fives courts built on their premises in a drive to bring in customers to either watch or play the game. This resulted in the game being played at many hostelries in London. The games played in London tended to be high-stakes games that attracted many onlookers. However, by the mid-19th century the popularity of fives in London had declined severely, and the game only really thrived in the southwest of the country and in the public schools that had started to play the game.

The first fives court was built at Eton College in 1840, with a further eight courts added in 1847, and the first codified rules of the game were devised and published by former Eton pupils A. C. Ainger and friends in 1877. By the end of the 19th century the game had become entrenched in the public school system and as a result also became popular at leading British universities such as Oxford. However, the advent of World War I in 1914 led to a decline in the playing of fives as students and schoolmasters were killed in battle. After the war ended in 1918, men who had been educated at the leading public schools and had survived the war began to tour England in order to reignite interest in the game. This ploy was successful to a degree, for in 1928 the first Oxford versus Cambridge varsity match was held, followed a year later by the Public Schools Handicaps tournament held at Queen's Club in London. Then in 1931 the Amateur Championship for the Kinnaird Cup was established by Lord Kinnaird as a competition for Old Etonians (the name given to men who have attended Eton). In March 1931 a new set of Eton fives rules was published by the Eton Fives Association to replace those established by Ainger. However, the popularity of Eton fives was again hampered by global conflict, for the coming of World War II saw the deaths of many players and the destruction of several courts, including that at Queen's Club. After the war ended fives competitions did not begin again until 1948, when the Kinnaird Cup resumed followed by the Public Schools Handicaps competition the next year. New fives competitions sporadically appeared over subsequent years, including the Midland Tournament that began in the 1960s and the Northern Championships and London Tournament, which both began in 1981. The first ladies' championships was held in 1984, and the first mixed-doubles championship took place in 1985. A national fives league for England was established in 1972. However, fives has never taken off as a mass-participation sport. and despite the recent introduction of fives to state schools in England, playing of the game tends still in the main to be limited to former pupils of leading English public schools.

Three variations of fives named after English public schools evolved over time—Eton, Winchester, and Rugby—and are all very similar to each other in that they each feature a ball being hit against the front wall of the court above a marked line. However, it is Eton fives, which is governed by the Eton Fives Association founded in the 1920s, which is most commonly meant by the term "fives." An Eton fives court is based on the design of a section of the chapel at Eton where the Eton variation on fives was first played.

An Eton fives court is divided into the backcourt and the frontcourt and has only three walls, with the front wall generally higher than those at the sides of the court. The top of the walls is marked by stonework called the coping, and a sloping ledge runs around the walls about 4.5 feet above the floor. The lowest edge of this slope is called the playline, and the ball must be played on or above this line to be considered in. The front walls feature an additional ledge about 2 feet from the floor.

As in real tennis, all Eton fives courts are unique, but all contain a number of universal features. One of the most striking universal features is a large shoulder-high L-shaped projection called the buttress (sometimes referred to as the pepperpot), which is very complex in shape, displaying many slopes and angles. The buttress extends into both the front and back courts and is located at the foot of another universal feature, the key step, which divides the court by stretching across from the buttress and is 6 inches high. Where the key step and the buttress converge, a small three-sided niche—called the dead-man's hole, the hole, or the box—forms. Players often display great accuracy by playing the ball into this hollow, as doing so usually results in an unreturnable shot. Another vertical feature is the blackguard line that travels from the floor of the court up the front wall about 30 inches from the right wall.

In Eton fives, players strike the ball with their gloved hand or wrist, aiming to hit the ball in such a way that it travels upward against the front wall in order to continue the rally. The ball can only bounce once before being struck. A point is played in the following way. At the start of play, the serving player stands between the buttress and the front wall. The player receiving the ball, known as the cutter, stands in the backcourt, along with the cutter's partner, who stands behind the cutter, and the server's partner, who stands in the bottom right-hand corner of the court. The server throws the ball up high so that it bounces off the front and right walls, coming to land behind the key step near the center of the court. The serve is not governed by any laws of the game; instead, the server must serve to the returner's requirements. However, a cutter may reject any serve, so it is beneficial to produce a serve that can be returned easily. The cutter then (usually) plays the ball overarm so that it travels up into a corner in such a way that the ball hits the right wall and then the front wall and then travels back to the server. Play continues with the cutter and the server attempting to volley the ball and the other two players playing the ball when the cutter or server misses it. Play continues until the ball is hit out of the court or is down, that is, beneath the playline. In fives only the serving team may score points, with a game won by the first team to reach 12 points. A match consists of five games.

The defining philosophy of all variations on fives is that the game be played in a spirit of fair play and honesty. Thus, in fives there is no referee or umpire. Indeed, a referee/umpire would not be able to adjudicate, as in fives only players can tell if the ball has bounced more than once. Players must admit foul shots and decide on other rule infringements, and disputes must be settled between players on the court. In this way fives promotes conflict resolution, for all players are taught to adopt a neutral standpoint and consider their opponents' feelings. This is achieved by observing the unwritten courtesy rules of fives, which are intrinsic to the game. These rules include players moving out of the way of opponents so as not to interfere with their shots and players querying their own shots if in any doubt that they may have traveled out or down. The game also encourages a sense of humor and a philosophical attitude toward losing, for in fives even the best shots can fly out of play after bouncing off the court's irregular playing surface.

See also: Cricket; Eton Wall Game; Handball; *Pelota;* Real Tennis

Further Reading

Birley, Derek. *Sport and the Making of Britain.* Manchester, UK: Manchester University Press, 1993.

Collins, Tony, John Martin, and Wray Vamplew, eds. *Encyclopedia of Traditional British Rural Sports.* Abingdon, UK: Routledge, 2005.

de Quetteville, Harry. "Eton Fives Becomes a State School Hit." *The Telegraph,* April 11, 2013, http://www.telegraph.co.uk/education/secondaryeducation/9973909/Eton-Fives -becomes-a-state-school-hit.html (accessed July 3, 2014).

de Quetteville, Harry. "The Fitness Workshop: Eton Fives." *The Telegraph,* August 23, 2010, http://www.telegraph.co.uk/health/wellbeing/7956117/The-Fitness-Workshop-Eton -Fives.html (accessed July 3, 2014).

Eton Fives Association. "A Brief History of Eton Fives." Fiveonline.net, June 21, 2001, http://www.fivesonline.net/oldefasite/about.fives/brief.history.html (accessed July 6, 2014).

Eton Fives Association. "A Brief Introduction to Eton Fives." Fiveonline.net, June 21, 2001, http://www.fivesonline.net/oldefasite/about.fives/brief.introduction.html   (accessed July 7, 2014).

Eton Fives Association. "Five Centuries of Fives: Extract from *Country Life*—March 25, 1976." Fiveonline.net, May 5, 2001, http://www.fivesonline.net/oldefasite/articles/five .centuries.of.fives.html (accessed July 7, 2014).

Fives Court Company. "About the Game." Fives Court Company, 2011, http://www.fives-courts.com/aboutthegame.html (accessed July 7, 2014).

Mangan, J. A., ed. *A Sport-Loving Society: Victorian and Edwardian Middle-Class England at Play*. Abingdon, UK: Routledge, 2006.

Mason, Tony, and Eliza Riedi. *Sport and the Military: The British Armed Forces, 1880–1960*. Cambridge: Cambridge University Press, 2010.

Wilson, Ed, ed. *The Sports Book: Fully Revised 4th Edition*. London: Dorling Kindersley, 2013.

Zug, James. *Squash: A History of the Game*. New York: Scribner, 2003.

Zuoz Fives Club Zurich. "Zuoz Fives Club Zurich." Zuoz Fives Club Zurich, http://www .zuozfives.ch (accessed July 3, 2014).

FOOTVOLLEY AND FUTNET

Footvolley is the English-language name for the Brazilian sport of *futevôlei*, a ball game for teams of two or four men or women that combines the rules and playing area of beach volleyball with the actions performed in soccer. The name "footvolley" derives from the fact that outside of the United States soccer is generally referred to as football. Footvolley is one of the world's fastest-growing sports,

Players compete for the ball during a Footvolley World Championship match between Italy and Brazil held in Rio de Janeiro on March 31, 2011. Footvolley is similar to beach volleyball except that footvolley players may touch the ball with any part of their body apart from their hands and arms. (AP Photo/Felipe Dana)

especially in countries already passionate about soccer and that have a sandy beach coastline, and the sport is rapidly gaining international recognition as a game that can be enjoyed cheaply by many people. Recently the sport has been played by professional soccer players and celebrities in exhibition matches and promotional events. Footvolley is popular in its home country of Brazil and is played across Europe and Asia. The sport is rapidly growing in popularity in the United States and Australia, and major footvolley tournaments have been held in a diverse range of countries including Spain, South Africa, Greece, Portugal, Paraguay, Thailand, France, the Netherlands, Aruba, and the United Arab Emirates. Though the Footvolley World Cup is usually hosted by Brazil, in 2011 when the United Arab Emirates hosted the tournament, 27 nations took part. This World Cup was also the first to take place under the auspices of the International Federation of Volleyball. However, the international governing bodies of footvolley are the International Footvolley Federation and the European Footvolley Federation. There is a movement within footvolley to have the sport included at the next Olympic Games to be held in Rio de Janeiro, Brazil, in 2016.

To play footvolley requires technical ball skills, physical fitness, agility, quick reflexes, and stamina.

Footvolley began as an informal beach game on Copacabana Beach in Rio de Janeiro, Brazil, in 1965 when Octavio de Moraes created the game as a way for soccer players to hone their ball-kicking skills during a strict ban on soccer played on Brazilian beaches—soccer players would head to the volleyball court when approached by police asking why they were carrying a ball. To begin with footvolley was called *pevoley*, which translates as "footvolley." However, this name was dropped in favor of *futevôlei*. From Rio de Janeiro the game spread to the Brazilian cities of Recife, Salvador, Brasília, Goiânia, Santos, and Florianópolis, and then during the 1970s footvolley spread beyond Brazil's borders to become an international sport.

Initially players tended to be professional soccer players, and footvolley teams consisted of five players per side. Due to the excellent soccer skills of the earliest footvolley players the ball rarely touched the ground, so it was decided that it would make for a better game if there were fewer players on each team. Thus, the number of players on each side was reduced from five to two. The first footvolley governing bodies started to form in the 1990s. For instance, the Brazilian Confederation of Footvolley (CBFv) was established in 1998 and organized the inaugural footvolley national championships, while the International Federation of Footvolley was formed in 2002. In 2003 the first Footvolley World Cup was held in Greece, with 18 pairs from 14 countries contesting the title. Women's footvolley was recognized in 2006 when the CBFv officially acknowledged the inaugural women's championship. The following year the debut World Circuit of Footvolley was held, starring Brazilian soccer hero Romário de Souza Faria.

Footvolley is played on a rectangular court made of leveled sand that is divided in two by a central net that is lower than the net used in volleyball, as it is strung at a height of 6 feet 10 inches. The court measures 18 meters by 9 meters (59 feet by 29.5 feet), with an area free from obstacles known as the free zone extending 3 meters (9.8 feet) around the court. The objective of footvolley is to maneuver the ball over the court's central net into the opponent's half of the court. Footvolley is played in much the same way as beach volleyball except that players may touch the ball with any part of their body apart from their hands or arms. Each team must touch the ball between one and three times before sending the ball back to the other side, though players are never permitted to touch the ball consecutively.

In footvolley, the ball enters play via a service that is executed by a player located behind the baseline who is allowed to construct a mound of sand in the free zone on which to place the ball before kicking it over the net and into play. The first touch after the ball has been served allows the server's teammate to find a position that lets him or her prepare to attack. Players may also kick the ball straight into the opposite side of the court after the initial touch, though this usually happens only if a player is injured or as a strategic maneuver. Players usually receive the serve on their chest, as this part of the body provides a large surface area on which to control the ball. The most common ways of scoring in footvolley are drop shots, which are formed close to the net; deep balls kicked close to the baseline; cross-ball attacks diagonally across the court; and parallel balls, which follow the side-lines of the court. Also, one of the most spectacular of all footvolley moves is the shark attack, in which a player jumps upside down and smashes the ball with the flat of the foot from above the height of the net. Other spectacular moves include the bicycle kick, in which a player's foot is above the level of the head when he or she strikes the airborne ball.

In order to defend against such attacks it is imperative that players have good communications skills and the ability to work well as a team.

In footvolley, points are awarded for several reasons. For instance, points are awarded if the ball touches the ground on the opponent's side of the net, if the opponent commits a fault. or if the opponent is unable to return the ball back over the net. Scoring follows the rally point system as in volleyball. The system of match scoring is decided by event organizers, who can choose between the best-of-three-sets option or the one-set format. The best-of-three-sets system means that the first team to win two sets wins. In this case the first team to reach 15 points by at least 2 clear points wins a set apart from in the third set, when teams need only reach 11 points to win the set. The one-set system means that teams need to score 18 points to win the set and thus the match.

While footvolley is normally played by teams of two, it can also be played in the 4x4 format in which two teams of four face each other over a lower net. This version of the game is particularly dynamic and entertaining and has helped to make the sport of footvolley more professional in general. The 4x4 format is played formally as World Cup Footvolley 4x4 in Brazil, Argentina, Uruguay, Thailand, the United Kingdom, France, Germany, Italy, Greece, the Netherlands, Croatia, Spain, and Austria, among other countries.

Related to footvolley is the sport of futnet, a team ball game for men, women, and children that combines speed, precision, skill, and strategy. While often used as a way of practicing soccer skills, futnet is also a popular leisure activity in many parts of Europe, particularly in the Czech Republic, France, Slovakia, Switzerland, Romania, and Hungary. Futnet was invented in the former country of Czechoslovakia (now divided into the Czech Republic and Slovakia) in 1922 as part of junior soccer training at the Slavia Prague soccer club. The game was intended to be a fun way of teaching soccer skills and was similar to a traditional Czech game called České Budějovice. Initially futnet was played over a wooden bench, then over a rope, and later over a net. Professional soccer players soon adopted the game, and futnet tournaments were held between 1939 and 1948. The official futnet rules were issued in 1940, when the sport was promoted alongside volleyball. In 1943 futnet spread to France, where it was taken up by the French national soccer side. Futnet tournaments increased in number during the 1950s and 1960s, and in 1961 futnet was recognized by the Czechoslovak Sports Organisation.

Futnet was further organized when in February 1987 Switzerland, England, Italy, Romania, and Germany established a world governing body, the International Football-Tennis Association (IFTA) located in Switzerland (in 2004 the IFTA was renamed the Fédération Internationale de Footballtennis Associationor). Soon more countries, including France, Brazil, the United States, Norway, Turkey, and Russia, joined the IFTA, while after the breakup of Czechoslovakia in 1993 the Czech Republic and Slovakia joined as two separate nations. In 1991 the first Men's European Championships were held in Switzerland and Hungary, and the first world championship was held in Slovakia in 1994. This was followed by the first world championship for women and juniors held in Slovakia in 2000. The next futnet milestones were the founding of two more governing bodies in 2010, the European Futnet Association founded in Marseille, France, and the Union Internationale de Futnet established in Geneva, Switzerland.

Futnet is played by two teams located on either side of a net that compete to score points by making the match ball bounce in the opponent's half of the court without the ball being returned. Players may touch the ball with any part of their body except their hands and arms and are forbidden to touch the net. There are three basic types of futnet: single, which is played on a smaller court by two individuals who may take two touches of the ball; double, which is played by two teams of two who may take three touches though not two consecutive touches by the same player, with one bounce allowed for men and two bounces for women and juniors, on a court measuring 12.8 meters by 9 meters (41.9 feet by 29.5 feet); and triple, which is played by three players per side who may take three touches though not two consecutive touches by the same player, with one bounce allowed for men and two for women and juniors. Triple futnet is played on a court the same size as a footvolley court.

The player or team that wins two sets wins a futnet match. A set ends on the 11th point. However, there must be a 2-point difference so a set may be won 11 points to 9, but if scores are tied at 10 points each, then the game must continue until one side wins the set by 2 points or reaches 15 points, for the game ends when a side earns 15 points without the need for a 2-point difference. Therefore, the maximum score in a set of futnet is 15:14.

See also: Aussie Rules Football; Bossaball; Elephant Sports; Kin-Ball; Korfball; Real Tennis; *Sepak Takraw*

Further Reading

"About Footvolley." Footvolley Australia, 2012, http://www.footvolley.org.au/about-footvo
   lley/ (accessed April 26, 2014).

"About Futnet." European Futnet Association, http://www.futnet.eu/about-futnet/ (accessed April 26, 2014).

"Footvolley." Cultures and Customs, September 26, 2013, https://sites.psu.edu/mgeitner-
   rcl/2013/09/26/footvolley/ (accessed September 26, 2014).

"Footvolley Rules." Footvolley Australia, 2012, http://www.footvolley.org.au/footvolley
   -rules/ (accessed April 26, 2014).

"Futnet at a Glance." Union Internationale de Futnet, 2011, http://www.unifut.net/futnet
   .php (accessed April 26, 2014).

"Futnet Scoring System and Single." European Futnet Association, http://www.futnet.eu
   /files/disciplines.pdf (accessed April 26, 2014).

"History of Futnet—Main Milestones." European Futnet Association, March 1, 2011,
   http://www.futnet.eu/about-futnet/historymilestones/ (accessed April 26, 2014).

Hulette, Elisabeth. "Footvolley Tourney Makes First Appearance in Va. Beach." Pilot Online, July 18, 2011, http://hamptonroads.com/2011/07/footvolley-tourney-makes
   -first-appearance-va-beach (accessed August 4, 2014).

"What Is Footvolley?" Aussie Footvolley, 2013, http://aussiefootvolley.com.au/wordpress
   /?page_id=32 (accessed April 26, 2014).

Wilson, Ed, ed. *The Sports Book*. Fully revised 4th ed. London: Dorling Kindersley, 2013.

FOXHUNTING

Foxhunting is a blood sport in which hunters on horseback chase a fox accompanied by a pack of specially trained dogs, usually foxhounds. The fox is then tracked and often killed by the dogs. Foxhunting is practiced in the United Kingdom, the United States, Canada, France, Belgium, the Netherlands, Italy, Portugal, Ireland, Australia, South Africa, Kenya, India, and Iraq. Though foxhunting is often considered a quintessentially English sport, the activity is banned in the United Kingdom and is a particularly divisive issue arousing strong emotions in those who are for or against the sport. Foxhunting with hounds is also banned in Germany and Switzerland.

In Europe it is the red fox, *Vulpes vulpes,* that is hunted. The red fox is hunted in North America too, together with the coyote, *Canis latrans,* and the gray fox, *Urocyon cinereoargenteus.* In the southern United States the bobcat, *Lynx rufus,* is targeted. In the United States the emphasis is placed on the fun of the chase rather than killing the animal. In Iraq and countries once belonging to the British Empire, such as India, it is the golden jackal, *Canis aureus,* that is the prey.

The first documented fox hunt took place in the county of Norfolk, eastern England, in 1534, when farmers took to hunting the animals as a form of pest control. This coincided with articles by writers such as George Gascoigne and Thomas Cockaine on the subject of hunting vermin and predators, particularly foxes. Antifox propaganda spread the notion that the fox was a sly creature that preyed on chickens and lambs belonging to poor farmers, and soon it was a common belief that the fox deserved to be hunted. Medieval writers declared that the foxhunting season should run from Christmas to the Feast of the Annunciation on March 25, though as foxes were now viewed as vermin these dates were usually ignored, with the fox hunted all year. To this day it is traditional (though illegal) for fox hunts in England to be held on Boxing Day, a national holiday held annually on December 26.

In the 16th century farmers routinely used snares and traps to hunt foxes, but the aristocracy of the time started to take an interest in hunting the animal too. However, the nobility thought of foxhunting as a sport rather than as a form of pest control. The nobility, however, realized that foxes, with their distinctive scent, made ideal prey for hounds to track aboveground using their sense of smell, and in order to ensure that the foxes could not hide underground during a hunt, huntsmen began to barricade the earth burrows in which the foxes took shelter using twigs and soil. The huntsmen took pride in rearing the dogs used in the sport and enjoyed watching them run. However, during the 16th and 17th centuries foxhunting was slow to thrive for several reasons. One problem was that the early fox hunts were slow-paced, as the dogs employed in the hunt were those used to hunt deer and tended to be too heavy to catch the fleet-footed foxes. Thus, fox hunts tended to be held unsociably early in the morning, when foxes were returning from their nightly prowl with full stomachs that slowed their running. While the full foxes were easier for the dogs to catch, the foxes were unwilling to run, which resulted in the hunt taking a long time to complete. Also, since the fox was ubiquitous, posed no threat to human life, and was inedible, there was little glory in hunting the animal. Thus, the fox was considered merely a pest, a wild animal that anyone with a pack of dogs could hunt. For this reason, during the early days of the sport foxhunting was generally considered a lower-class pursuit that doubled as a form of pest control. However, in the 18th century a wealthy huntsman named Hugo Meynell developed new breeds of hound that possessed enough stamina and speed to chase the fox successfully. This meant that hunts could now be staged midmorning when the fox was not too full to run, and hunts became fast-paced affairs offering excitement for onlookers and human participants. The hunt became a favorite pastime of Meynell and his wealthy neighbors, who realized that it was an excellent opportunity to make social connections and show off their horse-riding prowess. Eventually it became the norm in Britain to use fast hounds when foxhunting—only some areas of northern England and Wales resisted the change. Indeed, by the end of the century the sport had improved so much in terms of pace that it was taken up by royalty, for in 1793 the Prince of Wales began to foxhunt. Such royal approval meant that foxhunting became a key leisure pursuit of the gentry.

Two further innovations meant that the popularity of foxhunting continued to grow in the 19th century. First, by the end of the previous century most English counties had become enclosed. This meant that the vast tracts of open countryside through which fox hunters would once have ridden were now divided by fences and hedges used by individual landowners to enclose their land. Thus, it became necessary for hunters to make their horses jump fences and hedges as part of the chase, making the hunt much more exciting. The other innovation to affect foxhunting was the coming of the railway, for this allowed city dwellers to travel to the countryside in order to take part in hunts. Indeed, from the 1840s trains were equipped with horsecars that enabled hunters to take their horses to hunts all over

England. The popularity of foxhunting continued to grow, and by the start of World War I foxhunting's popularity was at its highest, and the sport had established a governing body, the Master of Foxhounds Association.

As the popularity of foxhunting rose so too did its social status, and many elements of the prestigious stag hunt were introduced into the fox hunt. For instance, on the death of the fox the hunter would declare "whoo-whoop" as stag hunters would on the death of their quarry. However, new rites particular to foxhunting were also invented, such as the tradition that parts of the fox should be cut from the carcass and given to the hunters present at the animal's death, as well as the custom of blooding, that is, smearing the fox's blood on the face of children and new hunt members.

Such traditions continue today, as does the procedure of the hunt. The hunt is overseen by the master, who may also double as the huntsman, that is, the person, male or female, in charge of the 20 to 30 matched pairs of hounds used in the chase, though more commonly the huntsman is the most senior-paid servant of the hunt. The huntsman controls the hounds through voice commands known as cheers and by using a copper horn measuring about eight inches long. The huntsman is assisted by two or three whippers-in, who keep the hounds together and carry out reconnaissance. The whippers-in, huntsman, and master have more authority over matters concerning the hounds than all other members of the hunt. Other hunt staff include grooms; second horsemen, who assist the master; the master's staff; leading followers; and earth stoppers, whose job it is to block off the foxes' dens. The adoption of foxhunting by the upper class led to the development of a foxhunting uniform that continues to be worn: the master, huntsman, and whippers-in wear a scarlet jacket, white cravat, and black velvet cap (women hunt members are also allowed to wear the cap). Important hunt followers are invited to wear scarlet jackets fastened with the buttons denoting that particular hunt plus a top hat. Other followers wear black jackets with either a top hat or bowler hat. At the more established ancestral hunts of the aristocracy, the scarlet jacket may be replaced by coats colored gray, green, or yellow.

At the start of a hunt the followers join the hounds and acknowledge the master, who commands the hounds to search the area in which a fox is suspected of hiding. This area is usually a field, gorse patch, or wood. When the whereabouts of the fox are discovered a cry of "Tally-ho" is shouted, and the chase begins. Once the fox is in sight a cry of "Holloa" goes up, and eventually the fox is killed. Traditionally once the fox is dead the master doles out the fox's head, feet, and tail to those they feel are particularly worthy of the prize. The rest of the fox's carcass is then thrown to the hounds.

After World War I foxhunting encountered several problems in the United Kingdom, particularly the further division of the countryside into multiple smallholdings. This division of the land resulted in a proliferation of barbed-wire fences to outline individual plots that proved dangerous to hunt participants, both human and animal. However, perhaps the greatest threat to the popularity of foxhunting was the growing belief that the hunt was a barbaric, antiquated, and elitist pursuit. Antifoxhunting sentiments had been expressed during the sport's rise in popularity during the 19th century. For instance, a character in Oscar Wilde's play *A Woman of No Importance* (1893) famously decries the pastime, and efforts to ban the sport intensified during the 20th and 21st centuries. Eventually in 2002, hunting wild animals with dogs was outlawed in Scotland, followed by the outlawing of the sport in England and Wales in 2004. Many legal challenges were pursued to overturn the ban, but it was enshrined in law in February 2005. Following the ban some hunts took up drag racing whereby hunters and hounds follow a previously laid scent trail rather than a live fox. If a living fox is chased during this type of hunt, law dictates that the fox must be shot dead by the hunters rather than ripped apart by dogs.

Foxhunting has appeared in many films, though it is often depicted in an unrealistic manner. For instance, the sport has appeared in several Disney films, such as *The Fox Hunt* (1938), *The Fox and the Hound* (1981), and, perhaps most famously, *Mary Poppins* (1964) that portrays foxhunting as a pursuit of the English aristocracy, which though somewhat silly is an inherent element of the English countryside and national identity. Paradoxically, the British film studio Hammer suggested that fox hunters are cruel and menacing in the horror film *The Plague of the Zombies* (1965) in which voodoo-practicing fox hunters chase a living woman rather than a fox.

The related sport of hound trailing takes place in certain areas of the United Kingdom, notably Cumbria, Yorkshire, and the Scottish Borders as well as parts of Ireland. Hound trailing, which is overseen by the Hound Trailing Association, was invented in the 18th century in order to settle an argument between the owners of two foxhound packs who quarreled over which pack had the faster-running dogs. In hound trailing, specially trained dogs, descended in part from foxhounds, follow a trail of aniseed across up to 10 miles of countryside without human guidance. The hounds race for a maximum of 45 minutes, and the dog that wins the most races is crowned the season's champion.

See also: Bearbaiting and Badger Baiting; Bull Running; *Buzkashi*; Camel and Yak Racing; Camel Wrestling; Cockfighting; Elephant Sports; Fell Running; Hare Coursing; Nonlethal Bullfighting; *Pato* and Horseball; Pigeon Racing; Sheepdog Trials; Spanish Bullfighting; Yabbie Races

Further Reading

Douglas, Ollie. "Fox Hunt: Looking at Motion, Animation and Film," University of Reading Weblogs, September 19, 2012, http://blogs.reading.ac.uk/what-to-look-for/tag/fox-hunt/ (accessed December 29, 2013).

"Fox Hunting Worldwide." BBC News, September 16, 1999, http://news.bbc.co.uk/1/hi/uk/428122.stm (accessed December 29, 2013).

"An Introduction to Fox Hunting," Countryside Alliance, http://www.countryside-alliance.org/ca/file/Hunting_for_Kids.pdf (accessed December 29, 2013).

Griffin, Emma. *Blood Sport: Hunting in Britain since 1066.* New Haven, CT: Yale University Press, 2007.

Walsh, John. "Racing Away." *LandScape Magazine,* March–April 2014, 80–83.

G

GILLI-DANDA

Gilli-danda is a folk game played by children and young adults, usually males, throughout the Asian subcontinent, especially rural areas of India and Pakistan, and resembles cricket or tipcat. The name of the game is a combination of two words from the Indian Hindi language that relate to equipment used in the game: *gilli,* which is a stick measuring between three and six inches in length with a center measuring one inch in diameter that tapers at both ends, and *danda,* which is a sticklike bat between two and three feet in length and one inch in diameter. These are used in place of the ball and bat employed in a game of cricket. The game is known by many different names throughout India, including *danguli* (in the Bengali language), *kitti-pul* (in the Tamil language), and *gulli danda* (in the Punjabi language). *Gilli-danda* is called *dandi-biyo* in Nepal and *alak-dolak* in Iran and Afghanistan.

Gilli-danda is thought to be a very ancient game dating back to the time of the Mauryan Empire, the first major dynasty to rule India, that held power between 323 BCE and 185 BCE. The antiquity of *gilli-danda* is such that the game is thought by some to be the originator of cricket, baseball, and softball. However, unlike these sports, *gilli-danda* does not have a governing body.

Unlike most games belonging to the Western Hemisphere, *gilli-danda* can be played by any number of players, though it is advisable for a game to be contested by just two teams so as to avoid disputes. *Gilli-danda* can also be played by individuals.

There are many ways of playing *gilli-danda,* but in general the game sees the two captains of both teams contest a toss of a coin to determine which side is on strike and which fields—the team that wins the toss chooses whether to bat or field first. Next a circle called the pillow is drawn on the ground in which the striker stands holding the *danda.* Meanwhile, the fielders spread themselves around the playing area. The *gilli* is placed inside the pillow, and the striker then taps the *gilli* at one end so that it becomes airborne, allowing the *danda* to be struck hard. Alternatively, the *gilli* may be placed on a stone in an inclined position so that one end of the *gilli* touches the ground and the other end is pointing into the air.

The striker aims to hit the *gilli* so that it travels as far as possible and out of the reach of the fielders. Once the *gilli* has been struck, the striker must leave the *gilli* in the pillow to act as a sort of wicket. Once the striker has hit the *gilli,* the next striker takes his turn to hit. The striker has three attempts to hit the *gilli.* If the striker fails to make contact with the *gilli* within the three attempts, then the striker is out. The striker is also out if the *gilli* is caught by the fielder immediately after being struck before it touches the ground and if a fielder manages to hit the *danda* resting inside the pillow with the *gilli,* with the *gilli* having touched the ground. A game of *gilli-danda* continues until all players have had a turn at being on strike. The winning team is the side that records the most *danda* lengths and thus scores the most points. A *danda* length is the distance between the pillow and where the *gilli* lands, measured using the length of the *danda,* and each length earns a team one point.

There are many variations of *gilli-danda.* In some versions, the points a striker scores depend on how many times the *gilli* is hit in the air in one strike. Alternatively, the total number of points earned may be doubled if the *gilli* travels past a certain distance as the result of two midair strikes. In another version of the game, the striker is required to run and reach a predetermined position outside the circle before the fielding side retrieves the *gilli.*

Gilli-danda is the subject of the multiaward-winning, Academy Award–nominated film *Lagaan: Once upon a Time in India* (2001).

A street game similar to *gilli-danda* is dainty, which is played in the Germantown community of Schnitzelburg in Louisville, Kentucky, where the World Dainty Championships are played over one day in mid-July. Dainty was introduced to the area by German immigrants who played a game in which a player uses a broom handle to hit into the air a small stick called a dainty that tapers at each end. The game disappeared for some time but was reintroduced to the area in 1971 by Charles Vettiner and George Hauck.

Today dainty may be played only by men over age 45, and as in *gilli-danda,* a swing and a miss counts as a strike, and after the third strike a player is declared out. To play dainty, a player taps the dainty so that it flips into the air and then, with a one-handed action, uses the broom handle to strike the dainty so that it travels as far as possible along the street in which the game is being played. It is quite common for hits to reach in excess of 80 feet, so sidewalks are lined with orange net to prevent injury to onlookers. The player who hits the dainty the farthest is the winner.

See also: Brännboll and *Pesäpallo;* Cricket; *Lapta;* Nipsy; Rounders

Further Reading

Bradley, Lloyd. *The Rough Guide to Cult Sport.* London: Rough Guides, 2011.

Carlisle, Rodney, ed. *Encyclopedia of Play in Today's Society,* Vol. 1. Thousand Oaks, CA: Sage, 2009.

"Dainty Played in Schnitzelburg." Daily News Journal, July 28, 2008, http://www.dnj.com /apps/pbcs.dll/gallery?Site=B2&Date=20080728&Category=ZONE01&ArtNo=80728 0817&Ref=PH&nclick_check=1 (accessed May 1, 2014).

Jadia, Rishika. "Gilli Danda." Indian Traditional Games, March 1, 2013, http://indiantradit ionalgames.wordpress.com/category/project-phase-1/gilli-danda/ (accessed May 1, 2014).

"Long Lost Childhood Games—Gilli Danda/Chinni Dandu." Niveditha's Blog, http:// nivedithatm.blogspot.co.uk/2014/02/long-lost-childhood-games-gilli-danda.html (accessed May 1, 2014).

Marshall, Anne. "Dainty World Championships: Louisville's Other Claim to Fame." *Only a Game,* August 25, 2012.

"Mauryan Empire (ca. 323–185 BC)." The Metropolitan Museum of Art, 2000–2013, http://www.metmuseum.org/toah/hd/maur/hd_maur.htm (accessed May 1, 2014).

RIC Publications. *India: A Cross-Curricular Theme.* Greenwood, Western Australia: RIC Publications, 2010.

GLIMA

Glima, which translates as "game of joy," is an umbrella term for forms of wrestling associated with Iceland in which both men and women compete and that favor technique over force. *Glima* originated over 1,000 years ago and was brought to Iceland by Viking settlers. *Glima* is currently enjoying a revival across Scandinavia and is often featured at festivals celebrating Viking culture.

There are three versions of the sport: *livtagsglima, lösatagsglima,* and *byxtagsglima.* The latter is the national sport of Iceland and is the version of the sport to which the umbrella term *glima* is most often applied. In earlier times there were three further variations of *glima:* formal *glima,* loose grips *glima,* and dueling *glima.* The latter form of the sport was used to settle major grievances and would see two men enter a field with a large, tapering slab of rock with the intention of bashing the opponent to death with the stone. This version of the sport is no longer practiced. Formal and loose *glima* are, however. Loose grips *glima,* which is akin to *lösatagsglima,* can be performed as a form of self-defense, and moves deemed illegal in formal *glima* may be used, such as the somersault throw. Formal *glima* is characterized by four key points and eight *bragd,* or tricks. The four key points are the erect stature of the wrestlers, the fixed grip on the opponent's waistband and the outside of the leg, the circular movement of the wrestlers, and the distinct throws achieved by means of hips, feet, and legs. The *bragd* include the hook, the cross-buttock, the outside stroke, the inside click, the cross-click, and the back-heel. The moves permitted in *glima* were formalized in 1916 when the Icelandic Sports Federation enshrined formal rules for the sport.

Glima is traditionally practiced outdoors between September and April, with competitors wearing appropriate dress for the cold winter weather. In the early days of *glima* the sport often took part on hillsides or in places offering natural shelter. Such places were given the name Glimuholl, meaning "Glima Hall."

One of the key characteristics of *byxtagsglima* is the belts worn by competitors. In the early days of *glima,* competitors wore trousers. However, in 1905 the decision was made to replace trousers with belts, and today *glima* wrestlers begin a bout by placing a wide belt called a *climubeltae* around their waist and two smaller separate belts around the lower thigh on each leg. The thigh belts are then connected to the waist belt by vertical straps. Wrestlers then grip the waist belt with one hand and place their other hand inside their trousers at thigh height. Wrestlers then stand facing one another and move clockwise around each other in a movement called *stigandi,* meaning "treading." All the while the wrestlers try to trip and throw the opponent by grabbing the opponent's belt, much as in Japanese sumo wrestling. If a wrestler is tripped but lands on his hands and feet, then it is not counted as a fall. It is also not a fall if both wrestlers land together in a move called a brother-fall. However, if a wrestler lands in such a way that a part of the body between the elbow and knee touches the ground, then a fall is said to have occurred, as it is if both a wrestler's arms touch the ground. The aim of the sport is to force an opponent to fall to the ground for the best of two out of three falls.

The belts worn by the wrestlers hark back to the heavy winter clothing worn when *glima* was contested in Viking times. Another echo of the sport's Viking heritage is seen in the areas of the body the wrestlers grab. For instance, the left hip and right thigh are both places where warriors would wear a sword or dagger. In addition to the belts, modern *glima* wrestlers wear sport-specific shoes.

The highest achievement for any *glima* wrestler is to win the Icelandic Glima Championship and thus be awarded the Grettir Belt, named after a famous character from Icelandic saga who, though an outlaw, is also courageous and physically strong. The highest honor for female *glima* wrestlers is to participate in the Freyjuglima event and win the title "Queen of Glima."

See also: Celtic Wrestling; Korean Wrestling; Mongolian Wrestling; *Pehlwani/Kushti; Schwingen;* Sumo Wrestling; *Varzesh-e Bastani; Yagli Gures*

Further Reading

"Glima." My Kick Boxing, http://www.mykickboxing.com/Sweden/glima.html (accessed August 11, 2013).

"Glima—The Icelandic Art of Wrestling Is Still Hot." The Martial Arts Reporter, December 22, 2011, http://themartialartsreporter.com/glima-the-icelandic-art-of-wrestling-is-still-hot/ (accessed August 11, 2013).

Green, Thomas A., ed. *Martial Arts of the World: An Encyclopedia,* Vol. 1, *A–L.* Santa Barbara, CA: ABC-CLIO, 2001.

Kautz, Pete. "The Gripping History of Glima." *Journal of Western Martial Art* (January 2000), http://ejmas.com/jwma/articles/2000/jwmaart_kautz_0100.htm (accessed August 11, 2013).

Young, Don, and Marjorie Young. *Reykjavik Iceland and Its Surroundings.* Edison, NJ: Hunter Publishing, 2009.

HANDBALL

The term "handball" can be applied to two different sports: court handball and team handball. Court handball, sometimes referred to as one-wall handball, three-wall handball, four-wall handball, or Irish handball, is a recreational game consisting of elements of squash, fives, real tennis, *pelota,* jai alai, and racquetball that requires speed, skill, strength, and agility, as players use a gloved hand to hit a ball against the walls of a court on which lines are marked. Court handball is played worldwide as a form of exercise and is played competitively at national and international levels, though unlike team handball, the game is not an Olympic sport.

Court handball is an extremely old game, with depictions of people hitting a ball with their hands found on the tombs of ancient Egyptian priests circa 2000 BCE and on sculpture and pottery dating from around 1500 BCE found at pre-Columbian sites in South America. In addition, images of people using their hands to hit a ball as it ricochets off a wall have been noted on artifacts found on the Mexican plateau on land populated by the Chichimeca peoples. More recently in Europe, court handball was a favorite pastime of King James I of Scotland, who in 1427 had blocked up a window that interfered with his handball playing. Unfortunately for James I, his love of court handball inadvertently led to his death, for when conspirators entered his castle intent on his destruction, the king hid in a sewer pipe but found that he could not escape his pursuers via the drain, as the end had been blocked to stop court handballs from being lost in the sewer. Thus, James I was discovered in the sewer and killed. Later during the 17th century, British church authorities took a stand against court handball, as they feared that striking a ball against church walls could lead to stained glass windows being broken. However, it was Catholic missionaries who helped spread court handball across the globe when they introduced the game to Australia, South Africa, and the Americas. Modern court handball has its roots in Ireland, for in 1884 the Gaelic Athletic Association was established, and the Irish settlers in New York City built a court for the playing of court handball. From New York the game soon spread across the United States. The sport became popular and counted as a fan Abraham Lincoln, who played the game regularly while living in Springfield, Illinois. In 1897 the U.S. Amateur Athletics Union (AAU) adopted the sport and held the first tournament. The AAU also organized the first four-wall handball tournament in 1919 and the first one-wall tournament in 1924. In addition to this, from 1925 to 1958 the Young Men's Christian Association (YMCA) built courts for court handball throughout the United States on which the organization hosted regular tournaments. In 1951 the Amateur Handball Association was founded, later

Heidi Loeke of Norway in possession of the ball against Spain in the final match of the women's team handball European Championship held in Budapest, Hungary, on December 21, 2014. The aim of the game is for teams to score more goals than their opponents. It is common for more than 50 goals to be scored during a match. (AP Photo/MTI, Tibor Illyes)

changing its name to the United States Handball Association (USHA). Together with the YMCA and the AAU, USHA helped establish standardized rules for four-wall handball in 1958.

Court handball may be played by two to four players on a court featuring one, two, or four walls. Players strike the handball ball so that it hits against the front wall, back wall, sidewalls, and ceiling in such a way that it rebounds with great velocity. In court handball only the serving side can score points, and the first team to reach 21 points or to earn a 2-point margin after 21 has reached is declared the winner. In a game of court handball, play begins when a serve is delivered from a marked zone so that it hits the front wall, ricochets off the floor beyond the service area, and then rebounds on to the back wall, the ceiling, or a sidewall. Opposing players then have to hit the ball back so that it hits the front wall and then the floor.

In contrast to court handball, team handball, also known as continental handball, European handball, and Olympic handball, combines elements of basketball and soccer. The most commonly played form of team handball is competitive team handball, which is played indoors by two teams of six and is particularly popular in continental Europe. However, an outdoor version featuring two teams of 11 also exists as a recreational pastime outside of Europe. The sport's governing body is the International Handball Federation (IHF) founded in 1946, with the founding members being France, the Netherlands, Switzerland, Poland, Norway, Denmark, and Sweden. Today, the IHF has around 170 members and oversees about 795,000 teams across the globe.

Team handball is known to be at least 3,000 years old, for the game was familiar to the ancient Greeks. This is evidenced by the fact that the great poet Homer in his epic poem *The Odyssey* describes how a Spartan princess named Anagalla invented the game, while Alexander the Great (356–323 BCE), king of the Greek kingdom of Macedon, is known to have played team handball. The origins of modern team handball are unknown. One suggestion is that the game was invented in Germany during the 19th century as a training regime for gymnasts. However, another theory suggests that team handball began in Scandinavia at the start of the 20th century, for there is documentary evidence of a seven-a-side version of team handball being played in Sweden in 1907, while Dane Fredrik Knudsen codified the rules of team handball in 1911. It should be noted, however, that other claims for the origins of team handball also exist, with some historians suggesting that the modern game was created by a Danish physical education teacher, Rasmus Nicolai, in 1897, though another Danish teacher, Holger Nielsen, is also credited with drawing up the rules in 1898, with the rules published in 1906. In Germany the rules of modern team handball were published in 1917 by Max Heiser, Karl Schelenz, and Erich Konigh.

Whatever the origins of team handball, by the early 20th century the game was played in Ukraine (as *gandbol*), Denmark (as *håndbold*), Germany (as *torball*), Slovakia (as *hádzaná*), and the Czech Republic (as *házená*), with the sport's first governing body, the International Amateur Handball Federation, founded in 1928. The first international game of handball for men was contested in 1925 by sides from Germany and Belgium. The first international game for women, between Germany and Austria, took place five years later.

Team handball was so popular in Germany that men's outdoor team handball was included in the 1936 Olympic Games held in the German capital of Berlin. However, it was not until the 1972 Olympics held in Munich, Germany, that men's handball was again part of the Games. Women's handball became an Olympic sport at the Montreal Olympics of 1976. After the inauguration of team handball as an Olympic sport, the first men's team handball world championship was held in 1938, though the advent of World War II put a halt to the world championship until the end of the conflict. However, World War II also helped spread knowledge of team handball, as prisoners of war brought the game to Canada, while immigrants from France and Eastern Europe who had fled the war and settled in Canada began to teach the game, especially in secondary schools in Quebec. After the end of World War II the newly formed International Handball Federation (which did not include Germany as a member) organized an international men's match between Sweden and Denmark, held in Gothenburg, Sweden, on November 6, 1946. The first women's outdoor team handball world championship was held in 1949, with the first indoor women's team handball world championship held in 1957. The world championship has been held biannually since 1995.

A game of team handball is contested by two teams, each consisting of six outfield players and a goalkeeper. Teams aim to score more goals than their opponents during the match's two 30-minute halves by throwing the ball into the goal belonging to the other team. It is common for over 50 goals to be scored during a match.

A goal is situated at either end of the team handball court, which is rectangular and divided into two. In front of each goal is an area into which only the goalkeeper may step, though all outfield players may jump over the zone as they relinquish the ball. This area stretches 6 meters, or just under 20 feet, from the goal and is marked by a 6-meter line. A court also features a 9-meter (29.6-foot) line.

In team handball, physical contact is not allowed between players except when a player sandwich occurs. This refers to times when a defensive player stands completely in front of an offensive player—if the defensive player stands behind the attacking player, the defensive player is not allowed to make contact with the offensive player. A foul is said to occur when illegal physical contact is made, with fouls classed as either offensive or defensive depending on whether an offensive or defensive player caused the contact.

See also: Fives; Hurling; *Pelota;* Real Tennis

Further Reading

"Handball." Handball09.com, 2014, http://www.handball09.com (June 18, 2014).
"History of Handball." Handball09.com, 2014, http://www.handball09.com/the-history -of-handball/ (accessed June 18, 2014).
Levinson, David, and Karen Christensen, eds. *Encyclopedia of World Sport: From Ancient Times to the Present.* Oxford: Oxford University Press, 1996.
"Women's World Championship." International Handball Association, 2014, http://www .ihf.info/IHFCompetitions/CompetitionsArchive/WomenWorldChampionships /tabid/4859/Default.aspx (accessed June 18, 2014).

HARE COURSING

Hare coursing is the pursuit of live hares using hounds that catch prey through a combination of speed and good sight as opposed to scent, particularly specially bred lurchers and greyhounds but also, depending on location, deerhounds, borzois, salukis, and whippets. As a competitive blood sport, hare coursing sees dogs assessed as to their skill in hunting the live hares. Hare coursing contests take place in Ireland and some areas of the United States as well as in Portugal, Spain, and Pakistan, though in Pakistan it is illegal to course for hares without a special license, but the extent to which this rule is adhered to is open to conjecture. Hare coursing is banned in most of Europe, including the United Kingdom and Australia. Meanwhile, pressure groups including the Irish Council Against Blood Sports, Animal Place, and PETA (People for the Ethical Treatment of Animals) have called for an end to hare coursing in Ireland and the United States.

Noncompetitive hare coursing is an ancient practice, with the oldest written reference to hare coursing dating from Greece in 180 CE and describing how all levels of society practiced the activity. In Europe this remained the case until medieval times, when the establishment of Forest Law meant that forests and the

A dog in pursuit of a hare at the last-ever Waterloo Cup hare coursing event held at Altcar, England, on February 14, 2005. In hare coursing, hounds' hunting skills are assessed as they chase the hares. The activity is controversial; a law banning the activity in the United Kingdom came into effect on February 18, 2005. (AP Photo/Jon Super)

hunting of animals living in the forests became the preserve of royalty. Competitive hare coursing was first codified in England by Thomas, Duke of Norfolk, in the 1560s who, according to legend, later revised the rules at the behest of Queen Elizabeth I (1533–1603) so that the hare was given a head start and the winning hound was awarded points. The first public hare coursing club was established at Swaffham, in the county of Norfolk in eastern England, in 1776. The popularity of hare coursing increased rapidly during the Industrial Revolution particularly on the open moorland of northern England, where competitive hare coursing took place in an informal manner among miners and farmers, and in the south of England at celebrated venues such as Ashdown Park, Epsom, Leatherhead, and Letcombe, where the coursing was much more formal and undertaken as a lavish event, though the United Kingdom's biggest and most prestigious hare coursing event, the three-day Waterloo Cup, which began in 1836, was held in Lancashire, northern England, until hare coursing was banned in the United Kingdom in 2005. The National Coursing Club was founded to regulate the sport in the United Kingdom in 1858. The popularity of hare coursing peaked in the United Kingdom during the 19th century, with more than 150 coursing clubs attracting up to 80,000 people. However, this surge of popularity meant that the activity lost its appeal for the upper classes, and by the late 19th century hare coursing had become a predominantly working-class pastime. The popularity of hare coursing in the United Kingdom declined further at the start of the 20th century, especially during the 1920s with the advent of greyhound racing, in which greyhounds chase a mechanical hare around a track. By the time the hare coursing ban came into effect in the United Kingdom, there were fewer than 30 coursing clubs operating. However, illegal hare coursing does still take place in some rural areas of the United Kingdom, usually at sunrise or sunset around the end of August or the beginning of September when crops have been harvested and fields are left bare, making it easy to spot the hares. As recently as April 2014, the British Parliament was warned that illicit hare coursing was on the rise in rural areas, with chases organized by illegal gambling gangs. During illegal hare coursing, human participants spread in a line across a field, drive a hare from its home, and then release their dogs so to chase the hare. Often large bets are made on which dog will catch the hare first. Once the hare is killed, its body is discarded and the chase continues until all the hares in the field have been caught. When this has happened, the chase moves to the next field.

The objective of legal coursing is to test and assess the athletic ability of the coursing hounds rather than to kill a hare. There are a number of hare coursing variations. Open coursing takes place in the open space, while closed coursing, also known as park- or Irish-style coursing, takes place in an enclosure fitted with an escape route. Open coursing is divided into two types: walked-up coursing, in which a line of people walk through the countryside to flush out the hare, and driven coursing, in which hares are driven by men called beaters whose role is to chase the hares out of wooded areas and toward the coursing field. This form of coursing was the basis of the Waterloo Cup. In both forms of hare coursing, when a suitable hare appears, a person known as a slipper uses a dual-collar slip to release two dogs simultaneously in pursuit of the hare, which is given a head start under a rule known as fair law. The head start is normally between 80 and 100 yards, with the hare sprinting at 24–26 miles per hour. The chase usually lasts for around 40 seconds over a third of a mile, with the hound pursuing the hare and, being the faster runner, gradually starts to catch up with the hare. However, since the hounds are significantly larger than the hare and also much less agile, the hound is unable to track the hare as it makes a series of sharp-angled turns while running, scared for its life. The hare's agility helps it evade the hound and, pro-coursing enthusiasts argue, usually escape. Judges mounted on horseback assess how many times the hound can make the hare turn and how closely they can follow the hare's course and award points accordingly. If a course is part of a knockout competition, then the winning hound proceeds to the next round of the tournament.

Hare coursing is popular in Ireland, with the most prestigious Irish event being the national meeting held in Clonmel, County Tipperary. This event attracts 10,000 spectators and, according to event organizers, brings €16 million to the local economy. There are around 70 formal hare coursing clubs in Ireland hosting around 80 meetings annually. The Irish Coursing Club has governed Irish coursing since 1916, and there are quite a few coursing rules that are particular to Ireland. For instance, as hares are not especially plentiful in Ireland, the Irish government permits coursing clubs to capture between 70 and 75 hares for events. Once captured, the animals are transported in boxes to the coursing venue and kept there for up to eight weeks, during which time they are trained to be chased. After the coursing event has finished, the hares are transported back to their natural habitat and released into the wild, though it has been noted that some hares have been coursed more than once at the same coursing event. The Irish Coursing Club has also tried to ensure hare safety by insisting, since 1993, that hounds must wear a muzzle while coursing. Also, Irish hare coursing only takes place in a secure enclosure over a set distance rather than on open land. Additionally, Irish coursing dictates that the first hound to turn the hare wins, with the win signaled by the use of either a red flag or a white flag, depending on the color of the collar worn by the winning hound.

Hare coursing in the United States began in the early 20th century when ranchers found coursing necessary to prevent the rabbit population from devastating crops. The first organized open field hare coursing event held in the United States, the Pacheco Hunt, took place in California in 1959 and was sponsored by the Borzoi Club of California. Two bodies govern hare coursing in the United States: the National Open Field Coursing Association (NOFCA) established in 1973 and the North America Coursing Association (NACA) founded in 1987. The NOFCA oversees courses held mainly in alfalfa fields near Merced, California, which are inhabited by the black-tailed jackrabbit. Meanwhile, the NACA governs courses held around Medicine Bow, Wyoming, where the white-tailed jackrabbit is native. The two associations are similar in their title requirements, with two championship titles available to win. The first title is the CC, or coursing champion, for which a hound must score 100 points in competition (10 of which must be scored in breed competition), plus either one first-place result or two second-place results and either two assisted kills or one unassisted kill. The second available open field coursing title is the courser of merit, for which, together with the other requirements, a hound must score 100 points in breed competition. A single judge scores the courses, assessing the hounds' speed, agility, and endurance (all of which earn 25 points) while directly controlling the hare. Points are awarded when a hound causes a rabbit to turn or goes for a kill (worth 10 points) or a near kill. The hounds' desire to course (worth 15 points) and touch (5 points) are also judged. Any hound that starts coursing before its official release receives a 10-point penalty.

In Spain, hare coursing is known as *caza* and uses a breed of hound called the *galgos* that is able to maintain a steady fast pace for over five minutes. Competitive coursing in Spain sees the *galgos* compete first at the regional level and then at the provincial level. Next, each province selects two champion hounds to compete at the national championships. In Spanish hare coursing, a dog that kills a hare during the course is not necessarily the winner. Instead, judges call a winner based on the amount of effort made by the hounds during the whole course. Therefore, hounds receive points according to their speed and stamina, their passing abilities, their tracking of the hare, and the nature of the hare's killing. Hounds are disqualified if they behave in an irregular manner, and any hound that is not considered to have tried its hardest at following the hare receives penalty points and will not be allowed to win. For the chase to be valid, the course must last for at least 55 seconds.

Kaninhop: The Gentle Sport of Bunny Hopping

Kaninhop, or rabbit hopping, which originated in Sweden around 1980, sees rabbits jump over small-scale obstacles as in horse show jumping. During competition rabbits are scored on the number of jumps they clear successfully, and there is often a time element to competition. *Kaninhop* clubs are established in Europe, the United States, Canada, and Japan, and competitions take place around the world. Breeders train rabbits to jump obstacles by walking them on harnesses from the age of eight weeks. This has led to protests from some animal rights groups.

During the 1970s the popularity of hare coursing in the United States and the United Kingdom dropped significantly, as the activity came to be considered inherently cruel. In the United Kingdom, hare coursing became a completely banned and illegal activity in 2005 when the Hunting Act (2004) came into force. This means that anyone convicted of involvement in hare coursing can be fined up to £5,000. While the ban has been welcomed by animal rights groups in the United Kingdom and by a majority of the British public, the ban has led to some discord between people living in the countryside and city dwellers. There have also been complaints that a significant aspect of British rural culture has been eliminated to appease those who do not fully understand the pastime.

See also: Bearbaiting and Badger Baiting; Bull Running; *Buzkashi;* Camel and Yak Racing; Camel Wrestling; Cockfighting; Elephant Sports; Foxhunting; Nonlethal Bullfighting; *Pato* and Horseball; Pigeon Racing; Sheepdog Trials; Spanish Bullfighting; Yabbie Races

Further Reading

Atkinson, Michael, and Kevin Young. *Deviance and Social Control in Sport.* Champaign, IL: Human Kinetics, 2008.

Bronner, Simon. *Killing Tradition: Inside Hunting and Animal Rights Controversies.* Lexington: University Press of Kentucky, 2008.

Clover, Charles. "Defiant Hare Coursing Fans Vow to Battle for Their Waterloo Cup." *The Telegraph,* February 15, 2005, http://www.telegraph.co.uk/news/uknews/1483542/Defiant-hare-coursing-fans-vow-to-battle-for-their-Waterloo-Cup.html (accessed April 20, 2014).

Collins, Tony, John Martin, and Wray Vamplew, eds. *Encyclopedia of Traditional British Rural Sports.* Abingdon, UK: Routledge, 2005.

"Coursing." Spanishdogs.com, http://www.spanishdogs.com/history/coursing.htm (accessed April 20, 2014).

"Hare Coursing." Racing-dog.com, http://racing-dog.com/hare-coursing.htm (accessed April 20, 2014).

Herbert, Ian. "Hare Coursers Gather for What Might Be Final Waterloo Cup." *The Independent,* February 26, 2003, http://www.independent.co.uk/news/uk/home-news/hare-coursers-gather-for-what-might-be-final-waterloo-cup-598864.html (accessed April 20, 2014).

"The Hunting Act 2004." The Crown Prosecution Service, https://www.cps.gov.uk/legal/h_to_k/hunting_act/#hare (accessed April 20, 2014).

Jones, Richard. *The Medieval Natural World.* Abingdon, UK: Routledge, 2013.

Levinson, David, and Karen Christensen, eds. *Encyclopedia of World Sport: From Ancient Times to the Present.* Oxford: Oxford University Press, 1996.

Norfolk Constabulary. "Hare Coursing." Norfolk Constabulary, 2012, http://www.norfolk. police.uk/safetyadvice/wildlifeprotection/wildlifeatrisk/harecoursing.aspx   (accessed April 20, 2014).

"Open Field Coursing with Borzoi." Borzoi Club of America, 1996–2006, http://www.borz oiclubofamerica.org/openfield.htm (accessed April 20, 2014).

Swinford, Steven, and Sarah Gallagher. "Poaching, Sheep-Rustling and Hare Coursing Are on the Rise, MPs Warn." *The Telegraph,* April 15, 2014, http://www.telegraph.co.uk /earth/10768669/Poaching-sheep-rustling-and-hare-coursing-are-on-the-rise-MPs -warn.html (accessed April 20, 2014).

HAXEY HOOD GAME

The Haxey Hood Game is a folk sport custom taking place on January 6 (or January 5 should January 6 fall on a Sunday) each year in the village of Haxey in the county of Lincolnshire, eastern England, that includes elements of soccer, rugby, and *la soule.* The ritual was first recorded in 1815, though according to local legend the tradition began in the 14th century when the silk hood of a local aristocrat, Lady de Mowbray, blew away as she was riding to an Epiphany church service on the hill that separates Westwoodside from Haxey. Thirteen local men gave chase to retrieve the hood, as they believed that whoever returned the clothing to her lady-ship would be well rewarded. Eventually one man prevailed, snatching the hood from his opponents. However, as he approached the lady he was overcome by shy-ness, enabling another man to snatch it from him and present it to her instead. The lady found the men's behavior entertaining and vowed to present half an acre of land to each of the 13 men on condition that the villagers would reenact the antics each year. Today the game takes on a riotous nature as a contest between the regular drinkers of the village pubs, causing streets to close to traffic and shop windows to be covered to prevent breakage. The game's main players are based on the event's original participants, with the men who chased the hood represented by players called boggins. The boggins perform stewarding duties and, starting on New Year's Eve, collect money from neighboring pubs to both defray the cost of staging the game and donate to local charities. A player known as the fool represents the man who was too shy to hand the lady her hood, and the man who took advantage of this bashfulness is known as the lord of the hood. The latter's costume is pink and includes a top hat adorned with flowers and pheasant feathers. To symbolize his importance, the lord of the hood carries a wand made of 13 osiers woven in a tra-ditional pattern.

The game begins in the morning with contestants drinking in their respective pubs and thereby entering into a combative mood. The players sing traditional En-glish folk songs such as "John Barleycorn," "The Farmer's Boy," and "Cannons" ("Drink England Dry"). At about 12:30 p.m. on the day of the game the lord of the hood carries his wand around the village accompanied by the fool and the chief boggin, stopping at each pub in turn. Each landlord gives the players free drinks as a token of good luck and to try to ensure that the hood will reach his pub first.

The fool's face is decorated with ceremonial markings at the first pub, allowing him to kiss any woman he desires.

At around 2:00 p.m. the boggins assemble at the gates of the village church and the fool tries to run away from the boggins, only to be caught and brought back to the church. Once he is returned, the fool climbs atop a mounting block called the Mowbray Stone, which is situated opposite the church and around which straw has been piled. The fool then recites the rules of the game, including orders not to cause physical injury. While the fool speaks the straw is set alight in a tradition known as smoking the fool, with the aim being to see how long the fool can speak before he is overcome by the smoke and flames from the fire and is forced to quit the mounting stone. This is a tamer version of the traditional smoking in which the fool was suspended over a fire and swung back and forth until he nearly suffocated. The fool was then dropped into the fire, from which he had to escape or be burned.

Next the lord of the hood leads the villagers to a field located equidistant between Haxey and Westwoodside where the game is traditionally held. The lord of the hood carries a heavy cylinder about 18 inches long that is made of leather-covered rope sealed at each end. This tube represents the lady's hood.

To start the game, 12 pieces of rolled-up sacking are thrown into the crowd by the boggins. These tubes represent hoods, and village children try to catch a tube and swap it for sweets or coins. Other villagers who catch these smaller hoods must keep hold of them and carry them away, passing the boggins who are stationed around the edge of the field. If by an opponent, the participant must throw the hood into the air again unless the tackler is a boggin, in which case the player is said to have been boggined and must return the caught hood to the lord of the hood, who relaunches it. After this family-friendly portion of the day, the lord of the hood signals the start of the more boisterous rugby-like game. Many male drinkers from the opposing pubs form teams and join in a dense scrum known as the sway. The men's aim is to get the leatherbound hood into their pub by pure physical force, though running, kicking, and throwing are not permitted. The sway has to pass through the village and may take many hours to reach a pub. Once the sway is under way, the men's wives and girlfriends join in to add strength to the teams. Victory can be achieved only by the landlord of a participating pub placing his hand on the hood. The landlord then provides free drinks to all players. The winning publican pours beer over the hood and suspends it from two special hooks behind the bar, where it remains until New Year's Eve, when it is collected by the boggins for use in the next game.

See also: Aussie Rules Football; Eton Wall Game; *La Soule;* Rugby League

Further Reading

Alexander, Marc. *The Sutton Companion to British Folklore, Myths and Legends.* Stroud, UK: Sutton, 2005.

Dunning, Eric. *Sport Matters: Sociological Studies of Sport, Violence and Civilization.* London: Routledge, 1999.

Pope, S. W. and John Nauright, eds. *Routledge Companion to Sports History*. Abingdon, UK: Routledge, 2010.

Simpson, Jacqueline, and Steve Roud. *Oxford Dictionary of English Folklore*. Oxford: Oxford University Press, 2000.

Wheewall, Adam. "Haxey Hood: 700 Years of Tradition." Wheewall.com, 2012, http://www.wheewall.com/hood/index.php (accessed November 7, 2012).

HELI-SKIING

Heli-skiing is a form of skiing in which skiers use helicopters rather than ski lifts to reach virgin powder snow. Heli-skiing takes place in the United States, Chile, Turkey, Japan, Switzerland, Russia, Nepal, India, Iceland, Norway, Sweden, Finland, New Zealand, and Austria and is a growing tourist industry. However, the 12,000-square-mile region of British Columbia in Canada is the most popular heli-skiing destination and accounts for over half of the world's heli-skiing. As a result, heli-skiing is worth in excess of $100 million each year and provides more than 2,000 jobs. Heli-skiing is banned in France on the grounds that it causes a great deal of noise pollution and environmental damage relative to the number of people who can benefit from the activity, though it is possible to be dropped off by helicopter in Italy and then ski into neighboring France.

The history of heli-skiing began with the use of airplanes rather than helicopters to transfer tourists in 1952 when pilot Al Gaetz flew a skiing guide and his clients to a ski lodge on Mount Assiniboine in the Canadian Rockies. The guide and the skiers then skied back down the mountain. This trip was possible because Gaetz's plane was equipped with a hydraulic gear that enabled the wheels of the craft to be retracted and replaced with skis. That summer Gaetz made many similar trips, and the activity of heli-skiing was born, albeit using an airplane rather than a helicopter. Then in 1955 a similar airplane service began in New Zealand's Southern Alps when Mount Cooke Ski Planes began a shuttle service, transporting skiers on to the Franz Josef and Tasman glaciers. Advances in aircraft technology revolutionized the activity during the mid-1950s, when the advent of short takeoff and landing (STOL) made mountain flying much safer. However, it soon became clear that helicopters could reach mountain ridges inaccessible to winged-aircraft, giving access to better powder snow. Also, helicopters are able to land in deep valleys and forested areas to pick up passengers, which airplanes would be unable to do. The earliest heli-skiing trips, which took place in the late 1950s, used Bell helicopters to ferry 2 skiers or 1 skier and a guide, plus the pilot. However, these trips were expensive compared to trips by plane, and heli-skiing became the preserve of the rich. This began to change when, in 1963, a Canadian geologist decided to hire a helicopter and a pilot without work to take him and his companions day-skiing near Banff, in the Canadian Rockies. Then in April 1965 a two-seater helicopter took over an hour to ferry 2 guides and 18 skiers to Bugaboos, British Columbia. The next winter 70 skiers traveled to Bugaboos by helicopter, increasing to 150 skiers the following year by which time organizers had invested in a four-seater helicopter to speed up the ferrying of passengers.

Indeed, so many skiers wanted to try heli-skiing that accommodation became an issue. The problem was solved when heli-skiing operator Hans Gmoser, who had started out as a ski guide, attracted the financial backing necessary to build a ski lodge for use by heli-skiing tourists. By the time the lodge opened in 1968, tours employing bigger helicopters equipped with turbine engines had started up, able to transfer increased numbers of skiers to higher, more remote destinations. Over time this would lead to skiers wanting to traverse up to 200,000 vertical feet of skiing in a week and compete informally to see who could record the most vertical skiing. The all-time record holders for nonguides achieving the most vertical feet are husband and wife Ned and Carolyn Damon. Ned holds the men's lifetime record of 19 million vertical feet of heli-skiing, and Carolyn holds the women's record of 16 million vertical feet.

In 1970 an 11-seater helicopter was developed, and from then on heli-skiing continued to grow, with more and bigger lodges being built in various resorts throughout British Columbia—today the province is home to at least 17 heli-skiing locations. One of the attractions for heli-skiing operators is that new ventures cost little in initial outlay or infrastructure. Therefore, heli-skiing began in the United States with operations opening up in Utah in 1973, Wyoming in 1974, and California in 1979 followed by Colorado in 1980 and Washington state in 1983. Meanwhile, heli-skiing was starting in the Himalaya Mountains in Russia and India. In 1991 the advent of the World Extreme Skiing Championship in the Chugach Mountains of Alaska highlighted the potential for heli-skiing in the region, and in 1995 Atlin, which is spread across British Columbia and the Yukon to the south of the Chugach range, began to allow heli-skiing.

During the earliest years of heli-skiing, the activity was reserved for advanced skiers who had the skiing ability to turn in deep snow the moment they left the helicopter. Today, however, with the invention of fat skis in the 1990s, this is no longer the case. Fat skis do not require the skill level of earlier skies, as their wide riding surface provides flotation, making skiing easier. As a result, heli-skiers need now only be proficient to intermediate in terms of skill, though physical fitness is required to ski off-piste or backcountry and make the journey back down the mountain. Similarly, it is also now possible to snowboard from a helicopter.

A variation on heli-skiing is snowcat skiing, in which skiers are transported by large truck-like vehicles that move on tracks rather than wheels and can access the powder snow, which would otherwise be inaccessible by ski lift.

As with all adventure sports, risks are involved with heli-skiing, including the danger of falling down a crevasse and being crushed by snow falling from overhead trees or cliffs, in addition to the usual skiing injuries. It has also been known for helicopters to crash while ferrying passengers, as happened when Walt Disney Company executive Frank G. Wells died in a crash in Nevada in 1994. However, perhaps the most fearful danger of heli-skiing is the risk of avalanches. The first death of an American recreational heli-skier, that of Geoff Taylor in 1969, came about when Taylor was crushed in an avalanche, and on March 12, 1991, nine skiers died when they were caught in an avalanche in Bugaboo. The avalanche was 100 yards wide and traveled almost 3,000 vertical feet. Deaths associated with heli-skiing have led campaigners to call for greater regulation of the activity, especially as technical innovations in ski equipment push skiers to take greater risks in search of greater thrills. However, despite the inherent dangers of heli-skiing, the activity attracts the rich and famous, including members of European royal families, prime ministers, tycoons, and film executives.

Another negative of heli-skiing is the impact of the activity on the environment, with environmental groups raising concerns about heli-skiing and related activities, arguing that such activity has a negative effect on the mountain environment. For instance, the environmental group Mountain Wilderness holds an annual protest against heli-skiing in Switzerland. While heli-skiing is strictly regulated in the Austrian Alps and is forbidden in France and Germany, neighboring Switzerland allows heli-skiing at 42 alpine locations, with over half these locations directly adjoining protected areas such as the UNESCO World Heritage Site Swiss Alps Jungfrau-Aletsch.

See also: Cresta Run; Extreme Ironing; Fell Running; Nordic Walking; Volcano Boarding; Wingsuiting; Zorbing

Further Reading

Admur, Neil. "Extreme Grief." *New York Times,* March 5, 2013, http://www.nytimes .com/2013/03/06/sports/skiing/grieving-families-of-extreme-sports-enthusiasts-are -left-to-wonder-was-the-thrill-worth-it.html (accessed March 11, 2014).

"Frank Wells, Disney's President, Is Killed in a Copter Crash at 62." *New York Times,* April 5, 1994, http://www.nytimes.com/1994/04/05/obituaries/frank-wells-disney-s-president -is-killed-in-a-copter-crash-at-62.html (accessed March 11, 2014).

Fry, John. "Up by Air! The Adventure-Filled Golden Years of Heli-Skiing." *Skiing Heritage Journal: Journal of ISHA the International Skiing History Association* 18(3) (September 2006): 8–13.

Mountain Wilderness International. "Stop Heliskiing in Switzerland." Mountainwildreness. org, April 4, 2012, http://www.mountainwilderness.org/2012/04/04/stop-heliskiing-in -switzerland/ (accessed April 11, 2014).

Pure Powder. "What Is Heli Skiing?" purepowder.com, http://www.purepowder.com /heliskiing/whatisheliskiing.cfm (accessed April 11, 2014).

Ritchie, Brent W., and Daryl Adair, eds. *Sport Tourism: Interrelationships, Impacts and Issues.* Clevedon, UK: Channel View Publications, 2004.

Whitetracks Ltd. "France: French Alps." Whitetracks Helicopters, 2002–2009, http://www .whitetracks.co.uk/Helicopter_Skiing_Heli_Skiing_Heliskiing_FRANCE.htm (accessed April 11, 2014).

HIGHLAND GAMES

The Highland Games are a series of traditional multisport events and social gatherings held annually across Scotland and in countries in which Scottish immigrants have settled, including the United States, Canada, Bermuda, Brazil, Panama, France, the Netherlands, Russia, Norway, Hungary, Indonesia, New Zealand, Sweden, Germany, Japan, and Switzerland. The Highland Games are intertwined with life in rural Scotland and hark back to political upheaval in the Scottish Highlands, a historical

A participant wearing a traditional kilt takes part in the throwing the hammer competition at a Highland Games event in Scotland. The hammer is made of iron, weighs either 16 or 22 pounds and has a rigid rod as a handle. During the competition participants aim to throw the hammer farther than their competitors. (Corel)

mountainous, sparsely populated region of northern Scotland. As such, the Highland Games are often viewed as a way of celebrating the cultural heritage of Scotland, particularly that of the Highlands, as well as a Celtic and Gaelic identity. As a festival of Scottish, Celtic, and Gaelic heritage, the Highland Games also include folk music played on bagpipes and harps and traditional dance, with the Cowal Highland Gathering hosting the annual World Highland Dancing Championship.

The governing body for the Scottish Highland Games is the Scottish Highland Games Association. The organization was founded in 1947 as the Scottish Games Association with the intention of popularizing events.

The origin of the Highland Games is unknown. Some historians suggest that the games are based on Druidic celebrations that involved fertility rites, harvest celebrations, and religious ceremonies. However, a less romantic theory is that the games evolved during medieval times as a series of contests testing accuracy, agility, strength, and stamina, such as archery, wrestling, and hill running, in order to find the most proficient professional men-at-arms.

The Ceres Games, held in Ceres, a village in Fife, eastern Scotland, claims to be the oldest continuous Highland Games, as it has been held every year since 1314 (except during 1746–1782, when the Act of Proscription prohibited clan activity, and during world wars), when Robert the Bruce (1274–1329), king of the Scots, allowed the village to hold the games as reward for the villagers' participation in the Battle of Bannockburn (1314), a very important battle in the history of Scottish independence. However, the prestigious Braemar Gathering, known locally as The

Games, is older still than the Ceres Games, for the Braemar Gathering can trace its roots back to the reign of Scottish king Malcolm Canmore (1031–1093), who according to Scottish folklore held a hill-running contest up Creag Choinnich, in Braemar, to determine which athletes ran the fastest and would therefore become his heralds. Braemar is also the home of the Highland Games as known today, the roots of which can be traced back to the reign of Queen Victoria, for in July 1815 the Braemar Wright's Society was founded as a charitable organization for wheelwrights and joiners, changing its name to the Braemar Highland Society in 1826. Part of the charity's remit was to function as a friendly society, and to this end the organization held an annual procession that ended with the Braemar Gathering. Queen Victoria attended the gathering in 1848 and took such a keen interest in the event that she declared that it should be known as the Braemar Royal Highland Society from 1866. Indeed, to this day it is traditional for members of the British royal family to attend the event, which is both the world's premiere Highland Games and a finale to the Highland Games season, as the Braemar Games are held in September.

After Queen Victoria visited the Braemar Games the concept of joint sporting and social gatherings spread, and many such events began to be held across Scotland. The invention of the Highland Games chimed with the romanticized ideal of Scotland promulgated by writers such as Sir Walter Scott (1771–1832), whose somewhat fanciful depictions of the Highlands in novels such as *Waverley* (1814) had helped start a mania for all things Scottish among the British upper classes.

Prior to the invention of the modern Highland Games, the 18th and 19th centuries had seen a series of political events transform the social structure of the Highlands. The first factor was the failure of the Jacobite Rebellion of 1745, an attempt by Charles Edward Stuart (1720–1788), sometimes referred to as Bonnie Prince Charlie or the Young Pretender, to regain the British throne for the House of Stuart. Stuart had been supported by a number of Highland clans, that is, tribal kinship groups whose members are often loosely related, and in the wake of the rebellion's failure the British government thought to make life extremely uncomfortable for the clans in general, curbing their power through regressive measures such as prohibiting the clansmen from wearing their traditional tartan kilts.

Another factor that helped transformed Highland life was the coming of the Industrial Revolution, which saw the large-scale voluntary migration of Highlanders to urban areas in search of work. In contrast, the infamous Highland Clearances saw the mass forced expulsion of Highland people from their land, usually by wealthy landowners who wished to enclose the land for agricultural purposes. Many of the expelled Highlanders immigrated to what is now the United States, Canada, and Australasia and took with them their traditions, including the idea of games and gatherings. As a result of this, Highland Games continue to be held across the United States and Canada. The first Highland Games to be held in the United States took place in New York in 1836, and over the next few decades American Highland Games became associated with Caledonian clubs. Indeed, the longest continuous running Highland Games in America is the one organized by the Caledonian Club of San Francisco since 1866. Sports historians recognize that the Highland Games have had a significant influence on the early development of track and field athletics in the United States and Canada, increasing interest in sport both at college and club levels and among the general public. Today there are over 200 Highland Games held across the United States and Canada annually, and many more are held across the globe.

By the beginning of the 20th century most of the Highland Games operating today had been established, and while sporting competition still takes place at the various Highland Games, the events have become major tourist attractions that have been criticized for being divorced from their original social context and for helping to propagate Scottish stereotypes. Nevertheless, the modern Highland Games retain many of the same sporting competitions as their Victorian predecessors. Men and women may compete in events, and competing athletes must wear traditional Highland dress, including a kilt. The events include athletic pursuits such as hill running, jumping, pole vaulting, and sprinting as well as strength competitions, known as heavy events, that include the caber toss, the stone put, the weight throw, the hammer throw, the sheaf throw, wrestling, and tug-of-war. The heavy events require great physical strength and power and recruit all the body's muscles. Over the years many international strongmen have taken part in the Highland Games' heavy events, including those who have entered the World's Strongest Man competition. For example, American power lifter Bill Kazmaier, the three-time World's Strongest Man, took part in the Highland Games in 1980 and 1984.

Perhaps the event most synonymous with the Highland Games is tossing the caber, which literally means "tossing the tree," as "caber" is the Gaelic word for "tree." While the origins of tossing the caber are unknown, one theory is that the event developed from men throwing tree trunks into the middle of rivers so the timber would float downstream to sawmills without becoming stuck on the riverbank. However, another theory suggests that the competition began as a way for foresters to prove their strength. The caber used today is usually a slightly tapering 18-foot-long log weighing between 100 and 150 pounds, though the caber used at the Braemar Gathering is 16 feet long and weighs only 132 pounds. Today athletes no longer throw the caber for distance. Instead, accuracy is the aim and is judged in relation to an imaginary clock face on the ground, with the winning toss being the one that lands nearest to 12 o'clock. Accuracy is determined by a judge who runs after the athlete and decides how near to perfect the throw is. To begin the toss, the caber is raised vertical to the ground in front of the competitor by helpers, who then place the athlete's clasped hands under the narrow end of the caber by resting the caber against the athlete's shoulders as the competitor stands up. The athlete, who must gain complete control of the caber before starting the run, then sprints as fast as possible before stopping and hurriedly hurling the caber so that the heaviest end of the log hits the ground first and the lighter end continues to fall into a 12 o'clock position. If the caber fails to flip over, then the angle that the caber would have reached had it flipped is noted in order to place the athlete in the competition. It is normal for more than one caber to be available at each Highland Games to allow different standards of athlete to compete and in case one of the cabers breaks during competition. Nearly identical log tossing events occur in

Portugal (under the name *jogo do panco*) and in Sweden, where log tossing is called *stang-störtning*. When the Olympic Games were held in the Swedish capital of Stockholm in 1912, *stang-störtning* was among the sports demonstrated, along with *pärkspel* and *glima*.

Another Highland Games event, the sheaf throw, is also a throwing event. The sheaf is a burlap bag filled with hay and weighing 16 pounds that is tossed over a suspended bar by a competitor equipped with a three-pronged pitchfork. Another throwing event, putting the stone or ball, is most probably the oldest Highland Games event and is akin to the modern shot put, for the competitor tries to throw the stone/ball, which is made of iron and weighs 17 pounds and has a circumference of 23 inches, as far as possible. Similarly, the throwing the hammer event is very like the modern hammer throw, with competitors vying to throw the hammer the farthest. The hammer is made of iron and weighs either 16 or 22 pounds, and the only difference between the hammer throw of the Highland Games and the modern hammer throw is that while the hammer in the latter event has a flexible chain, the Highland hammer has a solid, fixed bamboo rod as a handle.

An additional Highland Games throwing event is throwing the weight over the bar, in which the athlete stands under a bar suspended high above, swings the weight between the legs with one hand, and then releases the weight so that it travels up and over the bar to land inches from where the athlete is standing. Competing athletes repeat this process until the bar has been raised to a height over which only one winning athlete can throw or over which two athletes can throw to share the win. A related event is throwing the weight for distance. This event uses two standard weights weighing 28 pounds and 56 pounds in the form of a ball and chain (not measuring longer than 18 inches) with a handle at one end. To begin the event, the athlete stands behind a wooden trig position facing forward and then swings the weight around behind the body. Next the competitor pivots and spins repeatedly behind the starting position to build the momentum necessary to release the weight, aiming to make it travel as far as possible.

Like the Highland Games, the Redneck Games brings together members of a self-identifying white tribe for a multievent sporting and cultural gathering. The Redneck Games has been held annually in East Dublin, Georgia, since 1996 as a spoof of the Olympic Games and attracts large crowds to watch such events as hubcap hurling; redneck horseshoes, in which participants throw lavatory seats around a plunger; bobbing for pigs' feet; watermelon seed spitting; and the armpit serenade, in which participants, who come from as far afield as England and Australia, make noises by placing their hand in their armpit or behind their knee (the event is judged by onlookers). While proponents of the Redneck Games claim that such events are intended to critique and dispel disparaging stereotypes of lower-class white people living in the U.S. South, critics of the Redneck Games argue that the games actually cement the very racial stereotypes that the organizers of the games wish to eradicate.

See also: Celtic Wrestling; Cotswold Olimpicks; Curling; Fell Running; *Glima; Schwingen;* Stone Skimming

Further Reading

Barry, Kristy. "Down and Dirty at the Redneck Games." ESPN Page 2, July 19, 2010, http://sports.espn.go.com/espn/page2/story?page=barry/100719_redneck_games (accessed March 14, 2014).

Doane, Ashley "Woody," and Eduardo Bonilla-Silva, eds. *White Out: The Continuing Significance of Racism.* New York: Routledge, 2003.

Donaldson, Emily Ann. *The Scottish Highland Games in America.* Gretna, LA: Pelican, 1986.

"Games around the World." Scotland.org, http://www.scotland.org/features/games-around -the-world (accessed March 9, 2014).

"Heavyweight Events." Highland Games, http://www.highlandgames.org.uk/heavyweight _events.htm (accessed March 9, 2014).

"Highland Games." Scotland.org, http://www.scotland.org/features/highland-games (accessed March 9, 2014).

"History of the Society." Braemar Gathering, http://www.braemargathering.org/history.htm (accessed March 9, 2014).

Koch, John T. *Celtic Culture: A Historical Encyclopedia*, Vols. 1–5. Santa Barbara, CA: ABC-CLIO, 2006.

"The National Redneck Games." Redneck Olympics, http://www.redneckolympics.com (accessed March 14, 2014).

Nauright, John, and Charles Parrish, eds. *Sports around the World: History, Culture and Practice,* Vol. 1, *General Topics, Africa, Asia, Middle East, and Oceania.* Santa Barbara, CA: ABC-CLIO, 2012.

Rettie, Andrew. "Heavyweight Events." Highland Games, November 23, 2011, http://www.highlandgames.org.uk/heavyweight_events.htm (accessed March 10, 2014).

Tomlinson, Alan. *A Dictionary of Sport Studies.* Oxford: Oxford University Press, 2010.

Wiggins, David. *Sport in America: From Colonial Leisure to Celebrity Figures and Globalization,* Vol. 2. Champaign, IL: Human Kinetics, 2010.

HURLING

Hurling is the Anglicized name given to an outdoor team stick-and-ball game played by men that is native to Ireland but is also played where Irish immigrants have settled in large numbers, particularly in Australasia and North America but also England, Scotland, South Africa, and Argentina. Hurling, which has been likened to shinty, field hockey, bandy, and rugby, does not have a professional league, so all players are amateurs. Irish hurling, which is unrelated to Cornish hurling, was an unofficial sport at the 1904 Olympic Games held in St. Louis, Missouri.

Hurling is one of the world's oldest sports and is frequently referred to in Irish folklore. For example, hurling is mentioned in the tales of heroic Cú Chulainn, who is said to have killed the fearsome hound Culann by propelling a hurling ball, called a sliotar, through the dog's open mouth. Another example is the story of Grainne, daughter of the High King of Ireland, who is said to have fallen in love with the famous warrior Diarmuid after seeing him score a goal during a hurling match. The earliest surviving written references to hurling appear in Irish laws of the 7th and 8th centuries, which describe the sporting injuries incurred during hurling for which compensation should be paid. Hurling is also cited in the *Leabhar na hUidre* (Book of the Dun Cow), a manuscript dating from around the 12th century, while *Cath Mhaigh Tuireadh Chunga* (The Battle of Magh Tuireadh), a tale dating from the 13th or 14th century, tells of a vicious hurling game that was played at Moytura, County Mayo. As a result of the association between hurling and mythological heroes, the sport tends toward a very macho ethos favoring strength and aggression.

Hurling continues to feature in later medieval Gaelic Irish literature, often disparagingly. For instance, in 1367, County Kilkenny, which in the 20th and 21st centuries came to dominate the sport along with County Cork and County Tipperary, outlawed hurling to prevent the further dissemination of Gaelic culture, of which hurling was a major part. A similar law was enforced in Galway. Such laws had little effect, however, and hurling was played across Ireland in the late Middle Ages and continued to grow in popularity in the postmedieval period, even attracting the favor of the aristocracy. The high point of hurling's popularity came in the 17th and 18th centuries, by which time two distinct versions of hurling had been established. The first version was called *camán* (or commons) after the stick used in the game, the caman, from which the original Irish name for hurling, *camanaiocht*, derives. *Camán* was akin to shinty and modern field hockey, for players were not allowed to handle the ball and the game was played during the winter. This version of hurling was played in the northern half of Ireland and in Scotland. The second hurling variant was *iomán* or *báire,* which was confined to the southern half of Ireland. In this version the ball, called the sliothar, could be handled or carried on the stick, which was flat and rounded. Unlike *camán,* this form of hurling was played in the summer and was patronized by the gentry (who chose the teams, arranged the pitch, and supervised the matches) as both a spectator sport and a gambling sport. *Iomán* or *báire* was also played at public gatherings, such as country fairs, and was much more organized than its northern counterpart, even being advertised at country shows. Intercounty, and sometimes intervillage, hurling matches flourished briefly in the 19th century, but then suddenly the popularity of hurling dwindled to such an extent that the game (in any version) survived in only three places: the city of Cork, southeastern Galway, and the area north of Wexford town. One reason for this sudden decline was the coming of an age of political unrest that, partly influenced by the French Revolution, saw the rise of Catholic emancipation in 1829 and the disestablishment of the Church of Ireland in 1867 as well as greater general class-consciousness. This in turn led to antigentry feeling and a combative relationship between landlords and tenants. As a result of such political turbulence, authority figures including magistrates and priests began to turn against hurling, as they now associated the sport with social agitation and feared that matches might be used as cover for covert political meetings. Another reason for the sport's decline was the onset of the Great Famine of 1845–1852, also known as the Irish Potato Famine, a period of mass starvation and disease in Ireland primarily caused by the failure of Ireland's main agricultural product, the potato crop. It is thought that the famine killed around 1 million Irish and caused another 1 million to leave the country and settle abroad in countries including England, Scotland, America, Canada, and Australia, all areas of the world where hurling is still played today.

In order to save hurling from oblivion, the Dublin University Hurley Club established the first formal rules for the sport in 1870, and then in 1879 a governing body called the Hurley Union was founded, with matches played against English field hockey teams. Then in 1884 another governing body, the Gaelic Athletic Association (GAA) was formed in County Tipperary in the south of Ireland in order to standardize rules and establish parish, county, and national competitions, such as Ireland's premiere hurling competition the All-Ireland Senior Hurling Championship, an annual series of games that began in 1887, are played during the summer and autumn and are contested by the country's top intercounty teams. The GAA also sought to make the game less elitist and more nationalistic in nature. The creation of the GAA led to the disbanding of the Hurley Union, but the version of hurling promulgated by the GAA was a false, idealized version of the game inspired by the southern game of *iomán* or *báire* that members of the GAA had known as children. Thus, with the exception of the Glens of Antrim (an area in the northeast of Ireland), this new codified version of hurling never became popular in areas where *camán* had been played, mainly because the Protestant and Unionist communities of the north associated hurling with Catholicism and nationalism. Indeed, as well as reviving the game, the GAA also wished to use hurling as a vehicle for Irish nationalism and so removed the sport from any association with the English sports of cricket, soccer, and rugby. This led to hurling attracting the attention of Irish nationalists, and the sport gradually became very popular in regions that championed Irish nationalist politics, including southern Leinster and eastern Munster, which is still the hurling heartland. Other reasons for an upsurge in hurling's popularity after the establishment of the GAA include the increased wealth of the sport's followers, who tended to have jobs that allowed them to make use of leisure time; the desire for organized sport among working-class spectators; and improved mass transport facilities by which spectators could reach hurling events.

Hurling takes place on a pitch measuring between 130 and 145 meters (427 to 476 feet) by 80 to 90 meters (262 to 295 feet). The aim of hurling is for players, called hurlers, of whom there are 15 on each of two opposing teams, to use a wooden stick much like a wider, flatter shinty stick, called a hurley or caman, to propel a small, round, ridged cork and leather ball, called a sliothar or sliotar, between the opposing team's goalposts, which should not be less than 7 meters (23 feet) high. A match lasts for two periods of either 30 or 35 minutes in duration depending on the level of competition being played.

If the ball travels into the goal above the crossbar, then the scoring side receives one point, but if the ball enters under crossbar and into the net, which should be at least 6.5 meters (21 feet) wide and 2.5 meters (8 feet) high, guarded by the goalkeeper, then the team scores one goal, which is the equivalent of three points. Scores are recorded in the format goal total–point total.

Goalkeepers carry a stick with an extra wide and flat end with which to defend their goal. In order to maneuver the ball around the pitch, players may catch and carry the ball in the hand for no more than four steps, or the ball may be hit in the air or along the ground using the hurley. In order to move the ball a short distance, players may slap the ball with the hand in a move called a hand pass or kick the ball. To make the ball travel farther, players can bounce or balance the ball on the stick for not more than three paces, though the ball may be handled only twice while employing this tactic. Players are prohibited from throwing the ball, picking the ball off the ground with the hand, making more than four steps with the ball in their hand, catching the ball three times in a row without grounding it, or throwing their stick. Hurling is a semicontact sport in that players may charge side-to-side, but shoulder charging and bodychecking are not permitted. Despite this, protective clothing is not worn, and the wearing of a helmet is not mandatory. Overseeing play are eight officials consisting of the referee, two linesmen, four umpires (two at each end of the pitch) who signal points scored with a white flag and goals scored with a green flag, and, in intercounty games, a sideline official who is also a standby linesman.

The women's version of hurling is called camogie. The game has a different name because the women's game is played with a stick called a camog. Thus, the sport was first known as *camogaiocht,* which was Anglicized to camogie. Camogie was officially launched at a Gaelic League Fair in Meath, central eastern Ireland, in July 1904. There are several differences between camogie and hurling. For instance, in terms of clothing, all camogie players, including the goalkeeper, must wear the same top, while in hurling the goalkeeper must sport a distinctive jersey, and camogie is played in skirts, while hurlers wear shorts. In terms of equipment, the ball used in camogie is slightly smaller and lighter than that used in hurling, and the stick used is shorter. In terms of play, a goal may be scored by a hand pass in camogie but not in hurling, and in camogie the stick may be dropped to make a hand pass (as long as it is not dangerous to do so), while in hurling this would result in a foul being awarded against the player who dropped his stick. Also in camogie, a player may flick an opponent's stick into the air using her own stick, but in hurling such play would result in a penalty being awarded. Punishments also vary between the sports. For instance, in camogie a penalty called a 45-meter (roughly 148-foot) free is awarded for infringements, while in hurling it is a 65-meter (213-foot) free.

The two main camogie county competitions are the National League and the All-Ireland Championships. The National League takes place during the winter and spring, and the All-Ireland Championships takes place during the summer. The All-Ireland Championships Final is held at Croke Park stadium in September, with teams vying for the O'Duffy Cup.

See also: Bandy; Celtic Wrestling; Cricket; Curling; *La Soule;* Real Tennis; Rugby League; Shinty; Underwater Hockey

Further Reading

Collins, Tony, John Martin, and Wray Vamplew, eds. *Encyclopedia of Traditional British Rural Sports.* Abingdon, UK: Routledge, 2005.

Koch, John T. *Celtic Culture: A Historical Encyclopedia,* Vols. 1–5. Santa Barbara, CA: ABC-CLIO, 2006.

Matthews, George R. *America's First Olympics.* Columbia: University of Missouri Press, 2005.

Moriarty, Colm. "Hurling, Its Ancient History." Irish Archeology, http://irisharchaeology
.ie/2011/09/hurling-its-ancient-history/ (accessed April 7, 2014).

Nauright, John, and Charles Parrish, eds. *Sports around the World: History, Culture and Practice,* Vol. 1, *General Topics, Africa, Asia, Middle East, and Oceania.* Santa Barbara, CA: ABC-CLIO, 2012.

Whelan, Kevin. "The Geography of Hurling." *History Ireland* 1(1) (Spring 1993), http://www.historyireland.com/18th-19th-century-history/the-geography-of-hurling-11-2/ (accessed April 7, 2014).

J

JACKS AND KNUCKLEBONES

The game of knucklebones (which has a great many alternative English-language names including fivestones, alleygobs, checkers, dibs, dabs, snobs, and hucklebones, among others) and the game of jacks are very similar traditional children's pastimes. Knucklebones and jacks are played the world over. However, in developed countries such as England, the game is more popular among immigrant communities, such as the Pakistani community in Yorkshire, than it is among native English children. That said, much anecdotal evidence suggests that many people in England of middle age or older will have played a version of knucklebones or jacks at some point. In the United Kingdom during the 1950s knucklebones was extremely popular, and in the south of London, England's capital city, knucklebones and jacks were distinct individual games, with knucklebones played by boys and jacks played by girls. However, this was not true all over England, and the games of knucklebones and jacks are generally regarded as so similar that the name "jacks" is often used as an umbrella term for all forms of the knucklebones-type game.

The game of knucklebones is extremely old, having been played in ancient Egypt and Rome and in classical Greece. There is also some evidence of bones being used as part of a game in prehistoric Russia. Though the game has undergone revisions, it has stayed basically the same for thousands of years. The game requires little in the way of equipment except for five small stones or bones (usually animal anklebones rather than actual knucklebones) or bone-shaped replicas and possibly a ball. In earlier times knucklebones was played with actual animal bones, hence in ancient Rome the game was known as *astragals*, the Latin word for "anklebone." Roman emperor Augustus (63 BCE–14 CE) referred to knucklebones in a letter, and a Roman statue illustrating the game has been dated to 1 CE. Knucklebones was equally popular in ancient Greece. The game is depicted in a Greek sculpture dated to 330 BCE and is referred to in Aristophanes's play *Wasps* (422 BCE). In ancient times, knucklebones was played by a player rolling four animal bones as though they were dice. The bones were predominantly flat with four long sides between two rounded ends, with each side designated a different value from one, three, four, and six. Every time a dice rolled to reveal a side worth one, the player who rolled the one would have to put a silver coin called a denarius into a money pot. A penalty of one denarius was also incurred if a player threw and revealed a side worth six points. However, if a player rolled the four dice and each dice showed a different scoring side, then the player was said to have scored a Venus, named after the Roman god of love. The first player to achieve a Venus was

The Fresco of The Knucklebone Players from Hercula-
neum, Italy. Knucklebones is an extremely old game
that has changed little over the course of thousands of
years. The game requires little in the way of equipment
except for five small stones or bones (usually anklebones rather than knucklebones) or bone-shaped replicas and possibly a ball. (Mimmo Jodice/Corbis)

the winner and won the pot of
silver coins.

The later version of knucklebones, which is the version most
often associated with the name
and is still played today, is quite
complex and consists of five stages,
though as knucklebones has no
governing body there is no set way
of playing the game. All forms and
stages of the game require good
hand-eye coordination.

Stage one, sometimes called
the Beginnings, sees a player
throw five bones, or substitute
bones, into the air using one
hand and then try to catch as
many of the bones as possible on
the back of the throwing hand. It
is important that the bones are
not thrown up too high or too
fast or they will be difficult to
catch. Similarly, opening the fingers too far apart to catch the
bones means that they will fall
through the gaps; that said, if the fingers are too close together then the catching
surface will be insufficient. Bones that land on the ground during this stage of the
game must be left on the ground. Meanwhile, bones that land on the back of the
hand are then rethrown from the back of the hand, and the player then has to try
to catch the rethrown bones in the palm of the same hand. If the player fails to
catch any bones, then his or her turn is over temporarily—the player may resume play later, carrying on from where he or she left off. However, if the player
manages to catch at least one bone, then the player's turn continues and the ones
stage or onesies begins, in which the player selects one of the caught bones and,
throwing it in the air, then throws another of the caught bones on the ground.
While the thrown bone, known as the dab, is midair, the player picks up the
bone thrown on the ground and puts it to one side. The player must use the same
hand to both catch the dab and retrieve the bone from the ground. The player
repeats this pattern of throwing one bone in the air while throwing to the ground
and retrieving another bone until all the bones have been picked up one by one.
If the player drops the bone thrown in the air at any time, then the player is out.
Once all the bones have been retrieved, the twos stage or twosies begins in which
the player throws the dab and has to pick up two bones with the throwing hand
while the dab is in the air. The player continues the pattern of taking up two
bones for each throw of the dab until all the bones are retrieved. The process is

then repeated in the threes stage or threesies, in which three bones are picked up and then the dab is thrown twice, and finally in the fours stage or foursies the player picks up four bones with one throw of the dab. Some versions of the game omit the twosies, threesies, and foursies stages, and variations are played. For example, a one-off fivesies stage may be played in which the opponent places all five bones on the back of the player's hand, and the player must throw and catch all five bones in one go. Alternatively, a move called a bridge can be made. For a bridge, a player makes an arch with the left thumb and forefinger. A bone is thrown up, and while the bone is airborne the other bones are knocked through the finger arch. The player then catches the thrown bone, and play continues until all the bones have been caught. Another alternative stage is called crabs. To play the crabs version, once a player has caught bones on the back of the hand, the player picks up between the fingers any bones that were not caught and keeps them between the fingers while throwing and catching the bones on the back of the hand.

In addition to this pattern of play, two rules may be applied: the sweepsies rule and the nudgies rule. The sweepsies rule means that the correct number of bones must be collected in one sweep of the player's hand, while the nudgies rule maintains that a player may gather together the grounded bones while continuing to throw and catch the dab and then pick up the required number of bones from the ground all in one go.

In developed countries, animal bones have been largely replaced by mass-produced plastic bone-shaped replicas or pieces made of ivory, stone, ebony, clay, or metal. The manufactured pieces tend to be stylized natural bone shapes, except for when they are made of metal, for then they tend to be extremely angular. Mass-produced knucklebones stones have also been manufactured in the form of small cubes about half an inch square in size. The cubes are made of wood, clay, or chalk and are ribbed on four sides with a smooth top and bottom. The wooden cubes are strongly colored, while the clay and chalk cubes each come in different pastel tones.

The earliest recorded reference to the game of jacks dates to the 16th century, when a small pottery ball or a marble was introduced to knucklebones. By the 19th century, jacks had evolved into a game of many stages. By the 1800s, jacks was known in France as *passes-passes*, as through the arch in Australia, and as *kopru*, meaning "bridge" or "arch," in Turkey, which employed the bridge move from knucklebones.

Like knucklebones, the modern game of jacks features five bone pieces plus a bouncy ball that is bigger than the jacks. The word "jacks" applies equally to the game and the bone substitutes, which take the form of three-dimensional metal crosses, six-pronged and with a bobble on the end of each prong. To decide which player goes first, one player throws all the jacks in the air and tries to catch as many as possible on the back of his or her hand. The player then rethrows the jacks that landed on the hand and this time tries to catch as many as possible on the palm of the same hand. Each player repeats this pattern of play, and the player who catches the most jacks starts the game, with play continuing in a clockwise fashion thereafter.

The first player throws all five jacks on the ground and throws the ball into the air. With the same throwing hand, the player then picks up one of the jacks and catches the ball before it hits the ground. The jack is transferred to the player's other hand, and then the sequence of play continues until all the pieces have been picked up. Once all the jacks have been retrieved the player starts the sequence again, but this time two jacks at a time must be picked up except on the third and final throw, when one jack is picked up. This pattern of play continues for three jacks and four jacks and then, finally, for five jacks, which is when the player must throw the ball in the air and pick up all the jacks in one go before the ball is caught. If a player fails to catch the ball or does not pick up the correct number of jacks, then that player's turn is over and the next player begins to play. The winner is the player who progresses the furthest in the sequence. Variations in play can make the game of jacks easier or harder. For instance, allowing the ball to bounce once before it is caught makes the game easier. However, proficient players can introduce further challenges, such as bouncing the ball downward instead of throwing it upward or clapping the hands together before picking up the jacks from the ground or floor.

See also: Bunnock; Conkers

Further Reading

Dagonell the Juggler. "Game of the Month: Knucklebones." Canisius College, http://www
-cs.canisius.edu/~salley/SCA/Games/knucklebones.html (accessed August 12, 2013).

Opie, Iona, and Peter Opie. *Children's Games with Things.* London: Oxford University Press, 1997.

Roud, Steve. *The Lore of the Playground: One Hundred Years of Children's Games, Rhymes & Traditions.* London: Random House, 2010.

"The Rules of Fivestones and Jacks." Masters Traditional Games, 2012, http://www.masters games.com/rules/jacks-rules.htm (accessed August 12, 2013).

Schmauch, Alison. "Topic: The Role of Children's Games in Ancient Greece." Coming of Age in Ancient Greece, 2004, http://hoodmuseum.dartmouth.edu/exhibitions/coa /re_high_games.html (accessed August 12, 2013).

K

KABADDI

Kabaddi is a combative team game played by men and women that combines elements of rugby and wrestling. Variations of *kabaddi* are played all over Asia, but it is particularly popular in India as well as in Bangladesh, Iran, Japan, Nepal, Pakistan, and Sri Lanka. *Kabaddi* is also played in England, the United States, and Canada. In India *kabaddi* is played under many names, including *chedugudu* and *hu-tu-tu* in the south of the country, while in eastern India *hadudu* is the name given to men's *kabaddi* and *chu-kit-kit* to *kabaddi* played by women. *Kabaddi* is the name given to the sport in northern India and translates from the Tamil words *kai*, meaning "hand," and *pidi*, meaning "catch." Today *kabaddi* is played throughout all of India but is especially popular in rural areas, as *kabaddi* is a simple game requiring very little in the way of expensive equipment and a relatively small playing area that is divided in two by a central line known as the midline. The exact size of the court differs for males and females. Men and junior boys play on an area measuring 13 meters by 10 meters (43 feet by 33 feet), and women and junior girls play on a court that is 12 meters by 8 meters (39 feet by 26 feet). Subjunior boys and girls play on a surface measuring 11 meters by 8 meters (36 feet by 26 feet). Matches are arranged by sex, age group, and weight. Men are classified as being over 20 years of age and under 80 kilograms (176 pounds), while junior boys are males aged 20 years or under and weighing less than 65 kilograms (143 pounds). Women are classified as being over 20 years old and weighing under 70 kilograms (154 pounds), while junior girls are 20 years or under and weigh less than 60 kilograms (132 pounds). Subjunior boys and girls are both classified as being under 16 years of age and weighing less than 50 kilograms (110 pounds).

Little is known about the origins of *kabaddi*, but the sport has existed for at least 4,000 years. In earlier times the game was undertaken by individuals, groups, and teams to improve self-defense skills, heighten one-on-one fighting abilities, and improve reflex reactions. Modern *kabaddi* was first played in India in 1930, though the earliest standardized rules were invented in Maharashtra in 1921 and combined two early forms of the game to create a new version of the sport. The rules established in 1921 were modified two years later in time for the inaugural All India Kabaddi Tournament of 1923. The All India Kabaddi Federation was founded in 1950 with the aim of popularizing the game, and in 1952 the first senior national championship was held. Twenty years after this, the Amateur Kabaddi Federation of India (AKFI) was founded and affiliated with the Indian Olympic Association with the intention of spreading the game throughout Asia. The formation of the AKFI led

A *kabaddi* team member from Thailand, far right, takes on a team from India during a preliminary match at the 17th Asian Games held in Incheon, Korea on September 29, 2014. In *kabaddi*, teams score points by capturing or touching players from the opposing team within the time limits of the game. (AP Photo/Eugene Hoshiko)

to such a great surge in *kabaddi*'s popularity in India that new competitions were founded, including national contests at junior and subjunior levels for both boys and girls. The first Asian Kabaddi Championship was held in 1980, and the first World Cup of Kabaddi was held in Mumbai, India, in 2004, with India beating Iran in the final.

In *kabaddi,* teams compete to score the most points by capturing or touching players from the opposing team within the time limits of the game, two halves of 20 minutes divided by a 5-minute break to change sides. Teams consist of 12 players, 7 of whom actively take to the field of play and 5 of whom are reserves, and throughout the game the teams alternate between attack and defense. A coin toss decides which team starts the game as attackers and which as defenders. The team that wins the toss attacks first. The attacking side is known as the raiders and sends one of its players, a raider, into the opposing team's half of the court. Since *kabaddi* sees 1 player take on 7 players, the game is known as the game of struggle. The raider enters the court chanting the words "Kabaddi! Kabaddi! Kabaddi!" This chanting is called the cant and must be loud and clear and begin before the raider touches the opposite side of the court. To stop the clearly audible repetition of the cant in order to take a breath is known as loosing the cant—according to the rules of *kabaddi* the cant must be continued in one and the same respiration. In circle *kabaddi* the cant has a maximum duration of 30 seconds.

The aim of the raider is to touch as many players on the antis side—that is, the opposing, defending team—as possible and return to her or his own side of the court all in one breath. The attack made by the raider is known as the raid. The antis touched by the raider are declared out if they do not manage to catch the raider before the return to her or his own side of the court. If the raider cannot make the return while using one breath to chant "Kabaddi!" he or she is declared out. Players are also declared out if they move outside of the playing area or if any part of their body touches the ground, except in a struggle. If all of the opposing team is declared out, then a bonus of two points, called a *lona,* is scored. When a *lona* is awarded the game continues by putting all the players into play on both sides of the court. A *kabaddi* match is refereed by seven officials made up of two umpires, two line officials, a referee, a timekeeper, and a scorer.

In India three forms of *kabaddi* are played: *surjeevani, gaminee,* and *amar,* or circle *kabaddi. Surjeevani* is governed by the rules and regulations of the Kabaddi Federation of India. In *surjeevani kabaddi* a player is revived, that is, brought back into play, for a player who has been declared out. In contrast, *gaminee kabaddi* does not have a revival rule, so when all the players of one team are out the game ends. However, there is no time limit for a *gaminee* match. In *amar kabaddi* out players do not leave the field of play but stay inside, with one point awarded to the raiding side for touching the player. Unlike *gamine kabaddi, amar kabaddi* does have a fixed time limit. *Amar kabaddi* is played in the north of India in areas such as Delhi, Punjab, and Uttar Pradesh, where it is also known as circle *kabaddi* due to the variant's round court. The playing surface for circle *kabaddi* has a radius of 22 meters (72 feet) for men and junior boys and 16 meters (52 feet) for women, junior girls, and subjuniors. In the center of the circle is a concentric circle measuring 6 meters (20 feet) called the *pala.* This area acts as a gate in the middle of the field through which the raider must reach his or her home court. Circle *kabaddi* differs from other forms of the sport in that the raider may touch only one anti. If a raider breaks this rule, then a point is given to the anti team. Similarly, in circle *kabaddi* only one anti may tackle the raider. A fourth *kabaddi* variation, *goongi kabaddi,* is played without a court, but this variation is held in a degree of disdain as being more akin to one-on-one wrestling on the ground than true *kabaddi.*

Though *kabaddi* is a combative sport, it has a definite code of acceptable conduct. For instance, it is illegal for an anti to stifle a raider's cant by muffling the raider's mouth or pressing on her or his throat, violent tackling is not permitted, and players must have clipped fingernails to prevent them from scratching opponents. Players are also banned from applying oils to their skin so as to make themselves too slippery to hold. Players, coaches, and managers who break these rules are issued cards colored green, yellow, and red depending on the seriousness of their rule breaking. A green card denotes a warning, a yellow card results in a two-minute temporary suspension from a game, and a red card results in a player's suspension from a match or the player being banned from playing in the rest of a tournament.

There has been a gradual growth in *kabaddi*'s popularity worldwide, as the sport is included in an increasing number of important sporting occasions. For instance, *kabaddi* was included as a demonstration sport at the ninth Asian Games held in New Delhi, India, in 1982 and has been included in the South Asian Federation Games since 1984. In 1990 India won the gold medal for *kabaddi* at the Asian Games held in Beijing, China, and has gone on to win the last five consecutive Asian Games gold medals for *kabaddi*. The continued growth of *kabaddi*'s popularity seems assured. One of the reasons for this is that *kabaddi* is an inclusive sport that women are permitted to play. Indeed, India won the first Asian Women Championship held in Hyderabad, India, in 2005, while women's *kabaddi* was included in the South Asian Games for the first time in 2006. Another reason for the sport's growth is that *kabaddi* can be played on many different surfaces. For instance, in 2006 indoor *kabaddi* was included in the Asian Games in Qatar, and *kabaddi* was part of the second Asian Indoor Games held in Macau, China, in 2007. Similarly, *kabaddi* can also be played on sand, and in 2008 both men's and women's *kabaddi* was included in the first Asian Beach Games held in Indonesia, with India winning both events. As the sport is included in more and more tournaments, its popularity increases internationally. This growth in worldwide recognition can be seen by the list of nations entered in the 2013 World Cup Kabaddi tournament that includes competitors from Africa, Asia, Europe, the Middle East, and North America.

However, one factor that may hamper the rise *kabaddi*'s popularity is the doping scandals that have recently engulfed the sport. At the 2012 World Cup Kabaddi tournament 53 competitors tested positive for drugs, including 10 from the United Kingdom, 8 from both the United States and Canada, 7 from both Spain and Italy, 6 from Australia, 3 from Norway, and 1 each from India, Pakistan, Germany, and Argentina. While the variety of nationalities shamed during the championships attests to *kabaddi*'s growth as a worldwide sport, it also highlights the pressures that players feel to succeed, especially as prize money at top tournaments continues to grow in parallel with the sport's increasing popularity. As a result of drug scandals, Indian authorities are having to spend millions of dollars on antidoping measures to ensure that the sport stays as drug-free as possible.

See also: Aussie Rules Football; Celtic Wrestling; *Glima;* Korean Wrestling; *Lucha Libre; Mallakhamb; Pehlwani/Kushti;* Rugby League; *Schwingen; Varzesh-e Bastani*

Further Reading

"History." Amateur Kabbadi Federation of India, 2009, http://www.indiankabaddi.org/history.php (accessed August 12, 2013).

"Kabbadi." Sports in India, http://sports.indiapress.org/kabaddi.php (accessed August 12, 2013).

"Kabaddi: Canada Tries Again for World Title in Drug-Infested Sport." Vancouver Desi, August 9, 2013, http://www.vancouverdesi.com/news/india/kabaddi-canada-tries-again-for-world-title-in-drug-infested-sport/376159/ (accessed August 12, 2013).

Kumar, Ashok. *International Encyclopaedia of Sports and Games (in Four Volumes).* New Delhi: Naurang Rai for Mittal Publications, 2000.

"Rules & Regulations." Amateur Kabaddi Federation of India, 2009, http://www.indiankabaddi.org/rules.php (accessed November 30, 2014).

KIN-BALL

Kin-ball is a relatively newly developed team ball game originating in Canada that is unusual for two reasons. First, the ball used is very large, and second, a kin-ball match is contested by three teams of four players simultaneously rather than one side versus another. Kin-ball can be played indoors or outside. The sport is governed by the International Kin-ball Federation and has many millions of players in countries including Canada, the United States, Malaysia, Japan, the United Kingdom, Germany, France, Belgium, Spain, Switzerland, and Denmark. Kin-ball is played at a variety of levels from school physical education classes to international matches, with a European club championship called the Championnat Européen des Clubs de KIN-BALL® Sport, or CHECK, taking place annually and the Kin-Ball World Cup held every other year.

Kin-ball was created by physical education teacher Mario Demers in Quebec, Canada, in 1986 as a way of increasing the aerobic fitness, coordination, balance, and teamwork capabilities of children. Then in 1987 the idea was further developed by Omnikin Inc., which at that time consisted of a group of university physical education instructors. Today kin-ball is played to tackle childhood obesity levels and as a game that allows the integration of people with disabilities into sport.

A kin-ball match is played either over a set period of time, usually seven minutes, or to a certain number of points, usually 12 or 13. The aim of kin-ball is for players to catch and control the ball, which is 4 feet in diameter, weighs two pounds, and is covered in thick nylon, without it touching the playing surface, which in kin-ball is no larger than 60 feet by 60 feet. If the ball does touch the ground then a fault is said to have been committed, and points are awarded for a foul. Each team, called a cell, is designated a specific color, and the players must wear an appropriately colored jersey or pinny to identify their team. While playing, one of the teams is deemed to be in possession of the ball and is therefore the attacking side. To start the game, a team serves the ball in a manner specific to kin-ball, for three players from the serving side stand underneath the ball and support it with their hands. The fourth member of the team, who is the server, exclaims "Omnikin!" or "Kin-ball!" followed by the color of the opposing team of their choice. The server then hits the ball (with all other team members still in contact with the ball) with either or both of the hands or arms in an upward or horizontal direction so that it travels at least eight feet toward the team whose color identification was called by the server. Meanwhile, the team that is neither serving nor receiving must move out of the way and not interfere with play. The ball must reach this minimum distance or a fault is said to have been committed. The ball must also not be served in a downward direction, as this would be judged a foul. The same player may not serve the ball twice consecutively, as this too is considered a fault. A fault also occurs if, in an indoor match, the ball is served into the wall or any part of the gymnasium in which the match takes place.

Once the ball has been served, the team chosen to receive—that is, the team whose color was shouted by the server—must catch the ball before it touches the playing surface. Receiving players may catch and control the ball with any part of their body. The receiving side has five seconds to throw the ball to any of the other two teams and must do it immediately after three of its players have touched the ball. This is called contact, and after three contacts have been made the players on the receiving side are no longer permitted to move their feet; otherwise, a fault called walking is said to have occurred. However, if the receiving side is unable to catch the ball before it makes contact with the ground, a point is awarded to the other two teams, and the team that allowed the ball to touch the ground must restart the game as the attacking side.

To win a game of kin-ball, teams must serve the ball to the team with the highest score, as this increases the chance of the leading team committing a fault.

See also: Aussie Rules Football; Bossaball; *Brännboll* and *Pesäpallo;* Cricket; Eton Wall Game; Fives; Korfball; Netball; Real Tennis; Rounders

Further Reading

"Kin-Ball." University of Southern Indiana, www.usi.edu/media/1735560/KIN-BALL.doc (accessed November 22, 2014).
"Official Kin-ball Sport." Omnikin, http://www.omnikin.com/site/en/kin-ball-official/ (accessed April 17, 2014).
"Welcome to CHECK." CHECK, http://check.kinballsport.com/en/welcome-check (accessed April 17, 2014).
"What Is Kin-Ball Sport?" USA Kin-Ball Sport, http://usakinball.150m.com/overview.htm (accessed April 17, 2014).

KITESURFING

Kitesurfing, also known as kiteboarding, is a recently invented extreme surface water sport in which wind power is used to propel practitioners, known as kite-surfers, through water on a small board. In 2006 there were thought to be up to 200,000 kitesurfers in the world, but since kitesurfing is a fast-growing sport, with an estimated 60,000 new kitesurfers taking up the activity each year, the total number of global kitesurfers must now be in the millions, and in countries such as South Africa there are already more kitesurfers than there are wind surfers. This shift is reflected in the fact that kitesurfing will replace wind surfing at the 2016 Olympic Games to be held in Rio de Janeiro.

Kitesurfing is governed by the International Kitesurfing Association, part of the International Sailing Federation.

Kites originated in China around 478 BCE, and the Chinese used kites for propulsion as early as the 13th century. The history of kitesurfing can be traced to the 19th century, when English inventor and kiting enthusiast George Pocock used kites in a variety of exploits. In one famous stunt Pocock placed his young daughter in a wicker chair attached to a number of kites and hoisted her into the air with the kites, keeping her airborne, and then flew her across the Avon Gorge of western England. Then in 1827 Pocock published a book titled *The Aeropleustic Art or Navigation in the Air by the Use of Kites, or Buoyant Sails.* However, it was Pocock's 1826 patented invention of the *charvolant,* a horseless carriage powered by kites, that made him famous and earned him a cult following, for with the *charvolant* Pocock

A male kitesurfer takes to the ocean. Kitesurfing depends on the transfer of wind energy into speed through the use of the large kite that the surfer maneuvers using a handlebar. (yulkapopkova/iStockphoto.com)

discovered a way to harness two kites to a single line in order to provide enough power to propel a buggy carrying several passengers in a way similar to modern kite buggying. Pocock's invention of the *charvolant* is important to the history of kitesurfing, for it showed that is was possible for a kite flyer to actually control and pilot the kite in the sky. Then in November 1903 American showman Samuel Franklin Cody demonstrated the pulling potential of a kite when he successfully crossed the English Channel from Calais to Dover in a small boat drawn by kites. An anchor was dragged behind Cody's boat in order to provide resistance to the pull of the kites, as this made the kite cable remain taut.

The actual history of kitesurfing itself reached back to the 1980s, when Cory Roeseler of Oregon developed a kite ski system employing a rigid framed kite that he used with water skis. Meanwhile in France, the Legaignoux brothers were busy developing their wipika kite, the name of which broke down into "wi" for wind, "p" for power, "i" for inflatable, "k" for kite, and "a" for aircraft. The wipika was a tube kite, so-called because inner tubes gave the kite stability. Kitesurfing further developed in the 1990s with the invention of ram-air kites. By the late to mid-1990s any issues had been eradicated from the different forms of kitesurf, and kitesurfing became popular in places such as Hawaii, France, and Germany.

A kitesurf is a board similar to a wakeboard, snowboard, or surfboard that is typically between 120 and 170 centimeters (around 4 to 5.5 feet) in length. Despite the name "kitesurfing," the activity does not depend on the presence of water; rather, wind is the essential factor, for the kitesurfer stands on the board in order to transfer the wind's energy into speed through the use of a large movable kite that the kitesurfer maneuvers using a handlebar connected to the kite by four lines. One of these four lines is connected to the harness or wrist strap worn by the kitesurfer via a device called a kite leash that stops the kite from blowing away if the kitesurfer loses hold of the handle bar. The vertical lift generated by the kite allows the kitesurfer to accomplish jumps even in a light wind or surf conditions.

There are several different types of kitesurfing, some of which cross over. The most popular style is freeride kitesurfing, which is noncompetitive. This should not be confused with freestyle kitesurfing, which is the style used in most kitesurfing competitions. In freestyle competitions two or more kitesurfers vie to perform the best tricks or moves and are judged on the level of difficulty and style of their maneuvers. There are also specialized competitions for hang time, that is, the length of time spent in the air, and flat-out racing. Other types of competitive kitesurfing include course racing, in which kitesurfers follow a course and use their kitesurfing skills and tactical abilities to cover the course in the fastest possible time, and speed racing, in which kitesurfers aim to achieve the quickest speed (over 500 meters), which is then verified by the World Sailing Speed Record Council. In 2010 Rob Douglas became the quickest man on water when he set a new Outright World Speed Record in Luderitz, Namibia, by reaching a speed of 55.65 knots (103.1 kilometers, or 64 miles) per hour. International kitesurfing competitions take place across the world in countries as diverse as the Cayman Islands, England, the Philippines, France, Panama, China, and Morocco.

Aside from competition, kitesurfers can also aim to achieve records such as making long-distance journeys between countries. For example, a new distance record for kitesurfing was set in January 2014 when a team of six Dutch and American male and female sailors set a record for a relay crossing of the Atlantic Ocean by covering the 6,000 kilometers (around 3,728 miles) from the Canary Islands off the northwestern coast of Africa to the Turks and Caicos Islands in the Caribbean.

As an extreme sport, kitesurfing involves an element of danger. One of the main causes of injury among kitesurfers is the inability to release the kite from their harness, which results in blunt trauma as the kitesurfer is dragged into an obstacle such as a wall or boat, though kitesurfers using quick-release mechanisms report fewer injuries of this type. Other dangers include kitesurfers overestimating their swimming abilities, resulting in hypothermia or even drowning, or involve external factors, such as encountering dangerous animals (e.g., jellyfish) off the coast of Australia or changing water conditions. Ignoring weather warnings has been known to lead to the death of kitesurfers. For instance, in 2010 a male kitesurfer was killed in a horrific incident at the holiday resort of Saint-Jean-de-Luz, southwestern France, during a storm when a gale-force wind dragged the airborne man, who was unable to detach himself from his harness, inland along a beach at 100 miles per hour and then into a pier, the roof of a hotel, and a chimney stack. The Frenchman then fell 50 feet to the ground and died.

See also: Heli-Skiing; Round-the-World Yacht Races; Swimming the English Channel; Volcano Boarding; Wingsuiting

Further Reading

Allen, Peter. "Kite-Surfer, 28, Dies after Gale Drags Him 100mph across Beach and Drops Him from 50ft." MailOnline, November 8, 2010, http://www.dailymail.co.uk/news/article-1327705/Kite-surfer-28-dies-gale-drags-100mph-beach-drops-50ft.html (accessed April 19, 2014).

Currer, Ian. *Kitesurfing: The Complete Guide.* Penrith, UK: Lakes Paragliding, 2002.

Gittings, Paul. "Kiteboarders Evade Sharks to Conquer Atlantic." CNN International, January 2, 2014, http://edition.cnn.com/2014/01/02/sport/kite-surfing-atlantic-first/ (accessed April 19, 2014).

Nedim Doral, Mahmut, Reha N. Tandoğan, Gideon Mann, and René Verdonk, eds. *Sports Injuries: Prevention, Diagnosis, Treatment and Rehabilitation.* Berlin: Springer-Verlag, 2012.

"Pioneer Kite Runner." BBC: Inside Out, January 22, 2009, http://www.bbc.co.uk/insideout/content/articles/2009/01/19/west_pocock_kites_s15_w2_video_feature.shtml (accessed April 18, 2014).

"Rob Douglas (USA)." ISAF: The Official Website of the International Sailing Federation, 2014, http://www.sailing.org/worldsailor/2011/rob-douglas.php (accessed April 19, 2014).

"Samuel Franklin Cody and His Man-Lifting Kite." Design Technology, http://www.design-technology.org/military.htm (accessed April 18, 2014).

"What Is Kitesurfing?" KSA International, 2013, http://www.ksa-international.org/en-us/kitesport/whatiskitesurfing.aspx (accessed April 18, 2014).

KOREAN WRESTLING

Korean wrestling is the English-language term for *ssireum,* a traditional male-dominated Korean folk combat sport much like sumo wrestling. In Korean wrestling, two wrestlers employ various techniques using their arms, legs, and torso to bring the other down on the sand-covered circle that makes up the playing area. The sport takes place in both North Korea and South Korea as well as China. Little information is available about the history of *ssireum* in North Korea, but in South Korea the present structure and rules of *ssireum* were in place by 1953, and in 1962 UNESCO recognized *ssireum* as an intangible cultural asset.

It is generally believed that *ssireum* began as a form of self-defense against people and animals that evolved into a folk game and later became Korea's national sport. However, the origins of *ssireum* is not known, though it is certainly a very old activity. This is evidenced by the fact that a mural on the wall of the Goguryeo royal tombs in southern Manchuria/northwestern China (now called Tonggou, Jian Prefecture, and Jilin Province), believed to date from around the turn of 4th century, is thought to depict the sport. Meanwhile, the first official records on *ssireum* date from March 1330, when King Chunghye (1315–1344) is said to have delegated major affairs of state to his secretaries so that he could practice *ssireum* with an errand boy on the grounds of his palace. This led to the king being criticized for dereliction of duty, but he disregarded this condemnation and continued to practice the sport. Thus, it seems that *ssireum* was popular with the upper echelons of society—royalty and the fighting elite. However, at some point the sport became the preserve of the lower classes, for a report from around 1680 tells of a servant stabbing his opponent during a *ssireum* bout, and the 18th-century painting *Sangbak* by Kim Hong-Do portrays a *ssireum* match surrounded by spectators and sweets sellers redolent of the peasant class. Thus, it appears that after the Three Kingdoms period of Korean history (ca. 57 BCE–668 CE) *ssireum* went from being a form of military defense training to a folk sport for peasants, probably because changing military tactics meant that it was no longer necessary for soldiers to learn to grapple each other and also because the teachings of Confucius, which championed education over physicality, became fashionable among the elite. *Ssireum* was still important to the Korean elite, however, as it was included in upper-class burial ceremonies. The activity was also important in Korean life in general and was included in consecrations and agricultural events, with contests held on Daeborum (which falls on January 15 by the lunar calendar), Dano Day (May 5 by the lunar calendar), Jungwonjol (July 15 by the lunar calendar), and Chusok (the Korean version of Thanksgiving that falls in mid-August by the lunar calendar). The winners of such festive *ssireum* contests were traditionally awarded an ox, since most *ssireum* athletes were peasants and it was thought that the chance to win an ox would encourage the winner in his farming. During the 19th century *ssireum* was gradually shunned by the social and military elite, and by the beginning of the 20th century the sport was totally abandoned by the Korean military and was very much a lower-class pursuit.

The first commercially sponsored *ssireum* contest was held in a cinema in Seoul, the capital of South Korea, in 1912. From this time an increasing number of *ssireum* competitions began to evolve, including the first Pan Ssireum Championship Contest (1936), which would be the forerunner of the regular National Ssireum Champion Contest, broadcast of Korean television since 1972. Another milestone in *ssireum* history came in 1983 when the Korean Folk Ssireum Federation launched the inaugural Universal Hercules Contest, which drew huge crowds, including members of Korea's social and economic elite, and garnered 80 percent of the television audience. That same year the first Ssireum Champion Contest was held, and the esteem in which *ssireum* was held is indicated by the fact the winner took home ₩15 million (around US$14,265). At the time this was enough to buy an apartment in Seoul. Today the prize money is ₩10 million. Also during the 1980s, local governments and businesses began to create their own *ssireum* teams, leading to the sport gaining a new level of professionalism, with team sponsors including Samsung and Hyundai. However, after South Korea's banking crisis at the end of the 1990s, sponsorship from major corporations was less forthcoming. This coupled with the state's decision to cut back on funding for non-Olympic sports and the growing popularity of baseball and soccer in Korea mean that *ssireum* is rapidly falling out of fashion in the country. Indeed, today there are only 18 *ssireum* teams in South Korea, and in 2007 it was estimated there were 10 high school/university soccer players for each *ssireum* wrestler.

Originally, there were two different styles of *ssireum:* right-sided *ssireum,* which was popular in Gyunggi Province and Honam Province in the south of Korea, and left-sided *ssireum,* which prevailed in Hamgyung Province, Gyungsang Provice, and Choonchong Province. However, nowadays left-side *ssireum* is unanimously adopted as the one style of *ssireum* played by all competitors.

Each professional or semiprofessional *ssireum* wrestler represents one of two teams and wears either red or blue skintight shorts depending on which team the wrestler plays for. The shorts are emblazoned with the wrestler's name and team affiliation. Amateur wrestlers do not have a uniform but still wear either red or blue.

A *ssireum* contest sees two contestants enter a circular sand-filled ring and bow in front of the referee. The contestants then take hold of each other's *satba*, a belt and thigh strap that in earlier times was thought to posses magical properties—Korean women would often wear underwear made out of *satba* fabric in the belief that it would help them bear sons. Competitors then stand and, on the referee's signal, start to grasp, lift, pull, twist, turn, press, and tumble in an attempt to throw their opponent to the floor, as a wrestler wins the bout if he can force any part of the opponent's body above the knee to touch the floor. The referee declares the winner and may be supported in his decision by two assisting referees. Individual bouts tend to last less than a few minutes, though matches often use a best-of-three format. If three rounds end without a clear winner being announced, then both wrestlers are weighed and the lightest is declared the winner.

Ssireum requires great muscular strength and physical stamina in order for a wrestler to maneuver an opponent to the ground while using the *satba* to lift the opponent. *Ssireum* is not, however, purely a strength contest, as it is vital that a competitor take tactical advantage of an opponent's body position. *Ssireum* also fosters teamwork, for competitors have to interact with teammates in training. Training does not fall into specific schools of technique as in other martial arts, and training methods vary between institutions, though it is usual for wrestlers to train for several hours per day. As a result of this enforced teamwork, strong social bonds are built between wrestlers and coaches, who often remain friends after retirement—professional wrestlers tend to retire at around their mid to late 20s, having trained since primary school. Retired wrestlers often go on to become influential figures in politics, business, and entertainment. That retired wrestlers can achieve high-profile careers suggests that even if *ssireum* is not as popular as it once was, the sport continues to maintain a discernible presence in Korean life.

See also: Celtic Wrestling; *Glima;* Mongolian Wrestling; *Pehlwani/Kushti; Schwingen;* Sumo Wrestling; *Varzesh-e Bastani; Yagli Gures*

Further Reading

Green, Thomas A., and Joseph R. Svinth. *Martial Arts of the World: An Encyclopedia of History and Innovation,* Vol. 2. Santa Barbara, CA: ABC-CLIO, 2010.

Sang-Jun, Lee. "Traditional Korean Wrestling Faces Its Toughest Bout Yet." CNN Travel, July 28, 2011, http://travel.cnn.com/seoul/play/ssireum-legacy-old-days-727634 (accessed July 28, 2014).

"What Is Ssireum?" Korea Sirum (Ssireum) Research Institute, http://ynucc.yeungnam.ac.kr/~ssi/Introduction/What_is_Ssireum_/what_is_ssireum_.html (accessed July 28, 2014).

KORFBALL

Korfball is a fast-paced noncontact ball game similar to basketball that is played indoors or outdoors and is unique in being one of the world's only truly mixed team sports in which males and females play alongside each other on the same teams. The name korfball comes from the Dutch term *korf*, meaning "basket." Both children and adults play korfball from the level of school physical education classes up to international competition, with the majority of players being women. Indeed, of the 100,000 korfball club players worldwide, 60,000 are female. To begin with, korfball was played only in countries over which the Netherlands held a significant influence, such as the Dutch-speaking areas of Belgium and former Dutch colonies including Indonesia, Surinam, and Curacao. However, today korfball is played across Europe, Asia, and Australasia as well as in the United States, Canada, South Africa, and Zimbabwe. Despite the international spread of korfball, the sport remains in essence a localized sport, for with the exception of the Netherlands, which is home to over 600 korfball clubs, the number of players in other countries equals only a few thousand at most. The sport is governed by the International Korfball Federation, which was founded in the Dutch city of Rotterdam in 1933 and has in excess of 50 members. In 1938 korfball was granted a royal charter. The United States Korfball Federation was established in 1978.

Nico Broekhuysen, a Dutch teacher who had encountered a variation on women's basketball while staying in Sweden, invented korfball in 1902. At the turn of the 20th century women's basketball was played on a playing surface divided into three courts, as it was felt that this discouraged individualistic play and unladylike behavior. Players were not permitted to cross from one court into another and had to swap courts after each point scored. Dribbling with the ball was forbidden, as was obstructing a shot at goal. Broekhuysen wanted to create a game that boys and girls could play together on equal terms, encouraging teamwork and cooperation, and he decided to base his game on the women's basketball that he had seen in Sweden. The fundamentally mixed-sex basis of korfball together with the game's philosophy of favoring team play over the individual and cohesion over power, a strict notion of fair play, and the use of cane baskets similar to those found on the front of an old-fashioned ladies' bicycle attracts derision from some quarters, particularly macho sportsmen desperate to emphasize their overt masculinity.

Broekhuysen published the rules of his game in a booklet, and soon schools throughout the Netherlands adopted the game. However, korfball and women's basketball gradually grew apart. For instance, women's basketball dropped the court system in 1938 and became a full-court game in 1971. Korfball, on the other hand, became a two-court game in 1991 and has never switched to become a full-court sport. Another difference is that women's basketball has permitted dribbling since 1966, but korfball still forbids dribbling.

The objective in korfball is to score goals by depositing the ball, which is round and covered in leather, in the korf while preventing the opposition from doing the same. The principles of korfball are similar to those of netball, basketball, and handball, but korfball is unique in having mixed-sex rules that result in a much more varied game. In the earliest days of korfball two teams of 12 players, 6 boys and 6 girls over three courts, played the game. However, today korfball is played by two teams of 8 players divided into two sections—defense and attack. These sections each consist of 2 males and 2 females, and players swap roles throughout the game after every second goal scored, with players swapping sections so that attackers become defenders and defenders become attackers. Thus, unlike basketball, netball, and other similar games, there are no set playing positions in korfball. Korfball is based on the principle of cooperation within a team, and the rules aim to provide equality, since players can only mark, or be marked by, an opposing player of the same sex.

Korfball is played on a playing surface measuring 40 meters by 90 meters (44 yards by 99 yards) that is divided into two large squares joined along a centerline. Within each square is a korf, that is, a goal that stands 3.5 meters (11.5 feet) from the ground and is situated 10 meters (11 yards) inside from the end line in each half of the pitch, allowing players to shoot at goal from 360°. Within the 90 minutes of playing time in a korfball game, the ball is passed rapidly by hand only from player to player in order to gain a chance of shooting at the korf to score a goal. However, attacking players may not shoot if a defender of the same sex is within arm's length between themselves and the goalpost. Players may also not kick, fist, or strike the ball, and it is absolutely forbidden for a player to run with the ball; hence, a gifted athlete cannot sprint through the field to score, but rather teamwork must be employed to shoot at goal.

Korfball was included as an exhibition sport in the 1920 Olympic Games held in Antwerp, Belgium, and the Amsterdam Olympics of 1928. However, the sport has never caught on in a major way as either a game to play or as a spectator sport—only eight teams took part at the first annual world championship held in 1984, and championship final matches attract only around 7,000 to 10,000 onlookers.

See also: Canal Jumping; Kin-Ball; Netball

Further Reading

Connolly, Paul. *The World's Weirdest Sports.* Millers Point, Australia: Pier 9, 2007.

England Korfball. "What Is Korfball?" England Korfball, http://www.englandkorfball.co.uk /CMS/what-is-korfball.htm (accessed April 24, 2014).

Glasgow Korfball Club. "What Is Korfball?" Glasgow Korfball Club, http://www.glasgowkor fball.co.uk/korfball.html (accessed April 24, 2014).

Levinson, David, and Karen Christensen, eds. *Encyclopedia of World Sport: From Ancient Times to the Present.* Oxford: Oxford University Press, 1996.

Nauright, John, and Charles Parrish, eds. *Sports around the World: History, Culture and Practice,* Vol. 1, *General Topics, Africa, Asia, Middle East, and Oceania.* Santa Barbara, CA: ABC-CLIO, 2012.

KUBB

Kubb (pronounced koob) is a strategic Nordic throwing game played with wooden pieces. The game is designed to be played by two teams of up to six players. However, a team can consist of a single person so that, in effect, the match is one-on-one.

It has been suggested that *kubb* was invented by the Vikings around 1000 CE, and hence the game is sometimes referred to as Viking chess. However, there is little evidence to support this claim. Rather, it is known that *kubb* originated in the late 19th or early 20th century on the island of Gotland, Sweden, where the word *kubb* means "wooden block." The game is akin to bunnock, *kyykkä*, and *mölkky*, which all originated in Scandinavia or Russia, as well as the English game of Aunt Sally. *Kubb* is played in various forms across Scandinavia but is particularly popular in Sweden and Russia and is experiencing rapid growth in popularity in Western Europe, especially in the United Kingdom, Germany, Italy, Belgium, Holland, France, and Switzerland, as well as in the United States, Australia, and New Zealand.

A man preparing to throw a wooden *kaastpinne*, or casting block, during a game of kubb in Sweden. Kubb is a strategic throwing game designed to be played by two teams of up to six players, though a team may also consist of just one person, meaning a game is played one-on-one. (linus_forsberg/iStockphoto.com)

Kubb is usually played on a lawn or on level sand, though it can also be played on ice, snow, or concrete. The playing area is defined by four pieces known as *hornpinnar,* or the corner pins. *Kubb* is played on a large court that is divided in two much like a tennis court but without a net. The court measures 7 to 15 feet wide by 15 to 30 feet long. The short side is the baseline, and the long sides form the sideline boundaries inside which play must be kept.

To decide which team will throw first and from which side of the court each team will play, a player from each team throws one *kastpinne,* a single casting block, at the *kung,* or king piece. The team of the player who threw closest to the king but without knocking it over gets to play first and choose their end. Players hit the *kubbs* using six *kastpinnar,* or casting blocks, that are divided equally between the teammates. So, if playing one-on-one each player has six casting blocks, while a team of six players will each receive one block to throw. If the number of players in a team means the casting blocks cannot be divided evenly between the team members, then the spare block(s) are rotated among the team so that each member gets to throw for a second time. Players may only throw underarm, and though the block may rotate end-over-end in midair, it must be kept vertical in flight.

The rules of *kubb* vary from region to region, but in general the basic aim of the game is for players standing on their own baseline to knock over the five *kubbs,* or chopping blocks, that have been placed at each end of the pitch along the opposite baseline and then knock down the king piece that has been placed in the middle of the playing area. The team that takes the least number of throws to knock over all the *kubbs* and then the king is declared the winner.

One extremely popular variation on the basic *kubb* game is *faltkubbar,* or field *kubbs.* This variation begins in the same way as a basic game of *kubb,* but once all the casting blocks have been thrown, the opposing team collects any *kubbs* that have been knocked over and throws them from the baseline back across the field of play. The *kubbs* that are thrown back are the *faltkubbar.* The first team has to stand the field *kubbs* up again, placing them where they land after being thrown back by the second team. If a *kubb* is thrown but lands outside the playing area, then it is replaced after all the other thrown *kubbs* have been knocked over. The team can then throw at the replaced *kubb* once again. However, if the same *kubb* falls outside the pitch for a second time, then it becomes a punishment *kubb.* This means that the opposing team is allowed to place the *kubb* wherever they like within one casting block's length of the king piece. Play now switches so that the second team throws the six casting blocks at the replaced field *kubbs,* then at the baseline *kubbs,* and finally at the king piece. If the second team does not manage to knock over all the *kubbs* plus the king, then the first team picks up all the toppled *kubbs* and throws them back into play as field *kubbs.* The first team then throws again, attempting to knock down all the *kubbs.*

Play continues in this manner until the end of the game. If a team fails to knock over all the field *kubbs* on the opponent's side of the playing area, then the other team is allowed to move up to the *kubb* closest to the court's centerline and throw its casting blocks from there. Unlike the *kubbs,* which may only be thrown from the baseline, casting pieces may be thrown, temporarily, from midcourt.

The winning team is the one that knocks over all the *kubbs* on the opposite side of the court and on the baseline and then topples the king piece. However, if a team accidently knocks the king piece down before knocking over all the *kubbs,* then that team loses the game immediately. A game of *kubb* can last from a few minutes to well over an hour depending on the variations of play used. These variations usually pertain to when, if at all, a *kubb* is deemed out of play, when a team can move its throwing line and stacking, that is, the throwing back of the field *kubbs.* Time limits can be imposed to hurry the game along.

Championship-level *kubb* usually plays a best-of-three match system. Most tournaments, including the U.S. National Kubb Championship, play by the U.S. National Kubb Championship Rules. The U.S. National Kubb Championship has been held in July in Eau Claire, Wisconsin, since 2007, with all proceeds going to charity and to provide university scholarships for students studying Swedish. The championship has also established the Kubb Set Grant, which aims to inspire a new generation of *kubb* players by providing free *kubb* sets to community groups.

The U.S. championship has proven extremely popular, growing from a one-day event to a two-day tournament and having to move the location several times to accommodate growing attendance of both spectators and teams. This expansion is best illustrated by the fact that in 2007 40 players in total entered the competition, while in 2013 88 teams consisting of 310 players competed for the title. In addition to winning the championship team title, players also compete for the individual title of *basta inkastare,* or best tosser of the *kubbs.* In 2011 in addition to hosting the U.S. championship, Eau Claire declared itself the Kubb Capital of North America. The town is home to *Kubbnation Magazine* plus numerous *kubb* leagues and clubs.

The world championships have been held annually in Gotland since 1995 and play by very slightly different rules compared to the U.S. championship. For instance, at the world championship, teams must consist of at least six players, each of whom who can only throw once, while at the U.S. championships teams must have at least three players, and no player may throw more than two casting blocks.

See also: Aunt Sally; Bunnock; Chess Boxing; *Glima; Mölkky;* Nordic Walking

Further Reading

"Kubb—The Viking Game." Old Time Games, http://www.oldtimegames.com/howtoplay2 .html (accessed August 12, 2013).

Masters, James. "Kubb: History and Information." The Online Guide to Traditional Games, 1997, http://www.tradgames.org.uk/games/Kubb.htm (accessed August 12, 2013).

"Rules." Wisconsin Kubb, http://www.wisconsinkubb.com/rules.php (accessed August 12, 2013).

KYYKKÄ

Kyykkä is the name given to both an outdoor skittle-like folk game for children and adults of both sexes, also known as Karelian skittles, and a type of skittle used in the game. *Kyykkä* is popular in Finland, where it is played by people of Karelian extraction and as a leisure pursuit by students.

Kyykkä originated in the region of Karelia, which covers parts of Finland and Russia, and was first played many centuries ago by the Karelian population living in the land area between the coast of the White Sea and the Lake Ladoga region. After a period of civil unrest at the start of the 20th century, Karelian refugees left their homeland and fled to Finland, taking the game of *kyykkä* with them. Since then the game has become hugely popular in Finland, and many *kyykkä* tournaments are held every year. The governing body of *kyykkä* is the Finnish Skittles Association, which is part of the Finnish Sports Federation. The International Federation of Gorodki Sport organizes a world championship for three different skittle variations: *kyykkä, gorodki* (also known as Russian skittles), and Euro *gorodki.*

Kyykkä is played on a hard, flat playing surface that is usually made of leveled-off gravel, as playing on concrete risks breaking the playing equipment, and playing on grass will ruin a lawn. The playing area, which is known the *kyykkä kentta,* or *kyykkä* field, measures 5 meters by 20 meters (around 16 feet by 66 feet). The field is divided into two playing squares known as the throwing-square and the game-square, with an area between the two squares. For adults these squares have sides measuring 5 meters (16 feet) plus an area dividing the field in halves that measure 10 meters (about 33 feet). Children under 10 years of age play on squares measuring 3 meters by 3 meters (almost 10 feet by 10 feet), and the area between the squares is 6 meters (about 20 feet). A team's throwing square is also the opposing side's game square and vice versa.

Kyykkä is usually played by teams of four or two players, though singles competitions also exist. The rules of *kyykkä* vary from village to village and game to game, but the basic way to play *kyykkä* is for players to throw baseball bat–like clubs called *karttus* at small wooden cylindrical skittles with rounded corners called *kyykkäs.* Players aim to knock the *kyykkäs* out of their own game square. The *karttus* are rounded and made of wood and measure 85 centimeters (33 inches) in length with a maximum thickness of 8 centimeters (3 inches). There is no limit to how heavy a club may be. Meanwhile, the *kyykkäs* are 10 centimeters (4 inches) long with a diameter of 6.5 to 8 centimeters (2.5 inches to just over 3 inches).

At the beginning of the game, pairs of skittles are stacked vertically and placed on the front line of the playing square. In team games, 20 pairs of skittles are placed at intervals of 10 centimeters (4 inches). In one-on-one games, 10 pairs of skittles are similarly placed every 125 centimeters (49 inches). Once a skittle is knocked down, it is not righted. Before a game of *kyykkä* starts, the teams build the game area by placing the *kyykkäs* on the frontier line of the playing squares, at the interval determined by the type of match that is going to be played. In team and pair games, players have two bats per turn, while in singles matches, players have four bats per turn. Players take turns stepping up to the throwing square and throwing the club to try knocking the skittles out of the playing square. In men's competitions, the player throwing first stands 15 meters (49 feet) behind the throwing square while subsequent throws are taken from 10 meters (33 feet), that is, standing on the throwing square. In women's competitions the first player to throw stands at 10 meters (33 feet), with subsequent players throwing from 8 meters (26 feet). Thus, female players actually throw from in front of the throwing square, not from inside it. Throws can be overarm or underarm. The only rule is that players must throw from their own throwing square.

All players throw their *karttus* before the opposing side takes its turn, and thrown *karttus* must be left where they fall until all players have thrown. The winner is the team that is first to clear all of the *kyykkäs* out of their game square, with both teams throwing the same number of *karttus.* If both teams take the same number of *karttus* to clear their square, then the game is said to be a tie.

Games involving two teams continue until one team wins a predetermined number of ends, and once an end has finished, teams swap squares. However, if more than two teams are involved, then it is usual to play a tournament format in which every team plays two ends against all the other teams. When this format is employed, the winner of a game earns two points, a tie earns one point for both teams, and a loss earns no points. After all games have been played, the winner is determined by totaling all points received by each team. The team with the most points is the overall winner.

An alternative way of playing *kyykkä* sees teams agree on a number of throws per team prior to the match. After all the throws are taken, the winner is determined by adding up the number of *kyykkäs* left in each team's game squares. At the end of the game, every *kyykkä* that remains inside the game square leads to a one-point deduction from the number of points won. Remaining *kyykkäs* are known as crones. Also, two points are subtracted for each *kyykkä* left standing on the front line—remaining *kyykkäs* are known as priests. Skittles that land in the dividing zone between the playing squares also result in a team losing points. Under this rule a team can lose a match even though it removes more *kyykkäs* from the game square than its opponent.

In singles matches players may use 20 clubs per half, with each player taking turns to throw 4 clubs. Players receive points for the number of clubs that remain unused once they have cleared the playing square of skittles, with one point awarded per unused club. Once all the skittles have been removed from the field, players swap ends, and the second half of the match continues like the first. The final score is the sum of the player's number of unused clubs over both halves, with the winner being the player who uses the fewest clubs.

See also: Aunt Sally; Bandy; Bunnock; *Kubb; Lapta; Mölkky;* Nordic Walking; Orienteering and Rogaining; Skittles; Synchronized Skating; Wife Carrying

Further Reading

"Karelian Skittles—Kyykkä." Society of Karelian Language Friends, http://karelia.onegaborg.eu/eng/Sport.aspx (accessed May 3, 2014).

"Kyykkä—the Karelian Skittles Game." BBC, November 25, 2002, http://www.bbc.co.uk/dna/ptop/plain/A863336 (accessed August 12, 2013).

L

LAPTA

Lapta is a Russian folk game played with a bat and ball by two teams of six. The name *lapta* is derived from a Russian word for a bat, *lopatka*. The game is similar to cricket, rounders, and *pesapallo* and is thought by some to be a forerunner of baseball, brought by Russian immigrants to the United States and Canada during the 18th century. *Lapta* is known to have been played as far back as the 14th century, when Czar Peter the Great (1672–1725) ordered *lapta* to be played by his elite guards as part of their fitness regime. There is also some evidence that the game was played even earlier than this, as *lapta* bats and balls have been discovered at archaeological sites in Novgorod, Russia's capital city, between the 9th and 12th centuries. During the Soviet era (1917–1990) authorities endorsed *lapta* as the quintessential Soviet pastime, along with *gorodki*, a throwing game similar to bowling, bunnock, and skittles. *Lapta* was promoted as representing the best of Soviet values—resourcefulness, skill, strength, speed, and accuracy as well as loyalty.

The game's heyday came in the 1950s, when thousands of *lapta* teams were registered to play. In 1958 the first national *lapta* championship was held in Russia, and from 1959 *lapta* was included in the Spartakiads, sporting tournaments for Eastern bloc countries that were essentially a communist version of the Olympic Games. Even Leon Trotsky, the leader of the Bolsheviks, took time to play *lapta*.

The Soviet government's interest in *lapta* suddenly ceased, however, and the sport went unheard of for around 30 years. Though the game's rich folk tradition meant that the Russian people did not forget the game, it was only in the late 1980s, when the Soviet government announced that money would be spent on developing *lapta*, baseball, and softball, that the state began to take an interest in *lapta* once again. In the post-Soviet era the resurgence of interest in *lapta* has continued, and today around 10,000 Russians play *lapta* regularly.

Lapta is played on a field that is divided into three zones: the field itself, the round or *kon*, and the town or *gorod*. *Lapta* is played all year round, both outdoors and indoors. In the winter the *lapta* playing area is marked by lines drawn on top of snow-covered fields, while indoor *lapta* is played on a slightly smaller playing area, with adjustments made to the rules in case the ball hits walls or ceilings.

Lapta players use bats measuring 60 to 110 centimeters (24 to 43 inches) in length with a diameter of no more than 5 centimeters (2 inches) and weighing 1.5 kilograms (just over 3 pounds). A tennis ball is used for bowling. At the start of a game of *lapta*, lots are drawn by officials to determine the serving order, and players then take their positions on the field. The defending team—that is, the team that is not batting—takes to the field, and the batting side takes to the *gorod* area. A member of the batting team known as the server stands on a special pad. A member of the batting team then throws the server the ball, and the server hits the ball. If the server hits the ball and it travels out of the field without bouncing, the shot is called a strikeout. Once the server has hit the ball, the rest of the batting side rushes onto the field of play with the intention of reaching the *kon* line and then returning home to the *gorod* area while the ball is in play. Each successful player scores two points for the batting side. Members of the batting side can stay in the *kon* area until their team bats again and then run back. Fielders are not allowed to tackle runners. However, fielders can deduct points from the batting side's score by hitting runners with the ball. If a fielder tags a player with the ball, the fielder must run home without being tagged. Players on either team may be tagged as long as they are not in their home area. If there is no player to tag, then the ball is thrown back to the player who threw the ball to the server. The fielding side scores one point if a fielder catches the ball while it is in the air. A player is out of the game automatically if he returns home without completing his run. Once a player is out, the teams switch sides so that the defending team becomes the batting side.

In *lapta,* fouls are punished by the giving of a yellow card. Repeat offending, aggressive behavior, and fighting result in a red card, with players sent off the field. If a team dwindles to four players, then the team loses the game automatically.

The Swiss Alpine game of *hornussen* is akin to *lapta* in that it includes elements of baseball as well as similarities to golf. *Hornussen* is said to have originated when ancient Swiss beekeepers used large wooden pallets to swat menacing hornets away from their hives. The earliest written records of *hornussen* date to the 16th century, and the first competitive match is known to have been played in Trub in 1655. In its earliest form, competitive *hornussen* was a way for young farmers to prove their strength, and contests were also seen as a way to settle disputes between villages. As a result of this, *hornussen* matches often ended in brawls, in much the same way as *la soule.* In the 19th century a *hornussen* association established rules for the game in an attempt to prevent games from ending in violence, and in 1902 the *hornussen* governing body, Eidgenössischer Hornusserverband, was founded to organize leagues and the National Hornussen Festival, which is held every three years, plus the *hornussen* matches that accompany *schwingen* festivals.

In *hornussen* each team bats once and defends once. The batter hits twice, with three attempts permitted per hit. To start, the batter digs a foot well for the swing at one end of the playing surface, and into these hollows the batter places a small plastic puck called the *hornuss* atop a device called the *bock.* The *hornuss* is very light, weighing only 78 grams (just less than 3 ounces). The *bock* is a curved metal track that helps guide the club, called a *schingel.* The club is flexible and about 3 meters (nearly 10 feet) long. The main length of the bat is made of carbon fiber with a shorter length of pressed maple wood at the far end. The batter swings the club as though using a golf club, and as the club swings it bends and wraps itself around the batter's body. The club then hits the *hornuss,* which flies through the air at around 150–300 kilometers (93–186 miles) per hour. The opposing team members, who stand in a column starting 100 meters (109 yards) from the batter, each hold a large paddle called a *schindel,* which is shaped like a baker's shovel and painted with their team's emblem. The fielding team uses its paddles to try to intercept the *hornuss* as it hurtles overhead and before it touches the ground. A referee records the distance reached by the *hornuss* on a scoreboard, and then the next batter takes up position at the foot well. The winning team in the one that scores the fewest penalization points, that is, has the fewest failed interceptions of the *hornuss.* A game of *hornussen* has no set time limit and can take four hours to complete.

Hornussen teams are ranked, while individual strikers also receive a ranking accrued through the Swiss *hornussen* championships and one-off games held on special occasions.

See also: Brännboll and *Pesäpallo;* Cricket; *La Soule;* Nipsy; Rounders; *Schwingen;* Stone Skimming

Further Reading

Boroznova, Anislya. "Lapta: Russia's Own Bat-and-Ball Game." Russia beyond the Headlines, January 28, 2011, http://rbth.ru/articles/2011/01/28/russian_lapta_12321.html (accessed August 12, 2013).

Chambers, Lucas. "Swiss Know How to 'Schwingen.'" Straight.com, July 8, 2004, http://www.straight.com/life/swiss-know-how-schwingen (accessed August 9, 2013).

Chetwynd, Josh. *Baseball in Europe: A Country by Country History.* Jefferson, NC: McFarland, 2008.

Dickson, Paul. *The Dickson Baseball Dictionary.* 3rd ed. Jefferson, NC: McFarland, 2008.

"Games We Play—Lapta." *Moscow News,* July 5, 2010, http://themoscownews.com/arts/20100705/187912335.html (accessed August 12, 2013).

"Hornussen." Myswitzerland.com, http://www.myswitzerland.com/en-gb/hornussen.html (accessed September 23, 2013).

"Hornussen—Where the Nouss Flies from the Ramp and into the Playing Field." My Switzerland, http://www.myswitzerland.com/en-gb/hornussen-where-the-nouss-flies-from-the-ramp-and-into-the-playing-field.html (accessed September 23, 2013).

Keller, Bill. "Take Me Out to the Ballgame, Comrade." *Chicago Tribune,* July 27, 1987, http://articles.chicagotribune.com/1987-07-27/sports/8702250103_1_russians-moscow-chemical-technological-institute-american-national-pastime (accessed August 12, 2013).

Nauright, John, and Charles Parrish, eds. *Sports around the World: History, Culture and Practice,* Vol. 1, *General Topics, Africa, Asia, Middle East, and Oceania.* Santa Barbara, CA: ABC-CLIO, 2012.

LA SOULE

La soule, or *la choule,* is a loosely structured contact folk ball game generally thought to be the forerunner of rugby and soccer and is also related to lawn tennis. The game takes its name from the ball used, the *soule.* There are two theories as to how this name for the ball originated. One is that *soule* derives from the Latin word *cepulla,* meaning "onion," which was often used as a slang term for a ball. Another suggestion is that *soule* is a derivation of the Old High German word *kiulla,* meaning "leather pouch." *La soule* is played by at least two teams of varying numbers, each representing a different persona or identity associated with the locale. For example, games may involve married men versus bachelors, downtown dwellers versus uptown inhabitants, village versus village, or parish versus parish. Though the popularity of the sport waned somewhat during the 1930s and 1940s, *la soule* is enjoying a revival in certain French towns as a result of political regionalism, particularly in the Brittany region where anti-French separatist sentiments are prevalent. The game is also played annually in locations in northern France, especially in the towns of Vendôme and Tricot, and in Jersey, a Channel Island dependency of the United Kingdom that lies just off the coast of the northern French department of Normandy.

The influence of *la soule* can be seen throughout the north of France, where derivatives of the names *la soule* and *la choule* are evident in common family names such as Le Solleux, Chouleur, and Chollet as well as in northern place-names, including the Solle Valley near Paris, the French capital. The game even influenced linguistics, for in Norman French the phrase for setting a dog on someone is *chouler un chien contre,* which reflects the violence inherent in the game.

Nobody knows quite how old *la soule* is. According to the oral tradition of Brittany, the origins of *la soule* go back to Celtic prehistory, while records dating from 1374 mention a stick-and-ball version of the game, *shouler a la crosse.* Other documentary evidence of the game dates to the 12th century, when *la soule* was played either solely during the period leading up to Lent or once per year on the day of a religious festival, such as the feast day of a particular saint. This links *la soule* to competitive events held on religious feast days elsewhere, such as the English Shrove Tuesday Pancake Races, and, more particularly, to English street football events held once per year, such as the Ashbourne Shrovetide Football Game and Cornish Hurling, both of which are associated with Easter and feature goals located several miles apart. Another French game that seems to belong to the *la soule* family is *jeu de maille.* In this game players hit the ball along the ground toward a target using a wooden stick, or mallet. Another game similar to *la soule* is the ancient Swedish game *parkspel,* meaning "player's delight." *Parkspel,* which has been played for centuries on the Swedish island of Gotland, is thought to be an ancestor of both modern tennis and soccer, for the game sees players not only hit the ball with the palm of their hand, as in the earliest form of real tennis, *jeu de paume,* but also kick the ball.

The aim of *la soule* is to bring the ball to either your own goal or that belonging to the opposition. The ball, which is made of leather and filled with bran, straw, hair, fleece, or air, may be moved using sticks, hands, or feet. The version of the game using feet to propel the ball is known as *la soule au pied* and is extremely similar to modern soccer. Another version, played exclusively in Brittany, is called *melat* and is even more open and brutal than ordinary *la soule.*

A game of *la soule* begins with a ritualistic relinquishing of the ball, which happens three times. Players then try to catch the ball and form a scrum, as in rugby. Once a player succeeds in taking control of the ball, all the players run off across the local environs, which can take in rivers, urban areas, fields, and woods. The running is interrupted by further scrums, which are often rough in nature, as players try to reclaim the ball. When the ball finally reaches a goal, the winning team is given a prize. If the goal reached belongs to the team that scored the goal, then that goal area becomes the starting place for the game the following year. The game is governed by very few, if any, rules, with team numbers varying from dozens to many hundreds and with no restrictions placed on the size of the playing area; there are also no time limits. The only definite is that the game is accompanied by much eating, drinking, dancing, and general merrymaking, which engages the entire local community. During the 19th century, the rowdy nature of *la soule* resulted in authorities attempting to ban it, since a game of *la soule* often ended with players injured or even dead. One particularly notable game of *la soule* took place in Orne in 1851. The game, which involved hundreds of players and drew crowds in excess of 6,000, rapidly descended into a bloody fight that took four brigades of police to quell. Unsurprisingly, authorities took a dim view of such activity, and though the next match was held under a veil of secrecy, this removed the fun aspect from the Orne game, which eventually died out.

The continual attempts to control the ball while traveling through a wider landscape liken *la soule* to England's Haxey Hood Game and Cornish Hurling, also known as Hurling the Silver Ball. The latter is an ancient folk game that is at least 1,000 years old and thought to be Pagan in origin. It is unsurprising that a similar game should exist in both Brittany and Cornwall, the most southwesterly of all the English counties, as the two regions share strong religious and commercial ties dating back to medieval times, and both regions are recognized as sharing strong Celtic cultural and linguistic bonds. The link between Cornwall, Brittany, *la soule,* and soccer is illustrated by the fact that the old Cornish name for soccer is *chole.*

Cornish Hurling occurs in only two Cornish towns, St. Ives and St. Columb Major. The game sees two teams from different parts of the same parish, usually called the townsmen and the countrymen, aim to keep hold of a ball made of silver-coated apple wood. Touching the ball is said to bring fertility and good health. In St. Ives, the game is an essential part of the St. Ives Feast that takes place on the Monday after February 3 and today is mainly played by children and teenagers. In earlier times the game took place between the parishes of St. Ives and Lelant, with the church of each parish serving as a goal. However, when St. Ives's population grew much larger than that of Lelant, the game was restricted so that it only took place in St. Ives. At the start of the game the mayor of St. Ives throws the ball from the church steps into a scrum of players, who then seek to take possession of the ball in a rough, disorganized way, traveling across the region as they do so. The game ends at noon when the teams return to the town's Royal Square. The winning team, that is, the team carrying the ball, is rewarded with a prize of a five-shilling coin. In St. Columb Major, Cornish Hurling takes place on Shrove Tuesday and sees teams of local men snatch, tackle, and throw the ball through both public streets and private land with the aim of scoring a goal. To do this, the team of townsmen must carry the ball to a nearby ancient Celtic cross, while the team of countrymen must place the ball in a granite trough located in a nearby field. A team may also win if they manage to transport the ball over the parish boundary.

When a goal is scored, the game is won and the ball is taken back to the town's market square. From here the winners take the ball to visit every pub in the town, at each of which the ball is dunked in a pint of beer that is then shared by all those drinking in the pub.

A similar game, this time played on Good Friday, is the Chiddingstone Real Football match, played in Kent in southern England. At the start of the game, two teams meet at a local pub and from there proceed to score a goal by tapping the ball three times on the barrels designated as goals outside either a pub located to the north of the town or one to the town's south.

See also: Aussie Rules Football; *Buzkashi;* Dwile Flonking; Haxey Hood Game; *Kubb;* Pancake Races; *Pétanque;* Real Tennis; Rugby League

Further Reading

Baker, William Joseph. *Sports in the Western World.* Revised ed. Springfield: University of Illinois Press, 1988.

Chiddington Real Football. http://chiddingstonerealfootball.co.uk (accessed September 11, 2013).

Gillmeister, Heiner. *Tennis: A Cultural History.* London: Leicester University Press, 1997.

Gorini, Pietro. *Jeux et Fetes Traditionnels de France et d'Europe.* Rome: Gremese International srl, 1994.

"Hurling the Silver Ball." Cornwall Guide, 2014, http://www.cornwalls.co.uk/events /cornish_hurling.htm (accessed September 11, 2013).

"La Choule ou la Soule." Jeux Picards, http://www.jeuxpicards.org/choulemahon.html (accessed September 11, 2013).

Nauright, John, and Charles Parrish, eds. *Sports around the World: History, Culture and Practice,* Vol. 1, *General Topics, Africa, Asia, Middle East, and Oceania.* Santa Barbara, CA: ABC-CLIO, 2012.

Pereira-Palhinas, Clarisse. "Physical Culture and Sport." In *History of Humanity: The Twentieth Century,* Vol. 7, edited by Sarvepalli Gopal and Sergei L. Tikhvinsky, 447–463. Abingdon, UK: Routledge, 2008.

Smart, Barry. *The Sport Star: Modern Sport and the Cultural Economy of Sporting Celebrity.* London: Sage, 2005.

Weber, Eugen. *Peasants into Frenchmen: The Modernization of Rural France, 1870–1914.* Stanford, CA: Stanford University Press, 1976.

LAWNMOWER RACING

Lawnmower racing is a fairly new innovation in motorsport in which bladeless lawnmowers are ridden in races over a certain distance or in an endurance race format. The sport has grown rapidly in recent years and takes place in the United Kingdom, Ireland, Australia, the United States (particularly North Dakota), and Canada. As with all forms of motorsport, lawnmower racing is a fiercely competitive activity that is taken seriously by participants.

Lawnmower racing was invented at the Cricketers Arms pub in Wisborough Green, West Sussex, England, in 1973 when a group of beer drinkers, including motorsport consultant Jim Gavin, discussed how expensive it was to become

Competitors race bladeless lawnmowers during a lawnmower racing event. Lawnmowers can be raced over a certain distance or in an endurance race format. (buzbuzzer/iStockphoto.com)

involved in motorsport. The group began to consider potential alternative, cheaper, yet still enjoyable forms of motorsport and came upon the idea of lawnmower racing. That same year the first lawnmower-racing meeting, the British Grand Prix, was held at Wisborough Green, attracting 35 competitors driving lawnmowers ranging from a vintage Atco lawnmower from 1923 to a modern 8-horsepower tractor. The Grand Prix consisted of races for different types of lawnmower, including run-behind mowers, towed-seat mowers, and sit-on mowers. The year 1973 also saw the inaugural British Lawn Mower Racing Association (BLMRA) Endurance Championship. The event is held at a racing track in the English village of Five Oaks, near Horsham in West Sussex, and comprises 12-hour, 6-hour, and 3-hour races for teams of three. In 2013 the 12-hour race was started by British actor Warwick Davis, who was presenting a British television program on unusual family days out in Britain.

During the 1970s lawnmower racing in the United Kingdom saw an upsurge in popularity, with over 100 enthusiasts owning mowers used exclusively for racing. The sport was given a huge boost in 1975 when British Formula 1 legend Sir Stirling Moss made his return to motorsport after a near-fatal motor-racing crash when he entered and won the British Grand Prix for lawnmowers and also triumphed at the event the following year. In recent years other Formula 1 stars have also taken to the sport, including English drivers Martin Brundle, Anthony Davidson, and Johnny Herbert and Finnish Formula 1 world champion Kimi Raikkonen.

In America, the U.S. Lawn Mower Racing Association was established in 1992 and hosts around 15 events every year, including the STA-BIL Keeps Gas Fresh

Finals and the Challenge of Champions that takes place in Delaware, Ohio. The association also organizes a season-long points competition.

The lawnmower racing divisions established in the United Kingdom in 1973 form the present-day lawnmower racing classifications that are Group 1 (run-behind), Group 2 (towed-seat), Group 3 (sit-on), and Group 4 (lawn tractors). Group 1 mowers are the most basic form of self-propelled, roller-driven lawnmower designed to cut grass for domestic purposes, and their race speed is determined by the athletic ability of the person running behind the machine. Group 1 relay races tend to be particularly good for spectators to watch, as the drivers have to exchange places without losing control of their run-behind machine.

Group 2 lawnmowers are roller-driven cylinder mowers of the type used to prepare the grass at sporting venues such as cricket pitches but with the addition of a towed-seat at the back of the machine. Common makes of Group 2 mower include Atco, Webb, and Clio 2. Group 3 mowers are wheel-driven mowers with an original engine power up to 18 horsepower and with no obvious hood. This group of mower was originally designed and sold to mow domestic lawns, and like Group 2 mowers, Group 3 machines require a great deal of modification to become race-worthy. However, Group 3 mowers are generally the fastest, able to reach speeds up to 50 miles per hour. Wheel-driven lawn tractors used in Group 4 are very similar to the mowers in Group 3 except that Group 4 machines have a front-mounted engine encased within a hood. Like Group 3 machines, Group 4 mowers have a top speed of 50 miles per hour, and as is the case with Group 3 mowers, anybody adapting a Group 4 mower must check with the BLMRA to see that their modifications are "homologated," that is, that they conform to BLMRA standards.

Similar to lawnmower racing is the Weyerhaeser 200 World Championship Rotary Tiller Race, the only race of its kind, that has been held at the Purple-Hull Pea Festival in Emerson, Arkansas, since 1990. The race is run on a track measuring 200 feet in length, with competitors divided into two classifications: stock, for unmodified tillers, and modified, for tillers that have been adapted by their owners (there are eight divisions of modified tiller). The first-ever race was won by 16-year-old Jason Hines, driving a tiller modified for speed (Hines would go on to win the race three times). Indeed, today tillers are often built from scratch without any original tiller parts. Over the next couple of years the tillers entered into the race were increasingly modified to drive faster, leading race organizers to fear for racers' safety. As a result, in 1993 organizers took the contentious decision to hold the race on plowed soil in order to slow down the tillers. In 1994 festival organizers established the semiautonomous World Tiller Racing Federation. Since then the race has seen various changes to both rules and the tillers themselves, including the addition of a women's division in 2002. The current world record for tiller racing is held by Shane Waller of Junction City, who in 2009 completed the race in 5.59 seconds, while Erica Butler of Springhill, Louisiana, set the record for the women's race in 2005 with a time of 6.19 seconds.

Meanwhile, another sport similar to lawnmower racing is shovel racing, which was invented by off-duty ski lift operators in Angel Fire, New Mexico. Traditional shovel racing sees a driver sit in the bucket of a standard grain scoop, with the handle positioned between the pilot's legs in line with the face. The pilots then use their hands to control the shovel. In order to ensure that the shovel moves well, it is usual for competitors to wax their shovel using car wax, Teflon, or, bizarrely, ham luncheon meat. In addition to traditional shovel racing, competitors may also enter two other classifications of shovel racing: light-modified and super-modified snow shovels. Both types of shovel employ a nitrogen-filled pneumatic brake system and hand or foot brakes. A light-modified shovel, which resembles a street luge, weighs less than 100 pounds, can reach a speed of 74 miles per hour, and does not require a roll bar or that the pilot wear a harness, unlike a supermodified snow shovel, which must be fitted with a roll cage of harness, weighs between 100 and 500 pounds, and has a top speed of 79 miles per hour. The first Shovel Racing World Championship was held in Angel Fire in the 1970s, only to be discontinued in 2005 at least in part due to safety concerns. However, the world championship was restarted in 2010, with only traditional, unmodified shovels allowed to take part at the championships that saw helmet-wearing men, women, and children compete for cash and prizes by zooming down a 1,200-foot snow track at speeds up to 60 miles per hour. The dangerous nature of modified shovel racing resulted in the sport being removed from the X Games competition in 1997 after a competitor suffered a broken back and leg in addition to internal bleeding.

See also: Street Luge; Volcano Boarding; Wingsuiting; Zorbing

Further Reading

Adler, Jill. "Snow Shovel Racing Returns to Angel Fire Feb. 6." On the Snow, December 21, 2009, http://www.onthesnow.co.uk/news/a/10004/snow-shovel-racing-returns-to-angel-fire-feb—6 (accessed July 29, 2014).

BSkyB. "Lawnmower Racing with Kimi." Sky Sports, July 6, 2014, http://www1.skysports.com/watch/video/sports/f1/9373418/lawnmower-racing-with-kimi (accessed July 29, 2014).

Dailey, Bill. "Emerson PurpleHull Pea Festival & World Championship Rotary Tiller Race." The Encyclopedia of Arkansas History & Culture, October 8, 2009, http://www.encyclopediaofarkansas.net/encyclopedia/entry-detail.aspx?entryID=4391 (accessed July 29, 2014).

"Lawn Mower Racing: The Alternative Motor Sport?" British Lawnmower Museum, http://www.lawnmowerworld.co.uk/gallery.php?location=2 (accessed July 29, 2014).

"Lawn Mower Racing World Championship Takes Place in Sussex—Video." The Guardian, July 15, 2013, http://www.theguardian.com/sport/video/2013/jul/15/lawn-mower-racing-sussex-video (accessed July 29, 2014).

"Racing Groups." British Lawn Mower Racing Association, http://www.blmra.co.uk/racinggroups (accessed July 29, 2014).

Rosen, Michael J., and Ben Kassoy. *No Dribbling the Squid: Octopush, Shin Kicking, Elephant Polo and Other Oddball Sports.* Kansas City: Andrews McMeel, 2009.

"Sussex." *Weekend Escapes with Warwick Davis,* Season 1, Episode 2, April 18, 2014, ITV London.

"Sussex Hosts Annual Lawnmower Endurance Race." The Telegraph, August 12, 2013, http://www.telegraph.co.uk/news/newstopics/howaboutthat/10237921/Sussex-hosts-annual-lawnmower-endurance-race.html (accessed July 29, 2014).

LUCHA LIBRE

Lucha libre, meaning "free wrestling" or "free struggle," is a highly choreographed form of wrestling that emphasizes spectacle and theatricality. The sport is indigenous to Mexico and is popular in Spanish-speaking countries. *Lucha libre* is governed by the Consejo Mundial de *Lucha Libre* (Worldwide Commission of *Lucha Libre*), which requires wrestlers to undergo five years of training before being granted a wrestling license.

Today the term *lucha libre* is most often applied to professional wrestling, but in earlier times the term referred to an amateur wrestling style akin to Greco-Roman wrestling. A male *lucha libre* wrestler is known as a *luchador,* while a female wrestler is called a *luchadora. Lucha libre* began in 1933 when Salvador Lutteroth Gonzales founded the Empresa Mexicana de *Lucha Libre* (Mexican Company of *Lucha Libre*). The earliest fights featured foreign wrestlers, such as the American Bobby Sampson, together with native Mexican wrestlers. However, *lucha libre* soon flourished, and imported star wrestlers were no longer necessary to attract an audience, though wrestlers from the United States and Japan still compete in *lucha libre.* Indeed, in 1956 the Arena Mexico was opened, which was able to accommodate 20,000 spectators. Other important wrestling arenas include the Arena Revolucion, the Arena

Brazo de Plata launches himself from the top rope as he prepares to flatten two rivals during a *lucha libre* bout held in the historic Arena Coliseo in Mexico City, Mexico, in 2006. *Lucha libre* is big business with promoters battling to produce the most dramatic fights. (AP Photo)

Coliseo, and the Juan de le Barred Arena, all located in Mexico City, and the Arena Coliseo and Arena Victoria in Guadalajara. Wrestlers featured in inaugural fights at the Arena Mexico included El Santo, meaning "The Saint," the stage name of Rodolfo Guzman Huerto (1917–1984) who would go on to become an iconic figure in *lucha libre*. The most iconic female wrestler is perhaps Martha Villalobos (real name Martha Garcia Majia), who at 228 pounds cut a striking figure in the ring, where she was an expert at performing the *corbata,* the lock move most feared by female wrestlers.

Today *lucha libre* is big business, with promoters and companies battling to produce the most dramatic fights, of which there are four main types: one-on-one, pairs, trios, and tag-team events in which the number of wrestlers per tag team is uncapped. Bouts featuring quartets, women, and dwarves (referred to as minis) are also held. The four main categories are further divided into five weight divisions: heavyweight, light heavyweight, welterweight, cruiserweight, and middleweight. Several titles are disputed throughout the year, each relating to a different weight category.

Lucha libre sees wrestlers perform hand-to-hand combat with the intention of causing the opponent to surrender. To win a bout, which has no time limit, a wrestler must achieve two out of three falls. One particularly controversial aspect of *lucha libre* is that detractors question the sporting integrity of match results. In *lucha libre,* wrestlers or teams are assigned the role of either goodie and baddie, known as *technio* (pl. *technicos* and meaning "technical") and *rudo* (pl. *rudos* and meaning "crude"). The *technio* wrestlers aim to use skill and technique to achieve victory, while the *rudo* wrestlers employ illicit means to win, such as smuggling weapons into the ring or trying to escape the ring in order to avoid injury. However, it is quite usual for spectators of *lucha libre* to root for the *rudos* in a form of love-hate relationship rather than to cheer on the *technicos.* That said, the *technios* do have a loyal fan base consisting mainly of young children to whom the wrestlers are role models.

Irrespective of whether a wrestler is a *technio* or a *rudo,* all wrestlers assume a stage name, which is reflected in their costume. The stage personas may reflect a social type, such as El Mestizo, meaning a person of mixed race, or El Huichol, meaning an indigenous person. Other wrestlers use their persona to express political opinion. For example, stage names have included El Zapatista (The Zapatista) after the growth in popularity of the Ejercito Zapatista de Liberacion Nacional (Zapatista Army for National Liberation) in 1994.

One of the key elements of *lucha libre* is that the wrestlers wear masks, the color and design of which must coordinate with the rest of their costume and reflect the character of their stage persona. It is the ultimate shame for a wrestler to have his or her mask removed by an opponent; any wrestler who does unmask another is disqualified with immediate effect. In fact, such is the pride that wrestlers attach to their masks that Guzman Huerto was buried wearing his El Santo mask.

The flamboyance and good-versus-evil elements of *lucha libre* mean that the sport has been featured in many films. In Mexico the *Santos* film series, which spanned three decades (1961–1982), saw Guzman Huerto (in his guise of El Santo) play out a number of scenarios in which the costumed wrestler fought supernatural figures such as vampires in *Santo contra las mujeras vampiros* (Santo against the Vampire Women, 1962) and aliens in *Santo contra la invasion de los marcianos* (Santo against the Martian Invasion, 1966). These films helped the character of El Santo assume almost mythical status. In 1993 Guzman Huerto's son, who wrestles under the alias Hijo del Santo, or Son of the Saint, starred in *Santo, la layenda del enmascarado de plata* (Santo, Legend of the Man in the Silver Mask), in which he played his father. *Lucha libre* has also featured in Hollywood films such as *Nacho Libre* (2006), starring Jack Black.

See also: Celtic Wrestling; *Glima;* Korean Wrestling; Mongolian Wrestling; *Pehlwani/Kushti; Schwingen;* Sumo Wrestling; *Varzesh-e Bastani*

Further Reading

Grobet, Lourdes. *Espectacular de lucha libre.* Colonia Escandon, Mexico: Trilce Ediciones, 2004.

Levi, Heather. *The World of Lucha Libre: Secrets, Revelations and Mexican National Identity.* Durham, NC: Duke University Press, 2008.

Saragoza, Alex M., Ana Paula Ambrosi, and Silvia D. Zárate, eds. *Mexico Today: An Encyclopedia of Life in the Republic,* Vol. 1. Santa Barbara, CA: ABC-CLIO, 2012.

Shaw, Lisa, and Stephanie Dennison. *Pop Culture Latin America! Media, Arts and Lifestyle.* Santa Barbara, CA: ABC-CLIO, 2005.

MALLAKHAMB

Mallakhamb is a traditional Indian sport in which participants, both men and women as well as children, perform gymnastic moves and yogic poses known as asanas using a vertical wooden pole, a cane, and a rope or similar apparatus. The sport is sometimes referred to as Indian pole gymnastics and is most commonly played in Maharashtra, western India, though in ancient times the sport was also popular in the southern city of Hyderabad. The *mallakhamb* practitioner must shift around the pole or rope and demonstrate as many poses as possible without touching the ground. The word *mallakhamb* is derived from the words *malla,* meaning "gymnast" or "man of strength," and *khamb,* meaning "pole," and therefore can be translated as "pole gymnastics." The word *mallakhamb* refers to both the sport and the apparatus used to perform poses. *Mallakhamb* gymnasts are required to have great core strength, as the sport engages the abdominal muscles as well as the muscles in the back, legs, arms, and thighs. Great flexibility is also needed to achieve the yogic poses, as are balance, breath control, and concentration. *Mallakhamb* is also reported to improve the function of the circulatory system. Exponents of *mallakhamb* suggest that the sport is holistic in nature, for they believe that the unique combination of gymnastics and yoga represented by *mallakhamb* provides a perfect union of meditation and gymnastic exercise that allows the practitioner to achieve a healthy mind and body.

The origins of *mallakhamb* are somewhat clouded. The first written reference to *mallakhamb* can be traced back to the 12th century, when the sport was referred to in the Sanskrit text *Manasollas* written by Somesvara Chalukya in 1135. The sport then lay dormant for several centuries until it was revived by Balambhatta Dada Deodhar, the master wrestler to Peshwa Bajirao II, who ruled the Maratha Empire during 1796–1818. Legend has it that *mallakhamb* developed after two champion wrestlers came to Pune in the west of India and challenged the local wrestlers living at the Peshwa court to a wrestling bout. The strangers were considered unbeatable, and only Balambhatta accepted the challenge. In order to defeat the newcomers, Balambhatta decided to observe the movement of monkeys, which he considered to be nature's ultimate gymnasts, and having seen the way monkeys maneuvered through tree branches, Balambhatta opted to incorporate pole climbing into his preparations for the wrestling match. Balambhatta went on to win the bout, and thus *mallakhamb* was initiated as a training regime used in *kushti,* or Indian wrestling. *Mallakhamb* helped wrestlers build muscle and improve their flexibility, with the pole shaped vaguely like a man to remind the wrestlers of their

Indian army soldiers blow fire as they perform *mallakhamb* during a demonstration of skills held at the Officers Training Academy in Chennai, India, on March 15, 2013. *Mallakhamb* is a traditional Indian sport in which participants perform gymnastic moves and yogic poses using a vertical pole, a rope, or similar apparatus. (AP Photo/Arun Sankar K.)

ever-present opponent. The pole took the place of a training partner and was used to develop jumping leg locks.

As a form of body building, there were 16 forms of *mallakhamb* developed. However, as a sport there are around 6 common forms of *mallakhamb*. Plain *mallakhamb* uses a tapering wooden pole that is fixed to the ground. The pole is usually made of a tough yet smooth wood such as teak or sheesham (a rosewood native to the Indian subcontinent) and is 225 centimeters (89 inches) tall. The pole is 55 centimeters (22 inches) thick at its base, tapering to 45 centimeters (18 inches) in the center and 30 centimeters (12 inches) at the tip. The neck of the *mallakhamb* pole is 20 centimeters (8 inches) in height and 15 centimeters (6 inches) in circumference, and the upper knob is 26 centimeters (10 inches) in diameter. Hanging *mallakhamb* employs a smaller version of the plain *mallakhamb* pole suspended from hooks and chains. Performing *mallakhamb* poses on a swinging pole is much more difficult than on a fixed pole because of the increased instability of the equipment. Cane or rope *mallakhamb* became popular about 30 years ago, and in this version of the sport a cotton rope 2.5 centimeters (less than 1 inch) thick is used in place of the pole. In rope *mallakhamb*, performers create yogic poses without knotting the rope, and so rope *mallakhamb* is very close in nature to the Indian rope tricks of old. Like hanging *mallakhamb*, rope *mallakhamb* is more difficult to perform than plain *mallakhamb* because of the instability of the apparatus. Rope *mallakhamb* requires great focus and balance. A more recent from of *mallakhamb* is revolving bottle *mallakhamb*. In this form of the sport, 32 glass bottles are placed on a wooden platform, with the mallkhamb balanced on top of the bottles. Other recent innovations in *mallakhamb* include baseless *mallakhamb*, fixed-bottle *mallakhamb,* inclined *mallakhamb,* and suspended *mallakhamb.* A team version of the sport, pyramid *mallakhamb,* requires teams to build attractive human pyramids within a stipulated time limit.

Recently an artistic form of *mallakhamb* has begun to evolve in India after the *mallakhamb* troop Mallakhamb India won instant fame performing on the television show *India's Got Talent.* A choreographed *mallakhamb* sequence was also included in the 2005 Bollywood film *Kisna.* However, it is important to note that dance-inspired *mallakhamb* is not related to pole dancing.

Catalonia's Human Towers

For the past 200 years in the Catalonia region of Spain, teams have competed at the friendly sport of building the most elaborate human vertical structures possible, called *castells* (castles). A common sight at festivals in the region, *castells* can reach up to 10 floors high, usually with a small child (wearing a crash helmet) placed at the top of the construction. The tallest *castell* ever was a *3 de 10,* meaning a 10-floor *castell* with 3 people on each floor. In 2010 *castells* were added to the UNESCO Intangible Cultural Heritage List.

Despite the long history of *mallakhamb* in India, the sport is relatively unknown in the country, so regular *mallakhamb* championships are held to keep the sport alive. For the past 25 years, players from 29 Indian states have taken part in the national *mallakhamb* championships, and state-level contests have been held since 1990. One-day championships such as the All Orissa Mallakhamb Championship are also held, with practitioners taking part in four categories: senior, junior, sub-junior, and mini. However, while some worry about *mallakhamb's* future in India, the sport is gaining popularity in other parts of the world, particularly Europe. This is most likely because of the similarities between *mallakhamb* and yoga.

See also: Capoeira; *Parkour; Pehlwani/Kushti;* Rhythmic Gymnastics; Yoga

Further Reading

Bhave, Chinmaye. "Indian roots to gymnastics." December 6, 2007, NDTV Sports, http://sports.ndtv.com/othersports/athletics/34909-indian-roots-to-gymnastics (accessed July 23, 2013).

Boerema, Devi. "Mallkhamb: It's All about Strength and Flexibility." Radio Netherlands Worldwide, June 28, 2012, http://www.rnw.nl/english/article/mallakhamb-its-all-about-strength-and-flexibility (accessed July 23, 2013).

Dano, C. "Mallakhamb—Indian Pole Gymnastics." Yoga Horizons, April 20, 2011, http://yoga-horizons.com/2011/04/mallakhamb-indian-pole-gymnastics/ (accessed July 23, 2013).

"Mallakhamb." Sports in India, http://sports.indiapress.org/mallakhamb.php (July 23, 2013).

"Mallakhamb India—The Authentic Sport." Mallakhamb India, 2006, http://www.mallkhambindia.com/#home (accessed July 23, 2013).

"Mallakhamb Vies for Pole Position . . . Bottoms Up." The Sunday Indian, http://www .thesundayindian.com/article_print.php?article_id=2115 (accessed July 23, 2013).

Patnaik, Sunil. "Dying 12th Century Sport Gets a Lifeline." *The Telegraph,* November 3, 2011, http://www.telegraphindia.com/1111103/jsp/orissa/story_14698853.jsp (accessed July 23, 2013).

MÖLKKY

Mölkky is a Finnish throwing game played either on a one-on-one basis or by teams. *Mölkky* is most often played outside on grass or sand, though an indoor version called *tupa mölkky* is a recent innovation. The Keralian term *mölkky* means "baby's bottom," while *molkata* is a term found in 19th-century scientific dictionaries referring to something that moves back and forth making sound.

Mölkky is similar to the Keralian game of *kyykkä*, though playing *mölkky* requires less physical strength than playing *kyykkä*. *Mölkky* can be played by males and females of any age, with accuracy and hand-eye coordination more important than physical fitness when playing the game. A game of *mölkky* sees players throw a lightweight throwing pin, also called a *mölkky,* horizontally through the air using an underarm throwing action in order to knock over skittles of a similar size to that of the throwing pin. Both the pin and the skittles are made of wood hewn from trees grown in sustainable Finnish forests. The skittles to be knocked down are marked with numbers from 1 to 12, and at the start of a game of *mölkky* the skittles are stood upright and are arranged in a tight grouping of four rows about 10 feet from the throwing area, where the players stand to throw the pin. At the beginning of a game the skittles take the following formation: the first row consists of skittles marked with the numbers 1 and 2; the second row holds skittles 3, 10, and 4; the third row holds skittles 5, 11, 12 and 6, and the fourth row holds skittles 7, 9, and 8. A game of *mölkky* is won by the first player to reach exactly 50 points. Any player whose score exceeds 50 points is penalized by being docked 25 points. The *mölkky* scoring system is such that players must decide on the best tactics to reach the necessary 50 points, for knocking over a solitary skittle earns the number of points written on top of the skittle. So, for example, knocking down the skittle marked 9 will accrue 9 points, while knocking over multiple skittles with one throw of the *mölkky* earns a player the number of skittles knocked over; thus, knocking over four skittles at once scores 4 points. Therefore, using skill and judgment, players must decide how best to achieve 50 points exactly. Points are only earned if the skittle is knocked over in such a way that it lands parallel with the ground—if the skittle is knocked over so that it leans on the thrown *mölkky,* then no points are earned. Similarly, no points are earned for knocking a skittle so that it rests at an angle on another numbered skittle. If a player fails to hit any skittles three times in a row, he or she is disqualified from the game and must take on the role of scorekeeper. After each throw of the *mölkky* the skittles are lifted and replaced vertically in the exact spot where they fell, so during a game of *mölkky* the skittles spread across the playing area.

> ## The Finnish Sport of Cell Phone Throwing
>
> Cell phone throwing began in Savonlinna, Finland, in 2000. Since then the sport's popularity has increased, with annual national championships held in a number of countries. Competitors are judged on distance thrown and throwing technique and are usually divided into four categories: traditional, in which participants pitch over the shoulder to achieve the farthest throw; freestyle, in which contestants earn points for choreography; team original, which sees up to three competitors throw once each with their scores totaled; and a junior competition. The world record throw stands at 101.46 meters (332 feet 10 inches).

Since the mid-1990s *mölkky* sets and equipment have been manufactured by the Tuoterengas company using offcuts of wood left over from manufacturing other items, and the company owns the *mölkky* trademark.

The Mölkky World Championships were inaugurated in 1997 and take place in Lahti, Finland, with teams of four players competing for the title.

See also: Aunt Sally; Bandy; Bunnock; *Kubb; Kyykkä; Lapta;* Nordic Walking; Skittles; Wife Carrying

Further Reading

"Hard to Say, Easy to Play." Molkky, http://www.molkky.com (accessed July 30, 2013).
"Home." Molkyn MM—Kisat, http://mm-molkky.fi (accessed July 30, 2013).
"A Piece of History of Molkky." Molkyn MM—Kisat, http://mm-molkky.fi/historia-history/ (accessed July 30, 2013).

MONGOLIAN WRESTLING

Mongolian wrestling, also known as *bökh* (meaning "wrestling," "wrestler," "sturdiness," and "being strong"), is a form of folk wrestling found in Mongolia, Russia, China, and Inner Mongolia (an autonomous region of China). The sport is exclusively practiced by males. *Bökh* is an integral part of Mongolian culture and life, though the *bökh* practiced in Inner Mongolia differs from that practiced in Mongolia in general. *Bökh* is an important leisure activity of Mongolian children and teenagers and also makes up part of the Mongolian national Naadam festival and *ovoo* worship ceremonies. *Bökh* is also traditionally one of the "three manly skills" of the Mongols—wrestling, archery, and horsemanship—that are held in great reverence and are closely linked to the pastoral nomadic customs of the people of the Central Asian steppe region.

The roots of Mongolian wrestling can be traced back to the Xiongnu Empire (209 BCE–93 CE), while depictions of Mongolian wrestlers have been found on bronze tablets discovered in the Shanglin Garden of the Han Dynasty (206 BCE–220 CE) in Keshengzhuang, Xian, Shanxi Province, in neighboring China. In these early days *bökh* was an important way of keeping military forces physically fit, and the lack of ground work in Mongolian wrestling harks back to the time when wrestling was a military pursuit. As the Mongol Army consisted solely of cavalry units,

Mongolian wrestlers compete at the Nadaam Games in Mongolia. In general Mongolian wrestlers aim to force any part of their opponent's back, elbow, or knee to the ground using a variety of lifts, trips, and throws. (Pniesen/Dreamstime.com)

a soldier on the ground would most likely be trampled to death by horses or killed by the enemy; thus, soldiers were not expected to be on the ground at any point. During the era of Genghis Khan (ca. 1162–1227), the founder of the largest connecting empire in history known as the Mongol Empire, the favorite leisure activities of Mongolian warriors were wrestling, archery, and horsemanship.

Mongolian wrestling differs greatly from Western-style wrestling, for in Mongolian wrestling there are no weight categories or (usually) time limits (until recently matches could last as long as three hours). Also, matches take place outside on grass, usually during holidays. Wrestlers wear a highly distinctive outfit that varies between Mongolian and Inner Mongolian styles of *bökh*. Mongolian wrestlers wear a traditional Mongolian cap (which is removed by the referee before a match begins), traditional boots, briefs, and a cropped tight-fitting top, the latter two of which are made from silk and either heavy cloth or tear-resistant nylon. The top exposes a wrestler's chest but is held on by a length of rope that extends from both sides of the top's opening and is tied around the stomach. According to Mongolian folklore, the combination of briefs and frontless shirts came about when a woman disguised as a man won a wrestling event, and from then on wrestlers had to compete bare-chested and in skimpy attire on their lower body to avoid any future subterfuge. Inner Mongolians wear long, loose pants; a metal-studded leather top that exposes their chest; and more highly decorated boots. Inner Mongolian wrestlers do not wear a cap, though ranked wrestlers do sport a necklace called a *jangga*.

Mongolian wrestlers aim to force any part of their opponent's back, elbow, or knee to the ground using a variety of trips, throws, and lifts (in Inner Mongolian *bökh* a wrestler wins if he forces any part of his opponent's body above the knee to the ground). It is illegal for wrestlers to throttle or hit an opponent or to twist or hyperextend opponent's joints. In addition to this, Inner Mongolian wrestlers may not use their hands to grasp an opponent's leg. Two men who act as referees (and also as corner men) ensure that wrestlers adhere to the rules and declare the winner. However, if a match seems to be at a stalemate, with the wrestlers in a clinch and not moving, then the more aggressive wrestler of the two is awarded the win. It is important to note that while Mongolian wrestling is a full-contact sport requiring brute strength, great emphasis is placed on fair play and good sportsmanship.

Mongolian wrestling matches begin with a ritualistic dance in which each wrestler depicts a bird in flight, either a great falcon or, more usually, the mythical *khangarid* (known as the *garuda* in other cultures) that is the emblem of Ulaanbaatar, the capital of Mongolia, and is said to embody courage and honesty. In the Inner Mongolian wrestling style wrestlers depict an eagle, as in Mongolia eagles are greatly revered for their bravery and dignity. In both traditions the wrestler is supposed to imagine the sky and Earth while dancing—the sky because it symbolizes heavenly blessings and Earth for stability. The dance exhibits the wrestlers' strength and technique and also serves as a prematch warm-up to loosen the muscles. At the end of a match the winning wrestler performs a more flamboyant version of the dance. In addition to this, the losing wrestler must walk under the victor's right arm as he celebrates. Wrestlers who win several matches are given epithets, usually of noble or great beasts. A championship-winning wrestler is known as an *arslan,* or lion. The runner-up is a *dzan,* or elephant, and a third-placed competitor is a *nachin,* or eagle. The lowest-rated wrestler is likened to a hawk.

The finale of the Mongolian sporting year is the three-day annual festival of Nadaam, meaning "celebration" or "games," which is held the second week of July in Ulaanbaatar to mark the country's independence. At Nadaam, wrestling, archery, and horsemanship are celebrated, and though only wrestlers with a national ranking may compete in the Nadaam *bökh* contest, the event still features around 500 competitors. Before Nadaam, local and regional contests open to all are held across Mongolia to find competitors, and contestants and organizers spend around two months training and practicing before the festival starts. A few days prior to the beginning of Nadaam, preliminary wrestling bouts are held on an elimination basis to whittle down the number of competitors. Winners advance via a pyramid-style competition format of nine rounds so that the two last remaining wrestlers face each other in the final. The final is held at the 15,000-seat stadium in Ulaanbaatar, with all seats filled and an additional mass of spectators standing in a roped-off section of ground on the far side of the stadium. To start the final bout, the wrestlers enter the playing surface from opposite sides of the ring and perform the traditional prematch dance, only this time they imitate the animals indicating the top three ranks of wrestler—the lion, elephant, and eagle. After the bout the winning wrestler is paraded up to the grandstand, where he is proclaimed by government officials and others of note. The champion then returns to the site of his victory and is given fermented mare's milk, or *kumiss,* to drink, while sweets are thrown into the crowd. This prompts little boys to scramble for the confectionary, as Mongolian tradition holds that any boy who takes possession of this candy will share in the champion wrestler's strength and bravery.

Any wrestler who wins the Nadaam competition two years running is known as *avrag,* or titan, and wrestlers who achieve this level become national heroes and pass into legend. Mongolian wrestler Tuvdendorj, who competed during the 1950s and 1960s, was crowned titan three times, a lion four times, and an elephant six times.

A midwinter wrestling tournament is also held in Ulaanbaatar, and an Inner Mongolian wrestling tournament is part of the annual Minority People's Athletic Tournament held in the Inner Mongolian town of Tongliao. Mongolian wrestling also takes place at *ovoo* worship ceremonies. An *ovoo* is a type of pre-Buddhist Mongolian cairn made of rocks or wood that is usually found on top of mountains or at other high-altitude locations and is used in folk religious ceremonies, usually in shamanistic worship of the skies and ground. Annual *ovoo* ceremonies are held in Mongolia that take the form of social and sporting events and include traditional wrestling tournaments.

Bökh is a highly influential form of wrestling. It is thought to have been influential in the development of *shuai chiao,* the native wrestling of China, and the training received by Mongolian wrestlers has allowed some to compete in sumo wrestling and even to bring innovation to the Japanese sport.

Asashōryū, Mongolia's first-ever sumo grand champion, dominated the sport for three consecutive years and managed the unprecedented feat of winning all six major sumo tournaments in a calendar year. However, Asashōryū was considered pugnacious and violent by Japanese spectators for his seemingly disrespectful attitude toward the strict codes of sumo, and he was forced to retire after several controversial incidents. Many other Mongolian wrestlers who become sumo wrestlers because they are tempted to Japan by talent scouts also struggle to adapt to the world of sumo. However, some do succeed by gaining weight, learning Japanese, and conforming to sumo's strict cultural traditions. One Mongolian wrestler, D. Batbayar, has proved particularly successful in Japan by using wrestling moves that are frequently employed in Mongolian wrestling but have been forgotten by sumo wrestlers. Meanwhile, other Mongolian wrestlers are branching out and using their skills in other sports, including judo.

See also: Camel and Yak Racing; Celtic Wrestling; *Glima;* Korean Wrestling; *Lucha Libre; Pehlwani/Kushti; Schwingen;* Sumo Wrestling; *Varzesh-e Bastani; Yagli Gures*

Further Reading

Adams, Andy. "The Maulers of Mongolia." *Black Belt* 7(7) (July 1969): 22–27.

Bruun, Ole. *Precious Steppe: Mongolian Nomadic Pastoralists in Pursuit of the Market.* Lanham, MD: Lexington Books, 2006.

Cheng, Mark. "In Search of Mongolia's Fighting Arts." *Black Belt* 38(6) (June 2000): 20.

Dianwen, Du. "The Ovoo Worship Ceremony: A Grassland Festival." Translated by Zhu Meng. China's Ethnic Groups, 2011, http://www.ceg.com.cn/2011/11E-4Q/11ceg -4n3.htm (accessed July 30, 2014).

Green, Thomas A., and Joseph R. Svinth. *Martial Arts of the World: An Encyclopedia of History and Innovation,* Vol. 2. Santa Barbara, CA: ABC-CLIO, 2010.

Hanson, Jennifer L. *Nations in Transition: Mongolia.* New York: Facts on File, 2004.

Jung-Sheng, Chang. "Introduction to Mongolian Wrestling." *Mongolian and Tibetan Quarterly* 18(4) (2009), http://www.mtac.gov.tw/mtac_quarterly/quarterly_e/4/1376573586 .pdf (accessed July 30, 2014).

"Sumo on the Steppes." Aljazeera, August 16, 2013, http://www.aljazeera.com/programmes/101east/2013/08/201381210530145349.html (accessed July 30, 2014).

"Wrestling, Archery and Horse-Racing: Mongolia's 'Three Manly Games.'" CNN, August 22, 2011, http://edition.cnn.com/2011/TRAVEL/08/17/mongolia.naadam/ (accessed July 30, 2014).

NETBALL

Netball is a ball team sport involving running, jumping, throwing, and catching. Netball is predominantly played by women and tends to be played by teams of seven, depending on the version of the game being played. Netball is played across the globe. On the African continent netball is particularly popular in the countries of South Africa, Namibia, Botswana, and Lesotho, while in Asia netball is mostly played in India, Singapore, Malaysia, and Sri Lanka. Netball is played in Australia and New Zealand and in Pacific nations such as the Cook Islands, Samoa, and Fiji as well as in the United States, the West Indies, and the United Kingdom, where the Netball SuperLeague, which began in 2005, is the major elite club championship. Teams from England, Wales, and Scotland contest the Netball SuperLeague over a season lasting from November to June, and games from the Netball SuperLeague are often broadcast on satellite television, thanks to a major television deal signed in 2006. In Australasia the major elite club championship is the ANZ Championship, a joint venture between Netball Australia and Netball New Zealand that takes place between April and July. The ANZ Championship is contested by 10 teams, 5 from Australia and 5 from New Zealand, and the championship has had such an impact on the sport that netball has become a semiprofessional sport in both countries.

Netball is played at all levels from school physical education classes up to Olympic level, for in 1995 netball was recognized as a sport by the International Olympic Committee, though the game has never been included at the Olympic Games. Netball has, however, been included in the Commonwealth Games since 1988.

Netball developed when women's basketball spread to England from the United States at the end of the 19th century, for in 1893 a sports teacher in London, England's capital city, named Madame Osterberg introduced a version of basketball that was played outside using a net; hence, the game was called "net ball." In 1901 the first rules of the new game were published, and it quickly became popular across the British Empire, where knowledge of the game was disseminated via school systems. At the start of the 20th century the game began to be known as netball, and the sport's popularity grew, especially when it was introduced to Australia and New Zealand. Many leagues and competitions were established, and the first official netball governing body, the All England Netball Association, was established in 1926. However, no standard netball rules existed, and the game was played as both a nine-a-side game and a five-a-side game. Thus, it was extremely difficult to institute international competition. It was not until 1957 when England toured Australia that standardized netball rules were introduced. Subsequently in 1960, representatives from England, Australia, New Zealand, South Africa, the

South Africa's Amanda Mynhardt, right, tries to block New Zealand's Irene van Dyk during a quarterfinal of the Mission Foods World Netball Championships in Singapore, in 2011. Netball involves running, jumping, throwing, and catching as teams try to score as many goals as possible during a match. (AP Photo)

West Indies, and Sri Lanka formed the International Federation of Women's Basketball and Netball, subsequently renamed the International Netball Federation (INF). The new federation established a set of formal rules and decided that the Netball World Championships should take place every four years. The first world championship was held in Eastbourne, southern England, in 1963. Since this inaugural world championship, the tournament has been held in Australia (in 1967), Jamaica (in 1971 and 2003), New Zealand (in 1975, 1999, and 2007), Trinidad and Tobago (in 1979), Singapore (in 1983 and 2011), Scotland (in 1987), Australia (in 1991), and England (in 1995). The 2015 world championships are due to be held in Sydney, Australia. In the past Australia has dominated the tournament, winning in 1971, 1975, 1979, 1983, 1991, 1995, 1999, 2007, and 2011. The only other nation to win the title is New Zealand, in 2003. In 1988 a Netball Youth Tournament was held in Australia's capital city, Canberra, as part of the country's Bicentenary Celebrations. The event proved so popular that it was decided to hold a youth tournament for players under 21 years of age every four years. The youth tournament has been hosted by Fiji, Canada, Wales, the United States, and the Cook Islands, with the winners being Australia (in 1988, 1996, 2000, and 2009) and New Zealand (in 1992 and 2005).

The aim of the game is for a team to score as many goals as possible from within an area on the court called the goal circle. This is a semicircle centered on the goal line that has a radius measuring 16 feet. Only two players from each team—the goal attack and the goal shooter—are allowed to score goals. When a goal is scored, play recommences when a player called the center makes a move called a center pass. This move alternates between teams irrespective of which was the last team to score. Netball is played on a court measuring 100 feet long by 50 feet wide that is divided into thirds. Also marked on the court is a center circle with a diameter measuring 3 feet and two goal semicircles with a radius of 16 feet. All lines are part of the court and are 2 inches wide. If during play the ball touches the ground outside the legal playing area, a player from the team that was not the last team to touch the ball throws the ball back onto the court. Play then resumes. Goalposts are located at the midpoint of each goal line and are 10 feet tall. Each goalpost is fitted with a horizontally projecting goal ring that measures 6 inches in length, and each goal ring has an internal diameter of 15 inches. The ball used in netball is made of rubber, leather, or other similar material, weighs 14–16 ounces, and is 27–28 inches in circumference.

A game of netball is made up of four quarters lasting 15 minutes each, with the first and second quarters and third and fourth quarters divided by breaks lasting 3 minutes. Halftime is marked by an interval lasting 5 or 10 minutes.

In netball players are each assigned a playing position that determines the on-court areas in which they may play. The playing positions are indicated by identification letters worn on the front and back of a bib worn on the players' top half. The letters signify a player's objective, the areas of the court in which she may play, and her opponent on the opposite team. The positions are goal shooter (GS), goal attack (GA), wing attack (WA), center (C), wing defense (WD), goal defense (GD), and goalkeeper (GK). The goal shooter is a primarily attacking player whose job is to make herself available to shoot in goal-scoring areas of the court. The goal shooter, who may only operate in the opposing side's goal third, also acts as the first line of defense. The other player allowed to score is the goal attack, who must also defend by marking the opposing side's goal defense. Like the goal shooter, the goal attack may operate in the opposition's goal third but unlike the goal shooter may also work in the center. The wing attack, who operates in the center and the opposition's goal third (but not in the other side's goal circle), feeds the ball to the goal shooter and the goal attack. Since the wing attack players provide the ball for goal-scoring opportunities, players in the wing attack position are often marked by two players from the opposing team in order to prevent them from passing the ball forward to the goal shooter and goal attack. The center is a vitally important role, as the center connects defense and attack and is the only player who can work in all thirds of the court, though not in the goal circles. The center tries to prevent her opposite number from acquiring the ball and often combines with the wing defense to double-mark the opposing center. Wing defense works in both the center and in her own team's goal third but not in the goal circle and must eliminate the opposing wing attack to prevent her from feeding the ball to her own team's goal attack and goal shooter. The wing defense also turns defense into attack by maneuvering the ball up the court. The job of the goal defense, who may play in both the center and her own goal third, is to deny the opposing goal attack the ball to prevent her from scoring. The goalkeeper's role is to prevent the goal shooter on the opposing side from attempting goals, and the goalkeeper may only operate in her own goal third.

The type of passes that players may make can be categorized into one-handed passes and two-handed passes. One-handed passes include the shoulder pass and the hip pass, both of which may be made by all players and vary in length from midlength to long. Similar to the shoulder pass is the overhead pass, in which the player executes the pass above her head; the lob, which is an arching pass made by all players and can be any length; and the bounce, which is a short pass performed by all attacking players but most especially the center and wing attack. Another one-handed pass, the underarm flip pass, is used when an element of surprise is required, while the bullet pass is a fast and direct way of passing the ball that is used over short to medium distances. Two-handed passes include the chest pass and the side pass. The chest pass is performed by a player propelling the ball out from the chest area while stepping forward. This pass, which covers both long and short distances, is used when it is necessary to accurately throw the ball to another player who is in motion. The side pass is a straight throw used when a fast, direct pass is required.

The rules of netball are categorized in one of two ways. First, there are laws that deal with rule infringements that are called minor rules, despite the fact that they make up the majority of the rules. These minor rules include the infringements of holding the ball, stepping or breaking with the ball, and being offside or over a marked third. These infringements are penalized with a free pass. The other type of rule, called major rules, covers incidents that infringe the rights of an opponent. These rules pertain mainly to obstruction, intimidation, contact play, and ill discipline. Such illegal play is penalized with a penalty pass or shot. When a penalty is taken, the offending player must stand out of play until the ball has been thrown. During play, contact between players is only allowed if the contact does not impede another player or play in general, and players must remain at least three feet away from the ball while defending. If contact is made that impedes a player, then a penalty is awarded to the team of the impeded player, and the player who caused the impediment must stand out of play until the player taking the penalty has dispatched the ball.

In 2008 a new version of netball, the Fast Net World Netball Series, was launched. Fast Net is a six-a-side game that debuted at the World Netball Series in Manchester, northern England. Following consultation, Fast Net was further developed into a five-a-side game known as Fast5. This format was launched at the World Netball Series in Auckland, New Zealand, in 2012. Meanwhile, beach netball, as the name suggests, is netball played on a beach. An annual beach netball tournament is held in Singapore.

See also: Bossaball; Eton Wall Game; *Kabaddi*; Kin-Ball; Korfball

Further Reading

"Formats of the Sport." International Netball Federation, 2013–2014, http://www.netball .org/netball/formats-of-the-sport (accessed March 28, 2014).

"History of Netball." International Netball Federation, http://www.netball.org/images /documents/history/history-of-netball-download.pdf (accessed March 8, 2014).

International Netball Federation. "Netball Explained." Netball.org, September 5, 2013, http://www.netball.org/netball/netball-explained (accessed March 28, 2014).

"Netball—History." Teach PE, 2014, http://www.teachpe.com/netball/history.php (accessed March 28, 2014).

"Netball—Major Leagues & Competitions." Teach PE, 2014, http://www.teachpe.com /netball/leagues.php (accessed March 28, 2014).

Woodlands, Jane. *The Netball Handbook*. Champaign, IL: Human Kinetics, 2006.

NIPSY

Nipsy is a team club-and-ball game originating in the county of Yorkshire in the north of England. This is the area with which nipsy is most closely associated, in particular the town of Barnsley, where it is often played by men as a pub game, though it may be played by children too. The game is popular with working-class men and with children, as it requires little in the way of equipment, just a round or egg-shaped object to hit, a stick and a brick, and a playing area, such as a field. Nipsy is akin to other games originating in the region such as knur and spell, peggy and tipcat, and bat and trap, which is played in the south of England. Two similar games, *fiolet* and *la rebatta*, are played in Italy.

The word "nipsy" refers to both the game itself and the object, usually a ball, that players aim to hit as far as possible. To play the game, the nipsy is placed on a brick that tilts backward gently. Next the nipsy is risen, that is, made to shoot into air by clipping it lightly with a stick. Once the nipsy is airborne, the player who clipped it with the stick hits it again, this time with the aim of making the nipsy travel as far as possible. To ensure a good rise, a player may practice rising the nipsy six times before hitting it long distance.

The nipsy is usually made from one of two substances: lignum vitae, an extremely strong and dense wood generally considered to be the world's hardest and heaviest, or a wood substitute traded under the name Permali, as these are the only substances that are sufficiently strong to withstand the hard hitting common in nipsy. Nipsys made of ivory and of hard compound rubber used to be made too, but these are now outlawed mainly because they give an unfair advantage to their owners. Snooker balls were also played, though these too were illegal. In earlier days a miner's pick or a railway braking stick were used to hit the nipsy, as both implements provided a thick head with which to strike. However, these metal tools were superseded by wooden hitting sticks, as it was discovered that thinner hitting heads were more durable and played better. Today the stick used in nipsy is made of one continuous piece of hickory wood or a similar hardwood such as hornbeam and has a head about one inch in thickness with a metal hitting plate.

The future of nipsy looks uncertain at best, with nipsy leagues disbanding due to lack of interest. Another factor threatening nipsy is the difficulty of finding lignum vitae. The reason for the scarcity is twofold. First, the decline of the English coal industry in which picks made of lignum vitae were used to chisel through coal faces means that lignum vitae is difficult to come by. Second, lignum vitae is now an endangered species. The building of houses on public land also threatens nipsy, for it is increasingly difficult to find sufficiently large playing areas, though football pitches can be used in place of a field. However, one possible way of saving nipsy from extinction is initiatives such as that implemented by a Barnsley museum, which relaunched nipsy in Yorkshire schools as part of a project aiming to both celebrate the county's sporting heritage and attract a new generation to games of old.

Similar to nipsy is a team game called peggy, which was once very popular in the north of England, particularly in Yorkshire. Though mainly played by children, pub leagues devoted to peggy used to exist in Yorkshire towns, such as Castleford, in the 1960s. The name "peggy" refers to both the game itself and the small rectangular wooden block with tapering ends that is central to the game. The player places the peggy in the center of a square drawn with chalk and then hits one of its tapering ends with a stick. The stick is often made of an old broom handle. Hitting the peggy causes the wooden block to launch into the air, and the player then hits it again, as in nipsy. A player has three chances to hit the peggy, and making any contact with the peggy, however small, means the end of a player's turn. The biggest difference between peggy and nipsy is that once a player has struck the peggy, the batting side can offer the nonbatting team a certain number of strides in which to reach the hit peggy, starting from where the batting player stood to make the strike. The nonbatting side cannot refuse the challenge and so send its best strider out to reach the peggy. If the strider reaches the peggy in the set number of steps or fewer, then the batting team's score is nullified. However, if the strider fails, then the batting side gains as a score the number of yards to the peggy.

The team game of tipcat is very like both nipsy and peggy and was once played internationally but is now mostly forgotten. The earliest reference to tipcat in England dates to around 1440, but tipcat-playing equipment has been found in Egyptian ruins dating as far back as 2500 BCE. The cat of the game's title referred to a wooden block akin to the peggy that was laid on the ground and hit with a stick called a catstaff in such a way that the cat flew into the air and was then hit again over a long distance. The game was played inside a marked circle. A player who failed to make contact with the cat was immediately out of the game, but if the player managed to strike the cat then the distance the cat traveled in yards was converted into points, which were awarded to the batting side. A variation of tipcat was played inside a circle along the circumference of which were a number of evenly spaced holes. A batting player equipped with a stick was placed next to each hole. The cat was thrown at a player, and if the player hit the wooden block the player would have to run from hole to hole until a fielder recovered the cat. A point was scored for each hole the batter reached.

Other continental European games similar to nipsy also exist, including the old Italian game of *fiolet*, which is played exclusively in the Alpine region of Valle d'Aosta to the northwest of the country by over 400 players. *Fiolet* takes its name from the small, flattened, oval ball used in the game, the *fiolet*. A pebble used to be employed as the ball, but nowadays the *fiolet* is made either of aluminum or boxwood covered in metal nails. *Fiolet* is played on a triangle of grass of between 150 and 200 meters (492 and 656 feet) in length. The playing area is divided into increments every 15 meters (49 feet). *Fiolet* is played either by two teams of several players or by individuals. The game is similar to nipsy in that players use a club to hit as far as possible a ball that has not been placed on the ground.

When played as a team game, players take turns hitting the *fiolet*, which weighs 35 to 40 grams (1.2 to 1.4 ounces), into the triangular field. The *fiolet* is placed with the flat side facing upward on a type of tee called a *pira*, which consists of a large flat stone placed on a piece of cement. The player then hits the *fiolet* with a club called a *maccioca* measuring 40 to 70 centimeters (15 to 28 inches) in length. The player hits the *fiolet* twice. The first strike is a sharp hit that sends the *fiolet* spinning into the air, and then once the *fiolet* is airborne the player hits it again, this time aiming to launch the *fiolet* as far as possible into the field. The player then receives points depending on which 15-meter (49-foot) sector the *fiolet* lands in— the farther the *fiolet* travels, the more points the player receives. Once all the players have had their allotted number of turns (usually 10 turns each), the team or individual with the highest points total is declared the winner.

Also played in the Valle d'Aosta is the team game of *la rebatta*, which is played by 14 clubs in northern Italy. As in *fiolet*, players of *la rebatta* aim to hit a metal-covered boxwood ball as far possible into a field. The ball is placed in a hollow at one end of a wooden lever shaped like a pipe that serves as the tee. A player then hits the opposite end of the tee, which launches the ball into the air, and then hits the ball again using a reverse grip of the type used in baseball. As in *fiolet*, the player aims to hit the ball into the field of play, which is marked every 15 meters (49 feet), with the number of points scored dependent on which sector of the field the ball lands in. However, unlike *fiolet*, each *la rebatta* player has 20 turns at striking the ball. The winning team is the team that scores the most points.

See also: Cricket; *Gilli-Danda*

Further Reading

Brooke, Michael. "Miners above Ground." BFI Screenonline, 2003–2012, http://www
.screenonline.org.uk/film/id/1373265/index.html (accessed September 15, 2013).

Burnett, John. *Destiny Obscure: Autobiographies of Childhood, Education and Family from the
1820s to the 1920s*. Abingdon, UK: Routledge, 2013.

Hodgson, John. *Felling Colliery 1812: A Report of the Accident*. Wigan, UK: Picks Publishing,
1999, http://www.cmhrc.co.uk/cms/document/Felling_1812.pdf (accessed September
15, 2013).

Masters, James. "Knur and Spell, Nipsy Etc—History and Information." The Online Guide
to Traditional Games, 1997–2014, http://www.tradgames.org.uk/games/knur-spell
.htm (accessed August 12, 2013).

Meier, Eric. "Lignum Vitae." The Wood Database, 2013, http://www.wood-database.com/
lumber-identification/hardwoods/lignum-vitae/ (accessed September 15, 2013).

"Miscellaneous Stick and Ball Games." Ancient Golf, http://www.ancientgolf.dse.nl/stickball
.htm (accessed September 15, 2013).

"Nipsy Brought Forward for a New Generation." Wearebarnsley.com, December 5, 2011,
http://www.wearebarnsley.com/news/article/333/nipsy-brought-forward-for-a-new
-generation (accessed September 15, 2013).

Roud, Steve. *The English Year.* London: Penguin, 2006.

NONLETHAL BULLFIGHTING

In contrast to Spanish-style bullfighting, in nonlethal styles of bullfighting involve one or more humans taking on a bull or one bull facing another bull. One example of this occurs at a controversial 2,000-year-old bull-taming spectacle, *jallikattu,* held annually in Tamil Nadu, India, as part of the Pongal festivities. In *jallikattu* groups of men tackle an enraged bull and try to hang on to the animal until it passes a marker measuring 30 feet. Any man who can hold on to the bull for the duration of the animal's route from the arena's entrance to the marker wins a prize. If nobody achieves this feat, then the prize goes to the owner of the bull. While bulls have been killed accidently during the festivities, bulls have fatally gored many hundreds of spectator over the years. Another human-versus-bull contest is bloodless bullfighting, which takes place in towns in the San Joaquin Valley, California, from March to October, with fights drawing crowds of around 4,000 spectators. Azorean Portuguese immigrants brought this style of bullfighting to California, and the fights are of cultural significance to Portuguese Americans. However, as killing is simulated in bloodless bullfighting, this style is often mocked by bullfighting traditionalists. The bullfighting that takes place on the African island of Pemba (part of the Zanzibar Archipelago, a semiautonomous part of Tanzania) called *mchezo wa ngombe* is also the result of Portuguese influence, for Zanzibar belonged to the Portuguese Empire in the early 16th century. *Mchezo wa ngombe* is held in the village of Kengeja during the dry months of December and February, and the bullfighting ritual holds a spiritual significance. On the eve of the bullfight the villagers host a dance called *umund* and visit the graves of their relatives in order to seek help for the fight the next morning and to request the rain season to begin. The fight features three to six specially trained bulls that, to begin with, are tethered and then goaded by both pipe music and the raucous crowd that has gathered especially to see the spectacle. Once the bulls are sufficiently enraged, the crowd disperses and a male villager acting the role of chief bullfighter takes over as a show of bravado and to attest to his fearlessness. The villager uses a white flag to anger the bull and, as he is unarmed, has only his skill and agility to evade the charging beast. When the situation becomes too dangerous, the villager climbs a tree to escape the bull and then continues.

Another variation of nonlethal bullfighting sees one bull take on another as a form of wrestling. Bull wrestling takes place in Oman, the United Arab Emirates, the Balkan area of Europe, and Turkey, where bloodless bullfighting is known as *boğa güreşleri.* In Turkey such bull wrestling is seen as a variation on camel wrestling and features bulls that are naturally inclined to fight each other and are kept especially for the sport. As the bulls involved in bull wrestling are not working bulls, bull owners understand that they will need to spend a great deal of money to keep the animals, which must be fed a strict daily diet that is high in energy and protein and consists of corn flour, egg yolks, and dried fruit. Indeed, the bull owners will never earn enough prize money from the sport to pay for the bulls' upkeep. Instead the owners keep the animals for the kudos of owning a champion fighting bull and to gain the respect and honor of their peers. Bloodless bullfighting in the form of bull wrestling is central to the Caucasus Culture and Arts Festival held annually in the town of Artvin in northeastern Turkey. As in camel wrestling, the animals are paired with an opponent of a similar weight and size, with the smallest bulls starting the competition. The length of the bull wrestling match ranges from less than a minute to over several minutes, depending on how long it takes for one of the bulls to leave the arena either because it is bored or because it is so enraged that it bolts from the ring. The bull that leaves the arena first is the loser. The final contest of the Artvin festival is the title fight to decide which animal is the *bas boğa*, or head bull. The winner of the title wins a golden belt, and the owner is awarded a money prize.

Similar to *boğa güreşleri* is the Japanese sport of *togyu*, which is akin to taurine sumo wrestling and takes place in the cities of Ojiya and Uwajima. In *togyu* two bulls push against each other until one falls to the floor or is nudged out of the contest arena. The bull that yields first is the loser. Similarly, cow fighting has taken place since the 1920s in the canton of Valais, Switzerland, where there is a long history of dairy farming. In cow fighting, pregnant cows of the Eringer breed weighing half a ton battle for the title "Queen of the Alps" and the prize of a special cowbell by locking horns and attempting to push each other from a specially constructed ring in front of around 6,000 paying spectators. Cow fighting is a docile sport, as cows are usually more interested in chewing their cud than fighting, and there is little risk of injury to competing animals, as veterinarians file the cows' horns prior to fights. In fact, so lackadaisical are the fights that when a group of Austrian animal rights protesters arrived to protest at a cow fight in Martigny in 2005, the group watched one bout and then departed, withdrawing their objections. However, while the cows do not get very animated during fights, their owners are extremely keen for their animals to do well, for the calf of a prize-winning cow can sell for US$25,000—10 times the price of an ordinary calf. The ultimate cow fighting contest is the Combats de Reines (Battle of the Queens) competition held in Aproz, in Valais, where the winner of the grand finale is awarded the title "Queen of Queens."

See also: Bearbaiting and Badger Baiting; Bull Running; *Buzkashi;* Camel and Yak Racing; Camel Wrestling; Cockfighting; Elephant Sports; Foxhunting; Hare Coursing; *Pato* and Horseball; Pigeon Racing; Sheepdog Trials; Spanish Bullfighting; Sumo Wrestling; Yabbie Races

Further Reading

Dodd, Jan, and Simon Richmond. *The Rough Guide to Japan.* 2nd ed. London: Rough Guides, 2001.

Finke, Jens. *The Rough Guide to Zanzibar.* 3rd ed. London: Rough Guides, 2010.

Gayle, Damien. "Now That's a Beef! The Swiss Cows Battling It Out to Be Crowned 'Queen of Queens.'" MailOnline, May 11, 2014, http://www.dailymail.co.uk/news/article-2625601/Now-thats-beef-The-Swiss-cows-battling-crowned-Queen-Queens.html (accessed July 22, 2014).

Grushkin, Daniel. "Ringing in the New Year by Wrestling Bulls." *New York Times,* March 22, 2007, http://www.nytimes.com/2007/03/22/travel/21webletter.html?pagewanted=1 (accessed February 2, 2014).

Hayes-Gehrke, Melissa N. "In The Mood: Swiss Always Enjoy a Good Cow Fight." University of Maryland: Astronomy, http://www.astro.umd.edu/~avondale/extra/Humor/MiscellaneousHumor/CowFighting.html (accessed July 22, 2014).

Levine, Emma. *A Game of Polo with a Headless Goat and Other Bizarre Sports Discovered across Asia.* London: Andre Deutsch, 2003.

Lonely Planet. "Introducing Artvin." Lonely Planet, http://www.lonelyplanet.com/turkey/artvin (accessed February 19, 2014).

Soul of Japan. "Bull Sumo/Togyu." The Soul of Japan, October 6, 2013, http://thesoulofjapan.blogspot.co.uk/2013/10/bull-sumo-togyu.html (accessed February 2, 2014).

NORDIC WALKING

Nordic walking, also called Nordic pole walking, is a low-impact outdoor form of exercise enjoyed by men and women in which practitioners walk while actively using a pair of specially designed handheld poles. Nordic walking can take place in urban or rural areas and is particularly popular in Europe, where around 10 million people Nordic walk regularly, though the activity is most widespread in the European countries of Finland (sometimes referred to as the motherland of the activity), Germany, the Netherlands, and Austria. Nordic walking is also practiced in the United States and Canada. The International Nordic Walking Association (INWA), founded in Finland in 2000, oversees Nordic walking. The organization aims to further the development of Nordic walking, provide research on the activity, and promote Nordic walking as a means to a healthy lifestyle by providing an international network of trained instructors. As part of the INWA's drive to promote Nordic

Nordic walkers stride out in the countryside while actively using a pair of specially designed handheld poles. The poles propel the walkers along, making it easier for walkers to move quickly and cover long distances. (Lya_Cattel/iStockphoto.com)

walking and healthy living in general, the association organized World Nordic Walking Day, held on May 25, 2014, in which participants were encouraged to Nordic walk around city streets. At the time of this writing, the INWA has 20 officially affiliated member organizations and certified instructors in over 40 nations.

There is a great degree of disagreement over the origins of Nordic walking. It has been suggested that the exercise was invented in Finland in the 1930s when cross-country skiers wanted a training regime to keep active during the skiing off-season when there was no snow. The skiers decided to use their ski poles while taking long walks, as they felt that this would improve their cardiovascular health and strengthen the muscles in their upper and lower body. However, it has also been claimed that Nordic walking began in Helsinki, the capital of Finland, in 1966 when a physical education teacher, Leena Jääskeläinen, introduced walking with ski poles to her students. Similarly, it has been suggested that the technique of Nordic walking was invented in 1979 by former Finish cross-country skier Mauri Repo, who claimed that the walking style was a good way for cross-country skiers to keep fit when not skiing. Repo is credited with promoting Nordic walking as a sports-focused training regime. In 1998 an American, Tom Rutlin, promoted an exercise regime called Exerstriding in which walkers used poles, but both the equipment and technique of Exerstriding differed from that found in Nordic walking.

Whatever the origins of Nordic walking, there is no doubt that the activity is extremely beneficial to practitioners, for Nordic walking utilizes 90 percent of the body's skeletal muscles, thereby toning the upper and lower body simultaneously in a way that has low impact on the knees and other joints. The activity burns up to 50 percent more calories than normal everyday walking, partly because the use of poles propels the practitioner along, making it easier for walkers to move quicker than usual and over longer distances. The activity also improves core stability, flexibility, balance, coordination, and posture. Indeed, such are the cardiovascular and general health benefits of Nordic walking that the activity is claimed to be one of the most effective methods of cross-training for sportspeople. However, the health benefits of Nordic walking are not reserved solely for athletes. For example, the publicly funded health care system of the United Kingdom, the National Health Service, often referred to as the NHS, actively encourages the public to take up Nordic walking, citing the activity as a way of combating chronic illnesses such as type 2 diabetes, heart disease, asthma, strokes, and some cancers and as part of an exercise-based weight-loss program. Nordic walking also produces a calming effect on the practitioner that is similar to meditation, for the walker's body automatically sinks into a rhythm when Nordic walking, resulting in a feeling of relaxation and unity with the natural world that acts as a backdrop to the activity. For this reason Nordic walking is often likened to yoga, and indeed Nordic walking is called walking yoga by some practitioners. Advocates of Nordic walking claim that the activity comes naturally to practitioners, since it is in essence walking on all fours or on four legs, the way humans first learned to walk.

Nordic walking does not require a great deal of specialized equipment. Walking shoes and appropriate clothing are necessary, but the most important piece of apparel is a pair of carbon Nordic walking poles. There are five types of poles used in

Nordic walking: fixed length, extendable, adjustable, telescopic, and strapless. As the name suggests, a fixed-length pole is not adjustable, so a walker using this type of pole must be certain that the pole is at the correct height so as not to compromise the walking technique. An extendable pole is very similar to a fixed-length pole except that the pole can be extended to improve technique or if the walker's technique alters. On an extendable pole, the adjustable length of pole is located close to the handles in order to minimize vibrations. Adjustable poles are suitable for all walkers, as they allow for full flexibility when walking. Telescopic poles are best for traveling, as they can be folded down to fit into bags. However, telescopic poles necessarily have two adjustable sections and so may vibrate more, causing discomfort for users. Strapless walking poles are particularly good for walkers with balance or gripping problems, though it should be noted that if a pole does not have any straps attached it is not, technically, a Nordic walking pole.

The basic technique of Nordic walking is very similar to normal walking. The most basic form of Nordic walking sees participants walk as normal but carrying the poles. However, to work the upper body, participants should hold the poles vertically while walking in a specific way: the heel should touch the ground, and then the foot should roll forward so that the ball of the foot and then the toes touch the ground. Meanwhile, the walker's hands should be in the so-called grip-and-go position; that is, the walker should grip the pole every time the pole hits the ground and let go of the pole so that it is drawn behind the body, and the stride finishes with an open palm. As the walker's arms move the poles, the upper body and hips move in a swinging motion that is in the opposite direction to that of the lower body. This motion works the muscles of the midtorso, and it is possible to make the exercise more physically demanding by jogging, running, or taking longer strides.

There are several variations on basic Nordic walking. These include Nordic winter walking, in which walkers cross compacted snow; Nordic snowshoeing, in which walkers wear snowshoes while walking; Nordic hiking, in which walkers Nordic walk across dry ground; and Nordic fitness skiing, which is akin to traditional cross-country skiing but differs in that skiers use shorter, thicker poles. Another variation of Nordic walking, Nordic blading, sees practitioners wear in-line blades and employ a distinctive pole technique in which both poles are planted on the ground at once, while the practitioner's legs move alternately from side to side. This pole technique is also one of the two pole styles used in Nordic fitness skiing. The alternative Nordic fitness skiing technique sees practitioners move arms and legs forward and backward.

See also: Capoeira; *Kyykkä;* Orienteering and Rogaining; *Parkour;* Wife Carrying; Yoga

Further Reading

"About Us." INWA, 2014, http://inwa-nordicwalking.com/about-us/ (accessed June 22, 2014).

"Choosing Nordic Walking Poles—a Useful Guide." Nordic Walking UK, 2014, http://www.nordicwalking.co.uk/blog/2013/11/choosing-nordic-walking-poles-a-useful-guide/ (accessed June 22, 2014).

"The History of Nordic Walking." Nordic Walking UK, 2014, http://nordicwalking
.co.uk/?page=about_nordic_walking&c=22 (accessed January 7, 2014).

"Nordic Walking." NHS Choices, July 11, 2013, http://www.nhs.uk/Livewell/fitness/Pages
/nordic-walking.aspx (accessed June 22, 2014).

Schwanbeck, Klaus. *The Ultimate Nordic Pole Walking Book.* 3rd ed. Maidenhead, UK: Meyer
and Meyer Sport, 2014.

Svensson, Malin. *Nordic Walking.* Champaign, IL: Human Kinetics, 2009.

"Techniques." Nordic Walking Online, 2008–2014, http://www.nordicwalkingonline.com
/techniques.php (accessed June 22, 2014).

"World Nordic Walking Day." INWA, 2014, http://inwa-nordicwalking.com/events/world
-nordic-walking-day/ (accessed June 22, 2014).

0

ORIENTEERING AND ROGAINING

Orienteering is the term given to a family of related disciplines for men, women, and children in which competitors, known as orienteers, use navigation skills and a compass to navigate a path between unfamiliar locations, called control points, that are marked on a special topographical orienteering map. Participants must decide the best route to take in order to complete the course in the quickest time, for in orienteering the winner is (usually) the competitor to complete the course in the fastest time. Orienteering exists at local through international levels.

Orienteering began in Scandinavia at the end of the 19th century as a military training regime to teach soldiers how to navigate unknown territory using a map and compass. The mid-1890s saw an explosion of interest in organized sports, which in Scandinavia coincided with an increased interest in traversing unfamiliar terrain at speed. By 1895 both the Swedish and Norwegian militaries were competing in orienteering competitions, and soon orienteering clubs began to become established. In 1897 the Norwegian track-and-field club Tjalve Sports Club sponsored the first known public orienteering competition. The race's course, near Oslo, the capital of Norway, covered 19.5 kilometers (just over 12 miles) and featured three control points set against a wild terrain. The winner completed the course in 1 hour 47 minutes. Then in 1899, the first ski orienteering event was held in Norway, followed by the first Swedish orienteering competition in 1901, the first Finnish ski orienteering competition in 1904, and the debut Danish orienteering event in 1906. In 1918 Swedish scout leader Major Ernst Killander, who was seeking ways to attract more children to athletics events, decided to hold a cross-country running event that included elements of orienteering, for each competitor had to use a map and a compass to choose a route that took in various control points through to the finish. Over 200 runners took part in the 12-kilometer (almost 7.5-mile) race, with the winner completing the course in less than 1.5 hours. The race was a success, and subsequently Killander developed the basic rules of competitive orienteering. These rules included guidelines for choosing a course and control points as well as establishing age groups and other ways of organizing the competitions. For this reason, Killander is referred to as the Father of Orienteering.

The popularity of orienteering grew rapidly with the advent of the so-called back to nature movement that spread across Europe during the 1920s, idealizing nature in the face of the unnaturalness of growing industrialization and urbanization. By the outbreak of World War II, orienteering was practiced throughout Scandinavia, Hungary, Germany, Czechoslovakia, Estonia, and Switzerland and in

A couple consult a map while orienteering. In orienteering participants use their navigation skills and a compass to find a path between unfamiliar locations marked on a special topographical orienteering map. (leaf/iStockphoto.com)

parts of the United States. However, in the earliest years of the sport, orienteering was an exclusively male pursuit. This began to change in the 1920s, with the first women's orienteering event held in Sweden in 1925. By the end of the decade there were around 5,000 active Swedish male and female orienteers. Orienteering remains popular in Scandinavia, with an annual five-day orienteering festival, the O-Ringen, which attracts around 25,000 orienteers, held in Sweden.

Technical innovations have occurred throughout the recent history of orienteering. For instance, modern maps were introduced to orienteering during the 1950s—prior to this orienteering maps were simple black-and-white drawings of the course. Today orienteering maps are full color and include contour lines to show elevations and detail landmarks such as areas of water and roads. The compasses used have also evolved. Originally, orienteers used either rudimentary wooden box- or pocket watch–style compasses. However, in 1933 the more accurate Silva protractor compass was invented, and this style of compass is still in worldwide use today. More recently, electronic punching and Global Positioning System (GPS) tracking have been introduced. This has led to the sport becoming visible to audiences via broadcasts on television and the Internet.

Orienteering can take place in any location, including forests, the countryside, city parks, and school playgrounds. Four variations of orienteering—foot orienteering, trail orienteering, ski orienteering, and mountain bike orienteering—are governed by the International Orienteering Federation (IOF), which was recognized by the International Olympic Committee in 1977. The IOF, which is based in Finland, was founded in 1961 by a combination of orienteering associations from Bulgaria, Czechoslovakia, Denmark, Finland, Germany, Hungary, Norway, Sweden, and Switzerland. The first non-European nations to join the IOF were Japan and Canada, in 1969; and in 1973 the United States, Israel, and Australia joined. Today the IOF has 78 member nations and is divided into six regions: Africa, Asia, Europe, North America, South America, and Oceania. Most countries boast a national orienteering governing body as well as regional associations that coordinate clubs within a specified area. Local orienteering clubs also exist and are affiliated with national governing bodies.

Foot orienteering is an endurance sport that is as much mental as physical, since there is no marked route; therefore, the orienteer must navigate while running. The orienteer's map provides detailed information on the terrain, including the presence of hills, the type of ground surface, and any obstacles likely to be encountered. Thus, to be a successful foot orienteer takes excellent map-reading skills and concentration and the ability to make quick decisions while running at speed. Physical fitness, strength, and agility are also required, as foot orienteers usually have to navigate rough terrain and steep gradients.

There are a number of different foot orienteering events, including individual competitions and relays, ultrashort park races, and mountain marathon events. Night orienteering, in which orienteers compete wearing a headlamp, is also popular, while a recent innovation is the development of city sprints, in which participants race across urban parkland. The world's top foot orienteers compete at the World Cup and the world championships, where events include four competitions for both women and men: sprint, middle distance, long distance, and relay. Elite orienteers also take part in the World Cup.

The orienteering disciplines of mountain bike and trail orienteering have developed recently. Mountain bike orienteering, which began in the late 1980s, attracts fans of both orienteering and mountain biking. Participants must have excellent bike-handling skills and the fitness required to ascend vertiginous slopes. In order to protect the environment, competitors must not normally leave designated paths and tracks, though this is allowed in some countries. Mountain bike orienteering began at club level in countries where mountain biking was popular, and in 1997 national championships were run in 12 countries. By 2009 this number had increased to 58. The annual World Championships in Mountain Bike Orienteering attracts national teams from around 25 countries.

Trail orienteering focuses on map reading amid natural terrain and aims to offer everyone, including those with limited mobility, such as wheelchair users, those using walking sticks, and people needing assistance with movement, a chance to take part in an orienteering event in which speed is not an element of the competition. Instead, trail orienteers must identify at a distance ground control points shown on the map. Thus, both able-bodied participants and those with disabilities compete on level terms, especially as proof of correct identification of the control points does not require any manual dexterity. Thus, people with severely restricted movement are able to compete equally. Trail orienteers whose permanent disability is so severe that they cannot participate on reasonably equal terms are eligible for the Paralympic class of trail competition. Trail orienteering was recognized by the IOF in 1992. The first-ever World Cup in trail orienteering was held in 1999 but was then replaced with the World Trail Orienteering Championships in 2004. The world championships take place annually.

Ski orienteering combines navigation and cross-country skiing across rough terrain using specially prepared cross-country ski tracks, for ski orienteers use a map to navigate a network of trails in order to visit control points in the right sequence. Ski orienteers choose their route on the basis of the quality of the ski tracks and their gradient and distance, which they determine by reading their map, and the person to complete the course in the fastest time wins—an electronic card verifies that the orienteer has visited all control points in sequence. Ski orienteers marry physical stamina and strength with excellent skiing ability and the quick thinking necessary to choose the best cross-country route, and though ski orienteering takes place against a backdrop of the natural environment, events can make use of tracks used in biathlons and cross-country skiing events.

The World Cup is an official annual season-long series of events organized to determine the world's best ski orienteers, while the title "World Ski Orienteering Champion" is awarded at the World Ski Orienteering Championships, which take place every odd year. The championships includes sprint, sprint relay, and middle- and long-distance contests plus a relay for both men and women.

There are many different orienteering events. Annual international championships include the World Orienteering Championships, the Junior World Orienteering Championships, the World Masters Championships, and the European Orienteering Championships. In addition to these competitions there are also more than 100 world ranking events, and regional championships are held in five IOF regions: Europe, Asia, North America, South America, and Oceania. Orienteering is also part of multi-sport tournaments, including the World Games and the World Masters Games. The International University Sports Federation organizes the World University Orienteering Championships and the World University Ski Orienteering Championships, which take place every second year. Meanwhile, the International Military Sports Council (CISM) organizes the annual World Military Orienteering Championships, with ski orienteering part of the CISM Winter Military World Games.

Related to orienteering is the sport of rogaining, in which teams work together to amass the highest score possible through reaching checkpoints within a set time limit. Teams of two to five members traverse terrain on foot, often in both daytime and nighttime, with the aid of a topographic map and using an analogue compass.

Rogaining was invented in Australia, with rules established in 1968 and the first intervarsity 24-hour orienteering competition held in 1969. Traditionally a rogaining event, known as a rogaine, lasts 24 hours, and many rogaines feature a central base camp that provides hot food and to which teams may return at any time to eat or rest. Shorter events lasting 6, 8, and 12 hours also take place.

Before a rogaine begins, each participant receives a map of the course detailing the location and points value of the checkpoints. Teams choose their own route to reach whichever checkpoints they want and take the course at their own pace.

Once they reach a checkpoint, teams must then use a punch to make a hole at the corresponding numbered square on the competition control card. It is vital that teams return before the competition time limit expires, or they will be punished with a substantial point penalty.

Most rogaines take place a few hours' drive from a major city, and the terrain covered includes both open countryside and dense woodland. Rogaines in urban areas, known as metrogaines, are also held, as are cycling rogaines called cyclogaines and cross-country ski rogaines known as snograines.

The aim of rogaining is to encourage people to both respect and enjoy their surroundings and to encourage the development of navigational skills, self-reliance, physical fitness, and communication skills.

Another outdoor activity, geocaching, is partly descended from orienteering. Geocaching is akin to an Internet-based treasure hunting game in which participants, known as geocachers, navigate to a specific set of coordinates, known as waypoints, using mobile GPS-enabled devices or other navigational techniques and then attempt to find a container, called the cache or geocache, which is hidden, though never buried, at the specified location by a player called a hider (a geocacher who finds a cache is called a seeker). Several types of geocache exist, but a cache is usually a small waterproof box containing a logbook, a writing implement, and an item to be traded with the seeker, for once a geocache is found, it should be replaced with something else. The name "geocaching" is derived from the Greek *geo* (meaning "earth," as appears in the word "geography") and the term "caching," which is the process of hiding a cache. In computing terminology the term "cache" usually refers to information stored in a memory in order to make it faster to retrieve, and in hiking and camping parlance "cache" refers to a place for hiding and preserving provisions. Geocaching takes place across the globe, with geocaches located all over the world.

The recent history of geocaching can be traced to 19th-century England, for in 1854 a guide at Dartmoor National Park in Devon hid copies of his calling card inside a glass bottle at remote Cranmere Pool in order to prove that he had reached the location. Each subsequent visitor to the pool then left a letter or postcard inside a box that was addressed to themselves, a friend, or a relative, and the next person to discover the site would collect and mail the letters/postcards. This practice led to the pastime becoming known as letterboxing. Despite the advent of geocaching, letterboxing still takes place at Dartmoor and indeed across the world. Geocaching is also a descendent of orienteering. In the 1990s a group of Finnish orienteers started to use GPS systems to check accuracy while also using a map and compass to find locations. It has therefore been claimed that the members of this group were the original geocachers. However, the term "geocaching" has only been in use since 2000, when geocaching was called "GPS stash hunt." The GPS stash hunt was invented by David J. Ulmer, who hid the first geocache (a can of beans, a videotape, and a compass) in Oregon. The activity quickly became popular, but a month after creating the new craze Ulmer left the game, as he was fearful that geocaching might damage the environment. Before he left, however, he decided the game that should be renamed to remove the word "stash," thus avoiding any association with illegal drugs. After an online poll, the name "geocaching" was settled upon. The split between Ulmer and his fellow geocachers was acrimonious, and some histories of the game omit Ulmer and instead credit the creation of the activity to Mike Teague, who found the first geocache and created the first geocaching Web site. The popularity of geocaching continued to spread via online viral marketing, and the activity continues to be a major trend in adventure pursuits.

See also: Fell Running; Nordic Walking; *Parkour;* Ultramarathons

Further Reading

Baldwin, David. "More about Rogaining." Australian Rogaining Association, July 15, 2008, http://rogaine.asn.au/What-is-Rogaining-/More-About-Rogaining.html (accessed April 12, 2014).

Baldwin, David. "What Is Rogaining." Australian Rogaining Association, January 9, 2009, http://rogaine.asn.au/What-is-Rogaining-/ (accessed April 12, 2014).

Boga, Steve. *Orienteering: The Sport of Navigating with a Map & Compass.* Mechanicsburg, PA: Stackpole, 1997.

Cooper, Julia, Urs Niggli, and Carlo Leifert, eds. *Handbook of Organic Food Safety and Quality.* Abington, UK: Woodhead Publishing, 2007.

"Different Types of Geocaches." Caching Box, 2012, http://www.cachingbox.com/different-types-of-geocaches/ (accessed April 13, 2014).

Ferguson, Charles, and Robert Turbyfill. *Discovering Orienteering: Skills, Techniques, and Activities.* Champaign, IL: Human Kinetics, 2013.

"Foot Orienteering." International Orienteering Federation, 1995–2011, http://orienteering.org/foot-orienteering/ (accessed April 12, 2014).

Groundspeak, Inc. "Geocaching 101." Geocaching, 2000–2014, http://www.geocaching.com/guide/default.aspx (accessed April 13, 2014).

Groundspeak, Inc. "Geocache Types." Geocaching, 2000–2014, http://www.geocaching.com/about/cache_types.aspx (accessed April 13, 2014).

"History and Facts about Orienteering." Athletic Scholarships, 2001–2014, http://www.athleticscholarships.net/other-sports-orienteering.htm (accessed April 12, 2014).

"Letterboxing on Dartmoor." Dartmoor National Park Authority, http://www.dartmoor-npa.gov.uk/visiting/vi-enjoyingdartmoor/vi-letterboxing (accessed April 13, 2014).

Liebenberg, E. C., Peter Collier, and Zsolt Gyoso Török, eds. *History of Cartography: International Symposium of the ICA, 2012.* Berlin: Springer-Verlag, 2014.

"MTB Orienteering." International Orienteering Federation, 1995–2011, http://orienteering.org/mtb-orienteering/ (April 12, 2014).

Sherman, Erik. *Geocaching: Hike and Seek with Your GPS.* New York: Springer-Verlag, 2004.

"Ski Orienteering." International Orienteering Federation, 1995–2011, http://orienteering.org/ski-orienteering/ (accessed April 12, 2014).

"Trail Orienteering." International Orienteering Federation, 1995–2011, http://orienteering.org/trail-orienteering/ (accessed April 12, 2014).

"Welcome to British Orienteering." British Orienteering, http://www.britishorienteering.org.uk (accessed April 12, 2014).

P

PAINTBALL

Paintball is a strategic adventure sport for men and women similar to an armed version of the children's' game of tag in which players eliminate opponents by shooting them with paint pellets that explode on contact, leaving a brightly colored mark on the opponent and her or his clothes or equipment—once a player is marked, she or he is out of the game until a new round begins. Though usually played outdoors in the daytime, indoor paintball also exists, as does night paintball.

Paintball is played across the world and is growing in popularity. For instance, over 1 million new players take up paintball in the United Kingdom each year, and there are over 100 paintball centers throughout the United Kingdom. However, the legality of paintball varies between nations, mainly due to the use of guns in the sport; and in areas where the sport is regulated, it is common for players to have to wear safety masks. Paintball-related ocular injuries tend to be devastating, with some players blinded by being shot in the eye by pellets. Therefore, it is highly recommended that players wear eye protection as well as other safety equipment such as gloves and knee and elbow pads.

Paintball began in the United States in the 1970s when the Daisy Manufacturing Co. developed the gas-operated Nel-Spot 007, the first mass-market paintball gun, plus semipermanent marking pellets, for use in a variety of industries, including forestry and ranching, for the Nelson Paint Company. According to paintball lore, the game was invented by hunter Charles Gaines, sporting goods dealer Bill Gurnsey, and stockbroker Hayes Noel, friends from New Hampshire who decided to use the newly developed gun and pellets to test their individual survivalist and hunting skills against each other and thought that it would be beneficial to draw up rules to cover the activity, which they dubbed Survival Games. Thus, in 1981 Gaines, Noel, Gurnsey, and nine friends played the first-ever paintball game on a field measuring over 100 acres. Soon after this debut Gaines, Noel, and Gurnsey decided to rename their invention the National Survival Game, which was also the name of their new company, in order to reflect that paintball was a ruthless elimination game and to tie in with their newly formed company, which they hoped would sell paintball equipment. Soon paintball franchises began to pop up across the northeastern United States, and in 1982 rival paintball equipment firms, such as Pursuit Marketing Inc., began to sell paintballing supplies to companies wishing to start their own National Survival companies. This rapid industry growth soon led to an explosion in the number of people paintballing, and this in turn meant that National Survival Games evolved from the type of game played at the debut contest between Gaines, Noel, Gurnsey, and friends, in which one player had to take on all others, into a team sport, with the first-ever National Survival Games Championship held in New Hampshire in 1983. A year later the first outdoor paintballing facility opened in Buffalo, New York, and quickly became popular.

Paintball business owners found it necessary to develop new ways to keep players entertained, and this in turn led to innovations in play so that over the years paintball has become more complex, and different versions of the game now exist as well as competitive paintball leagues and tournaments, such as the Mediterranean Cup, the European Masters, and the World Cup Asia.

The main variations of paintball are woodsball and capture the flag. Woodsball is the name now applied to the original form of paintball in which teams compete in a wood or amid other natural surroundings rather than in a manufactured ground. Meanwhile, the most commonly played form of paintball is capture the flag, which is played by two teams of between 10 and 30 players. In this version teams guard their own flag, which is located at one side of the playing area, while simultaneously eliminating their opponents and trying to capture the other side's flag, which the first team then takes back to their own base.

Before any paintball game begins, the version of paintball being played, the time limit, and the allocation of players to each team must be established, as should the parameters of the playing area; the size of which depends on how many players are taking part in a game; and the location of both the dead zone, an off-field area where players go once they are out, and the home-base boundaries at either end of the field. It is advantageous to ensure that the bases are not in view of others by employing trees, bushes, and the like as barriers, though in the variation called speedball, a fast version of paintball played on a flat field with players in close proximity to each other, this will not be possible, for the only obstructions on the speedball field are manufactured bunkers.

A paintball game begins when both teams are at their home base and declare that they are ready to play. One team exclaims "Game on!" and the game starts. During the game a player is considered to have been hit if a paint pellet leaves a solid mark (as opposed to paint splatter that has ricocheted from a nearby surface) anywhere on the player's person or equipment. Some paintball variations allow players to be hit on the gun or require a player to be hit multiple times on the limbs before being dismissed from the game. Any player unsure of having been hit directly can request a paint check, whereby the nearest coplayer checks the nature of the paint mark. If the mark is a hit, then the player who initiated the check must leave the field by raising her or his gun above the head and entering the dead zone; otherwise all players resume their positions, and the player who asked for the check shouts "Game on!" to restart play.

A team achieves victory when it completes the objective of the version of paintball being played. When this occurs all players are informed of the win, though players should not remove safety equipment until barrel plugs or covers are placed on any loaded guns.

See also: Boomerang Throwing

Further Reading

Alliman, K. J., W. E. Smiddy, J. Banta, Y. Qureshi, D. M. Miller, and J. C. Schiffman. "Ocular Trauma and Visual Outcome Secondary to Paintball Projectiles." *American Journal of Ophthalmology* 147(2) (February 2009), http://www.ajo.com/article/S0002-9394(08) 00650-8/abstract (accessed April 15, 2014).

Billard, Mary. "The Executive Life; The Satisfying Silliness of the Paintball Wars." *New York Times,* October 20, 1991, http://www.nytimes.com/1991/10/20/business/the-executive -life-the-satisfying-silliness-of-the-paintball-wars.html (accessed April 15, 2014).

Delta Force. "What Is Paintball?" Delta Force, http://www.paintballgames.co.uk/what-is -paintball (accessed April 15, 2014).

"The History of Paintball." Empire Paintball, 2012, http://empirepaintball.com/the-history -of-paintball (accessed April 15, 2014).

"Industry Innovation." The Nelson Paint Company, 2013, http://www.nelsonpaint.com /about.html (accessed April 15, 2014).

Khan, Sami. "Paintball Games and Variations." The Paintball Times, 1993–2014, http:// www.paintballtimes.com/article.asp?ID=10 (accessed April 15, 2014).

Muhlstein, David. "How to Play Paintball (Basic Rules)." About.com: Paintball, 2007, http://paintball.about.com/od/howtoplay/ht/basicrules.htm (accessed April 15, 2014).

"Paintball and the Law." UK Paintball Sports Federation, 2014, http://ukpsf.com/paintball-and -the-law/ (accessed April 15, 2014).

Roza, Greg. *Paintball: Rules, Tips, Strategy, and Safety.* New York: Rosen, 2007.

PANCAKE RACES

Pancake races are a traditional English pre-Easter folk custom in which competitors race along a predetermined track while tossing a pancake in a frying pan. It is customary for pancake races to be held on Shrove Tuesday/Mardi Gras, the last day before Lent that marks the start of a period of abstinence meant to reflect the 40 days and nights that Jesus spent in the wilderness. Shrove Tuesday is therefore associated with emptying kitchen cupboards of food items such as sugar, fats, and eggs. In England, Shrove Tuesday is commonly known as Pancake Day, as making pancakes is a good way of using up such ingredients ahead of the fasting period. The exact date of Pancake Day varies, as the day must occur 47 days before Easter Sunday. However, the date of Easter Sunday is dictated by lunar cycles, so Pancake Day can occur anytime between February 3 and March 9. The association of pancakes with Shrove Tuesday is a very old one and dates from before 1619.

One of the most well-known pancake races is a charity run held in the town of Olney, in the county of Buckinghamshire near London, the capital of England. Olney's race is contested exclusively by females over the age of 16 who have resided in the town or the neighboring village of Warrington for more than six months. The tradition dates from 1445 and began when a woman was late for the parish church's shriving service, a church service during which sins are confessed ahead of Ash Wednesday. According to legend, on hearing the church bells calling townsfolk to the service, the woman ran from her home down the High Street and into the church still wearing her cooking apron and holding her frying pan. Today the Olney townswomen mark their forerunner's dash to church by completing the pancake

Schoolboys take part in a pancake race in Buckinghamshire, England, on February 12, 2013. Pancake racers must race along a course while flipping a pancake in a frying pan. (AP Photo/ Matt Dunham)

race wearing an apron and cap and carrying a frying pan bearing a real pancake. Competitors must toss their pancake three times during the race, including once at the start of the race outside the Bull Inn and then once at the finish line outside the church of St. Peter and St. Paul some 415 yards from the start line. If when tossed the pancake falls to the ground, it must be retrieved and then tossed again. The first competitor to reach the church with her thrice-tossed pancake is rewarded with a kiss from the church's bell ringer and a prayer book from the local vicar. When the race is over, competitors, officials, townsfolk, and tourists enter the church for the shriving service, and competitors place their frying pans around the church's font. During the service a prize-giving ceremony takes place, with prizes awarded to the race winner, the oldest competitor, and the runner who has raised the most money for charity. The Olney Pancake Race has a twin event held in the town of Liberal, Kansas, that began in 1950. The Liberal race is run on the same day as the Olney race and over the same distance, with the Kansas participants competing to better the time set by the fastest Olney woman. Representatives from Liberal attend the postrace church service in Olney, and this dual transatlantic pancake race is the only such race in the world.

A pancake race similar to the Olney race that is contested by men and children as well as women has taken place near Winster in the central English county of Derbyshire since 1870, though the pancakes used in Winster are specially made for toughness and are therefore inedible, unlike the pancakes used in Olney. Yarmouth on the Isle of Wight, a small island that lies off the southern coast of England, also holds a pancake race in the town square.

Another famous, though much more recent, pancake race is the Rehab Parliamentary Pancake Race in which British politicians from the House of Commons and the House of Lords compete as teams of members of Parliament and Lords against a team of political correspondents from the British media. In this race competitors run around College Green, a small area of grass opposite the Houses of Parliament in Westminster, central London. The race aims to raise awareness of the work that the Rehab organization does in helping people with disabilities and those who are socially excluded in the United Kingdom. The first Rehab Parliamentary Pancake Race took place in 1988, and since then the event has unsurprisingly achieved quite a large amount of press coverage, appearing in reports on television news broadcast by the BBC, ITN, and CNN. The Rehab Parliamentary Pancake Race takes the form of a relay race in which a team pancake instead of a baton is passed between competitors over a course of about 25 meters (just over 27 yards), during which competitors must wear an apron and a chef's hat over their work wear. The competitors must run carrying a frying pan and toss their team pancake three times so that the tossed pancakes reach a minimum height of 3 feet. If a competitor drops his or her pancake, the competitor must return to the starting line and start the race again. Each team member must run the course, and the team pancake must remain intact.

Relay pancake racing is also the basis of the World Pancake Racing Championship that takes place annually in Exeter, in the southern English county of Devon. Teams representing shops, businesses, and organizations compete in the event, which aims to raise money for local charities. The championship takes the form of several knockout relays during which team members run along a short course, pausing to toss their pancake four times along the track before passing the requisite frying pan to the next competitor. The first team to finish the race is declared the winner.

A related Shrove Tuesday pancake tradition takes place in English boys' public schools and sees the headmaster toss a pancake from a frying pan over a high bar on the other side of which stand the assembled schoolboys, who scramble to catch the pancake once it has been tossed. At Westminster School this pancake rite is called the Pancake Greaze, but the custom occurs under different names at other schools, including Eton College. Exactly how this tradition originated is unknown.

Jogging + Juggling = Joggling

Joggling (combining juggling with jogging) sees participants juggle at least three items constantly while running. If an item is dropped, the runner must resume running from the spot where the item fell. Most jogglers juggle balls, but clubs, beanbags, and even knives can be used. The first annual World Joggling Championships was held in 1980 and featured three-, five-, and seven-ball races ranging in length from 100-meter sprints to 5-kilometer distance races, plus relays. Jogglers have also competed in the New York Marathon as well as in ultramathons and triathlons.

Another English contest in which food throwing forms the basis of competition is the Knob Throwing competition held annually in Cattistock, in the county of Dorset in the southwest of England. This event, which began in 2008, sees competitors vie to toss a locally made savory biscuit called a knob as far as possible. The biscuits must be thrown underarm, and competitors must ensure that one foot stays in contact with the ground while performing the throwing action. Each competitor has three throws, with the farthest throw measured and recorded as the competitor's entry. The competition winner receives her or his winning biscuit as a prize, and the competitor's name is added to a board in the village hall. The record for the longest knob throw was set in 2012 at 96 feet. In 2013 more than 700 people took part in the competition, while over 5,000 spectators looked on.

See also: Barrel Races; Cheese Rolling; Cockfighting; Conkers; Eton Wall Game; Fives; Haxey Hood Game; *La Soule*

Further Reading

Albala, Ken. *Pancake: A Global History*. London: Reaktion Books, 2008.

Alexander, Marc. *The Sutton Companion to the Folklore, Myths and Legends of Britain*. Stroud, UK: Sutton, 2005.

BBC. "Dorset Knob Throwing Contest Attracts Thousands." BBC News Dorset, May 4, 2014, http://www.bbc.co.uk/news/uk-england-dorset-27259589 (accessed May 21, 2014).

Grout, Pam. *Kansas Curiosities: Quirky Characters, Roadside Oddities & Other Offbeat Stuff*. Guilford, CT: Morris Book Publishing, 2010.

Hallett, Emma. "Bank Holiday Weirdness: An Array of Strange English Events." BBC News England, May 4, 2014, http://www.bbc.co.uk/news/uk-england-27205244 (accessed May 21, 2014).

International Pancake Day of Liberal, KS. "The Story." Welcome to the Home of the International Pancake Race, 2013, http://www.pancakeday.net/#!the-story/c21kz (accessed April 28, 2014).

Le Vay, Benedict. *Ben Le Vay's Eccentric Britain*. 3rd ed. Chalfont St. Peter, UK: Bradt Travel Guides, 2011.

"Pancake Day in London." TimeOut London, http://www.timeout.com/london/things-to -do/pancake-day-in-london (accessed April 28, 2014).

"Pancake Race History." OlneyOnline.com, http://www.olneyonline.com/Pancake-Race -History (accessed April 28, 2014).

"A Parliamentary Tradition—Celebrating 17 Years of the Rehab Parliamentary Pancake Race." Rehab, http://www.rehab.ie/pancake-race/history.aspx (accessed April 28, 2014).

Porter, Laura. "Rehab UK Parliamentary Pancake Race Review." About.com London Travel, 2007, http://golondon.about.com/od/februaryannualevents/fr/parlracereview .htm (accessed April 28, 2014).

Roud, Steve. *The English Year*. London: Penguin, 2008.

"World Pancake Racing Championships." Wacky Nation, http://www.wackynation.com /pancake-race (accessed April 28, 2014).

PARKOUR

Parkour, sometimes referred to as *Le Parkour* or *L'art du Déplacement,* is a form of holistic physical training performed by individual men and women either alone or in groups in which participants aim to overcome any obstacle in their path by modifying their movements to suit the environment so that in effect, practitioners of *parkour* use only their bodies and their surroundings to propel themselves from one point to another. An individual who takes part in *parkour* is called a *traceur* (pl. *traceurs*), meaning "a person who draws a line or path." *Parkour* is particularly popular in France, the United Kingdom, the United States, Canada, Denmark, the Netherlands, Russia, and Germany, and though usually practiced in an urban setting, *parkour* can be performed anywhere.

Though *parkour* is an individualistic discipline, participants usually train and practice in small, nonhierarchical groups that meet up at gatherings organized via social media. Also, despite the individualistic nature of *parkour,* participants often have a keen sense that they belong to an increasingly multinational collective with a shared philosophy that is referred to as the *parkour* community. There are many *parkour* groups, both amateur and professional, within the *parkour* community across the world, of which perhaps the most famous is the Yamakasi. Other groups include Parkour Generations and Urban Freeflow, both of which are based in the United Kingdom, and Move Artistic and Pawa, based in Germany. Some of the biggest forces in modern *parkour* have united to establish the World Freerunning Parkour Federation (WFPF), which is influential not just in the United States but also worldwide after the success of the MTV television program *Ultimate Parkour*

A man performs a somersault after propelling himself from a wall during *parkour. Parkour* is a form of holistic physical training in which participants aim to overcome obstacles in their path by modifying their movements to suit the environment. (YouraPechkin/iStockphoto.com)

Challenge. The WFPF is dedicated to furthering the *parkour* philosophy and movement throughout the world. *Parkour* groups usually develop through word of mouth, social networking, and the activity's presence on the YouTube Web site.

It has been claimed that *parkour* is a sociopolitical concept in which *traceurs,* whom studies have shown tend to be young urban males displaying signs of marginalization, aim to reclaim control of their local urban landscape for their own purposes. That *parkour* has a somewhat anticonsumerist leaning is seen in the fact that it does not have a set uniform or look. Indeed, *traceurs* often wear cheap, comfortable, practical clothes that do not cost a lot of money to replace, as it is quite likely that clothing worn during *parkour* will be ruined quickly. Also, expensive high-fashion trainers are usually eschewed in favor of functional trainers suited to the discipline.

Movements employed in *parkour* include running, climbing, balancing, swinging, vaulting, jumping, rolling, and crawling, and so *traceurs* must possess great strength, physical fitness, balance and coordination, flexibility, imagination, and proprioception, that is, an awareness of the body's position in space. Despite the fact that many of the movements found within *parkour* are sports-like and demand rigorous physical and mental training, many *traceurs* regard *parkour* not as a sport but as an art form that consists of Eastern philosophical attitudes alongside physical discipline. *Parkour* is also often likened to the similar activity of free running in which many of the same actions are performed. Though the creators of *parkour* argue that the two disciplines are separate entities, *parkour* and free running are often referred to in tandem, and in 2009 the Parkour and Free Running Park was opened in Copenhagen, the capital of Denmark. Similarly, *parkour* and free running are combined at the Move Artistic Dome in Munich and at the indoor Parkour and Freerunning Hall in St. Petersburg, Russia.

Those who practice *parkour* argue that the activity instills in *traceurs* a sense of responsibility, self-reliance, and self-improvement and discourages the desire to behave recklessly. Though *parkour,* like free running, is traditionally a noncompetitive discipline, in recent times *parkour* competitions have begun. For instance, the inaugural Parcouring World Championships were held in Munich, Germany, in July 2007 in which *traceurs* had to complete a timed obstacle course. The championships began a debate within the *parkour* community between those who were pro- and anticompetition. The following year the Parcouring World Championships were extended to include a free running section.

Though *parkour* is often thought to have originated in France during the late 1980s, the history of the activity can be traced to an early 20th-century training regime called *méthode naturelle* ("natural method") or *hébertisme,* which was developed around 1906 by French naval officer Georges Hébert (1875–1957). Hébert believed that people should be physically fit and agile for the entire duration of their life so that they would be of benefit to their society, so he developed a training regime that he thought would foster physical fitness and dexterity while also reinforcing ideals of altruism and courage. Having left the navy, Hébert taught at the University of Reims in northern France, where he instigated a regime of sprinting and long-distance running, jumping, swimming, climbing, self-defense, throwing, lifting, and balancing, all performed outside on natural terrain. Hébert believed that this sort of physical training performed in a natural environment would provide his students with the stamina, strength, and speed to cope with all eventualities. However, he discouraged competition, as he believed that the very concept of competition would distract students from the philosophical focus of his regime. In time Hébert developed a series of drills and created equipment that substituted for natural terrain. Therefore, he became one of the first to teach physical training techniques and movements to overcome obstacles for nonmilitary reasons.

Modern *parkour* takes its name from the title Hébert gave to his obstacle course-style training, *parcours,* which translates from French as "course," "trail," or "route," and also from *parcours du combatant,* the French term for an obstacle course. Hébert's *méthode naturelle* had a strong hold on the French military during the Vietnam War, which utilized Hébert's regime during jungle combat. One of the French soldiers who taught the Hébert way of training was Raymond Belle, father of David Belle, often considered the creator of the modern *parkour* movement. Raymond Belle passed on his knowledge of *méthode naturelle* to his son, who was a keen martial artist and gymnast. During the 1980s David Belle moved to the Parisian suburb of Lisse, a multiracial area that had suffered from riots, and over time developed the principles of *méthode naturelle* and, in collaboration with others, most notably Sébastien Foucan, the founder of free running, developed modern-style *parkour.* Indeed, Belle and Foucan were founding members of the *parkour* group the Yamakasi. The name "Yamakasi," which derives from the Lingala language of Central Africa, translates as "strong body," "strong spirit," or "strong person" and was adopted by the nine members of the original *parkour* group (including Belle and Foucan) that was the first such group to come to prominence in the media.

In the late 1990s the media in England, France, and the Netherlands started to cover *parkour,* noting the activity's coolness, and in 2003 the British television station Channel 4 screened a documentary titled *Jump London,* which showed French *traceurs,* including Foucan, leaping across the landscape of England's capital city, London. However, after the program aired Belle apparently regretted that *parkour* had entered the media spotlight, and eventually a schism developed between Foucan and Belle as the two men disagreed over how *parkour* should evolve. Eventually Belle ensured that *parkour* would remain true to its roots in *méthode naturelle* and would retain an edge of risk while also being aesthetically pleasing. The schism also meant that *parkour* became distanced from free running, which placed an emphasis not on moving forward as in *parkour* but on moving the *traceur's* body in an individual and creative manner. Today free running is particularly associated with creative acrobatics and daring wall tricks, which do not meet the criteria of efficient movement as defined by Belle.

During the late 1990s and into the 2000s *parkour* became increasingly popular, as the activity was featured in numerous films, advertisements, and music videos. Though the activity had featured in films such as Luc Besson's *Taxi 2* (2000) and *Yamakasi—Les Samouraïs des Temps Modernes* (Yamakasi—The Modern Samurai, 2001) and its sequel *Les Fils du Vent* (2004, known in English as *The Great Challenge*), the popularity of *parkour* increased greatly after the James Bond film *Casino*

Royale (2006) featured a major fight scene at the beginning in which Bond chases an enemy, played by Sébastien Foucan, in the *parkour* style. The Jason Bourne films series (2002–2012) also features *parkour*-inspired chase sequences. Like Foucan, David Belle has also been involved with cinematic *parkour*, acting as *parkour* choreographer for the film *Prince of Persia: Sands of Time* (2010).

See also: Bull Running; Capoeira; *Mallakhamb*; Rhythmic Gymnastics; Yoga

Further Reading

Atkinson, Michael, and Kevin Young. *Deviance and Social Control in Sport*. Champaign, IL: Human Kinetics, 2008.

Cousineau, Phil. *The Painted Word: A Treasure Chest of Remarkable Words and Their Origins*. Berkeley, CA: Viva Editions, 2012.

Gerling, Ilona E., Alexander Pach, and Jan Vitfeld. *The Ultimate Parkour & Freerunning Book: Discover Your Possibilities*. 2nd revised ed. Maidenhead, UK: Meyer and Meyer Sport, 2013.

"Jump London 2003 FULL Video." YouTube, September 9, 2003, https://www.youtube.com/watch?v=l8fSXGP9wvQ (accessed March 18, 2014).

Wheaton, Belinda. *The Cultural Politics of Lifestyle Sports*. Abingdon, UK: Routledge, 2013.

PATO AND HORSEBALL

Pato is an Argentinean team ball game similar to *buzkashi* and includes elements of basketball, polo, and rugby that is played outside on horseback. In 1953 President Juan Peron declared *pato* the national sport of Argentina. Today the sport is popular in the pampas, grassland areas of the country where it is played by gauchos, the Argentinian equivalent of cowboys, and is enjoyed elsewhere in Argentina as an upper-class pursuit alongside polo. However, *pato* is in danger of losing its popularity to soccer, which is viewed as both accessible and cheap to play as opposed to *pato*, which is considered by many Argentinians as elitist and expensive, especially because as Argentina becomes increasingly urbanized, fewer people now own horses.

Pato developed as a folk sport around 1610 when residents of rural Argentina held competitions in which two teams on horseback from neighboring ranches would meet at the boundary of their properties and maneuver a live duck toward a predetermined point that served as a goal—the Spanish word *pato* means "duck." The teams would include many teammates who would bet money or land on which side would win. *Pato* thrived in Argentina despite being banned many times by the clergy and politicians, who feared that the game was too dangerous for both humans and animals—horses would be hurt, and it was common for players to be trampled as well as killed in knife fights resulting from disagreements over rule infringements. At one point during the 18th century, the Catholic Church decreed that any man caught playing *pato* would be excommunicated, and in 1739 the game was outlawed from the city of Santiago del Estero, followed by Buenos Aires, the capital city of Argentina, in 1822. However, theses bans were relaxed somewhat at the start of the 20th century, when the rules of *pato* were codified along the lines of polo, and in 1938 the ban was lifted altogether in Buenos Aires. In 1941 the Federación Argentina de Pato (FAP, Argentine Pato Federation) was established as the sport's governing body. Today the FAP has many responsibilities, including the promotion of the sport, regulating rules, organizing tournaments, and ensuring the implementation of special breeding and care regimes for the horses used in the sport, which exhibit the same characteristics as the horses used to play polo. There are over 30 *pato* grounds registered with the FAP.

Two teams of four players on horseback contest the modern game of *pato*, though a leather ball featuring six handles is used instead of a duck. The goal toward which the ball is maneuvered is a hoop attached to an upright post 2.4 meters (almost 8 feet) tall located at the end of the playing area, measuring 180 to 220 meters by 80 to 90 meters (590.5 to 722 feet by 626 to 295 feet), that is similar in size to a polo field. As in basketball, players aim to score more goals than their opponents by throwing the ball through the hoop. However, unlike in basketball, in *pato* players can hold on to the ball using the ball's handles and must offer the ball to the opposition when challenged. Possession of the ball is regained by pulling it away from the player holding it while simultaneously standing on the horse's stirrups. One of the game's most spectacular moves, which is facilitated by a special saddle, occurs when a player leans close to the ground to snatch the ball, demonstrating great balance and stability as well as excellent riding skills.

The sport is regarded as symbolic of Argentinean national identity and as a way of helping to marginalize foreign influence on the country's culture. However, in most areas of the Argentina *pato* is no longer a folk sport but has evolved into an elitist though amateur pursuit for the upper classes. This is evinced by the fact that in 2009 the 68th annual Abierto Argentino de Pato (Argentine Pato Open) was held at the celebrated Argentine Polo Ground in the Palermo area of northeastern Buenos Aires. The final of this championship attracted a crowd of around 4,000 people, which is small compared to the 70,000 who regularly watch soccer matches in the capital.

Snow Polo

The first official game of snow polo, a modified version of regular polo, was held in 1985 on Lake St. Moritz, Switzerland. The sport is played on an even layer of compacted snow or a frozen lake, a smaller playing area than that of mainstream polo.

The sport is an elitist leisure activity played across Europe, in the United States (exclusively in Aspen, Colorado), and in Argentina and Russia as well as China, where the Snow Polo World Cup took place in 2012. Teams from England, Australia, Chile, Canada, and New Zealand also compete.

Two variations of *pato* are *pato de picadero,* which is played by two teams of three on a smaller pitch, and *pato-snow,* which is *pato* played on snow. This version began as a demonstration sport for the amusement of tourists visiting Argentinian ski resorts. However, horseball is the most successful sport to develop from *pato.*

Horseball is a modified version of *pato* in which a ball is conducted across a field, and points are scored by shooting the ball through a high net. Horseball first became popular in France during the 1930s and subsequently spread across Europe and then the rest of the world. In 2006 the Federation International de Horseball (International Horseball Federation) and the FAP jointly revised the rules of horseball to bring the game in line with *pato,* though the sports remain somewhat distinct. Also in 2006 the inaugural World Cup of Pato–Horseball was held in Buenos Aires, with Portugal crowned champions. Horseball is recognized by the International Federation for Equestrian Sports.

See also: Bearbaiting and Badger Baiting; Bull Running; *Buzkashi;* Camel and Yak Racing; Camel Wrestling; Cockfighting; Croquet; Elephant Sports; Foxhunting; Hare Coursing; Nonlethal Bullfighting; Pigeon Racing; Rugby League; Sheepdog Trials; Spanish Bullfighting; Yabbie Races

Further Reading

DK Eyewitness Travel Guide: Argentina. London: Dorling Kindersley, 2010.

Moffett, Matt. "In Soccer-Mad Argentina, the National Sport Is a Lame Duck." *Wall Street Journal,* June 18, 2010, http://online.wsj.com/news/articles/SB1000142405274870350 9404575300403661697926?mg=reno64wsj&url=http%3A%2F%2Fonline.wsj.com% 2Farticle%2FSB10001424052748703509404575300403661697926.html (accessed April 24, 2014).

Nauright, John, and Charles Parrish, eds. *Sports around the World: History, Culture and Practice,* Vol. 1, *General Topics, Africa, Asia, Middle East, and Oceania.* Santa Barbara, CA: ABC-CLIO, 2012.

"Origins & Rules: Pato/Horse Ball." Poloconsult, http://www.poloconsult.com/index.php /en/le-polo/origines-a-reglements/153-pato-horse-ball (accessed April 24, 2014).

"What Is Horseball?" The British Horseball Association, http://www.britishhorseball.co.uk (accessed April 24, 2014).

PEHLWANI/KUSHTI

Pehlwani, also known as *kushti,* is a form of wrestling for men and women that is widespread across the Indian subcontinent and is also found in countries in which immigrants from the subcontinent have settled, particularly the United Kingdom and Australia. *Pehlwani* also occurs in Pakistan, Iran, Turkey, and various African nations. The sport transcends Indian society (including the caste system), culture, and religion, with Sikh, Muslim, Parsee, and Christian wrestlers competing. The sport is not limited by geography either, as it occurs in both rural and urban environs. Indeed, *pehlwani* is not just a sport but is also a way of life involving diet, exercise, training, ethics, and morality.

The origins of *pehlwani* can be found in Hindu mythology, and all Hindu holy books describe the sport. In addition, the ancient epic poem *Mahabarata* describes numerous *pehlwani* contests, including one match that lasted 27 days between Bhima, Lord Krishna's most faithful disciple, and Rajah Jarasandha, the enemy of righteousness who was ultimately torn in half as punishment for his immorality.

Another epic, the *Ramayana,* tells how Hanuman the monkey god taught the art of wrestling to humanity so that wrestling could be used to assist Rama in his battles against the demon Ravana. Hanuman is often depicted in religious art as the first *pehlwani* guru carrying a ceremonial *gada,* a large round rock attached to bamboo staff 1 meter (3 feet) long, that is often given to champion wrestlers and is also used in strength training. In actuality, *pehlwani* has a very long history, as *mallayuda,* traditional and extremely violent Indian combat wrestling, the sport from which *pehlwani* evolved, dates from the 5th century BCE. Meanwhile, the Greek invasion led by Alexander the Great in the 4th century BCE brought a revolutionary idea of interregional athletic contests called *samjya* to India, hence the similarities between the traditional Indian *akhara* wrestling gymnasiums and the *palaestra* or wrestling schools found in ancient Greece. Also during the rule of Ashoka the Great (265–238 BCE) of the Magadha Empire, wrestlers would journey across the subcontinent to compete in professional wrestling championships. Later, during the 8th century many small republics began to evolve in India's Ganges Valley, and it is chronicled that wrestling tournaments were held as peacekeeping exercises in which champion wrestlers faced against each other to avoid war. In the 12th century competitors began to be matched on the criteria of age, weight, and strength. During the British colonial period *pehlwani* continued to thrive, and because of the support of local maharajahs, the region of the Punjab, northern India, became the best wrestling area. It was from here that the greatest of all *pehlwani* wrestlers, Ghulam Muhammad, also known as Gama the Lion of Punjab, came. In 1898 Gama won the title of "Rustam i Hind" (Champion of All India), and in 1910 he traveled to England, where he won the John Bull World Championship for Catch as Catch Can Wrestling. Gama is the only wrestler to remain undefeated throughout his entire career, which consisted of over 5,000 matches.

In India, *pehlwani* takes place in a clay (*mitti*) or dirt pit, the soil of which is mixed with ghee (clarified butter), curd, limewater, Ayurveda medicines such as turmeric and honey, and, occasionally, minced meat and is tended to before each practice. The sport mainly consists of grappling matches and competitions called *dangals* in which wrestlers attempt to pin their opponent so that his back and shoulders are in contact with the floor for two seconds. There are no rounds in *pehlwani,* so it is common for fights to last between 20 and 30 minutes and sometimes as long as 90 minutes. Pehlwani consists of *paintra* (stance) and *daw-pech* (moves and countermoves). *Paintra* is the art of standing in the *akhara* and as such is the prelude to every *dangal.* The stance used in *pehlwani* allows a wrestler to attack or defend and is performed by fixing the feet in the ground, having made a move or counterattack. Though stance is extremely important, *pehlwani* features hundreds of moves and countermoves, feints and parries. Skilled wrestlers aim to achieve the best result from the least amount of motion, so they need to be able to anticipate their opponent's moves.

Pehlwani is organized around the institutional structure of a gymnasium called an *akhara.* Each *akhara* has between 40 and 60 *pehlwans,* wrestlers who are spiritually and physically strong, with an average age of 20 but ranging from 15 to 60 years old. Each *akhara* is run by a guru who teaches the *pehlwans* not just the art of wrestling but also the moral and ethical philosophy that underpins the physical training and exercise regimens that make up the *pehlwans'* everyday life. A wrestler wakes at 3:00 a.m., washes, and goes to the *akhara*, where he exercises until 8:00 a.m. Afterward he drinks a mixture of milk, ghee, and almonds. Later the wrestler eats—a *pehlwan's* expensive diet consists of milk, fruit, vegetables, almonds, ghee, eggs, and chapattis—and rests before returning to the *akhara* to perform strengthening exercises using equipment including *gadas*. Life at the *akhara* is extremely disciplined, with *pehlwans* told how to sleep, what to eat and wear, and even when to defecate. In addition, a wrestler must adhere to a strict morality of restraint and antisensuality. To this end a wrestler must be celibate, as semen is regarded as the main source of strength, so it is crucial that a wrestler abstain from sex. Wrestlers must also refrain from other things thought to enflame passions including smoking, spicy food, alcohol, tea, coffee, meat, and watching movies. This almost monastic lifestyle attests to the close association between religious mythology and *pehlwani* echoed by the suggested origins of the sport.

The future of *pehlwani* looks uncertain. In urban areas the sport is losing its popularity and having to modernize. For example, competitors in cities such as Mumbai now compete on rubber mats (rural economies tend not to be able to afford mats) rather than in pits and wear spandex uniforms and rubber shoes, while bouts now conform to time limits. Such innovations are partly in response to the fact that spectators are now used to watching American professional wrestling that is broadcast on Indian satellite television. *Pehlwani* purists, however, who call the choreographed wrestling bouts *noora kushti*, meaning "fixed fight," frown upon this style of televised wrestling. Other more TV-friendly sports such as cricket also receive increasing amounts of television coverage, thereby detracting from the reporting of *pehlwani*. Also, *pehlwani* may be a sport of strength and stamina but lacks glamour, meaning that it does not appeal to Westernized Indian men who now join *akharas* to get fit and attain the physique of Bollywood film stars. That having been said, major Bollywood star Akshay Kumar, the son of a wrestler, sponsors wrestlers in need in conjunction with the Maharashtra Wrestling Association. Another problem facing *pehlwani* is that the outlay to send a child to an *akhara* is often more than a rural or lower-class family can afford. In this case the boy's community may share some of the cost, believing that the wrestler's future earnings from appearing in *jatras* (fairs or festivals where many wrestling bouts are held) will be worth the expense in the long run. However, in reality there are few competitions where wrestlers earn between Rs20,000 and Rs50,000 (roughly US$328 to US$821).

On the upside, however, wrestling in general has become more popular in India after the success of Indian wrestlers at the last two Summer Olympics and the success of Geeta Phogat, the first Indian woman freestyle wrestler to qualify for the Olympic Games (London 2012) who won gold at the 2010 Commonwealth Games.

Pehlwani features in the 2010 Indian comedy film *Kushti*.

See also: Celtic Wrestling; *Glima; Lucha Libre;* Mongolian Wrestling; *Schwingen;* Sumo Wrestling; *Varzesh-e Bastani; Yagli Gures;* Yoga

Further Reading

Alter, Joseph. "Indian Nationalism and the World Wrestling Championships of 1910 and 1928." Academy of the Punjab in North America, 1988, http://apnaorg.com/articles /gama-1/ (accessed July 31, 2014).

Alter, Joseph S. *The Wrestler's Body: Identity and Ideology in North India*. Berkeley: University of California Press, 1992.

"The Art of Pahelwani." Pahelwani: The Art of Punjabi Wrestling, http://www.pahelwani .com/#/the-art-of-pahelwani/4544812677 (accessed July 31, 2014).

BBC Queen's Baton Relay Team. "Queen's Baton Relay: What Is Kushti Wrestling?" BBC News, October 24, 2013, http://www.bbc.co.uk/news/blogs-queens-baton-relay-2452 1084 (accessed July 31, 2014).

"Kushti—Traditional Indian Wrestling." Kushti Wrestling Blogspot, http://kushtiwrestling .blogspot.co.uk/search/label/kushti (accessed July 31, 2014).

Levine, Emma. *A Game of Polo with a Headless Goat and Other Bizarre Sports Discovered across Asia*. London: André Deutsch, 2003.

Rao, Mallika. "The Accidental Sensuality of Ancient Indian Wrestling." Huffington Post, July 2, 2014, http://www.huffingtonpost.com/2014/07/02/pehlwan-kushti-photography _n_5513303.html (accessed July 31, 2014).

Sainath, P. "The Culture and Crisis of Kushti." The Hindu, October 31, 2013, http://www .thehindu.com/opinion/columns/sainath/the-culture-and-crisis-of-kushti/article 5297790.ece (accessed July 31, 2014).

Sainath, P. "Wrestling with the Rural Economy." The Hindu, October 30, 2013, http://www .thehindu.com/opinion/columns/sainath/wrestling-with-the-rural-economy/article 5286230.ece?ref=relatedNews (accessed July 31, 2014).

Shah, Kunal M. "Kushti Inc." *Times of India,* January 29, 2008, http://timesofindia.indiatimes .com/entertainment/hindi/bollywood/news-interviews/Kushti-Inc/articleshow/273 8241.cms (accessed July 31, 2014).

"Sport/Activity: Wrestling: Pehlwani/Kushti." 4.4 Million Days, 2013, http:// 4point4milliondays.com/disciplines-sport-39–1048 (accessed July 13, 2014).

Wood, John. "The Great Gama: Lion of The Punjab." Oldtime Strongman Blog, March 4, 2012, http://www.oldtimestrongman.com/blogs/new-blog/2012-03/04-483-great-gama -lion-punjab (accessed July 31, 2014).

PELOTA

The word *pelota* refers to both the sport of *pelota,* sometimes called Basque *pelota* and called *pelote Basque* in France, and the ball used in that game. The sport of *pelota* is a folk court game played by men and women akin to handball. The sport originated in the Basque region of Europe that is made up of the area of the western Pyrenees mountains that form the border between northern Spain and the south of France. In the Basque area the popularity of *pelota* rivals that of soccer. *Pelota* is also popular in Latin American countries, including Chile, Argentina, and Uruguay, where the game has spread via Basque migration. *Pelota* federations also exist in countries as varied as the Netherlands, India, and the Philippines.

The sport is governed by the International Federation of Basque Pelota founded in Madrid, the capital of Spain, in 1929, though professional *pelota* is overseen by the League of Companies of Basque Pelota. Players, called *pelotaris,* wear white trousers and either a red or blue shirt or sash.

According to Basque folklore, the boulders of the Pyrenees were used as *pelotas* by the *jentilak,* giants who had rejected Christianity. However, the documented history of *pelota* reaches back to ancient Greece, as is evinced by the fact that Greek poet Homer refers to the game in his work *The Odyssey.* In the Basque region the game has been documented since the 13th century, and it is recorded that in 1331 King Felipe III of Evreux (in northern France) ordered a stand to be built in the cloister of the Dominican Order in Pamplona (in Spain) so he could watch a *pelota* match. Historians believe that the game may have adopted elements from both Aztec ball games brought to the Basque area by returning conquistadors and French *jeu de palme.* The Basque region was unique in Europe in that while the rest of the continent saw *jeu de palme* succeeded by lawn tennis, in the Basque region *jeu de palme* courts were transformed into *pelota* courts. The earliest documented *pelota* match was held during the early 1800s, and the popularity of the game grew considerably through the rest of the 19th century. Indeed, such was the popularity of the game during this period that tournament-winning *pelota* players were the highest-paid sportsmen of the era. In 1900 *pelota* was included in the Summer Olympic Games held in Paris, France. However, in 1924 (Paris), 1968 (Mexico City), and 1992 (Barcelona), *pelota* was included in the Olympics as a demonstration sport only. The first official professional *pelota* championship was held in 1925, leading to an increasing number of tournaments being established. The first amateur *pelota* world championships took place in San Sebastián, Spain, in 1952 and take place every four years.

In the past *pelota* was played on grass meadows called *pilota-soros* on isolated farms and in villages. Today village *pelota* is sometimes played on *plazas libres,* or free squares, that were originally bare earth but now tend to be paved areas. More commonly, however, *pelota* is played on a court called a fronton. These are classified as either short frontons measuring 30 and 36 meters in length (roughly 98 and 118 feet) or long frontons measuring 54 meters in length (117 feet).

In essence, *pelota* is contested either by two singles players or two teams of two who play the ball, which is normally made of leather or rubber, against the froton, aiming to move the ball out of the reach of their opponent/s so that the ball rebounds between the low line marking the low off-area and the high line indicating the high off-area. The ball may either be played so it rebounds directly off the front wall onto the floor of the court or struck onto the court's long side-wall. Opposing players may either play the ball straightaway after it ricochets off the front wall or the sidewall or after the ball has rebounded once from the court's floor. A team may score a point, or *tanto* (pl. *tantos*), for themselves by playing the ball so that the opposition cannot play it before it rebounds from the floor more than once or by playing the ball so that it ricochets off the front wall and then bounces off the floor and subsequently outside the playing areas. A team will also receive points if the opposing side hits the ball against the front wall but below the low line or above the high line or if the opposition strikes the ball but it fails to reach the front wall.

Pelota matches are played to different numbers of points depending on which version of the game is being played. More recently invented forms of the game, sometimes called indirect games, require various amounts of points to be scored to record a win. For instance, in *pelota a mano* the aim is to reach 22 points, while in *remonte* and *cesta punta* 40 points need to be reached, and 45 are needed to win *pelota a pala*. However, in the oldest styles of *pelota*, which are sometime classified as direct *pelota* games, the scoring system is very similar to that used in lawn tennis, proceeding as follows: 15-0, 15 all, 15-30, and 30 all. If both teams become level on 40 points each, a *dos* is declared, just as deuce is called in tennis. However, rather than proceed on to an advantage point as in tennis, when a *dos* occurs in *pelota* the first team to reach 40 points goes back from 40 to 30 points, and then both teams stay at 30 points all. The match then continues until one of the teams scores two consecutive points with which to end the match.

The various forms of *pelota* each employ different equipment, rules, and types of court. The game was simplified to a degree by the inauguration of the first professional championship, for the establishing of tournaments necessitated the standardization of *pelota* so that players around the world all played by the same rules. The standardization of *pelota* included the establishing of four modalities, that is, different types of court on which various styles of *pelota* are played, and 14 versions of *pelota* (of which all but 2 are played exclusively by men, with women permitted to play only *frontenis,* a Mexican hybrid of tennis and *pelota,* and rubber *pelota* in *trinquete*), plus set ball weights and court sizes. It should be noted that this move toward standardization was somewhat contentious, with critics arguing that the move erased the original traits of particular modalities.

The four standardized modalities are the *trinquete,* the 30-meter fronton, the 36-meter fronton, and the 54-meter fronton. The *trinquete,* which is a four-wall fronton measuring 28.50 meters (93.5 feet) in length with an inclined roof extending along the left wall from the front wall to the rear wall, is used to play the disciplines of *paleta* (with a rubber or leather *pelota*), *pelota a mano* in singles and doubles format, and *xare.* The 30-meter fronton is used to play *frontenis* as well as *paleta* (with a rubber *pelota*). The 36-meter fronton is used to play the disciplines of *pala corta, paleta* (with a leather *pelota*), and *pelota a mano* as singles or doubles, while the 54-meter fronton is used to play *cesta punta.* Of the 14 *pelota* disciplines, the most often played are *pelota a mano, pelota a pala,* and *cesta punta. Pelota a mano* is the most popular form of the sport and is played bare-handed or with hands protected by strips of material called *tacos* that reduce vibration and adhere to the hands with bandage strips. *Pelota a mano* is similar in nature to fives, as players hit the leather-covered ball (usually weighing 92–95 grams, or 3.2–3.3 ounces) against the end wall of the court with the intention of playing the ball out of their opponent's reach. *Pelota a pala* is a very physical version of *pelota* and is one of several forms of the game in which a wooden bat (usually made of beech wood) is used to hit the ball. *Cesta punta* (*zesta punta* in Basque), meaning "edged basket" in Spanish, is known outside of Europe as jai alai and is popular in Spain, southern France, Mexico, and the United States (especially Florida). The game is also played in the Philippines and was popular in Cuba until it was banned by Fidel Castro in 1960.

The earliest form of the game was played on Sundays and feast days in the court-yard of parish churches or against church walls, hence the term "jai alai" translates from Basque as "merry feast." Indeed, so close were ties between the church and jai alai that the game even has its own patron saint, St. Ignatius Loyola, who hailed from the Basque area and, according to some, invented jai alai.

As in other forms of *pelota,* jai alai involves hitting a ball between lines marked on the froton (in jai alai the 54-meter froton is used). However, in jai alai teams of gloved players propel the rubber ball using a curved basket measuring around 100 centimeters (39 inches), long called a cesta, hence the game's Spanish name. The cesta is usually made of chestnut wood and tightly woven wicker and features a pocket for holding the ball. When a player receives the ball in his basket, he im-mediately whips it back against the wall, generating a tremendous amount of speed and force. Indeed, in jai alai the ball travels at up to 300 kilometers (186 miles) per hour. For this reason, jai alai is often considered the fastest and most spectacular form of *pelota,* and for safety reasons professional players in the United States wear protective headgear. Jai alai is also unusual for *pelota* in that the game can be played between two teams of eight or eight teams of two players. Jai alai takes the form of a round-robin—a player or team that wins stays in the game, but losers are re-placed. This pattern continues until one player or team reaches seven points; sec-ond and third places in the contest are awarded to the two players or teams with the next highest scores. In the event of a tie, a play-off occurs. Thus, in jai alai punters may bet on wins, places, and show, as in horse-race betting. However, in jai alai punters can place quinella, exacta, trifecta, and perfecta bets.

Jai alai debuted in the United States at the St. Louis World Fair held in 1904, leading to frontons being erected nationwide. However, the game did not really become popular in the United States until 1937, when Florida adopted a law al-lowing parimutuel betting on the sport, that is, betting in which all bets are placed together in a pool, taxes are removed, and odds are calculated by sharing the bet-ting pool among all winners. Betting on the game has also been permitted in Las Vegas and Reno in Nevada (where the MGM Grand Hotels housed frontons until the mid-1980s) as well as in Connecticut and Rhode Island, but on the whole, bet-ting on the game has failed to take off across the United States.

It is not, however, only jai alai that attracts gambling, for *pelota* in general is as-sociated with betting. In the Basque region bookmakers called *corredores* call out odds as *pelota* matches progress, and a particularly curious traditional feature of *pelota* betting is that wagers are made on tiny strips of paper that the bookmaker throws at the punter using a hollowed-out tennis ball, which the punter subse-quently returns to the bookmaker, though today it is also possible to bet online.

See also: Bull Running; Fives; Handball; Real Tennis; Spanish Bullfighting

Further Reading

McKay, Brett, and Kate McKay. "The Return of Jai Alai." The Art of Manliness, November 19, 2009, http://www.artofmanliness.com/2009/11/19/the-return-of-jai-alai/ (ac-cessed July 13, 2014).

McNicoll, Kathryn. *Real Tennis.* Princes Risborough, UK: Shire Publications, 2005.

"Modalities." The International Federation of Basque Pelota, http://www.fipv.net/en/el-juego/modalidades (accessed July 13, 2014).

Nauright, John, and Charles Parrish, eds. *Sports around the World: History, Culture and Practice,* Vol. 1, *General Topics, Africa, Asia, Middle East, and Oceania.* Santa Barbara, CA: ABC-CLIO, 2012.

Shaw, Lisa, and Stephanie Dennison. *Pop Culture Latin America! Media, Arts and Lifestyle.* Santa Barbara, CA: ABC-CLIO, 2005.

Thompson, William N. *Gambling in America: An Encyclopedia of History, Issues, and Society.* Santa Barbara, CA: ABC-CLIO, 2001.

Wilson, Ed, ed. *The Sports Book.* 4th ed. London: Dorling Kindersley, 2013.

Woodworth, Paddy. *The Basque Country: A Cultural History.* Oxford: Oxford University Press, 2008.

"The World of the Ball." Kingdom of Navarre, 2014, http://www.turismo.navarra.es/eng/propuestas /naturalmente-deporte/ofertas/El_mundo_de_la_pelota.htm (accessed July 13, 2014).

PÉTANQUE

Pétanque is an outdoor folk bowling game played by both sexes on an individual or team basis. *Pétanque* belongs to the same family of traditional bowling games as the various forms of French *boules, bocce* (which is Italian in origin), *boccia,* and lawn bowls.

Locals playing *pétanque* in Ban Nong Luang, Laos, in September 2013. In contrast to many similar games, *pétanque* players throw the ball while standing with their feet anchored together on the ground. (mathess/iStockphoto.com)

In terms of individual players, *pétanque* is said to be the world's most played form of bowls. While *pétanque* is played across Europe, with players in Portugal, England, Monaco, Belgium, and Switzerland, the game is particularly associated with the Provence area of the south of France. Due to the French presence in Southeast Asia in earlier years, *pétanque* is also played in Thailand, Vietnam, Malaysia, Cambodia, Laos, Madagascar, and India, and for the same reason the game is also played in the United States and Canada. *Pétanque* is also popular in Australia and Singapore, where French migrants imported the game. *Pétanque* was recognized by the International Olympic Committee in 1986, and in 1987 66 teams took part in the inaugural Pétanque Open, held in Singapore.

There are several theories as to the origins of *pétanque*. It has been argued that the history of *pétanque* can be traced back to Roman times, for the Romans played a game in which flat stones, coins, or balls were thrown at a smaller target. Roman soldiers brought this game to Provence when they occupied the area around 125 BCE. *Pétanque* is also said to have evolved from an early more athletic version of *boules* particular to Provence called *jeu provençal*, the south of France counterpart of *boules Lyonnais*, which is played in Lyon in central France. *Jeu provençal* was invented at the end of the 19th century, and though the game is still played (particularly in the south of France) it has largely been overtaken in popularity by *pétanque*. The size and the weight of the *boules* and the jack in *jeu provençal* are the same as in *pétanque*.

The name *pétanque* derives from the Occitan language of southern France and Monaco, also spoken in parts of Italy and Spain, in which *petanca* or *ped tanco* translates roughly as feet together on the ground or feet anchored, for in contrast to other forms of *boules*, players throw or roll balls without moving their feet. The modern form of *pétanque* was created in 1907 in the town of La Ciotat, near Marseiles in southern France, most probably by Jules le Noir, whose rheumatism prevented him from running as he delivered the *boules*. In 1910 Ernest Pitiot organized the first *pétanque* tournament and then in 1945 established the Fédération Française de Petanque et Jeu Provençal (FFPJP, French Pétanque Federation). Until the founding of the FFPJP, *pétanque* and *jeu provençal* (and other forms of *boules* called *boule des berges* and *boule en bois*) had been governed by the Fédération Française de Boules (FFB). The FFB had been dominated by almost 130,000 *jeu provençal* players. However, in the lead-up to the creation of the FFPJP there had been many squabbles between players of *jeu provençal* and *pétanque* players. By the end of 1945 the FFPJP had gained about 10,000 members and today has more than 450,000 members in France, with more than 600,000 registered *pétanque* players in 86 countries, though as the game is often played informally, the actual number of *pétanque* players worldwide probably reaches into the many millions. The popularity of *pétanque* is most probably due to the game's simplicity, for the aim of *pétanque* (and similar *boules* games) is to either throw or roll a large ball, called the *boule* (pl. *boules*) at a smaller target ball known variously as a *bouchon* (meaning "cork"), *le petit* (meaning "the little"), the *cochonet* (meaning "piglet"), or at the *pallino* (meaning "small bat"). In English the target ball is known as the jack.

In *pétanque* there are competitions for singles in which two players face each other one-on-one (tête-a-tête), doubles (*doubletts*), and triples (*triplett*). In singles each player has three *boules*, in doubles and triples players have two *boules* each, and the individuals or teams take turns throwing or rolling the ball as close as possible to the target ball. In contrast to other *boules*-type games, *pétanque* players must keep their feet together and planted on the ground. The *boules* may be delivered in one of three ways—from an erect position, from a bending position, or from a squatting position. In *pétanque* the *boules* are thrown with the palm of the hand facing downward, as this allows for a greater degree of accuracy and control of power than if the *boules* were thrown with the palm facing upward. In terms of strategy, players must decide whether to shoot or to point. To shoot is to throw a *boule* so that it hits an opposing *boule* and moves it away from the jack. Players who choose this option are known as shooters. To point means to throw a *boule* so that it comes to rest as close to the jack as possible. Players who point are known as pointers and demonstrate accuracy; they are able to judge the correct amount of power necessary and show an ability to turn the *boule* to the left or right. Pointers may also use a backspin to stop the *boule* once it has hit the playing surface. When a pointer throws, the pointer keeps the arm fully extended and swings it back as far as possible and then forward again, releasing the *boule* as the hand rises in front of the body.

Before a game of *pétanque* begins a coin toss is held to decide which team plays first. The team winning the toss then draws a circle on the playing surface measuring about 35 to 50 centimeters (14 to 19.5 inches) across in which all players must stand in order to throw the *boules*, which are usually made of steel and are about 7 to 8 centimeters (2.75 to 3.15 inches) in diameter. The *pétanque* playing area is usually located in an open area such as a village or town square, a park, or a beach and on a playing surface covered in gravel, hard sand, or soil that measures 15 meters (49 feet) long by 4 meters (roughly 13 feet) wide. Though *pétanque* can be played on a closely cropped lawn, grass is not a good surface for *pétanque*, as the jack is so small that it can be difficult to spot among the turf.

A member of the toss-winning team throws the jack, which has a diameter of 2.5 to 3.5 centimeters (1 to 1.35 inches), forward so that it lands not less than 6 meters (about 20 feet) or more than 10 meters (33 feet) away. The team that throws the jack then throws the first *boule*. It is usual for a pointer to throw the first *boule*, as a player who is good at pointing is able to throw the *boule* so that it comes to rest in front of but not too close to the jack. In *pétanque* it is important that the opening throw should not land in too close a proximity to the jack, because if the opposing team has an talented shooter, a first *boule* that has come to rest very close to the jack will be removed by the shooter, and thus the accurate pointing demonstrated by the opening team will have been wasted.

After the first *boule* has been thrown, the opposing individual or team throws the second *boule*. From this point on the individual/team farthest away from the jack after each throw launches the next *boule*. However, if the closest *boules* from each individual or team are equidistant from the jack, then the individual or team that threw last throws again. If the *boules* are still the same distance from the jack, then the individuals or teams play alternately until the deadlock is broken. If the *boules* are still equidistant at the end of the game, then no points are awarded to either individual/team. This pattern of play continues until one individual/team has thrown all their *boules*. After this the other individual/team throws all their remaining *boules*.

Points are awarded for every *boule* of an individual/team closer to the jack than any *boule* of the opponent. In *pétanque* it is usual for the winner of the game to be the first to accrue 13 points. There are several ways for a player to ensure that her or his *boule* is nearer to the jack than that of the opponent. For instance, a *boule* can be thrown toward the jack, or the jack can be moved closer to an already played *boule* by the action of another *boule*. If necessary a player may use her or his *boule* to knock that of the opponent out of the way so that the player's own *boule* ends up nearest to the target—it is for this reason that good shooters throw after proficient pointers have played. An individual/team can claim as many points as they have *boules* nearer the jack than the opposing individual or team has. When the *boules* have been thrown for both sides and the points are assessed, a *mène,* or end, is said to have been played. The individual/team winning the end begins play in the next end.

As is the case with many folk sports, *pétanque* has many peculiar rituals of which perhaps the most well known, or infamous, is the custom of kissing the fanny, which occurs in Provence and Brittany. Kissing the fanny is the punishment awarded to any individual or team that loses a match by 13 points to 0, in what is known as a shutout game. The kissing the fanny custom sees the whitewashed loser made to kiss the bare bottom of a woman as depicted in a painting, sculpture, or similar object in public and with the opponent/s witnessing the punishment. According to legend, kissing the fanny originated in the eastern French region of Savoy during World War I when a café waitress called Fanny would try to cheer up players who had failed to score by allowing them to kiss her cheek. One day the local mayor failed to score during a match, but unfortunately Fanny disliked him intensely, and when he came to kiss her cheek as was customary, Fanny is said to have lifted her skirt and presented to the mayor her bare bottom to kiss. Undaunted, the mayor obliged, and the custom of kissing the fanny was born. Today it is customary for any team that is made to kiss the fanny to buy a round of drinks for the winning team, with the winners declaring "Fanny paie à boire!" ("Fanny pays for the drinks!").

An unusual form of *pétanque* in which participants play with color-coded square balls, *boules carrées,* occurs on the French Riviera. In 1980 three friends living in the old town of Cagnes-sur-Mer invented this variation, as they were frustrated at not being able to play *pétanque* on the town's steeply sloping roads. The friends decided to try playing with cubes, as once the square balls land on the stone roads they tend not to continue to roll downhill as round balls would, though they can veer bizarrely on landing. The balls' tendency toward an abrupt cessation of movement does, however, mean that luck more than skill is often a deciding factor when playing this variant. The 35th World Championship of Boules Carrées took place in the Montée de la Bourgade du Haut-de-Cagnes on August 16, 2014. The event, which used 1,218 *boules* and 474 jacks, attracted 330 participants from France, England, Italy, Denmark, Sweden, and Japan.

See also: Curling; *Kubb*; *La Soule*; *Mölkky*; Real Tennis

Further Reading

"History of Pétanque." Petanque.org, 1996–2013, http://petanque.org/around_the_world/french_games.shtml (accessed March 16, 2014).

Mr. Bordsenius. "Pétanque Beginners Pages: An Introduction." Pétanque.org, January 15, 2001, http://petanque.org/beginners/185.shtml (accessed March 16, 2014).

Mr. Bordsenius. "Pétanque for Beginners: Throwing Your Boule." Pétanque.org, January 15, 2001, http://petanque.org/beginners/187.shtml (accessed March 16, 2014).

Nauright, John, and Charles Parrish, eds. *Sports around the World: History, Culture and Practice*, Vol. 1, *General Topics, Africa, Asia, Middle East, and Oceania*. Santa Barbara, CA: ABC-CLIO, 2012.

Nicolas, Chloé. "Cagnes: À en perdre la boule . . . carrée." *Nice-Matin*, August 17, 2014.

Pagnoni, Mario. *The Joy of Bocce*. 3rd ed. Bloomington, IN: AuthorHouse, 2010.

PIGEON RACING

Pigeon racing is a sport in which specially trained pigeons are released in order for them to fly back to their lofts. The distance from the liberation site—that is, the point of release—to the loft is carefully measured, and the time it takes a bird to travel the distance is timed to calculate the pigeon's rate of travel. The speed of all the pigeons is compared, and the pigeon that returned at the quickest speed is declared the winner. The pigeon's velocity is measured in yards per minute or miles per minute. The velocity is calculated by dividing the distance traveled by the pigeon into yards and then dividing the number of yards by the amount of minutes it took the pigeon to return. A bird of optimum fitness can travel at 90 miles per hour and cover 500 miles in a day.

Pigeon racing is popular worldwide but most particularly in North and South America, Asia, Europe, and Africa.

A specific breed of pigeon, the racing homer, is used in pigeon racing. Around 60 pigeons are kept in a loft, with the birds ranging in age from young to old. Stock pigeons used to breed new birds also live in the loft. The pigeon racing season is split into two to accommodate both the young and old birds. In the United Kingdom old pigeons race from March to mid-July and young birds race from mid-July to September. Pigeon racers start to train their birds about three weeks before a race. Training involves allowing the birds to fly around the loft for an hour a day to begin with and then graduating to long-distance training that sees the birds released at increasing distances from their loft. On the day of the race, pigeons are driven in baskets to the marking station, where the numbered rubber band placed around one of each bird's legs has its number double-checked against the entry form. Next the pigeons are checked for good health. Once a pigeon has passed the fitness test, the bird's vaccination certificate is verified. Next the male and female pigeons are packed into separate crates and driven by transporter truck to the liberation site. It is quite usual for the truck to journey through the night to reach the designated launch site. Liberation sites are used more than once, and a decision on when to release the pigeons is made by the race organizers, the race controller, and the person in charge of conveying the birds. The decision on when to release the birds depends on the weather, for birds are not released during inclement conditions or when poor weather is forecast to occur on the line of flight back to the pigeons' home region. It is quite common for bad weather to delay a race by two days because fog, rain, and strong winds can affect the pigeons' performance. Indeed, it has been known for pigeons to fly into telephone poles and power lines when visibility is poor. Natural predators, particularly peregrine falcons and sparrow hawks, are another hazard faced frequently by racing pigeons.

When a pigeon arrives back at its loft, the rubber band is removed from its leg and placed into a timing clock. Most pigeons arrive home the day they are released, but some take up to two days to return. Any lost pigeons are returned to their owners if reported to racing authorities.

There are two long-held scientific theories to explain how racing pigeons find their way home. One theory proposes that pigeons have in-built magnetic and solar compasses that enable them to navigate. Magnetic contours are found on Earth's surface, and it has been argued that pigeons use these contours to fly by, as scientists have discovered that pigeon brains contain 53 cells that are influenced by Earth's magnetic field. This theory gained credence when recent large losses of pigeons coincided with periodic solar surface storms that subsequently disturb the planet's magnetic field. That pigeons also use the position of the sun to navigate by is perhaps borne out by the fact that pigeon racers make sure their pigeons learn the movement of the sun before they are released. Further, it has been suggested that pigeons navigate using the stars when flying longer distances. Another widely held belief is that racing pigeons combine their sense of smell with their ability to recognize landmarks such as rivers, motorways, and hills to chart a course home. Hence, fog and low levels of visibility can affect pigeons' racing performance significantly.

Pigeons have been used in communication since the days of the ancient Greeks, and pigeon fancying—the keeping of pigeons for their aesthetic appeal—was popular in England during the 1760s. However, the history of pigeon racing can be traced back to Belgium in the early 19th century, where the modern racing pigeon, the homer, was bred. The homer could reach high speeds and fly long distances. The first long-distance pigeon race was held in Belgium in 1818, while the first international race took place in 1820 when pigeons flew from Paris, France, to Liège, Belgium. Then in 1823, the first race across the English Channel took place from London to Antwerp. The Belgians conveyed their enthusiasm for pigeon racing to the British, for from as early as 1819, the Belgians would use England as a launch base for races. The English went on to import new faster, stronger breeds of pigeon from Belgium and France, and when the advent of the telegraph made carrier pigeons unnecessary in the 1840s, pigeons began to be bred for racing rather than for carrying messages. By the late 1870s pigeon racing clubs had started to form in the north of England, which is still the area of Britain most closely associated with the sport. During this time 150 racing clubs had been established in Belgium, which equaled 10,000 lofts. From Belgium the pigeon racing craze spread to neighboring Holland. The European love of pigeon racing continues to this day, for there are around 90,000 lofts in both Belgium and Holland and 100,000 lofts in England. Pigeon racing became popular in France and the United States during the second half of the 19th century. Today there are around 20,000 pigeon racing lofts registered in the United States. In terms of worldwide growth, the sport is becoming popular in China, Japan, Taiwan (which hosts more races than any other country), Australia, and South Africa, where the Million Dollar Pigeon Race is held.

Pigeons in World War II

When World War II erupted, thousands of Britain's pigeon fanciers allowed their pigeons to be used as message carriers, carrying communications either in special containers on their legs or pouches attached to their backs. The birds were frequently dropped by parachute to Resistance workers in France, Belgium, and the Netherlands, while Royal Air Force crews transported their pigeons in watertight baskets (in case the aircraft had to land in the sea). Of the 53 Dickin Medals presented to animals for displaying conspicuous gallantry and devotion to duty during World War II, 32 medals went to pigeons.

In recent years, however, pigeon racing has faced accusations of cruelty by animal rights groups such as People for the Ethical Treatment of Animals (PETA). Three main accusations of cruelty have been leveled at the sport. The first charge is that some breeders kill slow-flying birds. The second accusation concerns the practice of widowing. Male and female pigeons will, over time, form long-lasting relationships that produce offspring. Pigeon racers capitalize on this aspect of pigeon behavior, for they often take one of the pair of pigeons away from the loft to race, knowing that the bird will be frantic to return to its partner and so will fly home as quickly as possible. If the race is a sprint race, then the male is separated from the female. Males are the best choice for sprint races, as they are strongly territorial and surge back to their lofts. However, males are not a good choice for long-distance races, as they can become distracted by females other than their partner pigeons and set up home elsewhere. Instead, female pigeons are used for long-distance races, as their loyalty to their male is steadfast and they are not tempted by other males. Thus, it is female pigeons that participate in the sport's most prestigious race from Barcelona, Spain, to the United Kingdom. The females must fly the 740 miles over the Pyrenees mountains, which tires them greatly, and then across the English Channel. By the time the females reach the Channel they are exhausted, and it has been estimated that 75–90 percent of the birds from one race die crossing the water.

Another dark aspect of pigeon racing is bird doping. Random drug tests have been introduced to try to stop birds from being given endurance-enhancing drugs. The theft of prize-winning pigeons is another negative aspect of the sport. However, those who are pro–pigeon racing argue that any negatives are outweighed by the positives and highlight the documented restorative aspect that pigeon racing has been noted to have on children with learning difficulties and on young offenders.

See also: Camel and Yak Racing; Cockfighting; Fell Running; Sheepdog Trials

Further Reading

Brown, Paul. "Weatherwatch: How Do Racing Pigeons Find Their Way Back Home?" The Guardian, October 28, 2012, http://www.theguardian.com/news/2012/oct/28/weather watch-pigeons-racing-tracking (accessed August 4, 2013).

"Getting Started: A Beginners Guide." The Royal Pigeon Racing Association, 2014, http://www.rpra.org/about-rpra/getting-started/a-beginners-guide/ (accessed August 4, 2013).

Harrabin, Roger. "Is Pigeon Racing Cruel?" BBC News: Science & Environment, March 27, 2013, http://www.bbc.co.uk/news/science-environment-21938429 (accessed August 5, 2013).

Johnes, Martin. "Pigeon Racing and Working-Class Culture in Britain, c.1870–1950." *Cultural and Social History* 4(3) (2007): 361–383, http://www.niracingpigeon.co.uk/pdf/downloads/pigeon-racing-and-working-class-culture.pdf (accessed August 4, 2013).

Mora, Cordula V., and Michael M. Walker. "Do Release-Site Biases Reflect Response to the Earth's Magnetic Field during Position Determination by Homing Pigeons?" *Proceedings of the Royal Society of Biological Sciences* 276(1671) (September 22, 2009): 3295–3302, http://rspb.royalsocietypublishing.org/content/276/1671/3295.full (accessed August 4, 2013).

"Pigeon Racing—a History." Pigeon Racing UK & Ireland, 2014, http://www.pigeonracing uk.co.uk/about/pigeon-racing-a-history/ (accessed August 4, 2013).

Rowe, Mark. "Pigeon Power." Countryfile, February 25, 2013, http://www.countryfile.com/countryside/pigeon-power (accessed August 5, 2013).

"A Short History of Pigeon Racing." Canadian Racing Pigeon Union, 1944–2013, http://www.crpu.ca/our-sport/a-short-history/ (accessed August 4, 2013).

Q

QUIDDITCH

Quidditch, sometimes called muggle quidditch, is a contact sport combining elements of dodgeball, lacrosse, rugby, tag, and wrestling. The sport is based on the game of the same name played by pupils at Hogwarts School of Witchcraft and Wizardry and other wizzarding academies featured in the *Harry Potter* novels by J. K. Rowling. Quidditch was first played at Middlebury College, Vermont, in 2005, and it was here that the first intercollegiate Quidditch World Cup was held in 2007. Today there are around 300 quidditch teams governed by the International Quidditch Association. Teams tend to be based in universities and high schools in Australia, the United States, Canada, the United Kingdom, Italy, and France.

As in the *Harry Potter* books, quidditch is played by two mixed-gender teams of seven comprising three chasers, two beaters, one seeker, and one keeper. Each team member must play astride a broomstick, though unlike in the literary version of quidditch, the broomsticks used in real-life quidditch are not airborne but rather remain resolutely earthbound. The playing area features three raised hoops that act as goals and through which the chasers aim balls known as quaffles. It is the job of the keeper to defend the goal from the chasers while the beaters disrupt the opposing team by hitting opponents with another ball called a bludger. Teams aim to score the most goals before the game's end, which occurs when a seeker manages to capture the snitch; in nonmagical quidditch, a snitch is a tennis ball attached to the waistband of a neutral player know as the snitch runner whose role is to avoid capture by any means necessary. If scores are level when the snitch is captured, then the game continues into overtime.

Another activity inspired by children's literature is the gentle pastime of Pooh-sticks, a real-life version of a game played in A. A. Milne's *Winnie the Pooh* stories. Pooh-sticks is played very occasionally in England and sees two or more players simultaneously drop sticks from the upstream side of a bridge into the fast-flowing river below. Players then run to the other side of the bridge to see whose stick is first to emerge from under the bridge or whose is the first stick to pass a predetermined finish line. The rules of Pooh-sticks state that players must show their sticks to each other before the game begins to enable identification, and the stick must be made of natural wood. To start a game of Pooh-sticks, players stand side by side on the bridge facing upstream and then each player stretches his or her arm out over the river. As all sticks must start at the same height, a tall competitors must lower their arms to bring their sticks in line with the stick of the shortest player. Once all the sticks are aligned, the oldest or youngest competitor adopts the role of the starter and declares "Ready! Steady! Go!" At this announcement all the competitors

Silicon Valley Skrewts' Willis Miles IV, right, leads his team against the University of Ottawa Quidditch team at the Quidditch World Cup in Kissimmee, Florida, on April 12, 2013. Quidditch is a contact sport that combines elements of dodgeball, lacrosse, rugby, tag, and wrestling. (AP Photo/Phelan M. Ebenhack)

drop their sticks into the river. While some players claim that luck is the most significant factor in winning at Pooh-sticks, others assert that skill and judgment are needed to determine which is the fastest-flowing river current into which to throw the sticks.

The bridge featured in the Milne stories is thought to be located in Ashdown Forest in East Sussex, England. However, the Pooh-Sticks World Championships, which attract crowds of thousands, have been held annually on the Thames River in Oxfordshire for the past 30 years. Around 2,000 contestants (both children and adults) compete in the championships, which consist of individual and team heats, with winners going on to further heats and then a final. Though a particularly English event, the championships attract many foreign entrants (in 2004 the event was won by a team from the Czech Republic) plus global television interest.

See also: Eton Wall Game; Hurling; Korfball; Rugby League

Further Reading

Davies, Caroline. "Poohsticks Fans Club Together to Save the Game." *The Observer,* November 2, 2008, http://www.theguardian.com/uk/2008/nov/02/uk-news (accessed September 22, 2013).

Jalabi, Raya. "The Surprisingly Serious Quest to Make Muggle Quidditch a Real Sport." *The Atlantic,* April 12, 2013, http://www.theatlantic.com/entertainment/archive/2013/04

/the-surprisingly-serious-quest-to-make-muggle-quidditch-a-real-sport/274958/ (accessed December 8, 2013).

Le Vay, Benedict. *Ben Le Vay's Eccentric Oxford: A Practical Guide.* 2nd ed. Chalfont St. Peter, UK: Bradt Travel Guides, 2011.

"Rules." International Quidditch Association, 2013, http://iqaquidditch.com/about/rules (accessed December 8, 2013).

"Rules." Rotary Club of Oxford Spires, http://www.pooh-sticks.com/content/rules (accessed September 22, 2013).

R

REAL TENNIS

Real tennis, or *jeu de paume,* meaning "game of the palm," is a complex indoor racquet and ball sport enjoyed by around 8,000 players living in England, France, Australia, and the United States and is thought to be the ancestor of lawn tennis. In order to distinguish real tennis from lawn tennis, real tennis is sometimes referred to as royal tennis in England and Australia and as court tennis in the United States. In France the sport continues under its original name, *jeu de paume.*

The origins of real tennis are disputed. It has been suggested that the ancient Greeks and Romans played a version of the game on stone courts and that the game was transported to France when the Romans invaded Gaul (ancient France). It is, however, known for certain that real tennis was played as early as the 11th century in the south of France. Legend tells that real tennis developed in France during the 10th century when a wandering minstrel arrived at the French royal court and taught the inhabitants how to play the game. Whatever the truth behind this tale, by the 11th century real tennis was widely enjoyed as an outdoor pursuit by French monks, who would either string a rope across monastic quadrangles or play against castle walls. It is not too strong an assertion to say that the French clergy played the game with a fervor bordering on the religious. Indeed, provincial bishops received a tithe of real tennis balls as a gift each Easter Day.

At the beginning of the real tennis craze, monks played without a racquet, hitting the ball with their bare hand, hence the name *jeu de paume.* This early version of the game has led to the belief that real tennis is not just the ancestor of lawn tennis but is also a forerunner of handball and *pelota,* sports in which a ball is hit with the hand. The monks, however, soon graduated to wearing leather gloves to hit the ball, and in time strings were added to the gloves. Later still the monks began to play with bats that had a 6-inch handle. Today rackets are 27 inches long, tightly strung, and slightly curved.

The popularity of the game grew so that by the 13th century there were around 1,800 real tennis courts in France, and by the 14th century real tennis was one of the country's favorite pastimes. Meanwhile, real tennis had also become popular in England, for during this period England owned large parts of France, and so real tennis spread to the other side of the English Channel. It was, however, with the reign of King Henry VIII, who ruled from 1509 to 1547, that real tennis truly took off in England, as the king, who was devoted to the game, had real tennis courts built at four of his favorite palaces in or near London—Greenwich, Hampton Court, St. James's, and Whitehall—in an effort to outdo his French counterpart Francis I (1494–1547) who had had *jeu de paume* courts constructed at most of his royal residences. Henry VIII's court at Hampton Court still exists and is open to the public. Francis I meanwhile, who believed that imposing architecture was key to demonstrating monarchal power, had spectator galleries built at his courts so that visiting dignitaries could pay due homage to the magnificence of his sporting facilities.

Royalty in both France and England were keen to keep real tennis for themselves. However, this proved impossible, and the game's popularity continued apace. By the 17th century there were over 500 real tennis courts spread throughout France, though the sport was particularly associated with Paris, where everyone from the king down to the lowliest commoner played some version of the game. Seventeenth-century Paris was home to 250 real tennis courts and 7,000 players. William Shakespeare refers to the abundance of courts in France in his play *Henry V* (ca. 1599).

The popularity of real tennis began to wane in France during the reign of King Louis XIV (1638–1715). Rather than play the game, the French nobility at this time preferred to employ professional players known as *maître-paumiers* to play exhibition matches on their behalf. Aristocrats would then place huge bets on the outcome of matches. The French love of real tennis truly came to an end, however, with the advent of the French Revolution (1789–1799), when anything connected to royalty was despised. Indeed, in a deliberate affront to the aristocracy, on June 20, 1789, the real tennis court at the Palace of Versailles was chosen as the venue for the announcement that a new French constitution would be written. This announcement was a pivotal event in the early days of the French Revolution and became known as Le Serment du Jeu de Paume, or the Tennis Court Oath. The tennis court still survives but as a museum rather than a sporting venue. Today in France there are only three playable real tennis courts, two of which are in Paris.

Real tennis continued to be popular in England, however, where the game was played by the social elite. The association of real tennis with the royal family started by Henry VIII continued, for King George IV (1762–1830), Edward VII (1841–1910), and George V (1865–1936) all played the game. The husband of Queen Victoria, Prince Albert (1819–1861), also played real tennis at Hampton Court Palace, where the locker room bears his name to this day.

By the mid-19th century, however, real tennis in England was almost totally eclipsed by the new sport of lawn tennis. The main difference between lawn tennis and real tennis was that the latter was played on an enclosed court—though nascent lawn tennis was played on an hourglass-shaped court rather than the rectangle familiar today, the court lacked the side and end walls that surround a real tennis court. A real tennis court has a high ceiling and high walls, is asymmetrical, and consists of 16 parts including galleries built into a sidewall, sloping roofs, and a main wall featuring a protruding buttress called a tambour—when the ball hits the tambour it is propelled across the court. No two real tennis courts are identical, for they always differ in terms of the angle of the roof and the court dimensions. The reason for this is that real tennis courts were not built indoors until the 14th century, when cities were starting to develop, and courts were fitted in wherever space became available. The variance in court size is evident at Hampton Court Palace, where the court is wider than most, while the court at Fontainebleau, close to Paris, is longer than some. In theory French courts built during the Renaissance were supposed to meet certain standard dimensions and layout, with large courts, known as *jeu a dedans,* and smaller courts, known as *jeu quarré.* In actuality, however, all courts vary. Such disparity means that home advantage—knowing the dimensions of the court and how it plays—is much more important than power or speed when playing real tennis. For this reason many aficionados feel that real tennis is a game of nuance, precision, and guile.

A real tennis court is always divided in two by a net. The area from which spectators view the game is called the dedans. In front of the dedans is the side of the court called the service side. The other half of the court is the hazard side. The serve, of which there are around 50 variations, is only ever hit from the service side of the net. When players serve they must hit the ball so that it bounces once on the hazard side of the penthouse roof and then once on the floor of the service side. Points are won and lost when players make mistakes, such as hitting the ball out of the court or into the net. Points may also be claimed by striking the ball into winning areas of the court (including the dedans, the grille, and the winning gallery) in such a way that the ball bounces on the floor for a second time before the service line and the wall at the end of the hazard side. When the ball bounces twice anywhere else on the court or lands in any other gallery before another player touches it, a chase is said to have been laid. A chase is a complex rule unique to real tennis for which special lines, known as the chase lines, are marked on the floor of the court. The chase lines measure the length in yards from the back wall, so if a ball bounces for a second time on the six-yard line, then a chase 6 has been laid. If the ball bounces for a second time equidistant between two chase lines, then the numbers of both the lines are noted, for instance, "2 & 3" or "4 & 5." If the ball makes its second bounce between two chase lines but closer to one line than the other, then the phrases "better than" and "worse than" are used. For example, if a chase is "better than three yards" this means that the ball has bounced for the second time nearer to the dedans back wall than it has the three-yard chase line but farther than the dedans wall that a cry of "3 & 4" would denote.

Superficially, the scoring system of real tennis resembles lawn tennis, as the same terminology of love, 15, 30, and 40 are used. However, when a chase has been laid the score does not change. Instead the chase is noted and held in abeyance until the chase is played off. When a chase is played off, the player who is receiving (or serving if the chase is at the hazard end) strikes the ball so that the second bounce is nearer to the end wall than the chase that is being played. For example, if a six-yard chase is being played, the player must play to the one-, two-, three-, four-, or five-yard lines or forfeit the point. If the ball fails to reach the six-yard line on the second bounce, a shot need not be played and the point is awarded to the server. When two chases have been laid or one chase is outstanding and the score is at game point, that is, one player is at 40 points or has advantage, the players switch ends. After the change of ends, the chase or chases are played off in the order in which they were laid.

A player must win four points to win a game in real tennis, though sometimes, depending on the conditions under which the game is being played, the player must be two clear points ahead of the opponent to claim the game. Like lawn tennis, real tennis is played over the best of three sets consisting of six games each.

However, unlike lawn tennis, the score of the last player to win a point is announced first.

During the 19th century lawn tennis continued to eclipse real tennis in England. This lack of interest continued into the 20th century, with the number of English real tennis courts gradually declining. However, the number of courts began to pick up again at the beginning of the 21st century. Today in the United Kingdom there are 26 courts stretching from Dorset in the southwest of England to Fife in Scotland. The Fife court, a *jeu quarré* located at Falkland Palace, is the world's oldest, dating from 1539. There are 11 real tennis courts in use in the United States in locations as diverse as South Carolina and Virginia. Newport Casino in Rhode Island houses the International Tennis Hall of Fame and has a court open to the public.

See also: Handball; *La Soule; Pelota*

Further Reading

"About Real Tennis." Middlesex University Real Tennis Club, 2013, http://www.murtc
.co.uk/about/about-real-tennis/ (accessed August 12, 2013).
Brand, Jonathan. *"Jeu de Palme:* Holding Court in Paris." *Smithsonian Magazine,* May 19,
2010, http://www.smithsonianmag.com/travel/Jeu-de-Paume-Holding-Court-in-Paris
.html?c=y&page=1 (accessed August 12, 2013).
"The Court & Handicapping." Petworth House Tennis Court, http://www.petworthrealtenn
is.com/pages/rules.htm (accessed August 6, 2013).
"The Game." Cambridge University Real Tennis Club, 2001, http://www.curtc.net
/thegame/ (accessed September 6, 2013).
Gillmeister, Heiner. *Tennis: A Cultural History.* London: Leicester University Press, 1997.
Grasso, John. *Historical Dictionary of Tennis.* Plymouth, UK: Scarecrow, 2011.
"A History of the Royal Game of Tennis." The Tennis and Rackets Association Limited,
http://www.tennisandrackets.com/real-tennis-history.aspx (accessed August 12,
2013).
"Jeu de Paume (France)." Nederlandse Real Tennis Bond, http://www.real-tennis
.nl/?page=JeudePaume (accessed August 12, 2013).
"Les Maître-Paumiers: The First Tennis Professionals." Leamington Tennis Court Club,
http://www.leamingtonrealtennis.co.uk/history-of-the-game/les-maitre-paumiers
.html (accessed September 11, 2013).
Masters, James. "Origins of Tennis." Masters Traditional Games, http://www.tradgames.org
.uk/games/Tennis.htm (accessed August 12, 2013).

RHYTHMIC GYMNASTICS

Rhythmic gymnastics, also known as modern gymnastics, competitive gymnastics, and rhythmic sportive gymnastics, is an indoor Olympic sport combining elements of various styles of gymnastics, eurhythmics, and ballet and is particularly popular in Eastern Europe, Asia, and the United States.

There is evidence that a form of rhythmic gymnastics was present in ancient Egypt. However, the sport as it is known today truly developed at the end of the 19th century into the early 20th century as a marriage between art and sport when a Swiss woman, Emile-Jacques Dalcroze, built on the concept of dance as a form of aesthetic expression and exercise founded by Jean-Georges Noverre and Francois Delsarte. The exceptional grace with which rhythmic gymnasts move is often due to the gymnast's high degree of inherent flexibility or joint hypermobility, commonly thought of as double-jointedness. Indeed, some regard rhythmic gymnastics as a form of artistic contortionism. However, the physical elegance for which rhythmic gymnasts are noted can have a dark side. The artistic nature of rhythmic gymnastics has led to the sport being classified by some as an aesthetic sport, alongside figure skating and synchronized swimming, in which great emphasis is placed on physical appearance. This focus on physicality has in turn led to an overemphasis on gymnasts maintaining an extremely thin physique in order to increase performance and aesthetic appeal. As a result of this reverence for slenderness, rhythmic gymnastics is one of the most cited sports in relation to athletes and eating disorders.

A strong and flexible competitor uses a hoop during a rhythmic gymnastics competition. Rhythmic gymnastic routines consist of complex dance-inspired movements set to music and involve running, jumping, and throwing and catching apparatus, as well as movements such as pivots and leaps. (Dimitris66/iStockphoto.com)

Hypermobility

Hypermobility, sometimes called being double-jointed or referred to as joint hyperlaxity, means that a person can move some or all of her or his joints more than most people are able. Many people have some hypermobile joints, which can prove advantageous to dancers, musicians, and gymnasts. However, hypermobility can cause pain along with other symptoms—this is called joint hypermobility syndrome or benign joint hypermobility syndrome (BJHS). Hypermobility can be caused by several factors including shallow joint sockets, weak ligaments, or overly relaxed muscles. Hypermobility can be diagnosed by the Beighton score, which measures flexibility using a standard set of movements.

Rhythmic gymnastic routines are performed on a mat measuring 13 meters by 13 meters (roughly 43 feet by 43 feet) and consist of complex dance-inspired movements that must harmonize with and interpret the music accompanying the display. Basic rhythmic gymnastic movements are intended to show the skill and suppleness of the gymnasts and include running, throwing, jumping, and catching as well as moves that showcase basic body group movements such as pivots, leaps, balance, and flexibility. Though the moves must vary in direction, form, magnitude, speed, and level of difficulty, acrobatic movements such as tumbling are not permitted. The movements must be executed with the addition of a piece of apparatus that should be kept in motion for the duration of a routine. The apparatus used in rhythmic gymnastics are the rope, ribbon, ball, hoop, and clubs. The rope is made of hemp or a synthetic material, and its length is proportional to the gymnast's height. When using a rope, gymnasts must perform leaps, skips, and hops while throwing, catching, and rotating the rope. The ribbon, usually made of satin, is 6 meters (nearly 20 feet) long and 4–6 centimeters (1.5–3 inches) wide and is attached to a stick of between 50 and 60 centimeters (almost 20 inches to 24 inches) long that is made of wood, plastic, or glass. Ribbon work necessitates great arm and shoulder strength, as the apparatus must be used to create large sweeping movements while being thrown, tossed, caught, and spiraled as the gymnast pivots. The ball, made of plastic or a similar substance, has a diameter of 18–20 centimeters (7–8 inches) and weighs 400 grams (just over 14 ounces). Use of the ball requires elegance, lyricism, and great flexibility, for the ball must be thrown, caught, bounced, and rolled over the gymnast's body. The ball must not be gripped; rather, it should rest in the gymnast's hand. Extreme flexibility is also required to perform with the hoop, as is great balance. The hoop is made of wood or plastic, weighs 300 grams (10.5 ounces), and is rigid, for any vibration of the hoop when it is thrown in the air is penalized. The inner diameter of the hoop is 80 to 90 centimeters (about 31.5 to 35.5 inches). As gymnasts jump and pivot, they throw, catch, swing, and rotate the hoop. The hoop is the apparatus that best allows a gymnast to showcase her or his agility and the variety of the gymnast's technical abilities. The clubs meanwhile are between 40 and 50 centimeters (16–20 inches) in length and weigh 150 grams (5 ounces) each. The most important factors in club work are coordination and balance, as the gymnast performing with clubs must include mills, circles, throwing, catching, and tapping in the routine. Gymnasts are penalized for losing control of their apparatus or its breaking during a routine, hitting the ceiling of the competition hall, or leaving the area of the playing surface. If the latter occurs, the gymnast is permitted to use a replacement apparatus kept along the side of the designated floor space.

Competitive rhythmic gymnastics is performed as routines for either individuals or groups of five. Individual routines last from 1 minute 15 seconds to 1 minute 30 seconds, and individuals must perform four routines using a different apparatus each time. The individual is judged on overall performance and apparatus technique. Group displays last from 2 minutes 15 seconds to 2 minutes 30 seconds, and groups must perform two routines. In the first routine all gymnasts use the same apparatus, but in the second routine either all the gymnasts must use two different apparatus or three gymnasts must use one piece of apparatus and two others use another.

Rhythmic gymnastics was first included in the Olympics in 1928 as part of a combined artistic and rhythmic gymnastics competition, and in 1952 individual Olympic gymnasts had to perform rhythmic gymnastic routines, while a rhythmic team routine was mandatory. Gymnastics stopped being a combined event at the 1956 Olympics, as a growing number of gymnasts preferred to specialize in either rhythmic or artistic gymnastics. An individual competition did not, however, feature in the Olympics until 1984, and a group competition was included as recently as 1996.

Rhythmic gymnastics was, however, seen as a discipline separate from the artistic form of the sport as early as the 1920s in Russia. In 1942 Russia held its first national competition, and from then on the sport spread throughout Eastern Europe, hence Soviet and East European rhythmic gymnasts came to dominate the sport. The spread of rhythmic gymnastics as a distinct discipline meant that the Fédération Internationale de Gymnastique recognized rhythmic gymnastics as a separate sport in 1962. The first unofficial World Rhythmic Gymnastics Championship was held in Budapest, Hungary, in 1964, followed a year later by the first official world championships in Prague in the former Czechoslovakia (now the Czech Republic). The first European championship was held in Madrid in 1978. The breakup of the Soviet Union in the 1990s meant that medals are now shared among more countries, and new nations have emerged as rhythmic gymnastic champions, including Japan, China, Cyprus, South Korea, Switzerland, Italy, Greece, and Israel. However, Russia is still a powerhouse of rhythmic gymnastics. Indeed, in 2009 Russian Evgenia Kanaeva won all six world championship gold medals.

At this time, only rhythmic gymnastics performed by females is recognized officially in competition. However, a growing number of men are taking up the sport. This is especially true in Asia, where the men's portion of the sport evolved from Japanese stick gymnastics. Men's rhythmic gymnastics is also performed in such countries as Australia, Russia, America, Canada, and Mexico.

See also: Capoeira; *Mallakhamb;* Synchronized Skating; Trampolining; Yoga

Further Reading

Alter, Michael J. *Science of Flexibility.* Champaign, IL: Human Kinetics, 2004.

Bartlett, Roger, Chris Gratton, and Christer G. Rolf. *Encyclopedia of International Sports Studies.* Abingdon, UK: Routledge, 2010.

Dosil, Joaquin. *Eating Disorders in Athletes.* Chichester, UK: Wiley, 2008.

"Status of Men's Rhythmic Gymnastics." Men's Rhythmic Gymnastics, http://www.menrg.com (accessed August 12, 2013).

ROUNDERS

Rounders is an outdoor game sometimes considered the forerunner of baseball and also contains elements of cricket in which two teams aim to score points, called rounders. The winning team is the side that scores the most rounders. The game can be played by either sex and by all age groups. Rounders is particularly popular in the United Kingdom, especially in England and Wales, where the game is often played in school physical education classes during the summer term. Indeed, in England 2 million pupils play rounders regularly, with the game played in 87 percent of English schools. This makes rounders the third most played team game behind soccer and basketball (but ahead of both netball and cricket), with school teams competing in the National School Rounders Championships, first held over 30 years ago. Rounders is also played in areas of the world with strong links to the United Kingdom, including India, Ireland, and Australia.

Though most commonly thought of as a children's game, rounders provides an all-body workout and improves agility, hand-eye coordination, and muscle endurance, while actions such as throwing, catching, and sprinting burn up to 400 calories per hour. The game also develops communication and teamwork skills.

There are in excess of 40 rounders leagues in England and Wales. In England, over 24,000 adults play rounders once per week, and over 70,000 play the game once a month. The game is played at an international level by adults, under 14s, under 16s, and under 19s, with the first-ever rounders international between England and Wales taking place in 1983. In England the game is governed by Rounders England, which was established in 1943 as the National Rounders Association by a small committee of schoolteachers who wished to standardize the game's rules. The National Rounders Association was reorganized in 1999 after receiving a government grant allowing the association to move away from being volunteer-orientated to become an increasingly formal and structured body.

It is thought that rounders developed from the medieval English team game stool-ball, in which a batter would hit the ball using the hand and then gradually proceed around stools that were used as bases. Batters would advance one stool at a time each time a batter struck the ball. However, if a fielder managed to hit a batter with the struck ball as the batter ran between stools, then the fielder would take the place of the batter. In Tudor times (1485–1603) stool-ball was played by both sexes and was often associated with courtship rituals. This is evident in the Jacobean play *Two Noble Kinsmen* (1634), accredited to William Shakespeare and John Fletcher, in which the phrase "to play at stool-ball" is used as a double entendre. The earliest reference to rounders appears in *A Little Pretty Pocketbook,* published in 1744, that included an illustration depicting a batter, a bowler, and several rounders posts. Interestingly, in *A Little Pretty Pocketbook* the game is called "base-ball," the name used by English author Jane Austen when describing a game in her novel *Northanger Abbey* (1817). In 1828 *The Boy's Own Book* devoted a whole chapter to rounders, and in 1889 the Liverpool and Scottish Rounders Association was founded.

Rounders was one of several games brought to America by English colonists, though in America the game became known as town ball because it was usually played at town meetings. However, no official standardized town ball rules were ever established so the game varied from place to place, and over time the shape of the town ball playing area came to differ from that used in rounders. For instance, in Massachusetts the town ball pitch developed into a square.

The history of rounders in America includes a degree of controversy, for there is some dispute as to whether rounders should be considered the ancestor of baseball. Recent research suggests that the name "rounders" was used in England to refer to the game of baseball, which was becoming increasingly popular in America during the 1850s, while an American correspondent for a London newspaper makes clear that "rounders" is the English name for "baseball." Then in 1860, English-born sportswriter and baseball statistician Henry Chadwick, the so-called Father of Baseball, proclaimed rounders the progenitor of baseball in an edition of *Beadle's Dime Base-Ball Player*, the first annual baseball guide. However, Chadwick did not produce any evidence to back up his claim but merely cited the many similarities between the two games as proof. Later, renowned baseball scholar Robert Henderson would agree with Chadwick by stating in *Baseball and Rounders* (1939) that the game played in America as baseball was indeed directly, if remotely, descended from the old English game of base-ball, otherwise known as rounders. However, critics who do not agree with Henderson's hypothesis point to the fact that he bases his whole argument on the information presented in *The Boy's Own Book*. To further cloud the matter of baseball's connection to rounders (if any) in later works, such as *Ball, Bat, and Bishop* (1947), Henderson seems to de-emphasize the importance of rounders in the history of baseball. Proponents of baseball as a purely American sport invented in New York by U.S. Army general Abner Doubleday during the 19th century strongly disagree with the theory that rounders gave forth baseball. However, the notion that Doubleday invented baseball has also been contested and is known by some as the Doubleday Myth. It is therefore difficult to say with any certainty to what degree rounders is the antecedent of baseball, though the two games are undoubtedly extremely similar.

The equipment needed to play rounders consists of a truncheon-like rounders bat, a hard leather-covered rounders ball (sometimes an old tennis ball or cricket ball is used rather than a specific rounders ball), and four posts each about 4 feet tall and without fixed bases that are set out on the field of play in a diamond shape. On the pitch is marked a bowler's square that is about 25.5 feet from the batter's square. A backstop line is marked about 3 feet behind where the batter stands. Rounders pitches tend to have a batting area measuring 129 square feet.

In general, to play rounders each team should have between 6 and 15 players, and in a mixed team there should be no more than 5 males. Each team has two innings, with all team members having a go at batting—batters queue up one by one to take their turn in the batting square. Once there, the bowler bowls the ball at the batter using an underarm action. The bowled ball must not bounce before reaching the batter and must be thrown above the height of the batter's knees but below the height of the batter's head. The ball must not be bowled at the batter's body. In addition, the bowler's feet must be within the bowler's square when the ball is delivered. Contravention of these rules results in a no-ball being declared by the game's umpire. When the ball has been (legally) bowled, the batter hits the ball anywhere on the pitch and then runs to as many posts as possible before a fielder touches the ball to the post to which the batter was heading (the batter caught between posts is said to have been stumped). The batter must run even if unable to hit the bowled ball. If the batter does not strike the ball or hits the ball and it goes behind the batting square, then the batter may only run to the first post. However, if the batter hits the bowled ball and reaches the second or third post in one hit, then the batting team scores half a rounder. Similarly, if the batter manages to run all the way round to the fourth post in one hit, the batting side scores one rounder. The batting team also scores one rounder if the batter reaches the fourth post on a no-ball. However, the batting side only earns half a rounder if the batter reaches the fourth post without hitting the ball. Half a rounder is also scored if a fielder obstructs a batter running between posts. If the batter strikes the ball and arrives at the first, second, or third post without getting out, then the batter stays at the post reached, all the while keeping in physical contact with the post, until the bowler delivers the next ball. As soon as the bowler throws the ball, the batter may run to the next post (including on a no-ball). If the batter breaks contact with the post, then the fielding side can stump the next post by touching the ball to it so as to get the player out. Further, there can be no more than one runner at a post, so a player must run on to the following post if the next batter reaches the post at which the player was stationed. Once a player has proceeded around all the bases and reaches the fourth post, he rejoins the queue of batters and awaits another turn at batting.

As in cricket, there are many ways for a batter to get out. For instance, as in cricket, a batter is out if he or she strikes the ball that is then caught by a fielder before it hits the ground. A player is also out if he or she is stumped, runs inside the posts, overtakes a teammate when running around the posts, or obstructs a fielder when not running. Other ways of being out are if the player loses contact with a post while the bowler is within the bowler's square and holding the ball, and if the batter's feet are not within the batting square when the bowler delivers the ball. An innings ends either when all the batters are out or are at a base, meaning that there is no batter left to face the next ball. Other rules that are sometimes implemented are that the batter must carry the bat while running and must touch the fourth post to reach home safely.

Variations of rounders include indoor rounders and inclusive rounders. Indoor rounders is played on an area roughly equivalent to four badminton courts. The rules are much the same as for outdoor rounders, but the indoor variation of the game is played by two teams of six players and lasts a prearranged number of balls. Indoor rounders is exciting to play, as the ball bounces off the walls and ceiling at odd angles, making it easier to score rounders. The term "inclusive rounders" refers to a variation of the game geared toward people with disabilities. In this version the first post is moved closer to the batting square to allow for the amount of time it takes for the batter to let go of the bat, and a soft brightly colored ball fitted with a bell is used to aid partially sighted players. Wheelchair users are pushed around the posts, while powerchair users can also play. In inclusive rounders a batter is out if the bowled ball hits a batter's wheelchair, and if the wheel of a wheelchair traps the ball; then the game freezes, and the batter who hit the ball is only allowed to move on by one post. A batter is also out if a powerchair user stationed on a post catches the ball from another fielder—the powerchair user does not have to touch the ball to the post to get out the batter, as some powerchair users find it difficult to move their arms away from their body.

See also: Brännboll and *Pesäpallo;* Cricket; Kin-Ball; *Lapta;* Netball

Further Reading

Block, David. *Baseball before We Knew It: A Search for the Roots of the Game.* Lincoln: University of Nebraska Press, 2005.

Clark, Joe. *A History of Australian Baseball: Time and Game.* Lincoln: University of Nebraska Press, 2003.

"Evidence on Physical Education and Sport in Schools." Department for Education, United Kingdom, June 2013, https://www.gov.uk/government/uploads/system/uploads/att achment_data/file/226505/Evidence_on_physical_education_and_sport_in_schools .pdf (accessed August 2, 2014).

Furst, R. Terry. *Early Professional Baseball and the Sporting Press: Shaping the Image of the Game.* Jefferson, NC: McFarland, 2014.

Hershberger, Richard. "The Creation of the Alexander Cartwright Myth." *Baseball Research Journal* 43(1) (Spring 2014): 13–21.

"How to Get into Rounders." BBC: Get Inspired, October 1, 2013, http://www.bbc.co.uk /sport/0/get-inspired/24066823 (accessed August 2, 2014).

"Inclusive Rounders." Rounders England, 2013, http://www.roundersengland.co.uk/play /inclusive-rounders/ (accessed August 2, 2014).

"Information about Rounders." College Sports Scholarships, 2001–2012, http://www.colle gesportsscholarships.com/history-rounders.htm (accessed August 2, 2014).

"Rounders." Souters Sports Limited, http://www.souterssports.co.uk/dmdocuments /Rounders.pdf (accessed August 2, 2014).

"The Rules of Rounders." Masters Games, 2012, http://www.mastersgames.com/rules /rounders-rules.htm (accessed August 2, 2014).

Vlasich, James A. *A Legend for the Legendary: The Origin of the Baseball Hall of Fame.* Bowling Green, OH: Bowling Green State University Popular Press, 1990.

Wilkins, Sally E. D. *Sports and Games through History: Sports and Games of Medieval Cultures.* Westport, CT: Greenwood, 2000.

ROUND-THE-WORLD YACHT RACES

Round-the-world yacht races are international water-based endurance events in which yachts are raced along a specified long-distance ocean route. Round-the-world yacht races exist in various formats, and there are races for both professional and amateur sailors. International yacht racing is overseen by the International Sailing Federation, which provides a set of standardized rules and measurements and has established a list of 73 classes of yacht.

The first round-the-world yacht race to be held was the Sunday Times Golden Globe Race, a nonstop single-handed round-the-world yacht race held in 1968–1969. The race was sponsored by the British *Sunday Times* newspaper and aimed to capitalize on a number of individual round-the-world voyages that were already in preparation. For this reason, there were no qualification requirements to join the race, and competitors were allowed to join the race at any point between June 1 and October 31, 1968. The Golden Globe Trophy was offered to the first person to complete a nonstop, unassisted circumnavigation of the world via the great capes, which in sailing are Cape Good Hope in South Africa, Cape Leeuwin in Australia, and Cape Horn, the southernmost headland of the Tierra del Fuego archipelago belonging to Chile. A separate £5,000 prize was to be awarded for the fastest single-handed circumnavigation. The race proved controversial for several reasons, chief among them that only one entrant, Sir Robin Knox-Johnson, finished the race and therefore became the first person to sail single-handed nonstop around the world. Knox-Johnson was awarded both prizes but donated the £5,000 to a fund established to support the family of Donald Crowhurst, an entrant who committed suicide during the race.

The first round-the-world yacht race was a handicap fleet race, that is, a race in which different types of boats race against each other, with each boat having a handicap or rating so that its finish times can be adjusted (or its start time determined so that the slowest boats set off first). The Whitbread Round the World race began on September 8, 1973, when 17 boats from seven countries and carrying 167 sailors set sail from the Solent, a stretch of water off Portsmouth on the southern coast of England, bound for Cape Town in South Africa. The yachts were standard ocean cruisers measuring 32 to 80 feet, and in general the crews were either amateurs or military servicemen using the race as a training mission. The yachts followed paths used by 19th-century square riggers, also known as tall ships, by sailing four legs: Portsmouth to Cape Town, Cape Town to Sydney in Australia, Sydney to Rio de Janeiro in Brazil, and Rio de Janeiro back to Portsmouth. The race lasted 144 days, and the first yacht home was *Great Britain II,* which was captained by Chay Blyth and manned by paratroopers and arrived back on April 9, 1974. However, the *Great Britain II* was a 77-foot ketch and did not win the race, for a smaller vessel, a 65-foot Mexican boat called *Sayula II,* won on handicap, for the *Sayula II* took 150 days to complete the course, which after the size differential was taken into account, meant that the boat actually took only 133 days in corrected time. The inaugural race was not without incident. For example, three crewmen died while crossing the Southern Ocean, a stretch of water that no yacht had ever crossed before, and their bodies have never been found.

The Whitbread race went on to become the most prestigious round-the-world yacht race, attracting sponsorship and resulting in a new generation of professional yacht racers. The race also significantly boosted tourism in the port areas that hosted race stopovers. Since 1973 the Whitbread race has been held every four years, though the race was renamed the Volvo Ocean Race when race sponsorship was taken over by Swedish car manufacturer Volvo in 2001–2002.

Other round-the-world yacht races have been established as alternatives to the Whitbread/Volvo race. These include the Around Alone race (previously known as the BOC Challenge) for single-handed yachting; the Vendée Globe, which is contested by nonstop solo sailors; the Barcelona World Race for two-handed nonstop round-the-world racers; the Jules Verne Trophy, in which competitors aim to set nonstop round-the-world sailing records; and the Global Challenge for standard cutter-rigged sloops measuring 39 feet, which is divided into two classes for solo and double-handed sailing. The Global Challenge race is designed to test amateur sailors by taking a backward route sailing against the wind and prevailing currents. Another race, the Clipper Round the World Yacht Race, was created by Sir Robin Knox-Johnson in 1996 and sees a fleet of identical 70-foot yachts race along demanding routes selected for their downwind sailing potential. The yachts are provided by race organizers and are equipped with fully qualified captains, as most competitors are amateur sailors who have paid to compete in the race, with some competitors having no previous sailing experience at all. The Clipper Round the World Yacht Race attracts many land-based spectators. For instance, when the 2007 race started from the Albert Dock in Liverpool, northwestern England, 10,000 people watched from the dockside, while 200 million watched the race online. As a result, the race attracts a huge amount of advertising and sponsorship.

See also: Kitesurfing; Orienteering and Rogaining; Swimming the English Channel; Ultramarathons

Further Reading
"The Fleet." Clipper Round the World, http://www.clipperroundtheworld.com/fleet (accessed April 4th 2014).

"Fleet Racing." ISAF World Sailing, http://www.sailing.org/newtosailing/fleet_racing.php (accessed April 4, 2014).

"Global Ocean Race—Significant Changes in Store." Sailworld Cape Cod, April 2, 2014, http://www.sailworld.com/UK/index.cfm?SEID=0&Nid=120679&SRCID=0&ntid=0&tickeruid=0&tickerCID=0 (accessed April 4, 2014).

"History." Volvo Ocean Race, http://www.volvooceanrace.com/en/history.html (accessed April 4, 2014).

"History of the Square-Rigger." BBC: H2G2 Guide Entries, January 30, 2004, http://news.bbc.co.uk/dna/place-lancashire/plain/A1149257 (accessed April 4, 2014).

"History of the Whitbread." Kriter TV, http://www.kriter.tv/history/whitbread_history.pdf (accessed April 4, 2014).

Jennings, Gayle, ed. *Water-Based Tourism, Sport, Leisure, and Recreation Experiences.* Abingdon, UK: Routledge, 2011.

Laven, Karen, and Rod Gilmour. "Top 10 Volvo Ocean Race Moments: Page 3 Girls, Arrests, 'Rock Star' Sailors, All-Female Crews and Turning Turtle." *The Telegraph,* March 9, 2012, http://www.telegraph.co.uk/sport/othersports/sailing/volvo-ocean-race/9128778/Top-10-Volvo-Ocean-Race-moments-page-3-girls-arrests-rock-star-sailors-all-female-crews-and-turning-turtle.html (accessed April 4, 2014).

Lück, Michael, ed. *The Encyclopedia of Tourism and Recreation in Marine Environments.* Wallingford, UK: CAB International, 2008.

South, Mary. "Team Spirit." *Yachting,* August 2008.

RUGBY LEAGUE

Rugby league is a competitive, full-contact ball sport for men, women, and children played outdoors by teams of 13 (plus 4 substitutes called interchange players). Rugby league is one of the two codes of rugby football (the other being rugby union) and is played internationally and at the domestic club level. The sport originated

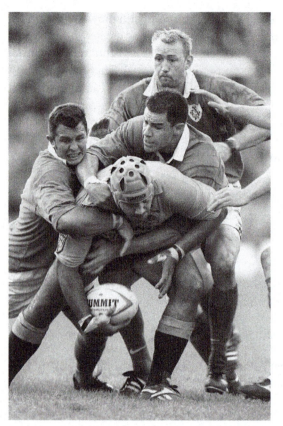

New South Wales Waratahs player Willie Ofahengaue, center, is tackled by three Ireland players during the Ireland vs. New South Wales Waratahs rugby union match in 1999. Teams aim to score more points through tries, goals, and field goals than the opposing side within 80 minutes of combative play. (AP Photo)

in England and is played across Europe (particularly the United Kingdom, Ireland, and France) and Australasia (Australia and New Zealand). However, rugby league is particularly popular with the South Pacific nations, especially Tonga, Fiji, Samoa, and the Cook Islands as well as Papua New Guinea, where rugby league is the national sport. Rugby league is also played in Jamaica, the United States, Canada, and South Africa. Today the sport is governed by the Rugby League International Federation, which organizes the international Rugby League World Cup. The premier club competitions are the European Super League and the Australian National Rugby League.

Rugby league began in 1895 when rugby union clubs in the north of England broke away from the Rugby Football Union (RFU), as the clubs wanted compensation for their working-class players for time spent not working when they were required to attend rugby matches played on Saturdays, during tours, and while injured. Players in the north of England tended to have low-paying jobs in mills, factories, and mining and could ill afford time off work. In comparison, rugby players in the south of England either had better-paying jobs or a second source of income that allowed them the luxury of being able to play as amateurs. This north-south divide was reflected in the fact that the new rugby code was known as the Northern Union, though it should be noted that many northern rugby clubs were run by wealthy former public schoolboys who defended amateurism. Thus, it is not the case that the conflict within rugby ran along purely geographical lines; rather, the cause of the schism was class-based attitudes to amateurism. The RFU refused to compensate working-class players, and over time the Northern Union moved away from the code of rugby union, bringing in rule changes that would render the two sports separate entities. One of the major modifications was that teams were reduced from the 15 players per team of rugby union to 13 players by removing 2 forwards. A second important innovation was that the play-the-ball rule was introduced so as to lessen the need for scrums and to replace the rucks and mauls found in rugby union. The play-the-ball rule allows a tackled player to place the ball in front of his foot and roll it backward with one foot to the next receiver on his team. All of the defending team, bar 2 defenders who guard the play-the-ball area, must retreat 10 meters (33 feet) from the play-the-ball area. The defending side may advance after the ball is rolled back, but if they move early, or encroach, a penalty is awarded.

Such changes made rugby league more popular in England, attracting increasing numbers of spectators. This in turn brought increased gate money, which allowed clubs to pay compensation to their players. The result of this division was that many rugby (union) clubs in the north of England lost key administrators and players to the new rugby code. Indeed, the England Rugby Union team took 18 years to regain the international championship title because the team had lost so many of its best players to rugby league. This created much animosity between the two codes.

Meanwhile in Australia, particularly in the states of New South Wales and Queensland, and in New Zealand, rugby was governed by bodies affiliated with the English RFU and consequently refused to pay compensation to their players, just as the RFU had refused. As in the north of England, rugby players in the Australian cities of Sydney and Brisbane were predominantly working class, and players and spectators alike were disappointed by the attitude of the rugby union authorities. Indeed, it seemed likely that the players and fans would defect to playing and watching Aussie Rules. The growing schism among Australian rugby authorities, players, and fans was exacerbated by the fact that at the start of the 20th century rugby suddenly became extremely popular, with matches attracting big crowds, and thus Australian rugby saw an increase in revenue. This led to increased discontent among the players and the public, as they felt that the increased revenue should be spent on the players as compensation for injuries and time away from work. Secret talks began to be held at which star rugby player Dally Messenger agreed to join the new professional rugby league being formed in Sydney, the New South Wales Rugby League. The formation of the rugby league and Messenger's decision to play in the breakaway code prevented Aussie Rules from obliterating rugby and monopolizing the loyalty of Sydney's huge working-class population. Over the next few years rugby leagues sprang up across Australia and club competitions were created, attracting ever-larger crowds. During this time many players from New Zealand joined Australian rugby league clubs, and rugby league teams were established in New Zealand too. Due to this cross-migration, rugby league has been the premier winter sport of New South Wales and New Zealand since 1910. In addition, the New South Wales Rugby League club competition gradually evolved into a national Australian competition, which in 1998 became known as the National Rugby League.

Rugby league is played on a rectangular grass pitch no more than 328 feet in length and 223 feet in width (though juniors play on pitches smaller than this). The pitch is covered in several markings to indicate the different boundary and position lines used in the game. However, the three most important lines are the goal lines (on which stand tall goalposts known as uprights that are connected by a horizontal bar), deadlines (which indicate where the ball is out of play behind the goals), and the halfway line. The pitch also has lines to indicate 10-meter (33-feet) intervals from the touchline to denote where scrums and restarts should occur. A rugby league team consists of defensive players known as backs and attacking players known as forwards, each of whom is assigned a standardized number. Forwards are usually chosen for their physical bulk, as they are required to run with the ball, attack, tackle, and make openings for the backs, thus improving the team's position in the field. Contrastingly, backs tend to be smaller and faster than the forwards, as backs have to take advantage of the field position gained by the forwards.

A team starts a rugby league match wearing numbers corresponding to playing positions—this only changes if substitutions are made or positions shift during the match. However, in some competitions, such as Super League, players are assigned a squad number that they keep all season, no matter which positions they play. Both playing positions and the numbers assigned to the positions are defined by the laws of the game. Player 1 stands behind the last line of main defense and is called the fullback. The fullback acts as both the last line of defense and the advancing player in an attack, as the fullback catches the ball after it has been kicked by the opposition, thereby turning defense into attack. The positions known as three-quarters consist of players called wings and centers. Players 2 and 5 are the wings positioned on each side of the pitch who use their sprinting ability to finish attacking moves. Therefore, wings often score tries. That said, wings also have to defend. Players 3 and 4 are the centers, who are positioned inside the wings and need to be fast runners, as they often provide the pass that enables the wing to score a try. Centers also tackle in defense. Players 6 and 7 are the halfbacks known, respectively, as the standoff half and the scrum half. The standoff makes tactical decisions and must be a strong kicker able to direct the ball in attack. For this reason, the standoff is sometimes known as the pivot. The scrum half is also a decision-making role. The position is sometimes referred to as the first receiver, as these players are often positioned in order to be the first to receive the ball from the dummy half after a play of the ball.

These are the backs. The rest of the 13 players make up the forwards. The front row of a rugby league side consists of the hooker and two props. Player 9 is the hooker, so-called because these players hook the ball back with the foot during a scrum. Traditionally the hooker plays in the dummy-half position, that is, standing behind the play-the-ball and collecting the ball before passing or running with it to continue the attack. Players 8 and 10, known as the props or prop forwards, flank the hooker. The props are often the heaviest players on a side, as they have to run directly at the opposition and act as the first line in a scrum. Props also use their size to defend. Players 11 and 12 are the second-row forwards, providing power to the front row during a scrum and also tackling. Player 13 is the lock, or loose forward, who stands behind the second row in a scrum making the ball available to the scrum half and also tackling opposing players. Also, each team may use its interchange players by making a maximum of 12 changes (involving any combination of players) during a match.

In rugby league the ball may be passed only in a backward or sideways direction. Therefore, players have to remain onside by not moving ahead of their teammate in possession of the ball. However, the ball may be kicked ahead for teammates, though if they are ahead of the kicker they will be judged offside. When infringements such as a forward pass or a knock-on—that is, losing the ball forward—occurs, the most senior match official, the match referee, awards a penalty. Other match officials may include touch judges and in-goal judges depending on the level of competition being played.

The side that is awarded the penalty must opt to restart play with either a kick or a scrum. A scrum sees eight players assume a formation known as the pack, with the hooker, the two props, the two second rows, and the lock all bound together in a 3-2-1 formation. The hooker is sandwiched between the two props, who ensure that no gaps exist between them. Next come the second-row forwards, who bind tightly together and stoop behind the front row, interweave their arms, and put their heads in the gaps between the hooker and the props. Finally, the lock stoops behind the second-row forwards, placing their heads in between the players immediately in front.

Play restarts when the ball is rolled in by the scrum half (from the side on which the referee stands) in such a way that the hooker can move the ball to the lock. The scrum half is forbidden from handling the ball until the ball has left the scrum. If the scrum is judged to have moved too far from where the ball entered the scrum, then the scrum may be retaken. A scrum is also awarded when the 40-20 rule is applied. The 40-20 rule began in Australia in 1997 and rewards accurate kicking by granting a scrum to the team whose player manages to stand behind the team's 40-meter line and kick the ball so that it bounces first in play and then passes the opposing side's 20-meter line and continues into touch, that is, travels out of play via the pitch's sidelines.

Teams aim to score more points through tries, goals, and field goals (also known as drop goals) than the opposing side within 80 minutes of playing time, divided into two halves of 40 minutes. If after 80 minutes the two teams are on level points, depending on the type of match format being played, a draw may be declared, or the game may enter extra time under the golden point rule. A try is the most common form of scoring and is worth four points. A team may manufacture a try in one of two ways, either by a player running and kicking the ball—which is large, oval in shape, and weighs up to 440 grams—farther upfield or by passing the ball from player to player in order to move around the opposing team's defense. To score the try, a player must touch the ball to the surface of the playing area on or beyond the defending team's goal line. The opposing side must attempt to prevent the attacking side from earning points by preventing their progress up the field by tackling the player carrying the ball. Tackling is a major component of rugby league, but only the player in possession of the ball may be tackled. An attacking player must try to avoid being tackled by using a combination of strength, speed, and skill; and a tackle is completed when the player being tackled is halted. An attacking team may be tackled a maximum of six times as they progress upfield before possession of the ball must switch to the opposing side—at this point most teams choose to kick the ball in order to gain as much ground as possible. After a tackle, the ball is played back along the ground to a player known as a receiver. After a try is scored, the team that scored the try is permitted to attempt a conversion, that is, a kick at goal for two extra points. A goal is worth two points and may be gained from either a conversion or a penalty. A drop goal, also known as a field goal, scores one point and occurs in open play when the ball is dropped and then kicked on the half volley between the uprights.

See also: Aussie Rules Football; Cricket; Eton Wall Game; Fell Running; Haxey Hood Game; *La Soule;* Pigeon Racing; Quidditch

Further Reading

"About Rugby League." South Australian Rugby League, 2013, http://www.sarugbyleague .com.au/ABOUT/ABOUTRUGBYLEAGUE.aspx (accessed March 23, 2014).

"The Basics of Rugby League." BBC Sport: Rugby League, 2009, http://news.bbc.co.uk /sport1/hi/rugby_league/rules_and_equipment/4216664.stm (accessed March 23, 2014).

Fagan, Sean. "History of Rugby League." National Rugby League, 2006, http://www.nrl .com/nrlhq/referencecentre/historyofrugbyleague/tabid/10440/default.aspx (accessed March 23, 2014).

"The Great Schism." Rugby Football History, 2007, http://www.rugbyfootballhistory.com /Schism.html (accessed March 23, 2014).

"A Guide to the Game: Official Laws." Rugby Football League Limited, http://www.therfl .co.uk/a_guide_to_the_game (accessed March 23, 2014).

"Rugby Field Dimensions." iSport: Rugby, http://rugby.isport.com/rugby-guides/rugby -field-dimensions (accessed March 23, 2014).

"Rugby League Rules." We Are Rugby, 2009–2010, http://www.wearerugby.com/rugby-101 /rugby-league-rules/ (accessed March 23, 2014).

"Understanding Positions." Rugby Football League Limited, http://www.therfl.co.uk/the -rfl/rules/understanding_positions (accessed March 23, 2014).

"When Is a Scrum Formed?" BBC Sport: Rugby League, 2009, http://news.bbc.co.uk /sport1/hi/rugby_league/rules_and_equipment/4216576.stm (accessed March 23, 2014).

SCHWINGEN

Schwingen is a form of folk wrestling native to Switzerland, particularly the tradition-led, rural German-speaking areas of the country, central Switzerland and the Mitteland, that is practiced by both men and women. *Schwingen* usually takes place outdoors in the summer, though during the winter it is also practiced in indoor *schwing* halls. The sport gets its name from the German word *schwingen,* meaning "to swing." *Schwingen* is also known as Swiss wrestling and as *Hoselupf,* which translates from the Swiss language of Schweitzer-Deutsch as "breeches lift." *Schwingen* is considered one of the national sports of Switzerland, along with *steinstossen* and *hornussen. Schwingen* is an exclusively Swiss pastime and is only practiced in Switzerland or by Swiss immigrants to Australia, North America, and South Africa. *Schwingen* is an amateur sport, and as such all forms of advertising and sponsorship are prohibited at venues.

As is the case with most folk sports, the origins of *schwingen* are hard to decipher. However, the sport has been part of the very fabric of Swiss folk culture for centuries, and an illustration of the sport dating to the 13th century can be found in Lausanne Cathedral, in the southwest of the country. The sport was often performed at Alpine folk festivals, where wrestlers would vie for the prize of a piece of trouser fabric, hence the sport's alternate name of *Hoselupf.* Other prizes included a sheep. However, the honor of victory was the main reward. One of the earliest *schwingen* competitions is the Easter Monday Schwingfest that has been held in Bern, the Swiss capital, since the 17th century. Switzerland holds around 30 *schwingen* festivals per year, each attracting over 100 entrants.

Originally *schwingen* was practiced exclusively by mountain farmers, known as Sennen, as a way of determining who was the strongest and most skillful wrestler. Over time agile, gymnastic wrestlers known as the Turners and living in Switzerland's flat regions joined in the sport. Thus, two styles of *schwingen* exist: Sennenschwinger and Turnerschwinger. The color of a wrestler's clothing reveals which form of the sport the wrestler practices.

Under the rule of the French emperor Napoleon I (1769–1821), *schwingen* was repressed. However, the sport was revived in 1805 at the inaugural Alpine shepherd's festival at Unspunnen in a deliberate act of Swiss patriotism. The event was organized with the express intention of strengthening Swiss national culture, so it was only fitting that *schwingen* be present at the festival. After the Unspunnen festival, *schwingen* grew in popularity through farmers' meetings, folk festivals, and wrestling events. In 1895 the Swiss Schwingen Association, or Eidgenossische Schwingerverband, was founded, and by the 19th century *schwingen* was practiced

Swiss wrestler Fabian Ruegg, top, competes against a wrestler from Guinea-Bissau during a friendly *schwingen* bout at the Olma Fair in St. Gallen, Switzerland, held on October 16, 2007. During a bout, wrestlers hold on to their opponent's shorts and make swinging moves in an attempt to make the opponent lose balance and fall to the ground. (AP Photo/Keystone/Regina Kuehne)

in urban areas as well as the countryside and was thought of as the country's national sport. Today the Swiss Schwingen Association presides over the sport, helping to organize and promote it. Over 5,000 wrestlers belong to the association, which is divided into 5 regional associations. The regional associations are further divided into 23 cantonal associations and 6 district associations.

Until 1980 *schwingen* was an exclusively male sport, but now women are permitted to take part. Indeed, *schwingen* is one of the most popular female folk combat sports practiced today, with hundreds of women competing. *Schwingen* is an unusual sport, for women competitors wrestle not just other women but also men. Before each bout, three to six judges organize the competitors. A distinct feature of *schwingen* is that after each bout, judges decide anew which competitor will face which opponent. As no weight divisions exist in *schwingen,* judges pair opponents on the basis of equivalent size and talent; thus, a strong woman may be matched against a smaller or younger male. The wrestlers wear shirts and shorts made of jute over long pants, with the color of the shirt denoting which variation of *schwingen* the wrestler employs. Those who wrestle using the Sennenschwinger style wear dark pants and a pale blue shirt, while Turnerschwinger-style competitors wear white pants and a white top. The legs of the shorts are rolled up to provide a handle for the wrestlers to grip, and this hold on the shorts material must be maintained throughout the bout. The grips used in *schwingen* are almost identical to those employed in Icelandic wrestling, or *glima,* for in *schwingen* the wrestler uses a right-handed grip to grasp the back of the belt on the opponent's shorts, while the left hand grips the cuff on the right of the opponent's shorts.

Schwingen takes place on a circular ring measuring 12 meters (39 feet) in diameter. The ring is covered in sawdust and is known as the *platz,* meaning "square." At the *schwingen* competition in Coire in Grisons, the easternmost canton of Switzerland, six rings are arranged in a circle so that six different bouts can occur simultaneously. At the start of a match the wrestlers move to the *platz* and shake hands as a sign of mutual respect. The wrestlers then assume the starting position, which is an extremely important feature of the sport. In the starting position the wrestler stands so that her or his weight is spread evenly between both legs, and the wrestler must also allow the opponent room to maneuver. This stance means that neither wrestler has an advantage over the other. Once the wrestlers are in the starting position, the referee cries out "*Gut!*" ("good"), and the wrestling begins.

During the bout wrestlers hold on to the shorts of their opponent and make swinging moves in an attempt to make the opponent lose balance and topple to the ground. If a wrestler loses her or his balance but falls outside the *platz* rather than onto the ground, then play is stopped and the wrestlers must resume the starting position. In order to topple their opponent, wrestlers employ a wide variety of throws. When *schwingen* first became popular only about 3 throws were used, but now there are 100 permitted throws. The 5 main throws are the Brienzer, Bur, Hufter, Kurtz, and Ubersprung throws.

A bout ends when one of the wrestlers touches the sawdust with her or his back, which in *schwingen* is classified as any area from the back of the head to the buttocks. For the result to count, both of the competitor's shoulder blades must come to lie within the circle of sawdust at the same time. A referee, often a former wrestler and located in the *platz,* umpires the bout, while two judges sit at a table to oversee the match. Each bout lasts five minutes. Once the win is given, the winner must wipe the sawdust from the loser's shoulders. The winner does not, however, receive a monetary reward. Instead, winners receive a wreath and prizes from what is known as the gift table. These prizes include a young bull called a Muni, cowbells, furniture in a rustic style, and other prizes associated with nature. Successful wrestlers are famous throughout Switzerland, where they are known as Bosen, or the Wicked Ones. The contest to find the champion *schwinger* is part of the two-day Eidgenössisches Schwing-Und Älperfest, or Festival of Wrestling and Alpine Sports, which is held in a different location every three years and attracts around 250,000 spectators, with more watching the event via extensive television coverage. The festival is a celebration of Swiss culture featuring folk dance, traditional Swiss music, yodeling, and flag spinning in addition to *schwingen*. Women *schwingers* are not permitted to take part in the festival but may enter a separate event at which a *schwinger* queen is crowned. The champion *schwingen* contest takes place alongside *steinstossen* and *hornussen*. Occasionally a supremely gifted wrestler is declared the king of wrestling. The first king, Johan Vogel, was crowned in 1735, and only 30 wrestlers have received this honor since 1895. The king is crowned at a *schwingen* festival by the festival's queen, who bestows upon the wrestler a garland of oak leaves or laurel. The king of *schwingen* enjoys great national celebrity. Indeed, a former winner of the title, Jorg Abderhalden, was voted Swiss of the Year in 2007. However, just as champion *schwingers* attract mass adulation, they can also garner nationwide condemnation if they are seen as disrespecting their sport. This was the case when Ruedi Hunsperger wrestled a bear during a televised *Night of Swiss Sport* in 1977 and received much criticism for bringing great shame on *schwingen*.

Schwingen is such an intrinsic element of Swiss culture that Swiss emigrants often bring the sport with them to wherever they settle. For instance, *schwingen* has a long history in the United States. Swiss immigrants started arriving in America soon after the end of the American Civil War (1861–1865), and by the late 19th century the immigrants had begun to establish societies with the aim of providing support for one another and to keep alive the traditions and customs of their homeland, including *schwingen*. The first American *schwingfest* was held in 1921 at McKim Bridge on the Von Moos and Ruchti Ranch in California. In 1957, a Swiss immigrant named Joseph L. Inderbitzin established the West Coast Swiss Wrestling Association. Inderbitzin had witnessed a *schwinger* incur a fatal broken neck during a bout and realized that it was necessary to form a governing body to oversee *schwingen* in the United States. The association standardized the rules and regulations of *schwingen* on the West Coast of America and organized an annual *schwingfest* for all *schwingen* clubs allied to the organization. Today the association continues to oversee *schwingen* in America, offering help to injured wrestlers, providing the means for American wrestlers to travel to Switzerland to compete, and enabling Swiss wrestlers to compete at *schwingfests* in America.

See also: Celtic Wrestling; *Glima;* Korean Wrestling; *Lapta; Lucha Libre;* Mongolian Wrestling; *Pehlwani/Kushti;* Shin Kicking; Stone Skimming; Sumo Wrestling; *Varzesh-e Bastani; Yagli Gures*

Further Reading

Chambers, Lucas. "Swiss Know How to Schwingen." Straight.com, July 8, 2004, http://www.straight.com/life/swiss-know-how-schwingen (accessed August 9, 2013).

"A Clash of the Alpine Titans." Swiss Info, August 20, 2010, http://www.swissinfo.ch/eng/culture/A_clash_of_the_alpine_titans_.html?cid=24853120 (accessed August 9, 2013).

"Federal Wrestling and Alpine Games Festival 2013." Bern Information, http://www.bern.com/en/region/emmental/events/schwingfest-2013 (accessed August 9, 2013).

LeVV. "Swiss Folk Wrestling Style 'Schwingen.'" Female Single Combat Club, 2000, http://www.fscclub.com/vidy/small-schwingen-e.shtml (accessed November 30, 2014).

Nauright, John, and Charles Parrish, eds. *Sports around the World: History, Culture and Practice,* Vol. 1, *General Topics, Africa, Asia, Middle East, and Oceania.* Santa Barbara, CA: ABC-CLIO, 2012.

"Schwingen." Wrestling Assistant, http://www.wrestlingassistant.com/C3I.html (accessed August 9, 2013).

"Swiss Wrestling (Schwingen)—From Herdsman's Pastime to Elite Sport." My Switzerland, 2014, http://www.myswitzerland.com/en/swiss-wrestling-schwingen-from-herdsman-s-pastime-to-elite-sport.html (accessed August 9, 2013).

"West Coast Swiss Wrestling Association History." San Joaquin Valley Swiss Club, http://www.riponswissclub.com/index_files/Page588.htm (accessed August 9, 2013).

SEPAK TAKRAW

Sepak takraw, sometimes written as *sepaktakraw,* is a competitive team ball sport for men, women, and children that combines elements of volleyball, football, gymnastics, and martial arts. The sport is native to the Malay-Thai Peninsula in Southeast Asia, but the game is popular across Asia, particularly in Malaysia and Thailand and in the Philippines. *Sepak takraw* is also played in India, Japan, Switzerland, Germany, the United States, and Canada. Indeed, competitive *sepak takraw* is played in 25 counties across five continents. However, the sport goes under different names in different countries. For instance, in Singapore the sport is called *bola sepak raga* or *sepak raga,* in Malaysia it is known as *sepak raga jaring* or *sepraga,* and in Brunei the sport is called *sepak raga jala.* Elsewhere *sepak takraw* is known as *rago* (Indonesia), *kat* (Laos), *ching loong* (Myanmar), *sipa* (the Philippines), and *takraw* (Thailand). The most commonly used name, *sepak takraw,* comes from the Malay word *sepak,* meaning "kick or smash," and the Thai word *takraw,* meaning "woven ball." This name very well describes the nature of the sport, for *sepak takraw* is a game of speed necessitating fast reflexes, balance, and flexibility as well as explosive jumping abilities. During a game, two teams of three players use their heads and feet to volley a rattan (or plastic) ball to and fro across a net standing

A young Thai person plays *sepak takraw* at the Thai temple in Homestead, Florida, on February 24, 2008. The sport combines elements of volleyball, soccer, gymnastics, and martial arts as players propel the ball over the net using their legs, head, and torso. (AP Photo/J. Pat Carter)

5 foot 1 inch tall, fitted over a regulation badminton court measuring 44 feet by 20 feet. The rules are the same as for volleyball.

The origins of *sepak takraw* are a subject of much debate. Some historians claim that a version of the sport was played across Southeast Asia in areas now known as the Philippines, Brunei, Myanmar, Indonesia, Singapore, Malaysia, and Laos during the 11th century. It has also been claimed that the explorer Marco Polo (1254–1324) brought back a game from China that was very similar to *sepak takraw* in that it saw village teams kick a ball-like object in the air. The aim of the game was to foster a teamwork ethic and a sense of community, for villagers had to maneuver the ball back and forth in the air between each other and count every time the ball was dribbled or kicked.

Other claims for the origins of *sepak takraw* are that the game was invented at the Malaysian royal court during the 15th century, and another theory suggests that early versions of the sport were played in Thailand during the 16th century. During the 18th century the Spanish colonial forces noted the cultural importance of *sepak takraw* in Southeast Asia, and in the 19th and early 20th centuries American forces occupying the region documented the playing of *sepak takraw* at feasts, weddings, and village festivals—a tradition that still continues. For the past 25 years the biggest annual international *sepak takraw* festivals have been the Khir Johari Cup, held in Malaysia, and the King's Cup, which takes place in Thailand and is organized by the Takraw Association of Thailand. The modern version of *sepak takraw* took shape during the late 19th and early 20th centuries, though exactly where and when is unknown. It has been suggested that the Malaysian state of Negeri Sembilan debuted the use of a badminton net and badminton rules in the game at an exhibition in 1915 to honor 50 years of the reign of King George V of England. However, it is doubtful that a major innovation, such as the introduction of a net, could have occurred overnight after one demonstration.

This new net-based version of *sepak takraw* continued to grow in popularity across Southeast Asia, particularly after the modified version was introduced to high schools. Then in 1945, three players from Penang in Malaysia wrote out the rules of *sepak jaring,* meaning "kick the net," and played the first exhibition match of this version of *sepak takraw.* In 1960 the rules of *sepak takraw* were codified when sporting bodies in Malaysia, Thailand, and Singapore decided to agree on both a common set of rules for the sport and a name—*sepak takraw.* Then in 1965, five years after the standardization of rules, *sepak takraw* was awarded medal status at the Southeast Asian Peninsular Games (the forerunner of the Southeast Asian Games, or SEA Games). Other milestone events in the history of *sepak takraw* include the founding in 1988 of the International Sepaktakraw Federation (ISTAF) and the recognition of the sport in 1990 by the Olympic Movement, which invited *sepak takraw* to be included at the 10th Asian Games in Beijing that same year.

Perhaps the most important piece of *sepak takraw* equipment is the grapefruit-sized ball. Traditionally woven rattan balls are used in *sepak takraw,* but in 1982 woven synthetic balls were introduced in Thailand. This change of material, which meant that balls could be mass-produced for the first time, revolutionized *sepak takraw,* for many more people could play the sport. *Sepak takraw* balls are made in different sizes and weights to suit various levels of expertise. The ball used by a novice male player weighs 140 grams, while an experienced male player's ball will weigh 175 grams. The balls used by women are generally smaller and lighter than the balls used by male players. The responsiveness of the ball relies on the tightness of its weave. For example, a tightly woven ball is the bounciest and will demonstrate the most amount of spring, while a more loosely woven ball will be soft and less bouncy. The footwear worn by players is also extremely important, with players opting for low-cut tennis or basketball shoes that have a flat instep. The uniforms worn by players are much like those worn in volleyball.

The basic rules of *sepak takraw* are simple, with players aiming to deliver the ball over the net into their opponents' court with the intention that the ball cannot be returned. Players may use any part of their legs, head, and torso to propel the ball, but they may not use their arms or hands. There are several forms of *sepak takraw*, but the most commonly played is the regu format, which is played by two teams of five members consisting of three on-court players and two substitutes; one substitution may be made per set. The on-court players consist of a striker, a server, and a feeder, and each has a distinct tactical role to play during a match. The service of the ball is often the determining factor in *sepak takraw* matches, with serves delivered by the server. Over the past 20 years many various styles of serving have evolved in different countries. In Vietnam the balletic and precise cartwheel serve is used, though the horse-kick serve, which originated in Thailand, is universally acknowledged to be both the most challenging to execute and the most difficult to return. Once the ball has been served by the server, the opposing side may touch the ball up to three times in order to return it back over the net. Usually the server and the feeder, who specializes in setting up the smash, receive the ball and try to set it up for the return over the net by using two touches. Once the ball has been set up for the return, it is smashed back over the net by the striker, whose hit on the ball constitutes the team's third touch of the ball. There are also various types of smashes, also known as spikes, in *sepak takraw*. For example, there are several variants of the sunback spike in which players jump with their back to the net and kick the ball over their shoulder in the manner of a soccer-style bicycle kick. The sunback spike sees the ball travel toward the opposing side at speeds in excess of 75 miles per hour. A team scores one point when the opposing team fails to return the ball across the net within three touches and when the ball is returned across the net but lands outside of the court.

New ISTAF tournaments use the regu scoring format in which teams play matches comprising five sets, with the match won by the team that is the first to win three sets. A set is won by the side that scores 15 points with a minimum lead of 2 clear points. If the score is tied at 14 points each, then the set is won either by the side that achieves a lead of 2 points or when a side reaches 17 points. A recent innovation in the scoring system that aims to ensure matches are not dominated solely by serve sees teams take turns at serving, and a service-over occurs after every 3 consecutive points scored regardless of which team has won the points. This means that after every 3 consecutive points, serving switches to the opposing team for the next 3 consecutive points. This pattern of play continues until a team obtains 15 points (or 17 points in the case of a deuce) and the set is won.

Over time new styles of *sepak takraw* have evolved. For instance, Beach Sepaktakraw is a recent innovation that led to the inclusion of *sepak takraw* as a medal sport at the inaugural Asian Beach Games 2008 in Bali.

Similar to *sepak takraw* is *jianzi,* an indoor or outdoor sport played by individuals, pairs, and teams of men and women. The name *jianzi* derives from *ti jian zi,* which translates as "kick little shuttlecock." The sport is also called shuttlecock or Chinese hacky sack. *Jianzi* is said to have originated in China during the fifth century BCE, though it was not until the sport was demonstrated at the 1936 Olympic Games in Berlin that it became known worldwide. Today *jianzi* is the national sport of Vietnam (where it is called *da cau*) and is played across Southeast Asia, India, Brazil, the United States, France, Greece, Germany, the Netherlands, Finland, Romania, Serbia, and Hungary. In *jianzi,* players aim to keep a shuttlecock-like weighted, feathered disk weighing about 15 grams in the air using any part of the body except the arms and hands. Points are won by successful passes and are lost when the disk touches the floor.

In individual matches, players may take two hits of the disk before launching it back over the net (or if not a net then a line drawn across the court), while in the team version of the sport (in which teams are made of six players, three on-court players and three substitutes) teams may take four touches. Competitive team matches are won by the first team to achieve 21 points. Casual games of *jianzi* resemble soccer-style keepy-uppy and are a common sight in parks in many Asian countries, where the game is considered excellent exercise for all, as it encourages flexibility, aerobic capacity, and joint strength.

Jianzi may be played competitively or as a form of artistry. Competitive *jianzi* is played on a court with rules very similar to those of badminton. The sport's governing body, the International Shuttlecock Federation, was founded in 1999, and the *jianzi* world championships have been held annually since 2000, when the contest took place in Hungary. The Shuttlecock Federation of Europe was founded in 2003, with the sport's first European Cup held the same year in Germany.

See also: Bossaball; Fives; Footvolley and Futnet; Real Tennis

Further Reading

Connolly, Paul. *The World's Weirdest Sports*. Millers Point, Australia: Pier 9, 2007.

Crego, Robert. *Sports and Games of the 18th and 19th Centuries*. Westport, CT: Greenwood, 2003.

"History and Heritage." Sepaktakraw Official Web site, 2014, http://www.sepaktakraw.org/about-istaf/sepaktakraw-heritage/#.UymcWxbna8q (accessed March 19, 2014).

"History of Shuttlecock Story." International Shuttlecock Federation, 2010, http://www.shuttlecock-world.org/site/news/history_of_shuttlecock_sport/ (accessed March 19, 2014).

Lopez, Lorna Fe P., McDonald D. Beldia, and Romulo J. Pangan. *Physical Education, Health, and Music III*. Manila: Rex Book Store, 2000.

"So What Exactly Is Sepaktakraw?" Sepaktakraw Official Web site, 2014, http://www.sepaktakraw.org/about-istaf/how-to-play-the-game/#.Uymf9Bbna8o (accessed March 19, 2014).

Wilson, Ed, ed. *The Sports Book: Fully Revised 4th Edition*. London: Dorling Kindersley, 2013.

SHEEPDOG TRIALS

A sheepdog trial is a competitive event in which a herding dog, such as a border collie, moves sheep into an enclosure as directed by its handlers. Sheepdog trials are often viewed as the ultimate test for the relationship between handler and dog, for the handlers may use only verbal commands and a whistle to control the animal. Handlers may be male or female, as may the dogs. Trials usually take place in hilly rural areas in the United Kingdom and Ireland; southern African nations including South Africa, Botswana, and Zambia; the United States and Canada; Chile; and Australia and New Zealand. Though it is commonly dogs of known herding breeds that take part in sheepdog trials, some competitions allow dogs of nonherding breeds to enter as long as the dogs have been trained to herd. The course used in sheepdog trials varies according to where the trial is taking place. Trials held in Africa, Europe, and North America employ the British-style course, while events in Australasian trials are split into several components, with the emphasis on dogs' timing and obedience.

The world's first sheepdog trial took place in Wanaka on New Zealand's South Island in 1867. The first UK sheepdog trial was held on October 9, 1873, near Bala in Wales. The competition was in two parts: penning and driving. Penning involved the dogs moving loose sheep into a pen, and driving saw the sheep driven toward the shepherd by the dog within a 20-minute time limit. Though most of the entrants in the first competition were Welsh, a Scottish shepherd and his dog, Tweed, won the contest. A year later the first sheepdog trial to be held in Scotland took place in Lanarkshire. The popularity of sheepdog trials grew swiftly in the United Kingdom during the latter stages of the 19th century, and in 1906 the International Sheep Dog Society was founded in Haddington, Scotland, in order to stimulate interest in shepherding and improve working conditions for sheepdogs. The society's aims remain the same today.

During the 19th century interest in sheepdog trials soon spread from the United Kingdom to the United States, and the sport continues in America, governed by the United States Border Collie Handlers Association, which was founded in 1979 and has 800 members. The first sheepdog trial in America was, however, held in 1880 as part of Philadelphia's centennial celebrations, and trials became a regular event in the United States from 1928. In 1969 sheepdog trials were incorporated in an American version of the Highland Games held at Fair Hill, Maryland. Today one of the most prestigious U.S. competitions is the Bank of the West Soldier Hollow Classic held annually on Labor Day in Utah. This competition attracts entrants from around the world as well as the world's largest number of spectators to a sheepdog trial. In 2009 a crowd in excess of 26,000 watched the trial.

The World Sheepdog Trials are held annually in the United Kingdom or Ireland and include competitions for individuals and teams. The first world trial was held in September 2002 in Bala, Wales, site of the first UK trial. There were 160 dogs from 13 countries entered in the event, which was won by Welshman Aled Owen and his dog, Bob. That the event has grown since the first world trial is evidenced by the fact that in 2008, 240 dogs from 22 countries entered the contest, which was also held in Wales at Llandeio. Incidentally, Aled Owen won the 2008 world trial too though with a different dog, Roy. The world trial is divided into qualifying rounds, semifinals, and the final. In the qualifiers and semifinals, dog and handler work together to move three unmarked sheep and two sheep wearing red collars around a course. Each course comprises seven components, and each component is scored by two or more judges of different nationalities.

The first component of the World Sheepdog Trials course is the outrun, for which 20 points per judge are available. For the outrun the dog is sent out to the left or right of a post while the handler stays at the post. The dog must not stop moving until it reaches the point of balance behind the sheep. The point of balance is where the dog will lift (i.e., cause to move in an orderly manner) the sheep in the direction of the course's first set of gates. Once the dog has reached the point of balance, it must stay sufficiently far from the sheep so as not to scare them. The lift is the second component and occurs at the end of the outrun, for when the dog has completed the outrun it must either come to a stop or slow down. The dog must then move toward the sheep in a smooth and steady manner so as not to worry them. The dog then has to take charge of the sheep and move the sheep in a direct line in the direction of the gates, which are the first obstacle encountered by either the dog or the sheep. The lift is worth 10 points per judge.

The third component of the course is the fetch, which scores 20 points per judge on completion. During this part of the course the sheep must be moved steadily in a straight line from the point of lifting, that is, where the dog slowed or stopped, to the first gates. The dog then moves the sheep from the gates to the handler, who is standing by the post. The dog must keep the sheep in as straight a line as possible when herding them toward the handler. However, if the sheep deviate from the line, the dog must bring them back into order as soon as possible. If the sheep refuse to move through the gates, then no points are scored for this section of the course, as no retry is permitted. The fourth course component is the drive, which is the highest-scoring part of the course, as it is worth 30 points per judge. During the drive the dog must move the sheep across a 450-yard triangular course consisting of two sets of gates through which the dog must maneuver the sheep. The drive starts as soon as the sheep have passed behind the dog's handler, who is still standing at the post, as in the fetch. The sheep must move in a straight line between obstacles and make a tidy turn at the post and the gates. A retry is not allowed should the sheep refuse to go through a gate. The drive concludes when the sheep enter the shedding ring. In the shedding ring unmarked sheep are kept apart from those wearing collars, and both handler and dog must combine to reunite the unmarked sheep with the others. The shed is the fifth component and is worth 10 points per judge.

Once all the sheep are brought back together the action moves to the pen, where the sixth part of the course, penning, takes place, for which 10 points per judge are available. For the penning, the handler moves to the pen and takes hold of a rope hanging from the gatepost, leaving the dog to bring the sheep to the pen. The handler continues to hold the rope, and once all the sheep have been moved to the pen, the handler closes the gate behind them. The handler then opens the gate, releasing the sheep. Having released the sheep, the handler recloses the gate and moves to the shedding ring once more. The final component of the course is the single, in which the dog moves the sheep from the pen to the shedding ring. The single is worth 10 points per judge.

Points are awarded for each component of the course completed within the time limit of 15 minutes per run. During the qualifiers each of the two judges awards points, so an aggregate score of 220 can be given. For the semifinal the aggregate score is 440. During the final, 170 points are available from each judge, which results in an aggregate of 680 points. The time limit during the final is 30 minutes.

During the final, handler and dog unite to move 20 sheep (15 unmarked and 5 wearing red collars) around the course. As in the semifinal, four judges award scores. The final also comprises seven sections, though some components combine more than one element. The first component is Outrun 1, which is worth 20 points per judge. For this outrun the judges decide which side of the post the dog must run, unlike in the qualifier in which the handler could choose which direction to send the dog. Next comes Lift 1, which is worth 10 points per judge. Lift 1 is carried out in the same way as the qualifier lift but is more difficult, as handler and dog must control a larger number of sheep than in the previous round. After Lift 1 comes Fetch 1, worth 20 points per judge. Fetch 1 sees the dog maneuver 10 of the sheep to a post called the turn-back pole and then through a set of gates. As in the qualifier, the sheep must move steadily and in a straight line. Fetch 1 is complete once the sheep have reached the turn-back pole. When the dog reaches the turn-back pole, the handler turns the dog back and directs it to the remaining 10 sheep that are located on the opposite side of the field to where the first 10 sheep stood at the start of Fetch 1. This is the first stage of the final's fourth component, which is called the Outrun, Lift, and Fetch 2. This component is worth 50 points per judge, with 20 for the outrun, 10 for the lift, and 20 for Fetch 2. During this phase of the competition the dog must direct the second lot of sheep through the gates so that they come to a stop parallel with the sheep that are already through the gates. The dog unites the two sets of sheep by moving the first 10 sheep toward the second. After the Outrun, Lift, and Fetch 2 comes the drive, worth 40 points per judge. The final's drive follows the same pattern as the qualifier drive but is more difficult, as it involves more sheep and is held on a course that is 600 yards long rather than 450 yards.

The shedding component of the final differs from that of previous rounds and is worth 20 points per judge. In the final the 15 unmarked sheep are separated from the 5 wearing red collars. The handler and dog then have to move the sheep between themselves so as to direct the unmarked sheep out of the shedding ring while leaving the collared sheep within the ring. If any of the collared sheep leave the ring with the unmarked sheep, then the shedding restarts from the beginning, with all the sheep brought back into the ring. Once all the unmarked sheep have been moved out of the shedding ring, the handler may proceed to the pen for the start of the final's last component, the penning. This final phase, worth 10 points per judge, sees the dog move the sheep to the pen. The handler waits for all the sheep to enter the pen and then closes the gate with a rope. The handler then releases the sheep and recloses the gate. The refastening of the gate concludes the run.

Individual winners receive a money prize and a solid gold shepherd's whistle, while all finalists receive a leather and brass dog collar. First-, second-, and third-place winners in the team event receive a small monetary prize and a gold, silver, or bronze medal. However, everyone who competes in the World Sheepdog Trials receives a competition medal.

A triennial World Sheepdog Trial also exists. Founded in 2002, the competition attracts entrants from countries as diverse as Brazil, Finland, Japan, and New Zealand.

Dog Surfing

Dog surfing has existed in America since the 1920s and sees specially trained dogs surf on surfboards or bodyboards either solo or with a human. Some dogs have also been taught to share paddleboards with their owners. In competitions, dogs are judged on their overall ability on the board, wave size, and ride length. Notable competitions include the yearly Surf City Surf Dog tournament held at Huntington Beach, California, and the annual Loews Coronado Bay Dog Surf Championships, also in California, that raises funds for the American Society for the Prevention of Cruelty to Animals.

In the United Kingdom, sheepdog trials are synonymous with the popular BBC television program *One Man and His Dog* that ran from 1971 to 1999 and attracted a large urban audience. The popular *Babe* films, about a pig that wants to herd sheep, brought sheepdog trials to a wider public consciousness. The films are based on Dick King-Smith's book *The Sheep-Pig* (1983) about sheepdog trials in northern England.

See also: Bearbaiting and Badger Baiting; Bull Running; *Buzkashi*; Camel and Yak Racing; Camel Wrestling; Cockfighting; Elephant Sports; Fell Running; Foxhunting; Hare Coursing; Highland Games; Nipsy; Nonlethal Bullfighting; *Pato* and Horseball; Pigeon Racing; Spanish Bullfighting; Yabbie Races

Further Reading

"The Association." USBCHA, 2011–2014, http://www.usbcha.com/assoc/association.html (accessed September 24, 2013).

Donaldson, Emily Ann. *The Scottish Highland Games in America.* Gretna, LA: Pelican, 1986.

"History." The International Sheep Dog Society, http://www.worldsheepdogtrials.org/history .html (September 24, 2013).

Midgley, Neil. "World Sheepdog Trials in Cumbria." *The Telegraph,* September 9, 2011, http://www.telegraph.co.uk/earth/countryside/8749386/World-Sheep-Dog-Trials-in -Cumbria.html (accessed September 24, 2013).

"World Trial Courses." The International Sheep Dog Society, http://www.worldsheepdogtrials .org/about-the-world-trials/world-trial-courses/ (September 24, 2013).

SHIN KICKING

Shin kicking, also known as hacking or purring, is a minority outdoor contact sport native to England usually practiced by men but occasionally by women. Shin kicking is practiced in the English town of Chipping Campden, in the county of Gloucestershire, as part of the Cotswold Olimpicks and at fairs and the like held in Pennsylvania in the United States.

The origins of shin kicking are unknown, but the sport dates from at least the 17th century, for shin kicking has been part of the Cotswold Olimpicks since 1612. Indeed, the World Shin Kicking Championship is perhaps the most famous aspect of the modern Cotswold Olimpicks. Usually between 12 and 20 contestants take part in shin kicking at the Cotswold Olimpicks, with entrants drawing lots to choose their opponent. Originally it seems that shin kicking did not have any rules, but today at the Cotswold Olimpicks the rules are enforced by a judge known as the stickler, who is responsible for ensuring the fairness of competition and whose decision is final.

In shin kicking, contestants, known as kickers, grasp each other's shoulders or coat lapels with straight arms and aim to weaken their opponent by kicking the opponent's shins to such a degree that the opponent may be thrown off balance and onto the ground while the contestant keeps one foot on the ground. It is illegal for contestants to throw an opponent over before a kick has been made, and the kicker must make contact for the kick to count. It is also illegal to kick or push an opponent to the ground. A throw is automatically awarded to a contestant if the opponent kicks him or her above the knee or trips the contestant so that he or she falls to the ground. It is therefore very important that contestants do not cheat, for in shin kicking a bout is won by the best of three throws; that is, two successful throws equals a win. As shin kicking is a knockout sport, a contest can last for two hours, with individual bouts lasting up to 10 minutes. The winner of the final bout wins the contest.

Kickers wear long trousers (or tracksuit bottoms) and may protect their shins by stuffing their trouser legs with the straw provided by competition organizers in the manner of a scarecrow and then tying the bottom of their trousers with rope in order to make sure the straw does not escape the trouser leg midfight. This element of protection is in contrast to the approach taken by competitors during the 19th century, when kickers would hit their lower legs with metal coal hammers before the competition in order to toughen up their shins. Above the waist competitors wear white coats that represent the white smocks traditionally worn by shepherds. The correct footwear is essential in shin kicking. Competitors must sport soft-toed shoes such as sneakers or unreinforced boots. During the 19th century competitors wore iron-tipped boots. However, it is now expressly forbidden for competitors to wear any form of metal-reinforced footwear—organizers check competitors' footwear both before and after bouts. If a competitor is found to sport illicit footwear, then he or she is immediately excluded from the contest and banned from all future shin kicking events.

Shin kicking is also synonymous with Norfolk and Devonian wrestling and Lancastrian clog fighting. The earliest written references to Norfolk and Devonian wrestling styles appear in *The Survey of Cornwall* by Richard Carew, which was published in 1602, while in the third edition of his *Progymnasmata: The Inn-Play, or Cornish Hugg-Wrestler,* dated 1727, Thomas Parkyns relates how women living in the eastern English county of Norfolk could not bear to watch local wrestling, as the shin kicking element of that wrestling style often resulted in broken legs. However, by 1840 it was Devonian wrestlers who had garnered a reputation as the fiercest shin kickers, for men from the southwestern English county of Devon were known to harden the soles of their shoes by baking them in order to inflict more painful blows on the legs of their opponents. Meanwhile during Victorian times in the north of England, particularly in the towns of Wigan and Rochdale, a working-class pastime called Lancastrian clog fighting was popular. Clog fighting was associated with gambling, which was illegal at the time, but as clog fighting had established rules and took place at specific locations, this variation of shin kicking was classed as a sport. Clog fighting saw men, naked except for their metal-trimmed wooden shoes, grapple and kick each other in the hope of winning £1 (about £60 in today's money). Some clog fighting bouts lasted for 45 minutes, and it was quite common for fighters to be severely injured during a fight, for the loser was the first kicker to either give up on the bout or bleed first. Indeed, a champion clog fighter called Ashworth even killed his opponent during a bout. Lancastrian clog fighting is thought to have originated in the 1700s but had died out by around 1910.

The 19th century also saw shin kicking sports exported to America by English and Welsh immigrants. In America the sport is known as purring. Newspaper reports of a purring contest held in Port Richmond, Pennsylvania, in January 1883 note the brutality of the contest, for the kickers wore copper-toed boots that resulted in cuts that exposed the bone of the shin. The bout lasted 16 minutes. Today shin kicking in America is all but extinct as a competitive sport, though it has been argued that it continues in the form of children's games known variously as shinning, cutlegs, cutlegging, and the more recent stampers, in which players aim is to stamp on their opponent's feet.

See also: Aunt Sally; Celtic Wrestling; Conkers; Cotswold Olimpicks; Cricket; Dwile Flonking; Foxhunting; Hare Coursing; *Schwingen;* Sumo Wrestling; Thai Boxing

Further Reading

Britton, Paul. "Exhibition Remembers Clog Fighting: The Victorian Martial Art." *Manchester Evening News,* January 7, 2014, http://www.manchestereveningnews.co.uk/news/greater-manchester-news/display-museum-wigan-life-tells-6476715 (accessed April 10, 2014).

Couch, Jason. "Purring." *Journal of Manly Arts,* August 2004, http://ejmas.com/jmanly/articles/2004/jmanlyart_couch_0804.htm (accessed April 10, 2014).

Curry, Neil. "Cotswold Olimpicks: Shin-Kicking at the 'Other' Games." CNN, June 9, 2012, http://edition.cnn.com/2012/06/07/sport/cotswold-olimpicks-shin-kicking/ (accessed April 10, 2014).

Daeschner, J. R. *True Brits.* London: Arrow Books, 2004.

Daeschner, J. R. "True Brits: A Tour of 21st Century Britain in All Its Bog-Snorkelling, Gurning and Cheese-Rolling Glory." http://www.daeschner.com/skab/naked.html (accessed April 10, 2014).

Polley, Martin. *The British Olympics: Britain's Olympic Heritage 1612–2012*. London: English Heritage, 2011.

Robert Dover's Games Society. "Get the Shin Kicked Out of You." Robert Dover's Cotwold Olimpicks, http://www.olimpickgames.com/shin-kicking/ (accessed April 10, 2014).

Sheckler Finch, Jackie. "Shin Kicking Competition Survives in Britain." Indianapolis International Travel Examiner, December 2, 2011, http://www.examiner.com/article/shin-kicking-competition-survives-britain (accessed April 10, 2014).

SHINTY

Shinty, also known as shindy, shinnie, shindig, and shintie, among other names, is a minority team stick and ball game played by men, women, and children. The name "shinty" is thought to derive from the Gaelic word *sinteag,* meaning "to leap." The Gaelic nature of the game is reflected in the parts of the world where shinty is enjoyed, for the sport is played mainly in Scotland, particularly the Scottish Highlands, Scottish universities, and those areas of the world where either the Scottish fought during world wars or Scottish emigrants have settled, including England (where the London Camanachd shinty club is based), Ireland, North America, and Australasia. Another theory is that the name "shinty" evolved from the cry of "Shin ye!" shouted during a game.

An 18th-century illustration depicting a game of shinty, the combative sport that is the national sport of Scotland. Shinty players use a broad, curved stick to toss, flick, and pass the ball in order to score goals for their team. (*Old England: A Pictorial Museum of Regal, Ecclesiastical, Baronial, Municipal and Popular Antiquities, Vol. 2, 1845.*)

Shinty is Scotland's national sport, though the game is played by only a few thousand men and women; the country's most popular sport to both watch and play is soccer. Traditionally shinty was a winter sport played between New Year and Easter and was part of the New Year's Eve festival of Oidhche Challuinn or Old New Year (January 11–13), which was a time of rituals and merriment that took precedence over Christmas. However, in 2003 it was decided that the shinty season should run from March to September in order to make the game more attractive to spectators who would rather avoid the harsh weather of the Scottish winter. The winter tradition does, however, live on through the annual Shinty Festival, which sees former shinty players take on current players on New Year's Day.

A game of shinty looks much like a game of field hockey at first glance, and the sport is thought to be the forebearer of ice hockey, for during the 19th century Scottish immigrants to Canada played shinty on ice. Indeed, to this day an informal game of ice hockey is known as a shinny in Canada. The game of golf is also thought to be related to shinty, for it has also been claimed that golf was born when shinty players practiced driving the ball with their long wooden curved stick, individually and in pairs. Shinty also shares ancestry with the game of bandy, for in Wales shinty is called bando.

It has been argued that shinty playing in England predates the game in Scotland, with games called variously shenty, shindy, and shinny played in many English counties, and the game was certainly played in England during the 19th century, when shinty clubs thrived in cities such as London, Nottingham, Manchester, and Birmingham. However, the history of shinty is generally thought to date back to the Middle Ages when Irish immigrants brought the game to northwestern Scotland, for shinty shares a common root with the Irish sport of hurling, and today an international shinty-hurling match is contested annually using compromised rules.

The first written reference to shinty can be found in the Kirk Session Records of Glasgow of 1589. During the earliest years of shinty the game was used to settle clan and parish rivalries and was a full-contact sport with few rules. Indeed, it was not unknown for games to be contested by teams of around 50 players. However, the rules of shinty developed rapidly in the 18th and 19th centuries, a time when Scottish nationalists supported the growth of shinty, as they saw the sport as a way of fostering traditional Scottish cultural values. The rules of shinty were ratified in 1879–1880; however, and the sport's governing body, the Camanachd Association based in the Scottish city of Inverness, was founded in 1893, with 33 clubs as founding members. The name of the association derives from the Gaelic word *caman* (pl. *camain*), meaning a stick with a hooked top. The name of the association also highlights that shinty is related to cammag, a team game played on the Isle of Man, a self-governing British dependency located in the Irish Sea. Cammag, which is a game of few rules and can feature teams of two to several hundred players, died out on the Isle of Man during the 20th century when soccer became popular on the isle, but the 21st century has seen a cammag revival, with an annual cammag match played in the village of St. John's every December 26.

The popularity of shinty declined after the outbreak of World War I in 1914, however, as people moved away from the shinty heartlands of the Scottish

Highlands and islands of the Inner and Outer Hebrides and settled in industrialized towns such as Glasgow or relocated to the north of England. This led to shinty becoming a minority sport played only in the eastern Highlands; at Scottish universities such as St. Andrews, Aberdeen, and Edinburgh; and among the Gaelic community living in Glasgow.

The modern game of shinty, as organized by the Camanachd Association, is played on a rectangular field sporting minimal markings. The size of the pitch varies from club to club but must measure 140 to 170 yards in length by 70 to 80 yards in width. A game of shinty is contested over two halves of 45 minutes with a 5-minute break at halftime and is contested by two teams of 12 players (plus 3 substitutes) that is made up of a hailkeeper (the goalkeeper), a fullback, three halfbacks, a center back, a center field, a center-forward, three half-forwards, and a full-forward. Players use their stick, which is broad and curved and resembles a field hockey stick, to toss, flick, and pass the ball aerially; the ball is round, made of cork and worsted, covered in leather or plastic, and is between 7.5 and 8 inches in circumference. Players must touch the ball with only their stick, chest, one foot placed on the ground, or both feet together, for only the hailkeeper may use her or his hands to touch the ball. Though a contact sport, pushing, hacking, charging, and blocking are illegal in shinty, and the rules are strictly enforced by the match referee, who is assisted by two lines persons and two goal judges.

Teams aim to score more goals than their opponents by maneuvering the ball into the hail, or goal, placed at each end of the pitch. The hail consists of two upright posts 12 feet apart that are joined by a horizontal bar placed just over 10 feet off the ground. As in soccer the goals, which lie equidistant from the pitch's corner flags, are netted.

Shinty games take place as part of national leagues and World Cup competitions. The national shinty league used to be based on a regional basis, with distinct leagues for the north and the south of Scotland. However, these leagues merged in the 1980s to form one league. In the modern era the league has been dominated by the Kingussie Shinty Club, based in Badenoch, which in 2005 was awarded the Guinness World Record for being the most successful team in the history of world sport, having won 20 league titles in a row. The premiere shinty cup competition is the Camanachd Association Challenge Cup. This competition too has been dominated by Kingussie Shinty Club, which won the first-ever Camanachd Association Challenge Cup in 1896, as well as its near neighbor, Newtonmore. Other shinty cup competitions include the Macaulay Cup (which began in 1947 and is organized in such a way that a team from the north of Scotland will always play a team from the south of the country), the MacTavish Cup for northern Scottish clubs, the Glasgow Celtic Society Cup for southern Scottish teams, and the Lovat Cup, an annual match held at New Year between the Lovat Shinty Club and the Beauly Shinty Club. The shinty grand slam is made up of the Macaulay Cup, the Camanachd Association Challenge Cup, the MacTavish Cup, and the league title. Unsurprisingly, the Kingussie Shinty Club has won the grand slam more often than any other club, winning it for a record seventh consecutive time in 2003.

See also: Bandy; Celtic Wrestling; Curling; Highland Games; Hurling; *La Soule;* Quidditch; Stone Skimming; Underwater Hockey

Further Reading

Be a Guid Sport: Teachers Book. Ulster-Scots Agency, http://www.ulsterscotsagency.com/fs /doc/teaching-resources/be-a-guid-sport-teacher-booklet.pdf (accessed April 6, 2014).

"Christmas on the Isle of Man." Celtic Life International, Winter 2012, http://www.celticlifeintl .com/christmas-on-the-isle-of-man/ (accessed May 22, 2014).

Cockburn, Craig. "Hogmanay Customs." Siliconglen, June 19, 2012, http://www.siliconglen .com/Scotland/12_16.html (accessed April 6, 2014).

Greig, Martin. "Shinty Stick: How Did a Tiny Highland Town Produce the Most Successful Team in the History of World Sport? Ronaldo of the Glens May Have Had Something to Do with It . . ." Herald Scotland, October 14, 2006, http://www.heraldscotland.com /sport/spl/aberdeen/shinty-stick-how-did-a-tiny-highland-town-produce-the-most -successful-team-in-the-history-of-world-sport-ronaldo-of-the-glens-may-have-had -something-to-do-with-it-1.7792 (accessed April 6, 2014).

"Kingussie Grand Slam Bid Reaches Round Two." *Inverness Courier,* November 25, 2011, http://www.inverness-courier.co.uk/Sport/Shinty/Kingussie-grand-slam-bid-reaches -round-two-13154.htm (accessed April 6, 2014).

Koch, John T. *Celtic Culture: A Historical Encyclopedia,* Vols. 1–5. Santa Barbara, CA: ABC-CLIO, 2006.

Levinson, David, and Karen Christensen, eds. *Encyclopedia of World Sport: From Ancient Times to the Present.* Oxford: Oxford University Press, 1996.

MacLennan, Hugh Dan. "Shinty." BBC Scotland, http://www.bbc.co.uk/scotland/sportscot land/asportingnation/article/0011/print.shtml (accessed April 6, 2014).

MacLennan, Hugh D. "Shinty in England Pre-1893." *Sports Historian* 19(2) (1999), http:// library.la84.org/SportsLibrary/SportsHistorian/1999/sh192e.pdf (accessed April 6, 2014).

MacLennan, Hugh Dan. "Shinty's Place and Space in World Sport." *Sports Historian* 18(1) (May 1998): 1–23.

"Shinty." Kingussie Business Forum, 2014, http://www.kingussie.co.uk/community/shinty (accessed April 6, 2014).

"Shinty: A Uniquely Scottish Sport." Scotland.com, 1995–2014, http://www.scotland.com /blog/shinty-a-uniquely-scottish-sport (accessed April 6, 2014).

Tomlinson, Alan. *A Dictionary of Sports Studies.* Oxford: Oxford University Press, 2010.

SHOE THROWING

The term "shoe throwing" covers several sports including welly wanging, clog cobbing, and horseshoe throwing.

Welly wanging is the sport of throwing a wellington boot as far as possible within set boundary lines from a standing or running start, much like a javelin event only using a rubber boot instead of a javelin. The sport originated in Upperthong Village in Yorkshire, northern England, where in the local dialect to wang means to throw and where the Official Welly Wanging World Championships are held annually as part of the Upperthong Gala. The Upperthong welly wanging takes place in the spirit of fair play and therefore without umpires, as a competitor is assumed to be honorable and honest. However, the competition, which is divided into four categories (men's, women's, and boys and girls under 14), is played by firm rules. For example, all thrown wellies must be Dunlop-make, green, size 9, and without a steel toe cap. In addition, the maximum permitted run-up is 42 paces and must end in a straight line of 10 feet. Once thrown, the welly must land within the marked area called the thong. Competitors may employ any action of the arm or foot to throw the welly and are allowed to wait for one minute if they think a beneficial gust of wind will arrive to help carry the welly farther. Winners of the men's and women's categories receive a trophy, while winners of the children's categories are awarded £5. A rival welly throwing world championship takes place in Wellington, Somerset, home to Arthur Wellesley, first Duke of Wellington (1769–1852), who gave his name to the wellington boot. Meanwhile, Taihape, New Zealand, has held an annual Gumboot Day since 1985 to honor the humble gumboot (gumboot being another name for the wellington boot). One of the main attractions of Gumboot Day is a gumboot throwing contest in which competitors aim to throw a gumboot the farthest.

A more formal version of welly wanging and gumboot throwing is boot throwing, which occurs in several European countries, particularly Germany, Poland, and Finland, as well as the United States. The International Boot-Throwing Association oversees major competitions including the world championships, a two-day competition for individuals and teams, and the World Cup. At the world championships the top 25 individual boot throwers compete over three rounds to determine which throwers go to the finals. The final consists of six rounds, with a cut after three rounds. The top 12 throwers continue on to the final three rounds. In the team event the top eight teams to emerge from qualifying go on to the finals, which consist of three rounds. The Boot-Throwing World Cup consists of six competitions—one each held in Estonia, Finland, Germany, Italy, Russia, and Sweden. At cup competitions, the top 15 competitors earn points ranging from 30 points for the winner to 1 point for the thrower in 15th place. Points earned from these events are added together, and the individuals and teams to have accumulated the highest scores are declared champions.

According to the Guinness Book of World Records, the farthest boot throws for both men and women were set on October 12, 1996, at Hämeenlinna, Finland. The men's record was set at 63.98 meters (roughly 210 feet) by Fin Teppo Luoma, while his fellow countrywoman Sari Tirkkon set the women's record at 40.87 meters (134 feet). New records may be set in the future, however, as scientists at Aberystwyth University, Wales, have created a welly wanging machine capable of propelling a welly up to 262 feet.

Another shoe throwing sport is clog cobbing, which sees competitors vie to throw a wooden shoe called a clog the farthest. The World Clog Cobbing Championship has been held on Easter Monday in Waterfoot, Lancashire, northern England, since the 1960s, when the event was inaugurated as a charity fund-raiser. The technique of clog cobbing involves cobbers (as clog throwers are known) swinging the clog between their legs to build up momentum and then hurling the clog backward.

Horseshoe throwing, also known as horseshoe pitching or just horseshoes, is an outdoor game in which competitors toss horseshoes or similar metal rings over a stake driven into the ground, though the rules vary from venue to venue. Horseshoe throwing is most popular in the United States, where regular competitions take place including the world championships, as well as in Britain and Ireland.

Horseshoe throwing is thought to have begun during the early part of the Roman occupation of Britain circa 43 CE when Roman officers played quoits (a game similar to horseshoes dating from around 2 CE) with specially made metal rings. The average Roman soldier could not, however, afford such expensive equipment and settled for throwing old horseshoes instead. In modern times the first horseshoe throwing contest took place in Manhattan, Kansas, in 1905, with the first official tournament, dubbed the World Tournament, held in Bronson, Kansas, in 1909. After this, tournaments were held frequently if not regularly. This changed in 1946, for in that year President Harry S. Truman was pictured playing the game on the lawn of the White House, leading to horseshoe throwing national championships being held annually.

Horseshoe throwing is played on a pitch by two players (or two teams of two) using four horseshoes. The pitch consists of two ends with a 6-foot-square pitching box marked on the ground at either end. Inside each pitching box is a smaller rectangle measuring 3 by 6 feet that is called the pit. The pit, which is filled with sand, is angled centrally so that its long side runs along the long edge of the pitch. In the middle of each pit is a metal stake 1 inch in diameter that protrudes 15 inches above the surface, which inclines toward the thrower. The two stakes are 40 feet apart. Players must stand in the area within the pitching box but outside the pit. The horseshoes used in informal games may be any size, but league competitions have strict regulations regarding horseshoe weight and size. For instance, horseshoes should weigh around 2 pounds 8 ounces and be 7⅝ inches long and 7 inches wide, and the gap should measure 3.5 inches wide.

To play horseshoe throwing, a coin is tossed to decide which player throws first, and thereafter players take alternate turns tossing horseshoes at the stake at one end. The score for the end is totaled, and the players play the next end by throwing at the other stake at the other end. However, scoring in horseshoes is surprisingly complicated for such an informal game, with the score calculated in the following way: any horseshoe that completely surrounds a stake is called a ringer. A ringer scores 3 points unless the opponent has also thrown a ringer. Similarly, if both players score two ringers each, the ringers cancel each other out and no points are scored. However, if one player throws one ringer but the opponent throws two ringers, then the opponent scores 3 points. Also, if one ringer is scored that player wins 3 points plus an extra point if the player's other horseshoe lands the closest of the remaining three horseshoes. If there is doubt as to whether or not a horseshoe is a ringer, a straight edge is placed against the open end of the horseshoe—if it fails to touch the stake a ringer is declared. If no ringers are adjudged to have occurred, then the nearest horseshoe to the stake earns 1 point. The winner is the first player to accrue 21 points.

Shoe throwing as political protest has also been known. In 2008 Iraqi journalist Muntazar al-Zaidi threw his shoes at U.S. president George W. Bush. Iranian officials declared this a heroic act and paid tribute to al-Zaidi by holding a number of shoe throwing contests in which competitors threw footwear at caricatures of President Bush—one of the competitions was named "Sock and Awe" as a pun of the U.S. shock-and-awe military tactics. In addition to the shoe throwing contests, Iran's main shoe-making federation promised a lifetime supply of shoes to al-Zaidi.

See also: Bunnock; Cotswold Olimpicks

Further Reading

Canocchi, Camilla. "From Cheese Rolling to Welly Wanging and Caber Tossing: The UK's Weirdest Tourist Events Revealed." MailOnline, May 18, 2014, http://www.dailymail .co.uk/travel/article-2631787/The-UKs-weirdest-tourist-events-From-cheese-rolling -welly-wanging.html (accessed July 25, 2014).

"Experts Make Robotic Welly Wanger." BBC News, August 24, 2006, http://news.bbc .co.uk/1/hi/wales/mid/5279884.stm (accessed June 25, 2014).

"Gumboot Day." Taihape, 2014, http://www.taihape.co.nz/information.php?info_id=36 (accessed July 25, 2014).

"International Boot-Throwing Association IBTA's Competition Rules of Boot-throwing 2013." International Boot-Throwing Association, http://bootthrowing.net/online/heitt ajanabc/tiedostot/engkilpsaannot.pdf (accessed July 25, 2014).

"International Horse Shoe Throwing Competition." GoKerry, 2014, http://www.gokerry.ie /international-horse-shoe-throwing-competition/ (accessed June 25, 2014).

"Iran to hold shoe-throwing competition." RIA Novosti, December 24, 2008, http://en.ria .ru/world/20081224/119160429.html (accessed June 25, 2014).

Levinson, David, and Karen Christensen, eds. *Encyclopedia of World Sport: From Ancient Times to the Present.* Oxford: Oxford University Press, 1996.

"New World Welly Record Set." Around Wellington, September 10, 2012, http://www .aroundwellington.co.uk/new-world-welly-records-set/ (accessed July 25, 2014).

"Preview: Clog Cobbing World Championships in Waterfoot." Lancashire Telegraph, March 29, 2010, http://www.lancashiretelegraph.co.uk/leisure/latest/5415187.Preview__Clog _Cobbing_World_Championships_in_Waterfoot/ (accessed July 25, 2014).

"The Rules of Horseshoe Pitching." Masters Traditional Games, 2012, http://www.masters games.com/rules/horseshoe-pitching-rules.htm (accessed June 25, 2014).

Tait, Rabert. "Shoe Reportedly Thrown at Iranian President Ahmadinejad." The Guardian, March 6, 2009, http://www.theguardian.com/world/2009/mar/06/shoe-protest-iran -ahmadinejad (accessed July 25, 2014).

"Throwing a Big Clog Cobbin' Bash." Rossendale Free Press, April 1, 2010, http://www .rossendalefreepress.co.uk/news/local-news/throwing-big-clog-cobbin-bash-1706031 (accessed June 25, 2014).

"Welly Wanging." Upperthong Village Community Web site, http://www.upperthong.org .uk/?page_id=404 (accessed June 25, 2014).

SHOVE HA'PENNY

Shove ha'penny is a traditional board game for two played by men and women in pubs in England either as independent games or as part of a league system. Variations of shove ha'penny are played across Europe and in America and Swaziland. Shove ha'pennny has been in existence since at least the 15th century, when under the reign of King Edward IV (1442–1483) the game was known as shoffe-grote, as the coinage of the time was called groats, while during the 16th and 17th centuries the game was called slype groat and slide-thrift. The modern game of shove ha'penny was first played in 1840. The game was named after the halfpenny, a coin used in the United Kingdom during the 19th century until decimalization of the British currency occurred in 1971.

A shove ha'penny board has markings denoting the playing area. These marking include 2 vertical lines running the length of each side of the board and a series of 10 horizontal lines across the width of the board, including across the vertical lines. The first horizontal line lies 4 inches from the front of the board, and the last line lies 5 inches from the rear of the board. The nine areas between the horizontal lines are called the beds, and each bed is 1.25 inches in width. In the 19th century shove ha'penny was played on any flat surface onto which lines could be drawn, but today the game is played on slates or boards made of hardwoods such as oak, teak, or mahogany or, very rarely, from glass or marble. The lines are not drawn onto modern boards; rather, horizontal indentations mark the beds.

As shove ha'penny is a traditional pub board game lacking a governing body, the rules of play vary from pub to pub. However, in general, to play shove ha'penny players take turns pushing five halfpenny coins confusing along the board so that they lie in the beds without touching any part of lines. Luxury shove ha'penny boards often feature brass rods housed inside the horizontal indentations that can be lifted from their slot via a hinge mechanism. If a coin moves when the rod is lifted from its position below the playing surface, then the coin is judged to have been touching the line and so does not score any points.

In order to prepare each coin to be shoved, a player places one coin at a time at the front of the shove ha'penny board with the rear of the coin just sticking out over the rim of the board. Once the coin is on the playing area, the player may use any part of her or his hand to shove the coin along the board. The most common technique for shoving the coins is to use the heel of the hand. However, the thumb, the fingertips, and the palm of the hand may all also be used. The shoving may be aided by rubbing the board with a slippery substance such as petrol, oils, paraffin, chalk, talcum powder, or even lead. The smoothest side of the coin should be used, as this too will help with the shoving. If a player shoves a coin but the coin does not reach even the first horizontal mark, then that turn does not count and the player may retake the shove. At the end of each player's turn each coin judged to be in a bed scores a point for that player, and the score is written in chalk in the square formed by the crossing of the vertical and horizontal lines at the end of each bed at the side of the board. The score for one player is written on the left-hand side of the board, and the other player's score is written on the right-hand side.

In order to win, a player must achieve three chalk marks in each of the squares by pushing a coin into a bed three times. However, if a player shoves a coin so that it lands in a bed that already has three scores marked in its square, then the point for that coin goes to the other player unless the opponent also has three scores marked in the same bed. For this reason it is advisable to avoid scoring three coins in one bed until near the end of the game so as to limit the number of times points must be donated to opponents. The only time the points donation rule is disregarded is when the donation of a point would result in a player winning. In shove ha'penny, a win can only be awarded by the scoring of a point.

A proficient player will often try to shove the coin so that it knocks on to one or more coin already on the board, as this improves the player's position and allows a point to be scored. If a player manages to push three coins into one bed in one go the player is said to have scored a sergeant; if a player manages to push all five coins into the same bed in one go the player is said to have scored a sergeant major or a gold watch.

The Shove Ha'penny World Championships is held annually in Cheltenham, southern England. However, the future of shove ha'penny leagues in England is uncertain, as the game has failed to attract a new generation of players, and pubs devote increasing attention to pool competitions, quiz nights, and gambling machines.

Two particularly notable versions of shove ha'penny are progressive shove ha'penny and penny-push. Progressive shove ha'penny is played in the Oxfordshire area of England and differs from regular shove ha'penny in that a player may retrieve and replay the coins with which he or she has scored. In this way a player can achieve a long, continuous turn of scoring opportunities as in billiards, snooker, and croquet. Push-penny is played in much the same way as shove ha'penny, but players use old English pennies, which are quite a bit larger than halfpennies, to play. Push-penny is mainly played in the county of Lincolnshire on the east coast of England, with the Push-Penny World Championship held each summer in the town of Stamford.

Sjoelbak or *sjoelen* is a 19th-century Dutch variation of shove ha'penny played frequently in Holland and Belgium and occasionally in England and America. In Germany *sjoelbak* is played under the name *jakkolo*. In *sjoelbak* players must propel 30 disks down a wooden table measuring six feet in length via four arches numbered 1 to 4. Players have to try to get an even number of disks through each of the arches, as achieving a set of disks in each arched compartment results in a doubling of the score. *Sjoelbak* is often played at Dutch family gatherings such as Christmas, and *sjoelbak* boards are regarded as cherished family heirlooms to be passed from generation to generation.

Shove ha'penny is an indoor version of the now-defunct game shovelboard. Shovelboard was extremely popular with the aristocracy of Tudor England (1485–1603). Indeed, King Henry VIII (1491–1547) is documented to have lost money when playing shovelboard. The game was played on a narrow table 30 feet in length along which players had to shove metal weights. The object of the game was to shove the weight as far along the table as possible without it falling off the far end of the playing area. Shovelboard had fallen out of fashion by the 18th century, and shovelboards are now seen in public only as a feature of English stately home museums. However, a close relative of shovelboard, shuffleboard, is still played today under various guises. Indoor shuffleboard, also known as table shuffleboard, is closely related to shovelboard and is often played in bars in America. The aim of indoor shuffleboard is to shove disks along a table measuring at least 10 feet in length so that the disks stop between target zones printed across the end of the table. Players aim to propel their disks into the target zones without their disks going past the scoring zones and thus falling off the end of the table, as any disk that falls off the table fails to score.

A shipboard version of shuffleboard existed in the 19th century, for wealthy passengers traveling aboard transatlantic liners heading to the United States in the 1870s played deck shuffleboard. These well-to-do immigrants continued to play shuffleboard once they had settled in America. As the immigrants were no longer at sea they decided to play on land, and the game of outdoor shuffleboard was born. To play outdoor shuffleboard, players stand at one end of the long narrow playing surface and use special cues to shove large disks along the playing area with the aim of propelling their disk into a triangular scoring zone marked at the opposite end of the playing area. The scoring zone is divided into sections, with each section scoring different amounts of points. The game became hugely popular in some parts of America, where it is still played today, as well as in Australia, Canada, and Japan.

See also: Aunt Sally; Croquet; Nipsy; Real Tennis; Snooker

Further Reading

Hoyle, Edmond, and Lawrence Hawkins. *The Complete Hoyle's Games.* Ware, UK: Wordsworth Editions, 1994.

Masters, James. "Shove Ha'penny—History and Useful Information." Masters Traditional Games, http://www.tradgames.org.uk/games/Shove-HaPenny.htm (accessed August 12, 2013).

Masters, James. "The Shovelboard Family—History and Useful Information." Masters Traditional Games, http://www.tradgames.org.uk/games/ShovelBoard.htm (accessed August 12, 2013).

"The Rules of Shove Ha'penny." Masters Traditional Games, 2012, http://www.masters games.com/rules/shove-hapenny-rules.htm (accessed August 12, 2013).

"Shove Ha'Penny League Forced to Disband." *The Telegraph,* May 19, 2009, http://www .telegraph.co.uk/news/uknews/5351197/Shove-hapenny-league-forced-to-disband .html (accessed August 9, 2013).

SKITTLES

Skittles, also known as nine pins, is a bowling target game for individuals or teams that is popular in the United Kingdom, particularly in western and central England, southern Wales, and southern Scotland. Variations of skittles are also played in France, the Netherlands, Germany, Austria, Switzerland, Liechtenstein, Hungary, Slovenia, Serbia, Croatia, Ireland, the United States, and Australia. In earlier times skittles was known as kittle-pins and later as skittle-pins. In England skittles is often played indoors in pubs. though it is also played outside on grass. In general, to play skittles players take turns throwing a round wooden object such as a ball down a lane called an alley in order to try to knock down several skittles, or pins, at the end of the lane opposite to where the player is standing. Originally skittles were made from bone, but today they too are wooden. There are a numerous versions of skittles found across the United Kingdom, and many more have been lost over the years. Indeed, the popularity of skittles in England is such that skittle terms have entered common usage and been applied to other sports. For example, in cricket when a bowler dismisses several members of the batting side in quick succession, the bowler is said to have "skittled" the opposition.

Though the Amateur Skittle Association, founded in 1900, specified both the dimensions of the generic skittle alley and the distance between each of the skittles within the diamond formation, the rules and scoring systems of skittles vary from place to place. However, usually the basic aim of the game is to bowl a ball made of either wood or rubber and weighing about 10 pounds at nine large oval-headed skittles, which are set in diamond formation 21 feet away. The player who knocks over all the skittles in the fewest throws is declared the winner. In some variations of skittles, particularly those found in London, the capital of England, players throw an object called a cheese instead of a ball. A cheese can vary in shape from barrel-shaped to an object shaped like an intact round cheese. The cheese is made from lignum vitae and weighs 12 to 14 pounds.

The history of skittles is unknown, however. One theory suggests that skittles originated in Germany, for during the 3rd and 4th centuries German monks played a game similar to skittles called *kegel,* after a club used in self-defense. In *kegel* the club represented temptation, and the monks would throw stones at the club until it was knocked over. Further, the modern German word for skittles is *Kegelen.* Skittles has been popular in England since at least medieval times, with references to the game found in art and literature. Manuscripts prove that skittles was played in England by the 14th century, for prayer books have been discovered that depict a game called club kayles. The name "club kayles" derives from the French *quilles,* meaning "skittles," and the game is very similar to skittles except that in club kayles one skittle is larger than the others and differently shaped. In club kayles the anomalous skittle is positioned so as to be the most difficult to knock over, and the large skittle was most probably a kingpin as featured in some modern versions of skittles. The manuscripts also reveal that players of club kayles threw a long club-like object at the skittles using an underarm action, as in the game of Aunt Sally. Similarly, illustrations of 17th-century Frost Fairs held on London's Thames River, that is, impromptu festivals held when the river froze over in England's capital city, show that skittles was included as one of the entertainments. The antiquarian Joseph Strutt (1749–1802), who wrote a chronicle of English games titled *Sports and Pastimes of the People of England* (1801), lists five main versions of skittles played during the 18th century—skittles, nine pins, pins, four corners and rolly polly—which reveals that in earlier times skittles and nine pins were separate games. In nine pins, players stood at a prearranged distance and tried to knock down all the pins in the least number of throws. By contrast, in skittles players both threw from a distance and performed a technique called tipping by which players began the game, standing at a distance from the skittles, and then took their final throw from point-blank range. The winner was the first player to topple a certain number of pins. Tipping also occurs in Dutch pins in which the ball is rolled both from a distance and from very close range. The balls used in Dutch pins differ from those in skittles, as they feature finger holes, while the pins are taller and thinner. Dutch pins also employs a kingpin, that is, a pin taller than the rest, which must be knocked over before the other skittles. It is thought that Dutch pins may have been the inspiration for Ten Pin Bowling, a form of skittles found in North America.

Four Corners, which is still played in Bristol and Somerset in western England, is very similar to basic skittles but differs in that only the four skittles at the corners of the square formation, that is, the front and back skittles and the two outside skittles, which are known as coppers, are used in play. Four Corners is usually played on an individual basis.

Rolly polly, also known as half-bowl, is occasionally played in Hertfordshire, a county north of London, and in variation in the Castillian area of Spain. In rolly polly a biased ball is rolled at 12 skittles in a circle formation. The ball travels past the skittles and also past another skittle set behind and then, because of the bias, returns in the reverse direction. Rolly polly, thought by some as the antecedent of table skittles, as is played on the floor, with the bias ball substituting for the suspended ball on a pole in the miniaturized tabletop version.

Over time, skittles evolved into many regional variations. Across England, new rules evolved and differences in the shape and size of the skittles and balls/cheeses developed, as did variations in the length of the skittle alley and the use of a kingpin. One of the most marked divisions is in the method for actually throwing the balls or cheeses. Today the most often played version of skittles is West Country Skittles, which is popular across southwestern England, particularly in the counties of Devon, Wiltshire, and Gloucestershire, as well as in Wales. The most played version of West Country Skittles is perhaps Western Alley Skittles, though as with nearly all versions of skittles, the game varies from location to location, even from pub to pub. Western Alley Skittles is the most basic form of skittles in which nine pins are arranged in a square formation at the end of an alley measuring about 24 feet in length. Each player's turn starts with all the skittles standing upright, and then the player has three throws with which to knock down the pins. Therefore, the maximum achievable score in one turn is 27. There are variations between the skittles used in West Country Skittles. For instance, in Devon all skittles bulge in the middle, but the regular pins are about 12 inches tall, with the kingpin standing at 15 inches tall. The skittles used in Gloucester also bulge in the middle but are shorter, at 10 inches. Shortest of all are the skittles used in Wales, which measure 6–8 inches tall and are also thin and lack a central bulge, though they are topped with a wooden bobble.

Long Alley Skittles is a game of skill played in central England. This variation is played along an alley measuring around 33 feet in length. Players must throw the ball along the length of the alley in such a way that it bounces once before reaching the skittles. The ball must make contact with a kingpin before hitting the other pins; otherwise, no score is awarded. In the county of Leicestershire, Long Alley Skittles is played with a barrel-shaped cheese, and the skittles are thin and tapering. This allows expert players to produce interestingly angled throws that bounce eccentrically, knocking over the pins in ways that could not be achieved with an ordinary round ball.

Long Alley Skittles is thought to be closely related to Old English Skittles, also known as London Skittles, as in both variations the ball/cheese is thrown rather than rolled. However, while Long Alley Skittles is still played frequently, the London variation is almost extinct, mainly because so many London pubs were destroyed during the German bombing raids of World War II. In recent times the playing of London Skittles has been confined to pubs in Hammersmith and Ealing in western London, Putney in southwestern London, Norbury in southern London, and, most famously, the Freemasons Arms in Hampstead, northern London. In London Skittles the heavy lignum vitae cheese, which varies from 8.5 to 12 inches in diameter, is flung full toss directly at the skittles that stand at the end of a 21-foot-long alley. The skittles are oval-shaped, 14.5 inches high and 6.5 inches across the middle, tapering to a diameter of 3 inches at either end. The skittles are made from hornbeam and weigh 9 pounds.

A five-pin variation of skittles has also evolved in Ireland, where players throw four clubs at the skittles that stand in a marked circle, with one skittle placed in the middle of the circle. In order to score, players have to knock the pin over and out of the circle.

See also: Aunt Sally; Bunnock; Cricket; *Kubb; Kyykkä; Mölkky;* Nipsy; Real Tennis

Further Reading

de Castella, Tom. "When the Thames Froze Over." BBC News Magazine, January 28, 2014, http://www.bbc.co.uk/news/magazine-25862141 (accessed March 7, 2014).

Masters, James. "Skittles—History and Useful Information." The Online Guide to Traditional Games, http://www.tradgames.org.uk/games/Skittles.htm (March 7, 2014).

Strutt, Joseph. *The Sports and Pastimes of the People of England.* London: Methuen, 1801.

Tomlinson, Alan. *A Dictionary of Sport Studies.* Oxford: Oxford University Press, 2010.

Tunnicliffe, Guy. "London Skittles: A Lost Recreation." The London Game—A History of Old English Skittles, 1987–1994, http://www.londonskittles.co.uk/content/docum ents/ALostRecreation.pdf (accessed March 7, 2014).

Tunnicliffe, Guy, and Paul Robinson. "A Brief History of Skittles." London Skittles, http://www.londonskittles.co.uk/content/history.htm (accessed March 7, 2014).

SNOOKER

Snooker is a cue and ball sport similar to billiards that is played by males and females on a baize-covered table. Snooker is especially popular in English-speaking countries, member nations of the British Commonwealth, Europe, Asia (particularly China), and the United States. Though not perhaps the most physically arduous of sports, snooker demands great concentration, stamina, and hand-eye coordination.

Snooker was invented in 1875 by Colonel Sir Neville Chamberlain, a British Army officer stationed at Jubbulpore in India (not the British prime minister of the same name) who decided to combine elements of the existing popular games pyramids, black pool, life pool, and English billiards. Chamberlain took the colored balls from life pool and the black ball from black pool and added them to pyramids in which 15 red balls are arranged in a triangle and players aim to hit the red balls with a white ball known as the cue ball. To the cue ball, the black ball, and the red

Japan's Atsutoshi Inoue prepares to play a shot at the International Billiards and Snooker Federation (IBSF) World Snooker Championship in Bangalore, India, on November 29, 2011. Though not as physically demanding as other sports, snooker demands great powers of concentration, stamina, and hand-eye coordination. (AP Photo/Aijaz Rahi)

balls, Chamberlain added a yellow ball, a green ball, and a pink ball. The blue and brown balls familiar today were added at a later date. The name "snooker" is taken from British Army slang, with a snooker being a first-year cadet. When Chamberlain saw a fellow soldier miss a shot while playing the new game, he is said to have likened the man to an inexperienced cadet.

Snooker spread quickly through the British army in India, for Chamberlain promoted his new game fervently when he was appointed to different postings throughout the country, introducing snooker to his colleagues. Having been injured in battle, Chamberlain was transferred to Ootacamund, where his colleagues were especially impressed with the new game, establishing the Ooty Club snooker society and posting the rules of snooker in the billiards room. A returning Englishman, John Roberts, who happened to be a champion billiards player and had made acquaintance with Chamberlain in Calcutta with the express intention of learning about Chamberlain's new game, then brought the game to England. Snooker soon became known throughout England, and manufacturers of billiards equipment soon saw a market for snooker cues and tables. By the end of the 19th century snooker as it is known today had evolved, with a governing body established in 1919 when the Billiards Association and the Billiards Control Club merged. Today, however, governance of snooker is divided into that for professional players and that for amateurs. The professional arm of the sport is governed by the World Professional Billiards and Snooker Association, founded in 1968 and based in Bristol, western England, a subsidiary of which, the World Snooker Association, organizes world ranking tour events. Amateur snooker is governed by the International Snooker and Billiards Federation.

It was not, however, until the 1920s and 1930s that snooker's popularity neared that of billiards with the English masses. During the 1960s the game's popularity began to increase further, and snooker tables began to be used in snooker clubs. Then in the 1970s the game received a further boost when star players including Ray Reardon, John Spencer, and Dennis Taylor began to emerge. However, perhaps the biggest boost to snooker's popularity came with the advent of color television, for as color television became available snooker players became national heroes, and demand for snooker tables surged throughout Britain. At the start of the 1980s it was commonplace for children to take up the game, and interest increased again when Steve Davies began to dominate the game by winning six world championship titles. Indeed, during the 1980s the final of the Snooker World Championships, which have been held at the Crucible in Sheffield, in Yorkshire northern England, since 1977, was routinely the most watched sporting event on British television. The popularity of snooker with British television audiences peaked with what is perhaps the most noteworthy event in snooker history, for in 1985 the winning of the world championship came down to the final black. On this occasion 18.5 million television viewers tuned in to see Dennis Taylor win the title at 12:30 a.m. The popularity of snooker on television also led to spinoff programs broadcast by the BBC, such as *Pot Black* (1969–1986) and *Big Break* (1991–2002). During the 1990s the international popularity of snooker increased, though the blanket coverage of snooker on British television caused interest among the public to wane a little except where the rivalry between players Jimmy White and Stephen Hendry was concerned, for this did still interest the viewing public. Nowadays, though, the final of the World Snooker Championships still attracts viewers watching at home on television; this is partly because the final occurs on the May Bank Holiday, when people are not in general at work and therefore have more opportunity to watch television. Today the television audience for snooker in Britain has suffered a small but noticeable decline, with twice as many viewers watching the world championships in continental Europe, especially in Denmark, Switzerland, Germany, and the Netherlands, as in Britain. However, though the popularity of snooker is not as great as during the heyday of the 1970s and 1980s, multiple championship-winning players such as the enigmatic Englishman Ronnie O'Sullivan, nicknamed "The Rocket" because of his attacking flair, mean that snooker still attracts new players and viewers.

Snooker is played on a table usually measuring 12 feet by 6 feet (though tables with other dimensions can also be used) with six pockets sunk into the cushioned wooden perimeter of the table—two on the top corners, two on the bottom corners, and two in the middle of the longer edges of the table. The table's playing surface stands between 2 feet 9.5 inches and 2 feet 10.5 inches from the ground. Balls, which usually have a diameter of 2 inches and are made of plastic resin, are potted when a snooker shot causes them to fall into these pockets. The object of the game is for a player to score more points than the opponent by potting balls in the correct order.

Snooker balls consist of 15 red balls worth one point each and six balls of various colors, which are worth two to seven points—yellow (two points), green (three points), brown (four points), blue (five points), pink (six points), and black (seven points). At the start of a game of snooker the balls are laid out in a specific manner, with all the reds gathered in a triangular formation near the bottom edge of the table and the colored balls placed on their spots, that is, positions marked on the playing surface. Snooker players use the chalked tip of a wooden tapering two-part stick, called a cue, traditionally measuring 4 feet 10 inches to strike the white cue ball so that they pot a red ball followed by a colored ball and so on until all the red balls have been potted, all the while amassing a score achieved by adding the points values of the balls potted successively. Once all the reds have been pocketed, the colored balls are potted in ascending order of points value so that the black ball is the last ball to be pocketed. In order to handle hard-to-reach areas of the table, players may employ additional equipment known as rests and spiders that come in a range of shapes and sizes and provide a raised bridge over the balls and adjacent to the cue ball. A player may also apply an extension to the cue in order to lengthen the stick in an attempt to reach a ball. It is important that a player try to reach the ball, for if a player fails to pot the necessary ball, then the opponent comes back to the table and plays the next shot.

As well as potting balls, a player may accrue points when fouls occur. There are many reasons why a foul occurs, such as a player failing to strike the correct ball or potting the white ball. A foul also occurs when a player fails to escape from a snooker. This is a defensive play whereby the cue ball is played in such a way as to make it conclude its run by lying behind another ball that must not be played first, for instance, behind a colored ball when a player needs to hit a red. Fouls are worth four points unless a foul affects a ball of a higher value, in which case the value of the ball is awarded. Another type of foul occurs when the cue ball is potted. Both points and fouls are announced by the match referee. The referee is an important element of a snooker match, as the referee is responsible for placing balls in their correct position at the beginning of a frame, replacing colored balls (not reds) when necessary, cleaning the cue ball, judging fouls, and handing out rests, spiders, and extensions.

A succession of balls potted by a player in one turn at the table is called a break, with the maximum possible break being 147 points—it is possible to achieve this score by potting all reds followed by blacks and then all colored balls in one visit to the table. The first officially ratified player to achieve a maximum break was Joe Davis in 1955.

The player who amasses the most points wins the game or the frame (i.e., an individual game), and the player who wins the most frames wins the match. A snooker match usually consists of a predetermined number of frames, with most professional matches requiring a player to win five frames. Such matches are called best of 9, as 9 is the maximum possible number of frames that can be played. Tournament final matches are usually best of 17 or best of 19 frames, though the world championships play longer matches, ranging from best of 19 played in qualifiers and the first round to the best of 35 frames played in the final, with the first player to win 18 frames declared the winner. The world championships final is played over two days, though this may be extended if necessary.

The World Professional Snooker Championship, commonly referred to as the World Snooker Championship, began in 1927 under the influence of leading snooker and billiard player Joe Davis, who did much to professionalize the game. Davis won every world title contested between 1927 and 1946 (15 in total) and was one of the first snooker stars. Over the years much of snooker's popularity has been due to a number of exuberant superstar players, often possessing evocative nicknames. For instance, Welshman Ray "Dracula" Reardon, who was so called because of his facial similarity to screen incarnations of Bram Stoker's vampire character; northern Irishman Alex "Hurricane" Higgins, whose fast playing style earned him his moniker; and Canadian "Big" Bill Werbeniuk, who was famous for drinking 40 pints of beer a day in order to quell a tremor that affected his playing ability. Other players who did not possess a nickname garnered attention for other reasons, such as Dennis Taylor, who was celebrated for wearing his spectacles upside down, as he claimed this improved his vision when playing a shot.

See also: Croquet; *Lucha Libre*; Shove Ha'penny

Further Reading

Bridle, Bob, and Richard Gilbert, eds. *The Sports Book*. 3rd ed. London: Dorling Kindersley, 2011.

"A Brief History of the Games of Billiards and Snooker." Nidderdale Pub Net, http://www.nidderdale.fslife.co.uk/gamehistory.html (accessed August 9, 2013).

Clare, Peter. "Origins of Snooker." Billiard & Snooker Heritage Collection, 2009 and 2011, http://www.snookerheritage.co.uk/normans-articles/days-of-old/origins-of-snooker/ (accessed May 5, 2014).

"History of Snooker." Snooker Clubs Dotcom, 2012, http://www.snookerclubs.com/history-of-snooker.htm (accessed August 9, 2013).

Masters, James. "Billiards and Snooker from England and the Commonwealth." The Online Guide to Traditional Games, 1997–2014, http://www.tradgames.org.uk/games/Billiards-Snooker.htm (accessed August 9, 2013).

Nauright, John, and Charles Parrish, eds. *Sports around the World: History, Culture and Practice,* Vol. 1, *General Topics, Africa, Asia, Middle East, and Oceania.* Santa Barbara, CA: ABC-CLIO, 2012.

Norridge, Julian. *Can We Have Our Balls Back, Please? How the British Invented Sport (and Then Almost Forgot How to Play It)*. London: Penguin, 2008.

"Snooker World Records." Snooker.org, April 27, 2014, http://www.snooker.org/Plr/records.shtml (accessed May 22, 2014).

Williams, Luke, and Paul Gadsby. *Snooker's World Champions: Masters of the Baize*. Edinburgh, UK: Mainstream Publishing, 2005.

SPANISH BULLFIGHTING

Bullfighting, also known as tauromachy, is a highly controversial spectacle in which a bull is baited, ceremoniously fought, and then usually killed by a male or female bullfighter for the entertainment of an audience. Those who advocate bullfighting

A bullfighter taunts a bull during a bullfight in Seville, Spain. The bullfighter uses the colorful cape to gradually gain control over the bull and choreograph the animal's movements. (Corel)

claim that the activity is not a sport but rather a spectacle central to the national identity of certain countries, particularly Spain, and point to the drama and ritual of the display. Indeed, in 2013 the Spanish government designated bullfighting the status of cultural heritage deserving of protection. However, opponents classify bullfighting as a form of animal cruelty. While lethal bullfighting is most closely associated with Spain, it is also a traditional spectacle in Portugal and the south of France, though in these countries it is illegal for the bull to be killed in the arena in which the fight takes place. Bullfighting also occurs in some Latin American countries with strong ties to Spain, including Mexico, Peru, Colombia, Ecuador, and Venezuela, as well as in the Philippines and Korea.

The exact origins of bullfighting in Europe are disputed. Some historians link the activity to a bull-taunting marriage rite of medieval Spain, while others see it as a continuation of the bull-taming rituals depicted in Minoan art circa 1500 BCE discovered on the Greek island of Crete. Others point to the games of Baetica (today the Spanish region of Andalucia) in which men would demonstrate great skill by using animal skins as a cape to goad a bull and then killing the animal using an ax or a sword. It has also been theorized that Spanish bullfighting may have evolved not from one particular source but rather from myriad customs that reflect the different peoples who have inhabited Spain, such as the Greeks who practiced forms of bullfighting and colonized the Iberian Peninsula, that is, the peninsula of Western Europe occupied by Spain and Portugal, around 1100 BCE, and the Moors of North Africa who invaded the peninsula in the 8th century, bringing with them religious feasts involving horseback bullfighters, whom some historians see as an early ancestor of the modern picador. Bull-lancing tournaments were a common feature of Moorish Spain, as Moorish chiefs and Christian knights vied to become the most adept bull killers. Special amphitheaters were built to accommodate the fights in most of Spain's major cities, including Cadiz, Cordoba, Seville, and Toledo. If an area did not have an amphitheater, then bullfights would take place in the town square or in a large field. By the 12th century organized bullfights had become common, with the most notable being perhaps the annual Fiesta de San Fermin in Pamplona that continues to this day, with the bulls to be used in the day's fights run through the town's streets to the bullring. When the Moors were driven from Spain during the 15th century bull-lancing tournaments became the preserve of the nobility, and by the 16th century the tournament had gained royal approval as signified by King Charles V, who lanced a bull to celebrate the birth of his son, Philip II. However, the king's wife, Queen Isabella, opposed bullfighting, as did the Catholic Church of the time, which felt that bullfighting went against the Christian teaching of kindness to animals. The reigning pope, Pius V, banned the spectacle and withheld Christian burial rights from any Catholic killed while fighting a bull.

The popularity of bullfighting continued, however, and eventually the Catholic Church overturned the ban and began to associate itself with the activity. For example, it became routine for fights to be held to celebrate holy days, and in some parts of Spain the bullfighting season begins on Easter Sunday. Some religious institutions even turned to bullfighting as a source of income. For instance, in 1744 the San Andres parish in Madrid, Spain's capital, used money made from fights to pay off debts incurred by repairs made to a church.

By the 18th century the popularity of bullfighting was such that the spectacle became big business, with herds of specialist bulls being bred for profit—the bulls used in bullfighting are a special breed of savage bull weighing 1,300–1,600 pounds and bred especially to attack humans. It was also at this time that Joaquin Rodríguez Costillares, one of the first professional bullfighters, introduced the pomp and ceremony of modern bullfighting. Costillares introduced the bullfighter's costume of the highly ornate *trajes de luces,* or suit of lights, so called because it is made of satin and decorated with sequins and reflective silver and gold thread. The suit consists of cropped, tight-fitting trousers; a vest; and a short jacket colored red, black, white, green, or blue. The suit is never yellow because the color is considered unlucky by bullfighters, who are particularly superstitious since their job involves the ever-present threat of injury or even death. Costillares also introduced the bullfighter's two-handed cape pass known as a *veronica* and the method of killing the bull known as the *volapié,* whereby the bull is so transfixed by the fighter's cape traveling low to the ground that it does not notice as the fighter lunges at him with a sword. Meanwhile, Costillares's main rival, Pedro Romero, popularized what is perhaps the bullfighter's most daring move, the *racibiendo,* in which the fighter stands immobile as the bull charges forward, only to impale itself on the sword.

By the 19th century the introduction of the railway across Spain, Portugal, and South America meant that an increasing number of bullrings were built, and during the 1880s and 1890s bullfighting became a cultural industry in Spain and continued to expand as a moneymaking venture not only for the fighters and fight promoters but also for the breeders, critics, and various enterprises for which bullfighting represented a source of income. The number of fights also increased greatly. For example, 400 bullfights were held during the 1860s, but over 700 fights occurred in 1895 alone. The frequency of fights continued to grow, and by 1912 more than 800 fights were held annually. This increase led in turn to an upsurge in the building of bullrings, the creation of additional ranches, and the rearing of more bulls, which sold at ever-increasing prices. The number of bullfighters increased too, as did their wages. Bullfighting continued to attract large numbers of spectators in the late 20th century and into the 21st century despite strong opposition. In 1996 40 million people attended bullfights worldwide, and the same year 650 fights were held in Spain (resulting in the death of 3,900 bulls), with Spanish television broadcasting several fights each week. Bullfighting is important to the Spanish tourist industry, and it is thought that over 200,000 Spaniards are employed in some aspect of the bullfighting industry. There is, however, a growing intolerance of bullfighting in some sections of Spanish society and the autonomous community of Catalonia, which in January 2012 became the first mainland Spanish region to ban bullfighting.

Today the bullfight, or *corrida,* is still accompanied by much splendor and ceremony. At midday on the day of the fight, six bulls are selected to take part in the event and are allocated in pairs to three individual bullfighters, known as matadors. Fight promoters known as impressarios contact the matadors, who, with the help of their assistant, go through a highly ritualistic donning of their bullfighting attire in a local hotel room. In addition to the *trajes de luces,* the matador also wears a white shirt, black tie and slippers, pink stockings, a black hat called a *montera,* and a clip-on pigtail that denotes his or her status as a matador.

The bullfight takes place in the late afternoon (hence there are two different ticket prices for the fight for seats that are in or out of the sun) when each matador, accompanied by her or his team of fellow fighters consisting of three older bullfighters, called banderilleros, and two lancers on horseback, called picadors, walks in procession across the *plaza de toros,* or bullring, to the president of the fight, usually a local dignitary, who controls the start and finish of each stage of the fight by waving a white handkerchief. The president then signals that the gates of the bulls' pen should be unlocked, and the bullfighters move behind a five-foot-high wooden wall called a *barrera* encircling the bullring with the exception of the matador set to face this particular bull. The matador hides behind one of four wooden shields, called *burladeros,* positioned along the perimeter wall that offer the fighters refuge during the fight.

Next a fanfare of trumpets signals the start of Act 1 and the entry of the first bull into the ring. In order to assess the bull's temperament, the banderilleros engage the bull by waving capes and take turns running at the bull. Next the matador enters the ring and uses a large colorful cape to make passes, particularly the veronica, at the bull. The matador uses the cape work to gradually gain control over the bull and eventually choreograph the animal's movements. After these theatrical passes, the picadors enter the ring on blindfolded horses with the intention of piercing the bull's neck with a lance in order to make the animal's head hang low enough for the matador to kill the beast later. The picadors protect their horses by stabbing the bull three times with a pike pole. The horses are also protected by protective clothing that prevent them from being disemboweled by bulls' horns. After the bull has made three charges at the horses, the matador assigned to this particular bull reenters the ring and distracts the bull with a series of cape passes. Next all three matadors work in the ring simultaneously, taking turns at using their cape against the bull. The matador assigned that particular bull does her or his cape work first followed by the other two, and all three compete to make the most graceful and daring passes of the cape. Act 2 sees the picadors and matadors leave the ring while the banderilleros aim to insert six decorated wooden sticks called banderillas into the bull's neck muscles again to force the bull to lower its head. The final act of the fight sees the assigned matador engage the bull alone. By now the bull is slower and weaker, making it easier for the matador to kill the animal. The act of killing usually takes the form of the matador performing a highly theatrical thrusting forward of a small red cape called a muleta with the left hand while using the right hand to sink a sword into the area between the bull's shoulders and neck on the diagonal, which severs the animal's aorta, causing almost instantaneous death. However, the bull's death is not always quick, and it can be necessary for two swords to be used. The matador has 10 minutes from the start of the muleta passes to kill the bull. If this does not happen the matador receives an official warning and is allowed a further 3 minutes. After this a second warning is issued and a further 2 minutes of killing time is allowed. If the bull is still alive after this the matador is booed from the arena, and the bull is taken away and killed. It has been known for the life of an exceptionally brave bull to be spared, but this happens very rarely.

The matador may dedicate the kill to the audience or to an individual spectator, and if the matador manages to kill the bull cleanly, spectators wave white handkerchiefs to try to persuade the president of the fight to award the matador the bull's ears, tail, or both as a reward. However, if the matador is injured during the fight, then it is left to the remaining fighters to kill the bull. Once the bull is dead, its carcass is removed from the ring by harnessed horses. The bullfight spectacle continues in the same manner until all six bulls that started the fight have been killed. Once all six are dead, the matadors and their teams cross the ring. If a matador has performed particularly valiantly in the eyes of the audience, then the spectators will carry the matador from the arena and through the main gates of the venue on their shoulders. This is the ultimate accolade for any matador. The matadors then returns to their hotel rooms to remove their *trajes de luces*. The next day's newspapers carry reports of the fight and publish league tables of the matadors' results, detailing the number of bulls each fighter has faced and the number of ears and tails awarded to each.

Bullfighting has a significant presence in popular culture in Spain and elsewhere. Unsurprisingly, many Spanish authors and artists have included bullfighting in their works. Perhaps the most famous Spanish literary work to feature the spectacle is *Sangre y arena* (1909) by Vincente Blasco Ibáñez, which has been adapted many times for the cinema, most notably as *Blood and Sand* (1941). Meanwhile, Spanish artists such as Francisco de Goya (1746–1828) and Pablo Picasso (1881–1973) have included many elements of bullfighting in their paintings, depicting the spectacle as either a potent symbol of good versus evil, life versus death, or as the embodiment of anger and misery. Spanish cinema has also explored bullfighting in films such as Pedro Almodovar's *Matador* (1986), which was criticized in Spain for portraying the bullfight negatively. Bullfighting has also influenced the world of music and dance. For instance, in ballroom dancing the *paso doble* represents the movement of a fight, and the opera *Carmen* (1875) features a bullfighter as a major character. However, perhaps the most accurate and influential depiction of bullfighting can be found in the work of American author Ernest Hemingway, who wrote nonfiction and fiction on the subject. Hemingway's 1932 nonfiction *Death in the Afternoon* focuses on the history and rituals of bullfighting, while scenes of bullfighting appear in his novels *The Sun Also Rises* (1926); *For Whom the Bell Tolls* (1940), which was made into a 1943 Hollywood film of the same name; and *The Dangerous Summer* (1960).

See also: Bearbaiting and Badger Baiting; Bull Running; *Buzkashi;* Camel and Yak Racing; Camel Wrestling; Cockfighting; Elephant Sports; Foxhunting; Hare Coursing; *Pato* and Horseball; *Pelota;* Pigeon Racing; Sheepdog Trials; Sumo Wrestling

Further Reading

"Bullfighting—Rough Guide." Andalucia.com S.L., http://www.andalucia.com/bullfight /roughguide.htm (accessed February 5, 2014).

Govan, Fiona. "Spain Grants Bullfighting Protected Status." *The Telegraph,* October 3, 2013, http://www.telegraph.co.uk/news/worldnews/europe/spain/10353287/Spain-grants -bullfighting-protected-status.html (accessed February 5, 2014).

Schubert, Adrian. *Death and Money in the Afternoon: A History of the Spanish Bullfight.* Oxford: Oxford University Press, 1999.

"Spanish Painting from El Greco to Picasso: Time, Truth and History; Blood and Sand." Guggenheim, http://www.guggenheim.org/new-york/education/school-educator-prog rams/teacher-resources/arts-curriculum-online?view=item&catid=724&id=71 (January 26, 2014).

STONE SKIMMING

Stone skimming is a gentle outdoor pastime practiced worldwide in which players throw a stone with a flattened surface across a body of water in such a way that the stone bounces on the water's surface. The term used to describe stone skimming varies from country to country. For example, in the United States stone skimming is called stone skipping, France uses the word *ricochets,* and the phrase "letting the frogs out" is used in Ukraine. In the United Kingdom the pastime is occasionally called skitting or ducks and drakes. Skimming objects across water for pleasure has a long history, for seashell skimming was a popular pastime in ancient Rome.

The sport of stone skimming requires skill and technique rather than power. For this reason, little special physical training is needed to prepare for a stone skimming competition, except maybe a few loosening arm stretches.

There are two forms of competitive stone skimming, each with its own world championship. In the United States players aim to achieve the highest number of bounces before the stone sinks, while in Europe players vie to bounce their stone the farthest. The reasoning behind the European choice is that it is impossible to count the number of times a stone bounces once it has started to aquaplane. However, this also means that even if a competitor bounces a stone an incredible number of times, that person will not win a contest if the stone fails to reach an impressive length. The world championship held in America takes place at Mackinac Island in Michigan, while the other world championship is held in a disused slate quarry on the tiny island of Easdale in Scotland. The abundance of slate pieces makes Easdale ideal for stone skimming, which on the island is known as skiting. The World Stone Skimming Championship at Easdale was first held in 1983 but then stopped, starting again as a charity fund-raiser in 1997. The championship is now held annually. At the Easdale championship, the stones to be skimmed must be no more than 3 inches in diameter and must have been formed naturally from slate found on the island. Each player has three throws, and for a throw to count the stone must bounce no more than three times on the surface of the water, though stones are scored on the distance traveled by the stone rather than the number of times the stone bounces. Distance judges are located every 5 meters (16 feet) along the walls of the quarry to help determine the distance covered by the stones. When a stone is thrown, it must stay within the lanes marked by buoys.

Around 300 competitors from around the world from ages 18 months to 80 years pay a small fee to enter the competition, which is split into four individual categories plus a team event. Individuals may enter categories for ladies, men, junior boys and girls, under 10s boys and girls, and the "Old Tossers" competition, a tongue-in-cheek title for a category exclusively for the over 60s. To enter into the team competition, team members enter as individuals and declare which team they belong to. Teams must consist of 4 players of either sex, and all must belong to the same age category. Each of the teammates' three throws counts toward both their individual result and that of the team, for the total length of a player's three throws are added together, and then the teammates' totals are added together to provide the team total. The winner of the team event is the team with the longest combined total length in meters.

The overall winner of the championship—that is, the entrant who throws a stone the farthest—wins the World Stone Skimming Cup. The woman who attains the longest distance receives the Sea-fari Salver, and the winning team is awarded the Puffer Trophy. Those who place second and third in each event receive a medal made from the Easdale's slate, as does the winner of the junior competitions. The winner of the Old Tossers contest receives a walking stick, and the islander who skims the farthest is presented with the Bertie, named after the event's founder, Albert Baker.

Another stone skimming competition held in the United Kingdom is the Welsh Open Stoneskimming Championships. One of the problems faced by stone skimming contests is that the competitions can plunder natural resources of local stone from riverbanks and beaches. The Welsh Open, however, resolves this problem by using artificial skimming stones made from reconstituted rock (entrants may also bring their own natural stones). This is not only an environmentally friendly option but also provides a consistency of performance between stones. The stones come in a variety of shapes and sizes to suit different age groups and abilities.

At the Welsh Open, competitors throw five stones four times, with the player who throws the farthest in each category declared the winner. In total there are six categories: children aged between 6 and 11 enter either the junior boys or junior girls competitions, while those aged 12 to 16 enter intermediate boys or intermediate girls competitions. Senior males and senior females are those aged over 17. Adult competitors are divided into two further categories: those who have won a regional or world skimming competition previously are entered into the Stoned category, while those who have never won a competition are regarded as Stoneless competitors. As in the Easdale championship, there is an Old Tosser category and a team competition into which Stoned competitors may not enter.

During the competition the top three competitors from the intermediate categories enter a toss-off in which each competitor throws five stones twice. The thrower who skims the farthest is the winner of the toss-off.

A great deal of academic research, particularly that by French scientist Lyderic Bocquet, has been carried out to establish the optimum conditions for stone skimming, and it seems that the secret to a winning skim is to pick the right stone. Oval, flat stones about the size of an adult palm seem to yield the best results, possibly because they are sufficiently large to be unaffected by wind and turbulence but are not so heavy that they are difficult to throw accurately. Champion skimmers aim to have their stone enter the water 30 meters out from the shore, as skimming the water too quickly saps energy from the stone, causing it to sink, while throwing it too far out means that the stone is vulnerable to the vagaries of the wind.

To achieve a lengthy skim, the stone should be thrown flat and fast so that it hits the water at an angle of 10–20 degrees. The texture of the stone's surface is important as well, though experts disagree as to what type of surface is best. On the one hand, some scientists believe that stones should be smooth-textured so as to skip across the water without hindrance. However, other experts assert that the best stones have multiple small holes on their surface, as this lessens drag from the water in much the same way as a golf ball has pimples to reduce drag in the air.

The reason that stones skim is down to the scientific principle of the conservation of momentum. This principle dictates that as the stone reaches the water, it pushes some of the water downward while the stone itself is forced upward. As long as the stone moves at a speed in excess of one kilometer per hour, the stone will continue its journey across the water. However, if the stone skims at a speed slower than this, it will surf along the top of the water for a short distance and then sink.

It is also important to spin the stone while throwing it. Spinning the stone produces a gyroscopic effect that in turn provides stability. As long as the stone rotates once during the time it makes contact with the water—that is, it reaches a certain minimum rotational velocity—the stone can remain stable on the surface of the water. Scientists have also theorized that to produce a particularly lengthy skim, a thrown stone should reach a speed of at least 80 kilometers per hour, which though quite fast is relatively slow when compared to a fast ball in baseball, which travels at 150 kilometers per hour.

While stone skimming employs small stones, the Swiss sport of *steinstossen,* or stone throwing, concentrates on the throwing of one huge stone. The most famous Swiss stone throwing event is the Unspunnen Festival, which is held every 12 years and is named after the Unspunnen Stone, the rough glacial boulder thrown by competitors. The boulder, which is named after the Swiss village of Unspunnen in Interlaken, has great symbolic political significance in Switzerland, for it is seen as a representation of the unification of the three main Swiss cantons, or states: Schwyz, Unterwald, and Uri. According to legend, nine shepherds united to lift the stone above their heads, each using one hand, and managed to throw the Unspunnen Stone 5 meters (16 feet). The first stone throwing event was held at Unspunnen in 1805 as part of the inaugural Alpine herdsmen festival. Thus, stone throwing is closely associated with Switzerland's national sport, *schwingen,* which also took place at the festival.

The original Unspunnen Stone was stolen from a museum in 1984 in an act of political protest. The replacement boulder weighs 83.5 kilograms (184 pounds), a weight so immense that most people have trouble even lifting the stone. To throw the Unspunnen Stone, competitors take a running jump and throw the stone as far as possible. The record for the longest throw was achieved in 2004 when the stone was thrown 4.11 meters (nearly 13.5 feet).

See also: Boomerang Throwing; *Schwingen*

Further Reading

"About the World Stone Skimming Championships." World Stone Skimming Championships, http://www.stoneskimming.com/about/index.htm (accessed August 12, 2013).

Chambers, Lucas. "Swiss Know How to Schwingen." Straight.com, July 8, 2004, http://www.straight.com/life/swiss-know-how-schwingen (August 9, 2013).

Foulkes, Imogen. "Stone Is Star of Swiss Festival." BBC News, September 2, 2006, http://news.bbc.co.uk/1/hi/world/europe/5308736.stm (accessed September 23, 2013).

Green Events. "Welsh Open Stoneskimming Championships." Green Events, http://www.green-events.co.uk/events.html?id=65 (accessed August 12, 2013).

"How Do You Skim a Stone 51 Times?" BBC News, October 2, 2007, http://news.bbc.co.uk/1/hi/magazine/7022464.stm (accessed August 12, 2013).

Piskie, Mike. "History of Sport." Stoneskipping.com, 2010, http://stoneskipping.com/about/history/ (accessed September 23, 2013).

"Scots Dominate in Stone Skimming." BBC News, September 25, 2005, http://news.bbc.co.uk/1/hi/scotland/4280078.stm (accessed August 12, 2013).

"Stone Skimming." World Alternative Games, http://www.worldalternativegames.co.uk/events/stone-skimming/ (accessed August 12, 2013).

Walker, Cameron, and Jeff Wilson. "The Physics of . . . Skipping Stones." *Discover Magazine,* August 1, 2003, http://discovermagazine.com/2003/aug/featscienceof#.UgUNyCKCr-Z (accessed August 12, 2013).

World and Its People: Germany and Switzerland. Tarrytown, NY: Marshall Cavendish, 2010.

STREET LUGE

Street luge, also known as land luge or road luge, is an extreme sporting activity in which participants, known as pilots, lie on a specially adapted skateboard to travel downhill over paved surfaces under the force of gravity. Street luge takes place in the United States, the United Kingdom, France, Switzerland, Germany, Austria, Canada, and South Africa in the form or either time trials for individuals or pairs or races for multiple entrants organized of a first-past-the-post basis.

The first official amateur street luge race took place in 1975. The sport evolved from the covert speed skateboarding races that were held in Signal Hill, California, in the mid-1970s when speed skateboarders realized that they could achieve much faster speeds by lying prone on their boards. This position produces increased speeds, as it reduces the effect of wind resistance on both the skater and the board, making both more aerodynamic. This is important, as the aim of street luge is to achieve the highest speed possible to win a race. In street luge it is common for pilots to reach speeds of 60 to 70 miles per hour, though a rate of 98 miles per hour is possible.

Bob Pereyra, perhaps the most celebrated pioneer of street luge, is credited with making the first street luge when he traced the outline of his body on a piece of cardboard and used this as a template from which to fashion a light metal sled, which he fitted with two sets of skateboarding wheels and then rode downhill. Ever

Street luge racers become airborne as they race downhill in the Potrero Hill district of San Francisco in the Streets of San Francisco street luge event held on July 27, 2002. Street luge sees participants lie on a specially adapted skateboard to travel downhill over paved surfaces under the force of gravity and often reach speeds of 60 to 70 miles per hour. (AP Photo/George Nikitin)

since Pereyra's innovation, the luges ridden in street luges are custom-made. This is because each pilot is a different height and weight and also because each street luge competition has its own rules regarding the specification of the luge. For instance, from 1997 to 2001 street luge was included in the ESPN X Games, an annual extreme multisport tournament organized by the American sports broadcaster ESPN, at which event luges were not allowed to be longer than 10 feet or heavier than 45 pounds. In general, however, the luge is much the same as a regular skateboard but is much longer, at around 8 feet in length and 16 inches wide. The luge is longer than a skateboard in order to allow pilots to adopt the street luge position of lying faceup along the board's length just inches from the ground. In the early days of the sport, street luges tended to be made of aluminum, wood, or steel. However, as the luge must be light, fast, and durable, today the luge is usually made of steel, aluminum, fiberglass, or carbon fiber and tends to weigh between 25 and 30 pounds. It is forbidden for a street luge to be fitted with brakes of any kind, so pilots must slow their luge by allowing their hands and feet to make contact with the surface over which they are traveling—the contact of the feet on the floor creates friction, which in turn slows down the luge. It is also illegal for a luge to be equipped with a steering mechanism other than sprung axles, so pilots direct their vehicle by leaning left or right.

Apart from speed, safety is a major concern for pilots. As pilots use their bodily extremities to slow down their luge, it is important that a pilot's hand and feet are encased in motor biking gloves and boots. Pilots wear full motor biking leathers over the rest of their body as well as a helmet and elbow, knee, and wrist protectors. The safety of spectators is also important. To this end, in 1990 Bob Pereyra created the Road Racers Association for International Luge (RAIL) to act as a liaison between the sport of street luge and city authorities. In 1993 RAIL organized the first professional street luge race, held in Laguna Seca Raceway in Monterey, California.

Street luge has continued to move away from its somewhat covert origins, and today the sport is organized by the International Gravity Sports Association (IGSA), which since 2002 has designated one event per year as the official IGSA World Championship. The pilot who wins her or his respective class at this event earns the title of IGSA world champion for the year. The IGSA also manages the IGSA World Cup Series that was founded in 2001 as a way of uniting the various different street luge events that take place around the world by creating an international series of street luge contests. The IGSA World Cup Series sees competitors awarded points based on their competition results, with some events worth more points than others. Pilots earn the most series points by taking part in World Cup contests followed by continental, national, and regional events. Each pilot's four highest scoring events are used to decide her or his individual IGSA world ranking, and the pilot who scores the greatest number of points between January 1 and December 31 each year is awarded the title of IGSA World Cup Series champion for that particular year.

See also: Bog Snorkeling World Championship; Cresta Run; *Parkour;* Volcano Boarding

Further Reading

Atkinson, Michael, and Kevin Young. *Tribal Play: Subcultural Journeys through Sport*. Bingley, UK: Emerald Group Publishing, 2008.

Belk, Sean. "Film Immortalizes Signal Hill's Downhill Skateboarding Competition as 'Birth of Extreme Sports.'" *Signal Tribune Newspaper,* February 1, 2013, http://www.signaltri bunenewspaper.com/?p=18306 (accessed January 12, 2014).

"IGSA World Champions." International Gravity Sports Association, http://www.igsaworld-cup.com/index.php/athletes/igsa-world-champions (accessed June 11, 2014).

"IGSA World Cup Series Champions." International Gravity Sports Association, http://www.igsaworldcup.com/index.php/athletes/igsa-series-champions (accessed 11t June 2014).

Murdico, Suzanne J. *Street Luge and Dirtboarding*. New York: Rosen Publishing Group, 2003.

Ryan, Pat. *Street Luge Racing*. Mankato, MN: Capstone, 1998.

Shipside, Steve. *Extreme Sports: Brilliant Ways for Taking Yourself to the Limit*. Oxford, UK: Infinite Ideas, 2006.

Williams, Frank. "Welcome to Street Luge PDX." Portland Underground Luge Society, 2013, http://streetlugepdx.com (accessed January 12, 2014).

SUMO WRESTLING

Sumo wrestling is a full-contact style of wrestling that takes place indoors. Sumo originated in Japan and is the country's national sport. The Ryogoku district of Tokyo, Japan's capital city, is the center of the sumo world and is home to the Kokugikan sumo stadium, which can accommodate up to 10,000 spectators and holds half of all Japan's annual sumo tournaments. The rules of sumo were codified during the Edo period (1603–1868), and today the sport is governed by the Kyokai, or Japan Sumo Association. Sumo is practiced at both professional and amateur levels, with some universities and high schools hosting sumo clubs. However, professional sumo wrestling is an all-male preserve, and women's tournament cannot receive official sanction partly because in sumo tradition women in the ring are thought to evoke evil spirits.

The origins of sumo are disputed. According to legend, sumo originated either as a fight between two deities for possession of Japan or as a battle between a Korean chieftain and a Japanese overlord. Some historians argue that the sport dates back to the eighth century, when sumo was performed annually at Japan's imperial court as a way of demonstrating the power of the Japanese emperor. Wrestlers, known as *rikishi* or *sumotori*, were called to court from across Japan, thus signifying the dominance of the emperor over his subjects and the centralized nature of his government. Over time the well-fed giant figure of the sumo wrestler became symbolic of Japanese imperial might and stability.

However, sumo is a highly ritualistic sport with many elements indebted to religion, and some historians believe that sumo dates from 250–552 CE, when the sport was performed to entertain the Shinto gods (*kami*) during festivals (*matsuri*). Today sumo is still greatly influenced by Shinto. For instance, the elevated ring, 15 feet in diameter, in which sumo bouts occur, the *dohyo,* is covered in sand, which

Sumo wrestlers compete in Tokyo, Japan. The ring in which sumo bouts occur is covered in sand as this symbolizes purity in the Shinto religion. Sumo wrestling matches are highly ritualistic yet the sport's rules are straightforward—the winner of a bout is the first wrestler to force his opponent out of the ring or to make the opponent touch the ground with any part of his body except the soles of his feet. (Imre Cikajlo/iStockphoto.com)

symbolizes purity in the religion. Also, the canopy above the ring, called the *yakata,* is designed to resemble the roof of a Shinto shrine. The four differently colored tassels on each corner of the *yakata* represent the four seasons—white for autumn, black for winter, green for spring, and red for summer. In addition, the purple bunting surrounding the roof represents clouds and the changing of the seasons. Meanwhile, the match referee, who is known as the *gyoji,* wears a robe reminiscent of the outfit worn by a Shinto priest, while chestnuts, cuttlefish, and kelp, which are thought to be purifying, are placed within the ring alongside prayers for the wrestlers' safety. Apart from the referee, other match officials include the *shinpan,* five former wrestlers who act as judges and sit surrounding the ring.

Sumo wrestlers live and train in stables, called *heya,* that tend to be located in Ryogoku. The stables are facilities where a stable master strictly controls all aspects of the wrestlers' lives, including sleeping, eating, training, and leisure time. As there are no weight restrictions or classes in sumo, a wrestler may find himself paired against an opponent many times his own size. Therefore, it is essential that sumo wrestlers maintain their bulk in order to fend off heavier opponents and to enhance their ability to force opponents from the ring. Since gaining weight is an essential part of sumo training, diet is necessarily a very important part of a sumo wrestler's regime, with the staple diet of sumo wrestlers being *chanko nabe,* a hot-pot dish consisting of vegetables, seafood, and meat. There are several restaurants in the Ryogoku area (often managed by former sumo wrestlers) that serve *chanko nabe*.

Professional sumo wrestlers are divided into six ranking classes, each of which is further divided into East and West Divisions. Wrestlers in each class are ranked within the East and West divisions, so wrestlers ranked East 1 and West 1 are the top wrestlers within each division. In practical terms, the East and West aspect of sumo means little other than determining from which side of the ring a wrestler will enter.

A wrestler's ranking is based on his tournament performance and is updated after each competition—wrestlers who win more bouts than they lose move up the hierarchy, while those who lose more than they win are demoted. The top division is called the Makuuchi and is made up of the best 42 wrestlers. The top wrestler is known as the *yokozuna*, meaning "grand champion," and throughout the history of sumo there have only been 70 *yokozunas*. A *yokozuna* cannot be demoted when his performance level begins to decline; instead, he is forced to retire when his powers wane. The second division of wrestlers is called the Juryo, which consists of 28 wrestlers. These top two divisions make up the *sekitori*, and wrestlers belonging to these divisions are distinguished from other wrestlers by their colorful belts called *mawashi*, which feature *sagari*, fringes of twisted string tucked into the belt that symbolize the sacred ropes found in front of Shinto shrines. The number of strings is odd and lie between 17 and 21, which are the lucky numbers of Shinto tradition. The top wrestlers also wear their hair in topknots, which are designed to resemble a ginkgo leaf. In addition, members of the *sekitori* are assigned a lower-ranked wrestler called a *tsuke-bito* whose job it is to act as a servant to the higher-ranked wrestler. The third division of wrestlers is called the Makushita, which consists of 120 wrestlers; the fourth division is the Sandanme, which consists of 200 hundred wrestlers; the fifth division is the Jonidan, which consists of 260 wrestlers; and the sixth division is the Jonokuchi, which consists of around 80 wrestlers. Professional wrestlers usually enter the sport at this level at age 16.

Six sumo wrestling tournaments, or *hon-basho* (often abbreviated to *basho*), are held every year, three in Tokyo during January, May, and September and one each in Osaka (in March), in Fukuoka (in November), and in Nagoya (in July). Each tournament lasts for 15 days, during which top wrestlers perform in one match per day, with lower-ranked wrestlers performing in fewer matches. Other sumo matches also take place outside of tournaments, including exhibition matches at shrines and during festivals such as the Crow Sumo Ceremony and at the retirement ceremonies of prominent wrestlers. Such ceremonies often include an exhibition sumo contest as well as a lengthy hair-cutting ritual, during which the topknot that is symbolic to an active wrestler is severed.

During a tournament, the first ceremony of a day's wrestling is called the *dohyo-iri*, or ring ceremony, which is a prematch purification ritual performed by Juryo and Makuuchi wrestlers that is reputed to cleanse their bodies and spirits. The lowest-ranked wrestler enters the ring first and completes a lap of the ring, followed by the other wrestlers who enter the ring in ascending order of rank, with each individual wrestler introduced to the spectators before entering the ring. Once the last wrestler has been introduced, the wrestlers turn away from the spectators and face each other in a circle around the ring. After clapping their hands once, they raise their right hand, lift the decorative aprons called *kesho-mawashi* that they wear specifically for the ring ceremony, and then raise both hands in unison. This tradition recalls the days of Japanese samurai warriors and is intended to show that none of the wrestlers carry weapons. Indeed, it has been argued that sumo is partly descended from the patriarchal martial arts practiced by samurai warriors, and the samurai influence on sumo is also evident in the stoicism demanded of wrestlers. Meanwhile, the *yokozuna* performs his own separate ring ceremony, for which he wears a white rope around his waist to denote his rank.

Just before a sumo bout starts, the two wrestlers spend some time lifting their legs high in the air and tramping heavily one leg at a time in a practice reputed to rid the match of evil spirits. The wrestlers also scatter several handfuls of salt, a Shinto symbol of purity, into the ring. Many wrestlers also throw salt around their bodies in order to ward off injury. To start a bout, a judge calls both wrestlers to two white lines, the *shikirisen*, marked in the middle of the ring, and when the signal to fight is given, both wrestlers crouch behind their *shikirisen* facing each other. The fight begins when both wrestlers place their fists on or behind their *shikirisen*. The rules of sumo are very straightforward, for the winner of a sumo bout is the first wrestler to force his opponent to exit the ring or to make his opponent touch the ground with any part of his body except the soles of his feet. A bout usually lasts only a few seconds, but occasionally a match may last more than a minute. If the outcome of a bout is in doubt, then the referee and *shinpan* can look at video footage for confirmation of the winner. The initial exchanges of a bout are very important, and during a bout a wrestler may employ any of 48 codified holds to win. However, a wrestler may not pull his opponent's hair, hit him with a closed fist, choke him, box his ears, or grab his crotch, though a wrestler may unbalance his opponent by holding the opponent's belt. After the last match of the day, a Makushita wrestler from the same stable as the *yokozuna* performs a bow-twirling ceremony called the *yumi-tori*. This represents the satisfaction felt by victorious wrestlers.

Matches attract many spectators, though sumo is arguably less popular in Japan than the imported sports of baseball and soccer, partly because admission tickets are very expensive. Spectators may buy one of three types of seat. Ringside seats are located closest to the ring, and despite the fact that ringside ticket holders sit on cushions on the floor and are exposed to the risk of injury if a wrestler is thrown from the ring, these are the most expensive seats. The rest of a sumo stadium's first floor consists of Japanese-style box seats, which usually seat four people. Spectators sitting in box seats sit on cushions and must remove their shoes. Box seats are divided into A, B, and C boxes according to how far the box is from the ring. On the second-floor balcony of a sumo stadium are several rows of Western-style seats known as balcony seats. These seats are also divided into A, B, and C seats depending on their distance from the ring. The cheapest sumo tickets are same-day tickets, which can only be purchased at the stadium on match day.

See also: Celtic Wrestling; Cotswold Olimpicks; *Glima; Lucha Libre;* Mongolian Wrestling; Nonlethal Bullfighting; *Pehlwani/Kushti; Schwingen; Varzesh-e Bastani; Yagli Gures;* Yoga

Further Reading

Adams, Andy. "Sumo Wrestling: Japan's Brutal National Sport." *Black Belt,* April 1985, 38–42.

Ceweb2. "The Bow Ceremony." A Guide to a Sumo Tournament, http://ceweb2.uml.edu /EW_Project2/fsome614/bowceremony.htm (accessed April 5, 2002).

Dunning, Eric, and Dominic Malcolm, eds. *Sport: Critical Concepts in Sociology.* London: Routledge, 2003.

Frédéric, Louis. *Japan Encyclopedia.* Cambridge, MA: Harvard University Press, 2002.

Hargreaves, Jennifer and Eric Anderson, eds. *Routledge Handbook of Sport, Gender and Sexuality.* Abingdon, UK: Routledge, 2014.

"The History and Traditions of Sumo." Sumo Talk, http://www.sumotalk.com/history.htm (accessed April 5, 2014).

Ray, Doug. "Living Gods: The Relationship between Sumo and Shinto." Doug Ray: Writer Photographer & Videographer, April 4, 2008, http://doug-ray.com/write/?p=35 (accessed April 5, 2014).

"The Rules of Sumo." Sumo Talk, http://www.sumotalk.com/rules.htm (accessed April 5, 2014).

"Ryogoku." Japan Guide, January 29, 2014, http://www.japan-guide.com/e/e3022.html (accessed April 5, 2014).

"The Structure of Sumo." Sumo Talk, http://www.sumotalk.com/structure.htm (accessed April 5, 2014).

"Sumo." Japan Guide, July 31, 2013, http://www.japan-guide.com/e/e2080.html (accessed April 5, 2014).

SWIMMING THE ENGLISH CHANNEL

Swimming the English Channel is an open-water endurance swimming event that sees a swimmer, male or female, navigate the narrow section of the Atlantic Ocean that separates southeastern England from northwestern France known in England as either the English Channel, the Straits of Dover, or as simply the Channel. The shortest swimmable distance across the Channel is an England-to-France swim starting from Shakespeare Beach in Dover, located in the county of Kent, to the French headland Cap Griz Nez that lies between the ports of Boulogne-sur-Mer and Calais. This swim covers a distance of 18.2 nautical miles (around 21 land miles). However, most swims take a more meandering course depending on factors beyond the control of the swimmer, such as weather and tides. Most England-to-France swims begin at either Shakespeare Beach or nearby Abbotts Cliff approximately 1 hour before high tide and 1 hour after high water, though, again, specifics depend on weather, tidal conditions, and the swimmer's ability. Swimming the English Channel has been likened to climbing to the summit of Mount Everest, as it is an extremely difficult feat to achieve for several reasons. One factor to consider is that Channel tides are strong, reaching a maximum speed of 4 nautical miles per hour, and vary every 6 hours. Most swimmers attempt their Channel swim during the weaker neap tide, that is, the time when the lowest tidal flow and height range occurs. Another difficulty of swimming the Channel is the variable and unpredictable weather conditions experienced in the strait, for the area is prone to localized weather that changes quickly, and a sudden wind can significantly alter swimming conditions. It is also important to consider that the English Channel is the world's busiest seaway, with 600 commercial ship sailings per day and between 80 and 100 passenger ferry crossings every 24 hours. Thus, swimmers must swim at 90°T to the traffic as they swim across the shipping lanes. It is the job of the pilot steering the boat that escorts the swimmer to keep the swimmer out of the way of commercial ships. Also, of course, swimming the English Channel is both physically and mentally grueling. Swimming the Channel exercises most of the body's muscle groups, but mental strength is as important as physical fitness, as the swimmer faces many hours of monotonous swimming in cold water. Taking all such factors into account, it is unsurprising that less than half of all Channel swims attempted each year succeed. However, in the history of cross-Channel swimming there have been only eight fatalities. This relatively small number of deaths is possibly due to the fact that swimmers are accompanied by an escort boat that provides the swimmer with as safe a passage as possible through the strait as well as food, drink, and encouragement.

Swimming the English Channel can be a solo or relay team event. Some swimmers even decide to do a two-way swim so that they cross the open water twice, that is, going from England to France and then back from France to England. A three-way swim has also been accomplished. Thus far 1,424 swimmers have swum 1,903 solo crossings, but the swimmer who has swum the Channel the most times is Alison Streeter, MBE, who has navigated the Channel 46 times and is known as the "Queen of the Channel." The male who has achieved the feat the most number of times and is known as the "King of the Channel" is Kevin Murphy, who has made 34 solo crossings. The fastest ever one-way swim was achieved by Australian Trent Grimsey, who took just 6 hours 55 minutes, while the slowest time ever posted was by Britain Jackie Cobell, who took 28 hours 44 minutes. Today most swimmers employ the front crawl, and the average crossing time is 13 hours 24 minutes.

Attempts at swimming the English Channel are overseen by two governing bodies, the Channel Swimming & Piloting Federation (CS&PF), which is the largest organization, and the Channel Swimming Association (CSA), which established a code of conduct for Channel swimming in 1927 in order to prevent swimmers from achieving the swim through artificial means, for instance, with the help of buoyancy aids. Today the CSA observes and authenticates swims to verify crossing times. A CSA observer monitors the swim and ensures that all appropriate rules are complied with, particularly that the swimmer does not touch anyone or anything other than a pole proffered by the support crew, at one end of which is a cup supplying the swimmer with hot drinks.

The first person to swim the English Channel was English seaman Matthew Webb (1845–1883) in an epic feat of endurance of 1875. Earlier the same year American Paul Boyton had made his way across the Channel as a publicity stunt to advertise the patented rubber lifesaving suit with built-in floatation device that he had invented and wore during his crossing. However, Webb, who swam breaststroke before the crawl had been invented, was the first person to actually swim the Channel unaided. Webb was a man inclined to acts of daring-do, having earned a living swimming out to shipwrecks sunk in shark-infested waters off the South African coast and having once jumped into the ocean to try to rescue a man who had fallen overboard in a gale during an Atlantic crossing. Webb's inherently heroic nature coupled with his physical strength, swimming ability, and marine knowledge meant that he was the perfect candidate to achieve the first swimming of the England Channel.

Having found the financial backing that allowed him to train for his Channel swim, Webb was offered a reward of £50 if he achieved his goal. With water temperatures at around 50°F to 60°F there was no certainty that Webb would be able to reach France, but at 27 years of age and weighing 240 pounds, he had the right physical makeup to achieve the feat. It was decided that Webb, dressed in a Victorian-era one-piece bathing suit, should be covered in porpoise oil as an insulator against the cold and would need to keep up his energy levels while in the water by drinking beef tea, brandy, cod liver oil, soup, and coffee and eating stale bread, meat, and eggs. Webb would have no eye protection, as goggles had yet to be developed fully. Today's swimmers follow the example set by Webb, for they are permitted to wear only a swimsuit, a cap, and grease. However, unlike Webb, swimmers may don goggles, and the grease is now a mixture of Vaseline and lanolin. Swimmers no longer eat solid meat during the crossing, though they do drink hot liquids such as chicken broth, liquefied bananas, tea, and watery oatmeal.

Apart from issues of hypothermia and lack of eye protection, Webb also had to consider which course to take from England to France, for while he could try to use the tide to his benefit, doing so would actually carry him parallel to the English coast, meaning that he made little progress on his journey, and he would also have to land at a point farther away from Cap Griz Nez, the point on the French coast that is nearest to England. Webb also had to consider the strength of the various coastal currents. However, as a sailor he realized that once he had swum around three miles out to sea, the tidal streams no longer go directly against the swimmer but instead come at the swimmer from the side. Therefore, Webb thought it sensible to swim across the tidal current in order to make headway and avoid fighting the tide. However, despite his careful planning, the unpredictable nature of the sea can be seen in the fact that this first attempt at swimming the Channel was aborted after Webb was swept along the English coast for several hours by a northeasterly current.

Undeterred, Webb decided to try again. On August 23, 1875, 11 days after his failed first attempt, with the Channel smooth and the weather set fair, he set out from Admiralty Pier in Dover accompanied by a boat crew, sightseers, and newspaper reporters. Webb started his swim two hours after high tide, and the ebb tide aided him by 1.5 miles per hour. However, during the second half of the swim his stroke rate dropped from 23 per minute to 20, so a journalist jumped into the sea and swam alongside Webb for 10 minutes in the hope that the company would lift his spirit. This worked and Webb continued on, swimming at 1 mile per hour. Four hours into his swim he was stung by a jellyfish. However, his steely nature showed through and he swam through the pain, even increasing his stroke rate to 1.5 miles per hour. By 2:00 a.m. Webb was starting to tire, and by 4:00 a.m. his stroke rate was reduced to 16 per minute. This was dangerously slow, for at that time in the morning the Channel tide changes, and Webb risked being swept away from the French coast rather than toward it. At 6:00 a.m. the wind blew up, making the sea turbulent; Webb's stroke rate dropped still further, and he was swept past his intended target of Cap Griz Nez toward Calais. By 10:00 a.m. Webb was 1.5 miles from the French coast, but his stroke rate dropped to 12 per minute, prompting one of his crew to dive into the water to spur him on. Eventually Webb reached the Calais shore, stumbling onto the sand after 21 hours 45 minutes. It has been estimated that taking into account tidal currents, Webb actually swam 39 miles in water averaging a temperature of 60°F, and his achievement stood for 36 years.

The first woman to swim the Channel was American Olympic gold medal swimmer Gertrude Ederle (1906–2003), who like Webb had failed at her first attempt. On August 6, 1926, Ederle set out from Cap Griz Nez wearing a two-piece swimsuit, a cap, and wrap-around goggles and smeared in lanolin and lard as protection against the cold and jellyfish stings. During her swim she encountered inclement weather and tides that forced her to swim 14 miles extra to reach Dover in 14 hours 31 minutes. On her return to America she was greeted by a ticker tape parade through New York and starred in the film *Swim Girl Swim* (1927). However, a consequence of her swim was that Ederle gradually became deaf, probably as a result of strong waves continually pounding against her head as she swam. The Gertrude Ederle Award, named in Ederle's honor, is awarded each year by the CS&PF to the woman who has achieved the year's most praiseworthy Channel swim.

The youngest person to swim the Channel, Thomas Gregory, was 11 years and 11 months old when he accomplished the feat. Since then an age limit has been introduced, so cross-Channel swimmers must now be at least 16 years old. In contrast, the oldest person ever to make the crossing is 73-year-old South African Otto Thaning, who in September 2014 swam the Channel in 12 hours 52 minutes. Thaning had previously completed the distance in 1994, taking 10 hours 29 minutes to make the crossing.

Swimming the English Channel has a strong presence in British popular culture. For instance, the British actor and comedian David Walliams raised over £1 million for the BBC charity Sport Relief in 2006 by swimming the Channel, and Channel swimming is the subject of the British film *On a Clear Day* (2005). Swimming the English Channel is also the subject of the Hollywood comedy-musical *Dangerous When Wet* (1953) starring Esther Williams.

See also: Round-the-World Yacht Races; Ultramarathons

Further Reading

"About the CSA." The Channel Swimming Association, http://www.channelswimmingass
    ociation.com/about (accessed January 19, 2014).
"Captain Webb 1848–1883." Shropshire Tourism, http://www.shropshiretourism.co.uk
    /captain-webb/ (accessed January 18, 2014).

"Channel Swimming—Introduction to the English Channel." Dover.uk.com, http://www
.dover.uk.com/channelswimming/ (accessed January 19, 2014).

Commings, Jeff. "Otto Thaning Claims Distinction of Oldest Person to Swim Across
English Channel." *Swimming World Magazine,* September 9, 2014, http://www.swimm
ingworldmagazine.com/news/otto-thaning-claims-distinction-of-oldest-person-to
-swim-across-english-channel/ (accessed September 14, 2014).

"The English Channel FAQ." NYC Swim, 2014, http://www.nycswim.org/Resource
/EnglChannelFAQ.aspx (accessed January 19, 2014).

Goble, Sally. "How I Swam the English Channel." The Guardian, August 9, 2013, http://
www.theguardian.com/lifeandstyle/the-swimming-blog/2013/aug/09/how-i-swam
-english-channel (January 19, 2014).

Nauright, John, and Charles Parrish, eds. *Sports around the World: History, Culture and Practice,* Vol. 1, *General Topics, Africa, Asia, Middle East, and Oceania.* Santa Barbara, CA:
ABC-CLIO, 2012.

Oram, Michael, and Angela Oram. "Frequently Asked Questions." Channel Swimming,
http://www.channelswimming.com/faq.htm (accessed January 19, 2014).

Tomlinson, Alan. *A Dictionary of Sports Studies.* Oxford: Oxford University Press, 2010.

Wennerberg, Conrad A. *Wind, Waves, and Sunburn: A Brief History of Marathon Swimming.*
New York: Breakaway Books, 1997.

"What Is the CS&PF?" Channel Swimming & Piloting Federation, http://cspf.co.uk/what
-is-the-cs-and-pf (accessed January 19, 2014).

SYNCHRONIZED SKATING

Synchronized skating, known as precision team skating until 1988, is a form of
competitive figure skating performed on ice by teams of 8 to 20, with teams of 16
taking part in adult competitions. Synchronized skating is a very technical form of
figure skating that demands a high level of accuracy and speed while executing
intricate holds, formations, and transitions. Unison is an important element of
synchronized skating; hence, all members of a team must wear the same costume.
Synchronized skating is an emerging discipline within figure skating and one that
is gaining rapidly in popularity. There are around 525 synchronized skating teams
in the United States alone, with 5,000 skaters taking part in the annual sectional
championships. Though usually performed by women, men are allowed to join
synchronized skating teams.

Synchronized skating includes several fundamental maneuvers. These include
blocks, in which skaters are arranged in parallel lines; no-hold blocks, which
differ from blocks in that the skaters are not connected to one another; circles, in
which the skaters form variations of a round; intersections, in which half the team
intercepts the other half; and lines, in which the team makes various types of
straight lines. Other maneuvers include movement in isolation, which sees some
of the skaters separate from the rest of the team in order to perform free skate elements. These free skate moves must have some relation to the choreography being
performed by the rest of the team and must enhance the team's musical interpreta-
tion. Moves in the field are also included and take the form of a series of at least
three free skating maneuvers connected by linking steps. Also incorporated is a

The Haydenettes synchronized skaters perform at the Skating Spectacular exhibition at the U.S. Figure Skating Championships on January 12, 2014, in Boston. Synchronized skating is a very technical form of figure skating for teams must display a high level of accuracy and speed while executing intricate holds, formations, and transitions in unison. (AP Photo/Steven Senne)

pair's element in which one skater attaches to another by using one or more hands, as in a lift or pivot such as a death spiral. All skaters must also perform a spin in unison as well as a wheel, in which all the skaters rotate around one central point.

In adult synchronized skating competitions, teams must perform two programs known as the short program and the free skate program, both of which must include these basic elements. The short program lasts 2 minutes 50 seconds and must include all the basic moves. Judges consider the degree of difficulty, presentation, and the unison with which teams perform the set maneuvers. The judging system employed is the same as in the other skating disciplines of singles, pairs, and dance. The free skate lasts 4.5 minutes and sees teams perform the basic moves interspersed with complicated step sequences that should include basic footwork such as choctaws and mohawks as well as more difficult moves such as twizzles. Artistry is a major component of the free skate, as moves are choreographed to a piece of music chosen by the team. The music must include at least one change of tempo and must not be a vocal work.

The sport of synchronized skating began in 1954 in Ann Arbor, Michigan, when Dr. Richard Porter organized a team of 16 girls into a troop called the Hockettes. The Hockettes performed tidy drill routines during the interval of ice hockey games at the University of Michigan, and in time the routines proved extremely popular with audiences locally, nationally, and internationally. The sport evolved from these drills, with synchronized skating clubs forming throughout the United States and Canada. In 1974 a team drill event took place at the Central Pacific Regional Championships, and in 1976 a precision team skating competition was held at the Ann Arbor Skating Club, with teams from the United States and Canada taking part. By 1984 the United States had begun to hold national championships, with the first national competition held in Bowling Green, Ohio. However, though the sport originated in the United States, the country did not dominate the discipline, for Canada soon became the world's leading synchronized skating nation. By the end of the 1980s synchronized skating had become popular in Japan, Australia, Sweden, and Finland. Indeed, the first international synchronized skating championships were held in Sweden in 1989, with seven teams from seven countries competing. Over time Finland and Sweden would go on to dominate the sport.

The International Skating Union officially recognized synchronized skating in 1990, and during the 1990s several synchronized skating championships were inaugurated. For instance, 1996 saw the first of four annual Challenge Cup events held in the lead-up to the inaugural world championships, which took place in Minneapolis in 2000. Teams from Scandinavia dominated the Challenge Cups, with Team Surprise from Sweden winning three out of four championships (1996, 1998, and 1999) and with the Canadian team, Black Ice, winning in 1997. Teams from Sweden and Finland have won 10 out of 11 world championships. In terms of medal accumulation, as of 2011 Team Surprise has the best competitive medal haul for teams, having won five gold medals. Marigold Ice Unity and the Rockettes, both from Finland, have the second-highest medal collection, with a combined total of five golds. Finland also has the highest combined national medal tally, with 14 golds. Next comes Sweden with 10 golds and Canada with 7. The United States has won 2 gold medals.

Similar to synchronized skating is theater on ice, known as ballet on ice in Europe. Theater on ice is a form of competitive skating in which teams of 8 to 30 skaters perform routines, with the emphasis on theatricality and artistry. Judges look for technical proficiency but also evaluate presentation, with the emphasis placed on originality, costuming, and musicality.

Neither synchronized skating nor theater on ice are Olympic sports. A team skating event was held at the Winter Olympics in Sochi, Russia, in 2014, with teams made up of six skaters—one solo male, one solo female, a pair's team, and an ice dance couple. Points were awarded to each skater or skating couple, and the team accruing the highest number of points was declared the winner.

See also: Bandy; Cresta Run; Curling; Rhythmic Gymnastics

Further Reading

Hines, James R. *Historical Dictionary of Figure Skating.* Plymouth, UK: Scarecrow, 2011.

Human Kinetics with Thomas Hanlon. *The Sports Rules Book.* 3rd ed. Champaign, IL: Human Kinetics, 2009.

"International Olympic Committee Announces Addition of Figure Skating Team Event for 2014 Sochi Olympic Winter Games." U.S. Figure Skating, 2014, http://www.usfsa.org /Story.asp?id=45988&type=media (accessed August 3, 2013).

"Synchronized Skating." U.S. Figure Skating, 2014, http://www.usfigureskating.org /Programs.asp?id=44 (accessed August 3, 2013).

"Theatre on Ice." U.S. Figure Skating, 2014, http://www.usfigureskating.org/Programs .asp?id=49 (accessed August 3, 2013).

THAI BOXING

Thai boxing, sometimes referred to as the art of eight limbs because it involves the use of fists, elbows, knees, and feet, is a full-contact martial art boxing style similar to kickboxing that originated in Southeast Asia. In theory the sport is open to both men and women, though in reality it is a very masculine pursuit (particularly in rural areas of Asia) in which few women take part. In Thailand the sport is called *muay thai,* and in Cambodia it goes under the name *pradal serey.* Thailand adopted the pastime as its national sport during the 1700s, and a Thai boxing bout is held every day at both the Lumphini Stadium and the Ratchadamnoen Stadium in Bangkok, the Thai capital, where over 250,000 professional Thai boxers live. Thai boxing is thought to be one of the world's fastest-growing sports and since the 1960s has been popular worldwide as both a competitive sport and a recreational activity, with many gyms and fitness centers holding Thai boxing classes. Indeed, it is estimated that only around 10 percent of those who join Thai boxing clubs actually fight but instead take up the activity purely as a form of exercise.

There is some dispute between rival governing bodies as to which body truly oversees Thai boxing, though it seems to be generally accepted that the International Federation of Muaythai Amateur is the leading Thai boxing association. Thai boxing has been part of the Southeast Asian Games and the Asian Indoor Games since 2005 and the Asian Martial Arts Games since 2009 and was a demonstration sport at the 1998 Asian Games held in Bangkok.

Thai boxing is an extremely physical activity that employs the knees, shins, and elbows and involves kicks, grappling, and swift footwork. It is therefore considered a good choice for those seeking to lose weight; increase their stamina, strength, and flexibility; achieve greater cardiovascular endurance and improved muscle tone; and enhance hand-eye coordination.

The origins of Thai boxing are unknown partly because the Burmese reportedly burned all documentation held by Thailand (then known as Siam) in 1767. Legend tells that the sport began in 1560 when Prince Naresuen of Siam fought a Burmese prince for a crown, defeating the Burmese prince by employing the fighting moves now associated with Thai boxing. Naresuen's fighting style is said to have deterred the King Bayinnaung of Burma (now Myanmar) from attacking Siam. Another story suggests that Thai boxing originated during a weeklong Buddhist festival held in Rangoon (now called Yangon), the capital of Burma, in 1774. According to this legend, a Thai boxer named Nai Khanom Tom overcame in excess of nine Burmese fighters in succession, earning the admiration of the Lord Mangra, the king of Burma. However, one surviving document suggests that the sport may date back further than these stories suggest, possibly to at least the 13th century.

However, it is a subject of much debate as to whether the sport was invented in Thailand or Cambodia, with the latter claiming that Thailand appropriated the sport. Indeed, so contentious is this issue that in the past Cambodia has boycotted Thai boxing events held as part of the Southeast Asian Games. The modern version of the sport developed during the early 20th century when the traditional martial arts form of the sport fused with Western-style boxing. Today the main difference between Thai boxing and Western boxing is that Thai boxers hold their guard up and away from their body to counter the kicks, elbows, and knees of their opponents. Indeed, the similarities between Western boxing and Thai boxing means that a number of Thai boxers have had success at Western boxing. For example, Khaosai Wanghompu boxed as "Galaxy" Khaosai and became the longest-reining bantamweight champion in the history of the World Boxing Association and was inducted into the Boxing Hall of Fame in 1999 after achieving 50 wins (and 1 loss) and defending his title on 19 occasions.

The urge to modify Thai boxing was triggered partly by the increasing popularity of Western-style boxing in the East and also because a significant number of Thai boxers were being seriously injured and even killed during Thai boxing bouts. The chief modifications to the sport were the adoption of a ring surrounded by ropes, the division of bouts into rounds with set time limits, the establishment of formal weight divisions, and the decree that all Thai boxers must wear gloves. Before 1929 it was traditional for Thai boxers to bind their hands with cotton cloth that had been dipped first into glue and then into ground glass rather than wear gloves.

Thai boxing fights last for five rounds of three minutes with two-minute rest periods between each round. Each fight is adjudicated by a center referee who declares knockouts through the use of a countdown from 10, as in Western boxing. The role of the center referee is important, as a fight can be won by three knockouts in a single round. A fight is also overseen by two judges who score Thai boxers on points. Therefore, in Thai boxing a fight may be won either on a points decision, through three knockouts occurring in one round, or by a single knockout. A fight may also end if it is stopped by the center referee.

To begin a bout, Thai boxers enter the ring wearing robes, while their trainers wear vests. However, during the bout the boxers sport trunks, groin protection, mouth guards, hand wraps, and gloves. In most bouts these gloves are the type worn by Western boxers. Boxers also wear magical amulets in the shape of the *mongkhon* headgear and *pra jiad* or *praciat* armband(s) during fights. The *mongkhon* is worn exclusively by boxers in Thailand and is given to a Thai boxer only after his trainer decides that the boxer has become an experienced and knowledgeable fighter. According to superstition, a *mongkhon* must never in any way come into close proximity to the ground or it will become worthless, and it may be handled solely by the fighter and his teacher or it will lose its special powers. The *pra jiad* is said to bestow a boxer with good luck and confidence and may be worn singularly or in pairs. Some Thai boxing schools use color-coded *pra jiads* to denote a boxer's rank, as belts do in karate. Traditionally, *pra jiads* must be kept in high places, as it was believed that if someone stepped over a *pra jiad*, the armband would lose its magic powers.

In Thailand a *mongkhon* must be worn during the *wai khru ram muay*, a warm-up routine performed by boxers in Thai fights in order to show respect for their opponents and their trainers. This reveals the extent to which Thai boxing is rooted in Buddhism, despite the various modifications and modernizations that have been adopted by Thai boxing. The name of the routine consists of *wai*, which refers to a praying-type action in which the boxers place their hands together; *khru*, meaning "teacher"; *ram*, which refers to a traditional Thai dance style; and *muay*, meaning "boxing." The tradition of the *wai khru ram muay*, which in Thailand is often abbreviated to *ram muay* or *wai khru*, originated as a way of apologizing to spectators, especially the onlooking king, for the brutality of the fight to come. To perform the *wai khru ram muay*, a boxer circles the ring three times and then kneels and bows three times in order to show his respect for God and man. The boxer also bows to Buddha in order to ask for protection for himself and his opponent and to ensure that the fight is honorable. The boxer then performs the highly ritualized prefight dance, the *ram muay*, on each side of the ring. Thai boxers perform the *ram muay* for several reasons: to demonstrate their abilities to the spectators, to display their body control and style, and to hex their opponents. Each boxer's *ram muay* is a personal ritual, often containing hints as to who trained the boxer and where the boxer originated. Another ceremonial aspect of Thai boxing is the music that accompanies fights. This fight music, known as *si muay*, is a vital inspirational element of every bout. A four-piece orchestra plays songs called *sarama* on instruments including a Javanese clarinet, called a *pi Java*; cymbals known as *shing*, and drums called *klong kaek kong*.

Once a Thai boxing bout begins, boxers deliver extremely forceful blows using their elbows, knees, and fists as well as kicks. Indeed, a characteristic move of Thai boxing is the roundhouse kick, in which a competitor swings his leg in a semicircular motion, striking low down, in the middle, or high up on his opponent's leg with the front of the leg or foot. This move is designed to weaken the opponent's leg, limit his mobility, and inhibit his ability to stand. Thai boxers are often taught to use this kick repeatedly, as the kicks produce a cumulative effect on the opponent, and during the opening round of a fight Thai boxers often trade low-line roundhouse kicks in order to prove which of them is the fittest. This is important, for it is after the first round that spectators place their bets on which boxer will prevail. The betting element of modern Thai boxing is somewhat controversial, for the activity is thought by some to bring a seedy aspect to the sport and to dehumanize the boxers. Other Thai boxing kicks include the front kick and the spinning kick, which is often the final kick of a bout.

Punching in Thai boxing consists of the basic moves found in Western boxing plus a long-range hook called a swing (among others). Elbows can be delivered downward (sometimes accompanied by a jumping motion), upward (akin to an uppercut), horizontally, driving (similar to a jab in Western boxing), and spinning. Meanwhile, there are three knee-attack deliveries—straight and round, which are the most frequently used, and jumping, which is employed against a cornered opponent and used to impress spectators.

While the sport features many types of attack, Thai boxing consists of just one standing posture—right-handed boxers lead with their left leg and then follow up with the right, while left-handers do the opposite. Thai boxers hold their hands high and protect their heads with their gloved hands and their elbows that are held inward, their arms protecting their body. Meanwhile, the boxer's head protrudes forward, and the body is angled slightly sideways. To move forward and backward, the boxer employs a shuffle step.

Thai boxers train in professional camps, practicing and training every day through stretching, running, swimming, kicking pads (as well as a special long, heavy type of punching bag called a banana bag), calisthenics, skipping, shadowboxing, sparring, and breath control. Boxers fight at least monthly, and it is traditional for boxers to carry the name of their training camp into the ring. Boxers are massaged regularly and eat a diet aimed at providing stamina. Training camps differ in their favored strategies. For instance, some, such as the Prapaisilp-Kitipitayangkul Camp located in Missouri, emphasize the importance of kicking an opponent's legs.

Thai boxing has featured in a number of films including *The Quest* (1996), the directorial debut of Belgian film star and martial artist Jean-Claude Van Damme, and James Bond film *The Man with the Golden Gun* (1974), parts of which were filmed at the Lumpini Stadium, the Thai boxing arena in Bangkok.

Other Thai martial arts include *lerdrit* (an empty-hand battlefield technique), *thaiplum* (grappling), *chuparsp* (fighting with an array of weapons), and *kemier* (a stealth art taught to head monks living at temples). Another Thai martial art, *krabi-krabong* (fighting with a sword and staff), belongs to *thaiyuth*, meaning "Thai skills," the same family of close-quarters combat martial arts as Thai boxing.

See also: Chess Boxing; *Glima;* Korean Wrestling; Mongolian Wrestling; *Pehlwani/ Kushti; Schwingen; Sepak Takraw;* Shin Kicking; Sumo Wrestling; *Varzesh-e Bastani; Yagli Gures;* Yoga

Further Reading

Alcock, Neil. "BlogalongaBond/The Man with the Golden Gun: The Girl with the Forgotten Story." The Incredible Suit, September 30, 2011, http://theincrediblesuit.blogspot. co.uk/2011/09/blogalongabond-man-with-golden-gun-girl.html (accessed July 5, 2014).

Green, Thomas A., ed. *Martial Arts of the World,* Vol. 1, A–Q. Santa Barbara, CA: ABC-CLIO, 2001.

"Jean-Claude Van Damme." Internet Movie Database, 1990–2014, http://www.imdb.com /name/nm0000241/?ref_=tt_ov_dr#director (accessed July 5, 2014).

"The Man with the Golden Gun: Filming Locations." Internet Movie Database, 1990–2014, http://www.imdb.com/title/tt0071807/locations?ref_=tt_dt_dt (accessed July 5, 2014).

Nauright, John, and Charles Parrish, eds. *Sports around the World: History, Culture and Practice,* Vol. 1, *General Topics, Africa, Asia, Middle East, and Oceania.* Santa Barbara, CA: ABC-CLIO, 2012.

"Wai Kru." Wech Pinyo Muay Thai, 2012, http://www.wechpinyomuaythai.com/waikhru .html (accessed July 5, 2014).

Wallis Simons, Jake. "Thai Boxing: Coming to a Gym Near You." *The Telegraph,* March 18, 2013, http://www.telegraph.co.uk/lifestyle/9937631/Thai-boxing-coming-to-a-gym -near-you.html (accessed July 5, 2014).

TRAMPOLINING

Trampolining is an acrobatic Olympic sport for males and females in which competitors, sometimes called trampolinists, perform gymnastic maneuvers in the air, having gained height by bouncing on a spring-suspended woven surface called a trampoline. Trampolining is popular across Europe, particularly in France and former Soviet states, especially Russia, as well as in China. In 1980 trampolining was introduced as a demonstration sport at the Moscow Olympics, and in the Sydney Olympics in 2000 trampolining became an Olympic event, with Russians Irina Karavaeva and Alexander Moskalenko becoming the first Olympic champions.

Trampolining takes place on a piece of apparatus called a trampoline, a padded steel frame with a sprung bed that aims to ensure that performers can land without injuring themselves. The bed is made up of narrow nylon strips that are sewn together to form a mesh. This allows air to pass through the bed when pressed, creating bounce. Springs or elastic attaches the bed to the inside of the frame. The basic aim of trampolining is for competitors to perform as many varied turns or twists, alone or in combination, as possible while in the air before landing back on the trampoline. Trampolining can be undertaken as a competitive sport or as a leisure

A North Korean athlete practices on a trampoline on September 2, 2014, in Pyongyang, North Korea. The basic aim of trampolining is for competitors to make as many different turns and twists, alone or in combination, as possible while in the air before landing back on the trampoline. (AP Photo/Wong Maye-E)

pursuit. In competition, individual competitors can perform as part of a team, while a synchronized event also exists for teams consisting of two men and two women. Men and women compete in their own separate divisions.

The roots of trampolining are unknown. One theory as to the origins of trampolining suggests the sport began when Inuit peoples used to launch each other into the air using walrus skin. However, there is also evidence that people in England used a blanket to throw each other into the air. This was certainly true at the start of the 20th century, when English stage acts used a springy trampoline covered in blankets (so that it resembled a bed) on which to bounce in order to amuse audiences with comic routines. Another theory argues that trampolining was invented by Italian trapeze artists known as "Due Trampoline" who used the bounce generated by their safety net to perform airborne acrobatics, later developing the trapeze safety net into a separate, smaller surface that could be used for both propulsion and landing. American professor of physical education and diving specialist George Nissen perfected the modern trampoline in the 1930s and marketed it for use at American universities, with the first collegiate championship held in 1946. At this championship a competitor had three minutes in which to achieve the greatest possible level of difficulty, with most competitors opting to repeat three or four moves. World War II saw trampolines used by the U.S. Navy Flight School to give it pilots and navigators practice in orientation. Trampolines were also used after the war by both American and Soviet space agencies to provide astronauts with experience of various body positions during flight.

At the end of the 1950s the sport of trampoling arrived in Europe, though recreational beach trampolining was already popular on the large, octagonal trampolines installed on the beaches on France's Atlantic coast. The first Nissen trampoline was delivered at the Institut National de Sport et de Éducation Physique (INSEP, National Institute of Sport and Physical Education), a center of sporting excellence in France that trains elite athletes, in 1959. However, trampolining only truly started to grow as a sport after 1961, when an international trampoline clinic took place in Macolin, northeastern Switzerland. The clinic was presided over by Bernard Ammon, coach of the Swiss society of gymnastics in Paris, and Pierre Blois, apparatus gymnastics professor at INSEP. Bernard Ammon, who did not have the necessary funds to buy a trampoline, asked Nissen to donate one to him. Nissen agreed to this on condition that a French trampoline federation was established. Ammon agreed, and on May 15, 1965, a meeting occurred at which it was agreed that the French Federation of Trampoline Sports (FFST) would be created. In 1985 tumbling and acrobatic gymnastics joined the FFST, which duly adopted a new name, the French Federation of Trampoline and Acrobatic Sports (FFTSA). Then in 1999 the FFTSA merged with the French Gymnastics Federation.

In 1964 a trampolining governing body, the International Federation of Trampoline (FIT), was established, and the same year the first world championship took place in London, with Judy Wills and Dan Millman becoming the first world champions. The first European championships were held in 1969, with titles awarded to Paul Luxon of England and Ute Czech of Germany. In 1998, however, the FIT merged with the International Gymnastics Federation, which now oversees the sports of gymnastics, trampolining, tumbling, and double minitrampoline (a discipline in which competitors sprint down a carpeted track and hurdle onto an apparatus, similar to two conjoined minitrampolines, before performing double and triple somersaults). Today most national trampoline federations have merged with national gymnastics federations, with a notable exception being Russia.

The European pioneers of trampolining were Englishman Ted Blake, who pioneered trampolining in England by making his own trampolines on which to demonstrate the activity and also worked with Nissen to introduce the trampoline to Europe, and Kurt Baechler of Switzerland. Baechler established a 10-skill routine system in which level of difficulty was emphasized rather than execution. In trampolining the term "skill" refers to combinations of somersaults and twists that must be executed with the arms held tight against the body and may be performed in one of three different positions: pike (in which the legs remain straight but are brought into the chest while the head and body stay straight), layout (in which athletes keeps their legs straight and in line with their hips), and tuck (a compact move in which athletes bend their knees and bring them into their chest with their feet and toes pointed). Pike and layout positions score the most points, as they are the most difficult skills to execute—one point is awarded to a total score per somersault executed in one of these positions. Perhaps the most difficult skill to execute is the full full full, a triple somersault with a twist in each somersault. In both individual and synchronized trampolining, competitors must perform three routines consisting of 10 skills as a nonstop sequence without repeating a move. The routines should be as testing as possible for the trampolinists to perform neatly while allowing them to maintain total control of their rebounds as they bounce. In synchronized trampolining the pair must try to perform their routine in absolute unison.

Competitors are awarded marks for demonstrating control, timing, and technique, with routines marked out of 10 points by five execution judges (who assess the athletes' ability to stay centered on the trampoline as well as uniformity of bounce and general style), two difficulty judges (who count the number of twists and somersaults and ensure that the skills have been executed in the positions announced before the athletes begin their routines), and a chair of judges panel whose role it is to oversee the whole competition. In both individual and synchronized trampolining, the top eight winners go to the finals to contest for titles.

Recent innovations in video technology and biomechanics have improved understanding of how the body moves in the air, resulting in trampolining becoming more technical and athletes attempting much more difficult routines. Similarly, the advent of synthetic fibers and metal alloys has changed the nature of the trampoline, allowing athletes to increase the height of their somersaults and twists. As athletes can now reach heights of 26 feet, they now have more time in the air in which to perform more difficult skills.

See also: Bossaball; *Parkour;* Rhythmic Gymnastics; Synchronized Skating; Yoga

Further Reading

Alswang, Joel. *The South African Dictionary of Sport.* Claremont, South Africa: Spearhead, 2003.

"History." Federation Française Gym, http://translate.google.co.uk/translate?hl=en&sl=fr&u=http://www.ffgym.com/decouvrir_les_gymnastiques/trampoline/decouvrir/l_histoire&prev=/search%3Fq%3Dbernard%2Bammon%2Btrampoline%26start%3D10%26client%3Dsafari%26sa%3DN%26rls%3Den%26biw%3D1245%26bih%3D619 (accessed March 21, 2014).

"History of Trampolining." Brentwood Trampoline, 2009–2012, http://www.brentwoodtc.org/history.htm (accessed March 21, 2014).

"The History of Trampolining." Trampolining-Online.co.uk, https://www.trampolining-online.co.uk/trampolining/history.php (accessed March 21, 2014).

Lefebvre, Guillaume. "History of French Trampolining." Acrobatic Sports, June 9, 2005, http://www.acrobaticsports.com/2005/06/09/history-of-french-trampolining/ (accessed March 21, 2014).

QA International. *Sport: The Complete Reference.* Montreal: QA International, 2000.

U

ULTRAMARATHONS

Ultramarathons, also known as ultrarunning, are endurance events that involve men and women running or walking farther than 26.2 miles, the traditional distance of a marathon. Most ultramarathons are 50 or 100 miles long, though some races are in excess of 100 miles. The winner of the distance-based races is the runner who finishes first, as is usual for a marathon. Alternatively, an ultramarathon can take the form of a fixed-time race, lasting 24 or 48 hours or 6 days and in which the winner is the athlete who completes the most miles within the time limit. During such races, competitors are allowed to take refreshments, rest, and even sleep. While all ultramarathons are arduous, some have additional trying factors such as changes of elevation, inclement weather, and rough terrain, the latter usually in the form of mountain paths or dirt roads. Ultramarathons take place across the globe, including areas of extreme geography such as Antarctica and the Arctic Circle, the Himalaya Mountains in Asia, the Namib and Sahara deserts in Africa, and the Amazon rain forest in South America.

It has been suggested that ultramarathons date back well into prehistory to a time when humankind evolved and, without transportation, had to walk. Ancient Greek writers knew of ultramarathons. The semihistoric story of the heroic herald Pheidippides is often cited as the inspiration for the sport of marathon running. However, in truth, Pheidippides ran an ultramarathon rather than a marathon, for he is reputed to have run the 240 kilometers (150 miles) from Athens to Sparta in two days in order to ask for help when the Persians landed at the Greek town of Marathon. According to some accounts, Pheidippides dropped dead after finishing his epic journey. This highlights the considerable physiological strain placed on the body by taking part in an ultramarathon. For instance, during an average 50-mile race a runner's foot will strike the ground around 25,000 times, thus placing great impact on the body's joints; hence, many ultramarathon runners develop joint problems over time, particularly in the knees. The blood sugar levels, heart rate, and core body temperature of an ultramarathon runner all become elevated during a race, as does levels of oxygen consumption. Therefore, the runner's body may take several days to return to normal after a race. Indeed, it may be several weeks before a runner's neuromuscular state and muscle function return to prerace conditions.

The earliest competitive ultramarathons date back to the 19th century, when the sport was known as pedestrianism. Pedestrianism involved competitors racing over extremely long distances, sometimes thousands of miles or almost continuously for many days. One of the most famous 19th-century pedestrians was Captain Robert Barclay Allardice, who once walked 1,000 miles in 1,000 consecutive hours (from June 1 to July 12, 1809) for a cash prize of 1,000 guineas, though in fact Barclay earned far more than this, probably in the region of 16,000 guineas (about £6 million today), as many bets were placed on the outcome of the race. Barclay's feat of endurance took place at Newmarket Heath in England and was watched by 10,000 spectators. Over the rest of the 19th century many pedestrians copied and even bettered Barclay's feat. For instance, at the Mozart Garden in Brooklyn between December 1878 and January 1879, Ada Anderson walked 2,700 quarter miles in 2,700 quarter hours, that is, 675 miles in 28.125 days.

Other 19th-century pedestrians preferred to walk 100 miles in less than 24 hours, winning huge cash prizes for completing the races, while in the 1870s the six-day race became popular. This type of race saw walkers compete to cover as great a distance as possible within a six-day time limit in order to win cash prizes. Six-day races attracted crowds in excess of 70,000, and eventually a series of six-day races called the Long Distance Challenge Championships of the World were instigated by race promoter Sir John Astley. Variations on the six-day race took place in cities across the United Kingdom and the East Coast of the United States, with formats including six days in 12 hours and six days in 10 hours events, which were more spectator-friendly than six days of nonstop walking. Over time these pedestrian races evolved into ultramarthons.

Barefoot Running

Barefoot running, also known as natural running, is the practice of running without shoes. Advocates argue that this corrects runners' form by fostering a forefoot strike technique, thereby resulting in fewer injuries. Critics, however, argue that the style is not suitable for all. In 1960 Ethiopian Abebe Bikila won the first of his consecutive Olympic marathon gold medals running barefoot. Other notable long-distance barefoot runners include Englishman Bruce Tulloh, American marathon runner Charlie Robbins, and Zola Budd, who competed for both Great Britain and her native South Africa and as a teenager in the 1980s set two 5,000-meter world records.

The International Amateur Athletic Federation recognizes ultramarathon running as an international sport, and the International Association of Ultrarunners oversees events throughout the world, including the 100-kilometer World Cup, the 50-kilometer Trophy, and the World Trail Challenge. In America, the grand slams of ultramarathons are the Leadville Trail 100, the Vermont 100, the Wasatch Front 100, and the Western States 100. Any runner who completes all four races will cover 400 miles. Some of the most prestigious ultramarathons include the Badwater Ultramarathon, which starts below sea level in California's Death Valley and finishes at an elevation in excess of 8,000 feet at Whitney Portal (the gateway to California's Mount Whitney in the Sierra Nevada) during the hottest part of July; the Marathon des Sables, in which competitors race across 151 miles of Morocco's Sahara desert over six days; the Ultra-Trail du Mont Blanc, in which competitors contend with snow, wind, and rain to race in a loop pattern at high altitude around

Mont Blanc (the highest mountain in the both the Alps and the European Union and located on the border of France and Italy); and South Africa's Comrades Marathon, which is both the world's oldest and largest ultramarathon. The Comrades Marathon takes place over a distance of around 90 kilometers (56.1 miles) between Pietermaritzburg, the capital of the Kwazulu-Natal Province, and the coastal city of Durban.

See also: Fell Running; Heli-Skiing; Nordic Walking; Orienteering and Rogaining; *Parkour;* Round-the-World Yacht Races; Swimming the English Channel; Volcano Boarding

Further Reading

"Beyond the Ultimate." Beyond the Ultimate, 2014, http://www.beyondtheultimate.co.uk /index.asp (accessed March 30, 2014).

Gocker, Ben. "Walk the Walk." Brooklyn Public Library, December 7, 2011, http://brooklynolo gy.brooklynpubliclibrary.org/post/2011/12/07/Walk-the-Walk.aspx (accessed March 30, 2014).

Godden, Keith. "Ultramarathon Running Resource." Ultra Marathon Running Resource, 2008–2014, http://www.ultramarathonrunning.com (accessed March 30, 2014).

Hayhurst, Chris. *Ultra Marathon Running.* New York: Rosen Publishing Group, 2002.

The Jockey Club. "Captain Robert Barclay Allardice (1779–1854) 'The Celebrated Pedestrian.'" Newmarket, http://www.newmarketracecourses.co.uk/about-the-home-of-racing/experi-ence-the-home-of-racing/did-you-know/captain-robert-barclay-allardice-1779–1854 -the-celebrated-pedestrian/ (accessed March 30, 2014).

Lambert, Mike. "Recovery after an Ultramarathon." *Marathon & Beyond,* September–October 2012, http://sporttudomany.hu/Hirlevel/pdf/15/Recovering_marathon.pdf (accessed March 30, 2014).

Liberman, Art, Stephen Pribut, and Carlo DeVito. *Running.* Cincinnati: F&W Media International, 2011.

Milroy, Andy. "The History of the 6 Day Race." Planet Ultramarathon, October 18, 2008, http://planetultramarathon.wordpress.com/2008/10/18/the-history-of-the-6-day -race/ (accessed March 30, 2014).

"The North Face Ultra-Trail du Mont Blanc." Ultra-Trail du Mont Blanc, http://www.ultratr ailmb.com/page/20/utmb_presentation.html (accessed March 30, 2014).

"Ultra Running." International Association of Athletics Federations, 1996–2014, http:// www.iaaf.org/disciplines/ultra-running/ultra-running (accessed November 30, 2014)

White, George. "A Very Pedestrian Subject." World Masters Athletics, May 17, 2013, http:// www.world-masters-athletics.org/news/397-a-very-pedestrian-subject (accessed March 30, 2014).

"The World's Greatest Ultramarathon." Comrades Marathon Association, 2014, http:// www.comrades.com (accessed March 30, 2014).

UNDERWATER HOCKEY

Underwater hockey, also known as octopush, is a noncontact team game played underwater in a swimming pool. The sport can be played by anyone able to swim. Underwater hockey is played in over 40 countries but is particularly popular in Europe, the United States, and Australasia as well as China, Indonesia, Japan,

South Africa (players wearing black caps) competes against Hungary in the qualifying round of the 18th CMAS Underwater Hockey World Championship held in Eger, Hungary, on August 23, 2013. Underwater hockey teams aim to maneuver the puck across the playing area with the intention of scoring goals. (AP Photo/MTI, Peter Komka)

South Africa, and Colombia. The sport is overseen by two governing bodies, the Confédération Mondiale des Activités Subaquatiques (CMAS, World Underwater Federation) and the World Aquachallenge Association. Underwater hockey competitions range from club level to world titles, with a world championship held every two years. The first world championship was held in Vancouver, Canada, in 1980 and was for men's teams only, with the tournament won by a team from the Netherlands. However, the second world championship, which took place in Brisbane, Australia, in 1982, had separate competitions for men and women's teams, both of which were won by the home nation. In addition to the world championship, every other year Australia, New Zealand, and South Africa compete in a trinations cup.

Underwater hockey was invented in Southsea, in the county of Hampshire in southern England, in 1954 by diving enthusiast Alan Blake, who was looking for a way to practice diving during inclement winter weather. Blake's sport involved two teams of eight players using a curved bat to propel a circular lead weight to the opposite end of the pool. Since the game was to be played by a team of eight, Blake named his game octopush, from *octo*, the Latin word for "eight." To continue the fishy theme, Blake dubbed the puck used in the game the squid and the goal the cuttle. The game was taken up by the Royal Navy, which was seeking a way of training sailors to work effectively underwater, and from England the game soon spread to Australia and South Africa, where the game was adopted by spear fishermen who were looking for a way to hone their skills when they were unable to get to sea.

As in ice hockey, underwater hockey sees two teams maneuver the puck across a playing area with the intention of scoring more goals than the opposing team scores. Underwater hockey is played in a pool 25 meters long by 15 meters wide (82 feet by 49 feet) that is between 2 to 4 meters (6.5 to 13 feet) deep. At each end of the playing area is a 3-meter-long (almost 10-foot-long) underwater goal tray, which slopes from the front into a shallow trough attached to the back wall of the swimming pool.

The game is made up of two halves lasting for 15 minutes with a 3-minute break at halftime. Each team is allowed one 60-second time out per half. The game clock stops for any infringements in the last 2 minutes of the game. Each team consists of 12 players, 10 of whom may play in any one game. During the game 6 players are in the water, with 4 interchange players waiting either out of the water at the side of the swimming pool or in the water but outside of the playing area. The interchange players may be called upon at any time. To take part in underwater hockey, players wear swimwear such as swim briefs for men and one-piece suits for women (baggy clothing is not recommended, as this causes drag and thus reduces swimming speed); a double-lens diving mask, which protects the players' eyes from injury if their face is hit by the puck; a snorkel, which allows players to breathe without having to remove their face from under the water; a thick glove made from latex, which protects the hand from scraping on the bottom of the swimming pool and the impact of hitting the puck; a cap with ear protection in the team color; and fins made of carbon fiber, plastic, fiber glass, or rubber that allow players to swim quicker. Players also carry a short stick, sometimes called a bat or pusher, with which to maneuver the puck. A player may hold the stick with one hand only.

A game of underwater hockey begins with the two teams at each end of the swimming pool, with each player placing one hand against the wall. The puck, which is made of plastic-coated lead, weighs about 1.5 kilograms (just over 3 pounds) and is placed in the middle of the pool. When the game's referee sounds a buzzer, both teams race to gain possession of the puck with the aim of passing the puck through the water to score a goal using a combination of skill, speed, agility, and breathe control, for underwater hockey, like free-diving, involves an element of dynamic apnoea, that is, the ability people to deliberately hold their breath. Therefore, underwater hockey is a supremely aerobic sport.

There are various underwater hockey team configurations, but in general a team is made up of three forwards, consisting of a strike and two wings, and three backs, consisting of two halfbacks and a fullback. The rules of underwater hockey are straightforward. Underwater hockey does not have an offside rule, but players may not shepherd or obstruct each other. Players are also not permitted to rest the puck on their glove or stick and may not stop the puck by using anything other than their stick. Also, as underwater hockey is a noncontact sport, players may not interfere with other players using their free hand.

When rule infringements are judged to have occurred, two referees in the water signal to an out-of-water referee to stop play by sounding the buzzer. For minor infringements referees can award an advantage puck, also known as a free puck, whereby the side who's player committed the foul is pushed back three meters from the puck, while the fouled team gets free possession of the puck. More serious transgressions of the rules, such as dangerous play or repeatedly and intentionally fouling, result in harsher penalties. For instance, a player can be ejected from the game for a specified amount of time (usually one or two minutes) or even for the rest of the game depending on the seriousness of the foul.

The CMAS also governs the related sports of fin swimming and underwater rugby. Underwater rugby is a contact team sport that was invented in Köln, Germany, in 1961 and became popular across Scandinavia under the name UW-Polo. Many different variations of the game evolved, but eventually official rules were standardized in order to hold an inaugural international tournament in 1978. Today underwater rugby is played at club, national, and international levels. Underwater rugby is played in a swimming pool measuring between 12 to 18 meters (39 to 59 feet) long by 8 to 12 meters (26 to 39 feet) wide. The water should be between 3.5 to 5 meters in depth (around 11 to 16 feet). Like underwater hockey, a game of underwater rugby consists of two 15-minute halves with a rest at halftime, and each team may take one 60-second time-out per game.

Underwater rugby teams consist of 15 players, 12 of whom play in any one game, with 3 substitutes available. During the game 6 players are in the water, with 6 exchange players available for substitution at any time. As in underwater hockey, players sport swimwear, fins, a diving mask, and a snorkel. Players aim to maneuver a slightly negatively buoyed plastic ball filled with saltwater into the opposing side's goal, which is made of steel and located on the bottom of each side of the swimming pool. The teams begin at each end of the swimming pool with one hand touching the wall. The ball is placed in the middle of the swimming pool floor. When the referee sounds a buzzer, both teams race to gain possession of the ball. As in underwater hockey, teams must use skill, speed, agility, and breath control to score more goals than their opponents. Various team configurations exist, but in general a team has two forwards, two backs, a goalkeeper, and a wing. As underwater rugby is a contact sport, a player may challenge another player who has the ball. However, kicking, hitting, and playing above the surface of the water are all punishable offenses that can be penalized by warnings, the awarding of a free throw, or the expulsion of a player for two minutes.

Fin swimming is a water sport in which competitors swim with the aid of one fin, known as a monofin, or two fins, called bifins, either on the surface of the water or underwater wearing a snorkel. The monofin was invented for use by the Russian Special Forces. Initially the device was strapped onto the feet of swimmers to allow them to move more quickly through water while keeping their hands free. It soon became evident that the easiest stroke to use while wearing a monofin is what is now known as the dolphin kick, a swimming method that requires a human to mimic the tail action of a dolphin. The sport was recognized by the International Olympic Committee in 1986 and has been staged at the Olympic Games as an exhibition sport ever since. Fin swimming is popular in Russia, China, Ukraine, France, Spain, Greece, and Colombia, and there are over 100,000 fin swimmers worldwide.

See also: Bandy; Bog Snorkeling World Championship; Curling; Rugby League; Shinty; Swimming the English Channel

Further Reading

"About Underwater Hockey." Confédération Mondiale des Activités Subaquatiques, http://www hand.cmas.org/hockey/about-hockey (accessed April 1, 2014).

"About Underwater Rugby." Confédération Mondiale des Activités Subaquatiques, http://www.cmas.org/underwater-rugby/about-2012032626 (accessed April 1, 2014).

Blake, Alan. "The Evolution of Octopush." Octopush, February 17, 2008, http://octopush .awardspace.com/fullenglish.htm (accessed April 1, 2014).

Bushell, Mike. *Bushell's Best Bits: Everything You Needed to Know about the World's Craziest Sports.* London: John Blake, 2013.

"FinSwimming: The Mono-Palm Meets the Dolphin Kick." FinSpirit, 2010, http://www .finspirit.com/what-is-finswimming-r12431.html (accessed April 1, 2014).

"World Championship Results," World Aquachallenge Association, http://www.thewaa .org/WAA_FILES/HTML/Results2.htm (accessed April 1, 2014).

V

VARZESH-E BASTANI

Varzesh-e bastani, meaning "sport of ancients" and sometimes called *varzesh-e pahlavani*, meaning "sport of champions," is an ancient form of wrestling in which pre-Islamic Persian (now Iranian) culture combines with physical strength, martial arts, morality, knowledge, and spirituality. The sport differs greatly from the forms of wrestling typically found in the West, as *varzesh-e bastani* is not intended as a form of entertainment. Rather, it is a highly ritualized activity that focuses on the spiritual aspects of Sufism, a mystical, philosophical branch of Islam that believes that purity of heart and prayer can bring adherents closer to God. Also, unlike Western wrestling, those participating in *varzesh-e bastani* do not truly fight an opponent but instead compete with a fellow wrestler in tests of flexibility and strength following ethical guidelines. *Varzesh-e bastani* includes the playing of ceremonial music and the recital of poetry as well as specific rites associated with the Mithraic religion (named after the Persian god Mithra) that spread through most of the Roman Empire before being displaced by Christianity and eventually Islam. Indeed, so great is the mystical dimension of *varzesh-e bastani* that the sport has been likened to a combination of yoga, personal development, and cultural heritage. While wrestling in the West portrays wrestlers as aggressive, individualistic, and ultracompetitive, *varzesh-e bastani* stresses that wrestlers are promoters of inner strength through might who embody the traditional traits of chivalry, kindness, humility, and resisting sin.

The form of *varzesh-e bastani* practiced today dates back to the rule of King Nassar al-Din Shah during the 19th century, when sporting competitions inspired by Persian mythology were held to celebrate the Persian New Year on March 21. However, from the 1920s to the 1960s the popularity of *varzesh-e bastani* declined significantly as Iran embarked on a program of modernization, and the sport was deemed a relic from a bygone era. The sport also fell foul of the Iranian Revolution of 1979 that overthrew the ruling Pahlavi dynasty and discouraged public gatherings, including sporting occasions.

Battle of the Nations: Medieval-Style Armed Combat Games

The Battle of the Nations is an international full-contact medieval battle world championship (first held in 2009 and held annually in Europe every April since) for competing national teams of 8 to 50 fighters equipped with metal weapons. Each national team comprises the country's best individual competitors as selected from qualifying tournaments held in accordance with the unified international rules of historical medieval battle. Battle categories include a one-on-one triathlon duel consisting of three rounds in which competitors use weapons such as swords and shields.

Somehow, however, the traditions of *varzesh-e bastani* have survived secular modernization and under the Islamic Republic of Iran have become a symbol of Persian national pride and cultural roots. Indeed, both modernizers and tradition-alists, though ideologically poles apart, promote the sport as a form of national physical education that reminds Iranians that during ancient times champion wrestlers known as the *pahlevans* defended their communities against Greek, Mongol, and Arab invaders. In Iran, *varzesh-e bastani* wrestler Gholamreza Takhti is idolized as a unifying figure who appeals to both Islamists and the more secular. That said, *varzesh-e bastani* only began to reemerge at the end of the 20th century and today is considered a noble Persian tradition imbued with nationalistic pride. The sport has also spread beyond Iran. On October 10, 2004, the International Zurkhaneh Sport Federation (IZSF) was established to promote *varzesh-e bastani* globally and organize regular competitions worldwide, including the Zurkhaneh Sports World Cup and the Asian Zurkhaneh Sports Championship. However, the success of the IZSF has been partial, with competing nations limited either to Iran's neighbors, including Tajikistan, Afghanistan, Iraq, India, Pakistan, and Azerbaijan, or to nations in which large numbers of Iranian immigrants have settled, including the United States, which is home to a number of Iranian immigrants. California in particular has a sizable Iranian community, as many Iranians fled there in the wake of the 1979 revolution.

Varzesh-e bastani usually takes place in a covered gymnasium called a *zurkhaneh* (or *zoorkhaneh*), meaning "house" or "home of strength," that is usually built and decorated in the style of the Mithraic era of 1 to 4 CE. The building is designed with a sunken octagonal or circular wrestling pit called a *gaud* sited in the center of the building. Exclusively male spectators sit around the *gaud*, separated from a sec-tion of drummers and Sufis who relate tales from Iranian mythology. A highly re-spected official called the *morshed*, who sits in a conspicuous position, signals the start of a wrestling session by sounding a drum. Next the competition ensues, with athletes performing calisthenics and acrobatics inspired by instruments resembling weapons, including metal shields called *sang*, iron weights shaped lie a bow called *kaman*, and stiff wooden sticks called *mil*. The wrestlers can attain three levels of membership of the *zurkhaneh*. The lowest rank is that of a *nocheh*, or a novice learning from a champion; then come the *nokhasten*, advanced students who have received substantial learning from a champion; and then there are the *pahlevans*, or champions, of which there are multiple grades. Traditionally, each school of pahla-vani has its own distinctive characteristics, based on the culture of the specific re-gion of Iran in which the school was based, and teaches slightly different exercises and wrestling techniques. However, all schools promoted similar codes of ethics and morality. Today the main schools of pahlavani are Tehran/Rey, Khorasan, Yazd, Qum, Mazandaran, and Western Regions. While the school of pahlavani in Kho-rasan is perhaps the oldest in Iran, the school at Tehran/Rey is the most important. It was founded by Nassar al-Din Shah, who ordered that a *zurkhaneh* be installed at the Golestan Palace and also participated in pahlavani rituals himself. The king was even accompanied on state visits to Europe and Russia by his official pahlavan, who would take on (and necessarily conquer) foreign wrestlers. Over time the

Tehran school became popular with the general public, not just royals, and as *varzesh-e bastani* championships were held in Tehran, many pahlavans from other parts of Iran came to Tehran and eventually enrolled at the school.

Some *varzesh-e bastani* champions are also members of the Iranian national mainstream wrestling team and compete at the Summer Olympic Games. That Iranian national pride is bound up with sport was evident in 1989, when just after the end of an eight-year war with Iraq, Iranian heavyweight mainstream wrestler Ali-Reza Soleimani beat an American wrestler to become world wrestling champion. This was the cause of great national excitement and struck a symbolic blow against the United States, as the United States had sided with Iraq during the war. As a result, state funding for mainstream wrestling increased.

However, it has been suggested that the future of *varzesh-e bastani* is uncertain. This is partly because *zurkhaneh* can seem quaintly traditional to the extent that they appear to be almost inauthentic or, conversely, because the schools have modernized but have evolved into leisure centers hosting corporate events rather than remained schools of learning. As a result, the *zurkhaneh* have little influence on their neighborhoods. Another problem is that the sturdy male physique traditionally associated with *varzesh-e bastani* is no longer one to which men aspire. However, the main threat to *varzesh-e bastani* is the huge popularity of soccer, for while *varzesh-e bastani* may be intrinsic to Iranian cultural, the sport is perhaps losing its grip on the attention of the nation, particularly in the face of the growing success of Iranian national soccer. According to official Fédération Internationale de Football Association (International Federation of Association Football, FIFA) rankings for June 2014, Iran is 2nd in Asia in soccer and 49th in the world. The team also qualified for the 2014 soccer World Cup finals in Brazil.

While *varzesh-e bastani* is an exclusively male preserve, a growing number of Iranian women are taking up the Japanese martial art of *ninjutsu*—of the 24,000 Iranians taking part in official *ninjutsu* classes, at least 3,000 of them are women. The first school to teach *ninjutsu* in Iran was opened in Karaj in 1989, and today *ninjutsu* is practiced in 22 provinces, including Tehran, Mazandaran, Qum, and Khorasan. The Karaj school faced some hostility to begin with, as the sport was deemed a Western import despite its Japanese origins. However, today the sport has largely been accepted, with *ninjutsu* students learning the traditional skills of the Japanese ninja, including unarmed self-defense; the use of weapons such as bows, swords, nunchucks, and *shuriken* (a concealed handheld blade); and the development of self-control, patience, and self-respect. Enthusiasts argue that *ninjutsu*, like *varzesh-e bastani*, instills respect, composure, and humility in practitioners.

See also: Camel Wrestling; Celtic Wrestling; *Glima;* Korean Wrestling; *Lucha Libre;* Mongolian Wrestling; *Pehlwani/Kushti; Schwingen;* Sumo Wrestling; *Yagli Gures;* Yoga

Further Reading

Bromber, Katrin, Birgit Krawietz, and Joseph Maguire, eds. *Sport across Asia: Politics, Cultures, and Identities: Politics, Cultures, and Identities.* Abingdon, UK: Routledge, 2013.

Farahani, Mansoureh. "The Lady Ninjas of Iran." The Majalla, November 12, 2013, http://www.majalla.com/eng/2013/11/article55246675 (accessed July 22, 2014).

Fisher, Max. "The Ancient Roots of Iran's Wrestling and Weightlifting Olympic Dominance." *The Atlantic*, August 9, 2012, http://www.theatlantic.com/international/archive/2012/08/the-ancient-roots-of-irans-wrestling-and-weightlifting-olympic-dominance/260919/ (accessed July 22, 2014).

Galvan, Javier A., ed. *They Do What? A Cultural Encyclopedia of Extraordinary and Exotic Customs from around the World.* Santa Barbara, CA: ABC-CLIO, 2014.

"Schools of Pahlavani: Tehran/Rey." Pahlavani.com, 2002, http://www.pahlavani.com/ish/html/ph/new/phskltrn.htm (accessed July 22, 2014).

VOLCANO BOARDING

Volcano boarding, also known as volcano surfing and ash boarding, is a recent innovation in adventure sports combining elements of snowboarding, sand boarding, and surfing. The origins of volcano boarding are somewhat clouded, as some suggest that the sport was invented by tour organizers in Nicaragua in 2005, while reports of volcano boarding on Pacific summits date back to 2002. Volcano boarding as an extreme sport that has become a tourist attraction is centered around Central America's youngest volcano, the extremely active and unpredictable Cerro Negro located in the Cerro Negro National Park in western Nicaragua. Once surfers reach the rim of the volcano's crater 2,388 feet above sea level, they then launch themselves back down the slopes of the volcano, which are made up of loose volcanic ash and rock. Participants can choose to either sit or stand as they surf back down, a descent of around 500 meters (1,640 feet) that has a slope of 41 degrees at its steepest. Interestingly, sitting surfers can reach speeds of up to 50 miles per hour, while a standing surfer can expect to reach a top speed of only around 10 miles per hour. Volcano boarding also takes place on the slopes of active Mount Yasur on the island nation of Vanuatu in the South Pacific Ocean.

Volcano boarding sees participants set out on a brief hike lasting about 45 minutes and of easy to moderate intensity up to the mountain's summit and then slide down the side of a volcano on a thin board made of plywood, metal, and formica and to which is attached a rope to aid steering. Typically a board weighs 5 to 10 pounds. Such is the stress placed on the board that it must be replaced every two weeks.

Volcano boarding differs from sand boarding, as the large size of the volcanic ash particles littering the volcanic slopes is such that sand-boarding maneuvers, such as carving, are not possible on the debris, as carving can only be performed on fine material. S-turns are also much more difficult to perform on ash than on snow or sand. The added difficulty of traveling over rocky volcanic ground makes volcano boarding an excellent workout for the legs, particularly the calf and thigh muscles.

However, like sand boarding, volcano boarding can be considered an extreme sport, as there is the ever-present danger of falling from the board and suffering cuts from the sharp volcanic gravel. Therefore, it is recommended that surfers wear protective clothing, including jumpsuits, knee pads, helmets, and goggles. The threat of a possible volcanic eruption adds an extra dimension of danger. Volcanoes such as Mount Yasur can emit multiple lava bombs, that is, masses of molten rock larger than 2.5 inches in diameter that cool into solid fragments of rock as they fly through the air. As volcano boarders head downhill once they are strapped to their board, it is impossible for them to dodge any bombs heading their way. In addition to lava, volcanoes are also liable to emit sudden bursts of sulfurous gas and thick smoke, which severely limit visibility.

See also: Bog Snorkeling World Championship; Cresta Run; Extreme Ironing; Heli-Skiing; Kitesurfing; Street Luge; Wingsuiting; Zorbing

Further Reading

Erfurt-Cooper, Patricia, and Malcolm Cooper, eds. *Volcano and Geothermal Tourism: Sustainable Geo-Resources for Leisure and Recreation.* London: Earthscan, 2010.

Fabricius, Karl. "Surfing on the Slopes of a Volcano." Environmental Graffiti, http://www.environmentalgraffiti.com/featured/volcano-surfing/11211 (accessed August 10, 2013)

Istvan, Zoltan. "Reporter's Notebook: Surfing the Volcano." National Geographic Today, November 5, 2002, http://news.nationalgeographic.co.uk/news/2002/11/1105_021105_TVVolcanoboarding.html (accessed August 10, 2013)

Sekula, Sarah. "The Seriously Hot Sport of Volcano Boarding." Fox News, June 27, 2013, http://www.foxnews.com/travel/2013/06/27/seriously-hot-sport-volcano-boarding/ (accessed August 10, 2013).

Siciliano-Rosen, Laura. "A Sport Erupts on a Live Volcano in Nicaragua." *New York Times,* April 16, 2009, http://travel.nytimes.com/2009/04/19/travel/19headsup.html?_r=0 (accessed August 10, 2013).

"Volcano Boarding: Adrenaline Junkies Think New Extreme Sport Is the Coolest Thing Going." MailOnline, May 8, 2009, http://www.dailymail.co.uk/news/article-1178850/Volcano-boarding-Adrenaline-junkies-think-new-extreme-sport-coolest-thing-going.html (accessed August 10, 2013).

W

WIFE CARRYING

Wife carrying is a minority endurance sport in which a male competitor carries a female teammate through an obstacle course in as fast a time possible. The man and woman do not have to be married to compete as a couple. The Finnish word for the sport is *eukonkanto,* which is translated politely as "wife-carrying race." However, a more precisely English translation is "old hag–carrying race." This combined with the sport's somewhat flippant preference for women competitors to be harmonious and gentle has been deemed politically incorrect by some. However, wife carrying is a fairly tongue-in-cheek sport.

Wife carrying is particularly associated with Sonkajarvi in Finland, where the sport originated. However, exactly how wife carrying evolved as a sport is unknown. It is thought that the sport may have developed from two aspects of Finnish history. First, 19th-century outlaw Ronkainen the Robber would set men who wished to join his band of brigands the challenge of completing an obstacle course while carrying a heavy load on their backs. Those who succeeded the initiation test were admitted to Ronkainen's criminal fraternity. Second, in earlier times, it was quite common for Finnish men to steal women from neighboring villages, carrying the women away and eventually marrying them.

The first wife-carrying competition was held in Finland in 1991, and foreign entrants were admitted to the competitions in 1995. The World Wife Carrying Championship has been held annually in Sonkajarvi since 1992. To qualify for the world championship, competitors must have won a wife-carrying competition in Finland or in Britain, Ireland, Australia, Estonia, Germany, or the United States. China (particularly Hong Kong) and India also hold wife-carrying competitions, but these do not count toward entry into the world championship. The sport remains a minority pastime, however—between 1992 and 2010 only 528 couples competed in the world championship.

The rules of competitive wife carrying state that the world championship obstacle course is 253.5 meters (832 feet) long and that competitors must overcome several obstacles including water, sand, forested terrain, and two hurdles made of logs. A further stipulation is that the woman teammate must not weigh less than 49 kilograms (108 pounds). If the woman does, however, weigh less than this, she is given a load to carry that will increase her weight to the required 49 kilograms. A scientific study has revealed that successful male competitors tend to engage in endurance and strength training to prepare for wife-carrying events, while women competitors are required to have great stamina.

Aleksander Pihlainen and Siiri Salli from Finland compete during the Wife Carrying World Championship in Sonkajarvi, Finland on July 6, 2013. Wife carrying is a fairly light-hearted endurance sport in which a male competitor carries a female teammate through an obstacle course in as fast a time possible. (AP Photo/Roni Rekomaa, Lehtikuva)

Over the years Estonians have proved to be the fastest wife carriers at the world championships. This may be because the Estonians have perfected the wife-carrying technique known as the Estonian Carry whereby the woman wraps her legs around the man's neck and shoulders and then hangs down the man's back, clasping her arms about his waist and with her face resting on his bottom. This is a particularly effective technique, as it keeps the man's arms free to enable him to run quickly. It is not, though, as comfortable for the woman, for when the couple negotiate a water trap the woman's head cannot avoid being forced underwater. Three other carrying techniques have also been employed at the championship, but these ways of carrying have not proved as successful for competitors or as amusing for spectators. For instance, instead of the Estonian Carry, a traditional piggyback position can be adopted by competitors, the man may throw the woman over his shoulder, or the woman can lay crosswise across the man's shoulders. Competitors may choose whichever carry they prefer, and they are also permitted to invent their own carrying position. Due to the nature of these positions, it is advisable for championship competitors to wear clothes that are easy to hold on to and that the man should wear a belt to give the woman something to grip. It is also a good idea for competitors to wear goggles in order to negotiate the water obstacles. Apart from the carry, another important factor in wife carrying is rhythm, for if the man and woman do not move in time together, they will record a slow time. Therefore, it is important for couples to practice moving and carrying before the event. The need for unison between the man and woman means that some wife-carrying experts believe it is beneficial for competing couples to be married, as this means it is more likely that they will intuitively understand what each other is going to do. The necessary interaction between man and woman in the event has led to the suggestion that wife carrying is an erotic activity, as man and woman find a mutual rhythm and move as one.

At the world championship, the winning couple is rewarded with a world title and the woman's weight in beer. This means that while it is advantageous in terms of speed for a man to carry a woman who does not weigh very much, as they will be able to traverse the course quickly, a light woman will result in a small amount of beer as a prize.

The first UK Wife Carrying Competition was held in 2008. The British National Championship race is particularly arduous, as it is run over 380 meters (1,247 feet), and with 15 meters (49 feet) of both ascent and descent. The North American Wife Carrying Championship was founded in 1999 at Sunday River Resort in Maine and is held at the resort annually in mid-October. Around 50 teams from around the United States and Canada navigate the obstacle course, which is 278 yards in length and made up of log hurdles, sand traps, and a water hazard known as the "Widow Maker." The winner of the North American title wins not only the woman's weight in beer but also five times the woman's weight in cash.

See also: Bandy; *Kyykkä; Lapta; Mölkky;* Nordic Walking; Synchronized Skating; Yoga

Further Reading

Ambers, Lou. "The Strange Sport of Wife Carrying." Bettor.com, http://blogs.bettor.com/The-Strange-Sport-of-Wife-Carrying-a15233 (accessed August 9, 2013).

Clarey. "Maine Couple Wins North American Wife Carrying Championship at Sunday River Ski Resort." The Ski Channel, October 9, 2010, http://www.theskichannel.com/news/20101009/maine-couple-wins-north-american-wife-carrying-championship-at-sunday-river-ski-resort/ (accessed August 9, 2013).

"How to Become a Master in Wife Carrying." Eukonkannon MM-kisat, http://www.eukonkanto.fi/en/How+to+Become+a+Master+in+Wife+Carrying.html (accessed August 9, 2013).

Lee, I-Min, Sylvia Titze, and Pekka Oja. "Wife Carrying for Health." Eukonkannon MM-kisat, December 2011, http://www.eukonkanto.fi/en/Wife+carrying+for+health.html (accessed August 12, 2013).

"North America Wife Carrying Championship." Sunday River, http://www.sundayriver.com/events-and-activities/events-calendar/north-american-wife-carrying-championship (accessed December 11, 2014).

WINGSUITING

Wingsuiting is an extreme sport that is popular in mountainous regions such as the European Alps as well as in New Zealand, Australia, and the United States. In wingsuiting, participants wear a special outfit called a wingsuit that features a

A wisBASE jumper wearing a wingsuit leaps from a high cliff in Norway. As soon as the jumper starts to fly, air rushes into the suit's inlets and the suit then stretches and acts as an airfoil allowing the jumper to fly down to the ground like a bird. (xof711/iStock-photo.com)

stretch of fabric linking the torso, arms, and legs that acts as a set of wings when the wingsuiter's arms are outstretched. This suit allows wingsuiters to jump from mountaintops and cliffs and then fly down to the ground in a bird-like manner—wingsuiters are also equipped with a single para-chute (but no reserve chute) that they use when they near the ground.

The first person to wear a winged suit to jump from a height was Austrian Franz Re-ichelt, who in 1912 donned a wingsuit to leap from the Eiffel Tower in Paris, the capital of France. Unfortunately, the jump resulted in Reichelt's death. Since then wingsuiting has only grown in popularity especially from the late 1990s onward, as technical innovations have allowed safer wingsuits to be made commer-cially available. Today's wingsuits allow jumpers to travel at speeds of up to 226 miles per hour. This is significantly faster than a typical skydiver's terminal velocity of between 110 and 140 miles per hour.

The design of the suit means that it is not vital that participants possess great physical strength, for as soon as a wingsuiter starts to fly, air rushes into the suit's inlets and the suit then stretches and acts as an airfoil, that is, a curved structure that provides the best possible ratio of lift to drag in flight. Indeed, recent develop-ments in wingsuit technology mean that suits can now allow wingsuiters to jump from lower peaks, as the latest wingsuits mean that for every meter (about 3 feet) a wingsuiter drops, he or she can fly horizontally for 3 to 4 meters (roughly 10 to 13 feet). Since physical strength is not a prerequisite to participating in wingsuit-ing, several of the top world's wingsuiters are women.

Wingsuiting enthusiasts have achieved several notable feats. For instance, Aus-trian adventurer Felix Baumgartner (the first skydiver to travel faster than the speed of sound, reaching a maximum velocity of 833.9 miles per hour) wingsuited from a height of 30,000 feet to cross the 22-mile-wide English Channel in July 2003. Baumgartner reached speeds of 220 miles per hour and made the crossing in just 14 minutes wearing a specially adapted wingsuit that featured a 6-foot carbon fin strapped at the back as well as an oxygen tank from which to breathe. However, wingsuiting hit the headlines for unfortunate reasons in August 2013 when Mark Sutton, the stuntman famed for impersonating James Bond as he parachuted into the Olympic Stadium from a helicopter during the opening ceremony of the 2012 London Olympics, died while wingsuiting from a helicopter 11,000 feet above the Grandes Otanes area of Switzerland, close to the French border. Sutton was traveling at about 125 miles per hour when he hit a ridge, causing injuries so severe that his body could only be identified by DNA testing.

A spin-off of wingsuiting is WisBASE jumping, also known as proximity flying, that began in 1999 and is a combination of wingsuiting and BASE jumping. BASE jumping refers to the sport of jumping from high places—BASE stands for building, antenna, span and earth, the four fixed structures from which a base jumper, wearing a parachute to break the fall, can jump. To begin with, WisBASE jumping was confined to a few very experienced jumpers. However, advances in wingsuit design and the materials from which the suits are made resulted in the suits being cheaper and more available for purchase. This in turn led to an uptake in WisBASE jumping, particularly among skydivers, and very soon there was an increase in mortality rates. The first WisBASE death occurred in 2002. Since 2008, there has been a 75 percent increase in WisBASE fatalities, mainly caused by jumpers misjudging their proximity to the ground or flying too close to rocks and cliffs.

BASE jumping is an extremely risky sport that is forbidden in many countries. In Switzerland BASE jumping is loosely regulated by the Swiss Federal Aviation Office and the Swiss Base Association. BASE jumpers in Switzerland are meant to possess a skydiving license and are advised to have completed at least 200 skydives before attempting to BASE jump. However, it has been claimed that the unparalleled visual experience offered by wingsuiting, BASE jumping, and WisBASE jumping as fliers travel within a few feet of cliffs, trees, and other landscape features means that some jumpers are allowing their enthusiasm to override their lack of experience, resulting in several deaths. Switzerland's Lauterbrunnen Valley is a hotspot of BASE jumping because of its vertical cliff walls that rise 2,300 feet from the valley floor. However, the valley has been dubbed "death valley" by the Swiss media after a number of deaths in the area caused by jumpers crashing into the sheer cliffs. Indeed, in April 2014 four deaths occurred in Lauterbrunnen Valley in a single week.

WisBASE jumping became particularly popular in 2011, the year that wingsuiting was featured in the hit film *Transformers: Dark of the Moon*. The wingsuiting scenes for the film saw wingsuiters jump from the 110-floor Willis Tower in Chicago.

See also: Heli-Skiing; Kitesurfing; Swimming the English Channel; Volcano Boarding; Zorbing

Further Reading

Ellsworth-Jones, Will. "She Swoops to Conquer." *Telegraph Magazine,* May 3, 2014.
Foulkes, Imogen. "The Girls Base Jumping Off Cliffs in the Swiss Alps." BBC News Europe, June 22, 2014, http://www.bbc.co.uk/news/world-europe-27785731 (accessed August 4, 2014).

Gallager, Paul. "Focus Turns to 'Wingsuiting' after Death of Olympic Stuntman Mark Sut-
    ton." The Independent, August 15, 2013, http://www.independent.co.uk/news/uk
    /home-news/focus-turns-to-wingsuiting-after-death-of-olympic-stuntman-mark
    -sutton-8763916.html (accessed August 4, 2014).
Mei-Dan, Omer, and Mike Carmont, eds. *Adventure and Extreme Sports Injuries: Epidemiol-
    ogy, Treatment, Rehabilitation and Prevention.* London: Springer-Verlag, 2013.
Metz, Nina. "'Transformers' Jumpers Up in Birdland." *Chicago Tribune,* June 29, 2011, http://
    articles.chicagotribune.com/2011-06-29/entertainment/ct-ent-0630-transformers
    -jumpers-20110629_1_willis-tower-office-buildings-jump (accessed August 4, 2014).
"Skydiver in Record Channel flight." BBC, July 31, 2003, http://news.bbc.co.uk/1/hi
    /uk/3112095.stm (accessed August 4, 2014).

YABBIE RACES

Yabbie, or yabby, is the Australian word for a small blue or brown freshwater crustacean resembling a crayfish. Yabbie races are events held in Australia to see which of a select group of yabbies is the quickest to run the distance of a purpose-built dry, indoor course. The races are fairly lighthearted events that aim to raise funds for local causes.

Yabbie races are occasionally held as part of school fetes in Australia, as they are very simple to set up. All that is needed are yabbies bought from a yabbie farm and then auctioned off to people attending the race. The yabbies are marked with a dot of white liquid paper and a numbered sticker and then placed in a box in the center of a flat piece of paper on which are drawn concentric rings. These circles mark the distance traveled by the yabbies, and the first yabbie to cross the outermost line is declared the winner. The outermost circle is usually 39 inches from the starting point. In hot weather, yabbies enjoy being squirted with water from a water pistol while racing.

The most famous yabbie races take place annually in the state of Queensland, particularly in the towns of Windorah and Moonie. The Windorah Yabbie Races began in September in the late 1990s as a way to attract tourists to the Birdsville Races (for horses). Local people caught the yabbies, and the first yabbie race meeting was extremely successful, raising AUS$6,000 that was split between prize money and local causes. Today the Windorah International Yabbie Races, as the event is now called, draws crowds in excess of 1,000 and is a major attraction for tourists journeying through Australia's Outback. The races close off the town center, for the yabbies are now raced down Windorah's main street. Bidding for yabbies begins at AUS$1,000 cash apiece, and the much-coveted Cooper Creek Cup is awarded to the person with the winning yabbie.

The Moonie Yabbie Races began in 2007 and are held in November, with around 400 people attending each year. When the Moonie races first started the yabbies were caught by local people, but nowadays they are purpose bred and cared for by seasoned yabbie handlers. The handlers are entrusted with keeping the crustaceans healthy and preventing any possible doping.

On the day of the races, the attendees form syndicates in order to win yabbies at the prerace yabbie auction. The yabbies are displayed before those bidding and their speed is noted, and syndicates bid for each individual yabbie. Bids for a quick swimming yabbie can reach as much as AUS$400 in cash. Once all the yabbies have been won at the auction, they then race in one of six race heats, with eight yabbies racing in each heat. To start the race, the yabbies are placed inside little wooden boxes at the top of the race course, which is usually a wooden rectangular structure divided into eight numbered straight lanes by high wooden sides. The course slopes downward to the finish line.

As a prize, the syndicates that own the yabbies in first, second, and third place share the total money raised by the yabbie auction. Once the heats have been completed, all the yabbies that won their heats are entered into the day's main race, the Moonie Cup. A second auction takes place in which all the yabbies entered into the Moonie Cup are again up for sale. The Moonie Cup race then takes place, with the winner basking in the kudos of becoming champion yabbie. The most celebrated yabbie ever at the Moonie races was called Blair Aplet and holds the record for completing the course in the fastest time. Blair Ablet was so quick that it won its race by four clear yabbie lengths, the official unit of measurement for yabbie races.

New yabbie race meets are inaugurated each year, with one of the newest races being the International Charity Yabby Race held on Easter Saturday at the Royal Shawsy Yabby Racing Club in Ballina, New South Wales. This race was first held in 2012, and after the event the yabbies are returned to their natural environment, as is the case with most yabbie races.

See also: Aussie Rules Football; Bearbaiting and Badger Baiting; Bull Running; *Buzkashi;* Camel and Yak Racing; Camel Wrestling; Cockfighting; Elephant Sports; Foxhunting; Hare Coursing; Nonlethal Bullfighting; *Pato* and Horseball; Pigeon Racing; Sheepdog Trials; Spanish Bullfighting

Further Reading

Keane, Lyndon. "Outback Punters Shell Out at Famous Yabbie Races." The Moonie Yabbie Races, 2012, http://www.moonieyabbieraces.com.au (accessed August 5, 2013).

McCormack, Robert B. "Keeping Pet Yabbies." http://www.rbmaqua.com.au/documents /KEEPINGPETYABBIES_000.pdf (accessed August 5, 2013).

Northern Star Ltd. "Yabbies Set to Race." Ballina Shire Advocate, March 23, 2013, http:// www.ballinaadvocate.com.au/news/yabbies-set-to-race/1797770/ (accessed August 5, 2013).

Price, Ethan "The Running of the Yabbies." The Horizon Sun, April 10, 2013, http://thehori zonsun.com/features-extras/2013/04/10/the-running-of-the-yabbies/ (accessed August 5, 2013).

Seinor, Blythe. "Windorah International Yabbie Races: The Color and the Catch." Australian Broadcasting Commission, August 31, 2012, http://www.abc.net.au/local/stories /2012/08/31/3579912.htm (accessed August 5, 2013).

YAGLI GURES

Yagli gures, also known as oil wrestling and grease wrestling, is an outdoor form of folk wrestling in which only men and boys compete. *Yagli gures* is the national sport of Turkey and is prevalent throughout the country, especially in the cities of Ankara, Antalya, and Karamursel. *Yagli gures* also takes place in those areas of the world in which Turkish migrants have settled and is becoming particularly popular in the Netherlands and Japan.

Yagli gures is very similar to the Persian form of wrestling called *kushti* and is thought to have developed simultaneously in ancient Egypt and Assyria around 2650 BCE. The first *yagli gures* tournament in Turkey is said to have taken place during the Persian era of Turkey's history, which began in 1065 BCE, when legend tells that the great *yagli gures* wrestler Rostam defended his people from the forces of evil.

Before a fight the wrestlers, known as *pehlivans*, are assessed on the basis of experience, talent, and weight and placed in 1 of 15 divisions. The wrestlers then cover each other in olive oil, probably because the oil helps to prevent friction burns caused by the wrestlers' skin rubbing on the grass playing surface. Next an important prebout ritual, the killing of an animal according to the Halal way, takes place accompanied by prayers to

Wrestlers compete in a bout of *yagli gures*, the national sport of Turkey. Wrestlers are covered in olive oil, as this helps to stop friction burns caused by the wrestlers' skin rubbing on the grass playing surface. (iStockphoto.com)

Allah, with the wrestlers standing in a line facing toward Mecca. After these rites the wrestlers face each other and, with a referee looking on, begin their bouts. As the *pehlivans* do not wear shirts or shoes, just black leather trousers known as *kispet,* the oil on the wrestlers' skin makes it very difficult for opponents to grip each other. The aim of *yagli gures* is for a wrestler to force his opponent into a position that exposes his belly button to the sky, for once a wrestler assumes this position he has lost. In order to achieve victory, a wrestler perform both holds and throws usually by either grasping the belt on his opponent's trousers or forcing his hand inside the opponent's trousers in order to gain leverage and affect his breathing. Wrestlers also try to keep an opponent's nose pressed into the grass, as this too limits the opponent's breathing.

In 2010 a points system was introduced to *yagli gures*. Before 1975, a bout would continue until either one of the wrestlers lost or conceded or the referee halted the match to protect a wrestler's health. This lack of a time limit resulted in extremely long bouts that sometimes lasted for two days. Today wrestlers have either 40 or 30 minutes to achieve victory depending on the division to which they belong. After that, extra time lasting 10 or 7 minutes is played. If no points are scored during this time, then the golden point rule is employed whereby the next wrestler to score a point wins the fight.

The most famous and important *yagli gures* tournament takes place on Kirkpinar Island in the city of Edirne at the end of June through the beginning of July each year. It is thought that the first *yagli gures* tournament was held in Kirkpinar in 1640, and the tournament claims to be the world's longest-running continuous athletic event.

See also: Celtic Wrestling; *Glima;* Korean Wrestling; *Lucha Libre;* Mongolian Wrestling; *Pehlwani/Kushti; Schwingen;* Sumo Wrestling; *Varzesh-e Bastani*

Further Reading

Connolly, Paul. *The World's Weirdest Sports.* Millers Point, Australia: Pier 9, 2007.

El-Fers, Mohamed. "History of Oil Wrestling." Kirkpinar News, http://www.kirkpinar.nl /oil05.htm (accessed December 31, 2013).

Foley, T. R. "Oil Wars—The Misunderstood World of Turkish Oil Wrestling." *Fight! Magazine,* August 2013, http://www.fightmagazine.com/mma-magazine/oil-wars-the-misun derstood-world-of-turkish-oil-wrestling-7467/ (accessed December 11, 2014).

Green, Thomas A. *Martial Arts of the World: An Encyclopedia,* Vol. 1, A–L. Santa Barbara, CA: ABC-CLIO, 2001.

Levine, Emma. *A Game of Polo with a Headless Goat and Other Bizarre Sports Discovered across Asia.* London: Andre Deutsch, 2003.

Sansal, Burak. "Turkish Oil Wrestling." All about Turkey, http://www.allaboutturkey.com /yagligures.htm (accessed December 31, 2013).

YOGA

Yoga is the umbrella term for a system of physical, mental, and philosophical practices originating in ancient India around 5,000 years ago and practiced in many different styles all over the world. The name "yoga" comes from the ancient Indian Sanskrit language, and while there is no one single accepted translation of the name, the word "yoga" is most commonly translated as meaning "union." However, the name derives from the root word *yuj,* which can be translated as meaning "to yoke, join, or concentrate or to put to active and purposeful use or as well formed, refined, perfect, and polished." Yoga is often associated with the Indian religion of Hinduism. Indeed, Hare Krishnas, that is, members of the Hindu religious organization the International Society for Krishna Consciousness, practice bhakti yoga, also known as the yoga of devotion. Elements of Hinduism are also evident in key yoga moves such as the *Surya namaskar,* more commonly called sun salutations or salute to the sun, a series of linked positions designed to greet Surya, the Hindu god of the sun. However, yoga forms an element of all the main religions originating in South Asia such as Sikhism, Buddhism, and Jainism, not just Hinduism; and yoga has in general been adopted by those of other faiths. For instance, yoga is extremely popular in Iran, where yoga has been stripped of any overt religious references and flourishes in a country with an Islamist political system. In Iran, yoga is referred to as the "sport of yoga" and is accredited to a yoga federation in the same way as other sports in the country, such as tennis and soccer, are accredited to federations. Similarly, in Kuala Lumpur, capital of Malaysia where Islam is the state religion, yoga is permitted as a physical activity once stripped of all overt religious references. Yoga is also permitted as a form of exercise without religious connotations in Indonesia, the world's most populous Islamic nation.

Despite the general acceptance that yoga is a form of exercise that can exist alongside various religious beliefs, it still encounters resistance from some sections of religious communities. For instance, in the United States yoga has been denounced by a Christian group called the National Center for Law & Policy, which claims that yoga instills religion through repetitive movement. The antiyoga sentiment felt by some American Christians has led to the creation of alternative exercise systems such as PraiseMoves, which combines stretching exercises with Christian worship, with practitioners reciting passages from the Bible as they assume poses.

An instructor adjusts a student performing a pose during a yoga class. Yoga poses aim to strengthen and stretch the body as well as ease chronic pain, lower blood pressure, improve core stability, and create a general sense of well-being. (Hongqi Zhang/Dreamstime.com)

Yoga is practiced by men (known as yogis), women (known as yoginis), children, and even some animals, especially dogs. Yoga is often taught in gyms and fitness centers, but practitioners can perform yoga anywhere once they have learned the correct techniques. Those who practice yoga believe that it creates strength, awareness, and harmony within the mind and body, as in general yoga comprises breathing exercises known as pranayamas, stretching, meditation, and strengthening postures known as asanas (from the Sanskrit word meaning "seat"), which are practiced barefoot, usually on a nonslip mat. The physical benefits linked to yoga include easing chronic pain, lowering blood pressure, increasing flexibility and core stability, improving posture, easing respiration, and improving energy levels and a general sense of well-being. However, people suffering from medical conditions such as joint hypermobility syndrome, for example, may find that yoga-type stretching aggravates their condition by increasing their flexibility, while certain yoga poses are not recommended for those suffering from high blood pressure.

Yoga lacks the clear historical development of other activities, and it is thought that many manuscripts dealing with yoga may have been lost over time. Some historians believe that there are references to yoga in the artwork of the Indus Valley civilization (ca. 3000 BCE), which seems to depict figures performing yogic meditation, while others feel that yoga originated from sacred Indian texts called the Vedas, which were written around 1900 BCE and from which came the religions of Hinduism, Jainism, and Buddhism.

However, it is widely thought that yoga emerged from the oral tradition of a teacher directly transmitting knowledge of the exercise system to a student, and in the second century the Indian sage Pantanjali collated the oral teaching of yoga into a written form known as the Yoga Sutra, which outlined the eight essential limbs, or elements, of yoga: the yamas (meaning restraints), the niyamas (observances), the pratyahara (withdrawal of the senses), dharana (concentration), the dhyani (meditation), and samadhi (absorption) as well as the pranayamas and asanas, with samadhi being the ultimate stage of enlightenment and liberation. Pantanjali presented yoga as a system in which every individual is divided into two parts—prakiti, or matter, and purisha, or soul—in which individuals aim to free the soul from the material world so that it may revert to its original form.

Antigravity Yoga

Antigravity or aerial yoga, a combination of aerial circus skills and vinyasa yoga with moves taken from Pilates, dance, and calisthenics, sees practitioners suspended several inches from the ground via a silk hammock hung from the ceiling. This allows participants to perform seemingly impossible yoga postures that are reputed to create a weightless body alignment, strengthening muscles and releasing pressure from compressed joints. Classes, which are taught in the United States and Europe, also use soft trapezes as props to create even deeper stretches. This form of yoga is favored by many celebrities, including actress Gwyneth Paltrow.

The style of yoga taught by Pantanjali is often referred to as classical yoga. Postclassical yoga, which is taught today, is not dualistic in nature and does not strive to remove the individual from the material world. Rather, its overriding philosophy is that the individual must live in the present reality. Postclassical yoga also looks at the body as an area of study, which is in contrast to classical yoga, which focused on the soul and so paid little attention to the physical body. During the 1960s the hippie movement in Europe and the United States embraced yoga along with other elements of Indian culture and mysticism, and gradually yoga was absorbed into mainstream Western culture, with a proliferation of printed media on the subject as well as television shows such as Richard Hittleman's *Yoga for Health,* first broadcast in 1961, that encouraged viewers to perform yoga at home in order to improve their posture. The 1970s and 1980s saw yoga firmly established in the West, with the establishment of yoga-specific institutions and centers that chimed with the onset of the New Age movement, which sought enlightenment and saw in yoga a manifestation of the movement's esoteric philosophies linking mind, body, and soul. By the 1990s yoga was fully assimilated in Western culture. This assimilation led to yoga becoming important commercially, with increasing amounts of yoga merchandise on sale including yoga-specific clothing, equipment, and instructional magazines, books, videos, and DVDs. Yoga also became a popular class at most gyms. The expansion of yoga as an industry paralleled the further codification of yoga, with spin-off forms of yoga appearing such as power yoga (an offshoot of the Ashtanga Vinyasa style of yoga). In the West the most commonly practiced form of yoga is hatha yoga, which corresponds to the third limb of yoga as set out by Pantanjali (i.e., the asanas), for hatha yoga is a system of physical postures designed to provide the physical strength and stamina necessary to perform lengthy spells of meditation with the aim of purifying the physical body. The poses found in hatha yoga aim to both strengthen and stretch the body, and this dual nature is reflected in the name "hatha," which derives from the Sanskrit words *ha,* meaning "sun," and *tha,* meaning "moon." The combination of *ha* and *tha* in the name "hatha" refers to the concept of balancing opposites that lies at the heart of hatha yoga, for the sun is seen as active and hot and therefore masculine, while the moon represents stability, coolness, and femininity. Thus, in hatha yoga opposites are united. The poses performed in hatha yoga are designed to align the bones, muscles, and skin while also freeing the spine, which practitioners of hatha yoga see as the body's main channel for energy. Hatha yoga poses can be divided into eight categories: seated and twisted, standing, arm balances, core, backbends, forward bends, inversions, and restorative poses intended to aid relaxation. Many hatha yoga poses are named after animals and include what are perhaps the most familiar poses in yoga, such as the downward-facing dog, the eagle pose, the crane pose, and the cobra pose. Poses are also named after the cow, the animal regarded as the most sacred by Hindus, including the cow face pose in which the participant sits with knees crossed one above the other and with hands clasped behind the back, with one elbow angled down and the other up in order to mimic the lips and ears of the cow. Other familiar hatha yoga poses include the handstand; the headstand; the bridge position, in which the performer lies on her or his back and lifts the hips while keeping the feet on the floor; and the backbend, called the wheel pose; and the lotus position. Some consider the lotus position to be the ultimate yoga position, as it usually requires consistent practice to be able to open the hips sufficiently in order to attain the full seated, cross-legged pose. Some hatha yoga positions also appear in other exercise systems. For instance, the boat pose, in which the individual balances on her or his sitting bones and tailbone while recruiting the abdominal and hip flexors to keep the feet raised to head height, is common to both yoga and Pilates, a fitness system that like yoga builds muscle strength and flexibility. Breathing exercises are also important in hatha yoga, as it is felt that using the breath in specific ways can help participants better achieve postures. A hatha yoga session usually ends with the reciting of a mantra, or sacred chant, consisting of the om sound. Om is the root mantra from which all other mantras derive, and many yoga practitioners believe that the om chant is a transcendental sound through which the soul is revealed and that both boosts energy and soothes. Hatha yoga practitioners often perform the om chant with an accompanying mudra, a hand position intended to produce a specific state of mind. There are many different mudras, each relating to a different quality, such as compassion or courage, and it is believed that practicing certain mudras can awaken such qualities with the individual and are a physical manifestation of an enlightened inner being.

Other popular styles of yoga include Iyengar, ashtanga, and bikram yoga. Iyengar yoga, which is named after its developer B. K. S. Iyengar and claims to be the most practiced form of yoga in the world, focuses on the need for precision and alignment when performing postures, and practitioners often use props such as fabric belts and foam blocks to achieve postures that are then held. Ashtanga yoga, literally meaning "eight-limbed yoga," follows the eight limbs of yoga outlined by Pantanjali in order to find the path of internal purification and involves a progressive series of poses accompanied by synchronized breathing. Bikram yoga, also known as hot yoga, was invented in Calcutta, India, in 1946 and is a series of 26 hatha yoga poses performed in a room heated to 43°C, or 109°F. It is believed that such excessive heat encourages the body's muscles to stretch more than they would when performing yoga at room temperature, thus improving the biodynamics of the body through encouraging the joints to open and balancing muscular alignment. It is also felt that the heat aids the body to detoxify, as it causes sweating. Bikram yoga is particularly popular with athletes, as practitioners believe that this form of yoga protects against injury.

Though yoga is usually thought of as a noncompetitive practice, there is a growing trend toward competitive yoga, with competitions taking place worldwide. Indeed, an international championship called the Bishnu Charan Ghosh Cup is held in Los Angeles every February. There is even a campaign for yoga to become an Olympic sport in time for the 2020 Olympic Games. While some may argue that competition is the antithesis of the yogic philosophies of spiritual and physical well-being attained through the journey of the individual, proponents of competitive yoga argue that yoga can be viewed as a competitive sport, pointing to the fact that yoga championships have been held in India for centuries. In these championships yogis performed extreme yoga poses and were awarded points for how well they executed their chosen asana. In modern yoga contests, competitors are scored on the quality of execution as they perform a three-minute routine comprising five compulsory asanas plus two optional poses. Competitors are awarded points for flexibility, strength, alignment, difficulty of chosen poses, execution, and overall demeanor.

See also: Capoeira; *Kabaddi; Mallakhamb; Parkour;* Rhythmic Gymnastics

Further Reading

"Ashtanga Yoga Background." Ashtanga Yoga, https://www.ashtanga.com/html/background .html (accessed February 23, 2014).

"The Benefits of Yoga." American Osteopathic Association, http://www.osteopathic.org/ osteopathic-health/about-your-health/health-conditions-library/general-health/Pages /yoga.aspx (accessed February 23, 2014).

Carrico, Mara. "The Roots of Yoga: A Beginner's Guide to the History of Yoga." *Yoga Journal,* August 28, 2007, http://www.yogajournal.com/basics/160 (accessed February 23, 2014).

Christensen, Alice. *The American Yoga Association's Beginners Manual: Fully Revised and Updated.* New York: Fireside, 2002.

Crangle, Edward Fitzpatrick. *Studies in Oriental Religions 29: The Origin and Development of Early Indian Contemplative Practices.* Wiesbaden: Harrassowitz, 1994.

Dhyansky, Yan Y. "The Indus Valley Origin of Yoga Practice." *Artibus Asiae* 48(1–2) (1987): 89–108.

"The History of Yoga." Yogi Nirmalendu, http://www.yoginirmalendu.com/History_of _yoga/History_Of_Yoga.html (accessed February 23, 2014).

"The History of Yoga." Zeenews India, January 27, 2011, http://zeenews.india.com/ayur veda/history-of-yoga_104.html (accessed February 23, 2014).

Jacobsen, Knut A., ed. *Theory and Practice of Yoga: Essays in Honour of Gerald James Larson.* Leiden, UK: Koninklijke Brill NV, 2005.

Kremer, William. "Does Doing Yoga Make You a Hindu?" BBC News Magazine, November 21, 2013, http://www.bbc.co.uk/news/magazine-25006926 (accessed March 1, 2014).

Lee, Cyndi. "Yoga Questions Answered." *Yoga Journal,* October 7, 2014, http://www .yogajournal.com/basics/820 (accessed December 11, 2014).

McGonigal, Kelly. "From Hand to Heart." *Yoga Journal,* August 1, 2008, http://www .yogajournal.com/practice/2668 (accessed February 23, 2014).

Rand, Hannah. "Downward-Facing Dogs for Upwardly Mobile Pets: How 'Doga' (That's Yoga for Your Pooch) Became a Hot New York Trend." MailOnline, January 11, 2012, http://www.dailymail.co.uk/femail/article-2084895/Doga-Yoga-dogs-hot-New-York -trend-upwardly-mobile-pets.html (accessed February 23, 2014).

Singleton, Mark. *Yoga Body: The Origins of Modern Posture Practice.* Oxford: Oxford University Press, 2010.

Stephens, Anastasia. "What HOT Yoga Can Do for You." MailOnline, September 27, 2008, http://www.dailymail.co.uk/health/article-1063237/What-HOT-yoga-you.html (accessed February 23, 2014).

Whitworth, Melissa. "Are You Cool Enough for Competitive Yoga." *The Telegraph,* June 7, 2012, http://www.telegraph.co.uk/health/wellbeing/7803435/Are-you-cool-enough-for -competitive-yoga.html (accessed February 23, 2014).

ZORBING

Zorbing, also known as globe-riding, orbing, and sphering, is a recreational activity in which participants roll around while encased in an inflatable orb made of a double layer of clear plastic. The sphere is equipped with a fully locking door to ensure that riders stay safely inside the orb as they roll. Orbs can either be harnessed or nonharnessed and can hold up to three riders, allowing them to roll simultaneously. Zorbing can take place on a range of surfaces including grass, snow, water, and indoor ski slopes and in wind tunnels. Competitive zorbing sees participants of both sexes vie to reach the fastest time for rolling along a specific route without deviating from a marked downhill course. In competitive water zorbing, competitors race the length of a swimming pool. Zorbing is most commonly associated with Rotorua in New Zealand, but the activity also takes place at multiple locations in North America, the United Kingdom and the rest of Europe, Asia, and Australia.

Zorbing is generally thought to have been invented in 1994 in Auckland, New Zealand, by Andrew Akers and Dwane van der Sluis, who had intended to use the inflatable ball to walk on water until they realized that it was more fun to use the sphere, which they called a zorb, on land. The two inventors found that financial investors were interested in the new activity, which eventually became commercialized with a worldwide franchise system put in place. It has, however, also been claimed that in the 1980s the originators of the modern bungee jump, the Dangerous Sports Club of Oxford, England, created a plastic ball 23 meters (75 feet) in diameter with two deck chairs fixed inside. This would predate the New Zealand invention of the zorb.

Most of the spheres used in zorbing are 8 to 10 feet in diameter, though the OGO (Outdoor Gravity Orb) brand of orb is larger (11 feet in diameter) and made up of 300 square feet of plastic.

There are several different types of zorbing. For instance, in hydro zorbing the inner surface of the sphere is slick with water so that riders slide side to side, backward and forward, while the sphere revolves around them. Air zorbing sees three riders placed inside a zorb eight feet in diameter that is then launched into a vertical wind tunnel with wind speeds reaching up to 150 miles per hour. In air zorbing, participants feel a similar downhill motion to that of plain zorbing as they twist, spin, and bounce around but with the added thrill of flight. Due to the turbulent nature of air zorbing, it is highly recommended that riders do not eat before they zorb. As with all extreme activities, an element of danger exists with zorbing. In January 2013, zorbing made worldwide news headlines when a zorb careered

A person rolls downhill inside a Zorb ball. Zorbing participants roll around while encased inside the inflatable orb. The sphere is equipped with a locking door to ensure that riders do not fall out of the orb as they roll. (Macsnap/iStockphoto.com)

off an unfenced snow slope in Russia, killing a man.

Since zorbing appeared during the closing ceremony of the 2010 Winter Olympics held in Vancouver, Canada, an image of a zorbing sphere has been chosen as the official symbol of the 2014 Winter Olympics to be held in Sochi, Russia.

See also: Street Luge; Volcano Boarding

Further Reading

McNeely, Scott. *Ultimate Book of Sports: The Essential Collection of Rules, Stats and Trivia for over 250 Sports.* San Francisco: Chronicle Books, 2012.

Shipside, Steve. *Extreme Sports: Brilliant Ideas for Taking Yourself to the Limit.* Oxford, UK: Infinite Ideas, 2012.

"Spheratoon." Noname Sport, http://www.nonamesport.net/ paintball_madrid/ingles_spher atoon_paintball_madrid.htm (accessed August 10, 2013).

"'Zorbing' Survivor Speaks of 'Fear' in Friend's Eyes before Death." *The Telegraph*, February 1, 2013, http://www.telegraph.co.uk/news/worldnews/europe/russia/9841403/Zorbing-survi vor-speaks-of-fear-in-friends-eyes-before-death.html (accessed August 10, 2013).

Selected Bibliography

Print Resources

Alswang, Joel. *The South African Dictionary of Sport.* Claremont, South Africa: Spearhead, 2003.

Alter, Michael J. *Science of Flexibility.* Champaign, IL: Human Kinetics, 2004.

Atkinson, Michael, and Kevin Young. *Deviance and Social Control in Sport.* Champaign, IL: Human Kinetics, 2008.

Baker, Steve. *Picturing the Beast: Animals, Identity, and Representation.* Champaign: University of Illinois Press, 1993.

Bartlett, Roger, Chris Gratton, and Christer G. Rolf. *Encyclopedia of International Sports Studies.* Abingdon, UK: Routledge, 2010.

Bekoff, Marc, and Carron A. Meaney, eds. *Encyclopedia of Animal Rights and Animal Welfare.* Abingdon, UK: Routledge, 1998.

Bingham, Jane. *The Cotswolds: A Cultural History.* New York: Oxford University Press, 2009.

Birley, Derek. *Sport and the Making of Britain.* Manchester, UK: Manchester University Press, 1993.

Blainey, Geoffrey. *A Game of Our Own: The Origins of Australian Football.* Melbourne: Black, 2003.

Blanchard, Kendall. *The Anthropology of Sport: An Introduction.* Revised ed. Westport, CT: Bergin and Garvey, 1995.

Block, David. *Baseball before We Knew It: A Search for the Roots of the Game.* Lincoln: University of Nebraska Press, 2005.

Bradley, Lloyd. *The Rough Guide to Cult Sport.* London: Rough Guides, 2011.

Bridle, Bob, and Richard Gilbert, eds. *The Sports Book.* 3rd ed. London: Dorling Kindersley, 2011.

Bronner, Simon. *Killing Tradition: Inside Hunting and Animal Rights Controversies.* Lexington: University Press of Kentucky, 2008.

Bushell, Mike. *Bushell's Best Bits: Everything You Needed to Know about the World's Craziest Sports.* London: John Blake, 2013.

Collins, Tony, John Martin, and Wray Vamplew, eds. *Encyclopedia of Traditional British Rural Sports.* Abingdon, UK: Routledge, 2005.

Connolly, Paul. *The World's Weirdest Sports.* Millers Point, Australia: Pier 9, 2007.

Craig, Steve. *Sports and Games of the Ancients.* Westport, CT: Greenwood, 2002.

Crego, Robert. *Sports and Games of the 18th and 19th Centuries.* Westport, CT: Greenwood, 2003.

Cumberpatch, Fiona. "Sliding Stones." *LandScape Magazine,* January/February 2014, 80–85.

Daeschner, J. R. *True Brits.* London: Arrow Books, 2004.

Davies, Huw. *The Games Book: How to Play the Games of Yesterday.* London: Michael O'Mara Books, 2008.

Delaney, Tim, and Tim Madigan. *The Sociology of Sports: An Introduction.* Jefferson, NC: McFarland, 2009.

del Valle, Teresa. *Korrika: Basque Ritual for Ethnic Identity.* Reno: University of Nevada Press, 1994.

Dils, Ann, and Ann Cooper Albright, eds. *Moving History/Dancing Cultures: A Dance History Reader.* Middletown, CT: Wesleyan University Press, 2001.

Donaldson, Emily Ann. *The Scottish Highland Games in America.* Gretna, LA: Pelican, 1986.

Dosil, Joaquin. *Eating Disorders in Athletes.* Chichester, UK: Wiley, 2008.

Dundes, Alan, ed. *The Cockfight: A Casebook.* Madison: University of Wisconsin Press, 1994.

Dunning, Eric. *Sport Matters: Sociological Studies of Sport, Violence and Civilization.* London: Routledge, 1999.

Dunning, Eric, and Dominic Malcolm, eds. *Sport: Critical Concepts in Sociology.* London: Routledge, 2003.

Essien, Aniefre. *Capoeira beyond Brazil: From a Slave Tradition to an International Way of Life.* Berkeley, CA: Blue Snake Books, 2008.

Federation of Gouren of the FALSAB. *Gouren: Breton and Celtic Wrestling.* Brittany, France: Fédération de Gouren et Institut Culturel de Bretagne, 1985.

Fox, John. *The Ball: Discovering the Object of the Game.* 1st ed. New York: HarperCollins EBooks, May 2012.

Furst, R. Terry. *Early Professional Baseball and the Sporting Press: Shaping the Image of the Game.* Jefferson, NC: McFarland, 2014.

Galvan, Javier A., ed. *They Do What? A Cultural Encyclopedia of Extraordinary and Exotic Customs from around the World.* Santa Barbara, CA: ABC-CLIO, 2014.

Gillmeister, Heiner. *Tennis: A Cultural History.* London: Leicester University Press, 1997.

Goodale, Greg, and Jason Edward Black, eds. *Arguments about Animal Ethics.* Lanham, MD: Lexington Books, 2010.

Green, Thomas A., and Joseph R. Svinth. *Martial Arts of the World: An Encyclopedia of History and Innovation,* Vol. 2. Santa Barbara, CA: ABC-CLIO, 2010.

Griffin, Emma. *Blood Sport: Hunting in Britain since 1066.* New Haven, CT: Yale University Press, 2007.

Grover, Kathryn ed. *Hard at Play: Leisure in America, 1840–1940.* Rochester, NY: Strong Museum, 1992.

Hargreaves, Jennifer, and Eric Anderson, eds. *Routledge Handbook of Sport, Gender and Sexuality.* Abingdon, UK: Routledge, 2014.

Herrera-Sobek, María, ed. *Celebrating Latino Folklore: An Encyclopedia of Cultural Traditions,* Vol. 1. Santa Barbara, CA: ABC-CLIO, 2012.

Hines, James R. *Historical Dictionary of Figure Skating.* Plymouth, UK: Scarecrow, 2011.

Hobson, Jeremy. *Curious Country Customs.* Newton Abbot, UK: David and Charles, 2007.

Hoyle, Edmond, and Lawrence Hawkins. *The Complete Hoyle's Games.* Ware, UK: Wordsworth Editions, 1994.

Hurley, John W. *Shillelagh: The Irish Fighting Stick.* Pipersville, PA: Caravat, 2007.

Jarrett, Derek. *England in the Age of Hogarth.*, New Haven, CT: Yale University Press, 1986.

Jones, Philip. *Boomerang: Behind an Australian Icon.* Kent Town, South Australia: Wakefield, 2004.

Koch, John T. *Celtic Culture: A Historical Encyclopedia,* Vols. 1–5. Santa Barbara, CA: ABC-CLIO, 2006.

Le Vay, Benedict. *Bradt Eccentric Britain.* 2nd ed. Chalfont St. Peter, UK: Bradt Travel Guides, 2005.

Levine, Emma. *A Game of Polo with a Headless Goat and Other Bizarre Sports Discovered across Asia*. London: André Deutsch, 2003.

Levinson, David, and Karen Christensen, eds. *Encyclopedia of World Sport: From Ancient Times to the Present*. Oxford: Oxford University Press, 1996.

Litt, W. *Wrestliana: Or, an Historical Account of Ancient and Modern Wrestling*. London: John Richardson, 1823.

Love, Christopher, ed. *A Social History of Swimming in England, 1800–1918: Splashing in the Serpentine*. Abingdon, UK: Routledge, 2008.

Mallon, Bill, and Jeroen Heijmans. *Historical Dictionary of the Olympic Movement*. 4th ed. Lanham, MD: Scarecrow, 2011.

Mangan, J. A., ed. *A Sport-Loving Society: Victorian and Edwardian Middle-Class England at Play*. Abingdon, UK: Routledge, 2006.

McNicoll, Kathryn. *Real Tennis*. Princes Risborough, UK: Shire Publications, 2005.

Nauright, John, and Charles Parrish, eds. *Sports around the World: History, Culture and Practice*, Vol. 1, *General Topics, Africa, Asia, Middle East, and Oceania*. Santa Barbara, CA: ABC-CLIO, 2012.

Norridge, Julian. *Can We Have Our Balls Back, Please? How the British Invented Sport (and Then Almost Forgot How to Play It)*. London: Penguin, 2008.

Opie, Iona, and Peter Opie. *Children's Games with Things*. London: Oxford University Press, 1997.

Polley, Martin. *The British Olympics: Britain's Olympic Heritage, 1612–2012*. London: English Heritage, 2011.

Pope, S. W., and John Nauright, eds. *Routledge Companion to Sports History*. Abingdon, UK: Routledge, 2010.

Reilly, Rick. *Sports from Hell: My Search for the World's Most Outrageous Competition*. New York: Doubleday, 2010.

Rosen, Michael J., and Ben Kassoy. *No Dribbling the Squid: Octopush, Shin Kicking, Elephant Polo and Other Oddball Sports*. Kansas City: Andrews McMeel, 2009.

Roud, Steve. *The English Year*. London: Penguin, 2006.

Roud, Steve. *The Lore of the Playground: One Hundred Years of Children's Games, Rhymes & Traditions*. London: Random House, 2010.

Schubert, Adrian. *Death and Money in the Afternoon: A History of the Spanish Bullfight*. Oxford: Oxford University Press, 1999.

Schwanbeck, Klaus. *The Ultimate Nordic Pole Walking Book*. 3rd ed. Maidenhead, UK: Meyer and Meyer Sport, 2014.

Shipside, Steve. *Extreme Sports: Brilliant Ideas for Taking Yourself to the Limit*. Oxford, UK: Infinite Ideas, 2012.

Simpson, Jacqueline, and Steve Roud. *Oxford Dictionary of English Folklore*. Oxford: Oxford University Press, 2000.

Stewart, Bob, Matthew Nicholson, Aaron Smith, and Hans Westerbeek. *Australian Sport: Better by Design? The Evolution of Australian Sporting Policy*. Abingdon, UK: Routledge, 2004.

Sumerling, Patricia. *The Adelaide Park Lands: A Social History*. Kent Town, South Australia: Wakefield, 2011.

Swaddling, Judith. *The Ancient Olympic Games*. 2nd ed. Austin: University of Texas Press, 2002.

Thomas, Jacques. "Why Boomerangs Boomerang (and Why Killing-Sticks Don't)." *New Scientist* 99(1376) (September 22, 1983): 838–843.

Thompson, William N. *Gambling in America: An Encyclopedia of History, Issues, and Society.* Santa Barbara, CA: ABC-CLIO, 2001.

Tomlinson, Alan. *A Dictionary of Sports Studies.* Oxford: Oxford University Press, 2010.

Weber, Eugen. *Peasants into Frenchmen: The Modernization of Rural France, 1870–1914.* Stanford, CA: Stanford University Press, 1976.

Wennerberg, Conrad A. *Wind, Waves, and Sunburn: A Brief History of Marathon Swimming.* New York: Breakaway Books, 1997.

Wiggins, David. *Sport in America: From Colonial Leisure to Celebrity Figures and Globalization,* Vol. 2. Champaign, IL: Human Kinetics, 2010.

Wilkins, Sally E. D. *Sports and Games through History: Sports and Games of Medieval Cultures.* Westport, CT: Greenwood, 2000.

Wilson, Ed, ed. *The Sports Book: Fully Revised 4th Edition.* London: Dorling Kindersley, 2013.

Woodworth, Paddy. *The Basque Country: A Cultural History.* Oxford: Oxford University Press, 2008.

Select Electronic Resources

AIS Sports Nutrition. "Australian Rules Football." AIS, 2014, http://www.ausport.gov.au/ais/nutrition/factsheets/sports/australian_rules_football.

Ashton Conker Club. "All About Conkers." World Conker Championships.com, 1965–2013, http://www.worldconkerchampionships.com/html/conkers_about.html.

Barkham, Patrick. "Badger Baiting Has Been Outlawed since 1835—So Why Is It Making a Comeback?" The Guardian, January 3, 2012, http://www.theguardian.com/world/2012/jan/03/badger-baiting-on-increase.

Baxter, Willie. "New Vigour in Our Oldest Sport." *Renfrewshire Local History Forum Journal* 8 (1997), http://rlhf.info/wp-content/uploads/8.2-Wrestling-Baxter.pdf.

"Boomerang Competition Events." Boomerang Association of Australia, http://boomerang.org.au/wp/articles/boomerang-competition-events/.

"Bullfighting—Rough Guide." andalucia.com, http://www.andalucia.com/bullfight/rough guide.htm.

Burchell, Helen. "A Handy Bandy Guide." April 2008. BBC, http://www.bbc.co.uk/cambridgeshire/content/articles/2006/02/15/bandy_sport_feature.shtml.

Cactus Ventures Ltd. "About Bunnock—the Game of Bones." The Original Bunnock, 2004–2014, http://www.bunnock.com/index.php?page=about-bunnock.

Chambers, Lucas. "Swiss Know How to Schwingen." Straight.com. July 8, 2004, http://www.straight.com/life/swiss-know-how-schwingen.

Chandler, Mark. "Chessboxing—The Bizarre Craze That Started in a Kidbrooke Youth Club." News Shopper, September 17, 2012, http://www.newsshopper.co.uk/news/greenwich/9933055.Chessboxing___the_bizarre_craze_that_started_in_a_Kidbrooke_youth_club/.

Davis, Simon. "The Cresta Run's 125th Anniversary." Country Life, December 27, 2009, http://www.countrylife.co.uk/countryside/article/435495/The-Cresta-Run-s-125th-anniversary.html.

Dellinger, Bob. "A History of Wrestling in the United States." New Milford Green Wave Wrestling, Spring 2014, http://newmilfordgreenwavewrestling.stackvarsity.com/cpage.asp?id=163294.

Goodheart, Benjie. "For the Real British Olympic Spirit, Visit the Cotswold Olimpicks." The Guardian, May 31, 2012, http://www.theguardian.com/sport/shortcuts/2012/may/31/british-olympic-cotswold-olympicks.

Hernandez, Raymond. "A Blood Sport Gets in the Blood; Fans of Cockfighting Don't Understand Its Outlaw Status." New York Times, April 11, 1995, http://www.nytimes.com/1995/04/11/nyregion/blood-sport-gets-blood-fans-cockfighting-don-t-understand-its-outlaw-status.html?pagewanted=all&src=pm.

Masters, James. "The Shovelboard Family: History and Useful Information." The Online Guide to Traditional Games, http://www.tradgames.org.uk/games/ShovelBoard.htm.

"Miscellaneous Stick and Ball Games." Ancient Golf, http://www.ancientgolf.dse.nl/stickball.htm.

Paton, Graeme. "Schools Banning Conkers and Leapfrog over Safety Fears." The Telegraph, April 19, 2011, http://www.telegraph.co.uk/education/educationnews/8458526/Schools-banning-conkers-and-leapfrog-over-safety-fears.html.

"The Rules of Fivestones and Jacks." Masters Traditional Games, 2012, http://www.mastersgames.com/rules/jacks-rules.htm.

Scriber, Brad. "Nat Geo Photographer Tells All about Buzkashi, the Afghan Sport Involving a Headless Goat (and the Subject of an Oscar-Nommed Film)." National Geographic, February 22, 2013, http://newswatch.nationalgeographic.com/2013/02/22/nat-geo-photographer-tells-all-about-buzkashi-the-afghan-sport-involving-a-headless-goat-and-the-subject-of-an-oscar-nommed-film/.

Tripp, Michael. "Persistence of Difference: A History of Cornish Wrestling." Volume 1 of 2. PhD dissertation, University of Exeter, 2009, https://ore.exeter.ac.uk/repository/bitstream/handle/10036/106560/TrippM_vol1.pdf?sequence=3.

"West Coast Swiss Wrestling Association History." San Joaquin Valley Swiss Club, http://www.riponswissclub.com/index_files/Page588.htm.

Select Filmography

Alice in Wonderland. 1951. Dir: Clyde Geronimi, Wilfred Jackson, Hamilton Luske.

Blood and Sand. 1941. Dir: Rouben Mamoulian.

Buzkashi Boys. 2012. Dir: Sam French, Martin Desmond Roe.

Casino Royale. 2006. Dir: Martin Campbell.

Dangerous When Wet. 1953. Dir: Charles Walters.

Extreme Ironing: Pressing for Glory. 2003. Dir: Martin Durkin.

The Fox and the Hound. 1981. Dir: Ted Berman, Richard Rich, Art Stevens.

Heathers. 1988. Dir: Michael Lehmann.

The Horsemen. (1971). Dir: John Frankenheimer.

Lagaan: Once upon a Time in India. 2001. Dir: Ashutosh Gowariker.

Mary Poppins. 1964. Dir: Robert Stevenson.

Nacho Libre. 2006. Dir: Jared Hess.

On a Clear Day. 2005. Dir: Gaby Dellal.

On Her Majesty's Secret Service. 1969. Dir: Peter Hunt.

The Plague of the Zombies. 1965. Dir: John Gilling.

The Quest. 1996. Dir: Jean-Claude Van Damme.

Santo contra las mujeras vampiros [Santo against the Vampire Women]. 1962. Dir: Alfonso Corona Blake.

Santo, la layenda del enmascarado de plata [Santo, Legend of the Man in the Silver Mask].
    1993. Dir: Gilberto de Anda.

Savages. 1972. Dir: James Ivory.

Taxi 2. 2000. Dir: Gerard Krawczyk.

Yamakasi—Les Samouraïs des Temps Modernes [Yamakasi—The Modern Samurai]. 2001.
    Dir: Ariel Zeitoun, Julien Seri

Index

Page numbers in **bold** reflect main entries in the book.

About the Author

Victoria Williams, PhD, is an independent writer and researcher living in London, England. She has written on a variety of subjects including Victorian literature and art, Martha Washington's Great Cake, the Culper Spy Ring, Hollywood film (for ABC-CLIO's *Movies in American History: An Encyclopedia* series), human sacrifice in Mesoamerica (for ABC-CLIO's *Conflict in the Early Americas*), and British folk customs (for ABC-CLIO's *They Do What? A Cultural Encyclopedia of Extraordinary and Exotic Customs from around the World*). She has also worked as an editorial assistant on a number of digital humanities projects, including the Nineteenth-Century Serials Edition, and was a long-term contributor to Routledge's Annotated Bibliography of English Studies. Williams wrote her PhD (King's College, London) on fairy tales in 19th-century British art and literature and on film, with special reference to the Brothers Grimm.

CPSIA information can be obtained
at www.ICGtesting.com
Printed in the USA
LVOW03*1429280616

494431LV00029B/254/P